The Data Warehouse Lifecycle Toolkit

Expert Methods for Designing, Developing, and Deploying Data Warehouses

Ralph Kimball

Laura Reeves

Margy Ross

Warren Thornthwaite

WILEY COMPUTER PUBLISHING

John Wiley & Sons, Inc.

New York • Chichester • Weinheim • Brisbane • Singapore • Toronto

Publisher: Robert Ipsen
Editor: Robert M. Elliott
Assistant Editor: Pam Sobotka
Managing Editor: Brian Snapp
Electronic Products, Associate Editor: Mike Sosa
Text Design & Composition: Publishers' Design and Production Services

Designations used by companies to distinguish their products are often claimed as trademarks. In all instances where John Wiley & Sons, Inc., is aware of a claim, the product names appear in initial capital or ALL CAPITAL LETTERS. Readers, however, should contact the appropriate companies for more complete information regarding trademarks and registration.

This book is printed on acid-free paper. ♾

This publication is designed to provide accurate and authoritative information in regard to the subject matter covered. It is sold with the understanding that the publisher is not engaged in professional services. If professional advice or other expert assistance is required, the services of a competent professional person should be sought.

Library of Congress Cataloging-in-Publication Data:

The Data warehouse lifecycle toolkit : expert methods for designing,
    developing, and deploying data warehouses / Ralph Kimball . . . [et al.].
        p.   cm.
    Includes index.
    ISBN 0-471-25547-5 (pbk. : alk. paper)
    1. Data warehousing.   I. Kimball, Ralph.
    QA76.9.D37D37   1998
    658.4′038′0285574—dc21   98-18853
                                                        CIP

Printed in the United States of America.

CONTENTS

Acknowledgments

The authors would first like to thank Julie Kimball for conceiving the idea of this book, corralling the four authors, and urging us onward when it seemed like too big a project. It wouldn't have happened without you, Julie.

The name *Lifecycle* for this book is apt in many ways because it reflects the accumulated experience all four of us have had in the course of our careers. It isn't possible to give proper credit to everyone who has influenced us over the years, but one group of very fine people stands out consistently: the employees of Metaphor Computer Systems. To them we owe our broadest thanks. We built a lot of data warehouses with these folks between 1982 and 1994.

We would like to thank several individuals from the publishing world for their support of this book. Bob Elliott of John Wiley & Sons has been a real pleasure to work with, both on this book and on the earlier *Data Warehouse Toolkit* by Ralph Kimball. Brian Snapp and Pam Sobotka, also with Wiley, have been patient and tireless in working with us to deliver a quality publication. Finally, Maurice Frank, formerly editor-in-chief of *DBMS Magazine*, was extraordinarily generous in working with us in those places where we adapted parts of Ralph Kimball's dimensional modeling articles from *DBMS Magazine* for recasting in this book.

This book profited significantly from professional reviews. Although it was tough to rewrite several of the chapters, we are sure the book is much better because it was reviewed so critically. If you ever want a book reviewed, here is a list of world-class reviewers. Our thanks (in alphabetical order) to:

- Cecelia Bellomo of Hewlett Packard
- Maurice Frank of IBM Global Services
- Bill Schmarzo of Sequent Computer Systems
- Mike Schmitz of Oracle
- Jerry Tattershall, Independent Technical Writer

We are profoundly grateful for the involvement of the business partners in each of our consulting businesses. Each of them has been enthusiastic and supportive of the book, and besides reading the book from cover to cover, they helped to write whole paragraphs and sections. Thank you to:

- Bob Becker of DecisionWorks Consulting
- Paul Kautza of StarSoft Solutions
- Julie Kimball of Ralph Kimball Associates
- Joy Mundy of InfoDynamics LLC
- Nancy Rinn of DecisionWorks Consulting

Finally, we long to thank our spouses, partners, and children for their support. We hope you will forgive us for only seeing the backs of our heads during much of the last year. Thank you to:

- Jennifer Finch
- Sara Hayden Smith, Brian and Julie Kimball
- Leah, Michael, Ryan, and Mark Reeves
- Katie and Scott Ross

The Data Warehouse Lifecycle Toolkit

Introduction

This book is for you, the designers, managers, and owners of the data warehouse. In most cases, you work in an information systems (IS) organization. No matter what your title is, you probably feel a big responsibility for creating and maintaining the data warehouse or for creating and maintaining some of the parts of the data warehouse we call data marts. This book is a field guide, a set of tools, for designing, developing, and deploying data warehouses and data marts in large organizations.

We have tried to distinguish this book from other data warehouse books by making the content very concrete and actionable. This book describes a coherent framework that goes all the way from the original scoping of an overall data warehouse, through all the detailed steps of developing and deploying the data warehouse, to the final steps of planning the next phases.

The data warehouse marketplace has definitely moved beyond its infancy. As of this writing, there are more than a thousand functioning data warehouse installations of one kind or another just in the United States. Many data warehouse owners now have a complete *lifecycle* perspective on their data warehouses. Probably the biggest insight that comes from this lifecycle perspective is that each data warehouse is continuously evolving and dynamic. A data warehouse cannot be static. It never stops evolving. New business requirements arise. New managers and executives place unexpected demands on the data warehouse. New data sources become available. At the very least, a data warehouse needs to evolve as fast as the surrounding organization evolves. Stable organizations will place modest demands on the data warehouse to evolve. Dynamic, turbulent organizations will make the data warehouse task more challenging.

Given the churning, evolving nature of the data warehouse, we must adjust our expectations and our techniques from the original idealistic, static view we had a few years ago. We need design techniques that are flexible and adaptable. We need to be half DBA and half MBA. We need to opportunistically hook together little pieces (like data marts) into larger pieces (data warehouses). And we need our changes to the data warehouse to always be graceful. A graceful change is one that doesn't invalidate previous data or previous applications.

This book has two deep underlying themes. The first is the Business Dimensional Lifecycle approach. The Business Dimensional Lifecycle starts with business requirements and builds a series of data marts that are understandable and have high performance. These data marts are based on star dimensional models.

The second theme is the Data Warehouse Bus Architecture. We will show you how to build a succession of data marts that will, in time, create an overall data warehouse. This approach will free you from the requirement to build a centralized, all-encompassing data warehouse that must be completed before you release your first data mart.

This book captures these perspectives. We will give you actionable skills and actionable tools for getting your job done. Along the way, we hope to give you the perspective and judgment we have accumulated in doing several hundred data warehouse installations and consulting assignments since 1982.

LEVEL OF UNDERSTANDING

The primary reader of this book should be a designer or a manager who really needs to get about the business of building and managing a data warehouse. Although the book contains some introductory material, we think it will be of most use to an IS professional who has already had some exposure to data warehousing. An appropriate background would be familiarity with *The Data Warehouse Toolkit*, by Ralph Kimball (Wiley, 1996). Certainly, the book you are reading, *The Data Warehouse*

Lifecycle Toolkit, can be viewed as one that builds on the original *Toolkit*'s foundation, but it then offers a deeper and more advanced treatment of the development methodology than the first book.

Alternatively, you may have developed your experience and formed your opinions by designing and delivering a real data warehouse. That is the best background of all! There is no substitute for having had the responsibility of delivering an effective data warehouse. We have all had the humbling experience of presenting our baby to a crowd of demanding end users. It is sometimes hard to accept the reality that most end users have real jobs that don't involve technology. They may not even like technology particularly. But end users will use our technology if it is easy to use and provides them obvious value.

This book is somewhat technical. The discussion of design techniques and of architectures will undoubtedly introduce terminology that you have not encountered. We have combed this book carefully to make sure that the more technical topics are ones we think you *must* understand. We have tried not to get bogged down in detail for its own sake. A good example is the fairly long section on data warehouse security. The discussion of security avoids describing the microscopic details of security technology, but it doesn't pull any punches. There are a number of security topics you simply have to understand if you are going to perform your job responsibly. Welcome to data warehousing.

HOW TO USE THE BOOK ACTIVELY

We recommend that the book be read in its entirety to understand the complete Business Dimensional Lifecycle. Hopefully, your past experiences and opinions will give you a personal framework on which to hang all these ideas. After reading Chapter 2, you will see that there are three parallel threads that must be pursued in building a data warehouse: the technical architecture, the data architecture, and the application architecture. We even show these three threads in all of the "You Are Here" diagrams at the beginning of each chapter. Although these threads clearly affect each other, they can be developed in parallel and asynchronously.

However, because a book is necessarily a linear thing, we have had to present the steps in the Business Dimensional Lifecycle as if they occur in one fixed order. Hopefully, as you work through the book, you will visualize the more realistic and complex real-world relationships among the various steps.

We have laced the book with practical tips, and we have formatted the tips like this:

 You can find all the tips in this book by flipping though the chapters and looking for this element, indicated by the light bulb icon.

To give you a snapshot of a particular part of the process, a spreadsheet of project plan tasks and responsibilities follows these elements:

 Key roles involved in the phases of the data warehouse lifecycle are collected at the end of appropriate chapters and are indicated by a key ring icon.

 Estimating considerations for each step of the process are collected at the ends of appropriate chapters and are indicated by an alarm clock icon.

 A list of supporting templates are collected at the ends of appropriate chapters and are indicated by a CD-ROM icon. Open your CD-ROM to obtain blank templates and instructions on how to use them.

Throughout the book we talk about various planning aids, lists, and templates. If it helps you, please use the samples we have provided on the CD-ROM. You probably have your own style, or maybe you have a planning framework in place already that is different from ours. Our objective is to get you started.

Our planning aids are meant to provide a moderate, but not excessive, amount of structure. We think that a data warehouse implementation is a big job, and anyone who does it needs to be a pretty good manager. A pretty good manager knows how to balance the methodology of managing a project with the human and logical issues of managing people and tasks. So we urge you strongly either to use our structure or your own equivalent, but not to depend on it slavishly. Your real job is to figure out what is important to do in your organization and then work with other people to get it done.

We have also divided this book into a basic thread and a "graduate" thread. The table of contents clearly labels three of the chapters as *graduate*. In your first reading of this book, especially if much of this material is new, we recommend that you simply skim the graduate chapters so that you know what is there. Then, when you are more comfortable with the entire Business Dimensional Lifecycle, we think you will find the graduate chapters very valuable. We believe these chapters represent state-of-the-art thinking in all three areas.

We hope you will return to each chapter and reread it very carefully when your project gets to that particular phase. That is why we called it *The Data Warehouse Lifecycle Toolkit*.

THE PURPOSE OF EACH CHAPTER

1. **The Chess Pieces.**   As of the writing of this book, a lot of vague terminology was being tossed around in the data warehouse marketplace. Even the term *data warehouse* has lost its precision. Some people are even trying to define the data warehouse as a non-queryable data resource! We are not foolish enough to think we can settle all the terminology disputes in these pages, but within this book we will stick to a very specific set of meanings. This chapter briefly defines all the important terms used in data warehousing in a consistent way. Perhaps this is something like studying all the chess pieces and what they can do before attempting to play a chess game. We think we are pretty close to the mainstream with these definitions.

Section 1: Project Management and Requirements

2. **The Business Dimensional Lifecycle.**   We define the complete Business Dimensional Lifecycle from 50,000 feet. We briefly discuss each step and give perspective on the lifecycle as a whole.

3. **Project Planning and Management.**   In this chapter, we define the project and talk about setting its scope within your environment. We talk extensively about the various project roles and responsibilities. You won't necessarily need a full headcount equivalent for each of these roles, but you will need to fill them in almost any imaginable project. This is a chapter for managers.

4. **Collecting the Requirements.**   Collecting the business and data requirements is the foundation of the entire data warehouse effort—or at least it should be. Collecting the requirements is an art form, and it is one of the least natural activities for an IS organization. We give you techniques to make this job easier and hope to impress upon you the necessity of spending quality time on this step.

Section 2: Data Design

5. **A First Course on Dimensional Modeling.**   We start with an energetic argument for the value of dimensional modeling. We want you to understand the depth of our commitment to this approach. After performing hundreds of data warehouse designs and installations over the last 15 years, we think this is the only approach you can use to achieve the twin goals of understandability and performance. We then reveal the central secret for combining multiple dimensional models together into a coherent whole. This secret is called conformed dimensions and conformed facts. We call this approach the Data Warehouse Bus Architecture. Your computer has a backbone, called the computer bus, that everything connects to, and your data warehouse has a backbone, called the data warehouse bus, that everything connects to. The remainder of this chapter is a self-contained introduction to the science of dimensional modeling for data warehouses. This introduction can be viewed as an appendix to the full treatment of this subject in Ralph Kimball's earlier book, *The Data Warehouse Toolkit*.

6. **A Graduate Course on Dimensional Modeling.**   Here we collect all the hardest dimensional modeling situations we can think of. Most of these examples come from specific business situations, such as dealing with a monster customer list.

7. **Building Dimensional Models.**   In this chapter we tackle the issue of how to create the right model within your organization. You start with a matrix of data marts and dimensions, and then you de-

sign each fact table in each data mart according to the techniques described in Chapter 5. The last half of this chapter describes the real-life management issues in applying this methodology and building all the dimensional models needed in each data mart.

Section 3: Architecture

8. Introducing Data Warehouse Architecture. In this chapter we introduce all the components of the technical architecture at a medium level of detail. This paints the overall picture. The remaining five chapters in this section go into the specific areas of detail. We divide the discussion into data architecture, application architecture, and infrastructure. If you follow the Data Warehouse Bus Architecture we developed in Chapter 5, you will be able to develop your data marts one at a time, and you will end up with a flexible, coherent overall data warehouse. But we didn't say it would be easy.

9. Technical Back Room Architecture. We introduce you to the system components in the back room: the source systems, the reporting instance, the data staging area, the base level data warehouse, and the business process data marts. We tell you what happened to the operational data store (ODS). We also talk about all the services you must provide in the back room to get the data ready to load into your data mart presentation server.

10. Architecture for the Front Room. The front room is your publishing operation. You make the data available and provide an array of tools for different user needs. We give you a comprehensive view of the many requirements you must support in the front room.

11. Infrastructure and Metadata. Infrastructure is the glue that holds the data warehouse together. This chapter covers the nuts and bolts. We deal with the detail we think every data warehouse designer and manager need to know about hardware, software, communications, and especially metadata.

12. A Graduate Course on the Internet and Security. The Internet has a potentially huge impact on the life of the data warehouse manager, but many data warehouse managers are either not aware of the true impact of the Internet or they are avoiding the issues. This chapter will expose you to the current state of the art on Internet-based data warehouses and security issues and give you a list of immediate actions to take to protect your installation. The examples

throughout this chapter are slanted toward the exposures and challenges faced by the data warehouse owner.

13. **Creating the Architecture Plan and Selecting Products.**   Now
    that you are a software, hardware, and infrastructure expert, you
    are ready to commit to a specific architecture plan for your organi-
    zation and to choose specific products. We talk about the selection
    process and which combination of product categories you need. Bear
    in mind this book is not a platform for talking about specific ven-
    dors, however.

Section 4: Implementation

14. **A Graduate Course on Aggregations.**   Aggregations are pre-
    stored summaries that you create to boost performance of your data-
    base systems. This chapter dives deeply into the structure of
    aggregations, where you put them, how you use them, and how you
    administer them. Aggregations are the single most cost-effective
    way to boost performance in a large data warehouse system assum-
    ing that the rest of your system is constructed according to the Data
    Warehouse Bus Architecture.

15. **Completing the Physical Design.**   Although we don't know
    which DBMS and which hardware architecture you will choose,
    there are a number of powerful ideas at this level that you should
    understand. We talk about physical data structures, indexing
    strategies, specialty databases for data warehousing, and RAID
    storage strategies.

16. **Data Staging.**   Once you have the major systems in place, the
    biggest and riskiest step in the process is getting the data out of the
    legacy systems and loading into the data mart DBMSs. The data stag-
    ing area is the intermediate place where you bring the legacy data in
    for cleaning and transforming. We have a lot of strong opinions about
    what should and should not happen in the data staging area.

17. **Building End User Applications.**   After the data is finally loaded
    into the DBMS, we still have to arrange for a soft landing on the
    users' desktops. The end user applications are all the query tools
    and report writers and data mining systems for getting the data out
    of the DBMS and doing something useful. This chapter describes the
    starter set of end user applications you need to provide as part of the
    initial data mart implementation.

Section 5: Deployment and Growth

18. **Planning the Deployment.**   When everything is ready to go, you still have to roll the system out and behave in many ways like a commercial software vendor. You need to install the software, train the users, collect bug reports, solicit feedback, and respond to new requirements. You need to plan carefully so that you can deliver according to the expectations you have set.

19. **Maintaining and Growing the Data Warehouse.**   Finally, when your entire data mart edifice is up and running, you have to turn around to do it again! As we said earlier, the data warehouse is more of a process than a project. This chapter is an appropriate end for the book, if only because it leaves you with a valuable last impression: You are never done.

Supporting Tools

- **Appendix A.**   This appendix summarizes the entire project plan for the Business Dimensional Lifecycle in one place and in one format. All of the project tasks and roles are listed.
- **Appendix B.**   This appendix is a guided tour of the contents of the CD-ROM. All of the useful checklists, templates, and forms are listed. We also walk you through how to use our sample design of a Data Warehouse Bus Architecture.
- **CD-ROM.**   The CD-ROM that accompanies the book contains a large number of actual checklists, templates, and forms for you to use with your data warehouse development. It also includes a sample design illustrating the Data Warehouse Bus Architecture.

THE GOALS OF A DATA WAREHOUSE

One of the most important assets of an organization is its information. This asset is almost always kept by an organization in two forms: the operational systems of record and the data warehouse. Crudely speaking, the operational systems of record are where the data is put in, and the data warehouse is where we get the data out. In *The Data Warehouse Toolkit*, we described this dichotomy at length. At the time of this writing, it is no longer so necessary to convince the world that there are really two systems or that there will always be two systems. It is now widely recognized that the data warehouse has profoundly different needs, clients, structures, and rhythms than the operational systems of record.

Ultimately, we need to put aside the details of implementation and modeling, and remember what the fundamental goals of the data warehouse are. In our opinion, the data warehouse:

- **Makes an organization's information accessible.** The contents of the data warehouse are understandable and navigable, and the access is characterized by fast performance. These requirements have no boundaries and no fixed limits. *Understandable* means correctly labeled and obvious. *Navigable* means recognizing your destination on the screen and getting there in one click. *Fast performance* means zero wait time. Anything else is a compromise and therefore something that we must improve.

- **Makes the organization's information consistent.** Information from one part of the organization can be matched with information from another part of the organization. If two measures of an organization have the same name, then they must mean the same thing. Conversely, if two measures don't mean the same thing, then they are labeled differently. Consistent information means high-quality information. It means that all of the information is accounted for and is complete. Anything else is a compromise and therefore something that we must improve.

- **Is an adaptive and resilient source of information.** The data warehouse is designed for continuous change. When new questions are asked of the data warehouse, the existing data and the technologies are not changed or disrupted. When new data is added to the data warehouse, the existing data and the technologies are not changed or disrupted. The design of the separate data marts that make up the data warehouse must be distributed and incremental. Anything else is a compromise and therefore something that we must improve.

- **Is a secure bastion that protects our information asset.** The data warehouse not only controls access to the data effectively, but gives its owners great visibility into the uses and abuses of that data, even after it has left the data warehouse. Anything else is a compromise and therefore something that we must improve.

■ **Is the foundation for decision making.**   The data warehouse has the right data in it to support decision making. There is only one true output from a data warehouse: the *decisions* that are made after the data warehouse has presented its evidence. The original label that predates the data warehouse is still the best description of what we are trying to build: a decision support system.

THE GOALS OF THIS BOOK

If we succeed with this book, you—the designers and managers of large data warehouses—will achieve your goals more quickly. You will build effective data warehouses that match well against the goals outlined in the preceding section, and you will make fewer mistakes along the way. Hopefully, you will not reinvent the wheel and discover "previously owned" truths.

We have tried to be as technical as this large subject allows, without getting waylaid by vendor-specific details. Certainly, one of the interesting aspects of working in the data warehouse marketplace is the breadth of knowledge needed to understand all of the data warehouse responsibilities. We feel quite strongly that this wide perspective must be maintained because of the continuously evolving nature of data warehousing. Even if data warehousing leaves behind such bedrock notions as text and number data, or the reliance on relational database technology, most of the principles of this book would remain applicable, because the mission of a data warehouse team is to build a decision support system in the most fundamental sense of the words.

We think that a moderate amount of structure and discipline helps a lot in building a large and complex data warehouse. We want to transfer this structure and discipline to you through this book. We want you to understand and anticipate the whole Business Dimensional Lifecycle, and we want you to infuse your own organizations with this perspective. In many ways, the data warehouse is an expression of information systems' fundamental charter: to collect the organization's information and make it useful.

The idea of a lifecycle suggests an endless process where data warehouses sprout and flourish and eventually die, only to be replaced with new data warehouses that build on the legacies of the previous generations. This book tries to capture that perspective and help you get it started in your organization.

VISIT THE COMPANION WEB SITE

This book is necessarily a static snapshot of the data warehouse industry and the methodologies we think are important. For a dynamic, up-to-date perspective on these issues, please visit this book's Web site at www.wiley.com/compbooks/kimball, or log on to the mirror site at www.lifecycle-toolkit.com. We, the authors of this book, intend to maintain this Web site personally and make it a useful resource for data warehouse professionals.

CHAPTER 1

The Chess Pieces

All of the authors of this book worked together at Metaphor Computer Systems over a period that spanned more than ten years, from 1982 to 1994. Although the real value of the Metaphor experience was the building of hundreds of data warehouses, there was an ancillary benefit that we sometimes find useful. We are really conscious of *metaphors*. How could we avoid metaphors, with a name like that?

A useful metaphor to get this book started is to think about studying the chess pieces very carefully before trying to play the game of chess. You really need to learn the shapes of the pieces and what they can do on the board. More subtly, you need to learn the strategic significance of the pieces and how to wield them in order to win the game. Certainly, with a data warehouse, as well as with chess, you need to think way ahead. Your opponent is the ever-changing nature of the environment you are forced to work in. You can't avoid the changing user needs, the changing business conditions, the changing nature of the data you are given to work with, and the changing technical environment. So maybe the game of data warehousing is something like the game of chess. At least it's a pretty good metaphor.

If you intend to read this book, you need to read this chapter. We are fairly precise in this book with our vocabulary, and you will get more out of this book if you know where we stand. We begin by briefly defining the basic elements of the data warehouse. As we remarked in the introduction, there is not universal agreement in the marketplace over these definitions.

But our use of these words is as close to mainstream practice as we can make them. Here in this book, we will use these words precisely and consistently, according to the definitions we provide in the next section.

We will then list the data warehouse processes you need to be concerned about. This list is a declaration of the boundaries for your job. Perhaps the biggest insight into your responsibilities as a data warehouse manager is that this list of data warehouse processes is long and somewhat daunting.

BASIC ELEMENTS OF THE DATA WAREHOUSE

As you read through the definitions in this section, please refer to Figure 1.1. We will move through Figure 1.1 roughly in left to right order.

Source System

An operational system of record whose function it is to capture the transactions of the business. A source system is often called a "legacy system" in a mainframe environment. The main priorities of the source system are uptime and availability. Queries against source systems are narrow, "account-based" queries that are part of the normal transaction flow and severely restricted in their demands on the legacy system. We assume that the source systems maintain little historical data and that management reporting from source systems is a burden on these systems. We make the strong assumption that source systems are not queried in the broad and unexpected ways that data warehouses are typically queried. We also assume that each source system is a natural stovepipe, where little or no investment has been made to conform basic dimensions such as product, customer, geography, or calendar with other legacy systems in the organization. Source systems have keys that make certain things unique, like product keys or customer keys. We call these source system keys *production keys,* and we treat them as attributes, just like any other textual description of something. We *never* use the production keys as the keys within our data warehouse. (Hopefully that got your attention. Read the chapters on data modeling.)

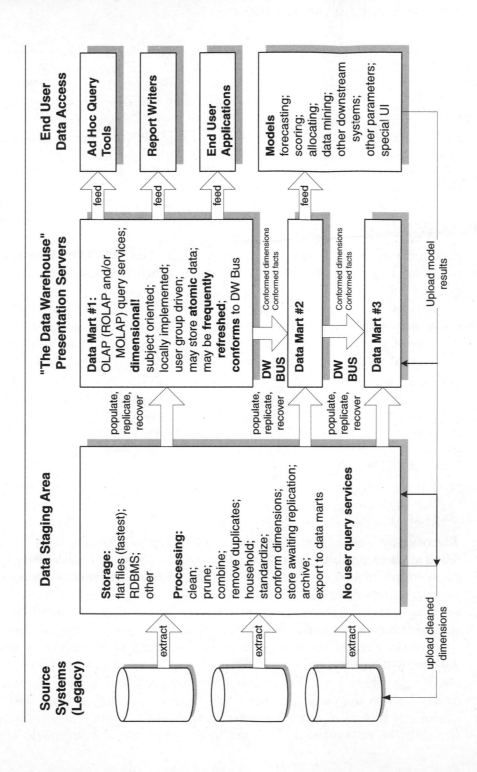

FIGURE 1.1 The basic elements of the data warehouse.

Data Staging Area

A storage area and set of processes that clean, transform, combine, deduplicate, household, archive, and prepare source data for use in the data warehouse. The data staging area is everything in between the source system and the presentation server. Although it would be nice if the data staging area were a single centralized facility on one piece of hardware, it is far more likely that the data staging area is spread over a number of machines. The data staging area is dominated by the simple activities of sorting and sequential processing and, in some cases, the data staging area does not need to be based on relational technology. After you check your data for conformance with all the one-to-one and many-to-one business rules you have defined, it may be pointless to take the final step of building a full blown entity-relation-based physical database design.

However, there are many cases where the data arrives at the doorstep of the data staging area in a third normal form relational database. In other cases, the managers of the data staging area are more comfortable organizing their cleaning, transforming, and combining steps around a set of normalized structures. In these cases, a normalized structure for the data staging storage is certainly acceptable. The key defining restriction on the data staging area is that *it does not provide query and presentation services.* As soon as a system provides query and presentation services, it must be categorized as a presentation server, which is described next.

Presentation Server

The target physical machine on which the data warehouse data is organized and stored for direct querying by end users, report writers, and other applications. In our opinion, three very different systems are required for a data warehouse to function: the source system, the data staging area, and the presentation server. The source system should be thought of as outside the data warehouse, since we assume we have no control over the content and format of the data in the legacy system. We have described the data staging area as the initial storage and cleaning system for data that is moving toward the presentation server, and we made the point that the data staging area may well consist of a system of flat files. It is the presentation server where we insist that the data be presented and stored in a dimensional framework. If the presentation server is based on a relational database, then the tables will be organized as star schemas. If the presentation server is based on nonrelational *on-line analytic processing* (OLAP) technology, then the data will still have recognizable dimensions, and most of the recommendations in this book will pertain. At the time this book was written, most of the large data marts (greater than a few gigabytes) were implemented on relational databases. Thus, most of the specific discussions surrounding the presentation server are couched in terms of relational databases.

Dimensional Model

A specific discipline for modeling data that is an alternative to entity-relationship (E/R) modeling. A dimensional model contains the same information as an E/R model but packages the data in a symmetric format whose design goals are user understandability, query performance, and resilience to change. The rationale for dimensional modeling is presented in Chapter 5.

This book and its predecessor, *The Data Warehouse Toolkit*, are based on the discipline of dimensional modeling. We, the authors, are committed to this approach because we have seen too many data warehouses fail because of overly complex E/R designs. We have successfully employed the techniques of dimensional modeling in hundreds of design situations over the last 15 years.

The main components of a dimensional model are fact tables and dimension tables, which are defined carefully in Chapter 5. But let's look at them briefly.

A *fact table* is the primary table in each dimensional model that is meant to contain measurements of the business. Throughout this book, we will consistently use the word *fact* to represent a business measure. We will reduce terminology confusion by not using the words *measure* or *measurement*. The most useful facts are numeric and additive. Every fact table represents a many-to-many relationship and every fact table contains a set of two or more foreign keys that join to their respective dimension tables.

A *dimension table* is one of a set of companion tables to a fact table. Each dimension is defined by its primary key that serves as the basis for referential integrity with any given fact table to which it is joined. Most dimension tables contain many textual *attributes* (fields) that are the basis for constraining and grouping within data warehouse queries.

Business Process

A coherent set of business activities that make sense to the business users of our data warehouses. This definition is purposefully a little vague. A business process is usually a set of activities like "order processing" or "customer pipeline management," but business processes can overlap, and certainly the definition of an individual business process will evolve over time. In this book, we assume that a business process is a useful grouping of information resources with a coherent theme. In many cases, we will implement one or more data marts for each business process.

Data Mart

A logical subset of the complete data warehouse. A data mart is a complete "pie-wedge" of the overall data warehouse pie. A data mart represents a project that can be brought to completion rather than being an impossible galactic undertaking. A data warehouse is made up of the union of all its data marts. Beyond this rather simple logical definition, we often view the data mart as the restriction of the data warehouse to a single business process or to a group of related business processes targeted toward a particular business group. The data mart is probably sponsored by and built by a single part of the business, and a data mart is usually organized around a single business process.

We impose some very specific design requirements on every data mart. Every data mart must be represented by a dimensional model and, within a single data warehouse, all such data marts must be built from conformed dimensions and conformed facts. This is the basis of the Data Warehouse Bus Architecture. Without conformed dimensions and conformed facts, a data mart is a stovepipe. Stovepipes are the bane of the data warehouse movement. If you have any hope of building a data warehouse that is robust and resilient in the face of continuously evolving requirements, you must adhere to the data mart definition we recommend. We will show in this book that, when data marts have been designed with conformed dimensions and conformed facts, they can be combined and used together. (Read more on this topic in Chapter 5.)

We do not believe that there are two "contrasting" points of view about top-down vs. bottom-up data warehouses. The extreme top-down perspective is that a completely centralized, tightly designed master database must be completed before parts of it are summarized and published as individual data marts. The extreme bottom-up perspective is that an enterprise data warehouse can be assembled from disparate and unrelated data marts. Neither approach taken to these limits is feasible. In both cases, the only workable solution is a blend of the two approaches, where we put in place a proper architecture that guides the design of all the separate pieces.

When all the pieces of all the data marts are broken down to individual physical tables on various database servers, as they must ultimately be, then the only physical way to combine the data from these separate tables and achieve an integrated enterprise data warehouse is if the dimensions of the data mean the same thing across these tables. We call these conformed dimensions. This Data Warehouse Bus Architecture is a fundamental driver for this book.

Finally, we do not adhere to the old data mart definition that a data mart is comprised of summary data. Data marts are based on granular data and may or may not contain performance enhancing summaries, which we call "aggregates" in this book.

Data Warehouse

The queryable source of data in the enterprise. The data warehouse is nothing more than the union of all the constituent data marts. A data warehouse is fed from the data staging area. The data warehouse manager is responsible both for the data warehouse and the data staging area.

Please understand that we (and the marketplace) have departed in a number of ways from the original definition of the data warehouse dating from the early 1990s. Specifically, the data warehouse is the *queryable* presentation resource for an enterprise's data and this presentation resource *must not* be organized around an entity-relation model because, if you use entity-relation modeling, you will lose understandability and performance. Also, the data warehouse is *frequently updated* on a controlled load basis as data is corrected, snapshots are accumulated, and statuses and labels are changed. Finally, the data warehouse is precisely the *union of its constituent data marts*.

Operational Data Store (ODS)

The term "operational data store" has taken on too many definitions to be useful to the data warehouse. We have seen this term used to describe everything from the database that underlies the operational system to the data warehouse itself. There are two primary definitions that are worth exploring in the context of the data warehouse. Originally, the ODS was meant to serve as the point of integration for operational systems. This was especially important for legacy systems that grew up independent of each other. Banks, for example, typically had several independent systems set up to support different products—loans, checking accounts, savings accounts, and so on. The advent of teller support computers and the ATM helped push many banks to create an operational data store to integrate current balances and recent history from these separate accounts under one customer number. This kind of operational lookup is a perfect example of the useful role an ODS can play. In fact, this need for integration has been the driving force behind the success of the client/server ERP business.

Since this kind of ODS needs to support constant operational access and updates, it should be housed outside the warehouse. That is, any system structured to meet operational needs and performance requirements will be hard pressed to meet decision support needs and performance requirements. For example, you don't want someone to launch a complex scoring model that requires full table scans and aggregation of the customer history at the same time 1,000 catalog phone reps are trying to view customer history to support a one-to-one marketing relationship. This would not be good.

In the second definition, the purpose of the ODS has changed to include what sounds like decision support access by "clerks and executives." In this case, the logic seems to be that since the ODS is meant to contain integrated data at a detailed level, we should build one to support the lowest layer of the data warehouse.

In our view, these two definitions are very different. The original ODS is truly an operational system, separate from the data warehouse, with different service levels and performance requirements it must meet. The second ODS is actually the front edge of the kinds of data warehouse we design, really a part of the data warehouse and not a separate system at all.

If you have an operational data store in your systems environment, or in your plans, examine it carefully. If it is meant to play an operational, real-time role, then it truly is an operational data store and should have its own place in the systems world. If, on the other hand, it is meant to provide reporting or decision support, we encourage you to skip the ODS and meet these needs directly from the detailed level of the data warehouse. We provide additional discussion on including this detailed level in the warehouse in Chapter 9.

OLAP (On-Line Analytic Processing)

The general activity of querying and presenting text and number data from data warehouses, as well as a specifically dimensional style of querying and presenting that is exemplified by a number of "OLAP vendors." The OLAP vendors' technology is nonrelational and is almost always based on an explicit multidimensional cube of data. OLAP databases are also known as multidimensional databases, or MDDBs. OLAP vendors' data designs are often very similar to the data designs described in this book, but OLAP installations would be classified as small, individual data marts when viewed against the full range of data warehouse applications. We believe that OLAP-style data marts can be full participants on the data warehouse bus if they are designed around conformed dimensions and conformed facts.

ROLAP (Relational OLAP)

A set of user interfaces and applications that give a relational database a dimensional flavor. This book is highly consistent with both ROLAP and MOLAP approaches, although most of the specific examples come from a ROLAP perspective.

MOLAP (Multidimensional OLAP)

A set of user interfaces, applications, and proprietary database technologies that have a strongly dimensional flavor.

End User Application

A collection of tools that query, analyze, and present information targeted to support a business need. A minimal set of such tools would consist of an end user data access tool, a spreadsheet, a graphics package, and a user interface facility for eliciting prompts and simplifying the screen presentations to end users.

End User Data Access Tool

A client of the data warehouse. In a relational data warehouse, such a client maintains a session with the presentation server, sending a stream of separate SQL requests to the server. Eventually the end user data access tool is done with the SQL session and turns around to present a screen of data or a report, a graph, or some other higher form of analysis to the user. An end user data access tool can be as simple as an ad hoc query tool, or can be as complex as a sophisticated data mining or modeling application. A few of the more sophisticated data access tools like modeling or forecasting tools may actually upload their results into special areas of the data warehouse.

Ad Hoc Query Tool

A specific kind of end user data access tool that invites the user to form their own queries by directly manipulating relational tables and their joins. Ad hoc query tools, as powerful as they are, can only be effectively used and understood by about 10 percent of all the potential end users of a data warehouse. The remaining 90 percent of the potential users must be served by pre-built applications that are much more finished "templates" that do not require the end user to construct a relational query directly. The very best ROLAP-oriented ad hoc tools improve the 10 percent number to perhaps 20 percent.

Modeling Applications

A sophisticated kind of data warehouse client with analytic capabilities that transform or digest the output from the data warehouse. Modeling applications include:

- *Forecasting models* that try to predict the future
- *Behavior scoring models* that cluster and classify customer purchase behavior or customer credit behavior
- *Allocation models* that take cost data from the data warehouse and spread the costs across product groupings or customer groupings
- Most *data mining* tools

Metadata

All of the information in the data warehouse environment that is not the actual data itself. We take an aggressive and expansive view of metadata in this book. Chapter 11 enumerates all the forms of metadata we can think of and tries to give you some guidance about how to recognize, use, and control metadata. You should catalog your metadata, version stamp your metadata, document your metadata, and backup your metadata. But don't expect your metadata to be stored in one central database. There is too much that is metadata, and its formats and uses are too diverse.

BASIC PROCESSES OF THE DATA WAREHOUSE

Data staging is a major process that includes, among others, the following subprocesses: extracting, transforming, loading and indexing, and quality assurance checking.

- **Extracting.**   The extract step is the first step of getting data into the data warehouse environment. We use this term more narrowly than some consultants. Extracting means reading and understanding the source data, and copying the parts that are needed to the data staging area for further work.
- **Transforming.**   Once the data is extracted into the data staging area, there are many possible transformation steps, including
  - Cleaning the data by correcting misspellings, resolving domain conflicts (such as a city name that is incompatible with a postal code), dealing with missing data elements, and parsing into standard formats
  - Purging selected fields from the legacy data that are not useful for the data warehouse
  - Combining data sources, by matching exactly on key values or by performing fuzzy matches on non-key attributes, including looking up textual equivalents of legacy system codes
  - Creating surrogate keys for each dimension record in order to avoid a dependence on legacy defined keys, where the surrogate key generation process enforces referential integrity between the dimension tables and the fact tables
  - Building aggregates for boosting the performance of common queries
- **Loading and Indexing.**   At the end of the transformation process, the data is in the form of load record images. Loading in the data warehouse environment usually takes the form of replicating the dimension tables and fact tables and presenting these tables to the bulk loading facilities of each recipient data mart. Bulk loading is a very important capability that is to be contrasted with record-at-a-time loading, which is far slower. The target data mart must then

index the newly arrived data for query performance, if it has not already done so.

- **Quality Assurance Checking.**   When each data mart has been loaded and indexed and supplied with appropriate aggregates, the last step before publishing is the quality assurance step. Quality assurance can be checked by running a comprehensive exception report over the entire set of newly loaded data. All the reporting categories must be present, and all the counts and totals must be satisfactory. All reported values must be consistent with the time series of similar values that preceded them. The exception report is probably built with the data mart's end user report writing facility.

- **Release/Publishing.**   When each data mart has been freshly loaded and quality assured, the user community must be notified that the new data is ready. Publishing also communicates the nature of any changes that have occurred in the underlying dimensions and new assumptions that have been introduced into the measured or calculated facts.

- **Updating.**   Contrary to the original religion of the data warehouse, modern data marts may well be updated, sometimes frequently. Incorrect data should obviously be corrected. Changes in labels, changes in hierarchies, changes in status, and changes in corporate ownership often trigger necessary changes in the original data stored in the data marts that comprise the data warehouse, but in general these are "managed load updates," not transactional updates.

- **Querying.**   Querying is a broad term that encompasses all the activities of requesting data from a data mart, including ad hoc querying by end users, report writing, complex decision support applications, requests from models, and full-fledged data mining. Querying never takes place in the data staging area. By definition, querying takes place on a data warehouse presentation server. Querying, obviously, is the whole point of using the data warehouse.

- **Data Feedback/Feeding in Reverse.**   There are two important places where data flows "uphill" in the opposite direction from the traditional flow we have discussed in this section. First, we may upload a cleaned dimension description from the data staging area to a legacy system. This is desirable when the legacy system recognizes the value of the improved data. Second, we may upload the results of a complex query or a model run or a data mining analysis back into a data mart. This would be a natural way to capture the value of a complex query that takes the form of many rows and columns that the user wants to save.

- **Auditing.** At times it is critically important to know where the data came from and what were the calculations performed. In Chapter 6, we discuss a technique for creating special audit records during the extract and transformation steps in the data staging area. These audit records are linked directly to the real data in such a way that a user can ask for the audit record (the lineage) of the data at any time.

- **Securing.** Every data warehouse has an exquisite dilemma: the need to publish the data widely to as many users as possible with the easiest-to-use interfaces, but at the same time protect the valuable sensitive data from hackers, snoopers, and industrial spies. The development of the Internet has drastically amplified this dilemma. The data warehouse team must now include a new senior member: the data warehouse security architect. Data warehouse security must be managed centrally, from a single console. Users must be able to access all the constituent data marts of the data warehouse with a single sign-on. In Chapter 12, we present an in-depth discussion of security issues in the data warehouse and what you should do about them.

- **Backing Up and Recovering.** Since data warehouse data is a flow of data from the legacy systems on through to the data marts and eventually onto the users' desktops, a real question arises about where to take the necessary snapshots of the data for archival purposes and disaster recovery. Additionally, it may be even more complicated to back up and recover all of the metadata that greases the wheels of the data warehouse operation. In Chapter 9, we discuss the various kinds of backup activities, and what a realistic recovery operation would entail.

THE BIG DATA WAREHOUSE DEBATES

At the time of writing this book, the data warehouse market is in the middle of a number of evolutionary changes. As an industry, we have thousands of working data marts and data warehouses under our belts. We must now revisit some of the original assumptions and restrictions we placed on ourselves in the late 1980s and early 1990s. And of course, we have very different technology to work with. In early 1998, $10,000 could buy a machine with twin 300 MHz processors, 512 MB of random access memory, and 50 GB of fast disk drive. This machine can sit on a fast Ethernet system and run any of the major relational databases, even DB2. Although many data marts need a bigger machine than this, one wonders if terabyte data marts on PC class machines are just around the corner.

At the same time, the data warehouse market has reacted strongly to the difficulty of planning and implementing a single, undifferentiated, master data warehouse for the whole enterprise. This job is just too overwhelming for most organizations and most mortal designers to even think about.

The future of data warehousing is modular, cost effective, incrementally designed, distributed data marts. The data warehouse technology will be a rich mixture of large monolithic machines that grind through massive data sets with parallel processing, together with many separate small machines (i.e., maybe only terabyte data marts!) nibbling away on individual data sets that may be granular, mildly aggregated, or highly aggregated. The separate machines will be tied together with navigator software that will serve as switchboards for dispatching queries to the servers best able to respond.

The future of data warehousing is in software advances and design discipline. Although the largest machines will continue to be even more effective at parallel processing, the smallest machines will become proportionally more powerful due to hardware advances. The biggest gains in performance, analysis power, and user interface effectiveness, however, will come from better algorithms and tighter, more predictable data designs. By adhering to the discipline of dimensional modeling, a data warehouse will be in a much better position to ride the advances being made in database software technology.

At the time of this writing, the most visible discussions in data warehousing included the topics listed in the next section. We will not develop the full arguments in this chapter, but we make our summary positions clear.

Data Warehouse Modeling

As we have already remarked several times, we believe strongly in dimensional modeling for the presentation phase of the data warehouse. Chapter 5 leads off with a detailed justification for this approach. To summarize, dimensional modeling should be used in all the presentation servers of a data warehouse because, compared to entity-relation (E/R) modeling, this approach yields predictable, understandable designs that users can use and assimilate and that can be queried with high performance. Understandability and performance are the twin, nonnegotiable requirements of the data warehouse. The dimensional approach, unlike the E/R approach, does not require the database to be restructured or the queries to be rewritten when new data is introduced into the warehouse or when the relationships among data elements must be revised. A dimensional data mart, unlike the E/R data mart, does not need to anticipate the user's queries and is very resilient to changes in user analysis patterns.

Data Marts and Data Warehouses

Again, as we have already described, the data warehouse is nothing more than the union of its constituent data marts. These data marts avoid being stovepipes by being organized in a Bus Architecture around conformed dimensions and conformed facts. The main data design task for the data warehouse team is identifying and establishing these conformed dimensions and facts. The opposite perspective, which we disagree with, is that the data warehouse is a nonqueryable, E/R structured, centralized store of data and that data marts are disjoint and incomplete summarization of the central data warehouse that are spun off when the users demand a particular kind of analysis.

As a historical footnote, the idea that a data warehouse can be built incrementally from a series of data marts with conformed dimensions was fully described by Ralph Kimball in a DBMS magazine article in August 1996. Other descriptions of this technique, notably the "Enterprise Data Mart Architecture" with "common dimensions" and "common facts," appeared in the literature a year later. These descriptions are virtually identical to Kimball's work. The original terms "conformed dimensions" and "conformed facts" were described by Nielsen Marketing Research to Ralph Kimball in 1984, and referred to Nielsen's practice at that time of tying together syndicated scanner data with customers' internal shipments data. The terms "dimension" and "fact" originated from developments conducted jointly by General Mills and Dartmouth University in the late 1960s. It is clear that these ideas for combining data marts had been invented and introduced into the commercial marketplace long before the current generation of industry experts and consultants, even if we didn't call them data marts.

Distributed versus Centralized Data Warehouses

We feel that the tide has been coming in for some time in this industry. The idea that an organization's data warehouse is supported by a single, centralized mainframe-class machine is about as realistic as the 1950s idea that you only need one computer in an organization. At the personal computing level, we already have tens of thousand of computers in large organizations. The data warehouse is already following suit. Future data warehouses will consist of dozens or hundreds of separate machines with widely different operating systems and widely different database systems, including all flavors of OLAP. If designed correctly, these machines will share a uniform architecture of conformed dimensions and conformed facts that will allow them to be fused into a coherent whole.

We think that these last two topics, namely data warehouses consisting of many data marts and the enterprise data warehouse being a distributed system, will fuse together into a single architectural view. This view allows both the "hub and spoke" view of an overall data warehouse as well as a fully distributed view of the warehouse. We don't in any way oppose the idea of a large monolithic machine at the middle of a data warehouse operation. Some organizations will find that this makes most sense for them. Inside that monolithic machine will be hundreds of tables, organized by subject areas. We will call these groups of tables "data marts," and they will only function as a seamless whole if they possess conformed dimensions.

SUMMARY

We have defined all the parts of the data warehouse environment shown in Figure 1.1, and we have described how they work together. We have briefly touched on the big discussions taking place in the data warehouse industry today. In the next chapter it is time to turn our attention to the Business Dimensional Lifecycle, which is the framework for the rest of the book.

Project Management and Requirements

CHAPTER 2

The Business
Dimensional Lifecycle

Before we delve into the specifics of data warehouse design, development, and deployment, we will provide an overall methodology by introducing the Business Dimensional Lifecycle. The Business Dimensional Lifecycle provides the framework that ties together the content of this book. It sets the stage and provides placeholders for the detailed information that unfolds in the following chapters.

This chapter begins with historical background on the evolution of the Business Dimensional Lifecycle. We formally introduce the steps of the lifecycle and the associated diagram. Each high-level task or component of the Business Dimensional Lifecycle is then described. Finally, we provide general guidelines for effectively using the lifecycle throughout your project.

We recommend that all readers take the time to peruse this brief introductory chapter, even if you are involved in only a single facet of the data warehouse project. We believe it is beneficial for the entire team to understand the overall methodology. This chapter is written to help you see the big picture. For now, we will focus on the forest; subsequent chapters will get down to the tree, leaf, bark, and root level.

LIFECYCLE EVOLUTION

The Business Dimensional Lifecycle presented in this book first took root at Metaphor Computer Systems in the mid-1980s. Many of you have probably heard of Metaphor as it has found a place in data warehousing folklore, but you may not be aware of the specifics. Briefly, Metaphor was a pioneering decision support vendor that was founded in 1982. At that time, Metaphor's product was based on LAN technology with a relational database server platform and user-friendly GUI client. Sounds strangely familiar, doesn't it? At any rate, Metaphor focused on this industry when it was called "decision support," long before the term *data warehousing* came into use.

The authors of this book worked together during the early days at Metaphor implementing decision support solutions. At the time, there were no industry best practices or formal written methodologies. The authors and other Metaphor colleagues began developing techniques and approaches to deal with the idiosyncrasies of decision support. We had been groomed in traditional development methodologies, but we modified and enhanced those practices to address the unique challenges of providing direct data access to business end users while considering growth and extensibility for the long haul.

Over the years, the authors have been involved with literally hundreds of data warehouse projects. Many have been wildly successful, some have met minimum expectations, and a few have failed in spectacular ways. Each project taught us a lesson. In addition, we have each had the opportunity to learn from many talented individuals and organizations over the years. Our approaches and techniques have been refined and honed over time—and distilled into *The Data Warehouse Lifecycle Toolkit*.

Successful implementation of a data warehouse depends on the appropriate integration of numerous tasks and components. It is not enough to have the perfect data model or best-of-breed technology alone—you need to coordinate the many facets of a data warehouse project, much like a conductor must unify the many instruments in an orchestra. A soloist cannot carry a full orchestra. Likewise, the data warehouse implementation effort needs to demonstrate strength across all aspects of the project for success. The Business Dimensional Lifecycle is similar to the conductor's score. It ensures that the project pieces are brought together in the right order and at the right time.

In spite of dramatic advancements in technology since the early days of Metaphor in the 1980s, the basic constructs of the Business Dimensional Lifecycle have remained strikingly constant. Our approach to designing, developing, and deploying data warehouses is tried and true. It has been tested with projects across virtually every industry, business function, and technology platform. The Business Dimensional Lifecycle approach has been proven to work.

LIFECYCLE APPROACH

The overall Lifecycle approach to data warehouse implementation is illustrated in Figure 2.1. This diagram depicts the sequence of high-level tasks required for effective data warehouse design, development, and deployment. The diagram shows the overall project roadmap, in which each box serves as a guidepost or mile (or kilometer) marker.

Project Planning

The Lifecycle begins with project planning, as one would expect. Project planning addresses the definition and scoping of the data warehouse project, including readiness assessment and business justification. These are critical early tasks due to the high visibility and costs associated with most warehouse projects. From there, project planning focuses on resource and skill-level staffing requirements, coupled with project task assignments, duration, and sequencing. The resulting integrated

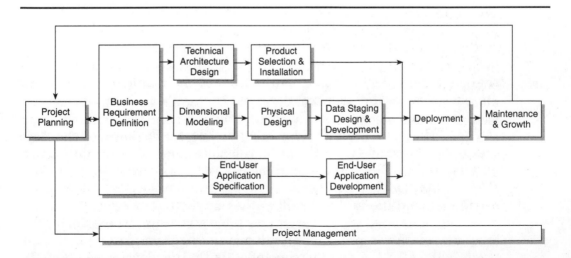

FIGURE 2.1   The Business Dimensional Lifecycle diagram.

project plan identifies all tasks associated with the Business Dimensional Lifecycle and notes the parties involved. It serves as the cornerstone for the ongoing management of your data warehouse project. Project planning is dependent on the business requirements, as denoted by the two-way arrow between these activities.

Business Requirements Definition

A data warehouse's likelihood for success is greatly increased by a sound understanding of the business end users and their requirements. Without this understanding, data warehousing will likely become an exercise in futility for the project team. The approach used to gather knowledge workers' analytic requirements differs significantly from more traditional, data-driven requirements analysis. Data warehouse designers must understand the key factors driving the business to effectively determine business requirements and translate them into design considerations. The business requirements establish the foundation for the three parallel tracks focused on technology, data, and end user applications. Chapter 4 provides a comprehensive discussion of gathering business requirements.

Data Track: Dimensional Modeling

The definition of the business requirements determines the data needed to address business users' analytical requirements. Designing data models to support these analyses requires a different approach than that used for operational systems design. We begin by constructing a matrix that represents key business processes and their dimensionality. The matrix serves as a blueprint to ensure that your data warehouse is extensible across the organization over time.

From there, we conduct a more detailed data analysis of relevant operational source systems. Coupling this data analysis with our earlier understanding of business requirements, we then develop a dimensional model. This model identifies the fact table grain, associated dimensions, attributes, and hierarchical drill paths and facts. The logical database design is completed with appropriate table structures and primary/foreign key relationships. The preliminary aggregation plan is also developed. This set of activities concludes with the development of the source-to-target data mapping.

Dimensional modeling concepts are discussed in Chapters 5–7. Chapter 5 provides an introduction and justification for dimensional modeling, while Chapter 6 covers advanced dimensional modeling topics. Chapter 7 describes the recommended approach and process for developing a dimensional model.

Data Track: Physical Design

Physical database design focuses on defining the physical structures necessary to support the logical database design. Primary elements of this process include defining naming standards and setting up the database environment. Preliminary indexing and partitioning strategies are also determined. Physical database design is addressed in Chapter 15.

Data Track: Data Staging Design and Development

The data staging design and development process is typically the most underestimated data warehouse project task. The data staging process has three major steps: extraction, transformation, and load. The extract process always exposes data quality issues that have been buried within the operational source systems. Since data quality significantly impacts data warehouse credibility, you need to address these quality problems during data staging. To further complicate matters, you need to design and build two warehouse staging processes—one for the initial population of the data warehouse and another for the regular, incremental loads. Details about developing the data staging process are provided in Chapter 16.

Technology Track: Technical Architecture Design

Data warehouse environments require the integration of numerous technologies. The technical architecture design establishes the overall architecture framework and vision. You will need to consider three factors —your business requirements, current technical environment, and planned strategic technical directions—simultaneously to establish the data warehouse technical architecture design. Chapter 8 provides an introduction to data warehouse technical architecture. Specific architecture discussions for the back room and front room are presented in Chapters 9 and 10, respectively. Chapter 11 highlights the architecture's infrastructure and metadata. Finally, a "graduate course" on data warehouse security and the impact of the Internet is provided in Chapter 12.

Technology Track: Product Selection and Installation

Using your technical architecture design as a framework, specific architectural components such as the hardware platform, database management system, data staging tool, or data access tool will need to be evaluated and selected. A standard technical evaluation process is defined along with specific evaluation factors for each architectural component. Once the products have been evaluated and selected, they are then installed and thoroughly tested to ensure appropriate end-to-end integration within your data warehouse environment. Chapter 13 highlights the architecture design, technology evaluation, and subsequent selection and installation processes.

Application Track: End User Application Specification

We recommend defining a set of standard end user applications since not all business users need ad hoc access to the data warehouse. Application specifications describe the report template, user driven parameters, and required calculations. These specifications ensure that the development team and business users have a common understanding of the applications to be delivered. Details regarding these specifications for end user applications are provided in Chapter 17.

Application Track: End User Application Development

Following application specification, the development of end user applications involves configuring the tool metadata and constructing the specified reports. Optimally, these applications are built using an advanced data access tool that provides significant productivity gains for the application development team. In addition, it offers a powerful mechanism for business users to easily modify existing report templates. Chapter 17 describes the end user application development process.

Deployment

Deployment represents the convergence of technology, data, and end user applications accessible from the business users' desktop. Extensive planning is required to ensure that these puzzle pieces fit together properly. Business user education integrating all aspects of the convergence must be developed and delivered. In addition, user support and communication or feedback strategies should be established before any business users have access to the data warehouse. As emphasized in Chapter 18, it is critical that the deployment be well orchestrated—deployment should be deferred if all the pieces are not ready for release.

Maintenance and Growth

Plenty of work remains following the initial deployment of the data warehouse. You need to continue focusing on your business users by providing them with ongoing support and education. You also need to focus attention on the back room, ensuring that the processes and procedures are in place for effective ongoing operation of the warehouse. Data warehouse acceptance and performance metrics should be measured over time and logged to support marketing of the data warehouse. Finally, your maintenance game plan should include a broad-reaching communication strategy.

If you have used the Business Dimensional Lifecycle thus far, your data warehouse is bound to evolve and grow. Unlike traditional systems development initiatives, change should be viewed as a sign of success, not failure. Prioritization processes must be established to deal with this business user demand for evolution and growth. After the project priorities are identified, we go back to the beginning of the lifecycle, leveraging and building upon what has already been established in the data warehouse environment, with a focus on the new requirements. Chapter 19 details our recommendations to address the long-term health and growth of your data warehouse.

Project Management

Project management ensures that the Business Dimensional Lifecycle activities remain on track and in sync. As illustrated in Figure 2.1, project management activities occur throughout the lifecycle. These activities focus on monitoring project status, issue tracking, and change control to preserve scope boundaries. Finally, project management includes the development of a comprehensive project communication plan that addresses both the business and information systems organizations. Ongoing communication is absolutely critical to managing expectations, and managing expectations is absolutely critical to achieving your data warehousing goals. Chapter 3 also details these project management activities.

GUIDELINES FOR USING THE BUSINESS DIMENSIONAL LIFECYCLE

The Business Dimensional Lifecycle diagram lays out the general flow that occurs during a data warehouse implementation. It identifies high-level task sequencing and highlights the activities that should be happening concurrently throughout the technology, data, and application tracks. For example, you should not attempt to complete your physical data design and begin building your data staging area without a clear understanding of the business requirements, overall technical architecture design, and specific technical architecture selections, including the end user data access tool.

The Business Dimensional Lifecycle, however, does not attempt to reflect an absolute project timeline. As you likely noticed, each box or mile marker in Figure 2.1 is the same width, with the exception of project management. If you have any experience with data warehousing, you know that the magnitude of resources and time required for each lifecycle box is *not* equal. Clearly, the reader should not lay a ruler along the bottom of the diagram and divide the tasks into timeline months. Focus on sequencing and concurrency, not absolute timelines.

As with most project methodology and management tools, you may need to customize the Business Dimensional Lifecycle to address the unique needs of your organization. If this is the case, we applaud your adoption of the framework, as well as your creativity. Truth be told, we usually tailor the specific lifecycle tasks for each new project. Throughout this book, we attempt to describe nearly everything you need to think about during the design, development, and deployment of a data warehouse. Don't let the volume of material overwhelm you. Not every detail of every lifecycle task will be performed on every project. We understand that all systems development is based upon compromises. However, in our experience, successful projects will perform all the tasks at some point—it's just a matter of when and how.

Finally, as we'll further describe in Chapter 3, the Business Dimensional Lifecycle is most effective when used to implement projects of manageable yet meaningful scope. It is nearly impossible to tackle everything at once, so don't let your business users, fellow team members, or management force that approach. On the other hand, it is extremely doable to design, develop and deploy your data warehouse environment through multiple iterations using the Business Dimensional Lifecycle.

BUSINESS DIMENSIONAL LIFECYCLE MILE MARKERS AND NAVIGATION AIDS

You'll find references to the Business Dimensional Lifecycle throughout the book. For starters, each chapter title page will include a miniature graphic version of the Business Dimensional Lifecycle diagram (Figure 2.1), which highlights where you are within the overall Lifecycle framework. You should view this as your Lifecycle mile marker. Be forewarned that there is not always a one-to-one relationship between mile markers and book chapters. In some cases, a single chapter will address multiple markers, as in Chapter 3, which covers both project planning and project management. In other cases, multiple chapters will cover a single mile marker, such as Chapters 5–7, which discuss dimensional modeling.

In addition to the you-are-here mile marker, the process-oriented chapters will include the following common elements as appropriate:

- **List of detailed project plan tasks and associated responsibilities with the mile marker.**   These listings are then pulled together into a complete integrated project plan in Appendix A.
- **Key project team roles.**
- **Estimating considerations.**   Every project is so unique it's nearly impossible to provide specific time estimates for each mile marker. Instead, we provide a list of variables or dependencies you should consider as you allocate time to each mile marker on your project plan.
- **Listing of the supporting templates associated with the mile marker.**   We have provided sample templates to support your use of the Business Dimensional Lifecycle. The templates are included on the companion CD-ROM.

SUMMARY

The Business Dimensional Lifecycle provides the framework to organize the numerous tasks required to implement a successful data warehouse. The Business Dimensional Lifecycle has evolved through years of hands-on experience and is firmly grounded in the realities you face today. Now, with the Lifecycle framework in mind, let's get started!

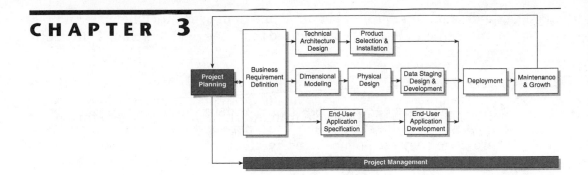

CHAPTER 3

Project Planning and Management

Now that you have a high-level understanding of the Business Dimensional Lifecycle, it is time to dig in and get started. This chapter explores the considerations and activities associated with the project planning and project management boxes of the Lifecycle diagram.

The chapter is organized into three major sections. The first section focuses on defining your data warehouse project. It provides advice and guidelines for getting started with your data warehouse initiative, from assessing readiness through scoping and justification for funding. The middle section concentrates on detailed project planning activities, including staffing and project plan development. Last, we discuss considerations for running your data warehouse project, focusing on the unique aspects of a warehouse initiative.

This chapter is geared toward people who are responsible for the overall data warehouse project, regardless of whether they are part of the information systems (IS) or the functional business organization. Both IS and business management should read the chapter to better understand the overall data warehouse project landscape and their essential role. Other project team members would also benefit from a common understanding of these project planning and management challenges and recommendations, but it is not required that they read this chapter in depth.

DEFINE THE PROJECT

So you have been asked to spearhead the data warehouse project at your company. What does that mean and where do you start? Unfortunately, there is no easy recipe for the early, up-front activities associated with defining the warehouse project and securing funding—there is a very low degree of repeatability in this phase of the lifecycle because it varies so greatly from one organization to another. To further complicate matters, the activities associated with project definition are seldom linear. You will find yourself looping between activities in the real world.

Nevertheless, chances are your organization fits one of the following scenarios:

- **Demand from a lone business zealot.**   In this scenario, one business executive has a vision about getting better access to better information to make better decisions. We probably encounter this situation in more than half of our engagements. In many ways, this is the most desirable and manageable situation—unless the zealot doesn't have what it takes to be an effective sponsor or leaves to take a new job with a different organization in the middle of the project.

- **Too much demand.**   In this scenario, multiple business executives are voicing a need for better information. This scenario is slightly more complicated than the first, because you need to prioritize the requirements before proceeding, but that can typically be accomplished without too much difficulty.

- **In search of demand.**   This scenario might also be viewed as demand from a lone CIO. Your CIO doesn't want to be the only kid on the block without a data warehouse. This is by far the most challenging scenario to deal with. Based on our experience, most if not all organizations can benefit from a decision support solution, even if the demand doesn't currently exist. However, it will require effort to ferret out the demand before you can get rolling with your data warehouse.

Regardless of your situation scenario, we suggest that you take a moment to assess your organization's readiness for a data warehouse before proceeding full steam ahead with the project. The following material on readiness factors is intended to help you, your management, and your sponsors understand what it takes for an organization to achieve success with data warehousing. You don't necessarily need glowing marks in each area to "pass" and move forward. However, all involved parties should be keenly aware of any shortfalls or vulnerabilities and work together to devise strategies to shore them up.

 Before beginning a data warehouse or data mart project, make sure you understand whether there is demand and where that demand is coming from. If you have no strong business sponsor and no eager users, postpone the project.

Assess Your Readiness for a Data Warehouse

Based on our experience, five key factors must be in place before you begin detailed work on the design and development of your data warehouse. These factors establish the foundation to ensure you can successfully build your data warehouse. If you are unable to confidently give your organization a relative passing grade on the combined factors, we strongly suggest slowing down and reconsidering whether your organization is ready for a data warehouse. Our experiences indicate that readiness factor shortfalls will *not* correct themselves over time. It is far better to pull the plug on the project before significant investment has been made than it is to continue marching down a path filled with hazards and obstacles.

Strong Business Management Sponsor(s)

Strong support and sponsorship from business management is the most critical factor when assessing data warehouse readiness. Strong business sponsors share a number of key characteristics. First of all, they have a vision for the potential impact of a data warehouse. Strong sponsors possess a firm personal conviction about their vision, which is generally demonstrated by their willingness to be accountable for it.

Strong business sponsors are influential leaders within the organization. Typically, they have demonstrated a solid track record of success and are well respected by others. In other words, they have organizational clout. Strong business sponsors are typically politically astute and well connected. Interestingly, the lone zealot sponsor described in the situation scenarios is often new to an organization—they come on board and have gung-ho visions of changing the organization. We have seen the new kid achieve success with a data warehouse, but it is a riskier proposition given their lack of knowledge about the culture, players, politics and process.

The ideal business sponsor is not only strong, but realistic. It helps if they have a basic understanding of data warehousing concepts, including the iterative development cycle, to avoid unrealistic expectations. Effective sponsors are able to accept short-term problems and setbacks because they are focused on a long-term success of the project. Realistic sponsors are willing to compromise. They are also able to make the tough decisions and live with the consequences.

Finally, successful data warehouse teams typically cultivate several strong business sponsors within their organization—in other words, don't put all your eggs in one basket. It is not uncommon for a data warehouse to stall in the wake of the departure of a sole business sponsor. The sponsor's replacement typically doesn't have much time for their predecessor's pet project.

 Your project will live and die with your business sponsor. Be sure you have a business sponsor, and stay in communication with that individual.

Compelling Business Motivation

A data warehouse is an enabler to address specific critical business requirements. Period. Organizations that have successfully implemented data warehouses often share a common characteristic: an organizational sense of urgency caused by a compelling business motivation. Sometimes competition and changes in the competitive landscape are the motivators. Internal crisis has motivated other organizations. Elsewhere, the strategic vision of a potential marketplace opportunity is the overpowering motivator. If your executives have determined that survival over the next decade is dependent on being a customer-centric organization, who is going to question a data warehouse initiative that brings the vision of an entirely new way of conducting business to reality. Some organizations have historically grown through acquisition, and the integration necessary to understand performance across the organization is nearly impossible without developing an integrated data warehouse.

Data warehouses that align with these strategic business motivations stand a good chance of succeeding. Likewise, business justification becomes nearly a nonissue if the data warehouse is poised to support a compelling business motivation. In these situations, the organization also likely possesses the economic willpower to continue investing in the data warehouse for the long haul. Organizations in the midst of complete upheaval, such as significant downsizing or unfriendly merger discussions, are probably too distracted to launch a successful data warehouse initiative.

IS/Business Partnership

Successful data warehouses result from a joint business and IS effort in which both groups share responsibility for the initiative. Neither group is likely to achieve success if they try to build a warehouse on their own. The good news is that a data warehouse project is the perfect opportunity to fix a broken relationship between IS and the business community, assuming both parties are willing to come to the table and talk.

Current Analytic Culture

Data warehousing is all about providing improved access to better information to support decision making. If your business community does not currently place value on information and analyses, its readiness for a data warehouse is questionable. The adage "you can bring a horse to water, but you can't make it drink" certainly applies to data warehousing. The most successful data warehouses are deployed in organizations in which fact-based decision making is encouraged and rewarded. If your business users prefer to rely on gut feelings, think twice before investing resources to construct an elegant data warehouse environment. At a minimum, be prepared for the additional burden of shifting the cultural mindset.

Feasibility

The term *feasibility* commonly refers exclusively to technical feasibility. Today's technology offerings seem to make almost anything possible, although you are in far better shape if the overall infrastructure to support your data warehouse is already in place and robust.

The primary feasibility concern with data warehousing relates to the data itself. If the data required to support the compelling business motivation is too filthy, overly complex for the initial effort (e.g., located in twenty unique manufacturing systems at sites around the world), or not even collected, you have a significant feasibility issue on your hands. Likewise, your data warehouse timeline will expand if common business rules and definitions have not already been agreed to across the organization.

Take the Readiness "Litmus Test"

Let's now see how your organization stacks up against the five strategic readiness factors. It is all too easy to *say* that you have a strong sponsor, but do you really? Take the following self-check test to bring these strategic readiness factors into focus so you can determine if you are ready to move forward with a data warehouse initiative—you can pull out your pink and blue highlighters if you want to better visualize the litmus paper readings (Figure 3.1).

Evaluate your Combined Readiness Factors

As we indicated earlier, the five readiness factors are not equally weighted in importance. Strong business management sponsorship bears a disproportionate share of the overall importance—around 60 percent of the total in our experience. Compelling business motivation and feasibility each receive about 15 percent of the weighting, and the remaining two factors split the remaining 10 percent.

Business sponsorship is critically important for a number of reasons. Strong sponsors can formulate and articulate the necessary vision for data warehousing and its impact on the organization. Data warehouses tend to be expensive, with support and growth costs that never end. Strong sponsorship, coupled with a solid financial return, is needed to sustain the economic willpower for the long haul. A strong sponsor is also able to command the appropriate resources even when competing with other mission-critical projects. Finally, warehouses are often the

Readiness Factor	Low Readiness		High Readiness
Strong Business Management Sponsor			
	Not well respected	⇕	Considerable organizational clout
	Can take weeks for team to gain access	⇕	Readily available to team
	"I'll get back to you on that"	⇕	Quick, decisive resolution to issues
	Hope "you" get it done	⇕	Active, vocal and visible supporter—willing to put own neck on the line
	You can deliver this to 250 users next month, right?	⇕	Realistic expectations
	"A data whatta?"	⇕	Data warehouse savvy
Compelling Business Motivation			
	"And your point is?"	⇕	Survival dependent on data warehouse
	Funding is a big problem	⇕	Cost is not an issue—we can't afford not to do this!
	"Shifting sands" vision	⇕	Clearly articulated vision
	Ten different views of the solution	⇕	Consistent view of the solution
	Tactical issue	⇕	Strategic issue
	Cost savings opportunity	⇕	Revenue enhancement opportunity
	Unable to quantify the payback	⇕	Huge payback
IS/Business Partnership			
	Business engages outside consultant without IS knowledge	⇕	Business and IS work hand-in-hand
	Business unit creates own pseudo-IS team to build a data warehouse	⇕	IS actively engaged with business unit
	"We can't trust any numbers from our systems"	⇕	Strong confidence in existing reporting environment
	It takes "years" to get a new ad hoc request turned around	⇕	Quick IS response to ad hoc requests
	Users don't even submit requests anymore	⇕	Short existing user request backlog

FIGURE 3.1   Data warehouse readiness litmus test.

Readiness Factor	Low Readiness		High Readiness
Current Analytic Culture			
	"Gut feel" decision making	⇕	Decision making relies on facts and figures
	Users don't ask for data	⇕	Business users clamor for access to data—"Just get me the data and I'll figure it out"
	Users don't look at current reports	⇕	Current reports are consistently rekeyed into spreadsheets for analysis and historical trending
	Current reports used as doorstops until the recycling bin comes by	⇕	Current reports are dog eared, highlighted and filled with yellow self adhesive notes
	Users have secretaries log on and print off e-mail to read it	⇕	Users are very computer literate
	Finance is extremely possessive of bottom line performance figures	⇕	Information shared openly throughout the organization
Feasibility			
	Data warehouse would require purchase of all new technology	⇕	Robust technical infrastructure in place
	Everyone and their uncle is committed to the year 2000 project	⇕	Experienced resources available
	Reliable data won't be available until after the enterprise resource planning (ERP) implementation	⇕	Quality data available

FIGURE 3.1 *Continued.*

catalyst for cultural change—a strong sponsor will embrace and facilitate this change.

Strong business sponsorship can cover a multitude of shortcomings elsewhere on the project. Conversely, if your project has everything going for it but lacks a strong business sponsor, you have a very steep hill to climb. Even the most elegantly designed data warehouse cannot overcome a lack of business sponsorship.

Research conducted by Barbara Haley of the University of Virginia confirms our experienced-based assertions. In her 1997 doctoral dissertation titled "Implementing the Decision Support Infrastructure: Key Success Factors in Data Warehousing," she states that "management support is a critical factor impacting the success of a data warehouse implementation."

At this point, you need to evaluate your combined readiness factor score giving consideration to the weightings described earlier. As we mentioned, with the exception of business sponsorship, you don't need high marks in each area to pass, but any shortcomings represent risks to the project. Risk-reduction strategies and contingency plans should be developed in conjunction with your management and sponsors to address any shortfalls.

Your next step depends on your level of data warehouse readiness, coupled with your specific situation scenario. If you originally described your situation as "in search of demand," you clearly have significant work to do before you can start building the data warehouse. On the other hand, you may have a lone business zealot requesting a data warehouse, yet still have significant work to do if the zealot lacks the sponsor characteristics described earlier.

We outline several alternatives for addressing readiness shortcomings in the following section. If you are confident of your readiness, with a strong business sponsor targeting a specific, compelling, high-payback business requirement, you can bypass this section and proceed directly to developing your preliminary scope. However, if you have any doubts, the following techniques will help relieve your concerns, in addition to supporting the subsequent scoping and justification efforts.

Techniques to Address Readiness Shortfall

We describe the following techniques to address your data warehouse readiness shortfall as isolated activities; however, they are frequently used in conjunction with one another.

High-Level Business Requirements Analysis

This first approach is effective in numerous situations—whether you are in search of demand, trying to better understand requirements to prioritize overwhelming demand or looking for new demand due to a poorly positioned or focused lone zealot.

Chapter 4 spells out detailed tactics and techniques for effectively gathering business requirements. Rather than repeat that material here, we suggest you jump forward to Chapter 4, since these techniques apply here with a few minor adjustments. For now, we want to focus on high-level business issues and the business value impact—we don't need to drop down to 500 feet to gather gory details for designing the dimensional data model. In general, you will want to uncover the following during a high-level requirements analysis with business management:

- Understand their key strategic business initiatives.
- Identify their key performance indicators or success metrics for each of the strategic business initiatives.
- Determine the core business processes they monitor and want to impact.
- Determine the potential impact on their performance metrics with improved access to improved business process information.

You will also need to conduct preliminary data discovery sessions, as described in Chapter 4, to identify any gaping data feasibility issues.

Business Requirements Prioritization

The next technique, prioritization of the business requirement opportunities, is often a follow-on activity to the high-level business requirements analysis just described. This business-centric technique is appropriate when you are evaluating several alternatives, struggling with justification, attempting to build organizational consensus on a warehouse game plan, or trying to mend a broken relationship between the business community and IS.

We first observed the highly effective facilitation-based technique described next while working with Sequent Computer Systems. In this scenario, key business and IS influencers participate in a facilitated session sponsored by either the CIO or business sponsor. The facilitation team and attendees must be well prepared to ensure an effective session similar to the pre-interview prep work described in Chapter 4.

The facilitated session begins with a review of meeting objectives, participant introductions, and session ground rules. The results of the high-level business requirement analysis are then presented as business "themes," that is reasonably well-defined, manageably sized opportunities to impact the business. Everyone at the meeting should have a consistent understanding of the requirements themes. The themes often focus on a single core business process, although not always.

The facilitator helps the group prioritize the business requirement themes based on two considerations—potential impact on the business and feasibility/readiness. The business influencers assign a priority to each theme depending on it is importance to the business based on potential dollar payback to the organization, strategic significance, availability of alternatives, political willpower, and so on. Optimally, the priority is expressed in a quantified dollar impact; alternatively, a "high/medium/low" or "1 to 10" ranking is assigned.

The business influencers at this meeting need to both represent their own departmental or divisional interests as well as those of the overall organization. We worked with one client who brought two baseball caps to the prioritization session. One was labeled with the corporation's name, and the other was labeled "divisional." The hat props were used by everyone in the meeting to encourage a focus on the needs of the overall entity, rather than the needs of a single user group.

After the business priorities have been set, the requirement themes are prioritized in terms of feasibility. Typically, the IS representatives apply similar "high/medium/low" or "1 to 10" feasibility rankings. Feasibility is largely a function of data availability, perceived ease of development and deployment, and resource availability and experience.

Finally, the business impact and feasibility priorities are brought together. As illustrated in Figure 3.2, quadrant analysis is used to diagram the combined priorities. Sometimes the themes are written on yellow self-adhesive pads for easy manipulation on the quadrant grid while interactively reaching group consensus on the combined priorities.

Optimally, the group has identified a requirement theme that has high business impact and a high feasibility score. If multiple themes receive a high business impact score, then the feasibility score is the tiebreaker.

Requirements themes in the upper-right quadrant, such as Theme B, are the ones you should initially focus on—they are highly feasible with high potential business impact. The remaining themes are less de-

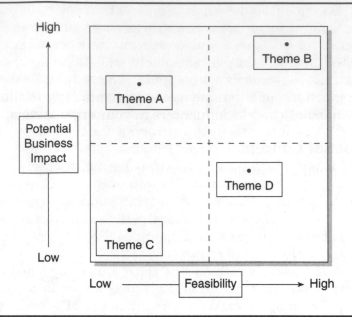

FIGURE 3.2   Quadrant analysis for requirement prioritization.
Chart from Sequent Computer Systems' Business Benefit Analysis offering.

sirable for various reasons. Theme A has high business impact but is extremely difficult to implement. It still warrants attention given its impact, but should not be the first one tackled by the data warehouse initiative. Theme D is more feasible, but it has little impact on the business. Requirement themes like C in the lower-left quadrant should be avoided like the plague—they have very little impact on the business and are difficult to implement.

This technique is effective for numerous reasons. First, it identifies a specific requirement that represents the highest impact that can be delivered in a reasonable time frame—what more could you ask for at this point? We have associated a measure of business benefit, in conjunction with feasibility, for each requirement so we avoid tackling pipe dreams. From the start, a business-based focus for data warehousing initiatives that boosts the long-term probability for success has been established. The session generates a prioritized roadmap for future development as the themes frequently translate into phased warehouse deliverables. The technique relies on consensus, so the attendees leave the session with buy-in and a sense of ownership for the direction, rather than the sponsor dictating a course of action. It also demonstrates and strengthens the partnership between the business and IS. Last, but not least, the scoping and business justification activities just got much easier if you have conducted an early facilitated session with key business and IS influencers in your organization.

Proof of Concept

The proof of concept is a small, low-cost effort to demonstrate the potential impact of a data warehouse project to the business community. Again, this technique may be used in conjunction with the others, perhaps to illustrate a high-priority business requirement that was uncovered using the earlier techniques.

Vendors have adopted the proof-of-concept technique to accelerate their sales cycle as it is difficult to sell something people don't understand or realize they need. Vendors often offer proof-of-concept packages that bundle software and services at a reduced price. They are usually presented under an attractive marketing name that starts with a descriptive word like *quick* or *fast* and ends with an action verb like *start* or *strike*. These bundled packages can be a valuable way to educate your organization and generate enthusiasm, but don't be fooled by the marketing hype. It is not possible to build a robust, business-based data warehouse with a flexible infrastructure and repeatable data staging process in four weeks.

 The proof of concept should be positioned as a "disposable" effort. While quick results are very positive, don't let the proof-of-concept development cause expectations to rise to unattainable heights.

Develop the Preliminary Scope

By now, you should be comfortable with your organization's overall readiness to proceed with a data warehouse. We need to begin putting a fence around the project scope and getting it justified so you have the funding to proceed. In reality, scope and justification go hand-in-hand—

it is nearly impossible to complete one without the other, so teams often loop between the two activities. For clarity, we will present the concepts separately in the next two sections, but these activities will probably be intermixed on your project.

Before we get started with specifics, it is important to first discuss *what* we are scoping. Once again, this varies widely by organization. Are we scoping and requesting funding to cover the short-term requirements definition and design phases? Or the first delivery of data warehouse information to the business community? Or the whole three-year enchilada? It is almost certain that the farther you try to see, the worse your vision becomes. Consequently, defining the scope and building the justification becomes much more perilous the further you need to predict into the future.

Project managers are most frequently asked at this stage to put together a scope and justification for the initial delivery of warehouse information to business users. Throughout the remainder of this section, we will proceed with this assumption. Scoping is still a best-guess exercise at this point, but you need funding to further explore business requirements and feasibility in order to more crisply define scope. In general, we are attempting to make as few promises as possible with this preliminary scope, yet fill in enough of the picture to identify benefits and costs associated with going forward.

Here are general guidelines for developing the preliminary data warehouse project scope:

 Define your scope based on your business requirements, not calendar deadlines.

- **Defining scope is a joint effort performed by IS and business representatives.**   Scope is usually established to address a specific business requirement. Obviously, a reasonable understanding of these requirements is a prerequisite to defining scope. Scope is occasionally established by a given target delivery date, and then the deliverables are managed to meet the delivery date. While we have seen this approach work, it is a riskier path.
- **The initial data warehouse project scope should be meaningful yet manageable.**   *Meaningful* typically translates into busi-

ness value or impact derived from addressing a well-defined business requirement. Many teams' first instinct is to start where no one will notice, but the data warehouse project will go nowhere if no one notices.

Manageable means doable. In other words, start small. The Lifecycle is intended to support iterative development of your data warehouse. We encourage launching smaller, quicker-to-market, four-to-eight month development projects rather than tackling the monolithic multiyear effort in one big gulp. There are two key variables to consider in terms of satisfying the "small" recommendations: the number of source systems and the number of users. The source data variable is the one most likely to cause uncontrollable scope creep.

- **Focus initially on a single business requirement supported by data from a single source process.**   It is much too broad to say that you are going to serve the needs of the marketing or actuarial departments. Their analyses look at information from multiple business processes. Instead, try to define your scope in terms of a single business process, like customer orders or claims payments, rather than extracting and integrating information from multiple business processes generated by multiple source systems. The data staging effort grows exponentially with each additional major source system. Don't get greedy and attempt multiple concurrent initial projects to satisfy political pressures. No one will be satisfied with this approach.
- **Limit the number of users who will initially access the data warehouse.**   On average, a user count somewhere around 25 supports this manageability requirement, with a plan to roll out quickly after this core user base has been established.
- **Begin establishing success criteria for the project while scope is being defined.**   It is extremely important to understand what business management expects from the data warehouse project. More details will be described in Chapter 4 about establishing specific, measurable project success criteria.

 Your biggest risk is not understanding the difficulty of sourcing your data.

Once IS and business management have agreed on scope, it should be documented. Given the unknowns at this stage of the project, scope is destined to change. Regardless, write it down so everyone has a consistent understanding of the project's preliminary focus and motivating business requirements, anticipated data, target users, and estimated completion date at this time. It may also be appropriate to explicitly list data and analyses that will not be addressed with the initial project. By identifying what is outside of the scope, you are demonstrating that you have heard the users' requests and are not just ignoring them. Figure 3.3 shows a sample preliminary project scope.

The scope of your data warehouse project will likely change several times before your first business end users access the data warehouse. This is to be expected, since the scope becomes more clearly defined and more clearly negotiated with each step you take toward delivery. The project scope statement should not sit on a shelf—it should be reviewed frequently, revised as needed, and republished. Finally, it is important to recognize that scope *refinement* is different from scope *creep*. The goal of scope refinement is to retain the same sized box, although the contents may change; the dimensions of the box expand in the case of scope creep.

ADJUST SCOPE BASED ON PROJECT MAGNITUDE

Data warehouse projects take on many different forms. Although we have participated in hundreds of them, no two have been identical. As we mentioned in Chapter 2, you need to adjust scope and adapt the Lifecycle accordingly depending on the magnitude of your project.

Throughout this chapter and book, we have attempted to describe nearly everything you need to think about throughout the lifecycle of a data warehouse implementation. Don't let the weight and depth of the material overwhelm you. You can still deliver valuable information to business end users in less than six months, but you may not be able to dot all your *i*'s in the process.

Background
ACME wants to maximize its return on promotion investments. It currently spends approximately $40 million annually in promotional efforts. ACME's goal is to reduce promotion spending by 25% in three years.   The Promotion Data Mart project will create a decision support environment containing promotion information, complementing the earlier warehouse project focused on sales information. Brand teams, sales operations, and marketing research will have access to both the sales and promotion information to enable more effective promotion spending to improve ACME's return on promotion investments.

Phase 1 Scope
The initial phase (Phase 1) of the Promotion Data Mart is defined as follows: • Three years of historical internal promotion detail information. • Maximum of 25 initial users, with roll-out plans for 150 ultimate users in brands, sales operations, and marketing research. • Technical architecture for Phase 1 of the Promotion Data Mart will be based on . . . • Current project timeline calls for initial production deployment by the end of second quarter. • . . .

Exclusions From Phase 1 Scope
The following items are specifically excluded from the Phase 1 scope: • External data such as competitive sales and promotions information. • Support for nondomestic promotion programs. • . . .

Success Criteria
Several key success criteria have been designated for the Promotion Data Mart Project: • Provide a single source to support promotions-related analysis. • Reduce the time required to perform an promotions-related analysis. • Increase the effectiveness of promotion programs due to improved allocation decisions based on insights from the Promotion Data Mart. • . . .

Risks and Risk Reduction Action Plan
Phase 1 poses the following risks: • . . .

FIGURE 3.3   Sample initial project scope.

Build the Business Justification

Now that the project scope has been established with the business and IS sponsors and management, the project's business justification needs to be built. Justification is another joint activity that depends on a strong IS/business partnership; IS cannot develop the data warehouse justification in a vacuum.

Building the justification simply means that you are identifying the anticipated costs and benefits associated with the data warehouse project over time. You shouldn't let terms like *return on investment* (ROI) intimidate you—basically you are comparing the predicted financial return (i.e., business benefits) against the predicted investment (i.e., costs). Other traditional financial performance measurements such as net present value (NPV) or internal rate of return (IRR) are essentially variations on the theme. If you are unfamiliar or uncomfortable with these concepts, enlist the help of others in your organization who are seasoned veterans of this process.

In this next few sections, we will begin by reviewing the investment or cost side of the equation, followed by the more challenging return or benefits. Finally, we will pull the two components together to create the justification. Your organization probably has a standardized financial model for consistently analyzing project justifications; we will focus on deriving or estimating the numbers to input into your model.

Determine the Financial Investments and Costs

We will start first with the easier side of the equation. You should consider the following cost components when developing your financial justification. These costs begin now and continue for the foreseeable future. When in doubt, it is preferable to err on the side of overestimating costs rather than underbudgeting.

- **Hardware and software license purchase or lease expenses.** You should include all hardware components and/or upgrades, including database servers, application servers and client desktop hardware. On the software side, consider the database management system software, data staging tools, connectivity software, and desktop licenses. If you are unfamiliar with the technology components required for a data warehouse, refer to Chapters 8–13.

- **Ongoing maintenance expenses.**   Most hardware and software purchases will be accompanied by ongoing maintenance expenses. Be certain whether these maintenance charges are based on list price or your negotiated discount price.

- **Internal development resources.**   You need to do preliminary project planning to estimate resource headcount requirements at a high level.

- **External resources as required.**

- **Education for both the project team and business community.**

- **Ongoing support.**   You can't presume that the existing user help desk will suffice for data warehouse support. Also, unlike many systems, user support will not decline over time with the data warehouse.

- **Expenses to support scaleable growth.**   Depending on your planning horizon, you may need to consider ongoing expenses to support changing business requirements, loading of additional data, expanded user populations, new release upgrades, technology to support higher performance demands, and so on.

Determine the Financial Returns and Benefits

Now that the costs have been estimated, we will turn our attention to the business returns or benefits. Unfortunately, the financial benefits are much more difficult to quantify up front than the associated costs.

Business end users typically struggle to provide specific business impact numbers before building a data warehouse. They will request better access to better information. Unfortunately, this frequently heard request does not translate immediately into bottom-line business impact. Any personnel productivity gains provided by better access are likely to be negligible when compared to the potential impact of improved decision making. The layers of the onion need to be peeled back to understand the why, what if, and how much behind this seemingly innocent user request.

"A priori" data warehouse justification typically focuses on revenue or profit enhancement, rather than reducing costs. It is very difficult to justify a data warehouse by eliminating the costs associated with a mainframe-based reporting system. Unfortunately, the benefits that can be easily quantified typically aren't the significant ones. Instead, we focus on opportunities such as the following:

- Increasing revenue due to new sales to new customers, increased sales to existing customers (either cross-selling additional products or up-selling more expensive products), and so on.
- Increasing profit due to increased response rate to mailings, increased average sale per mailing, elimination of low-margin products, decreased raw material costs, decreased promotional spending, reduced fraudulent claim expense, reduced customer churn or turnover, and so on.
- Increasing customer service or quality levels due to improved service levels, reduced defect rates, increased closure rate on first call, and so on.
- Enabling a new information-based capability or market opportunity never before possible.

The key to ferreting out quantified business benefits from statements like the preceding is to keep asking probing questions. What would it mean to the business if you had . . . ? Would you be able to . . . ? How much is . . . worth? You need to continue questioning and searching for the component numbers that can be extrapolated into business benefits.

For example, assume the direct marketing manager said that better-targeted mailings would allow them to increase response rates by 20 percent. There is not enough information in that statement alone to derive the financial impact. You need to ask the follow -up questions to bring that high-level impact prediction down into dollars and cents. If you simply asked "On average, what is the revenue generated by a direct mail campaign?" and "How many campaigns to you run each year?" you would have the data needed to derive the financial impact from this 20 percent increase in response rate. Take the $700,000 average revenue per campaign times 12 campaigns per year times 20 percent increased response rate to come up with $1,680,000 in incremental revenue attributed to the 20 percent improvement in response. You will find additional quantification examples in the "Crunch the Numbers" sidebar.

CRUNCH THE NUMBERS

We have provided several additional benefit quantification examples to help convey how these elusive numbers are derived.

Reduce time to market.   Development estimates the average revenue derived from new products following launch is $50,000 per month. They believe they can reduce the development cycle and bring products to market six weeks sooner on average with better access to information. Fifteen new products are typically introduced each year.

The financial benefit is calculated as follows:

Each new product generates $50,000 revenue each month times 1.5 months due to the six-week cycle time reduction times 15 new products per year, which results in $1,125,000 incremental revenue per year.

Facilitate movement to new store format.   The Store Operations group believed that implementing a more effective fact-based selling approach would allow them to transition between 300 and 400 franchise stores to a new format each year. Store Ops agreed that the new format stores would show an average sales increase of $50,000 the first year. The company determined a 10 percent margin rate on the increased revenues.

The financial benefit is calculated as follows:

300 impacted stores per year times $50,000 increased revenue per store results in $15 million in increased sales revenue. Given a 10 percent profit margin rate, this results in increased profit of $1.5 million.

Improve customer acquisition capabilities.   Marketing believes improved customer segmentation analysis will enable the company to better target its marketing efforts on more appropriate candidates. They think they can reduce the cost of acquiring new customers by $75 each. In addition, they believe they can add 125,000 new customers per year.

The financial benefit is calculated as follows:

$75 reduction per customer in acquisition costs times 125,000 new customers per year results in $9,375,000 improved profitability per year.

Improve seasonal merchandise stocking. Merchandising has determined that it can improve its seasonal merchandise sales through better stocking strategies if given better access to information. Merchandising estimated the company could positively impact seasonal sales by 10 to 20 percent. Seasonal products represent approximately one-third of the company's $750 million in sales or about $250 million of sales revenues. The company determined a 12 percent margin rate on the increased revenues.

The financial benefit is calculated as follows:

A 10 percent improvement in seasonal sales represents an increase of $25 million in revenues. Multiplied by a 12 percent margin rate results in a $3 million profit improvement.

Focus catalog mailings more accurately. Large catalog retailers spend enormous sums of money on catalogs sent to prospective purchasers. If the retailers can more accurately understand the recipients of the catalogs, they can usually trim the mailing list significantly, while retaining the same marketing effectiveness. Sending fewer catalogs causes savings in production to go all the way to the bottom line.

Combine the Investments and Returns to Calculate ROI

At this point, your investments and returns figures are entered into a financial model to calculate the return on investment. The resulting ROI percentages tend to be very large—so large, that even taking a fraction of the predicted return will probably be satisfactory to provide adequate justification and obtain funding approval.

You can also look at the financial justification in terms of "opportunity cost." If the projected benefit of the data warehouse is $100,000 in incremental revenue per month, then it costs the organization $100,000 each month the project is delayed.

Once again, a strong partnership between IS and business is required to complete the justification task. IS can determine the investment or cost side of the equation, but the business users must drive the returns or benefits side. Going back to our early readiness factors, justification is much easier if you are working with a strong sponsor on a strategic business issue. If you are really struggling with financial justification, then you are probably still in search of the right sponsor and business problem.

Some organizations are much more rigorous in their justification process than others. As a division president at a $14 billion company recently explained, justification was merely a test to ensure that the people in his organization were committed to making the initiative work. The raw numbers weren't particularly important—he viewed the justification as a measure of organizational buy-in. Other organizations examine costs and benefits rounded to the nearest whole dollar.

We have tried to help you estimate a justification or return on investment before the data warehouse is built. It is worthwhile to remember that it is much easier and much more believable to provide the justification and return on investment after the data warehouse is implemented.

For instance, if the Credit department decides to grant more liberal credit to a group of customers after using the data warehouse, this decision should be claimed by the data warehouse. Or, if the Store Operations group decides to merchandise the stores differently as a result of using the data warehouse, this decision should also be claimed as belonging to the data warehouse. Once these kinds of decisions are claimed by the data warehouse, calculating the ROI is relatively straightforward. As the data warehouse manager, be sure that you are on the alert for these kinds of decisions, which you can legitimately claim.

 The key step is providing the after-the-fact analysis is to *claim the decisions* made as a result of using the data warehouse.

PLAN THE PROJECT

Congratulations, you have defined the initial project and gained approval and funding to move forward! What next? You are now ready to do detailed project planning.

In this section, we will describe key considerations for getting the project staffed and building your overall project plan. But first, we will deal with the project's identity crisis.

Establish the Project Identity

Your data warehouse project needs to have a name. Like most systems projects, the name you select is often reduced to an acronym, such as PAM for the Pricing Analysis for Marketing project—perhaps it should have been called Strategic Pricing Analysis for Marketing instead. In any case, this task requires creativity—it is a good time to collaborate with your business cohorts. Some organizations even create project logos, which then appear on presentations, deliverables, T-shirts, coffee mugs, and so on. As anyone who has been to the vendor booths at a data warehouse conference knows, you can never have too many T-shirts or coffee mugs.

Staff the Project

A data warehouse project requires a number of different roles and skills, from both the business and IS communities, during its lifecycle. The various roles on a data warehouse project are actually somewhat analogous to those in a professional sports team. The team starts with a front office of owners and general managers—in the data warehouse world, these are the sponsors and drivers, who set the direction and foot the bill. The front office relies on the coaching staff to establish a regular starting lineup—in our parlance, the business project lead and project manager are the coaches who lead the core project team charged with developing the data warehouse. Along the way, specialty players are added to the team roster—as does the warehouse team. Finally, the professional sports team wouldn't last long if it weren't for the fans—if we do our job right, the business end users are analogous to these fans. Unfortunately, this analogy falls apart completely when we get to player salary negotiations.

In this section, we will review the major categories of people involved in the data warehouse—front office, coaches, regular lineup, and special teams. We will briefly describe the tasks each role is responsible for; however, this will be illustrated in much greater detail in the project plans located at the end of appropriate chapters, as well as in Appendix A and on the CD-ROM.

Before we get started, remember that there is seldom a one-to-one relationship between data warehouse roles and individual people. Like the regular lineup running back who also returns kickoffs, the same player may fill multiple roles on the data warehouse project. The relationship between project roles and actual headcount varies by organization. We have worked with data warehouse teams as small as two people—a project manager (who also handled the dimensional modeling, end user application development, and user support) working with a part-time data staging programmer. At the other end of the spectrum, we have occasionally worked on project teams with more than 25 members. One project had almost a dozen data modelers alone. The vast majority of the data mart projects fall somewhere in between, say, between two and five full-time members, with access to others as required.

 Although there are many roles in a data warehouse project, individual staff members will wear several hats at once. Don't be daunted by the number of roles!

Front Office: Sponsors and Drivers

As we described extensively earlier in this chapter, business sponsors play an extremely critical role on the data warehouse team in a number of areas. They are the business owners of the project and often have financial responsibility for the project. Business sponsors help make and then support key project scope decisions. In addition, business sponsors fill both high-level cheerleader and enforcer roles for the warehouse. As cheerleaders, their enthusiasm encourages others to share the vision for the impact of improved access to information. At the other end of the spectrum, their reinforcement is important as it encourages apprehensive users to jump on the bandwagon.

There is usually a complementary sponsorship role from the IS organization. The IS sponsor carries the project budget in cases where the business sponsor does not. The IS sponsor works closely with the business sponsor to ensure a joint success. The IS sponsor also works closely with the data warehouse project manager to assist with dispute resolution, especially when the disputes pertain to resources.

The data warehouse team often does not have continuous access to the business sponsor due to the sponsor's typical stature within an organization. The business sponsor often designates a "business driver" to tactically serve in their place. The business driver is accessible, engaged, and empowered to make the difficult decisions regarding priorities and dispute resolution that are bound to come up on a data warehouse project. Business drivers must have a solid understanding of their surrounding business organization.

Some organizations use a business user steering committee instead of a business driver. This group makes the tough decisions on behalf of the business community at large. This group needs to meet frequently to avoid becoming a project bottleneck.

Coaches: Project Managers and Leads

In professional sports, there are several coaches who direct day-to-day activities with a slightly different focus. The same is true for a data warehouse project.

- **Project manager.**   The project manager is responsible for day-to-day management of project tasks and activities, including resource coordination, status tracking, and communication of project progress and issues, working closely with the business project lead. This role is typically staffed from among the best and brightest of the IS organization—project managers should possess a broad knowledge of technology and system development in order to comprehend the full lifecycle. The project manager should have strong communication skills, as well as a strong affiliation with and the respect of the business community. The project manager should also have a good sense of balancing the mechanics of project management with the needs of the people working on the project.

  Ideally, a project manager is also skilled in navigating the political environment of the organization. While project management skills are important, overall drive can be even more critical to the project's success.

This is a full time position—it just doesn't work to have a part-time data warehouse project manager. However, as described earlier, sometimes the project manager is a player/coach who both leads the charge and plays specific roles on the data warehouse project.

- **Business project lead.**   This business community representative works with the project manager on a day-to-day basis, jointly monitoring project progress and communicating to the rest of the organization. The business project lead should have a solid understanding of the business requirements. Optimally, the person who fills this role is well respected by the business community. Sometimes the same person fills the business driver role. This is typically a part-time role, but the business project lead is expected to attend status meetings and be extremely accessible to the team, just as every coach would attend team meetings.

Regular Lineup: Core Project Team

This team bears the bulk of the responsibility for the design and development of the data warehouse. We will introduce the players in approximately the order that they come onto the scene.

Some team members are assigned to the project full time. Others, like the business project lead, are needed on a part-time or sporadic basis. Part-time team members are expected to attend regular status meetings and actively assist the team as needed.

Before you start hyperventilating, remember that *each core project team member often plays more than one role* on the project team. For example, the business system analyst may also be responsible for end user application development and education. The data modeler and database administrator roles may be handled by the same individual. The roles listed correspond to a set of project *tasks*—they do not correspond to actual headcount. We described the roles individually because each organization combines the roles differently depending on prior experiences, skill sets, and workloads.

- **Business systems analyst.**   The business systems analyst is responsible for leading the business requirements definition activities and then representing those requirements as the dimensional model is developed. The business systems analyst role is often filled by an IS resource who is extremely user-centric and knowledgeable about the business. Alternatively, it may be staffed with a resource who currently resides in the business organization but has a solid technical foundation. On smaller projects, the project manager or business project lead may fill this position. Regardless, the person in this role must have strong communication skills; it is certainly beneficial if they are respected by the business community as the business systems analyst, along with the business project lead, will be representing their requirements to the rest of the team.

- **Data modeler.**   The data modeler is responsible for performing detailed data analysis and developing the dimensional data model. Knowledge about existing corporate data models is extremely valuable. Strong data modeling skills are beneficial, but the individual must be able to break away from traditional OLTP and E/R design practices and embrace data warehouse design techniques. It is also helpful if this person has a solid understanding of the business rules; he or she often participates in the business requirements definition activities in a secondary role. Finally, this role is often responsible for also developing an overall data architecture strategy; in larger organizations, a data architect role may be established to handle these responsibilities.

 The data modeler in a data warehouse project should be equally interested in the data relationships in the data and in the users' ability to understand the data models.

- **Data warehouse database administrator (DBA).**   The DBAs translate the dimensional model into physical table structures. In many cases, they are involved in the dimensional modeling process; at a minimum, they should be knowledgeable of these data warehouse design techniques and be open to new approaches. The DBA also determines initial aggregation, partitioning, and indexing strategies. The DBA is often responsible for the day-to-day operational support of the database, ensuring data integrity, database availability, and performance. In larger organizations, this role is sometimes divided into separate design and production DBA roles.

- **Data staging system designer.** The data staging system designer is responsible for the end-to-end design of the production process to extract, transform, and load the data in preparation for the data warehouse. While many aspects of data warehousing differ from traditional development, the development of the data staging process requires strong modular system design skills. Too often this role is not identified, and programmers just begin coding.

- **End user application developers.** This role creates and maintains the end user applications, typically using off-the-shelf data access software. The end user application developer is also responsible for loading the data access tool metadata. The end user application developer needs moderate PC knowledge and a deep interest and understanding of the business. If complex applications are required, technical proficiency equivalent to writing Excel macros is typically adequate. Like the business system analysts, this role may be filled from either the IS or business organizations; resources that currently reside in the business organization, but behave as systems professionals by developing databases and creating ad hoc reports, are prime candidates for this role. The business systems analyst may handle this responsibility on smaller projects.

 Data staging system design and end user application design are both software development activities, and these activities need to be planned and managed with a traditional software development perspective.

- **Data warehouse educator.** The business end users must be educated on the data content, the prebuilt end user applications, and the data access tool itself. Clearly, the educator must have in-depth knowledge of each of these areas. This role typically develops the initial education course materials, as well as delivers the education on an ongoing basis. Responsibility for user education is sometimes split between players in the IS and business communities—an IS resource teaches tool mechanics and the business representative covers the data and end user application topics. Alternatively, the data access tool vendor assumes responsibility for the tool education component. Again, this role is often filled by another team member, such as the business system analyst or end user application developer.

Special Teams

These data warehouse team players contribute to the project on a very specialized, limited basis. These special team players may become part of the core team during specific parts of the project lifecycle. For example, data staging programmers may be treated as core team members during the development of the data staging process, but they are not required to attend all status meetings during the requirements analysis phase. As we mentioned earlier, these special roles may be assumed by resources who are already members of the core team.

- **Technical/security architect.** This architect is responsible for the design of the technical infrastructure and security strategy to support the data warehouse. This role does not need to be an expert in all the infrastructure and security technologies, but he or she must provide the overall cohesiveness to ensure that the components will fit together within your organization. The security architect is a new member of the data warehouse team and must represent the special needs and risks of the data warehouse to the rest of IS. This role is described in detail in Chapter 12.

- **Technical support specialists.** Depending on your environment, there may be specialists focused on mainframe systems software, client/server systems, and networking. These specialists are involved in early stages of the warehouse to perform resource and capacity planning. During product selection, they ensure compatibility with the existing technical environment. Once technology has been selected, they are involved in the installation and configuration of the new components. The specialists also provide ongoing production support.

- **Data staging programmer.** Programmers are needed to construct and automate the data staging extract, transformation, and load processes under the direction of the data staging system designer. Optimally, this resource has an intimate knowledge of the source systems as well as a basic understanding of the target dimensional models. Obviously, the requirement for this resource drops significantly if you are using an automated data staging tool.

- **Data steward.** The data steward, sometimes called the data administrator, is responsible for gaining organizational agreement on common definitions for conformed warehouse dimensions and facts, and then publishing and reinforcing these definitions. This role is often also responsible for developing the warehouse's metadata management system.

- **Data warehouse quality assurance analyst.** The QA (quality assurance) analyst ensures that the data loaded into the warehouse is accurate. This person identifies potential data errors and drives them to resolution. The QA analyst is sometimes also responsible for verifying the integrity of prebuilt end user applications. Since the business side must take responsibility to identify fundamental data errors, this role is typically staffed from within the business community, often with resources who straddle the business and IS organizations. Once a data error has been identified, the IS organization takes responsibility for correction. This role has a significant workload during the initial data load to ensure that the data staging process is working properly. However, the QA analyst role does not end once the warehouse is put into production as the data must be reviewed with each load for accuracy.

Now that you understand the required roles, you must determine how to fill those roles. Once again, the readiness assessment reviewed earlier comes into play. If the warehouse ties to overall organizational priorities, we often find a "whatever it takes" mentality supported by senior management. On the other hand, some projects need to beg, borrow, and steal to get things done.

Once your team is staffed, the coaches need to turn their attention to team cohesiveness and development. Team building activities are important to ensure that the team gels—personality issues can quickly undermine a talented roster. In terms of player development, chances are that the team lacks the first-hand experience necessary to build a successful data warehouse. You need to acknowledge that data warehousing demands new techniques and skills, and then allocate the time and money to get your team up to speed on general data warehousing concepts and methodologies, dimensional modeling, and technology-specific topics, either through specialized courses or industry conferences.

  It is far cheaper to invest in education than it is to fund rework due to lack of knowledge.

ROLE OF EXTERNAL CONSULTANTS ON YOUR PROJECT TEAM

Admittedly, the author team provides data warehouse consulting services. However, putting our biases aside, you should be aware of several considerations before enlisting consultants to participate in one of the most visible systems projects under development in your organization.

Like most systems development projects, you obviously want to work with experienced people. However, the unending nature of a data warehouse project and its business orientation warrants additional requirements of external consultants:

1. Don't let consultants fill all the key roles on your core project team. You should retain ownership of the data warehouse project and not let an external organization build it for you.
2. Demand extensive skills and knowledge transfer from your consultants.
3. Clearly understand if you are buying a consultant with specialized knowledge or whether you are augmenting your regular staff. When possible, it may be valuable to bring in an external resource to offload the existing staff's routine responsibilities. This would free up internal resources with critical knowledge about your business and underlying systems for the data warehouse project.
4. Don't let a consultant talk you into a data- or technology-centric warehouse development approach, even if it feels more comfortable to both you and your consultants. Your development should always be based on business requirements

Managing the expectations of the data warehouse project team is often overlooked. Due to the iterative nature of data warehouse development, frustrations can mount on the team. Think about traditional incentives offered to systems personnel. When given a design specification, they developed programs, tested them, and released them for production. If major rework was required, either the design was wrong or the programmers did a poor job. These same resources are now invited to join the data warehouse project where change is good—rework is a fact of life and necessary to address changing business requirements and growth. The data warehouse team needs to be reminded of this mindset shift, or morale is certain to plummet.

We have worked with teams that have been extremely creative with incentives and bonuses to compensate the data warehouse team for its heroic efforts. In addition, many teams members often find motivation from working with the business users and/or hearing of their enthusiasm for the data warehouse.

Develop the Project Plan

Obviously, the data warehouse project needs a project plan given its complexity, both in terms of task and player counts. There are two key words that need to describe this plan—*integrated* and *detailed*. Unfortunately, data warehouse teams often have multiple project plans that don't tie together. There may be a plan for the modeling tasks, another for the data transformation process, and perhaps yet another for defining the technical architecture. Without a single integrated plan, the likelihood of completing the many discrete tasks on time is greatly reduced.

The level of detail tracked is another common problem with data warehouse project plans. A single task called "Develop the Data Transformation Process" is not sufficient given the many underlying subtasks required. The goal is to provide enough detail to be able to track progress on key tasks and to identify issues or delays as soon as possible. If a single task will require more than two weeks, subtasks should be identified.

Many organizations have already established methodologies and supporting software for systems development projects. We encourage you to use the resources available to you. However, we want to remind you that the best project management software package will be worthless unless the time is invested to input *and maintain* the project plan, including detailed dependencies.

Too often, significant time is spent developing the initial plan, but then it is not updated and used throughout the lifecycle. The key to effective project management is to employ tools that you and the team will actually use—even if that means resorting to a spreadsheet for project task tracking.

Figure 3.4 illustrates an excerpt from a project plan. We recommend you track the following information for each project task:

- **Resources.** Individuals responsible for completing this task. There should be one and only one person with primary responsibility for each task, and that person should be listed first.
- **Original estimated effort.** Original estimated number of days to complete this task. This number should never be revised.
- **Start date.** Date task is estimated to begin.
- **Original estimated completion date.** Original date when this task is to be completed. Again, this date should never be revised.
- **Current estimated completion date.** Current estimated completion date for this task.
- **Status.** Indicates current status as a percentage of the total effort required based on the current estimated effort.
- **Effort to complete.** Currently estimated number of work days required to complete this task.
- **Dependencies.** Identification of other tasks that must be completed prior to beginning this task.
- **Late flag.** Simple math between the estimated completion date and current date to identify tasks that are behind schedule.

A template that outlines high-level project plan tasks and each roles' responsibilities is located in Appendix A, and it is included on the CD-ROM. Specific project plan tasks are described in the subsequent chapters, if applicable.

We suggest you identify and list all the tasks associated with the entire lifecycle. The task should be included even if you do not yet know when, who, or how effort will be required. You can estimate approximate dates, but make sure that others are aware that this is an estimate. Otherwise, you can list the tasks but only complete the other pertinent information as you develop greater visibility with project progress.

The project plan should include formal user acceptance tasks following each major deliverable.

Overall task estimating guidelines and considerations are provided at the end of the appropriate chapters. In general, there is no single variable that drives the amount of time required to build a data ware-

Project Task	Resources	Original est. effort	Start date	Original est. complete date	Current est. complete date	Status	Effort to finish	Depend	Late flag
1. PROJECT PLANNING									
1.1 Establish Project Identity	PM/Business Proj Lead	0.5	1/1/01	1/1/01	—		0.5		
1.2 Identify Project Resources			1/1/01	1/1/01	—		0.0		
1.2.1 Determine Required Roles	PM	0.5	1/1/01	1/1/01	—		0.5		
1.2.2 Identify Resources	PM/Business Proj Lead	1.0	1/1/01	1/1/01	—		1.0		
1.2.3 Assign Roles to Resources	PM	0.5	1/1/01	1/1/01	—		0.5		
1.3 Prepare Draft Project Plan	PM	2.0	1/1/01	1/1/01	—		2.0		
1.4 Conducted Project Team Kick-Off and Planning									
1.4.1 Discuss Project Scope	PM/Business Proj Lead	1.0	1/1/01	1/1/01	—		1.0		
1.4.2 Review Generic Project Plan	PM/Team								
1.4.3 Review Roles and Responsibilities	Team								
1.5 Revise Project Plan	PM/Team	2.0	1/1/01	1/1/01	—		2.0		
1.6 Establish Project Management Procedures									
1.6.1 Establish Change Management Process	PM	0.5	1/1/01	1/1/01	—		0.5		
1.6.2 Create Issue Resolution Process	PM	0.5	1/1/01	1/1/01	—		0.5		
1.6.3 Establish Enhancement Tracking Process	PM	0.5	1/1/01	1/1/01	—		0.5		
1.7 Develop Project Communication Plan			1/1/01	1/1/01	—		0.0		
1.7.1 Determine Communication Audiences	PM/Team	0.5	1/1/01	1/1/01	—		0.5		
1.7.2 Establish Frequency, Vehicle, and Key Content	PM/Team	0.5	1/1/01	1/1/01	—		0.5		

FIGURE 3.4 Sample project plan excerpt.

Continues

Project Task		Resources	Original est. effort	Start date	Original est. complete date	Current est. complete date	Status	Effort to finish	Depend	Late flag
1.8	*Develop Program to Measure Success*									
1.8.1	Define Measurement Criteria	PM/Mgmt	0.5	1/1/01	1/1/01	—		0.5		
1.8.2	Criteria	PM/Business Proj Lead	1.0	1/1/01	1/1/01	—		1.0		
1.8.3	Implement Program to Measure Project Success	PM/Business Proj Lead	2.0	1/1/01	1/1/01	—		2.0		
1.9	*Ongoing Project Management*									
1.9.1	Conduct Status Meetings	PM/Team	—	Ongoing	Ongoing	Ongoing		—		
1.9.2	Document Project Status Reports	PM	—	Ongoing	Ongoing	Ongoing		—		
1.9.3	Update Project Plan	PM	—	Ongoing	Ongoing	Ongoing		—		
1.9.4	Manage Issue Resolution Process	PM/Team	—	Ongoing	Ongoing	Ongoing		—		
1.9.5	Coordinate Project Changes	PM/Business Proj Lead	—	Ongoing	Ongoing	Ongoing		—		
1.9.6	Coordinate Project Communication	PM	—	Ongoing	Ongoing	Ongoing		—		
1.9.7	Appropriate	PM/Business Proj Lead	—	Ongoing	Ongoing	Ongoing		—		
1.9.8	Deliverables	PM/Vendor/ Consultant	—	Ongoing	Ongoing	Ongoing		—		

FIGURE 3.4 *Continued*

house. The number of business users is an estimating variable that drives the time spent collecting requirements and deploying the data warehouse. However, the business user count has virtually no impact on the effort required to design and develop the data staging process; that effort is the same for one or one hundred users.

As you are building your project plan, remember to inflate estimates for unknowns. Due to all the unknown data realities hidden in your source system data, data staging processes have a well-earned reputation of being nearly impossible to estimate and deliver on time—at a minimum, double your best-guess estimate to construct the data staging processes (and then double it again). You may also need to inflate estimates due to cultural issues. We worked with one client where it typically took three weeks lead time to get three managers in same room at the same time—they needed to incorporate this cultural reality into their project plan. Don't forget that data staging development is a classic software development task with five distinct phases: development unit testing, system testing, trial deployment, and final rollout with documentation. Inexperienced project managers may focus most of their attention on what turns out to be the first of these five steps.

The project manager typically develops a skeleton project plan prior to the project team kickoff meeting, perhaps starting with the template provided in this book. The project manager then meets with key representatives for each major lifecycle activity for their input on tasks. These representatives should be responsible for developing the estimated effort and preliminary schedule for their tasks, working in conjunction with the project manager. Their participation in this up-front planning encourages buy-in from the people who will actually be doing the work.

More often than not, we witness a lack of project planning and management on data warehouse projects, but we have also seen the opposite extreme. Don't delay the start of the project for six weeks while the project manager develops an overly detailed project plan. Projects need to be defined and tracked but not just for the sake of project management.

MANAGE THE PROJECT

In this final section, we discuss techniques for keeping your data warehouse project on track as it begins to unfold, starting with the team kickoff, through monitoring status and managing scope, and finally, focusing on your ongoing communication strategy. Many of these concepts are rooted in basic project management techniques. However, data warehouse projects have a few unique characteristics that cause some of these concepts to warrant additional discussion:

- **Cross-functional implementation team.** The sheer number of players with varying responsibilities throughout a data warehouse project drives the need to monitor status closely and communicate effectively.

- **Iterative development cycle.** The development of the data warehouse never ends. This causes a greater need for communication to keep everyone in sync, issue tracking for future enhancements, and detailed project documentation to support an evolving data warehouse team. All projects should go through cycles in which the requirements are "open" and the requirements are "closed." Both the project team and the business users should be aware of these characteristic phases.

- **Inevitable data issues.** Project scope is vulnerable to unknown data issues, driving more focus on scope containment. Data issues *will* wreak havoc on anyone's best laid project plans.

- **Elevated visibility.** Organizational expectations of a data warehouse typically run high. Effective communication is required to keep them in check.

In general, we assume you are familiar with basic project management concepts. However, based on our experience with numerous clients, these basics are often forgotten or ignored. We feel compelled to review the basics at a high level, focusing on the unique aspects of managing a data warehouse project whenever possible.

Conduct the Project Team Kickoff Meeting

The data warehouse project officially begins with a project team kickoff meeting. The purpose of this meeting is to get the entire project team on the same page in terms of where the project currently stands and where it hopes to go. Attendees should include the coaches, members of the core project team, and all specialty players if possible. A separate launch meeting, described in Chapter 4, will be held for the business community.

As illustrated in the sample agenda in Figure 3.5, the meeting begins with a brief introduction by the business sponsor, who describes the over-

Project Team Kickoff Meeting Agenda	
Project Introduction ■ Goals and Objectives ■ Project Scope	Business Executive Sponsor
Data Warehousing Overview	Project Manager
Team Roles and Responsibilities	Project Manager
Project Management ■ Project Administration Tools ■ Project Milestones ■ Draft Project Plan Review	Project Manager
Questions and Answers	
Next Steps	

FIGURE 3.5   Sample project team kickoff meeting agenda.

all goals for the project and its business relevance. From there, the project manager assumes responsibility for the remainder of the meeting. If appropriate, based on team members' exposure to data warehousing, a brief primer is often presented next. The project team roles and responsibilities are then discussed. The project plan is presented at a high level, probably without estimated effort and due dates, and general project management expectations are reviewed. Finally, the next steps are identified.

The project manager typically compiles a project kickoff packet for distribution at the meeting. The packet should include copies of the project scope document, a project team contact list with responsibilities, an initial project plan and sample status meeting agenda, status report, issue log, and change control documents.

Monitor Project Status

Like all systems development projects, the project status should be formally monitored on a regular basis. As we described in Chapter 2, the data warehouse project lifecycle requires the integration of numerous resources and tasks that must be brought together at the right time to achieve success. Monitoring project status is key to achieving this coordination.

We have observed many teams that initially have fine intentions concerning status monitoring, but these status-related activities take a back seat once the project is in crunch mode. Unfortunately, that is when status should be monitored most closely during the project.

Project Status Meetings

We recommend regular status meetings for the core project team—typically these meetings should be scheduled for a one-hour time slot at the same time and place each week. Attendance will eventually suffer if you allow the meeting to overrun or stray off course. As illustrated on the sample status meeting agenda in Figure 3.6, the status meeting should focus on accomplishments and current task progress, particularly tasks that are past due. In addition to reviewing the project plan, the status meeting is a forum to raise concerns that have become visible since the last meeting. In general, these issues are identified, but their resolution is frequently handled off-line.

The project manager plays an important role in setting the tone of the status meeting and running an efficient meeting without numerous discussion tangents. In addition, the project manager should create an atmosphere of openness within the team. While no one wants tasks to

---

Status Meeting Agenda

Review Project Plan

- Review completed tasks
- Review milestones completed and pending
- Review major deliverables status
- Task assignments for the next period

Review Issues and Follow-up

- Review issues resolved since last meeting (resolution, who, when, move to closed)
- Review new issues (determine steps to resolve, responsible party, priority, date to be resolved by)
- Review open issues and determine if a change in status is needed

Review Change Requests

- Review change requests closed since last meeting
- Review new change requests (determine responsible party for analysis, impact analysis, priority)
- Review open change requests to determine if a change in status is needed

Announcements and General Comments

FIGURE 3.6   Sample status meeting agenda.

overrun the estimate, it far preferable to know about it sooner rather than later. Often the missed deadline is caused by other demands on the resources' time—a problem the project manager should be well suited to tackle.

Project Status Reports

Status reports provide a high-level snapshot of project progress. They go hand-in-hand with regularly scheduled status meetings. The status reports capture key accomplishments, significant decisions, planned activities for the next period, and major issues. The status report should not be overly detailed. Keep it relatively brief so that people will actually read it. Figure 3.7 provides a sample format.

Status reports should be distributed to the entire project team and key IS and business management. Be aware that even if the status re-

---

Data Warehouse Status Report

To: Tim Barnes   Business Proj Lead
      Leah Andrews   Business System Analyst
      Julie Hustead   Data Modeler
      Michael Kells   DBA
      Paul Leaf   End User Appl Devel

From: Mark Emerson   Project Manager

CC: Susan Reed   Business Driver

Period: Week of 1/13

Work Accomplished during week of 1/13

- Completed project team kick-off meeting.
- Revised project plan based on team input—see attached.
- Conducted four interviews as scheduled with Sales, Sales Support, Financial Analysis, and Market Research.

Work Planned through 1/27

- Document and deliver individual interview write-ups.
- Begin drafting the requirement findings document.

Open Issues/Change Control

- Schedule additional interview requested by Sales. Tim responsible, due by 1/30.

FIGURE 3.7   Sample data warehouse status report.

ports are brief and summarized, they may not be the most effective tool for communicating with your executive business sponsor but more on that later in this chapter.

Maintain the Project Plan and Project Documentation

The integrated project plan should be updated weekly to accurately reflect progress and then shared with the core project team. As we mentioned earlier, the project plan should reflect reality, whether it is good, bad, or ugly. Early flagging of project plan problems allows the team to develop strategies to adjust as well as minimize downstream ripple effects.

Like most system projects, you need to understand and evaluate your options if your project falls behind schedule. Working with your business sponsor, you may be able to reduce the project scope. Alternatively, you may need to obtain an extension on the project deliverable date. Finally, you could obtain more funding to supplement the project team with additional resources. This final alternative is probably the least effective option for dealing with data warehousing project delays. Regardless of the alternative selected, the important thing is to have the courage to acknowledge to your management and sponsors that you are behind.

It is only worse if expectations continue gaining speed with hopes that the team will make up the schedule shortfall during the two weeks before the target deliverable date. It won't happen. Pretending that it will and continuing to go through the motions with user education and deployment is typically a fatal mistake.

The unending nature of a data warehouse generates demand for detailed project documentation. In addition, the data warehouse project team is bound to evolve—additional players will come on board and others will head for greener pastures now that they have warehousing on their resumes. Robust documentation will help ease the burden of getting the new team members up to speed. Documentation is also invaluable in the event that the warehouse does not meet expectations. It may be necessary to refer to key project assumptions and decision points. Document every step.

Unfortunately, documentation is not usually anyone's favorite task. When time pressures mount, the first item that gets eliminated is typically formal documentation. We recommend that you avoid falling into this trap. While it may seem like you are getting the warehouse delivered faster, you are probably costing the organization more in the long run.

Data warehouse project documentation is often stored in a set of official project binders as well as in electronic format with a section corresponding to each major activity in the Lifecycle. The official binders should contain copies of all project communication and all major deliverables. Obviously, all project documentation should be dated and/or versioned appropriately.

Manage the Scope

There is only one guarantee for any data warehouse project and that is that there will be change! There are two major sources of these changes—previously unidentified issues and additional user requests. Each issue or request may be manageable and doable on its own, but when they are added all together, they become mission impossible.

The data warehouse project manager has the unenviable job of managing scope changes. Out of one side of our mouths, we encourage you to focus on the business users and their requirements, while the other side is reminding you to stay on track. In general, the project manager has several options when facing a previously unidentified issue or additional user request:

- Just say no.
- Adjust scope assuming a zero-sum. In other words, the overall effort remains the same, but what is in and out of scope is modified.
- Expand the scope. In this case, the fence around the project grows. It is then mandatory to expand timeline and/or budget appropriately.

The right choice depends on the specific situation. Regardless of the situation, it is certain that the data warehouse project manager should not make scope decisions in a vacuum. We have observed numerous data warehouse project managers ignore this warning—and their solo decisions regarding scope changes were inevitably second guessed. Don't bear the burden of adjusting scope alone. A strong IS and business partnership is invaluable when evaluating these scope alternatives.

In the next section, we will provide you with tools and techniques to track issues and change requests. Once again, many organizations have already adopted issue tracking or change management methodologies and software. You should use the resources available to you (and that you are expected to use).

Track Issues

Tracking issues on a data warehouse project is probably similar to issue tracking you have done on other systems projects. However, the data warehouse poses greater challenges given its elevated visibility. In addition, the required integration of numerous resources, data, and technologies in a data warehouse project tends to generate numerous issues.

Issue tracking is critical to ensure that nothing slips between the cracks, that everyone's concerns have been heard, and finally, that the rationale used to resolve issues has been captured for future reference. Identifying issues or roadblocks is the first step toward resolving them. The data warehouse project manager should establish a team mindset that having numerous issues is allowed and preferable to simply pretending they don't exist.

There are two classes of issues—project issues that impact the overall project and task-related issues that must be resolved to complete a major task but may have no impact on the project budget and/or schedule. In addition to an overall project issue log, several individual task issue logs are typically developed, each corresponding to the major lifecycle activities such as dimensional modeling, data staging, end user application development, and deployment.

A simple issue log format can be used for both project- and task-level issue logs, as illustrated in Figure 3.8. The issues are typically captured in a table within a word processing software package or spreadsheet; alternatively, some teams log the issues in a database. Your issue-tracking technology choice is irrelevant, as long as you do it somewhere.

The project issue log should be reviewed at each status meeting. The task issue log should be reviewed at major design sessions. It is helpful to shade all closed issues to maintain group focus on open issues in these forums.

Control Changes

Formal acknowledgment of project changes is critical to overall project success. Any issue resolution that impacts the project schedule, budget,

Issue Tracking Log

Issue #	Topic	Issue	Id Date	Resp	Date Closed	Status	Priority	Rptd By
DM001	Time	Which time hierarchies (calendar and/or fiscal) are needed?	3/12	JAK	4/10	Closed	High	PAK
DM002	Client	Franchisee is not included in the Business model. This should be processed properly, but not explicit in the data model.	3/12	Rqmts	4/15	Closed	High	MER
DM003	Client	This is a slowly changing dimension. Represent this in the model.	3/15	LJK	4/15	Closed	High	LLR
DM004	Client	How would Region Country be used for analysis?	3/15	KLK		Open	Low	BTK
DM005	Household	National DMA equivalent—geography equivalent. Explore additional geographic attributes. Make sure block group is in the model.	3/26	MER	4/28	Closed	Med.	PAK
DM006	Consumer	Investigate end user defined demographic groups. Can a person belong to more than one Group?	3/28	MSR		Open	Low	LLR
DM007	Geo	Understand business use/analysis of district and division. Determine how to support this in the model.	3/28	LMR		Open	High	PAK

FIGURE 3.8 Sample issue tracking log.

or scope should be considered a change. If a change does not affect the schedule or budget, it is often not documented. However, these changes may still impact the overall scope. By formally documenting and communicating the change, users' expectations will be readjusted as well.

Many organizations and project managers have mechanisms in place to handle major changes. These major changes are typically scrutinized and then a collective business decision is made.

 The changes that often cause the biggest impact on a project are the little ones, cumulatively applied.

Individually, the minor requests might be quite simple to implement. However, problems develop if there are too many small requests. If a small change is estimated to take half a day, but ten different team members independently agree to make only two changes each, those few small changes could impact the schedule by several weeks.

Figure 3.9 shows a sample of a change control log. Each change should be documented in detail and entered in the log. Priorities, often described in terms of business impact, should be assigned to every change request.

Document Enhancement Requests

As the data warehouse implementation effort progresses, additional user requests and enhancements will inevitably arise. Like issues and changes, these enhancements should be documented in a database or log. The enhancement log provides a mechanism to capture requests for future action, rather than expanding the current project's scope. Documentation regarding each request should identify the "value" of the enhancement; asking what the enhancement is worth will facilitate future enhancement prioritization.

Develop Communications Plan to Manage Expectations

Last, but certainly not least, successful data warehouse project managers establish a robust communications game plan to address the needs of their various audiences or constituencies. Communication

Change Control Log

Change #	Change Request	Req. By	Date Req.	Priority	Resp.	Est. Effort	Est. Cost	Date Closed	Status
CCR001	Need to interview five additional users.	LLR	3/26	High	LLR	3 Days	$1.2K	4/10	Closed
CCR002	New data source required to complete customer attributes.	PAK	4/12	High	JAK	TBD	TBD		Open
CCR003	DSS Tool Selection process delayed.	MER	4/12	High	Rqmts	20 Days	None	4/15	Closed
CCR004	Daily data required for analysis, currently planning weekly	LLR	4/15	High	LJK	40 Days	$80K		Open

FIGURE 3.9   Sample change control log.

allows the project manager to consistently establish and manage expectations of the data warehouse project; expectation management is an absolute key to success for a data warehouse project. Regular, ongoing communication essentially makes the "black box syndrome" disappear.

The overall communication plan should outline general message content, format, and frequency for communicating with each group of constituents. Developing a communication plan forces the project manager to fully consider the organization's requirements—otherwise, it is far too easy to just let communication slip through the cracks. This section will review communications recommendations for the common constituency groups.

Project Team

Naturally, most project managers tend to focus on communication within the project team, much as a sports team's coach reviews the play book and game plan with the team regularly. Many of the tools described in this chapter, such as the project scope document, status meetings, status reports, and project plans, facilitate communication within the team. These communication vehicles should be shared with both the core team and specialty players as appropriate, especially on large data warehouse teams.

Sponsor and Driver Briefings

Obviously, you need to keep your business and IS sponsors and drivers in the loop. Generally, we find that face-to-face communication with these players is more effective than merely copying them on project communication documents. Everyone in the front office certainly has access to the coach's playbook, but most aren't interested in that level of detail. Clearly, these communication briefings need to be well planned—don't wing it with the business sponsor. The briefings should focus on progress to date and any issues requiring higher-level assistance. In general, project managers typically schedule monthly sponsor briefings and weekly sessions with the business driver, although this varies by organization.

 Communicate face to face with your sponsors. Don't rely exclusively on project memos.

We believe it is absolutely imperative that you develop a "no surprises" communication strategy with the sponsors and drivers. Based on our experience, this approach is not often employed in most organizations. Regardless, we have personally found it more effective to communicate honestly. The problem you are trying to ignore will surface eventually, so you should tell all early—your sponsors and drivers might even have the wherewithal to make the problem go away permanently.

Business User Community

Perception is reality, as they say. It is important that the business users' perception of the data warehouse matches reality. Communication is key to accomplishing this goal. In addition, communication with your business user community helps maintain their involvement with the data warehouse project. Greater involvement typically translates into a greater likelihood of acceptance and usage.

The first formal communication with the business users involved in the project, the user kickoff meeting, will be described in Chapter 4. It is important that you follow up this launch meeting with regular communication on an ongoing basis. As with communication to the sponsor and driver constituency, it is helpful to tailor your message to the audience, so once again we discourage you from merely distributing the status reports to the user community. Chances are slim that they will take the time to read a status report; the chances are even greater that they will be confused if they do.

 Business users should be reading the front page of the sports section, not the detailed game plan.

We recommend that user communication focus on what's in it for them in terms of capabilities, exclusions, and timeframes—expectations, in other words. You should let them know what is expected of them in terms of involvement, feedback checkpoints, and so on. Finally, business users should be reminded every so often about the iterative nature of data warehouse development. Let them know that the warehouse is going to evolve, just as their business does.

Business user communication is broadcast in a variety of formats—one-page monthly memos or e-mails, newsletters, or a regularly updated Web page on the organization's intranet. Regardless of the communication medium, the message should be brief, pointed, and free of any technical vocabulary. Involved business users should also receive the project scope document as it is updated and republished. Finally, in addition to written communication, the business driver and project lead should routinely communicate informally with the business community regarding the data warehouse.

Communication with Other Interested Parties

In addition to the key communication constituencies just described, several other audiences should be kept in the loop:

- **Executive management.** Like all high visibility projects, data warehouse projects are of great interest to your company's executive team. A briefing, often part of a regular staff meeting, is the best way to keep them informed. The joint business and IS sponsors typically spearhead this briefing. Depending on organizational factors, these executive briefings sometimes occur one on one. As we mentioned earlier, you will need acceptance of the data warehouse across the organization if it is to grow and thrive—these briefings are a start.

- **IS organization.** Naturally, other IS professionals in the organization will be interested in data warehousing as it is one of the more popular buzzwords in the IS industry today. To start, interested resources in the IS organization should receive a general briefing on data warehousing in addition to a few specifics about the project, including scope, timelines, and resource requirements. In addition, the project manager often provides a monthly status briefing to other IS managers. This communication is important to ensure that the warehouse is integrated with other development activities, and it helps establish expectations for the warehouse across IS. It seems that the data warehouse often becomes the answer to everyone's problem in an IS organization—year 2000 issues with the antiquated batch reporting systems, ERP reporting, integration of newly acquired businesses, implementation of activity-based costing systems, and so on.

The sooner proper project boundaries are established, the less you will need to deal with misperceptions. You will gain as much respect for saying what you will not do as for saying what you will do.

- **Organization at large.**   Finally, there are probably others within your business community who are interested in the data warehouse. Data warehousing has become so popular today that many people hear about it through nontechnical publications and other business contacts. Again, a short newsletter or Web page can publicize data warehouse news to the rest of the organization. With this approach, the data warehouse team conveys a consistent message across the organization rather than let the corporate rumor mill serve as the primary source of information.

SUMMARY

The up-front definition of your data warehouse initiative plants numerous stakes in the ground that have downstream implications on your ultimate success. We encourage you to assess your overall readiness, paying extra attention to the requisite business sponsorship. This sponsorship is essential as you define project scope and build the financial justification.

Once the initiative is funded, the project manager needs to focus on resource staffing and detailed project task and timeline planning. Ongoing management of a data warehouse project is similar to more traditional system development efforts, but the realities of a cross-functional project team working on a highly visible initiative imposes additional demands on status monitoring, documentation, scope control, and, most importantly, communication. Be sure to consult the project plan tasks spreadsheet at the end of this chapter for a summary of the tasks and responsibilities for project planning and management (Figure 3.10).

KEY ROLES

The key roles for project planning and management include:

- The project manager and business project lead drive the project definition activities, with heavy involvement from both business and IS management.
- Project planning is also guided by the project manager and business project lead, with active participation and input from all other team members.
- Ongoing project management responsibilities rest primarily on the shoulders of the project manager again with assistance from the business project lead.

ESTIMATING CONSIDERATIONS

The effort required to define your data warehouse is highly dependent on your readiness and situation scenario. At one end of the spectrum, it may require only a few weeks to establish scope and build the justification. However, if you identify a significant readiness shortfall, it may require several months of effort to conduct a high-level business requirements analysis and construct a proof of concept before you can proceed.

The initial project plan should be developed in less than two weeks. This plan will continue to be revised every step of the way.

The ongoing project management effort is directly related to the project's size and scope. As we mentioned earlier, the data warehouse project manager should be assigned full time to the initiative although he or she may also perform non–project-management tasks depending on his or her availability and skill set.

TEMPLATES

The following templates for project planning and management can be found on the CD-ROM:

- Template 3.1 Project Scope Document
- Template 3.2 User Acceptance Form
- Template 3.3 Project Kickoff Meeting Agenda
- Template 3.4 Status Meeting Agenda
- Template 3.5 Status Report
- Template 3.6 Project Issue Log
- Template 3.7 Change Control Log
- Template 3.8 Change Request Form

Project Task	Fans	Front Office			Coaches		Regular Line-Up						Special Teams				
	Business End Users	Business Sponsor	IS Sponsor	Business Driver	Bus. Project Lead	Project Manager	Bus. Sys. Analyst	Data Modeler	DW DBA	Data Staging Designer	DW Educator	E/U Appl Devel	Tech/Security Architect	Tech. Sppt Specialists	Data Staging Programmer	Data Steward	DW QA Analyst
PROJECT DEFINITION																	
1 Assess Data Warehousing Readiness		○	○	○	●	●	◗	◗	◗	◗			◗				
2 Develop Preliminary Project Scope		○	○	○	●	●	◗	◗	◗	◗			◗				
3 Build Business Justification	◗	◗	◗	●	●	○	◗										
PROJECT PLANNING & MANAGEMENT																	
1 Establish Project Identity				◗	●	●											
2 Identity Project Resources		○	○	○	●	●											
3 Prepare Draft Project Plan				◗	◗	●	◗	◗	◗	◗	◗	◗	◗	◗	◗	◗	◗
4 Conduct Project Plan	□	□	○	○	○	●	○	○	○	○	○	○	○	○	○	○	○
5 Revise Project Plan				◗	◗	●	◗	◗	◗	◗	◗	◗	◗	◗	◗	◗	◗
6 Develop Project Communication Plan		◗	◗	◗	○	●	◗	◗	◗	◗	▲	◗	◗	▲	◗	▲	▲
7 Develop Program to Measure Success		○	○	○	●	○											
8 Develop Process to Manage Scope				○	○	●											
9 Ongoing Project Management					○	●											

LEGEND:
Primary Responsibility for the Task = ●
Involved in the Task = ○
Provides Input to the Task = ◗
Informed Task Results = □
Optional Involvement in the Task = ▲

FIGURE 3.10   Project plan tasks for project planning and management.

CHAPTER 4

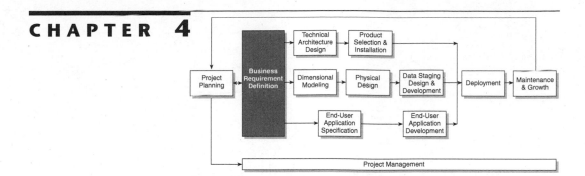

Collecting the Requirements

Business users and their requirements impact almost every decision made throughout the implementation of a data warehouse. From our perspective, business requirements sit at the center of the "data warehouse universe" as illustrated in Figure 4.1. As you read in Chapter 3, the scope of your data warehouse initiative must be driven by business requirements. Requirements determine what data must be available in the data warehouse, how it is organized, and how often it is updated. Although architecture design sounds like a technology-centric activity, business-driven requirements, such as the number of warehouse users and their locations, have a large impact on the architecture. Clearly, the end-user application templates are defined by requirements. Finally, your deployment, maintenance, and growth plans must be user-driven. You begin to formulate answers to all these lifecycle questions based on your understanding of users' business requirements.

This chapter provides tips and techniques for effectively uncovering business requirements. It begins with a recommended overall approach, focusing on interviewing techniques for requirements gathering and the preliminary data auditing. Specific tactics to prepare for the interview, including research, questionnaire development, interviewee selection,

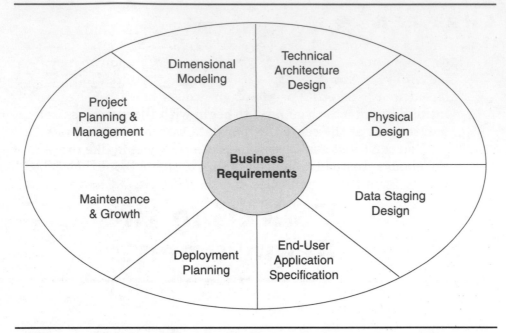

FIGURE 4.1   Business requirements impact virtually every aspect of the data warehouse project.

and scheduling, are detailed. The interview flow is then outlined, along with interviewing ground rules and common obstacles. Analysis of the interview findings and deliverable development are discussed. Finally, we review the use of facilitation, particularly for prioritizing and consensus-building at the conclusion of requirements analysis.

This chapter is a must-read for project managers and business system analysts who are leading requirements definition activities. Likewise, any other team members who are participating in the requirements process should become familiar with the techniques and guidelines outlined in this chapter. Business and IS project sponsors should also peruse this material to help manage organizational expectations appropriately.

OVERALL APPROACH TO REQUIREMENTS DEFINITION

To better understand business requirements, we recommend you begin by talking to your business users. Although this may sound obvious, we have seen many organizations try alternative approaches. Unfortunately, we all prefer to operate within our comfort zone; we are at ease looking at copy books and talking with DBAs and source system experts. On the other hand, business users can be intimidating and demanding. They also speak a language that the typical IS person may be unfamiliar with—for example, the word *index* means something completely different to a marketing person than it does to a DBA. Regardless of the intimidation factor, you need to begin with the business users. Remember, they sit at the center of your data warehouse universe.

You can't just ask users what data they would like to see in the data warehouse. Instead, you need to talk to them about their jobs, their objectives, and their challenges and try to figure out how they make decisions, both today and in the future.

As you gather requirements from the business users, you should also intersperse some data reality into the process by interviewing key IS personnel. You must consider what the business needs in tandem with the availability of data to support these requirements. It's a balancing act, but failure is inevitable if you consider one without the other. As we conduct business user meetings, we begin interweaving sessions with the data side of the house, typically DBAs or operational source system experts. These meetings tend to start out as informal discussions with knowledgeable project team members. Once you begin to hear consistent themes from users, it is time to formally sit down with the data gurus and get into the gory details of their source systems. In these data audit interviews, you are trying to understand whether the data is there to support what users are asking for and whether the data is complete and reliable. You are also trying to understand where the land mines are hidden in the data. For example, there might be indicator fields that were never populated or were labeled one thing but then used for something completely different. These kinds of land mines will invariably expode when loading years of history into your data warehouse.

Interviews versus Facilitated Sessions

There are two basic techniques for gathering requirements and investigating the underlying operational data: interviews and facilitated sessions. Interviews are conducted either with individuals or very small groups. One advantage of this approach is that you need to schedule a relatively limited amount of time on the interviewees' calendars. You don't need to try to coordinate ten people for a full off-site meeting. Interviews also encourage a high degree of participation from the interviewees, which generates tremendous detail data. There is no way an interviewee can just listen without participating in one of these meetings. Interviews ensure that every voice is heard.

The alternative approach is to schedule larger group sessions led by a facilitator. Facilitated sessions can be used to encourage creative brainstorming with a limited number of participants. Although they require a greater time commitment from each participant, facilitated sessions can actually reduce the elapsed time required to gather information, assuming you can schedule a convenient time to meet with ten to twelve people within a reasonable time period. Based on our experience, facilitation is more appropriate after you have gathered enough baseline information to understand the general business and its vocabulary. Teams will often tell us that they fully understand the business, only to be amazed after sitting through an interview by all that was uncovered and learned.

We don't believe that one technique is necessarily always better than the other. We recommend that you use the technique that is most effective given your organization's expertise, challenges, and what you have already subjected your users to. No two organizations are identical, so there is no right approach.

Having acknowledged that different approaches should be used in different situations, we are going to describe the approach that seems to "fit" most often. It is actually a hybrid of the two techniques. Interviews are used to gather the gory details, and then facilitated sessions are used to agree on priorities and next steps. We believe the "interview first" approach ensures effective, productive facilitated group sessions.

The reader should note that most of the recommendations throughout this chapter will be applicable regardless of the technique chosen.

PREPARE FOR THE INTERVIEW

We believe the prerequisite setup activities prior to gathering business requirements are often overlooked. We want to review the techniques to position you for success by eliminating as many unknowns during the requirements gathering process as possible. These are all common-sense activities, but are frequently forgotten.

Identify the Interview Team

First of all, you need to determine roles and responsibilities within the interview team. We strive to have the same team conduct both the business user requirements and IS data audit meetings for continuity. We typically structure a team with the following team members.

Lead Interviewer

The primary responsibility of the lead interviewer is to direct the questioning. The lead interviewer also takes notes, primarily as the basis for the next questions to be asked. A key candidate for this role is the business systems analyst described in Chapter 3. Desirable characteristics include basic business knowledge and good verbal communication skills. It helps if the lead interviewer has a genuine interest and curiosity about the business. The best lead interviewers are "quick studies" who can think on their feet and are nimble enough to go with the flow.

This is a relatively risky role. Not everyone is cut out to be a lead interviewer. We caution against coercing potential candidates into working beyond their personally deemed competence levels. The lead interviewer's relationship with interviewees and the user community should be taken into consideration. The requirements analysis process depends on open, honest communication between the lead interviewer and interviewees.

Scribe

The scribe's primary responsibility is to take copious notes during the interview. The scribe should capture as much detail as possible regarding the interview content, regardless of whether it is news to them. These notes serve as the documentation base for the entire data warehouse team, many of whom may not be as familiar with the subject matter. The scribe also asks for clarification if a disconnect or misunderstanding between the lead interviewer and interviewee occurs. The scribe is the safety net that catches any points missed by the lead interviewer and can intervene if the interviewee is becoming frustrated with the process. Finally, the scribe asks questions during interview lulls.

Although it sounds like a relatively easy role to fill, again, not everyone is destined to be an effective scribe. Good scribes must be willing and able to capture excruciating details. Also, the scribe typically develops the initial draft of deliverables from the requirements definition activities, so solid written communication skills are necessary. Finally, some people may find the scribe's naturally passive role frustrating and be tempted to barge onto the lead interviewer's turf and establish themselves as the expert. Potential conflicts like these between the lead interviewer and scribe should be avoided as they are distracting to everyone in the interview.

We are generally opposed to using tape recorders instead of human scribes during the interviewing process.

We are sometimes asked about using a tape recorder instead of a human scribe. Generally, we discourage this practice for several reasons. First of all, tape recorders change the dynamics of the meeting. Users are often uncomfortable with the notion of being taped. Also, they might want segments of the meeting to be off the record, which makes for awkward transitions during the meeting. Second, the lead interviewer's written notes will inevitably not capture the full content of the interview. Someone will need to listen to the tape recordings and take supplemental notes from them. This process is somewhat like watching a television rerun. It is not very interesting but consumes large chunks of time. We believe it is better to have two people with two brains and two sets of eyes and ears actively engaged in the session rather than using a tape recorder as your partner.

However, tape recorders may be used to supplement the scribe, depending on their experience and comfort level with physical note taking. You will not want to listen to the whole tape, but it can be useful as a backup. If an interviewee is really on a roll, the recorder may be helpful to ensure that the complete content is captured without slowing down the interviewee. If you choose to use a tape recorder, you should inform the interviewee during the interview introduction that the tape will only be used by the interview team; the tape is not part of the permanent project files and will be erased once the interview has been documented.

Observers

Observers are an optional part of the interview team. Other data warehouse team members, such as data modelers, DBAs, or technical support specialists involved in tool evaluations, are often interested in sitting in on interviews. We frequently have observers during our interviews since we are transferring interviewing skills to our clients' data warehouse teams. Optimally, there should be no more than two observers during an interview. It is important to remember that the role of observers is to observe—they are spectators.

Conduct the Pre-interview Research

It is important to do your homework before starting the requirements gathering process. We recommend you start by reading your company's annual report. The letter from senior management provides clues about strategic corporate initiatives. If initiatives are mentioned by the president, you can usually bet it's important to know about them. You should also focus on the narrative review of business operations. You can usually skip the detailed financial statements as the important financial highlights have probably already been presented elsewhere in the report. Finally, the last couple of pages of the annual report may provide insight regarding organizational structure and reporting hierarchies.

If it is available, get a copy of your sponsor's internal business plan. You are inevitably going to discuss the business plan during the interviews, so you might as well read it ahead of time.

The interview team should also read the organization's external marketing literature, if appropriate. The Internet is another resource that should be leveraged. Take a look at your organization's Web site to understand the messages your company is trying to project to the marketplace, as well as your internal intranet for insight on organizational personnel changes and other company initiatives. Finally, you should use the Internet to research some of your key competitors. Understanding where your competitors are focused will probably provide insights into your own organization.

 Try to thoroughly understand any earlier attempts at data warehousing within your organizations.

The saying "those who forget the past are condemned to repeat it" certainly applies to data warehousing initiatives. Chances are that earlier efforts were not called "data warehousing" since that is the latest buzzword—maybe it was the "management reporting system" or "marketing information system" or some cleverly constructed acronym for a business-oriented reporting and analysis system. It is in your best interest to find out what worked, what didn't, and why. Most importantly, you need to determine who was involved in these prior initiatives. You will want to use a different approach when dealing with any interviewees who were involved in a recent data warehouse attempt.

Select the Interviewees

Working with your business and IS management sponsors, you need to determine who should be interviewed. It is inefficient, not to mention impossible, to speak with everyone, so you need to select a cross section of representatives. You need to have a documented organization chart to review with your sponsors or a trusted coach. It is important that you understand both the formal organization structure, as well as the more informal, undocumented organization. You need to know who is highly influential, who is considered a visionary, who is the departmental mover and shaker, who is a supporter, and finally, who is a naysayer when it comes to information-based decision making. You also need to consider the political ramifications of not interviewing someone. It may be easier to conduct an extraneous interview for political reasons than to risk alienating someone within the organization. Depending on the number, you may need to work with your sponsors to prioritize potential interviewees.

Select the Business Interviewees

Even though you may be focused on a single primary business area for your initial data warehouse project, you should interview horizontally across the organization beyond the initial group. This horizontal, cross-functional perspective helps build a blueprint to ensure that your warehouse will be extensible across the enterprise, especially when it comes to common data such as product or customer information. For example, Marketing may be designated as the initial user group. We suggest you speak with representatives from other functional areas, such as Sales, Customer Service, Logistics, Manufacturing, and Finance to better understand the big picture—in other words, the organization's value chain. This horizontal perspective is absolutely critical to developing the Data Warehouse Bus Architecture matrix, as we'll learn in Chapter 7. You want to make sure you have an enterprise-wide understanding of common vocabulary during the early development phases so you can integrate data in the warehouse over time and ensure that you are not building those dreaded "data islands" or "stovepipes." That doesn't mean you should take six months to speak with representatives from every function within your organization—focus on the core business processes.

You should strive for vertical representation from your target business user area. You need to meet with executive business management to understand high-level strategy and overall vision. However, you shouldn't just stay in the treetops. You need to venture into the middle management trenches of the target user area to add reality to your interview findings. Middle management understands how those high-level strategies are translated into business tactics. They also have a realistic perspective of where they'd like to be going with information and analysis versus where they are today. Finally, you should meet with business analysts from the target area. These individuals will have great insight into existing information usage. Naturally, we are all attracted to the "best and brightest" analysts, but you should meet with a cross-section of business analyst representatives to understand the needs of the masses, not just the empowered, privileged few.

Select the IS Data Audit Interviewees

Every organization has key IS people who know the data inside and out. You definitely want to interview these data gurus, kings, queens, and czars. You will also want to speak with the people who are responsible for the core operational systems. You need to conduct preliminary interviews with the programmers who support the likely candidate source systems, as well as key database administrators and data modelers. Finally, you should meet with IS liaisons to the user community.

The data audit interview has a different flavor than the business user interviews.

 The data audit is a systematic exploration of the underlying legacy source systems, not a free-wheeling discussion of where the business would like to go.

In addition, we also often meet with senior IS management during the interviewing process. IS management sometimes offers a vision for the potential use of information within the organization for competitive advantage. In other cases, these interviews offer guidance regarding overall plans for information dissemination throughout the organization. Although senior IS management may have already approved funding for the data warehouse initiative, depending on the size of the organization and communication channels, the data warehouse team may not fully understand IS management's vision or perspective on the project. It is important that the team allocate time to meet with these players to ensure they are in sync with general direction and strategies related to the data warehouse.

Develop the Interview Questionnaires

The lead interviewer must develop an interview questionnaire before interviewing begins. Actually, the lead interviewer should develop multiple questionnaires because the interview questioning will vary by job function and level. You are not going to ask a marketing executive the same questions you would a financial analyst. Also, the questionnaires for the data audit sessions will differ from business user requirements questionnaires. Though data audit meetings are more within our comfort zone, it is still important that the lead interviewer generate a more IS- and data-oriented questionnaire prior to sitting down with the data gurus.

The interview questionnaires should be structured to align with your intended interview flow. The questionnaire should fit on one page so you are not flipping through pages if the interview comes to a lull. It is important that the lead interviewer view the questionnaire as a fall-back device, not a rigid script. The questionnaire can help you organize your thoughts before the interview, but it shouldn't be followed like a cookbook during the interview. The lead interviewer needs to be mentally prepared for on-the-fly questioning to be successful. Figure 4.2 provides a sample questionnaire for a business manager or analyst. Questionnaire content for interviews with business executives and IS representatives are detailed later in this chapter.

Schedule the Interviews

Once it is time to actually schedule the interviews, we strongly suggest you get an administrator to help you. Even with electronic calendars, scheduling can become a nightmare. Also, don't be surprised by the lead time that is sometimes required. Especially with rigorous travel sched-

A. INTRODUCTION
- Discuss data warehouse project objectives and overall status.
- Discuss interview goals (e.g., focus on business requirements, talk about what you do, what you want to be doing, and why) and interview flow.
- Introduce interview team and roles.
- Confirm time available.
- Describe next steps following interview.

B. RESPONSIBILITIES
- Describe your organization and its relationship to the rest of the company.
- What are your primary responsibilities?

C. BUSINESS OBJECTIVES AND ISSUES
- What are the objectives of your organization? What are you trying to accomplish? What are your top priority business goals?
- What are you success metrics? How do you know you're doing well? How often do you measure key success factors?
- What are the key business issues you face today? What prevents you from meeting your business objectives? What's the impact on the organization?
- How do you identify problems/exceptions or know you're headed for trouble?
- Describe your products (or other key business dimension such as customer, vendor, etc.). How do you distinguish between products? Natural way you categorize products? How would you narrow a list of thousands of products?
- How often do these categorizations change? What should happen with your business analysis following a change?

D. ANALYSES REQUIREMENTS
- What type of routine analysis do you currently perform? What data is used? How do you currently get the data? What do you do with the information once you get it?
- What analysis would you like to perform? Are there potential improvements to your current method/process?
- What type of on-the-fly analysis do you typically perform? Who requests ad hoc analysis? What do they do with the analysis? Do you have time to ask the follow-up questions?
- Which reports do you currently use? What data on the report is important? How do you use the information? If the report were dynamic, what would the report do differently?
- What analytic capabilities would you like to have?
- Are there specific bottlenecks to getting at information?
- How much historical information is required?
- What opportunities exist to dramatically improve your business based on improved access to information? What's the financial impact?

E. WRAP-UP
- Summarize findings heard.
- What must this project accomplish to be deemed successful? Criteria must be measurable.
- Thank participants.
- Describe next steps (e.g., draft interview write-ups available within week) and upcoming opportunities for user involvement.

FIGURE 4.2   Sample interview questionnaire for a business manager or analyst.

ules, it might be two to three weeks before you can conduct an interview. You should plan for this inevitable down time. For example, it may be useful to use this time for data warehouse team education.

Sequence the Interviews

We recommend you begin the requirements definition process by first meeting with your business sponsorship. Optimally, you would interview the business driver, followed by a meeting with the business sponsor. You should understand the playing field from their perspective. From there, our preference is to initially interview in the middle of the organizational hierarchy, rather than leading off at the top or bottom. The bottom is a disastrous place to begin because you have no idea where you are headed. The top is an appropriate place to grasp the overall vision, assuming you have the business background, confidence, and credibility to converse at those levels. If you are not adequately prepared with in-depth business familiarity, the safest route is to begin in the middle of the organization.

If you are interviewing several marketing teams, several finance teams, several teams from the field, and conducting several source system data audits, you should scramble the interviews so that you don't complete one type of interview before you start another type. It is very typical to hear certain messages from marketing and then get quite a different perspective from finance or from a data audit interview. If you have completed all your marketing interviews, it is difficult to return to these people and try to resolve the discrepancies you have uncovered.

 Scramble the sequence of interviews so that you have a mix of departments and perspectives throughout the interview process.

Establish the Interview Time and Place

As for logistics, we suggest you schedule executives for private interviews. They can handle being a lone interviewee with a two- or three-person interview team. If an executive insists on bringing anyone else to the interview, their lieutenant will either participate sparingly or monopolize the interview. If they do contribute, it probably won't be at the level of detail that you need, so it is better to interview these people separately. Executives should be interviewed in their own offices or an adjacent conference room. It is always best to meet with users on their turf.

The remaining interviews should either be scheduled in candidates' offices, assuming there is adequate space for the interview team, or in a conference room in their department. We have been asked to do user interviewing in an IS conference room that was a 20-minute hike across campus from the user community. It may have been an easy room for the administrator to reserve, but users struggled to locate it. We wasted valuable interview time waiting for, or searching for, lost interviewees. When they finally found the room, they didn't have ready access to their key resources, like a binder of monthly reports. You should make sure the interview space is large enough to accommodate the interviewees and interview team, including the observers. No one wants to be shoved together like sardines. If you do meet in an office, you should shut the door to minimize disruptions.

 All interviews should be conducted on the users' turf. This minimizes delays, and allows the users to fetch supporting documents at the end of the interview. Make sure disruptions such as phone calls are minimized.

Interviews with nonexecutive business users may be set up as individual interviews or small group sessions. Middle management can handle an interview team, but the team may overwhelm a lone individual contributor. If you are scheduling small groups, the groups must be homogenous. The fact that all the interviewees "come from Marketing" is not homogeneous enough. You want the interview group to come from the same function and/or job focus. In small group interviews, no more than four people should be interviewed at once, representing no more than two organizational levels.

 Having their boss's boss in the same meeting is enough to squelch most users' candor and enthusiasm for the process.

Sometimes even two levels of organizational hierarchy in the same interview is too much, depending on the working relationship between the interviewees. Data audit interviews with IS representatives typically focus on a single source system.

Business requirements and data audit interviewing is exhausting. It requires intense concentration to listen, take notes, and formulate the next brilliant question. You shouldn't schedule more than three or four interviews in a day. Executive interviews typically require about thirty minutes, unless you have hit upon their hot button. You should allow a minimum of an hour for analytic users and one and a half to two hours for small groups. Last but not least, you need to reserve at least thirty minutes between interviews. You need this break between interviews to debrief, allow for "overruns" begin to fill in your meeting notes, and deal with biological requirements. Interviewing can be an extremely painful process otherwise.

Although you can't schedule eight interviews a day, we do suggest that you attempt to schedule the interviews in a relatively short period of time, remembering to allow adequate time for interview absorption, analysis, and documentation. As you saw in Figure 4.1, the requirements you gather impact almost every aspect of the implementation. Since you can't immerse yourself in dimensional data modeling until the completion of the interviews, you don't want to drag out the entire process. Interviewing is a critical path. We recommend you get it scheduled and finished in a reasonable period of time so that you can move on to the next step of the data warehouse implementation.

Prepare the Interviewees

Even before you start scheduling interviews, it is important that the project be appropriately launched. We recommend conducting a user kickoff meeting to disseminate a consistent message. All business users potentially impacted by this project, as well as their management, should be invited to reinforce their role and importance to the data warehouse. This meeting is similar to the project team kickoff meeting described in Chapter 3, but the focus and emphasis is shifted.

 Schedule all interviewees for a single large kickoff meeting at the start of the project.

A sample agenda for the user kickoff meeting is shown in Figure 4.3. We suggest the business sponsor start the meeting by communicating the *why* behind the data warehouse project. Everyone at the meeting needs to understand the importance of this initiative and the high-level level of commitment behind it. The joint IS and business project leads should then discuss the *how*s and *when*s of the project to help everyone understand the general approach without getting mired in the detail.

This meeting is a critical tool for managing your users' expectations. Everyone should get a consistent message regarding the preliminary scope and general timeframes. It is also an opportunity to set expectations regarding the amount of time users will need to invest in this project for interviews, requirements validation, checkpoint reviews on the data model or application specifications, and education. One of the indirect benefits of this meeting is to communicate that this is a joint user/IS project, not a technology-driven IS initiative. Rather, the data warehouse is a user system that is driven by user requirements. All users should walk away from the kickoff with a sense of ownership and commitment to make the project successful.

Sometimes the geographic dispersion of people makes a physical kickoff meeting impossible. If that is the case, you still shouldn't skip this step. The project still must be launched and all the information just described must be conveyed, even if it can't be accomplished face-to-face. You will waste valuable minutes at the beginning of every interview explaining this general launch information if it is not communicated up-front.

PROJECT NAME
User Kickoff Meeting Agenda

♦ **Introductions**

♦ **Project Overview**   Business Sponsor
   Goals & Objectives

♦ **Project Detail**   Project Manager &
   Scope   Business Project Lead
   High-Level Plan
   Project Team Roles and Responsibilities
   Users' Roles and Responsibilities
   Project Milestones
   Next Steps

FIGURE 4.3   Sample user kickoff meeting agenda.

As soon as requirements and data audit interviews are scheduled, you should send a pre-interview letter or e-mail message to the interviewees to set their general expectations regarding their meeting. You probably already met most of the interviewees during the user kickoff. The letter is another opportunity to reiterate the overall project and its objectives. This correspondence should be sent by someone they know and respect such as the business sponsor. Otherwise, it should be sent out jointly by the project manager and business project lead.

The pre-interview letter, illustrated in Figure 4.4, should let the interviewee know what to expect during the interview. You should explain

---

Dear ATTENDEE,

Thank you for participating in user meetings for the PROJECT NAME data warehouse project. As a reminder, the PROJECT NAME project is focused on . . .

The objective of the user meetings is to better understand your area's business goals and priorities which translate into data and analyses needs. Your insight during these meetings is crucial to defining the requirements for PROJECT NAME.

Specifically, project team members intend to discuss the following topics during their meeting with you:

- **Responsibilities**
  Individual and departmental responsibilities
- **Business Objectives and Issues**
  Business metrics, industry and competitive trends, opportunities and obstacles
- **Analyses and Data Requirements**
  Key reports and analyses, frequencies and current limitations
- **Project Success Criteria**

Please **bring copies of the analyses** you are currently performing and/or requesting.

ATTENDEE, thanks in advance for your participation. The project team looks forward to meeting you on DATE at TIME in MEETING ROOM. Please call me if you have any questions in the meantime.

Sincerely,

Executive Sponsor or Joint Project Managers

CC:

FIGURE 4.4   Sample pre-interview letter.

that the goal is to understand their job responsibilities and business objectives, which then translate into the information and analyses required to get their job done. The interviewees may be asked to bring copies of frequently used reports or spreadsheet analyses.

 If there is any resistance from the users to sharing reports, don't push. The users will almost always give you stacks of reports *after* the interviews.

Finally, you should remind them of the interview time, duration, and location. A variation of the pre-interview letter should also be sent to the IS interviewees.

We typically advise against attaching a list of the fifty questions you might ask in hopes that the interviewees will come prepared with answers. It is nearly inevitable that they won't take the time to prepare responses to your list of questions. It is also likely that some interviewees will cancel because they've been overly intimidated by the volume of your questions. However, the interviewees' reaction to the "laundry list" approach varies by corporate culture.

CONDUCT THE INTERVIEW

Before we delve into the actual interview, we want to review some general interviewing ground rules.

Remember your Interview Role

The first ground rule for effective interviewing is to abide by your designated roles and responsibilities on the interview team. The lead interviewer is supposed to ask unbiased questions; the user is to answer; the scribe should take notes and everyone else should listen. The entire interview team should be absorbing like a sponge. Unfortunately, people seem to often forget their job assignments.

We have witnessed lead interviewers ask very leading questions of the user rather than the classic, open-ended why, how, what-if, and what-then questions. We have seen scribes get so caught up in the conversation that they forget to take notes. Finally, we have seen observers answering the questions rather than letting the user respond or defending the current systems using highly technical terms in response to criticism.

In each of these scenarios, someone on the interview team has missed the point, and they are not going to uncover what they need to be successful.

Verify Communications

During the interview, it is important to make sure you comprehend what the interviewee is saying. Paraphrasing what you have heard in your own words is one technique to ensure comprehension. It is also critical that you address any confusion during the interview.

You shouldn't wait until the interview is over to confide to your team members that you didn't understand what the interviewee was referring to during a fifteen-minute segment. The lead interviewer and scribe should have the courage to acknowledge that they are lost and resolve these miscommunication points during the meeting.

Define Terminology

As you are conducting interviews, it is important that vocabulary not be taken for granted. The exact definition of terminology will have a huge impact on the grain and dimensionality of your data model. We often find that the same word has multiple meanings and that different words are frequently used to mean the same thing. For example, we worked with a client on a data warehouse focused on customer revenue. Even though the board had approved a multimillion dollar budget for this project, no one seemed to have a consistent view or definition of *customer revenue*. Was it what the customer paid, what they paid less taxes, what they paid less commissions to third parties, or some combination of the above? Vocabulary standardization issues become especially apparent as you conduct interviews horizontally across the organization. You should be identifying and making note of inconsistencies in vocabulary during the interviews, but don't attempt to resolve them in the interview forum. You have just sent up a red flag that more work awaits you down the road as you attempt to define common vocabulary in the data warehouse. This type of issue is best resolved by a facilitated session with cross-department empowered decision makers.

Establish Peer Basis

It can be intimidating to conduct an interview with executive management. After all, we are mere mortals, and they are division presidents. If possible, the interview team should try to ignore those hierarchical differences and assume they are equals. It helps the flow of the interview if you are able to establish a peer relationship with the interviewee. A key to establishing this type of relationship is to use the interviewees' vocabulary. It is also helpful to demonstrate general business acumen, especially when you are trying to get the interviewees to think outside of the box. You may integrate general learning from earlier interviews to illustrate your understanding without forgetting that the interview is all about them talking and you listening. Finally, the attitude of the lead interviewer is also important. Within the same day, the lead interviewer may need to demonstrate the confidence to converse with an executive without being condescending to analysts.

Maintain Interview Schedule Flexibility

During the interview process, the number of interviews typically grows from 10 to 25 percent. It is very common for an interviewee to suggest that you meet with someone else in the organization. The interview team should anticipate these additional interviewees and view them as a bonus rather than a burden. Based on our experience, these additional interviewees frequently have keen insights to add. Since it is inevitable, the interview team should mentally prepare for the additions.

Avoid Interview Burnout

Having just suggested that the interview team stay flexible about adding interviews to the schedule, it is also important to remember that user interviewing is very draining. You will probably be exhausted and uncertain what you asked whom by the third or fourth interview in a day. It is a waste of everyone's time to attempt to conduct thirty interviews in a week due to the diminishing returns. Depending on the players involved, you may want to rotate the lead interviewer and scribe responsibilities.

You will know the interview process is nearly complete when you begin to hear significant repetition during the interviews, although you may still need to conduct some interviews for political or organizational reasons. Hearing the same answers repetitively is good news. It means that you have encircled the organization's business requirements.

Manage Expectations Continuously

The final interview ground rule is to manage user expectations during the course of the interview. Data warehouses are typically very high-visibility projects. The user kickoff meeting and interview process reinforce that visibility. Throughout the interview as appropriate, the data warehouse initiative should be presented positively, without overselling and making promises that can't be delivered on. Users should be informed that the data warehouse will evolve. The users are probably used to a more traditional, one-time requirements gathering process following by frozen specifications and a lengthy enhancement queue. Now is the time to set the expectation that data warehousing is an iterative process. There will be an ongoing process for gathering requirements and releasing functionality in the data warehouse. This leaves the door open for a return visit to gather more requirements for the next phase.

START THE INTERVIEW

We are now ready to begin interviewing. Every interview starts with introductions to remind the user who we are and why we are here. Depending on the interview team composition, the project manager or business project lead may communicate this high-level project information; otherwise, the lead interviewer takes responsibility for this part of the interview. Both the project and interview objectives should be reviewed. It is also appropriate to introduce the team players in attendance and explain their roles during the interview. Otherwise, the interviewees may wonder why the scribe isn't asking any questions. The overall requirements analysis process should also be communicated to the interviewees during the introduction. You should let the interviewee know that you will be documenting the interview, providing documentation to the interviewee for their review and feedback, and then publishing the consolidated findings. Finally, it is always wise to reconfirm the time available for the interview.

The first couple of minutes of the interview are critical as they set the tone for the rest of the meeting. We strongly suggest that you use organized notes or a pseudo-script for this segment of the meeting and rehearse what you are going to say in advance. It is important that you convey a crisp and clean message. You want the users to feel at ease and comfortable talking with you openly. At the same time, you want them to understand the importance of the requirements-gathering activity. In part, you convey this importance by being organized and prepared for the meeting. This is not the time or place to "wing it." It is also essential that you use the interviewee's vocabulary during the introduction. You should tell them that this will not be a technical meeting. Unfortunately, we have been on teams where the user interview introductions were littered with techno-babble, including hardware model numbers, network protocols, and so on. These comments were totally inappropriate and did not set a productive tone for the user interview.

 The one question you never ask in an interview is "what do you want in your computer system?" That answer is your job, not theirs.

Following the introduction, the lead interviewer jumps into the substance of the meeting by getting users to talk about what they do and why. The initial questions should focus on their jobs and where they fit. It is similar to the name and address block on a consumer survey. The questions are very simple, nonthreatening, and don't force the interviewee to think very hard from the start. You should ask them what their responsibilities are. Although you already know their official title from the organization charts, it is typically enlightening to hear them describe their key responsibilities.

From this point, there are forks in the road depending on the general responsibilities of the person you are interviewing. We describe each of these forks in the following sections. However, you should be aware that there are gray lines distinguishing these various routes. Some executives will have specific analytic requirements; some business analysts will have intimate knowledge of the underlying source systems. The interview content questions should be used as general guidelines.

You should strive to peel back the layers of the onion by asking high-level questions and then follow the interviewee's lead to get into the details. The ability to follow the interviewee's lead and ask follow-up questions distinguishes a mediocre interviewer from an outstanding one.

First of all, you are building credibility by demonstrating that you are listening and absorbing what they saying. It also gets you to the ultimate level of detail you need to build a dimensional model. If you stay at the treetops level of questioning, you will never get users to tell you what they need on a dimension table and which aggregates will be used most frequently. Finally, it is a very comfortable flow for the interviewee because it is conversational. People typically don't mind taking the time to tell you what they do. However, it is not much fun to be pelted with questions from a five-page questionnaire whether they make sense to ask at this time or not. We provide sample questions, but every interview flows differently. Don't expect to ask all of these questions or to ask them in this order; you need to go with the flow.

Business Executive Interview Content

The objective of the executive interview is to get an overall understanding of the organization and where it is headed. This perspective helps tie together the data collected elsewhere throughout the organization. High-level questions you might ask of an executive include the following:

- **What are the objectives of your organization? What are you trying to accomplish?**   These questions provide insight into the key business processes that they monitor and attempt to impact, such as increasing sales, decreasing direct mail expenses, and so on.

- **How do you measure success? How do you know you are doing well? How often do you measure yourselves?**   It is absolutely critical that you understand the organization's success metrics. These are the core data elements that must be tracked in the data warehouse. Depending on the situation, this data might be sales volume, market share, response rate, profit, quality, length of stay, and so on. The response to "How often do you measure yourself" has implications on the update strategy for the data warehouse.

- **What are the key business issues you face today? What could prevent you from meeting these objectives? What is the impact on the organization?**   This is the classic "What keeps you awake at night?" question, which may be a challenge for some interviewers to pose to their senior executives.

You need to be brave enough to ask executives what keeps them awake at night.

- **How do you identify problems or know when you might be headed for trouble? How do you spot exceptions in your business? What opportunities exist to dramatically impact your business based on improved access to information? What is the financial impact? If you could . . . , what would it mean to your business?**   These are key questions, especially if you still need to financially justify the data warehouse initiative. Even if quantified business impact isn't a current project concern, ask the questions anyway. The answers will probably be extremely useful at some point down the road.

- **What is your vision to better leverage information within your organization? Do you anticipate that your staff will interact directly with information?**   With this question, you are getting an understanding of their vision, and assessing whether they have the political willpower to encourage and reinforce fact-based decision making instead of the more prevalent gut-based process that is currently used. You will also gain an understanding of their expectations regarding their staff's interaction with data. Some executives don't want their staff to "play" with the data. If that is a concern for them, it is better to know it sooner rather than later.

Business Manager or Analyst Interview Content

The business manager or analyst interview is similar to the business executive interview, but the lead interviewer asks more detailed questions. As with the business executive interview, we begin with departmental objectives and goals following introductions.

- **What are the objectives of your department? What are you trying to accomplish? How do you go about achieving this objective?**

- **What are your success metrics? How do you know you are doing well? How often do you measure yourselves?**

- **What are the key business issues you face today? What limits your success today?**

- **Describe your products (or other key business dimensions such as customers, vendors, manufacturing sites, etc.). How do you distinguish between products? Is there a natural way to categorize your products? How often do these major categorizations change? Assuming you can't physically look at a list of all your thousands of products, how would you narrow the list to find the one product you are looking for?** Users' responses to these questions provide insight into how they describe key aspects of their business. The data warehouse must support "slicing-and-dicing" on these descriptive characteristics. The example question assumes you are interviewing someone focused on a product set. It could just as easily be a customer-oriented database marketing question, such as "How do you distinguish between your customers?"

  The team should also try to understand the relationship between these key business attributes. For example, "Is there only one broker associated with an account?" or "Can a rep cover more than one territory?" The team needs to pay close attention to the exceptional relationships. A red flag should go off if the answer is "Not usually" to questions like these.

Following these higher-level business objectives and overview questions, we typically move onto analysis requirements with questions such as the following:

- **What types of routine analysis do you currently perform? What data is used? How do you currently get that data? What do you do with the information once you get it?**

- **What analysis would you like to perform? Are there potential improvements to your current methods/process?**

- **Currently, what on-the-fly analysis do you typically perform? Who requests these ad hoc analyses? What do they do with the analyses? How long does it typically take? Do you have the time to ask the follow-on question?**

- **What analytic capabilities would you like to have? Is there much re-creation of the wheel across the organization?**

- **Are there specific bottlenecks to getting at information?**
- **How much historical information is required?**
- **What opportunities exist to dramatically improve your business based on improved access to information? What is the financial impact? If you had the capability just described, what would it mean to your business?**   These are key questions that should be asked regardless of whether quantified business impact is a current project concern. Sometimes it is easier for users, especially analysts, to describe their existing key reports and analyses, than respond to more free-form questioning. Rather than simply collecting copies of their current standard reports and spreadsheets, you should ask for details about how they currently use these documents. Inevitably, they rekey data into a spreadsheet program, where they are then building their personal "data warehouse."
- **Which reports do you currently use? Which data on the report is important? How do you use the information? If the report were dynamic, what would it do differently?**   Unfortunately, there is an abundance of data on current standard reports that is never looked at. The lead interviewer should try to identify opportunities for improving current reports. Maybe there should be additional data on the report, such as calculated ratios, additional summarization, and so on.

 The interview team needs to resist the temptation to focus only on the top five reports or top ten questions.

As you analyze the results of input based on current reports and analysis, it is important to remember than you are designing an analytic environment with the data warehouse, not a reporting system.

You need to understand the larger picture so you can construct an analytic platform that will allow users to build today's top five reports without running into a brick wall three months from now when they want a different set of top reports.

Interviews with business managers and analysts typically provide most of the detailed content derived from the requirements definition process. Unfortunately, deciphering the interview and translating it into a dimensional data model is more art than science. It takes practice to become comfortable with the free-form questioning while listening for key user information, including:

- Business objectives and key processes.
- Performance metrics such as revenue, share, variance, and so on.
- Vocabulary and business dimensionality. For example, a business manager may tell you that they want to look at monthly revenue by customer by product by sales territory. In this case, customer, product, and sales territory reflect the business dimensionality. We often refer to the "by words" as the *business dimensions* because the business users describe their analytic needs using these words. You should also listen for dimension hierarchies as the user describes their business. In this example, the manager may want to look at sales territories rolled up into their respective sales districts and regions, too.
- General information and analytic needs representing the business questions that must be answered, the data required to answer the questions (including information integration), the process used to answer the questions, and the frequency.

Inevitably, you will hear about constraints and problems with the current environment. "The data's not accessible, we are rekeying everything into Excel, the data doesn't match, . . ." This is all valuable insight, but it doesn't replace the need to fully understand the fundamental business requirements.

IS Data Audit Interview Content

The goal of the data audit interviews is to assess whether the data exists to support the themes you are hearing from the user interviews. The IS interviews are intended to provide a reality check. You should view these data audit meetings as surface scratchers. There will be subsequent meetings to really pour into the data and better understand the field definitions, granularity, data volumes, data demographics, and so on as described in Chapter 7. At this stage, you are merely trying to assess the feasibility of addressing users' requirements with existing operational data.

Following a discussion of their job responsibilities, we generally focus on several key data access and analysis requirements:

- **Request an overview of their key operational source systems.** Discuss the update frequency and availability of historical data.
- **What is the current process used to disseminate information to users? What tools are currently used to access and analyze information?** Review documentation (file layouts, copy books, or a data model) on existing reporting or analysis systems focused on this business process, including a demonstration if available.
- **What types of analyses are routinely generated?**
- **How are ad hoc requests for information handled? How are business users' data access and analytic requirements currently supported? Do multiple IS or business analyst resources support the same business users?**
- **Are there any known data caveats or quality issues?**
- **What is the biggest bottleneck or issue with the current data access process?**
- **What are your concerns, if any, about data warehousing? What roadblocks do you see to its success in the organization?**
- **What do you want the data warehouse to accomplish within the organization?**

At this stage of the lifecycle, the interview team should conduct data audit interviews until they are confident that source data exists to support the business requirements themes. You need not understand every nuance of the data, but you must be comfortable with the availability of data to address users' requirements.

We strongly caution that this may require more data digging than you might initially imagine. For example, profitability analysis, whether by product, customer, vendor, shipper, or agent, is a very common business request. Through a relatively superficial review, you'll inevitably learn that both revenue and cost information exists in your source operational systems. Based on this cursory understanding of revenue and cost information, you might jump to the conclusion that you can deliver profitability data to your business users. In most cases, you would have leapt to an erroneous conclusion and gravely mismanaged user expectations. In fact, upon further data interrogation, you probably would have discovered that your operational source systems don't capture cost information at the appropriate granularity or that it can't be appropriately allocated to support profitability analysis by a key business dimension. This is the classic data audit horror story. We encourage you to resist being overly hasty with your data audit interviews—it's imperative that you keep digging until you're reasonably confident about the availability of the core data needed to support the frequently requested business requirements.

WRAP UP THE INTERVIEW

The final step of the interview is its closure. The lead interviewer should watch the time and allocate at least five minutes at the end of the session to bring the interview to an orderly conclusion. The wrap-up should begin with a summarization of what has been discussed during the session.

Determine the Success Criteria

This is the time to ask about project success criteria. You have established rapport during the meeting. Now is the perfect opportunity to get a better understanding of their attitudes and expectations. The lead interviewer should ask what is the number-one thing this project must accomplish to be deemed successful. You should try to get them to articulate measurable, quantifiable success criteria. "Easy to use" and "fast" are not adequate success criteria because they mean something different to everyone. Based on our experience, this bare-your-soul success criteria question sometimes makes members of the interview team uncomfortable. They may worry that users will want subsecond response time to deem the project successful. If users' success criteria are unrealistic, it is better to know it now when you still have time to react and reset their expectations rather than learn of their expectations as you are about to deploy the warehouse. Acceptable success metrics include the following:

- **Implementation metrics.**   These metrics include the number of gigabytes of data available to users, number of users trained or number of users with installed end user software. Each of these could be tracked as of the end of a given time period.

- **Activity and usage metrics.**   For a given time period, such as a day, week, month, or quarter, you might track the number of queries, number of logons, total number of logon minutes, or average number of logon minutes.

- **Service level metrics.**   Some organizations establish service level agreements with their users that are based on the following types of measures:

  - Availability based on database and application server down time.
  - Data quality based on the number of errors (e.g., completeness or adherence to transformation business rules) per gigabyte of data.
  - Data timeliness based on the amount of time following the close of business before the data is available in the data warehouse.
  - Data warehouse responsiveness based on the average response time to a standard set of queries and applications.
  - Support responsiveness based on the average response time to service requests or average time to resolve service requests. Both these measures are extremely cumbersome to track.

- **Business impact metrics.**   Business impact metrics include the financial impact associated with cost savings or incremental revenue generation. This financial impact can then be used to calculate a return on investment. These are typically the most important success metrics for a data warehouse, although they are difficult to capture. Even if your numbers aren't absolutely precise, you should strive to capture and calculate these business impact metrics.

- **Performance against "pre–data warehouse" baseline.**   For example, you may hear that it took a week to perform a given analysis prior to the data warehouse; following the implementation of the data warehouse, the same analysis could be completed in less than an hour. These "before and after" examples are typically useful and impressive, although they presume that you had a pre–data warehouse baseline measurement for comparative purposes.

As you're wrapping up the interviews, you should thank interviewees for their participation and valuable insights. It's a good idea to request their permission for future contact to clarify any key points.

AVOID REQUIREMENTS INTERVIEW OBSTACLES

There are several common interviewing obstacles that you might run into as you gather business requirements:

- **Abused user.** This is an uncooperative business user who claims "we already told IS what we want." These users have been interviewed in the past but have yet to see anything result from their efforts. They are frustrated by these past false starts and will probably refuse to meet with an interview team again.

  As we mentioned earlier, you should proactively determine who was involved and interviewed in earlier attempts at data warehousing. Any documentation relating to business requirements from the prior project should be reviewed. Unfortunately, documentation is seldom sufficient to take the place of a face-to-face meeting with the user again. When scheduling meetings with these abused users, it is helpful to first of all acknowledge their participation in previous efforts and let them know that you have already reviewed the resulting documentation. The new session should be presented to the interviewees as a "validation" rather than as another interview. Naturally, users will resist going back to the very beginning, but may be more willing to meet if you are focused on understanding current priorities. Finally, this is probably a good time to select an alternative forum for gathering requirements. If interviews were conducted previously, use the earlier requirements documentation as a baseline and grounding for a facilitated session to gather details on changes within their business.

- **Overbooked user.** These uncooperative business users are simply too busy to meet anytime soon. If this is a contagious malady within your primary user organization and executive management is unwilling to acknowledge and address the condition, we suggest you stop now before expending more effort on this initiative. It is a safe bet that users who don't have time to meet and share their requirements won't have time to attend education and incorporate new information and analyses into their daily jobs. This results in a never-ending uphill struggle for data warehouse teams. We strongly recommend that you get off this slippery slope now before any damage is done. You will probably be able to find a more cooperative business partner elsewhere within your organization.

- **Comatose user.** These business users respond to your classic, open-ended questions with monosyllabic, one-word responses. Fortunately, this is a relatively rare syndrome. It is sometimes effective to ask these people questions from a more negative perspective. For example, rather than trying to get them to envision life outside the box, they sometimes find it easier to tell you what is wrong inside the box. We try to pry information out of interviewees like this, but it is senseless to prolong everyone's pain as these interviews are no fun for anyone involved. We suggest you make a valiant attempt, but if it is still not effective, abort the interview. You should schedule a replacement representative if this user is in a critical function or position.

- **Overzealous user.** This is the opposite end of the spectrum. This condition manifests itself when you think you are interviewing two business users, but seven people arrive in the conference room. The users are excited and want to be heard by the data warehouse team. It is great news that the users are engaged and enthused. However, that won't last long if you try to interview seven people in a single one-hour meeting. We suggest you quickly assess the homogeneity of the crowd. Are they all doing the same job and can build off of one another's ideas, or do they represent various jobs and functions? It is almost always the latter, so you should break them into smaller groups and give them slots on the interview schedule. This results in a more efficient use of everyone's time and ensures that adequate time is allocated for each meeting to gather the details you need.

- **Nonexistent user.** The final obstacle is typically fatal to a data warehouse initiative. This condition results when members of IS organizations say they know what the business users need, "in fact, we know it better than they do." These are the IS organizations that attempt to model their data warehouse based on existing data copy books exclusively and then don't understand why business users aren't clamoring to use the data warehouse. The good news is that this obstacle is totally within the ability of the IS organization to overcome.

You should also let them know what to expect next in terms of deliverables and opportunities for user feedback. As we stated in Chapter 3, communication with your users is extremely important but too often forgotten. Rather than leaving them in the dark, you should take advantage of every opportunity to let them know what to expect next. For example, tell them that you will have the documented interview write-up to them by a certain date and that you will need their review and comments returned by another specific date. It is then important that you meet the deadline you have established. You are building your credibility with the users at every point of contact.

Finally, we suggest you include a general disclaimer at the end of each interview, reminding the interviewee there is no firm commitment that what was discussed will be delivered in the initial release. Again, let the interviewee know about the high-level process you will be using to prioritize requirements. Also, they should be informed of general timeframes when these priorities will be communicated back to them.

REVIEW THE INTERVIEW RESULTS

Just because the interview is over doesn't mean that your requirements definition work is done. The team should informally debrief with each other right after the interview. It is very helpful to confirm that everyone on the team is on the same page regarding common, repetitive user requirements "themes." You should also identify areas where there is any misunderstanding so these points can be clarified in subsequent interviews. The lead interviewer should keep a running list of unresolved questions or open issues. If any team member has experience with the source operational systems, they should share their thoughts regarding the feasibility of the requirements being heard. There is no sense in letting these requirements gain momentum if they can't possibly be supported by data captured in the current operational systems. Finally, as you are defining requirements to drive the data model, you are also gathering insights about the users' comfort level with data, analysis, and technology. Users' expectations regarding their level of direct interaction with the data will have an impact on tool selection and the need for standard analysis templates and customized data-specific user education. These insights should be shared with other data warehouse team members.

As soon as possible following each interview, we recommend reviewing your interview notes and completing any partial remarks. Inevitably, your notes will be littered with dangling thoughts or stubs followed by white space as you jumped to capture the interviewee's next point. We also suggest that you comb through your notes and highlight key findings. We often supplement our notes with margin tags to identify business issues, information requirements, success criteria, and so on. These activities should occur immediately following the debriefing, if possible. Your interview notes will become an indistinguishable blob after even one full day of interviews.

 Summarize and flush out your notes within a few hours of your interviews.

You should also review the key reports and analyses gathered following the interviews. These reports and analyses typically provide a rough translation into your dimensional data model. As illustrated in Figure 4.5 and further described in Chapter 7, dimension tables will supply the values for the report headings and row or supercolumn headings. The reported numeric measures are represented as facts. In this example, the fact is sales dollars, while the month and region, district and sales rep hierarchy are supported by dimension tables. It is often helpful to review the gathered reports off-line for further insight on the business' dimensionality and users' analytic requirements. Sometimes you will see dimensions or attributes in these reports that never came up in interviews. Deeper granularity or more dimensionality should then be discussed in follow-up conversations with business users. Finally, you should label these key reports with the name of the end user who provided it and the date. These should then be filed with other project documentation.

 Don't forget to ask for key reports at the end of each interview. You will be amazed at what you will receive after a positive interview. Mark each received report with the donor's name, department, and the date received.

Sales Rep Performance Report
Central Region

	February 1998	January 1998
Chicago District		
Adams	$ 990	$ 999
Brown	990	999
Frederickson	990	999
Minneapolis District		
Andersen	950	999
Smith	950	999
Central Region Total	$4,780	$4,995

⇧
"Dimensions"
Report, row, and
super-column headings

⇧
"Facts"
Numeric report values

FIGURE 4.5   Analysis of business dimensions and facts from users' key reports.

PREPARE AND PUBLISH THE REQUIREMENTS DELIVERABLES

Formal documentation seems to be everyone's least favorite activity, so it is consequently the most frequently skipped task. We strongly recommend that you develop formal documentation from the requirements analysis process.

It is absolutely essential to write down the information gathered for several reasons. First of all, documentation becomes the encyclopedia of reference material as resources are added to the data warehouse team. Likewise, critical information will be lost if people roll off the team without documenting their findings. You won't have the opportunity to send the replacement resources back for a tour of the users world just because of team attrition. Secondly, documentation helps the team crystallize and better understand the interview content. It is one thing to listen passively to an interviewee, but another to actively document what was said. Finally, documentation allows you to validate the findings with users. It closes the loop with the users by confirming that we accurately heard and documented what they said. This checkpoint further reinforces the users' role as the driver for the entire data warehouse project.

Interview Write-Ups

As the first level of documentation, we recommend writing up each interview as soon as possible following the interview session. The write-up, shown in Figure 4.6, should organize the interview content by topic.

INTERVIEW WRITE-UP

BACKGROUND AND BUSINESS OBJECTIVES

John is Vice President of Outcomes Management at Healco. His organization focuses on analyzing patient outcomes in order to improve the quality of patient care, as well as operational efficiencies at Healco. . . .

ANALYTIC REQUIREMENTS

—Outcomes analysis
John wants the ability to analyze performance by diagnosis codes at a specific facility versus the company baseline broken down by patient age, cost, and diagnosis. He needs to evaluate functional improvement/decline based on a variety of key indicators including . . .

—Operative performance analysis
John's group analyzes operative performance by procedure, procedure type, and surgeon. Key monthly metrics include surgical procedure counts, patient counts, length of stay, and operative mortality. John's group wants the ability to probe deeper into the information. Are the exceptional outcomes isolated to a given surgeon? Is it due to unusual risk factors in their case load?

INFORMATION REQUIREMENTS

—Patient information
Patient demographics include age, gender, date of birth, risk factors, history of prior procedures. . .

—Diagnosis codes
Outcomes analysis requires all diagnosis codes including primary diagnosis, admitting diagnosis, discharge diagnosis, and secondary diagnosis. . .

—Acuity measures
Acuity measures are captured several times during a patient stay. . .

SUCCESS CRITERIA

John identified the following success criteria for this project:

1. Access to three years of history to support trending.
2. Productive usage of the warehouse with no more than two days of initial user education.

FIGURE 4.6   Sample business manager interview write-up.

It is important to provide a well-organized interview summary—this is not meant to be an interview transcript. Depending on the situation, it might include sections on business background and objectives, analytic and information requirements (including potential business impact), and success criteria. You should review this document with the interviewee and get their sign-off before publishing it for others' consumption.

Requirements Findings Document

In addition to the individual interview write-ups, the data from all the interviews should be consolidated and synthesized into a requirements findings document. This document is organized similarly to the interview write-ups to facilitate its creation:

- Executive overview
- Project overview (including requirements definition approach and participants)
- Business requirements:
  - High-level review of business objectives
  - Analytic and information requirements (typically organized by business process, as illustrated in Figure 4.7)
- Preliminary source system analysis (tied as often as possible to a business requirement)
- Preliminary success criteria

Depending on the breadth of interviews, we sometimes use a spreadsheet to consolidate information across interviews and assist in the development of the requirements findings document. The spreadsheet allows you to track the frequency of a response or requirements and to categorize and group the interview findings.

 The business requirements findings document is immensely important because it establishes the relevance and credibility of the data warehouse project. It also is probably the first time anyone has tied the business requirements to the realistic availability of data.

REQUIREMENTS FINDINGS EXCERPT

Sales Performance Analysis

Business users in the Sales Division want to leverage existing sales order information to better understand customer, product, and sales channel performance. They need to see the impact of pricing changes or promotional trade offerings on sales volumes and sales mix by product or customer grouping. Users currently receive summary monthly sales performance reports, but are unable to drill into the detail information. They also need to see sales trends over time, rather than just viewing a single month's activity compared to last year. Due to the lack of timely, actionable information, sales business users may be unaware of customer opportunities and problem situations. They need access to sales information on a daily basis in order to react to performance problems or opportunities *before* the close of the current month.

Typical analytic questions that could be answered with access to more timely sales order information include:

- How much volume have we done with a specific customer or group of customers over the last 6 months?
- Has my customer participated yet in a promotion which ends in two weeks?
- What is the sales mix by market and customer? Is there an opportunity to up-sell or cross-sell? Has that mix changed over the last 12 months?
- How does the sales mix for a given store compare with similar stores in the chain?
- What other products are frequently ordered with lower-productivity SKUs—are they dragging along sales and creating a larger "market basket"?

FIGURE 4.7   Sample requirement findings excerpt.

It is important that you communicate both the requirements and realities back to the users in this consolidated document. The data warehouse will not be a panacea for a twenty-five-year-old operational system that is wrapped in layers of bandages. A draft of the requirements findings should be reviewed with the joint IS and business project leads and sponsors and then distributed to the interviewees, their management, the data warehouse team, and IS management.

AGREE ON NEXT STEPS AFTER COLLECTING REQUIREMENTS

At this point, you have listened to users' requirements and conducted a high-level investigation of likely source systems. You have a sense of what users want and what it is going to take to deliver against those requirements. Depending on your organization, one or more of the following activities should take place now. First, users need to confirm that the synthesized requirement findings are accurate. Second, unless your users differ significantly from most we have worked with, they inevitably want more than can be delivered in a single phase of your data warehouse implementation. The data warehouse team needs input from the business community regarding priorities, and then the joint IS and business team needs to reach consensus and agree on scope before going forward.

Facilitation for Confirmation, Prioritization, and Consensus

Approaches for confirmation, prioritization, and consensus-building seem to vary from one organization to the next. We typically rely on a facilitated session with business and IS management representatives. Although it requires more coordination and effort, facilitation makes everyone part of the decision. The attendees walk away with a sense of ownership of the solution.

We suggest you use the business requirements prioritization technique described in Chapter 3. In this approach, the facilitation attendees should have already received and read a copy of the requirements findings prior to the session.

Following the prioritization as described in Chapter 3, the session concludes with next-step action planning as appropriate focused on realistic, measurable tasks in a specified time frame. Of course, any scope changes should be reflected in the project scope document as described in Chapter 3 and then redistributed.

Even if the initial project has already been firmly scoped, we still suggest a joint checkpoint session to confirm that the project team and business community are still in sync. It also brings the requirements definition tasks for this phase of warehouse development to closure.

Facilitation as an Alternative to Interviewing

As we said at the beginning of this chapter, facilitation is another viable approach for gathering user requirements. Although people often consider facilitation and interviewing to be dramatically different approaches, you will see that they are fairly similar by reviewing the following tasks associated with the facilitation process:

- Identify the facilitation team and roles (facilitator, cofacilitator/scribe).
- Prepare the facilitation team with background information and pre-workshop briefings.
- Determine workshop participants.
- Determine workshop schedule and coordinate logistics.
- Develop workshop materials.
- Prepare the participants with a pre-workshop packet sent by the workshop sponsor, outlining the project and workshop objectives and their roles to manage participant expectations.
- Conduct the workshop, beginning with a structured introduction, followed by interaction driven largely by the facilitator's style, skills, and prior experience, and concluding with a session wrap-up.
- Document the workshop results.
- Distribute to the participants for validation.

As you can see, the task flow for a successful facilitated session is similar to our recommended interview flow. Most of the techniques described in this chapter are applicable to the facilitation process with a few minor adjustments.

SUMMARY

The Business Dimensional Lifecycle approach is anchored in a fundamental belief that data warehouses *must* focus on the business and its requirements. This chapter provided specific tips and techniques to establish that focus with your business community. The information gathered using the tools described in this chapter will be invaluable as your data warehouse development effort unfolds, especially as you embark on the design of your dimensional model. Be sure to consult the project plan tasks spreadsheet at the end of this chapter for a summary of the tasks and responsibilities for collecting the requirements (Figure 4.8).

KEY ROLES

The key roles for collecting the requirements include:

- The business system analyst drives the process to gather and document requirements. The project manager, business project lead, data modeler, and end user application developer often assist with these requirements definition activities.
- Representative business users and management are actively involved in the interviews and prioritization activities. IS resources knowledgeable about the source systems also participate as data audit interviewees.

ESTIMATING CONSIDERATIONS

The effort needed to collect the requirements is obviously impacted by the project magnitude and scope. In general, we try to complete the requirements definition tasks within a four to six week window. Dependencies include:

- **Number of interviewees.**   Assume a maximum of three interviews can be conducted in a single day. Add 60 to 90 minutes for each interview, plus 30 minutes for debrief and recovery.
- **Ability to get on interviewees schedules.**   If possible, try to avoid conducting requirements definition interviews or facilitated sessions during the "busy season," while the annual planning process is taking place, or in the midst of some other time-consuming corporate initiative. These competing activities will have a large impact on your ability to schedule the requirements sessions and on the quality of the sessions given the distractions.
- **Number of source systems involved.**   The number of IS data audit sessions that must be scheduled is impacted by the number of source systems.
- **Level of documentation produced.**   Allocate a minimum of four hours per interview to produce a draft interview write-up. Addi-

continues

ESTIMATING CONSIDERATIONS (*continued*)

tional time should be allocated for the review process and incorporation of changes. Also, be sure to allocate time in the project plan for the analysis of the interview findings and development of the overall findings document.

- **Ability to schedule a facilitated session for prioritization and consensus.** You should begin lining up calendars for this wrap-up facilitated session prior to the completion of your overall findings document. Travel schedules can severely impact the timeliness of this meeting. Also, don't forget to allow time to prepare materials for this meeting.

- **Commonality of needs.** This variable impacts the effort required to reach consensus.

TEMPLATES

 The following templates for collecting business requirements are found on the CD:

- Template 4.1 User Kickoff Meeting Agenda

- Template 4.2 Pre-Interview Letter

- Template 4.3 Business Executive Questionnaire

- Template 4.4 Business Manager or Analyst Questionnaire

- Template 4.5 IS Data Audit Questionnaire

- Template 4.6 Interview Write-Up

- Template 4.7 Requirements Findings Document

Project Task	Fans	Front Office			Coaches		Regular Line-Up						Special Teams				
	Business End Users	Business Sponsor	IS Sponsor	Business Driver	Bus. Project Lead	Project Manager	Bus. Sys. Analyst	Data Modeler	DW DBA	Data Staging Designer	DW Educator	E/U Appl Devel	Tech/Security Architect	Tech. Sppt Specialists	Data Staging Programmer	Data Steward	DW QA Analyst
USER REQUIREMENT DEFINITION																	
1 Identify and Prepare Interview Team						●	○	○									
2 Select Interviewees		◗	◗	◗	●	●											
3 Schedule interviews					○	●											
4 Conduct User Kick-Off & Prepare Interviewees	○	○	○	○	○	●	○	○									
5 Conduct Business User Interviews	○	○		○	○	▲	●	▲				▲					
6 Conduct IS Data Discovery Interviews						▲	●	●	○	○		▲			○		
7 Analyze Interview Findings					○	○	●										
8 Document Findings and Review	◗			◗	○	○	●	○				▲					
9 Publish Requirements Deliverables	□	□	□	□	○	○	●	○	□	□	□	□	□	□	□	□	□
10 Prioritize and Revise Project Scope	◗	◗	◗	○	●	○	○	○	○	○	▲	○	▲	▲	○	▲	▲
11 User Acceptance/Project Review	▲	□	□	○	●	○	○	○	○	○	▲	○	▲	▲	○	▲	▲

LEGEND:
Primary Responsibility for the Task = ●
Involved in the Task = ○
Provides Input to the Task = ◗
Informed Task Results = □
Optional Involvement in the Task = ▲

FIGURE 4.8   Project plan tasks for collecting the requirements.

SECTION 2

Data Design

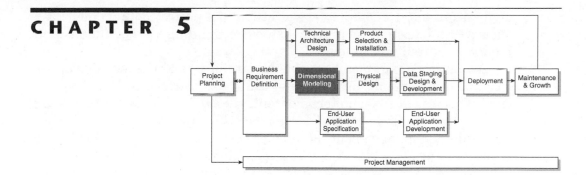

CHAPTER 5

A First Course on Dimensional Modeling

Now that we have gathered the business requirements and performed the data audit, we are ready to start on the logical and physical design of our data warehouse. This design will transform the legacy data resources into final data warehouse structures. The logical and physical designs are the cornerstone of the data warehouse. From these designs we will be able to plan the data extraction and transformation steps. We will able to estimate the overall size and administrative needs of the central DBMS, and we will be able to plan and begin prototyping the final applications.

The authors of this book have spent most of their professional careers designing and using databases for decision support. From this experience, we have concluded that the dimensional modeling approach is the best way to model decision support data. Dimensional modeling provides the best results for both ease of use and high performance. We start this chapter with an impassioned argument for the benefits of dimensional modeling. Then we show how a set of dimensional models can be fitted together into a Data Warehouse Bus Architecture.

This chapter provides a good introduction to dimensional modeling. Chapter 6 is a "graduate course" that explores a series of challenging design situations. In Chapter 7, we return to a project management perspective and discuss the practical steps for building a set of dimensional models in a real environment.

All project team members should carefully read the sections on the case for dimensional modeling and the Data Warehouse Bus Architecture. The rest of the chapter's content, the basic dimensional modeling techniques, should be well understood by the data modelers. If there are remaining questions about these basic concepts, it would be worthwhile to refer to *The Data Warehouse Toolkit*. Although the rest of the team does not need to have the same detailed level of understanding as the modelers, it may be useful for them to peruse the second half of this chapter.

THE CASE FOR DIMENSIONAL MODELING

Dimensional modeling is the name of a logical design technique often used for data warehouses. It is different from entity-relationship modeling. This section points out the many differences between the two techniques and makes the clearest possible case for dimensional modeling:

 Dimensional modeling is the only viable technique for delivering data to end users in a data warehouse.

Entity-relationship modeling is very useful for transaction capture and can be used in the data administration phases of constructing a data warehouse, but it should be avoided for end user delivery.

What Is Entity-Relationship Modeling?

Entity-relationship modeling is a logical design technique that seeks to eliminate data redundancy. Imagine that we have a business that takes orders and sells products to customers. In the early days of computing, long before relational databases, when we first transferred this data to a computer, we probably captured the original paper order as a single fat record with many fields. Such a record could easily have been 1000 bytes distributed across 50 fields. The line items of the order were probably represented as a repeating group of fields embedded in the master record. Having this data on the computer was very useful, but we quickly learned some basic lessons about storing and manipulating data. One of the lessons we learned was that data in this form was difficult to keep consistent, because each record stood on its own. The customer's name and address appeared many times, since this data was repeated whenever a new order was taken. Inconsistencies in the data were rampant, since all the instances of the customer address were independent, and updating the customer's address was a messy transaction.

Even in the early days, we learned to separate the redundant data into distinct tables, such as a customer master and a product master, but we paid a price. The software systems used for retrieving and manipulating the data became complex and inefficient because they required careful attention to the processing algorithms for linking these sets of tables together. We needed a database system that was very good at linking tables. This paved the way for the relational database revolution where the database was devoted to just this task.

The relational database revolution took place in the mid-1980s. Most of us learned what a relational database was by reading Chris Date's seminal book, *An Introduction to Relational Databases* (Addison Wesley), first published in the early 1980s. As we paged through Chris' book, we worked through all his Parts, Suppliers, and Cities database examples. It didn't occur to most of us to ask whether the data was completely "normalized" or whether any of the tables could be "snowflaked," and Chris didn't develop these topics. In our opinion, he was trying to explain the more fundamental concepts of how to think about tables that were relationally joined. All the issues of entity-relationship modeling and normalization were to be developed in the coming years as the industry shifted its attention to transaction processing.

Entity-relationship modeling is a discipline used to illuminate the microscopic relationships among data elements. The highest art form of entity-relationship modeling is to remove all redundancy in the data. This is immensely beneficial to transaction processing because it makes transactions very simple and deterministic. The transaction of updating a customer's address may devolve to a single record lookup in a customer address master table. This lookup is controlled by a customer address key that defines the uniqueness of the customer address record and allows an indexed lookup that is extremely fast. It is safe to say that the success of transaction processing in relational databases is mostly due to the discipline of entity-relationship modeling.

However, in our zeal to make transaction processing efficient, we lost sight of the original, more important goal of relational databases.

 We have created transaction-oriented databases that cannot be queried.

Even our simple order-taking example creates a database of dozens of tables that are linked together by a bewildering spider web of joins (see Figure 5.1). We are all familiar with the big chart on the wall in the IS database designer's cubicle. The entity-relationship model for the enterprise has hundreds of logical entities. High-end enterprise resource planning (ERP) systems like SAP have *thousands* of entities. Each of these entities usually turns into a physical table when the database is implemented. This situation is not just an annoyance, it is a show stopper:

- End users cannot understand or remember an entity-relationship model. End users cannot navigate an entity-relationship model. There is no GUI (graphical user interface) that takes a general entity-relationship model and makes it usable by end users.
- Software cannot usefully query a general entity-relationship model. Cost based optimizers that attempt to do this are notorious for making the wrong choices, with disastrous consequences for performance.
- Use of the entity-relationship modeling technique defeats the purpose of data warehousing, namely intuitive and high performance retrieval of data.

From the beginning of the relational database revolution, IS shops have noticed this problem. Many who have tried to deliver data to end users have recognized the impossibility of presenting these immensely complex schemas to end users, and many of these IS shops have stepped back to attempt "simpler designs." We find it striking that these "simpler" designs all look very similar. Almost every one can be thought of as "dimensional." In a natural, almost unconscious way, hundreds of IS designers have returned to the roots of the original relational model because they know a database cannot be used by end users unless it is packaged simply.

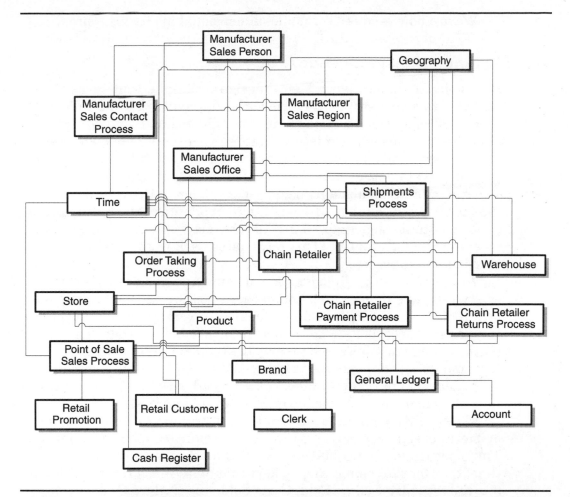

FIGURE 5.1   An entity-relationship model of an enterprise that manufactures products, sells products to chain retailers, and measures the retailers' sales.

 It is probably accurate to say that this natural dimensional approach was not invented by any single person. It is an irresistible force in the design of databases that will always appear when the designer places understandability and performance as the highest goals.

We are now ready to define the dimensional modeling approach.

What Is Dimensional Modeling?

Dimensional modeling is a logical design technique that seeks to present the data in a standard framework that is intuitive and allows for high-performance access. It is inherently dimensional and adheres to a discipline that uses the relational model with some important restrictions. Every dimensional model is composed of one table with a multipart key, called the *fact table,* and a set of smaller tables called *dimension tables*. Each dimension table has a single part primary key that corresponds exactly to one of the components of the multipart key in the fact table (see Figure 5.2). This characteristic star-like structure is often called a *star join*. This term dates back to the earliest days of relational databases.

Interestingly, the dimensional modeling approach may predate the entity-relationship modeling approach. As best we can determine, in the late 1960s General Mills and Dartmouth University developed vocabulary consisting of "facts" and "dimensions." We believe that this allowed Nielsen Marketing Research to carry these techniques forward with grocery and drug store audit data in the 1970s and later with grocery and drug store scanner data in the late 1970s and early 1980s. The authors first became aware of these ideas from Nielsen in 1984.

A fact table, because it has a multipart primary key made up of two or more foreign keys always expresses a many-to-many relationship. The most useful fact tables also contain one or more numerical facts that occur for the combination of keys that define each record. In Figure 5.2, the facts are Dollars Sold, Units Sold, and Dollars Cost.

 The most useful facts in a fact table are *numeric* and *additive*.

Additivity is crucial because data warehouse applications almost never retrieve a single fact table record. Rather, they fetch back hundreds, thousands, or even millions of these records at a time, and the only useful thing to do with so many records is to add them up.

Dimension tables, by contrast, most often contain descriptive textual

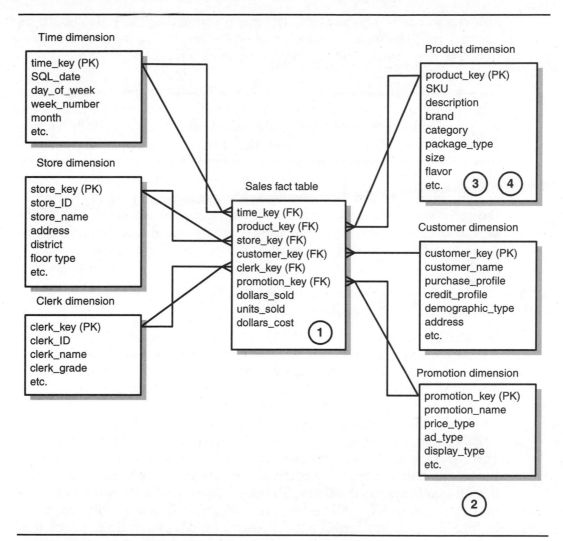

FIGURE 5.2   **A dimensional model isolating the retail sales process from the first figure. The facts and dimensions can be found in the entity-relationship model.**

information. The dimension attributes are the source of most of the interesting constraints in data warehouse queries and are virtually always the source of the row headers in the Structured Query Language (SQL) answer set. In Figure 5.2, we constrain on the lemon-flavored products via the Flavor attribute in the Product table, and radio promotions via the AdType attribute in the Promotion table. It should be obvious that the overall power of the database in Figure 5.2 is proportional to the quality and depth of the dimension tables.

 Dimension tables are the entry points into the data warehouse.

The charm of the database design in Figure 5.2 is that it is highly recognizable to the end users in the particular business. We have observed literally hundreds of instances where end users agree immediately that this is "their business."

The Relationship between Dimensional Modeling and Entity-Relationship Modeling

Obviously, Figures 5. 1 and 5.2 look very different. Many designers react to this by saying that there must be less information in the star join or that the star join is only used for high-level summaries. Both of these statements are false.

The key to understanding the relationship between dimensional modeling and entity-relationship is that *a single entity-relationship diagram breaks down into multiple fact table diagrams*. Think of a large entity-relationship diagram as representing every possible business process in the enterprise. The master entity-relationship diagram may have Sales Calls, Order Entry, Shipment Invoices, Customer Payments, and Product Returns, all on the same diagram. In a way, the entity-relationship diagram does itself a disservice by representing on one diagram multiple processes that never coexist in a single data set at a single consistent point in time. No wonder the entity-relationship diagram is overly complex. Thus the first step in converting an entity-relationship diagram to a set of dimensional modeling diagrams is to separate the entity-relationship diagram into its discrete business processes and to model each one separately.

The second step is to select those many-to-many relationships in the entity-relationship model containing numeric and additive non-key facts, and designate them as fact tables.

The third step is to denormalize all the remaining tables into flat tables with single-part keys that connect directly to the fact tables. These tables become the dimension tables. In cases where a dimension table connects to more than one fact table, we represent this same dimension table in both schemas, and we refer to the dimension tables as "conformed" between the two dimensional models.

The resulting master dimensional model of a data warehouse for a large enterprise will consist of somewhere between 10 and 25 very similar-looking star-join schemas. Each star join will have 5 to 15 dimension tables typically. If the design has been done correctly, many of these dimension tables will be shared from fact table to fact table. Applications that drill down will simply be adding more dimension attributes to the SQL answer set from within a single star join. Applications that drill across will simply be linking separate fact tables together through the conformed (shared) dimensions.

 Even though the overall suite of star-join schemas in the enterprise dimensional model is complex, the query processing is very predictable because at the lowest level, we recommend that each fact table should be queried independently.

The Strengths of Dimensional Modeling

The dimensional model has a number of important data warehouse advantages that the entity-relationship model lacks. First, the dimensional model is a predictable, standard framework. Report writers, query tools, and user interfaces can all make strong assumptions about the dimensional model to make the user interfaces more understandable, and to make processing more efficient. For instance, since nearly all of the constraints set up by the end user come from the dimension tables, an end user tool can provide high-performance "browsing" across the attributes within a dimension via the use of bit vector indexes. Metadata can use the known cardinality of values in a dimension to guide the user interface behavior. The predictable framework offers immense advantages in processing. Rather than using a cost based optimizer, a database engine can make very strong assumptions about first constraining the dimension tables, and then "attacking" the fact table all at once with the Cartesian product of those dimension table keys satisfying the user's constraints. Amazingly, using this approach it is possible to evaluate arbitrary n-way joins to a fact table in a *single pass* through the fact table's index. We are so used to thinking of n-way joins as "hard" that a whole generation of DBAs doesn't realize that the n-way join problem is formally equivalent to a single sort-merge. Really.

 The predictable framework of a dimensional model allows both database systems and end user query tools to make strong assumptions about the data that aid in presentation and performance.

A second strength of the dimensional model is that the predictable framework of the star join schema withstands unexpected changes in user behavior. Every dimension is equivalent. All dimensions can be thought of as symmetrically equal entry points into the fact table. The logical design can be done nearly independent of expected query patterns. The user interfaces are symmetrical, the query strategies are symmetrical, and the SQL generated against the dimensional model is symmetrical.

A third strength of the dimensional model is that it is gracefully extensible to accommodate unexpected new data elements and new design decisions. By that, we mean several things. First, all existing tables can be changed in place either by simply adding new data rows in the table or by executing an SQL ALTER TABLE command. Data should not have to be reloaded. Graceful extensibility also means that that no query tool or reporting tool needs to be reprogrammed to accommodate the change. And finally, graceful extensibility means that all old applications continue to run without yielding different results. In Figure 5.2, we have labeled the schema with the numbers 1 through 4 indicating where we can make the following graceful changes to the design after the data warehouse is up and running by:

1. Adding new unanticipated facts, as long as they are consistent with the fundamental grain of the existing fact table.

2. Adding completely new dimensions, as long as a single value of that dimension is defined for each existing fact record.
3. Adding new unanticipated dimensional attributes.
4. Breaking existing dimension records down to a lower level of granularity from a certain point in time forward.

 Dimensional models can be changed gracefully.

A fourth strength of the dimensional model is that there are a number of standard approaches for handling common modeling situations in the business world. Each of these situations has a well-understood set of alternatives that can be specifically programmed in report writers, query tools, and other user interfaces. These modeling situations include:

- Slowly changing dimensions, where a "constant" dimension like Product or Customer actually evolves slowly and asynchronously. Dimensional modeling provides specific techniques for handling slowly changing dimensions, depending on the business environment.
- Heterogeneous products, where a business like a bank needs to track a number of different lines of business together within a single common set of attributes and facts, but at the same time needs to describe and measure the individual lines of business in highly idiosyncratic ways using incompatible facts.
- Pay-in-advance databases, where the transactions of a business are not little pieces of revenue, but the business needs to look at both the individual transactions as well as report on revenue on a regular basis.
- Event-handling databases, where the fact table usually turns out to be "factless."

A final strength of the dimensional model is the growing body of administrative utilities and software processes that manage and use aggregates. Recall that *aggregates* are summary records that are logically redundant with base data that is already in the data warehouse, but are used to greatly enhance query performance. A comprehensive aggregate strategy is required in every medium- and large-sized data warehouse implementation. To put it another way, if you don't have aggregates, then you are potentially wasting millions of dollars on hardware upgrades to solve performance problems that could be otherwise addressed by aggregates.

 All of the available aggregate navigation software packages and utilities depend on a very specific single structure of fact and dimension tables that are absolutely dependent on the dimensional model. If you don't adhere to the dimensional approach, you cannot benefit from using these tools.

MYTHS ABOUT DIMENSIONAL MODELING

There are a few myths floating around about dimensional modeling that deserve to be addressed.

Myth #1 is that *implementing a dimensional data model will lead to stovepipe decision support systems*. This myth sometimes goes on to blame denormalization for supporting only specific applications that therefore cannot be changed. This is a short-sighted interpretation of dimensional modeling that has managed to get the message exactly backwards. First, we have argued that every entity-relation model has an equivalent set of dimensional models that contain the same information. Second, we have shown that even in the presence of organizational change and end-user adaptation, the dimensional model extends gracefully without altering its form. It is in fact the entity-relation model that whipsaws the application designers and the end users by requiring SQL to be rewritten.

A source of this myth, in our opinion, is the designer struggling with fact tables that have been prematurely aggregated. For instance, the design in Figure 5.2 is expressed at the individual sales ticket line item level. This is the correct starting point for the retail database because it is the lowest possible grain of data. There just isn't any further breakdown of the sales transaction. If the designer had started with a fact table that had been aggregated up to weekly sales totals by store, then there would be all sorts of problems in adding new dimensions, new attributes, and new facts. However, this isn't a problem with the design technique, this is a problem with the database being prematurely aggregated.

Myth #2 is that *no one understands dimensional modeling*. We have seen hundreds of really good dimensional designs done by people we have never met or had in our classes. There is a whole generation of designers from the packaged goods retail and manufacturing industries who have been using and designing dimensional databases for the last 15 years. We personally learned about dimensional models from existing A.C. Nielsen and IRI applications that were installed and working in places like Procter & Gamble and Clorox as early as 1982.

Incidentally, although this section has been couched in terms of relational databases, nearly all the arguments in favor of the power of dimensional modeling hold perfectly well for proprietary multidimensional databases, such as Oracle Express, Arbor Essbase, Microsoft's SQL Server OLAP component, and others.

Myth #3 is that d*imensional models only work with retail databases*. This myth is rooted in the historical origins of dimensional modeling but not in its current-day reality. Dimensional modeling has been applied to many different business areas, including retail banking, commercial banking, property and casualty insurance, health insurance, life insurance, brokerage customer analysis, telephone company operations, newspaper advertising, oil company fuel sales, government agency spending, manufacturing shipments, health care, and many more.

Myth #4 is that *snowflaking is an alternative to dimensional modeling*. Snowflaking is removing low-cardinality textual attributes from dimension tables and placing them in "secondary" dimension tables. For instance, a product category can be treated this way and physically removed from the low-level product dimension table. While we believe this compromises cross-attribute browsing performance and may interfere with the legibility of the database, we know that some designers are convinced that this is a good approach. Snowflaking is certainly not at odds with dimensional modeling. We regard snowflaking as an embellishment to the simplicity of the basic dimensional model. We think that a designer can snowflake with a clear conscience if this technique improves user understandability and improves overall performance. The argument that snowflaking assists the maintainability of the dimension table is specious. Maintenance issues are indeed leveraged by entity-relation–like disciplines, but all of this happens in the data staging area, before the data is loaded into the dimensional schema.

A data model that cannot gracefully accommodate new sources of data has probably been prematurely aggregated.

In summary, we firmly believe that dimensional modeling is the only viable technique for designing end user delivery databases. Entity-relationship modeling defeats end user delivery and should not be used for this purpose.

Entity-relationship modeling does not really model a business, rather it models the micro-relationships among data elements. Entity-relationship modeling does not have business rules, it has data rules. Few if any global design requirements in the entity-relationship modeling methodology speak to the completeness of the overall design. For instance, does your entity-relationship computer-aided software engineering (CASE) tool try to tell you if all the possible join paths are represented and how many there are? Are you even concerned with such issues in an entity-relationship design? What does entity-relationship have to say about standard business modeling situations like slowly changing dimensions? In a sense, entity-relationship techniques model the structure of data, whereas dimensional techniques model the semantics of the data.

Entity-relationship models are wildly variable in structure. Predict in advance how to optimize the querying of hundreds of interrelated tables in a big entity-relationship model. By contrast, even a big suite of dimensional models has an overall deterministic strategy for evaluating every possible query, even those crossing many fact tables. (Hint: you control performance by querying each fact table separately.) The wild variability of the structure of entity-relationship models means that each data warehouse needs custom-written and fine-tuned SQL. It also means that each schema, once it is tuned, is very vulnerable to changes in the user's querying habits, because such schemas are asymmetrical. By contrast, in a dimensional model, all dimensions serve as equal entry points to the fact table. The visual symmetry that is obvious in Figure 5.2 is mirrored in the query strategies that should be used with such a physical model. Changes in user's querying habits don't change the structure of the SQL or the standard ways of measuring and controlling performance.

Entity-relationship models do have their place in the data warehouse. First, the entity-relationship model should be used in all legacy OLTP applications based on relational technology. This is the best way to achieve the highest transaction performance and the highest ongoing data integrity. Second, the entity-relationship model may possibly be used in the back room data cleaning and combining steps of the data warehouse. This is the data staging area.

However, before data is packaged into its final queryable format, it must be loaded into a dimensional model on the presentation server. The dimensional model is the only viable technique for achieving both user comprehension and high query performance in the face of ever-changing user questions.

PUTTING DIMENSIONAL MODELS TOGETHER: THE DATA WAREHOUSE BUS ARCHITECTURE

One of the most widely debated issues in data warehousing is how to plan the warehouse construction. Do we build the whole data warehouse all at once from a central, planned perspective (the monolithic approach) or do we opportunistically build separate subject areas whenever we feel like it (the stovepipe approach)? We need to demolish two powerful myths. First, nobody believes in a totally monolithic approach, and nobody defends a totally stovepipe approach. All the leading data warehouse practitioners use some kind of architected step-by-step approach to build an enterprise data warehouse. We describe a specific variation of that step-by-step approach called the Data Warehouse Bus Architecture.

Second, we have moved beyond the phase in data warehouse development where a data mart must be restricted to being a highly aggregated subset of a nonqueryable data warehouse. This view of data marts is the source of many problems and misunderstandings. In Chapter 1 we defined a data mart to be a natural complete subset of the overall data warehouse.

 Every useful data mart should be based on the most granular (atomic) data that can possibly be collected and stored.

The Planning Crisis

The task of planning an enterprise data warehouse is daunting. The newly appointed manager of the data warehousing effort in a large enterprise is faced with two huge and seemingly unrelated challenges. On the one hand the manager is supposed to understand the content and location of the most complicated asset owned by the enterprise: the legacy data. Somehow (usually overnight) the new data warehouse manager is supposed to become an authority on exactly what is contained in all those VSAM, ISAM, IMS, DB2, and Oracle tables. Every field in every table must be understood. The data warehouse manager must be able to retrieve any such element of data and, if necessary, must be able to clean it up and correct it. On the other hand, the data warehouse manager is supposed to understand exactly what keeps management awake at night. The data warehouse is expected to contain exactly the data needed to answer the "burning questions." Of course, the data warehouse manager is "free" to drop in on senior management at any time to discuss current corporate priorities. Just make sure you get this data warehouse done pretty soon.

The pressure of this daunting task has built up to the point where its relief has a name. The name is *data mart*.

 The term *data mart* means avoiding the impossibility of tackling the enterprise data warehouse planning job all at once.

Data warehouse planners take refuge in carving off a little piece of the whole data warehouse and bringing it to completion, calling it a data mart.

Unfortunately, in many cases building separate data marts rather than a single data warehouse has become an excuse for ignoring any kind of design framework that might tie the data marts together. Vendors' marketing claims for a "data mart in a box" and a "15-minute data mart" pander to the marketplace's demand for a simple solution, but these claims are a real disservice to the manager of data warehousing who must make these data marts fit together into a coherent whole.

Isolated stovepipe data marts that cannot usefully be tied together are the bane of the data warehouse movement. They are much worse than a simple lost opportunity for analysis. Stovepipe data marts perpetuate incompatible views of the enterprise. Stovepipe data marts enshrine the reports that cannot be compared with one another. And stovepipe data marts become legacy implementations in their own right, where, by their very existence, they block the development of an integrated enterprise data warehouse.

So if building the data warehouse all at once is too daunting and building it as isolated pieces defeats the overall goal, what is to be done?

Data Marts with a Bus Architecture

The answer to this dilemma is to start planning the data warehouse with a short overall data architecture phase that has very finite and specific goals and then to follow this architecture phase with a step-by-step implementation of separate data marts, where each implementation step closely adheres to the architecture. In this way the data warehouse manager gets the best of both worlds. The data architecture phase produces specific guidelines that the separate data mart development teams can follow, and the data mart development teams can work fairly independently and asynchronously. As the separate data marts come on line, they will fit together like the pieces of a puzzle. At some point, enough data marts exist to make good on the promise of an integrated enterprise data warehouse.

Any successful data warehouse implementer who succeeds in implementing an enterprise data warehouse will inevitably perform the following two steps:

1. Create a surrounding architecture that defines the scope and implementation of the complete data warehouse.
2. Oversee the construction of each piece of the complete data warehouse.

Now stop and consider step 2. The biggest task in constructing the data warehouse is designing the extract system that gets the data from a specific legacy system into the data staging area where it can be transformed into the various load record images needed by the final database that presents the data for querying. Since the implementation of the extract logic is largely specific to each original data source, it really doesn't matter whether you think of the task as one task or whether you break it into pieces. Either way, you have to put your pants on one leg at a time. You will, in effect, be implementing your data marts one at a time no matter how you plan your project.

Conformed Dimensions and Standard Fact Definitions

In the architecture phase that precedes the implementation of any of the data marts, the goals are to produce a master suite of conformed dimensions and to standardize the definitions of facts. The resulting set of standards are called the Data Warehouse Bus Architecture. We are assuming here that you have a proper dimensional design for all of the data marts. Any given data mart is assumed to consist of a set of fact tables, each with a multipart key made up of dimension key components (foreign keys joining to the dimension tables). Recall that the fact tables all contain zero or more facts that represent measurements taken at each combination of the dimension key components. Every fact table is surrounded by a halo of dimension tables, where the dimension keys are primary keys in each respective dimension table. This design is also called a *star join*. These dimensional modeling constructs are defined carefully later in this chapter.

 A conformed dimension is a dimension that means the same thing with every possible fact table to which it can be joined.

Generally this means that a conformed dimension is identically the same dimension in each data mart. Examples of obvious conformed dimensions include customer, product, location, deal (promotion), and calendar (time).

 A major responsibility of the central data warehouse design team is to establish, publish, maintain, and enforce the conformed dimensions.

The establishment of a conformed dimension is a very significant step. A conformed customer dimension is a master table of customers with a clean customer key and many well-maintained attributes describing each customer. It is likely that the conformed customer dimension is an amalgamation and a distillation of data from several legacy systems and possibly outside sources. The address fields in the customer dimension, for instance, should constitute the best mailable address that is known for each customer anywhere within the enterprise. It is often the responsibility of the central data warehouse team to create the conformed customer dimension and provide it as a resource to the rest of the enterprise, both for legacy use and for data warehouse use.

The conformed product dimension is the enterprise's agreed-upon master list of products, including all product rollups and all product attributes. A good product dimension, like a good customer dimension, should have at least 50 separate textual attributes.

The conformed location dimension should ideally be based on specific points on the map, like specific street addresses or even precise latitudes and longitudes. Specific points in space roll up to every conceivable geographic hierarchy, including city, county, state, country, and zip code, as well as idiosyncratic sales territories and sales regions.

The conformed calendar dimension will almost always be a table of individual days, spanning a decade or more. Each day will have many useful attributes drawn from the legal calendars of the various states and countries the enterprise deals with, as well as special fiscal calendar periods and marketing seasons relevant only to internal managers.

Conformed dimensions are enormously important to the data warehouse.

 Without a strict adherence to conformed dimensions, the data warehouse cannot function as an integrated whole.

If a dimension like customer or product is used in an nonconformed way, then either the separate data marts simply cannot be used together, or worse, attempts to use them together will produce wrong results. To state this more positively, conformed dimensions make the following possible:

1. A single dimension table can be used against multiple fact tables in the same database space.
2. User interfaces and data content are consistent whenever the dimension is used.
3. There is a consistent interpretation of attributes and, therefore, rollups across data marts.

Designing the Conformed Dimensions

The task of identifying and designing the conformed dimensions should take a few weeks. Most conformed dimensions will naturally be defined at the most granular (atomic) level possible. The grain of the customer dimension will naturally be the individual customer. The grain of the product dimension will naturally be the lowest level at which products are tracked in the source systems. The grain of the time dimension will usually be individual days.

We recommend that conformed dimensions always have an anonymous (surrogate) data warehouse key that is not a production system key from one of the legacy systems. There are many reasons for the data warehouse keys to be independent from production. The administrative goals of the production systems are different from those of the data warehouse. Sooner or later, the production system will step on the data warehouse, either by reusing the same key or by changing the administrative assumptions in some way. Also, the data warehouse has to produce generalized keys for various situations, including the problem of slowly changing dimensions. We discuss slowly changing dimensions later in this chapter.

Taking the Pledge

If the central data warehouse team succeeds in defining and providing a set of master conformed dimensions for the enterprise, it is extremely important that the data mart teams actually use these dimensions. The commitment to use the conformed dimensions is more than a technical decision. It is a business policy decision that is key to making the enterprise data warehouse function.

 Since the creation of conformed dimensions is as much a political decision as it is a technical decision, the use of the conformed dimensions should be supported at the highest executive levels. This issue should be a sound bite for the enterprise CIO.

Using data effectively in a large enterprise is intimately connected to how the enterprise is organized and how it communicates internally. The data warehouse is the vehicle for delivering the data to all the affected parties. Changing the way an enterprise is organized, how it communicates, and how it uses its data assets is mainline business reengineering. The CIO of the enterprise should make all the separate data mart teams take the pledge to always use the conformed dimensions.

Establishing the Conformed Fact Definitions

Thus far, we have talked about the central task of setting up conformed dimensions to tie our data marts together. This is 80 percent of the up-front data architecture effort. The remaining effort goes into establishing conformed fact definitions.

Fortunately, the task of identifying the conformed fact definitions is done at the same time as the identification of the conformed dimensions. We need conformed fact definitions when we use the same terminology across data marts and when we build single reports that drill across the data marts as described in the last section.

Examples of facts that must be conformed include revenue, profit, standard prices, and standard costs. The underlying equations that derive these facts must be the same if they are to be called the same thing. These conformed fact definitions need to be defined in the same dimensional context and with the same units of measurement from data mart to data mart. Revenues and profits need to be reported in the same time periods and in the same geographies.

Sometimes a fact has a natural unit of measure in one fact table and another natural unit of measure in another fact table. For example, the flow of product down a typical manufacturing value chain may best be measured in shipping cases at the manufacturer, but it should be measured in scanned units at the retailer. Even if all the dimensional considerations have been correctly taken into account, it would be difficult to use these two incompatible units of measure in one drill-across report. The usual solution to this kind of problem is to refer the user to a conversion factor buried in the product dimension table and hope the user can find the conversion factor and use it correctly. This is unacceptable overhead in our opinion. The correct solution is to carry the fact in both shipping cases and in scanned units in the manufacturer's table or in a view of the manufacturer' table. That way a report can easily glide down the value chain, picking off comparable facts.

 If it is difficult or impossible to exactly conform a fact, be sure to give the different interpretations different names.

A similar unit-of-measure conflict can occur when reporting financial figures. Revenue is a very important measure but it can have slightly different interpretations. For instance, we must distinguish Month End Revenue from Billing Cycle Revenue. The most serious mistake is to seriously call both of these facts Revenue.

The Importance of Data Mart Granularity

The conformed dimensions will usually be granular (atomic) because each record in these tables most naturally corresponds to a single description of a customer, a product, a promotion, or a day. This makes it quite easy to bring in the associated fact tables at the intersection of all these granular dimensions. In other words, the base level fact tables in each data mart should be at the natural lowest levels of all the constituent dimensions.

There is tremendous power and resiliency in granular fact table data.

 By expressing the bedrock data of the data mart at the lowest grain, the data mart becomes almost impervious to surprises or changes.

Such a granular fact table can be gracefully extended by adding newly sourced facts, by adding newly sourced dimension attributes, and by adding whole dimensions. When we say "gracefully extended" we mean specifically that all old queries and applications continue to run after a graceful change has been made, no fact tables have to be dropped and reloaded, and no keys have to be changed. This notion of graceful extension is one of the strong characteristics of the dimensional modeling approach.

An unfortunate practice of some designers is to state that the atomic data in the data warehouse should not be in a dimensional format but should be highly normalized. This is confusing the data staging area with the data marts that make up the main, queryable data warehouse.

The main, queryable data warehouse must remain dimensional all the way down to the most granular data. It is impractical to drill down through dimensional data "almost" to the most granular data and then lose the benefits of a dimensional presentation at the last step.

When the fact tables are granular, they serve as the natural destination for current operational data that may be extracted very frequently from the operational systems. The current rolling snapshot of an operational system finds a happy home in the granular fact table defined at the Account by Day by Transaction level. In Chapter 6 we describe a common business situation calling for two companion tables, a transaction fact table, and snapshot fact table, that can be the bedrock foundation of many of our data marts.

A new and growing justification for extreme granular data is the desire to do data mining and to understand customer behavior. Data mining is generally much less effective on aggregated data.

Multiple-Source Data Marts

This discussion has mostly focused around single-source data marts that are recognizable images of legacy applications. In other words, if we have an orders system, then we have an orders data mart. If we have a payments and collections system, then we have a payments and collections data mart.

We recommend starting with these kind of single-source data marts because we believe it minimizes the risk of committing to an impossible implementation that is too ambitious. Most of the risk comes from biting off too big an extract programming job.

An efficiently implemented single-source data mart will provide users with enough interesting data to keep them happy and quiet while the data mart teams keep working on harder issues.

After several single-source data marts have been implemented, it is reasonable to combine them into a multiple source data mart. The classic example of a multiple-source data mart is the profitability data mart, where separate components of revenue and cost are combined to allow a complete view of profitability. Profitability data marts at a granular level are tremendously exciting because they can be rolled up through the customer dimension to generate customer profitability. They can be rolled up through the product dimension to generate product profitability. And they can be rolled up through the promotion dimension to generate promotion profitability. The lesson here is to be disciplined. Don't try to bring up a complete profitability data mart on the first try or you will drown in extract programming as you struggle to source all the separate components of revenue and cost.

Later, when you have time to source the cost detail correctly, you can bring up an Activity-Based Profitability multiple source data mart to supersede your single-source data mart.

 If you are absolutely forced to bring up profitability in your first data mart, then you may need to assign costs with simple rule-of-thumb allocations rather than by doing the complete job of sourcing all the underlying cost detail.

Rescuing Stovepipes

Can you rescue your stovepipes and convert them into architected data marts? You can do this only if the dimensions used in the stovepipes can be mapped one-to-one or one-to-many with the proper conformed dimensions. If you can, the stovepipe dimension can be replaced with the conformed dimension. In some cases the conformed dimension can gracefully inherit some of the special attributes of the stovepipe dimension. But stovepipe data marts usually have one or more dimensions that cannot easily be mapped into the conformed dimensions. The stovepipe sales geographies may simply be incompatible with the conformed sales geographies. Be careful about assuming that you can decompose something simple like stovepipe weeks back into conformed dimension days. While this sounds simple logically, you are probably making an unfounded assumption that you can spread a stovepipe week over weekdays and then turn around and add up again into months.

As difficult as it is to admit, stovepipe data marts usually have to be shut down and rebuilt in the proper conformed dimensional framework.

When You Don't Need Conformed Dimensions

If you have several lines of business where your customers and products are disjoint, and you don't manage these separate business lines together, there is little point in building a data warehouse that tightly integrates these businesses. For example, if you are a conglomerate business whose subsidiaries span food businesses, hardware businesses, and services, it probably doesn't make sense to think of your customers as leveraging your brand name from product to product or service to service. Even if you tried to build a set of conformed product and customer dimensions in a single data warehouse spanning all the lines of business, most of the reports would end up weirdly "diagonalized" with the data from each business line in rows and columns not shared by the other lines. In this case your data warehouse would mimic your management structure, and you would be better off building separate, self-contained data warehouses for each subsidiary.

In this section we have described a rational approach to decomposing the daunting task of planning an enterprise data warehouse. We have achieved the best of two worlds. We have created an architectural framework that guides the overall design, but we have divided the problem into bite-sized data mart chunks that can be implemented by real human beings. Along the way, we have adjusted the conventional definitions of the data mart. We see now that a data mart is a complete subset of the overall data warehouse and almost always based on the most granular possible data we can extract from our legacy systems. Every data mart is a family of similar tables sharing conformed dimensions.

These conformed dimensions have a uniform interpretation across the enterprise. Finally, we see the overall data warehouse for what it is: a collection of separately implemented data marts bound together with a powerful architecture based on conformed dimensions and conformed facts.

The Data Warehouse Bus

Conformed dimensions and conformed facts are the "bus" of the data warehouse. The word *bus* is an old term from electrical power plants that is now used commonly in the computer industry. A bus is a common structure that everything connects to and derives power from. The bus in your computer is a standard interface that allows many different kinds of devices to be connected to your computer. If all the devices conform to the standard interface definition imposed by the bus, then these devices can usefully coexist with the rest of the computer.

It should be obvious from this section that conformed dimensions and conformed facts play the role of a bus in the data warehouse.

 By defining a standard bus interface for a given data warehouse environment, a new data mart may be brought into the data warehouse where it can usefully coexist with what is already there.

Almost certainly the new data mart will derive power from the bus, because the bus offers an array of standard dimensions and parallel facts that increase the expressiveness of the new data mart.

BASIC DIMENSIONAL MODELING TECHNIQUES

Having made the case for dimensional modeling, let us review the standard techniques that define this data modeling discipline. This chapter discusses most of the important dimensional modeling situations without motivating the discussions with specific business examples. The grounding of these situations with examples is extremely important, but this grounding was done originally in *The Data Warehouse Toolkit*, and it is assumed that the reader is familiar with that material.

Fact Tables and Dimension Tables

The fundamental idea of dimensional modeling is that nearly every type of business data can be represented as a kind of cube of data, where the cells of the cube contain measured values and the edges of the cube define the natural dimensions of the data. Of course, we allow more than three dimensions in our designs, so we technically should call the cube a *hypercube*, although the terms *cube* and *data cube* are used by almost everyone.

Real dimensional models in the business world seem to contain between 4 and 15 dimensions. Models with only 2 or 3 dimensions are rare, and often lend the suspicion that more dimensions should be added to the design, if only the designer would stop and think. Models with 20 or more dimensions, for different reasons, seem unjustified. A 20-dimension design usually has superfluous dimensions that should be combined. Although the final choice of dimensions is the prerogative of the designer, there is a fundamental sense that the identity of the dimensions is rooted in the reality of the business environment, and not in the designer's taste. Few of us really believe that we live in a world in which 20 or more independent variables affect every observation.

Facts

A dimensional model distinguishes between facts and attributes. A fact is usually something that is not known in advance. A fact is "an observation in the marketplace." Many facts in the business world are numeric, although a few can be text valued. The designer should suspect that any numeric data field, especially if the value is a floating point number, is probably a fact, not an attribute. Sometimes a numeric value like a "standard price" seems to be an attribute of the product dimension, and it seems to be a constant that is known in advance. But on closer examination, the standard price attribute turns out to be adjusted once or twice per year. In these cases, late in the design phase, we change our minds and make the standard price a "measured" fact. We can ensure that there is ultimately no difference in the information content of the database, but we have made a typical (and correct) decision to make nearly all floating point number fields into facts.

Attributes

Attributes, by contrast, are usually text fields, and they usually describe a characteristic of a tangible thing. The most obvious attributes are the descriptions of products. The flavor of a product is a well-known attribute of the product, and it is probably displayed in a prominent way on the product packaging. We don't measure the flavor attribute of a product, we know it in advance. If we create another product with a new flavor, we create a new product record. Creating a new product record for a new flavor is a fundamental data warehouse activity, and does not require the production OLTP system to assign a new product ID to the new flavor, although they usually do.

Dimensions

The textual attributes that describe things are organized within the dimensions. In a retail database, at a minimum, we have a product dimension, a store dimension, a customer dimension, a promotion dimension, and a time dimension. A dimension is a collection of text-like attributes that are highly correlated with each other. There is a degree of designer judgment in the choice of dimensions. In a retail database, we could attempt to combine the product dimension with the store dimension and make a single monolithic product-store dimension. If we had 1000 products and 100 stores, we must ask how many product-stores we ended up with when we tried to combine these dimensions. If there was no meaningful correlation between product and store, and every product was sold in every store, then our combined product-store dimension would be the Cartesian product of the two original dimensions, and we would have 100,000 product-stores. Although this new combined dimension would contain exactly the same information as the original dimensions, we would reject this design immediately because the new larger dimension would be unwieldy and would present performance problems and no user interface advantages. Conversely, if the combined dimension contained only 2000 product-stores, it would indicate that products were branded to sell in very specific stores. In this case the combined dimension would be very useful. Not only would it be very compact, but the dimension itself would reveal much interesting information about the relationship between products and stores and it would be a desirable "browsing" target. In most cases the designer can use his or her intuition about separate dimensions to determine whether they should be combined, but in some cases the dimensions are abstract, and the designer may have to perform a series of COUNT DISTINCT operations on combinations of attributes to see whether they are really independent or not.

Inside Dimension Tables, Drilling Up and Down

Drilling down is the oldest and most venerable kind of drilling in a data warehouse.

 Drilling down means nothing more than give me more detail by, for instance, adding a row header to an existing SQL request.

In a dimensional model, the attributes in the dimension tables play a crucial role. These attributes are textual, or they behave like text, they take on discrete values, and they are the source of application constraints and row headers in the final report. In fact, one can always imagine creating a row header in a report by opportunistically dragging a dimension attribute from any of the dimension tables down into the report, thereby making it a row header. See Figure 5.3. The beauty of the dimensional model is that all dimension attributes are revealed to be equal candidates to become row headers. The process of adding row headers can be compounded, with as many row headers from as many dimension tables as the user wishes. The great strength of SQL is that these row headers simply get added to the SELECT list and the GROUP BY clause and the right thing happens. Usually we add these row headers to the ORDER BY clause also so that we get the grouping in a prescribed order.

From the preceding discussion we see that the precise definition of drilling down is to add a row header. A few query tool vendors have tried to be overly helpful, and they have implemented Drill Down commands in their user interfaces that adds specific row headers, usually from the product hierarchy. For instance, the first time you press the Drill Down button, you add a Category attribute. The next time, you add the Subcategory attribute, and then the Brand attribute. Finally, the detailed product description attribute is at the bottom of the product hierarchy. This is very limiting and often not what the user wants! Real drill down mix hierarchical and nonhierarchical attributes from all the available dimensions.

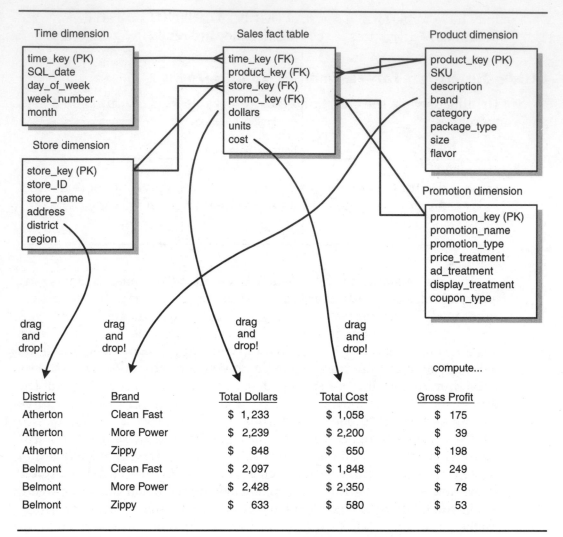

FIGURE 5.3   The relationship of a star schema model to a report.

In fact, there is almost always more than one well-defined hierarchy in a given dimension. In some companies, Marketing and Finance have incompatible and different views of the product hierarchy. Although one might wish that there was only a single product hierarchy, all of the Marketing-defined attributes and all of the Finance-defined attributes are well defined in the detailed master product table. See Figure 5.4.

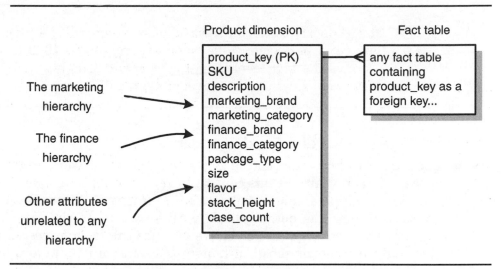

FIGURE 5.4 **A product dimension table showing two incompatible hierarchies and attributes unrelated to any hierarchy.**

Users must be allowed to traverse any hierarchy and to choose unrelated attributes that are not part of the hierarchy, like flavor.

Large customer dimension tables often have three simultaneous hierarchies. If the grain of the customer table is the Ship To location, we automatically have a geographic hierarchy defined by the customer's address (city, county, state, and country). We probably also have a hierarchy that is defined by the customer's organization, such as Ship to, Bill To, Division, and Corporation. Finally, we may have our own sales hierarchy that is based on assigning sales teams to the customer's Ship To location. This sales hierarchy could be organized by Sales Territory, Sales Zone, and Sales Region. In a richly defined customer table, all three hierarchies could coexist happily, awaiting all possible flavors of end user drill down.

If drilling down is adding row headers from the dimension tables, then drilling up is subtracting row headers. Of course, it is not necessary to subtract the row headers in the same order that they were added. In general, each time a user adds or subtracts a row header, a new multitable join query must be launched. If we have an aggregate navigator, each such multitable join query smoothly seeks its proper level in the space of explicitly stored aggregates.

In a properly tuned data warehouse, there will be little difference in performance between bringing back 1000 answer set rows at a high level of aggregation and bringing back 1000 answer set rows at a low level of aggregation.

The Importance of a Good Browser

The data warehouse marketplace has been using the word *browsing* for at least fifteen years. In this context, it means interactively examining the relationships among attributes in a dimension table. Data warehouse browsing has nothing to do with browsing on the Internet. At least for this section of the book, we will use the term *browsing* in the older data warehouse sense, although we realize our claim to this word is a lost cause.

A good browser should allow the user to explore an unfamiliar dimension table and reveal the relationships in it. The user should be able to enumerate all the distinct values of an attribute as a user interface action that takes place within one or two seconds. There should be a threshold number of distinct values above which the browser simply returns the COUNT DISTINCT rather than each distinct value. The results of a browse request must be affected by other constraints that may have been set in the dimension table during the browse session. Finally, a set of constraints that have been carefully specified during a browse session must be able to be saved with a user defined name so that this set of constraints can be used at various times in the future in queries and reports. Please ask your favorite query tool vendor for this set of features. If you get a blank stare, ask why the vendor's developers don't spend time building queries against real dimension tables with their customers.

Permissible Snowflaking

A dimension is said to be *snowflaked* when the low cardinality fields in the dimension have been removed to separate tables and linked back into the original table with artificial keys. An example snowflaked product dimension table is shown in Figure 5.5. Generally, snowflaking is not recommended in a data warehouse environment. Snowflaking almost always makes the user presentation more complex and more in-

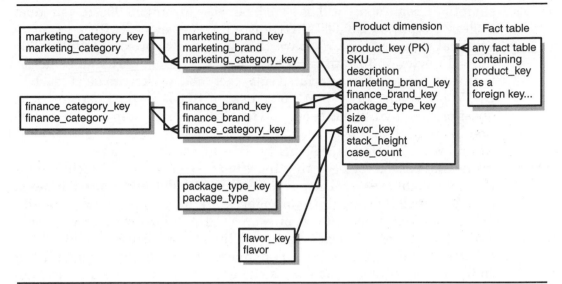

FIGURE 5.5 **The same product dimension table as in Figure 5.4, this time snowflaked to remove low cardinality attributes and place them in separate tables. Note the presence of many new keys to implement the new joins.**

tricate. Database designers often like this intricacy, but users are often intimidated by the detail. Snowflaking also makes most forms of browsing among the dimensional attributes slower. Remember that most browses involve selecting the distinct values of a dimension attribute *subject to one or more other attributes in the dimension being constrained.* Obviously a snowflaked category table will perform extremely well if the user is asking only for the distinct values of category with no ancillary constraints, but if the user is constraining on package type at the same time, then the query needs to join the snowflaked category table back through to the product dimension table and possibly out through another snowflake link to the package-type table where the constraint has been placed. In a realistic product dimension with 250,000 records, this query could run for several minutes on well-known relational databases. And yet this simple query is supposed to be a user interface action that responds in one or two seconds.

Some database designers snowflake because they are trying to save space on the disk. Surely by eliminating all those nasty text fields, we will save space. Granted, if the artificial key required for each snow-flaked entry is shorter than the text string it replaces (a reasonable assumption), some space will be saved. Suppose in our 250,000-row product table, we replaced 250,000 fifteen-byte category names with a two-byte artificial category key. We have thereby saved approximately 250,000 times 13 bytes or 3.25 MB. Our overall product table may well be larger than 100 MB, and the associated sales fact table is likely to be at least 10 GB. We have just saved 3 MB on a base of 10 GB, or 0.03 percent. This questionable savings has been paid for with an extra step of administration in creating and populating the artificial keys, as well as an almost certain severe performance penalty for cross-attribute browsing.

A final reason for not using snowflaking as a standard technique is that it probably defeats the purpose of a new and useful class of indexes called *bitmap* indexes. Bitmap indexes are meant for low cardinality fields, like our category field, or even Yes/No indicator fields with only two values. Bitmap indexes encourage the DBA to directly index all low cardinality fields. The best bitmap indexes may even perform a kind of "internal snowflake" that makes the enumeration of the distinct, unconstrained list of attribute values extremely fast. It is virtually certain that if the snowflaked value resides off in a remote table connected to the primary dimension table through one or more joins, then the ability to cross browse the original unsnowflaked dimensional attributes while using the bitmap indexes will be lost.

 Snowflaking (the removal of low cardinality attributes from a dimension table) almost always interferes with user understandability and cross-attribute browsing performance. Snowflaking probably interferes with the use of the new bitmap indexes in a dimension.

In spite of this prohibition against snowflaking, there are still some situations where we urge you to build a "subdimension" that has the appearance of a snowflaked table. See Figure 5.6. Subdimensions have some special requirements that make it different from a simple snowflaked attribute. In our example, the subdimension is a set of demographic attributes that have been measured for the county that the customer is in. All the customers in the county will share this identical set of attributes, and thus the dimension attributes are all at a different

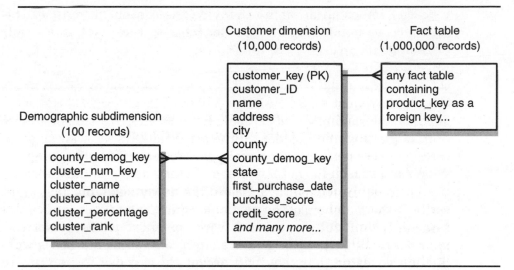

FIGURE 5.6 An example of permissible snowflaking where a large cluster of relatively low cardinality attributes can be removed all at once.

level of granularity. Furthermore, since the demographic data consists of the names and population counts and population percentages of 50 different demographic groupings, we have 150 fields in the subdimension. Now, for many reasons, it makes sense to isolate this demographic data in a snowflaked subdimension. First, the demographic data is available at a significantly different grain than the primary dimensional data and is administered and loaded at different times than the rest of the data in the customer dimension. Second, we really do save significant space in this case if the underlying customer dimension is large. And third, we may often browse among the attributes in the demographics table, which strengthens the argument that these attributes live in their own separate table.

Another similar example of permissible snowflaking occurs when we use a dimension like location or business entity or time in a "role." The creation of role dimensions, which are actually views on a single underlying dimension is described in Chapter 6.

The Importance of High-Quality Verbose Attributes

Dimension attributes are the entry points into the data warehouse. Dimension attributes are where most of the interesting constraints are placed. Dimension attributes provide the content of most of the user interface responses when the user asks to see what is available by browsing.

 In many ways the quality of the data warehouse is measured by the quality of the dimension attributes.

An ideal dimension table contains many readable text fields describing the members of the particular dimension. These text fields contain individual fully expanded words or short phrases, not codes or abbreviations. Data designers are often convinced that users want production codes or that they will accept these codes in lieu of full-text equivalents. A major responsibility of the data warehouse team is to source the full text for each code and to quality assure this text. It is helpful to remember that user interface responses and final reports themselves usually are restricted to the precise contents of the dimension table attributes. Incomplete or poorly administered text attributes lead directly to incomplete or poorly produced final reports.

The data warehouse team should eliminate attributes that look like

C001AX247

or

GRN PAPR TOWLS 3OZ MULTIPCK RVS

The first attribute is obviously a code, and only rarely would something like this be a desirable constraint or report row header. Perhaps it can serve as a semiautomated link for jumping through a 3270 screen back to the production system. The second attribute is a typical multifield abbreviation. While it may be useful for report headings, it cannot be used as a target for constraining and it is incomprehensible. What does RVS mean? This long field must also be presented as a series of separate fields with complete words in them, preferably mostly in lowercase letters.

The goal of the data warehouse team should be to make dimension table attributes:

- Verbose (full words)
- Descriptive
- Complete (no missing values)
- Quality assured (no misspellings, impossible values, obsolete or orphaned values, or cosmetically different versions of the same attribute)
- Indexed (perhaps B-tree for high cardinality and bitmap for low cardinality)
- Equally available (in a single, flat-denormalized dimension)
- Documented (in metadata that explains the origin and interpretation of each attribute)

Recommended Time Dimension

The Time dimension occupies a special place in every data warehouse because virtually every data warehouse fact table is a time series of observations of some sort. We always seem to have one or more time dimensions in our fact table designs. In *The Data Warehouse Toolkit,* we discussed a recommended standard time dimension table at a daily grain that contained a number of useful attributes for describing calendars and for navigating. We present that table in Figure 5.7 for reference. This table lets us compare comparable days and weeks across separate years, lets us find month ends, and lets us label our private seasons and fiscal periods. Remember that the big reason for this detailed time table is to remove every last vestige of calendar knowledge from our actual applications. We drive calendar navigation through the time dimension table, not through hard coded logic.

As data warehouses serve increasingly multinational needs, we can generalize the domestic view of this standard time table to handle multinational calendars as shown in Figure 5.7. In this case we include day names, month names, and holidays for all of the countries we must deal with.

Recommended Name and Address Coding for People

Any data warehouse that stores names and addresses of individual human beings faces a number of similar issues. Most of the current designs for name and address storage are too simple and lack structure that would be very helpful. Since so many data warehouses are trying to support detailed views of customer behavior and customer profitability, it is time for data warehouse designers to upgrade their designs.

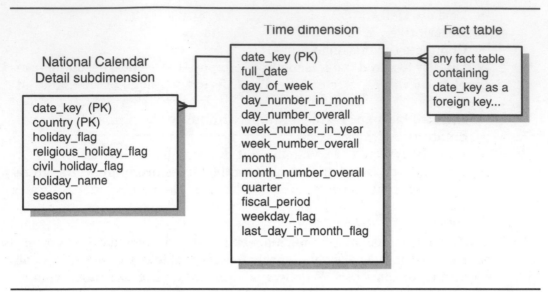

FIGURE 5.7   A subdimension for calendar details specific to a number of different countries.

The main application issues for names and addresses are to support the following:

- High-quality mailable addresses (i.e., creation of valid domestic and international address labels).
- Sufficient detail to support international mailing idiosyncrasies.
- Address parsing to support written or telephone greetings.
- Name part recognition to accommodate cultural idiosyncrasies.
- Address parsing to support easy to use geographic area queries.
- Address parsing to support address consistency analysis for data cleaning.
- Address parsing to support automated demographic and latitude/longitude matching.
- Alternate or multiple mailing and legal addresses.
- Alternate communication addresses, including telephones, fax, telex, and Internet.

Lacking a discipline or a design framework, most data designers allocate a few general-purpose fields for names and addresses, such as Address-1 through Address-6. The designer feels that "any eventuality can be handled with a liberal design with six fields. If anything, this is too elaborate."

 A good name and address record should be broken down into as many parts as possible.

It is too easy to design the name and address fields in a generic way that actually contributes to data quality problems. Consider a typical design with the following fields:

Field	*Example*
Name	Ms. R. Jane Smith, Atty
Address1	123 Main Rd, North West, Suite 100A
Address2	PO Box 2348
City	Kensington
State	Ark.
Zip Code	88887-2348
Phone Number	509-555-3333 x776 main, 555-4444 fax

The name field is far too limited. There is no consistent mechanism for handling salutations, titles, or suffixes, or for identifying what the person's first name is. Ad hoc abbreviations are used in various places. The address fields may contain enough room for any address, but there is no discipline imposed by the fields that will guarantee conformance with postal authority regulations, such as the Coding Accuracy Support System (CASS) guidelines from the United States Postal Service. This design may all too easily contain unmailable addresses and will not support downstream systems that use the data warehouse to automate customer greetings or create address labels.

The key to a proper design is a full breakdown of names and addresses with as much detail as possible. Very few individual records will have every attribute filled in. The extract process must perform significant parsing on the original dirty names and addresses. Ideally, the extract system will flag records with questionable parsing or unrecognizable elements. Abbreviations in the original data must be replaced with full text words. In other words, *Chas.* becomes *Charles* and *Str.* becomes *Street*.

Numbers rendered as words should become numbers in street addresses. A recommended set name and address fields for individuals in a business context are shown next. Some of the business organization fields could be omitted in a database of residential customers. Examples of the fields are shown, but one should not treat the entire set of examples as comprising a realistic *single* example of an address!

Field	*Example*
Salutation	Ms.
Greeting Style	Professional
Informal Greeting Name	Jane
First and Middle Names	R. Jane
Surname	Smith
Suffix	Jr.
Name Ethnicity	English
Gender	Female
Title	Attorney
Relationship	Trustee for John Doe
Organization	ABC Generic International
Sub Organization	Estate Planning Division
Second Sub Organization	Analysis Department
Street Number	123
Street Name	Main
Street Type	Road
Direction	North West
Post Box	2348
Suite	100A
City	Kensington
District	Cornwall
Second District	Berkeleyshire
State	Arkansas
Country	United States
Continent	North America
Primary Postal Code	88887
Secondary Postal Code	2348
Postal Code Type	United States
Contact Telephone Country Code	1
Contact Telephone Area Code	509
Contact Telephone Number	5553333

Contact Extension	776
FAX Telephone Country Code	1
FAX Telephone Area Code	509
FAX Telephone Number	5554444
(perhaps others, like home	
phone and pager numbers)	
E-mail	RJSmith@ABCGenInt.com
Web Site	www.ABCGenInt.com
Public Key Authentication	Type X.509
Certificate Authority	Verisign

Recommended Commercial Customer Address Coding

Commercial customers are represented in the data warehouse quite differently than individual people are. Commercial customers have complex names and multiple addresses. Commercial customers usually have a hierarchy of identities ranging from individual locations or organizations up through regional offices, international headquarters, and parent companies. These hierarchical relationships change frequently as customers reorganize themselves internally or are involved in acquisitions and divestitures. In our experience, the best representation of this complex picture is to make a separate customer record for each level of this kind of hierarchy. Doing this allows us to focus on the issues of describing a single customer entity without also trying to represent the hierarchy itself. In Chapter 6, we will return to the larger issue of representing and navigating the hierarchy.

A single commercial customer may have multiple addresses, such as physical address and shipping address. Each address follows much the same logic as the address structure for people we developed in the previous section:

- Organization name
- Post name
- Post name abbreviation
- Role
- Street name
- Street type
- Street number
- Street modifier
- Location 1

- . . . Location 5
- City
- Pre-city modifier
- Post-city modifier
- District (area, county)
- Primary postal code
- Secondary postal code
- State
- Country
- Continent

Slowly Changing Dimensions

In *The Data Warehouse Toolkit,* we discussed the classic techniques for handling a slowly changing dimension like a product or a customer. The key assumption is that the production product key or the production customer key does not change, but the description of the product or customer does. In response to these changes, the data warehouse has three main options:

1. Overwrite the dimension record with the new values, thereby losing history.
2. Create a new additional dimension record using a new value of the surrogate key.
3. Create an "old" field in the dimension record to store the immediate previous attribute value.

These three options are referred to as the Type 1, 2, and 3 responses to a slowly changing dimension. The Type 1 response is used whenever the old value of the attribute has no significance or should be discarded. Certainly, the correction of an error falls into this category. The Type 2 response is the primary technique for accurately tracking a change in an attribute within a dimension.

 The Type 2 response *requires* the use of a surrogate key because we are assuming that the production product key or customer key has not been allowed to change.

It is permissible in this case to place an effective date and an end date in the record, but this should be done with caution. These dates do not have the same meaning as a date key in a fact table. For instance, the begin effective date and the end effective date in a product record might refer to the span of time during which the particular formulation of the product was being manufactured. But the date in a corresponding fact table might indicate when the product was sold, and this selling date does not have to lie within the span of times defined in the dimension record. These various dates simply have different meanings. Also, one needs to be careful about the interpretation of the effective dates in the dimension if there are several possible dimension attributes that might get updated. In such a case, what do the effective dates refer to? A general solution to this dilemma of effective dates is presented in the human resources tracking example in Chapter 6.

The Type 2 response to a slowly changing dimension is used when a true physical change to the dimension entity (like a product or customer) has taken place and it is appropriate to perfectly partition history by the different descriptions. Each of the separate surrogate keys governs a unique description of the product or customer that was true for a span of time. Thus each particular surrogate key is naturally used during the time when the particular instance of the product or customer was valid. Simply by constraining on any combination of attributes in the dimension, the query does the right thing. If the query constrains directly on the attribute that was changed, then it can very precisely pick out the version of the product or customer that is needed. But if the query naturally constrains on other attributes in the dimension unaffected by the slow changes, then several versions of the product or customer will be swept into the query. This is what we want to happen.

The Type 3 response to a slowly changing dimension is used in a different business situation than the Type 2 response. Usually in the Type 3 response we do not have a change that perfectly partitions history. We may have a change, like the redrawing of sales district boundaries or the redefinition of product category boundaries that is a "soft" change. In other words, although the change has occurred, it is still logically possible to act as if the change had not occurred. We may want to track the sales offices for a while with either the old or the new sales district definitions. We may want to track the sales of products for a while with either the old or the new category definitions. In this case, we cannot partition history disjointly as in Type 2 response, but we simultaneously provide both the old description and the new description in the same record. This lets us choose between the two versions of the sales district or the product categories at will.

 The Type 3 response is used when a change is "soft," or tentative, or when we wish to keep tracking history with the old value of the attribute as well as the new.

If we are using the Type 3 response to a slowly changing dimension, we push down the old attribute value into the "old" attribute and we write the new attribute value into the regular current field. This has the effect of causing all existing standard queries and reports to switch seamlessly to the new attribute assignment, but allows a query or report to return to the old attribute assignments (the old sales district boundaries or the old category boundaries) by changing the query or report to use the old dimension attribute. In using this technique, no new dimension record needs to be created and no new surrogate key needs to be created. It should be obvious that this technique works best for one such soft change at a time. If your environment really has a succession of many soft changes, and you really believe that the requirement is for the user to switch back and forth amongst more than two alternative sales district maps or more than two category definitions, then you need a more complex design. Make sure you really need such complexity because your application may be confusing to end users.

Rapidly Changing Small Dimensions

Although we have used the term *slowly changing* to refer to the occasional and sporadic changes that occur to dimensional entities like product and customer, this description is more a pedagogical aid than a real guide for the designer. After all, what is slow? What if changes are fast? Must I use a different design technique?

Even if your changes are rapid and happen every day or at least many times per year, you should probably use the Type 2 slowly changing dimension technique to track all the versions of your product or your customer. In Chapter 6, we describe a human resources tracking example where the profiles of 100,000 employees are each tracked through many changes per year. Even though the employee dimension is relatively large and each employee record is quite verbose (2000 bytes), we find it very attractive to use the Type 2 response, together with beginning and ending effective dates for each transaction. Please see the next chapter for the details of this example.

There is a certain self-consistency in the need to track rapid transactional changes to a product or a customer dimension. If you are a business like a telecommunications company that has thousands of rate structure–oriented products and services, and you are constantly tinkering with their definitions, then you almost certainly need to track each version of each product or service accurately. Especially if the definition of the product or service is independent from its provision, you must record these products or services in a dimension table. In other words, we don't want to lose track of a product or service just because we never actually provided it to any customer.

Similarly, if you are a human resources department or agency or are an insurance company, then you are very motivated to capture the descriptions of your employees or customers accurately. Again, this requires a large human being dimension table administered using the Type 2 response, as described in the human resources example in Chapter 6.

Finally, at some point we have to cry "uncle" and stop creating new dimension records for every measured change. This occurs in the extreme realm of monster dimensions and rapid changes. To handle this case, we must make some compromises. But first let us discuss these very large dimensions more broadly.

Large Dimensions

Data warehouses that store extremely granular data may require some extremely large dimensions. Any enterprise or agency that deals with the general public needs an individual human being dimension. The biggest retailers and the biggest government agencies have monster people dimensions whose size approaches the population of the United States (100 million records or more). Other, "more reasonable" dimensions in normal-sized enterprises may contain five or ten million human being records.

The biggest commercial customer dimensions, such as those in telecommunications, may contain up to ten million records. The biggest product dimensions, such as those in department store retail environments, may contain several million records. Big insurance companies may, in addition to their monster human being dimensions, have automobile or house dimensions with millions of records.

We are now in a position where in most cases we can support these very large dimensions with the current generation of relational databases. We must, however, adopt a conservative design to keep these dimensions under control. In particular, we must choose indexing technologies and data design approaches that:

- Support rapid browsing of the unconstrained dimension, especially for low cardinality attributes.
- Support efficient (if not rapid) browsing of cross-constrained values in the dimension table.
- Do not penalize the fact table query for using a large and "expensive" dimension.
- Find and suppress duplicate entries in the dimension (e.g., with name and address matching).
- Do not create additional records to handle the slowly changing dimension problem.

The first three bullets are requirements you should take to your RDBMS vendors.

The Worst Case: Rapidly Changing Monster Dimensions

Unfortunately, huge customer dimensions are even more likely to change than the medium-sized product dimensions. Retailers are anxious to periodically update information about their customers. Insurance companies *must* update information about their customers, their insured automobiles, and their insured homes, because it is critical to have an accurate description of these items when a policy is approved and when a claim is made. Figure 5.8 shows a typical customer dimension, with hot demographic fields that are especially interesting to track on a changing basis. It would seem like we are between a rock and a hard spot. We must track the slowly changing nature of the customer dimension, but we don't dare use either of the techniques appropriate for medium-sized dimensions because of the size of the table.

The solution to this dilemma is to break off the hot customer attributes into their own separate dimension table as in Figure 5.8. We will call this new dimension Demographics. We leave behind constant infor-

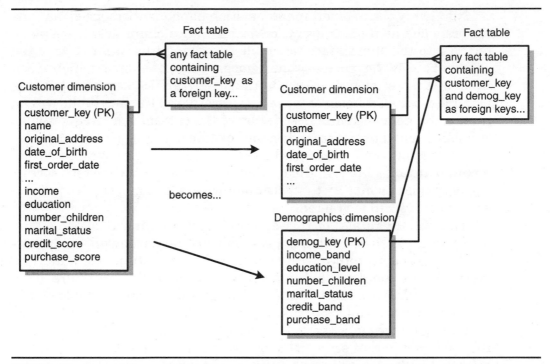

FIGURE 5.8   A modeling solution for a rapidly changing monster dimension, such a huge customer dimension with continuously revised demographics.

mation in the original customer table. We gain the advantage of being able to track the changing nature of the customer descriptions, but we make some compromises as well.

First, we need to make a subtle change in order to successfully create this new demographics dimension. All of the continuously variable demographic facts, such as income and total purchases, must be converted to banded values. In other words, we force the attributes in this new dimension to have a relatively small number of discrete values. We then build the demographics dimension with all possible discrete attribute combinations. For example, in Figure 5.8, if each of the five attributes has ten possible values, then the demographics dimension will have exactly $10^5 = 100,000$ records. We also need to construct a surrogate demographics key for this dimension. It may as well consist of the consecutive numbers from 1 to 100,000.

Now every time something interesting happens with one of our customers, such as a sales event, or an insurance claim event, we put a record into the appropriate fact table describing this event. Two of the keys will always be customer and demographics, as shown in Figure 5.8. Because the decision to associate the demographics key with the customer key occurs whenever we place a record into the fact table, we can change the demographics description of the customer as frequently as we wish. Amazingly, there is no added overhead in the dimension tables with this approach because we built every possible demographics combination at table creation time. All we do is plug in the current correct demographics profile for that customer whenever an event occurs, and a fact table record is created.

The big advantage of this approach for handling these changing monster dimensions is that we can support very frequent "snapshotting" of customer profiles with no increase in data storage or data complexity as we increase the number of snapshots. But there are some trade-offs. First, we have been forced to clump the demographic attributes into banded ranges of discrete values. This places a limit on the specificity of the data (such as income), and makes it impractical to change to a different set of value bands at a later time. Once you decide on your bands, you are stuck with them. Second, the demographic dimension itself cannot be allowed to grow too large. The 100,000 predetermined values in our example is a reasonable number of possible values. In some cases it may make sense to support up to a million predetermined values in the demographics dimension. There are certainly some cases where we need more than five demographic attributes with ten values each. Surprisingly, a workable solution to this problem is to build a second demographics dimension, as shown in Figure 5.9. At a large retailer recently, we faced the problem of two sets of demographics facts. One set related to traditional income, family, and education measures of the customer, and the other related to volatile purchase and credit behavior measured while buying the retailer's products. All of these attributes combined together resulted in several million possible combinations. We were worried that the demographic dimension approach was not going to work. Somewhat reluctantly, we proposed a two-demographics dimensions approach. To our surprise, the resulting data warehouse was very successful. The retailer was very pleased with the flexibility of the data model and the ability to very responsively track the changes both in family demographics and customer behavior.

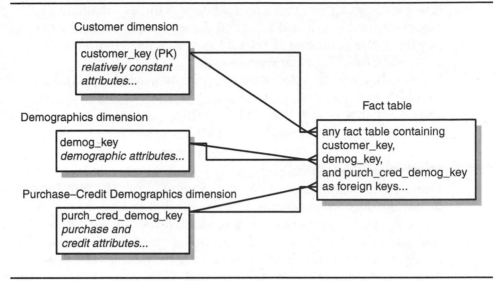

FIGURE 5.9 **A rapidly changing customer dimension with two separated demographics dimensions, one for traditional customer attributes and one for purchase/credit behavior.**

A third potential drawback of this approach is that we have separated the hot demographics data from the more constant descriptors of the customer, such as geographic location and birth date. Now it is harder to browse the data as if it were a single dimension implemented as a flat file. The demographics data now can be browsed only along with the more constant customer data by linking through the fact table. This will usually be a slower and more expensive browse than if all the data were in a single dimension table. We do not think this is a major criticism, however. A relational system will give the correct answer to the browse, but it may be a little slow. This seems like a reasonable price to pay for the freedom to track the customers so responsively.

Finally, a sharp eyed reader may point out that by using this approach we can associate demographics with the customer only when we actually generate a fact table record, such as a sales event or an insurance claim event. Theoretically, if there are no sales, the fact table is empty. If the fact table is empty, we will never be able to link the demographics to the customer. While this is technically true, there are easy ways around this problem. If sales are so sparse that we are in danger of missing a demographics measurement, all we need to do is define a demographics transaction event. This event has no sales dollars associated with it, but it is a good place to register a new demographics profile of the customer. Fact table records are cheap—we have billions of them in our fact tables, anyway.

Another way to associate current demographics with the customer is to add a current demographics key to the customer dimension table. This supports stand-alone demograhic analysis of your full customer base without traversing the fact table.

Degenerate Dimensions

Many of our dimensional designs revolve around some kind of control document like an order, an invoice, a bill of lading, or a ticket. Usually these control documents are a kind of container with one or more line items inside. A very natural grain for a fact table in these cases is the individual line item. In other words, a fact table record is a line item, and a line item is a fact table record. Given this perspective, we can quickly visualize the necessary dimensions for describing each line item.

But what do we do with the order number itself? Or by extension, the invoice number, the bill of lading number, or the ticket number? These numbers are the old parent keys that we used when we designed parent-child transaction systems. The answer is not to discard these parent numbers. The order number, for instance, should go directly into the fact table, right after the dimensional keys and right before the normal numeric facts. This order number looks like a dimension key (even though we don't make a surrogate key for it) but when we are done with the design of the other dimensions, we usually discover that we have stripped out all the old parent or header information like the order date and the customer identification from the order number and placed this information in the other dimensions. At the end of the design, the order number is sitting by itself, without any attributes. We call this a *degenerate* dimension.

 Degenerate dimensions usually occur in line item–oriented fact table designs.

Degenerate dimensions are normal, expected, and useful. The degenerate dimension key should be the actual production order number (or invoice number, etc.) and should sit in the fact table without a join to anything. There is no point in making a dimension table because it would contain nothing. The degenerate key can be used to group line items on a single order, and it is required to answer even broad questions, like what the average number of line items on an order is. The degenerate key can be used as a link through a 3270 screen to access an operational system to place real-time transactions against an order.

If for some reason, one or more attributes are legitimately left over after all the other dimensions have been created, and they seem to belong to this header entity, you should simply create a normal dimension record with a normal join. You don't have a degenerate dimension any more. Make sure in this case that you create a surrogate key, just as you do with all your other dimensions.

Junk Dimensions

Sometimes when you are extracting from a complex production data source, after identifying source attributes for a number of obvious dimensions, you are left with a number of miscellaneous flags and text attributes. These flags and text attributes do not seem to be organized in any coherent way. Often the meaning of the flags and text attributes is obscure. Many of the fields are filled in sporadically, or their content seems to vary depending on the context of the record. This situation leaves the designer with a number of bad alternatives, all of which should be avoided, including:

- Leaving the flags and attributes unchanged in the fact table record.
- Making each flag and attribute into its own separate dimension.
- Stripping out all of these flags and attributes from the design.

Leaving the flags and attributes in the fact record is bad because it might cause the fact table record definition to swell alarmingly. It would be a shame to create a nice tight dimensional design with five dimensions and five facts, and then leave several uncompressed 20 byte text fields in the fact record. It could be prohibitively expensive to build indexes for constraining and browsing on these fields as well.

Making each separate flag and attribute into its own dimension doesn't work either. A 5-dimensional design could balloon into a 25-dimensional design.

Finally, stripping out this information could be a mistake if there is demonstrated business relevance to any of these fields. It is worthwhile, of course, to examine this question carefully. If the flags and text attributes are incomprehensible, noisy, inconsistently filled in, or only of operational significance, they should be left out.

The key to fixing this type of problem is to study these flags and text attributes carefully and to pack them into one or more *junk* dimensions.

A simple example of a useful junk dimension would be taking ten Yes/No indicators out of the fact table and putting them into a single dimension. It is assumed that these indicators are left over after the other more obvious dimensions like Time, Product, Customer, and Location have been designed. Perhaps there seems to be no correlation among these ten indicators or between these indicators and any of the other dimensions. This is okay! You simply pack all ten indicators into one dimension. At the worst, you have $2^{10} = 1024$ records in this junk dimension. It probably isn't very interesting to browse among these flags within the dimension, because every flag occurs with every other flag if the database is large enough. But the junk dimension is a useful holding place for the flags, and it provides a home for the user interface that the user will use when constraining or reporting on these flags. Obviously, the ten fields in the fact table have been replaced with one little short surrogate key. A subtle issue in the design is whether you create all the combinations of these flags in your dimension beforehand or whether you create junk dimension records for the combinations of flags you encounter in the data. The answer depends on how many possible combinations you expect and what the maximum number could be. Generally, when the number of theoretical combinations is very high and you don't think you will encounter them all, you should build a junk dimension record at extract time whenever you encounter a new combination of fields.

 A *junk* dimension is a convenient grouping of random flags and attributes to get them out of a fact table and into a useful dimensional framework.

Sometimes the choice of a junk dimension is much less obvious. In our experience, however, some analytic digging into the real data pays off. Many times what look like independent junk attributes in the fact table turn out to be correlated. A whole group of junk attributes may turn out to have values only in certain transactional situations. When this happens, all of these attributes may be able to be grouped into a single dimension and removed from the fact table. The data designer needs to pose a number of test queries against the source data to tease out these relationships. Most of the messy source data sets we have encountered have yielded to this kind of analysis.

A final kind of messy attribute that fits well into the junk dimension approach is the open ended comments field that is often attached to a fact record, especially at the line item level. If you decide that the contents of the comments field are good enough to justify inclusion in the data warehouse, then you should proceed with the design. Hopefully, only a few of the comments fields have anything in them. In this ideal case, the junk dimension simply contains all the distinct comments. But the junk dimension is noticeably smaller than the fact table because the comments are relatively rare. Of course you will need a special surrogate key that points to the "no comment" record in the dimension. Most of your fact table records use this key.

Foreign Keys, Primary Keys, and Surrogate Keys

All dimension tables have single part keys, which, by definition, are primary keys. In other words, the key itself defines uniqueness in the dimension table.

 All data warehouse keys must be meaningless surrogate keys. You must not use the original production keys.

In this book, we presume a surrogate key is a simple integer. As the data warehouse administrator, you assign the first key the value 1, the next key the value 2, and so on. You simply assign the keys as you encounter the need for them. The keys themselves have no meaning. If all you have is a key for a dimension, you can tell absolutely nothing about the underlying record. You must use the key to retrieve the record to see what it contains. In most cases, a 4-byte integer makes a great surrogate key. A 4-byte integer can contain 2^{32} values, or more than two billion positive integers, starting with 1. Two billion is enough for just about any dimension, including customer, product, or time.

Surrogate Date Keys

The mandate to use surrogate keys applies to date keys as well as other types of keys. It is a significant mistake to use an SQL-based date stamp as the join key between the time dimension table and a fact table. First, a SQL-based date key is typically 8 bytes, so you are wasting 4 bytes in the fact table for every date key in every record. Second, the only excuse for actually using a date-meaningful key is that you intend to bypass the join to the time table and constrain directly on the date key in the fact table. This is an example of relying on smart keys in your application. You are now bypassing the information in the time dimension table, and you are almost certainly embedding knowledge of your corporate calendar in your application, rather than querying this knowledge from your time dimension table. Finally, by using an SQL-based date stamp as the key, you are giving up the possibility of encoding a date stamp as "I don't know," or "it hasn't happened yet," or "a date stamp is not possible in this case." All of these special cases can be handled gracefully with a surrogate date key, which can point to special records in the time table that cover these cases.

If, in addition to the calendar date, you are recording the precise time of day, you should split off the time and make it an SQL time stamp fact or simple integer fact that is not part of the date key.

Avoid Smart Keys

The data warehouse designer should always avoid smart keys with embedded meaning. In other words, resist the temptation to make a primary dimension key out of various attributes in the dimension table. You will never actually program an application to use the components of such a smart key for constraints, and you should not consider making the join to the fact table be a double-barreled or triple-barreled join that employs several fields at both ends of the join. You should always have these components broken out as separate fields in the dimension tables anyway.

Avoid Production Keys

If you use production defined attributes as the literal components of your key construction, sooner or later you will get stepped on. Several bad things can happen. First, production may decide to reuse keys. If they purge their version of the dimension every year, then they may have no compunction about reusing a key after two years. You as the owner of the data warehouse may be left in an impossible position by this decision because you may be storing three or more years of data.

Another possibility is that your company might acquire a competitor, and the rules for building the production key may be thrown out the window. You may suddenly get handed ugly 14-byte alpha codes instead of the nice 6-byte integers you have been relying on. If you have been too literal in your use of production codes to build your dimension key, you will be sorry. Finally, the worst possibility is that you may be handed a revised dimension record from production, where *the production key was deliberately not changed.* If you decide that you must track this revised description as a legitimate new version of the dimension record, you are between a rock and a hard spot unless you have surrogate keys.

Additive, Semiadditive, and Nonadditive Facts

Whenever possible, the facts in the fact table should be chosen to be perfectly additive. That means it makes sense to add the facts along all of the dimensions. Discrete numerical measures of activity, such as retail cash register sales in either dollars or units, are often perfectly additive. Numerical measures of intensity, however, are not perfectly additive. The most important measures of intensity are account balances and inventory levels. These facts are snapshots of something taken at a point in time. Unlike the measures of activity, they do not represent a flow past a point. Measures of intensity are usually additive along all the dimensions except time. To combine account balances and inventory levels across time, the query tool or reporting tool must add these facts across time and then divide by the number of time periods to create a time-average. This is not the same as using the SQL AVG (average) function. Most of us are familiar with this technique because most of our banks report the average-daily-balance in our accounts.

Some numeric measures of intensity cannot be added across any dimension. Measurements of room temperature might make a good fact for a fact table, but these temperatures would have to be averaged across every dimension over which they were combined. For measures of intensity that are averaged across all dimensions, it would be appropriate to use the SQL AVG function.

It is possible for a measured fact to be textual. This condition arises rarely because in most cases a textual measurement is a description of something and is drawn from a discrete list of alternatives. The designer should make every effort to put textual measures into dimensions because they can be correlated more effectively with the other textual attributes in a dimension, and they will require much less space, especially if the proposed fact table text field is a wide fixed-width field that is often empty. An example of a textual fact is the condition of the weather as written down by the police officer at the scene of an accident. If this weather description were free text with widely varying descriptions, it would be hard to store in a dimension without making every single accident into a dimension record. Assuming that the accident itself is the grain of the fact table (presumably with various dimensions like time, driver1, driver2, car1, car2, officer, location, type, severity, and status), then the weather phrase might well end up as a textual fact. Textual facts can be counted and constrained upon, but if, as in this example, they are unpredictable free text, the usual dimensional activities of constraining and grouping on these text values will be of little value. A true "text fact" is not a very good thing to have in a data warehouse.

The Four-Step Design Method for Designing an Individual Fact Table

The detailed logical design of a dimensional schema is driven by four steps. This methodology is discussed in more detail in *The Data Warehouse Toolkit*, and it is also discussed in Chapter 7 of this book in the larger context of managing an overall data warehouse project. The four logical design steps for a single dimensional schema consist of four choices, made in order. We choose

1. The data mart
2. The fact table grain
3. The dimensions
4. The facts

Step 1. Choosing the Data Mart: Single-Source and Multiple-Source Data Marts

Choosing the data mart in the simplest case is the same as choosing the legacy source of data. Typical data marts include purchase orders, shipments, retail sales, payments, or customer communications. These would be examples of single-source data marts. In more complex cases, we can define a data mart that must include multiple-legacy sources. The best example of a multiple-source data mart is customer profitability, where legacy sources that describe revenue must be combined with legacy sources that describe costs. We recommend strongly that the data warehouse designer limit risk by implementing only single-source data marts at first, so as to reduce the number of lengthy extract system development tasks. We also recommend implementing these separate data marts only in the context of a set of conformed dimensions, so that the data marts can plug into the Data Warehouse Bus. Using conformed dimensions guards against building stovepipe data marts.

 Start your portfolio of data marts with a single-source data mart.

Step 2. Declaring the Fact Table Grain: Styles of Fact Tables

Although it seems like a detailed technical step, it is crucial to define very clearly exactly what a fact table record is in the proposed dimensional design. Without this definition, the design cannot proceed, and without a clear definition, the data architects will waste valuable time arguing about what a dimension is and what a fact is. We call this step "declaring the grain."

 Be very precise when defining the fact table grain. Do not leave this step out. The grain is the answer to the question "What is a fact record, exactly?"

Generally, the fact table grain is chosen to be as low, or as granular, as possible. There are many advantages to choosing a low-level grain, such as individual transaction, or individual day snapshot, or individual document line item. The lower the level of granularity, the more robust the design. We have seen that a very low level of granularity is far better at responding to unexpected new queries and far better at responding to the introduction of additional new data elements than higher levels of granularity.

Typical choices for the grain of the fact table could be expressed as follows:

- Each sales transaction is a fact record.
- Each insurance claims transaction is a fact record.
- Each ATM transaction is a fact record.

- Each daily product sales total in each store is a fact record.
- Each monthly account snapshot is a fact record.
- Each line item on each order is a fact record.
- Each line item on each shipment's invoice is a fact record.
- Each coverage in each individual insurance policy is a fact record.

Although all of these choices sound similar, the preceding list represents three common styles of fact tables. The first three choices of grain are *individual transactions*. In a given day or month, we can measure any number of transactions for a given product or against a given account. The number can be zero or a million. We are not guaranteed to find a transaction against a product or against an account in the database. The individual transactions typically have a very simple structure, with a single amount field as the value of the transaction.

The next two grain examples in the list are *snapshots*. We wait until the end of the day or the end of the month, and we take a snapshot of the activity that occurred during that period. This snapshot is more complex than the individual transaction perspective. We may have many measures of the activity during the period, including total sales, total number of transactions, and semiadditive facts, such as the ending account balance. In some cases, like retail sales, it may be easy to move from the individual transaction perspective to a daily snapshot because we can summarize the transactions to the daily level. In this case we would probably build the daily snapshot only if we needed to construct a summary table for performance reasons. In other cases, like the monthly account snapshot, the pattern of transactions is potentially very complex, and the creation of the snapshot is not a simple aggregation. The calculation of revenue, for example, may depend on how a transaction like a deposit or an advance payment is booked. In this case, the monthly snapshot is absolutely required to give management a flexible and quick view of revenue. Later in this chapter we will contrast the snapshot table more specifically with the transaction table, because in many cases we will need both at once.

The final three examples are all *line items* on various control documents like orders, shipments, or policies. There is exactly one record in each of these fact tables for each line item on a control document. In this design, each fact table record represents the entire existence of a line item. These fact table records can be thought of as a rolling, evolving snapshots of the line items. We saw in *The Data Warehouse Toolkit* that line-item fact tables typically have multiple time keys representing various phases that the line item goes through. Line-item fact tables usually need a status dimension to record the current status of the line item. Finally, line-item fact table records are revisited for updating far more frequently than records in the other types of fact tables because they have a possibly long history that may need to be updated many times.

 The three most useful fact table grains are individual transactions, higher-level snapshots, and line items from control documents like invoices.

Step 3. Choosing the Dimensions

Once the grain of the fact table is firmly established, the choice of dimensions is fairly straightforward. The grain itself will often determine a primary or minimal set of dimensions. For instance, the minimal set of dimensions for a line item on an order would have to include the order date, the customer, the product, and a special degenerate dimension consisting of only the order number. Within this framework the designer can add a potentially large number of additional dimensions. In almost every case, these additional dimensions take on a unique value in the context of the primary dimensions. Thus additional dimensions, like delivery date, contract terms, order status, and delivery mode, can be added at the designer's discretion if the source data is available. In many of these cases, a dimension can be added gracefully to the design because the addition does not change the grain of the fact table. An example of a gracefully added dimension might be a causal dimension that is added to the design to explain exogenous market facts like promotions, competitor actions, or the weather.

The fact table in a dimensional model is a set of simultaneous measurements at a particular granularity. The most useful measurements are numeric, but they don't have to be numeric. Many times the dimensional designer is handed a set of measurements as a *fait accompli,* and the designer must decide which dimensions are valid in the context of these measurements. At this point the dimensional designer "decorates" the set of measurements with *all* of the dimensions he or she can find, driven by business requirements, of course. The best dimensions are those that take on a single value in the context of the proffered set of measurements. The powerful idea here is that there is no sense of anticipating queries or planning the schema based on user needs at all. This is just physics.

 The designer examines all the data resources at his or her disposal and preferentially attaches the single-valued descriptors as dimensions.

The single-valuedness of the chosen dimensions has a couple of implications. The best single-valued dimension to be attached to a set of measurements is the *lowest* level of granularity of that dimension that is still single valued. Thus if our measurements are truly at a daily grain, the associated time dimension should also be at a daily grain. We could alternatively attach the year to the measurements as a dimension, but that is rather dull.

We can actually attach many-valued dimensions to a set of measurements, but it is hard to build useful reports and queries across a many-to-many relationship. One needs a many-to-many bridge table in between the dimension table and the fact table, and to get things to add up properly, some kind of allocation or weighting fact is required, and that is controversial and a lot of work. One example of this is the many values of diagnosis that a patient can simultaneously have when undergoing a single treatment. There is no easy way out of that one. It's the physics, not the model.

The measurement-centric view of dimensional modeling makes it easier to see what to do if new descriptive data becomes available. If that new data is single valued in the presence of some of the measurement sets, then you can gracefully attach the new source of data to these measurements. For instance, if you have daily data measurements according to some geography, you may be able to add daily weather data to the set of measurements in a graceful way. Just attach the weather key to the list of keys in the fact table. No tables need to be dropped or redefined, and no existing applications change in any way.

Each dimension has its own granularity. The granularity of an individual dimension cannot be lower than the overall fact table granularity. In other words, if the fact table granularity specifies a monthly time, the time dimension cannot be days or weeks. Interestingly, the granularity of an individual dimension can be coarser than the granularity of the fact table without causing a logical contradiction. For instance, the delivery mode dimension could be limited to "air" and "land" even though the underlying data contained much more detail. The product dimension could even be stated at a higher level than individual stock keeping unit (SKU), such as brand. In both these cases it would seem that there was a loss of useful information to the end users, but the design by itself has not introduced any logical contradictions.

Step 4. Choosing the Facts

The grain of the fact table also allows the individual facts to be chosen, and it makes it clear what the scope of these facts must be. In the case of individual transaction fact tables, we have already pointed out that there is usually only one fact, namely the amount of the transaction. Snapshot fact tables have the most open-ended number of facts because any summary of activity during the snapshot period is fair game for the fact table. Snapshot fact tables can be gracefully extended with additional facts when additional useful summaries are identified. Line-item fact tables also can contain several facts since, for example, an individual line item may be broken down into quantities, gross amounts, adjustments, discounts, net amounts, and taxes.

 Facts should always be specific to the grain of the fact table.

In other words, do not mix in facts from other time periods or other aggregations to make calculations convenient. Any facts that do not match the exact grain of the fact table record will wreak havoc when a query tool or reporting tool attempts to combine these facts along various dimensions. It is fine to create aggregate or summary records for performance and other reasons, but these facts are always stored *in different records in different fact tables*. We discuss systems for building and loading aggregates later in Chapter 14.

Families of Fact Tables

Although the preceding sections have focused on building a single fact table surrounded by a set of dimension tables, in reality even a single data mart is a coordinated set of fact tables, all with similar structures. Throughout this book we stress that the secret of a successful incremental data warehouse design is the use of conformed dimensions. Conformed dimensions are common dimensions that are the same from fact table to fact table.

In this section we discuss four different fundamental reasons for building families of fact tables within a single data mart or across a complete data warehouse. In complex environments, like insurance, we can have combinations of all of these separate kinds of fact tables.

Chains and Circles

Many businesses have a logical flow that has a beginning and an end. An order, or a product, or a customer characteristically evolves through a series of steps. Often, we capture transactions or snapshots for each step. Usually, it makes the most sense to build a separate fact table for each step. In the manufacturing world, a product moves from the acquisition of raw materials through to the finished good. This is often called the *supply chain*. We may have a series of legacy systems that are data sources for each step of the supply chain:

- Raw material production, such as mining or growing
- Ingredient purchasing
- Ingredient delivery
- Ingredient inventory
- Bill of materials
- Manufacturing process control
- Manufacturing costs
- Packaging
- Trans-shipping to warehouse
- Finished goods inventory

After a product enters finished goods inventory in a warehouse, it is thought of as being part of the demand chain, or value chain. The legacy systems in the demand chain may include:

- Finished goods inventory
- Manufacturing shipments
- Distributor inventory
- Distributor shipments
- Retail inventory
- Retail sales

A budgeting process for a large organization also presents a kind of value chain (see Mike Venerable and Chris Adamson's wonderful book *Data Warehouse Design Solutions* (Wiley, 1998) for a complete explanation of this particular value chain):

- Budgets
- Commitments
- Payments

Insurance companies have a very important value chain:

- Marketing
- Agent/broker sales
- Rating
- Underwriting
- Reinsuring
- Policy creation
- Claims processing
- Claims investigation
- Claims payments
- Salvage
- Subrogation

All of these examples can be approached in a similar way. A fact table and a set of associated dimensions is defined for each step in the chain. When this is done, the requirements for a set of conformed dimensions becomes obvious. The conformed dimensions are carefully designed, and these dimensions are used as the framework (the bus) for separately implementing each step in the chain. In the insurance example, perhaps the two most interesting steps in the value chain would be agent/broker sales and claims processing. These two dimensional models could be implemented prior to the others, with the full confidence that the framework of conformed dimensions would always give guidance to the subsequent implementation efforts and would guarantee that all the fact tables would work together in the future.

 Multiple fact tables are needed to support a business with many processes. Each process spawns one or more fact tables, When the processes are naturally arranged in order, we often call this a *value chain*.

Other kinds of businesses may be thought of as being organized in a *value circle*, rather than a linear chain. In these kinds of businesses, all the entities may be performing or measuring the same kind of transaction. A good example of a value circle is a large health care organization, which might consist of the following:

- Hospitals
- Clinics
- Long-term care facilities
- Physician offices
- Pharmacies
- Pharmaceutical manufacturers
- Laboratories
- Employers
- Insurance companies
- Government agencies like Medicare

In this value circle, all the organizations around the circle are either generating patient treatments or measuring patient treatments. These organizations will be able to share data successfully if and only if the various sources of patient treatment data can be conformed. Specifically, this means that all these organizations must use the following typical set of conformed dimensions:

- Time (calendar)
- Patient

- Provider (physician)
- Location
- Treatment
- Diagnosis
- Employer
- Payer

When this set of dimensions has been conformed, the patient treatment records across this group of organizations will snap together on the Data Warehouse Bus in a simple way that will make it possible for all of them to effectively share data.

Heterogeneous Product Schemas

In many financial service businesses, a dilemma arises because of the heterogeneous nature of the products or services offered. For instance, a retail bank may offer checking accounts, savings accounts, mortgage loans, personal loans, credit cards, retirement investment accounts, and safe deposit boxes. In this environment there are usually two perspectives on the account activity that are difficult to present in a single fact table. The first perspective is the global view that needs to slice and dice all the accounts of all types at the same time. The global view wants to plan cross-selling and up-selling against the aggregate customer base spanning all the possible account types. Since in a big retail bank, there may be 25 lines of business, it is impractical to query 25 separate fact tables each time the customer base needs to be profiled. Thus the global view needs to be a single *core fact table* crossing all the lines of business. See Figure 5.10. Note that the core fact table can present only a limited number of facts that make sense for virtually every line of business. The core fact table also turns out to be useful to inquire about a specific customer's complete account portfolio, since all the accounts are linked to the same customer dimension.

The second, and conflicting, perspective is the line-of-business view that focuses on one line of business like checking. In this case there is a long list of special facts that only make sense for the checking line of business. These special facts cannot be included in the core fact table because if we did this for each line of business in a real retail bank, we would have 200 special facts, most of which would have null values in any specific record. The solution to this dilemma is to create a custom fact table for checking that is limited to just checking accounts (see Figure 5.11). Now

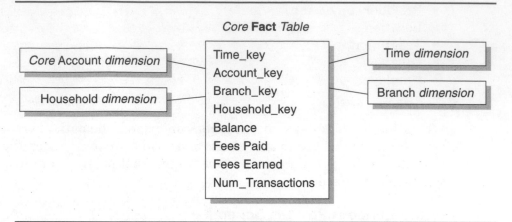

Core **Fact** *Table*

Core Account *dimension*	Time_key	Time *dimension*
Household *dimension*	Account_key	Branch *dimension*
	Branch_key	
	Household_key	
	Balance	
	Fees Paid	
	Fees Earned	
	Num_Transactions	

FIGURE 5.10   A core fact table for a retail bank.

both the fact table and the account table may be extended to describe all the specific facts and attributes that make sense only for checking. We go ahead and build a custom fact table and custom account table for each line of business.

If the lines of business in our retail bank are physically separated so that each one has its own data mart computer, the custom fact and dimension tables will not reside in the same space as the core fact and dimension tables. In this case, the total base of account activity in the core fact table must be duplicated exactly once to implement all the custom tables. Remember that the custom tables provide a disjoint partitioning of the account space, so that there is no overlap between the custom tables.

 Multiple fact tables are needed when a business has heterogeneous products that have naturally different facts but a single customer base.

If the lines of business are able to share the same database partition on the same physical machine, then the copying of the primary fact table can be avoided. In this case, a special join key is added to each core fact table record. The requesting query tool or application must know to use

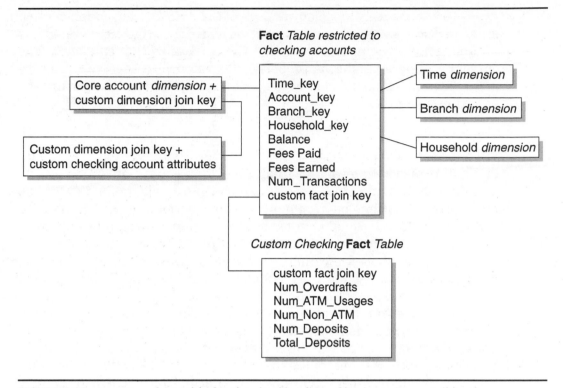

FIGURE 5.11   A custom fact table for the checking line of business in a retail bank.

this special join key to link to the correct extended fact table for each line of business. This is quite natural, since by the definition of the heterogeneous facts, it would almost never make sense to attempt in a single SQL expression to join to more than one extended fact table representing more than one line of business. The names of the facts in the separate extended fact tables are by definition different and no single SQL expression can "talk" to multiple extended fact tables. Thus a requesting application analyzing a specific line of business like checking would always be hard-coded to link to the correct extended fact table.

Transaction and Snapshot Schemas

When we take an operational view of our data warehouse, we find that there are some characteristic structures that are probably independent of the specific kind of business we are in. Virtually every data mart needs two separately modeled versions of the data: a transaction version and a periodic snapshot version. Furthermore, the snapshot version has an additional special feature called the *current rolling snapshot*. The current rolling snapshot is properly integrated into the overall enterprise data warehouse. Let's tease apart the transaction schema and the snapshot schema.

The Transaction Schema

We hope that the most basic view of our operational system is at the individual transaction level. In a financial services environment the transactions may be individual deposits and withdrawals against accounts. In a communications environment the transactions may be individual calls placed or individual charges against accounts. In a retail environment the transactions may be individual line items on sales tickets. And in some cases where we cannot get a proper transaction feed, we may have to construct pseudotransactions by examining the daily status of accounts and seeing what changed since yesterday.

In any case, the flow of low-level transactions is often quite easy to place into a good dimensional framework for querying in our data warehouse. Remember that the lowest-level data is the most naturally dimensional data. For instance, the raw feed of ATM transactions in a retail bank environment contains the information needed to identify time, location, account, and transaction type. The extract process must convert the original legacy system identifiers into proper data warehouse keys that link to the respective data warehouse dimensions. This is basically a lookup process. The structure of the extracted ATM transaction would look like Figure 5.12.

In addition to the obvious physical keys of Time, Location, Account, and Transaction Type, we almost always add additional key-like information to the transaction fact record. See Figure 5.12. It is useful to add an audit key that points to a special dimension record created by the extract process itself. This audit dimension record can describe data lineage of the fact record itself, including the time of the extract, the source table, and the version of the software that ran the extract.

We may also include the original transaction record production identifiers, like account number and transaction reference, so that we could open a terminal connection back to the transaction system and perform a direct on-line administrative operation.

The fact record for an individual transaction frequently contains only a single "fact," which is the value of the transaction. In most cases we must simply label this fact Amount, as in Figure 5.12. Since there may be many kinds of transactions in the same table, we usually cannot label this fact with anything more specific.

The design of the transaction fact schema is not nearly as open-ended as the snapshot schema will turn out to be. We almost never need to add more numeric facts to a transaction schema because the transaction capture system usually returns only one amount in a transaction. More often we will add more transaction types to the transaction dimension, but that is not a schema change, it is a data content change.

Once we have built the transaction component of our data warehouse, we can perform many powerful analyses that cannot be done on any form of summarized data. Transaction-level data lets us analyze *behavior* in extreme detail. Using our ATM example, we can perform *behavior counts* such as the number of times users of ATMs make mortgage payments at ATM locations not near their homes. We can perform exquisite *time-of-day analyses* such as the number of ATM transactions that occur during the lunch hour or before work. Time-of-day analyses may allow us to do a fairly accurate *queue analysis*.

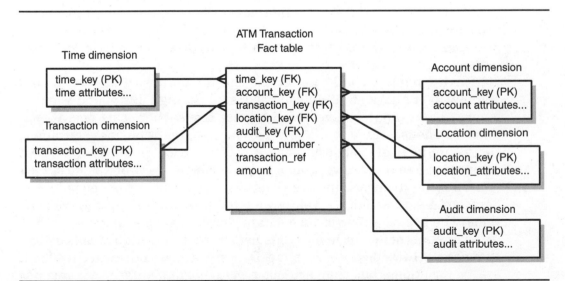

FIGURE 5.12   The fact and dimension tables that represent a set of ATM transactions.

The gap between certain kinds of transactions is usually very interesting. In insurance companies one of the most important measures is the *time gap* between the original claim and first payment against that claim. This is a basic measure of the efficiency of the claims process.

Transaction detail also lets us look at *sequential behavior*. In the insurance example, we want to look at how many times we opened and closed the reserve against a claim, and whether there were any intervening changes in the claim made by the claimant. Interesting applications of sequential behavior analysis include *fraud detection* and *cancellation warning*. Banks are interested in predicting cancellation warnings because they would like to intercept the customer who is about to empty the account and ask them what is wrong or how the bank can better serve them.

Finally, transaction detail allows an analyst to do *basket analysis*. The obvious example is the retail environment, where we might ask what products naturally sell with 12-ounce bottles of 7-Up. A less obvious example of basket analysis is to ask what additional satellite television channels we are likely to sign up for in the month following a purchase of season football watching. A very tough version of basket analysis is to ask what didn't sell in the market basket when we bought 7-Up. We might call this *missing basket analysis*.

Many of the preceding examples are good, classic data mining. Most analysts agree emphatically that to do data mining, you need extreme, granular, unaggregated data. In other words, you need individual transactions.

Having made a solid case for the charm of transaction-level detail, you may be thinking that all you need is a fast, big DBMS, and your job is over. Unfortunately, even with a great transaction-level operational data warehouse, there is still a whole class of urgent business questions that is impractical to answer using only transaction detail. These urgent business questions revolve around quick, accurate views of *current status*.

When the transactions are themselves little pieces of revenue, the boss can ask how much revenue we took in by adding up the transactions. The best example of such a data source is cash-register sales in a retail environment, but in most businesses, there are many transactions that are not little pieces of revenue. Deposits and withdrawals in a bank are transactions, but they are not revenue. Payments in advance for subscriptions and for insurance coverage are even worse. Not only are they not revenue, but their effect must be spread out over many reporting periods as their organizations *earn the revenue* by providing the subscription or providing the insurance coverage. This complex relationship between individual transactions and the basic measures of revenue and profit often makes it impossible to quickly please the boss by crawling through individual transactions. Not only is such crawling time-consuming, but the logic required to interpret the effect of different kinds of transactions on revenue or profit can be horrendously complicated.

Businesses that have a rich transactional history but whose transactions are not little pieces of revenue usually need two fact tables to represent all the activity. One fact table captures the transactions, and the other captures the periodic snapshots. Hopefully, the snapshot data is provided from a legacy system, because if it is not, the data warehouse must contain very complex logic to correctly interpret the financial impact of each transaction type.

The Snapshot Schema

The solution to this problem is to create a second, separate fact table, called the *snapshot table,* that is a companion to the transaction table. The companion to our first example is shown in Figure 5.13. We add records to the snapshot table at the end of specific reporting time periods, often monthly. The application that creates the snapshot records must crawl through the previous period's transactions to calculate the correct current status, which is the snapshot, but at least this crawling occurs only once.

Often we find it convenient to build the monthly snapshot incrementally by adding the effect of each day's transactions to a *current rolling snapshot*. If we normally think of our data warehouse as storing 36 months of historical data in the snapshot table, then the current rolling month should be month 37. Ideally, when the last day of the month has been reached, the current rolling snapshot simply becomes the new regular month in the time series and a new current rolling snapshot is created the next day. The current rolling month becomes the leading breaking wave of the data warehouse.

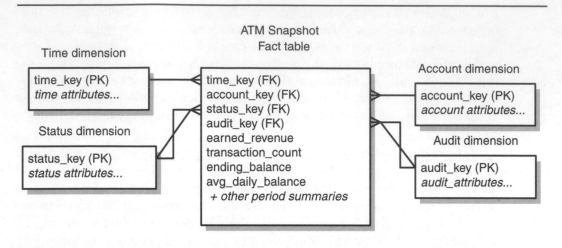

FIGURE 5.13   The ATM transactions rolled up to a companion ATM snapshot schema.

The design of the snapshot table is closely related to the design of its companion transaction table. Usually the snapshot table is explicitly account-specific. In the snapshot we keep the Account and Time dimensions, but we suppress several of the other dimensions found in the transaction table. Location, Employee, and Transaction Type are all suppressed in Figure 5.13. We can keep the production identifier that refers to the account itself. We can keep an audit dimension, but we now refer to an aggregate status of the extract covering the entire reporting period. Finally, we introduce a status dimension that flags this account in this time period according to various useful indicators like New Account, Regular Account, Account Under Scrutiny, and Account About To Close.

The fact structure in the snapshot table is much more interesting and open-ended than that of the transaction table. Basically we can introduce as many facts, counts, and summaries as we wish. It is important that all the facts refer to the current period. Some of the facts will be completely additive across all the dimensions, such as Earned Revenue and Total Transaction Count. Other facts will be semiadditive, such as Ending Account Balance and Average Daily Balance. These particular semiadditive facts add across all the dimensions except time. Semiadditive facts must be *averaged across time* when used across time periods.

Because of the open-endedness of the snapshot table design, we may progressively add more facts to this table as we understand our user's needs in more detail. Obviously, there is a trade-off at some point. Obscure or rarely used summaries are not worth putting in the snapshot table and must be computed from underlying transaction detail every time they are needed. Other basic facts like earned revenue and account balance absolutely must go in the snapshot table and are the reason for the table's existence.

There may be times when we want a snapshot-like summary of a business at some intermediate point in time, not at the end of a reporting period. In such a case, it may make sense to start with the immediately preceding snapshot and add the effect of the incremental transactions between the beginning of that period and the desired date. This will be fairly straightforward if the fact you are interested in (say, account balance) exists within the snapshot table. If the fact is more obscure (say, the cumulative number of times a request for credit was denied), and it is not part of the snapshot, then you may have no choice but to crawl through that account's transaction history from the beginning of time because otherwise you have no starting point.

Transactions and snapshots are the yin and yang of a data warehouse. Transactions give us the fullest possible view of detailed behavior, and snapshots allow us to quickly measure the status of the enterprise. We need them both because there is no simple way to combine these two contrasting perspectives. Used together, transactions and snapshots provide a full, immediate view of the business, and when they are part of the overall data warehouse, they blend gracefully into the larger views across time and across the other main dimensions.

Aggregates

The fourth and final reason for creating families of fact tables is the creation of aggregates. Aggregates are stored summaries built primarily to improve query performance. We won't say a lot about them in this section because the issues of designing, loading, and updating aggregates are more related to the physical design issues of the data warehouse, and we will treat aggregates in detail in other chapters. However, to complete our current topic, the creation of aggregates introduces a family of fact tables that are usually derived from the most granular fact table in each data mart. Each member of the family represents a particular degree of summarization along one or more of the fact table's dimensions. A mature and full set of aggregates could involve a dozen separate aggregate fact tables, all echoing the original structure of the base fact table. Each aggregate fact table will have one or more shrunken dimension tables together as well as other regular dimension tables.

 Aggregates are meant to improve performance. Aggregates are stored in separate tables, not in the original fact tables containing the unaggregated data.

Occasionally an aggregate fact table is built for reasons other than performance. Certain facts in the environment may not be expressible at the lowest granularity. In this case, an aggregate table is required to present these new aggregate facts. The regular aggregate facts can also be placed in the aggregate table if the granularity is correct. The best example of the need for an aggregate table beyond simple performance considerations is when costs are available to match with revenue data (hence providing a view of profitability), but the cost data cannot be expressed at the lowest grain of the fact data. For instance, shipping cost may be available at the customer level of the shipping invoice but not at the line item or product level. If your organization cannot reach agreement on allocating the shipping cost to the individual line items of the invoice (and it is strongly recommended that you try to do so), then the data mart designer may have no choice but to express the shipping costs at a higher level. Another example might be advertising costs that can be expressed for a brand or a category but cannot be expressed at the individual SKU.

Factless Fact Tables

There are two modeling situations in which the designer engages in normal design process but fails to find any facts to go into the fact table. These factless fact tables are very useful to describe *events* and *coverage*, so we can ask what did not happen.

The first kind of factless fact table is a table that records an event. A good example of an event-tracking table is shown in Figure 5.14. Here we are tracking student attendance at a college. Imagine that we have a modern student tracking system that detects each student's attendance event each day. Plausible dimensions include:

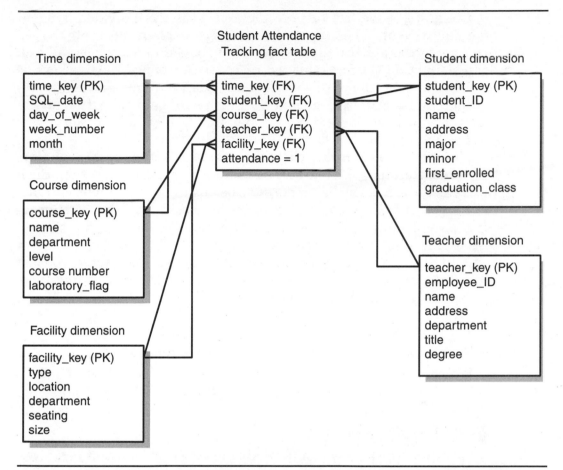

FIGURE 5.14   A factless fact table that represents student attendance events at an institution of higher learning. Every record contains the dummy attendance field whose value is always 1.

- **Date.** One record in this dimension for each day on the calendar.
- **Student.** One record in this dimension for each student.
- **Course.** One record in this dimension for each course taught each semester.
- **Teacher.** One record in this dimension for each teacher.
- **Facility.** One record in this dimension for each room, laboratory, or athletic field.

The grain of the fact table in Figure 5.14 is the individual student attendance event. When the student walks through the door into the lecture, a record is generated. It is clear that these dimensions are all well defined and that the fact table record, consisting of just the five keys, is a good representation of the student attendance event. Each of the dimension tables is quite deep and rich, with many useful textual attributes on which we can constrain, and from which we can form row headers in reports.

The only problem is that there is no obvious fact to record each time the student attends a lecture or suits up for physical education. Such things as the grade for the course don't belong in this fact table. Our fact table represents the student attendance process, not the semester grading process or even the midterm exam process. We are left with the odd feeling that something is missing.

Actually, this fact table consisting only of keys is a perfectly good fact table and probably ought to be left as is. A lot of interesting questions can be asked of this dimensional schema, including:

- Which classes were the most heavily attended?
- Which classes were the most consistently attended?
- Which teachers taught the most students?
- Which teachers taught classes in facilities belonging to other departments?
- Which facilities were the most lightly used?
- What was the average total walking distance of a student in a given day?

To make the SQL for these queries more readable, we may add a dummy fact-like field to each record called Attendance. Since we make a record every time the student attends, all of these attendance fields are set equal to 1. If we ever build aggregates on this data, we will find this attendance field quite useful, because unlike the base table, the attendance field in the aggregate tables will contain interesting values that are not obvious.

A second kind of factless fact table is called a *coverage* table. A typical coverage table is shown in Figure 5.15. Coverage tables are frequently needed when a primary fact table in a dimensional data warehouse is sparse. In Figure 5.15 we also show a simple sales promo-

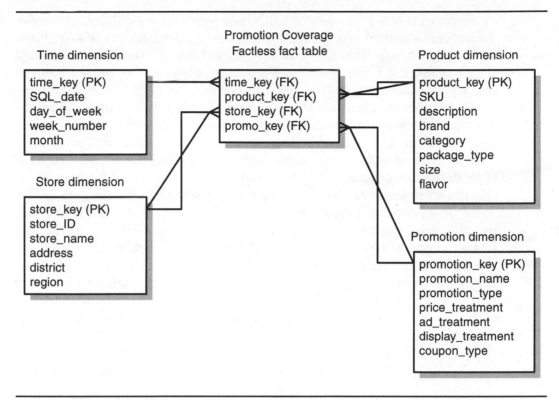

FIGURE 5.15   A factless fact table representing the products sold on promotion by store by time period.

tion fact table that records the sales of products in stores on particular days under each promotion condition. The sales fact table answers many interesting questions, but it cannot answer questions about things that didn't happen, such as which products were on promotion but didn't sell.

The sales fact table cannot answer this question because it contains only the records of products that did sell. The coverage table comes to the rescue. A record is placed in the coverage table for each product in each store that is on promotion in each time period. Notice that we need the full generality of a fact table to record which products are on promotion. In general, which products are on promotion varies by all of the dimensions of product, store, promotion, and time.

Perhaps some of you are wondering why we don't just fill out the original fact table with records representing zero sales for all possible products. This is logically valid, but it expands the fact table enormously. In a typical grocery store, only about 10 percent of the products sell on a given day. Including all the zero sales could increase the size of the database by a factor of ten. Remember also that we would have to carry all the additive facts as zeros.

The coverage factless fact table can be made much smaller than the equivalent set of zeros. The coverage table needs only to contain the items on promotion. The items not on promotion that did not sell can be left out. Also, it is likely for administrative reasons that the assignment of products to promotions takes place periodically, rather than every day. Often a store manager will set up promotions in a store once each week. Thus we don't need a record for every product every day. One record per product per promotion per store each week will do. Finally, the factless format keeps us from storing explicit zeros for the facts as well.

Answering the question of which products were on promotion but did not sell requires a two-step application. First, we consult the coverage table for the list of products on promotion on that day in that store. Second, we consult the sales table for the list of products that did sell. The desired answer is the set difference between these two lists of products.

 Factless fact tables are the preferred method for recording events in a data warehouse where there is no natural numeric measurement associated with the event. Factless fact tables also are used to guarantee coverage.

SUMMARY

In this chapter we defined what dimensional modeling is and why it works. We covered the need for developing data marts where your dimensions and your facts are conformed. We called this the Data Warehouse Bus Architecture. Finally, the fundamental design techniques for dimensional modeling were reviewed. In Chapter 6, we delve into more advanced design techniques. If you are not responsible for modeling the data and do not need to understand these advanced topics, you may move directly to Chapter 7, which covers how to build dimensional models in a real data warehouse project.

CHAPTER 6

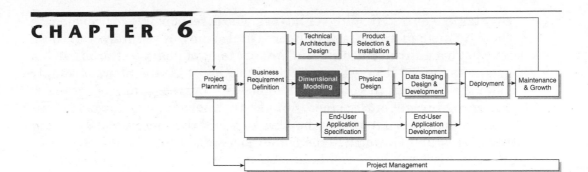

A Graduate Course on Dimensional Modeling

Dimensional modeling techniques have been applied to nearly every kind of business. As the body of accumulated modeling experience has grown, designers have recognized many recurring themes driven by common business situations. Businesses in health care and financial services have fundamental dimensions that show a many-to-many relationship rather than the usual one-to-many relationship to the major fact tables. Many businesses find that one or more of their dimensions seem to be repeated multiple times in their designs as if these dimensions played different roles. As businesses extend their reach internationally, characteristic calendar and currency issues always seem to arise.

This chapter identifies a number of advanced dimensional modeling issues and provides specific guides for handling each situation. The first section discusses a set of extended dimension table designs, and the second section discusses specific fact table issues. The last section discusses some of the most challenging possible queries in a data warehouse environment.

The reader should have a solid grasp of the material covered in Chapter 5 prior to reviewing the advanced topics in this chapter. This chapter is required reading for anyone who is responsible for developing the data model for a data warehouse. It also may be of interest to those who have a natural curiosity and are not faint of heart—after all, it is a graduate course. It may be useful for the other team members to simply skim the headings to know which topics are covered. If any of these situations apply to your business, you know where to turn for help. This chapter is targeted to those who have digested the contents of *The Data Warehouse Toolkit* and are ready for more!

EXTENDED DIMENSION TABLE DESIGNS

In this section we describe a number of common modeling situations where a specific dimension structure is very effective or conversely where the designer may risk choosing an inefficient design.

Many-to-Many Dimensions

In a number of classic design situations the existence and grain of the fact table is easily understood and very fundamental, and the existence of each of the dimensions attached to the fact table records is obvious and not controversial. But one of the dimensions can legitimately have many values. Often, the offending dimension can legitimately have zero, one, or many values for a given record. The number of dimension values for such a fact record is not knowable before the fact table record is created. In some sense, the number of values for this dimension is a measured fact. We call this kind of dimension a *many-to-many dimension.*

Health care offers a clear example of a many-to-many dimension. If we build a fact table record for each line item of a hospital bill or each line item of a treatment performed in a physician's office, the dimensions would look something like Figure 6.1.

The problem for the designer is what to do with the diagnosis dimension. Real patients sometimes have more than one diagnosis. Really sick patients in a hospital may have as many as ten diagnoses. To handle this open-endedness, we cannot add multiple diagnosis dimensions to the schema. Not only do we not know what the extreme upper bound is for the number of diagnoses, but such a schema would be awkward to query. OR joins across dimensions are anathema to relational systems, and SQL's GROUP BY logic fails.

We resolve the design problem and provide for an arbitrary number

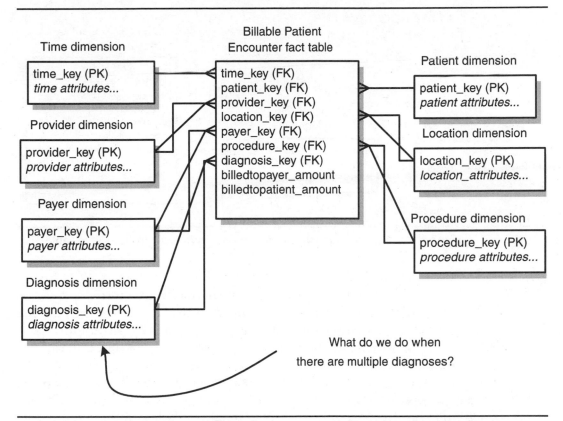

FIGURE 6.1   A billable patient encounter schema with a diagnosis dimension that can take only one value at a time.

of diagnoses by inserting a bridge table in between the fact table and the diagnosis dimension, as in Figure 6.2. We must generalize the original diagnosis key in the fact table to be a special diagnosis group key. The diagnosis group table, which is our bridge table, contains a specific set of records (a diagnosis group) for each patient. Each record in the diagnosis group table contains the diagnosis group key, an individual diagnosis key, and a weighting factor. A patient with three diagnoses will have three records in their respective diagnosis group. Within a given diagnosis group, the sum of all the weighting factors must be 1.00.

The individual diagnosis key joins to the diagnosis table, which contains a full description of the diagnosis. With this structure, the user can perform two important kinds of queries. First, the user can ask for a cor-

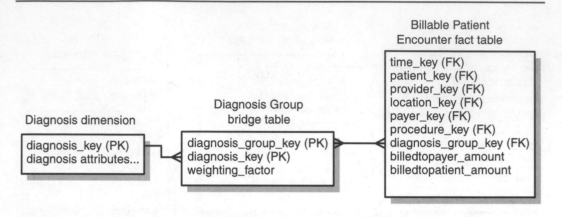

FIGURE 6.2   Solving the multiple diagnosis problem with a diagnosis group bridge table.

rectly weighted summary of all charges (the main fact in the fact table) grouped by diagnosis. The join through the bridge table picks up the weighting factor for each diagnosis and multiplies it by the amount fact. The use of the weighting factor guarantees that the bottom line total of amounts adds up correctly.

Alternatively, the user can request an impact report that performs the same join across the tables but does not use the weighting factor. Such an impact report deliberately double counts the amounts, but correctly totals the impact each diagnosis has in terms of total amounts associated with that diagnosis. The user decides which kind of report, correctly weighted or impact, to run.

Notice that over a period of time, a patient will have different diagnosis groups. Thus an embellishment to this design adds the patient key, a begin effective date, and an end effective date to the diagnosis group record, although these extra fields are not required for the basic navigation we are describing here.

A fact table representing account balances in a bank has an exactly analogous problem. Each account may have one or more individual customers as account holders. To join an individual customer dimension table to an account balances fact table, we build an account to customer bridge table that has the same structure as the diagnosis group table in the last example (see Figure 6.3). With the account-to-customer bridge

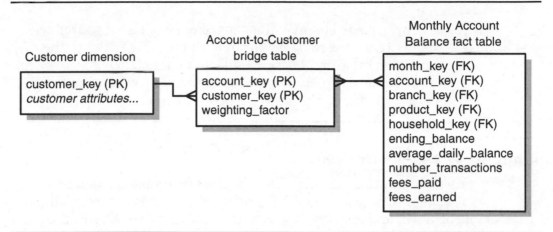

FIGURE 6.3   Solving the multiple customers per account problem with an account-to-customer bridge table.

table, we can build a correctly weighted account balance report by any attribute within the customer table, or alternatively, we can build a customer impact report by ignoring the weighting factors. These contrasting styles of reports are both of interest in banking environments.

A fact table that represents revenue received from commercial clients also faces the many-to-many problem. Each commercial customer may be represented by one or more standard industry classification codes (SICs). A large diversified commercial customer could have as many as ten SICs. Again, by building an SIC group bridge table with the same structure as the last two bridge tables, we can report total revenue by any attribute found within the SIC table, either correctly weighted or as an impact report.

All of the examples discussed in this section would usually have one or more entries in the outlying dimension for each fact table record. None of these examples would have a lot of cases where no dimensional entry was valid. Nevertheless, to handle the case of no valid value, we simply create special diagnoses, special bank customers, or special SICs that represent "we don't know," "no value in this case." and "hasn't happened yet." The bridge table then has just one record entry for that fact record, and this bridge record points to the special diagnosis, customer, or SIC.

An open-ended many-valued attribute can be associated with a fact table record by means of a bridge table between the dimension table and the fact table, but summarizing facts from this dimension requires the assignment of weighting factors to get the numbers to add up correctly.

Many-to-One-to-Many Traps

It is worth pointing out that there are some simple situations where what appear to be the obvious joins between tables do not return the correct results in any relational system. Consider the case where customers create orders for products, and the same customers return the products. There is a one-to-many relationship between customer and order and another one-to-many relationship between customer and return. The orders and returns tables are assumed to have different cardinalities. In other words, not every return corresponds exactly to a single order. It would seem obvious to create a report showing orders and returns by customer by joining the tables together as shown in Figure 6.4. This simultaneous join does not return the correct answer in a relational database management system (DBMS). Fortunately, this problem is easily avoided. We simply issue multipass SQL and query the orders table

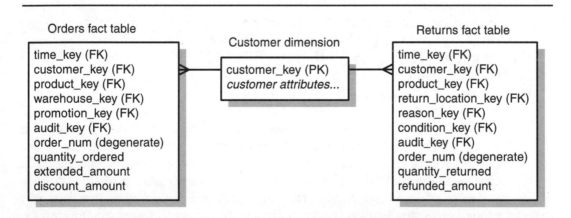

FIGURE 6.4   A many-to-one-to-many schema that should not be queried with one SELECT statement.

and the returns table in separate queries, outer-joining the two answer sets on the customer row header. Of course, these two queries probably come back faster when issued separately than if the DBMS processes the combined SQL, anyway.

 Be very careful when simultaneously joining a single dimension table to two fact tables of different cardinality. In many cases, relational systems will return the "wrong" answer.

Role-Playing Dimensions

A *role* in a data warehouse is a situation where a single dimension appears several times in the same fact table. This can happen in a number of ways. For instance, in certain kinds of fact tables, time can appear repeatedly. For instance, we may build a fact table to record the status and final disposition of a customer order. This kind of fact table is called an *accumulating snapshot* fact table. The dimensions of this table could be the following:

- Order date
- Packaging date
- Shipping date
- Delivery date
- Payment date
- Return date
- Refer to collection date
- Order status
- Customer
- Product
- Warehouse
- Promotion

Each of these dimensions is a foreign key in the fact table record that points to a specific dimension table. Dimension tables contain the descriptive textual attributes of the data warehouse and are the source of most of our interesting constraints.

The first seven dimensions in the design are all dates! However, we cannot join these seven foreign keys to the same table. SQL would interpret such a seven-way simultaneous join as requiring all the dates to be the same. That doesn't seem very likely.

Instead of a seven-way join, we need to fool SQL into believing that there are seven independent time dimension tables. We even need to label all the columns in each of the tables uniquely. If we don't, we get into the embarrassing position of not being able to tell the columns apart if several of them are dragged into a report.

Even though we cannot literally use a single time table, we still want to build and administer a single time table behind the scenes. For the user, we can create the illusion of seven independent time tables by using views. We create seven SQL views of the time table, being careful to make each of the view field names unique.

Now that we have seven differently described time dimensions, they can be used as if they were independent. They can have completely unrelated constraints, and they can play different roles in a report.

The scenario described in the last few paragraphs is the classic role model exercise in a data warehouse. Although the other examples we are about to describe have nothing to do with time, they are handled in exactly the same way.

The second example occurs in data marts that represent voyages or networks. In such a fact table, we need to have at least four "port" dimensions to properly describe the context of a journey segment. The dimensions of a frequent-flyer flight segment fact table need to include the following:

- Flight date
- Segment origin airport
- Segment destination airport
- Trip origin airport
- Trip destination airport
- Flight
- Fare class
- Customer

The four airport dimensions are four different roles played by a single underlying airport table. We build and administer these exactly the way we did the seven time tables in the previous example.

The telecommunications industry has lots of situations that require role models. With the advent of deregulation, a number of competing entities may all extract revenue from a single phone call. On a single call these entities might include the following:

- Source system provider
- Local switch provider
- Long-distance provider
- Added value service provider

These four entities may need to be dimensions on every call. In the complex and evolving telecommunications industry, it may be very difficult and confusing to maintain four different partially overlapping tables of business entities. Some business entities will play several of these roles. It will be much easier to keep a single business entity table and use it repeatedly within a data warehouse role model framework.

Actually, in building a full-blown call revenue analysis fact table, we would also recognize that there are at least two more business entity roles that should be added to the design. The fifth and sixth business entity dimensions could be:

- Calling party
- Called party

The telecommunications industry also has a very well-developed notion of location. Many telecommunications dimensions have a precise geographic location as part of their description. This location may be resolved to a physical address or even to a highly precise latitude and longitude. Using our role-modeling skills, we can imagine building a master location table and then using it repeatedly. The location table could be part of a working telephone number, billing telephone number, equipment inventory, network inventory (including poles and switch boxes), real estate inventory, service location, dispatch location, right of way, and even business entity. Each record in the location table is a point in space. Points in space are great because they roll up to every conceivable geography. Points in space roll up just as easily to area codes as they do to counties, census tracts, and sales territories. A single location record should probably include all these rollups simultaneously.

However, you will have noticed a little different emphasis in this discussion of location. Location is more naturally thought of as a component of a dimension, not as a standalone dimension. The working telephone number dimension is the most basic description of where all the phone numbers are actually located, but this dimension also needs to describe the customer who owns this working telephone number and perhaps something about the type of service this number represents. For instance, is it part of a Centrex system? This larger description seems to confuse the issue of creating a role for the location table.

 A single dimension may play several simultaneous roles when used with a fact table. The underlying dimension may exist as a single physical table, but each of the roles must be presented in a separately labeled view.

The use of an embedded role, like location, in a variety of unrelated larger dimensions, is one of the few places where we encourage and support snowflaking. In other words, we recommend creating a join from each of the tables that need to describe location to a clone of the location table. The issues in creating location clones are exactly the same as creating the time, airport, and business entity clones described earlier in this section. We need separate views for each use of the location table, being careful to create distinguishable column names. These views are then used to join into their respective larger dimensions, like working telephone number.

Organization and Parts Hierarchies

Representing an arbitrary organization structure or an arbitrary parts hierarchy is a difficult task in a relational environment. For example, we may wish to report the revenues of a set of commercial customers who have relationships with each other. See Figure 6.5. We may sell our products or services to any of these commercial customers, and at different times we want to look at them individually or as families arranged in a hierarchical structure.

The computer scientist in us would try to model such a hierarchical

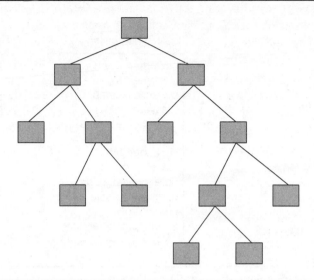

FIGURE 6.5 A schematic diagram of a set of parent companies and subsidiaries, all of whom may be customers.

structure with a recursive pointer in each customer dimension record containing a customer key of the parent organization as shown in Figure 6.6. Although this is a compact and effective way to represent an arbitrary hierarchy, this kind of recursive structure cannot be used effectively with standard SQL. The GROUP BY function in SQL cannot be used to follow the recursive tree structure downward to summarize an additive fact like revenue in an organization. Oracle's CONNECT BY function also cannot be used because although it is able to navigate a recursive pointer in a dimension table, the CONNECT BY phrase cannot be used in the presence of a join to another table. This prohibits connecting a recursive dimension table to any fact table.

As a guide to a more effective SQL-oriented design, let's pose a number of desirable requirements for an organization structure (or parts hierarchy) design. We would like to:

- Keep the original grain of the customer dimension, so that the customer key from this dimension when desired can be joined directly to the fact table, bypassing any bridge table we might build to navigate the hierarchy.

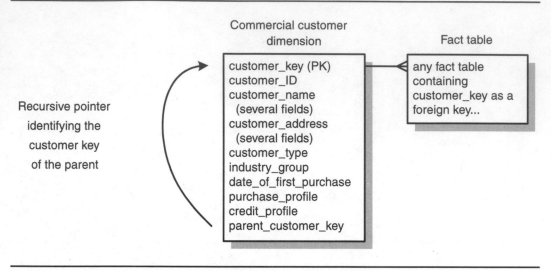

FIGURE 6.6   A commercial customer dimension with a recursive parent_customer_key link.

- Be able to additively summarize an additive fact across the entire subtree of an organization, using standard SQL GROUP BY logic.
- Be able to additively summarize an additive fact across either the set of immediate subsidiaries of a customer or, alternatively, the lowest-level subsidiaries of an organization, regardless of the depth or complexity of the organization tree, using standard SQL GROUP BY logic.
- Be able to find the immediate parent as well as the top-most parent of any customer in the organization hierarchy in one step by using standard SQL logic.

We can meet all these objectives simultaneously by building a special kind of bridge table between the customer dimension and the fact table as depicted in Figure 6.7. Neither the customer dimension nor the fact table has to be modified in any way. The use of the bridge table is optional. If it is left out, the customer dimension joins to the fact table in the usual way, and there is no information available to navigate the organization hierarchy. If the bridge table is used, it is inserted between the customer dimension and the fact table and can be used in two different modes.

The organization bridge table contains one record for each pathway in Figure 6.5 from a customer entity to each subsidiary beneath it. There

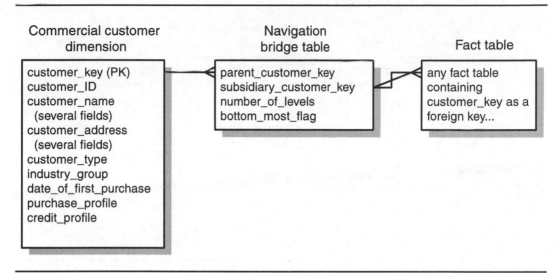

FIGURE 6.7   A commercial customer dimension with a navigation bridge table that allows natural SQL reporting at all levels of the tree. This join configuration supports descending the tree.

is also a record for the zero-length pathway from a customer to itself. Each pathway record contains the customer key of the customer entity (called the *parent* entity), the customer key of the specified subsidiary entity, the number of levels between the parent and the subsidiary, and finally a flag that identifies a subsidiary as being at the bottom-most possible level.

When we want to descend the organization hierarchy, we join the tables together as shown in Figure 6.7. We can now GROUP BY or constrain on any attribute within the customer table, and we can request in one step any aggregate measure of all the subsidiaries at or below all the customers implied by the GROUP BY or the constraint. We can use the number of levels field in the organization bridge table to control the depth of the analysis. A value of 1 would give all the direct subsidiaries of a customer. A value of "greater than zero" would give all subsidiary customers but not the original parent. We can use the bottom-most flag field to jump directly to all of the bottom-most customer entities but omit all higher-level customer entities.

When we want to ascend the organization hierarchy, we join the tables as shown in Figure 6.8. By constraining the number of levels field

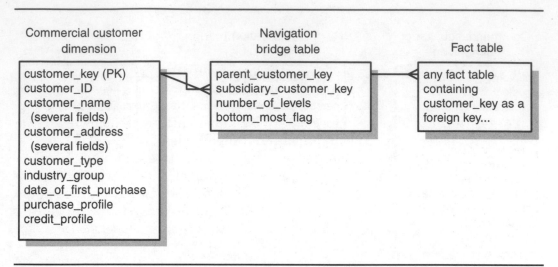

FIGURE 6.8 **This different configuration of joins between the navigation bridge table and the other tables is used to climb up the tree.**

in the organization bridge table to the value of 1, we find the unique single parent of the customer in the customer dimension. By searching for the maximum value of the number of levels field, we find the top-most parent customer. Alternatively, we could add a top-most flag to the organization bridge table to accomplish the same purpose.

There are a number of administrative issues in building and maintaining an organization bridge table. Perhaps the biggest question is where does the original organization information come from? How is the information captured and what happens when an organization change occurs? If a complete history of old organizational relationships needs to be maintained, then the organization bridge table can be generalized to include begin and end effective dates on each record. If these dates are properly administered, then every requesting application would have to constrain on a specific date between the begin and end effective dates. In this way, old organizational relationships can be tracked.

Updating the organization structure would require a simple program, perhaps written in Visual Basic, that would perform the functions of Add, Delete, and Move subtrees within the organization bridge table. These manipulations are not difficult, but these operations are not single SQL statements. To move a subtree from one place to another, all the customer entities within the subtree would first have to be enumerated as a set. Then all the records in the bridge table that referred to any member of this set as a subsidiary entity would have to be adjusted so that the parent entity key was the new destination parent entity.

The number of records in the organization bridge table is several times the number of records in the customer dimension table. For the organization shown in Figure 6.5, 13 customer entities are shown, and we need 43 records in the organization bridge table.

Small- and medium-sized parts explosions in a manufacturing application can be modeled using the same kind of bridge table in between a part/assembly dimension table and a fact table. Some caution should be taken to estimate the size of the bridge table before trying to build it automatically. A really large manufacturing parts explosion, such as for a Boeing 747, taken all the way down to tiny individual components would almost certainly be impractical because the bridge table would probably have hundreds of millions of rows.

 Organization hierarchies and parts explosion hierarchies may be represented with the help of a bridge table. This approach allows the regular SQL grouping and summarizing functions to work through ordinary query tools.

Unpredictably Deep Hierarchies

In some situations a hierarchy exists within a dimension, but its use is inconsistent. A dimension describing financial services may have an elaborate hierarchy that only makes sense for some of the products. If the differing hierarchical descriptions are obviously dependent on the type of the product, it is probably because of heterogeneous products. As described in Chapter 5, in this case one normally makes a core schema describing all products and their associated measured facts on a lowest common denominator basis (the core tables), but then a set of custom tables are built for each grouping of products that have similar sets of extended attributes and measured facts.

However, sometimes the variable depth of the hierarchical description is due to the unique history of the individual product and not due to the surrounding family of similar products. For instance, among a large group of retail electronic products, we may have products that have manufacturing profiles like the following:

- Locally manufactured, locally tested
- Remotely partially assembled, locally finally assembled, locally tested
- Remotely partially assembled, locally finally assembled, locally tested, sent to retail, returned, refurbished

A kind of hierarchy is implied by these sequential operations. The simplest situation only has one or two levels. We recommend modeling this situation as kind of many-to-many table attached to the product dimension as shown in Figure 6.9. Each record in the manufacturing profiles table contains a possible manufacturing step associated with that product. All the steps for a specific product are placed in sequence via the step sequence field. The user can constrain on a specific step like "locally tested" without having to know which step to constrain. This has an advantage over a fixed-field design where up to ten fields might be reserved in the product dimension table and these fields are filled in with the manufacturing steps for a specific product. In such a case, the requesting query would not know which field to constrain.

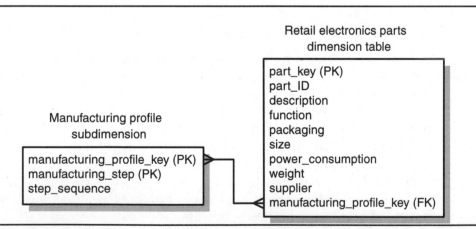

FIGURE 6.9   A manufacturing profile subdimension is used to model an unpredictably deep hierarchy.

Time Stamping the Changes in a Large Dimension

To frame the problem, let's describe a typical human resources environment. We assume that we are the human resources department for a large enterprise with more than 100,000 employees. Each employee has a complex human resources profile with at least 100 attributes. These attributes include all the standard human resources descriptions, including date of hire, job grade, salary, review dates, review outcomes, vacation entitlement, organization, education, address, insurance plan, and many others. In our large organization, there is a constant stream of transactions against this employee data. Employees are constantly being hired, transferred, promoted, and having their profiles adjusted in various ways.

In our design, we will address three fundamental kinds of queries we want to run against this complex human resources data. In the first kind of query, we want to rapidly report summary status of the entire employee base on a regular (monthly) basis. In these summaries, we want counts, instantaneous totals, and cumulative totals, including such things as number of employees, total salary paid during the month, cumulative salary paid this year, total and cumulative vacation days taken, vacation days accrued, number of new hires, and number of promotions. Our reporting system needs to be extremely flexible and accurate. We want these kinds of reports for all possible slices of the data, including time slices, organization slices, geographic slices, and any other slices supported in the data. Remember the basic tenet of dimensional modeling: If you want to be able to slice your data along a particular attribute, you simply need to make the attribute appear in a dimension table. By using the attribute as a row header (with SQL GROUP BY), you automatically slice the data. We demand that this database support hundreds of different slicing combinations.

The hidden, difficult reporting challenge in this first kind of query is making sure that we pick up all the correct instantaneous and cumulative totals at the end of each month, even when there is no activity in a given employee's record during that month. This prohibits us from merely looking through the transactions that occurred during the month.

In our second kind of query, we want to be able to profile the employee population at any precise instant in time, whether or not it is a month end. We want to choose some exact date and time at any point in our organization's history and ask how many employees did we have, and what their detailed profiles were on that date. This query needs to be simple and fast. Again, we want to avoid sifting through a complex set of transactions in sequence to construct a snapshot for a particular date in the past.

Although in our first two queries, we have argued that we cannot depend directly on the raw transaction history to give us a rapid response, in our third kind of query we demand that every employee transaction be represented distinctly. In this query, we want to see every action taken on a given employee, with the correct transaction sequence and the correct timing of each transaction. This detailed transaction history is the "fundamental truth" of the human resources data, and it should be able to answer every possible detailed question, including questions not anticipated by the original team of data mart designers. The SQL for these unanticipated questions may be complex, but we are confident the data is there waiting to be analyzed.

In all three cases, we demand that the employee dimension is always a perfectly accurate depiction of the employee base for the instant in time specified by the query. It is a huge mistake to run a report on a prior month with the current month's employee profiles.

Now that we have this daunting set of requirements, how on earth can we satisfy all of them and keep the design simple? Amazingly, we can do it all with a single dimensional schema with just one fact table and a powerful dimension table called the Employee Transaction dimension. Take a moment to study Figure 6.10.

The human resources data mart consists of a fairly ordinary looking fact table with three dimensions: employee transaction, month, and organization. We show all three dimensions in Figure 6.10 although we only explode the employee transaction table in detail because that is the interesting part of the design. The month table contains the usual descriptors for the corporate calendar, at the grain of the individual month. The organization dimension contains a description of the organization that the employee belongs to at the close of the relevant month.

The employee transaction dimension table contains a complete snapshot of the employee record for each individual employee transaction. The employee transaction key is an artificial key made during the extraction process, and it should be a sequentially assigned integer, starting with 1. Resist the urge to make this a smart key consisting of employee ID, transaction code, and effective date/time. All of those attributes are valuable, but they are simply attributes in the employee

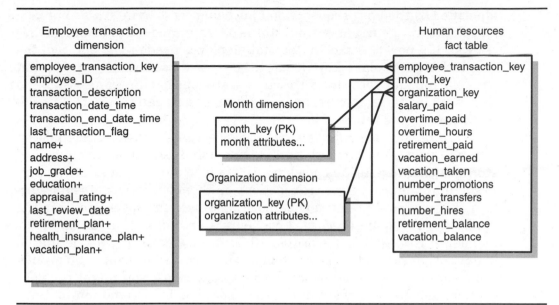

FIGURE 6.10   A model for a human resources environment with an employee transaction dimension time stamped with current and next transaction dates and times.

transaction record, where they participate in queries and in constraints like all the other attributes.

The employee ID is the normal human resources EMP ID that is used in the production system. The transaction description refers to the transaction that created this particular record, such as Promotion or Address Change. The transaction date/time is the exact date and time of the transaction. We assume that these date/times are sufficiently fine-grained that they guarantee uniqueness of the transaction record for a given employee. Therefore, the true underlying key for this dimension table is employee ID plus transaction date/time.

A crucial piece of the design is the second date/time entry: transaction end date/time. This date/time is exactly equal to the date/time of the *next* transaction to occur on this employee record, whenever that may be. In this way, these two date/times in each record define a span of time during which the employee description is exactly correct. The two date/times can be one second apart (if a rapid sequence of transactions is being processed against an employee profile) or many months apart.

The current last transaction made against an employee profile is identified by the Last Transaction Flag being set to True. This approach allows the most current or final status of any employee to be quickly retrieved. If a new transaction for that employee needs to be entered, the flag in this particular record needs to be set to False—we never said that we don't update records in the data warehouse. The transaction end date/time in the most current transaction record can be set to an arbitrary time in the future.

Some of you may object to the storage overhead of this design. Even in a pretty large organization, this approach doesn't lead to ridiculous storage demands. Assume we have 100,000 employees and that we perform 10 human resources transactions on them each year. Assume further that we have a relatively verbose 2000-byte employee profile in the employee transaction record. Five years' worth of data adds up to $5 \times 100,000 \times 10 \times 2000$ bytes or just 10 GB of raw data. If your definition of employee transaction is much more fine-grained so that a job promotion requires dozens of low-level tiny transactions, you might consider creating a small set of super transactions like Job Promotion to make the data sizing realistic. Admittedly, this makes the extraction task more complex.

This compact design satisfies our three categories of queries beautifully. The first kind of query, which wants fast high-level counts and totals, uses the fact table. All of the facts in the fact table are additive across all of the dimensions except for the ones labeled as balances. These balances, like all balances, are semiadditive and must be averaged across the time dimension after adding across the other dimensions. The fact table is also needed to present additive totals, like salary earned and vacation days taken.

The particular employee transaction key used in a fact table record is the precise employee transaction key associated with the stroke of midnight on the last day of the reporting month. This guarantees that the month end report is a correct depiction of all the employee profiles.

The second query is addressed by the employee transaction dimension table. A time-based cut through the employee database can be made by choosing a specific date and time and constraining this date and time to be greater than or equal to the transaction date/time and less than the transaction end date/time. This is guaranteed to return exactly one employee profile for each employee whose profile was in effect at the requested moment. The query can perform counts and constraints against all the records returned from these time constraints.

The third kind of query can use the same employee transaction dimension table to look in detail at the sequence of transactions against any given employee.

 The design for the slowly changing Type 2 dimension may be embellished by adding begin and end time stamps and a transaction description in each instance of a dimension record. This design allows very precise time slicing of the dimension by itself.

Some of you may be wondering if the employee transaction dimension table isn't really a kind of fact table since it seems to have a time dimension. While technically this may be true, this employee transaction table mainly contains textual values, and it is certainly the primary source of constraints and row headers for query and report-writing tools. So it is proper to think of this table as a dimension table that serves as the entry point into the human resources data mart. The employee transaction table can be used with any fact table in any data mart that requires an employee dimension as long as the notion of employee key is extended to be the employee transaction key. This design is really an embellishment of the standard slowly changing dimension we routinely use when dimensions like Product change at unexpected intervals. The key idea that makes this human resources database fit into our familiar dimensional framework is making each dimension record an individual employee transaction and then tying these records to precise moments in time.

Building an Audit Dimension

An interesting dimension to add to a fact table is an audit dimension that records the lineage of each fact record. The audit dimension is constructed during the extract process in the data staging area. An ideal audit dimension design is shown in Figure 6.11. There is one record in the audit dimension for each separate run of software during the extract operations. The records of the runs are assembled into a single audit record describing the major phases run, the status of each phase upon

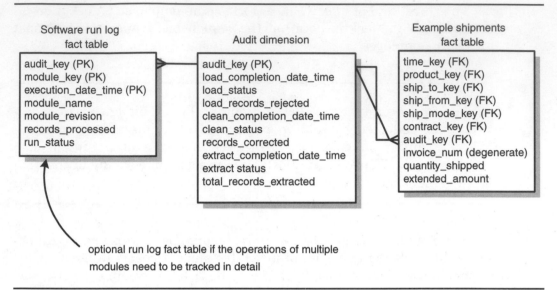

FIGURE 6.11 An audit dimension can be used to accurately track the lineage of individual records in the fact table.

completion, and the exact time of completion of each phase. If individual software modules need to be tracked in more detail, then an optional Run Log fact table can be added that records the run results of as many individual software modules as desired.

If a fact record is subject to updating, then the design needs to be generalized an additional step. A many-to-many bridge table must be added between the audit dimension and the fact table in much the same way we described bridge tables for patient diagnoses and customers within accounts earlier in this chapter.

Too Few Dimensions and Too Many Dimensions

Most dimensional models end up with between five and fifteen dimensions. At the low end, there is a strong suspicion that dimensions have been left out. The designer should carefully think whether any of the following kinds of dimensions should be added presuming there is business demand:

- Causal dimensions, like promotion, contract, deal, store condition, or even the weather.

- Additional time-stamp dimensions, especially when the grain of the fact table is a line item in a control document such as an order, a shipment, an invoice, a bill of lading, or a ticket. See *The Data Warehouse Toolkit* for examples of fact tables with a large number of time stamps.
- Dimensions that implement multiple roles. Often even a single transaction may have several business entities associated with it. As described earlier in this chapter, a telephone call may have a local service provider, a backbone carrier, a long-distance provider, and an added value service provider. All four of these can be dimensions on the single call record. Similarly, sometimes a single transaction may have multiple employee role dimensions, or multiple responsible organization dimensions such as sales organizations associated with the transaction. Each of these can be a separate dimension.
- Status dimensions that flag the current status of a single transaction or monthly snapshot within some larger context, like New Customer or In Collections.
- An audit dimension, as described in earlier in this chapter.
- One or more degenerate dimensions that identify header control numbers usually of significance to an operational system.
- A junk dimension, as described in Chapter 5.

Most of these dimensions can be added gracefully to the design even after the data warehouse has gone into production. The addition of these dimensions usually does not alter the existing dimension keys or the measured facts in the fact table, and it does not cause the grain of the fact table to change. In this case, all existing applications should continue to run without any changes being required. Remember that any descriptive attribute that is single valued in the presence of the measurements in the fact table is a good candidate to be added to an existing dimension or to be its own dimension.

At the high end of the spectrum, especially if the design seems to have 20 or 30 dimensions, one should look for ways to prune the dimension list.

 Usually a very large number of dimensions is a sign that several dimensions are not at all independent and should be combined into a single dimension.

Either the dimensions are obviously related to each other, such as brand, category, and department in a typical product table, or the dimensions have a mathematical correlation that may have to be uncovered by analysis, as described in the section on junk dimensions in Chapter 5.

EXTENDED FACT TABLE DESIGNS

In this section we describe a number of common modeling situations where a specific fact table structure is very effective or conversely where the designer may choose an inefficient design.

Facts of Differing Granularity and Allocating

The dimensional model gains power as the individual fact records become more and more atomic. At the lowest level of individual transaction or individual snapshot in time, the design is most powerful because:

- More of the descriptive attributes have single values.
- The design gracefully withstands surprises in the form of new facts, new dimensions, or new attributes within existing dimensions.

    These new data elements can usually be added to the existing design without unraveling existing administrative procedures or existing queries and reports.

- There is usually more expressiveness at the lowest levels of granularity, and, thus, more dimensions make sense at this level. For example, one can often attach an employee dimension to a customer transaction that represents the clerk, the customer agent, or the loan officer, but this employee dimension may not make logical sense on a monthly summary record or across multiple customers.

When the designer is faced with facts of differing granularity, the first response should be to try to force all of the facts down to the lowest level. We can broadly refer to this procedure as "allocating" the high-level facts to the low level. There are many, many examples of the need to allocate in a data warehouse. The most pervasive example is the need to allocate costs. For example, on a shipment invoice, there may be a shipping cost for the whole invoice that is initially not allocated down to the individual line item.

The data architect working with the business should make a significant effort to allocate invoice shipping costs down to the line-item level, even if the process of allocating involves some degree of compromise or controversy. If the design does not successfully allocate this shipping cost, two bad things happen:

- The shipping cost must be presented in a higher-level table, such as at the invoice level. Perhaps the situation is even worse, and the measured shipping costs are simply standards or rates that are not even specific to the invoice, but rather exist at a regional or product category level. In any case, the design of a profitability reporting schema that combines revenues and costs will be more complicated due to the presence of multiple fact tables at differing levels of granularity.
- A worse problem may arise because of the refusal to allocate shipping cost to the line item level. If the line item distinguishes one product from another on a shipping invoice, this refusal may mean that product profit and loss (P&L) statements may not be possible because the shipping cost can only be represented independently from the product dimension. Such a refusal is usually unacceptable, and it forces the end user groups to agree on an allocation scheme.

If we are successful in allocating all cost facts down to the lowest level, our problem goes away. In Figure 6.12, we show a successfully allocated set of revenues and costs that is the basis of the classic "most powerful" schema discussed in *The Data Warehouse Toolkit*. The items that had to be allocated are indicated in the figure. Incidentally, it is wonderful if the whole issue of allocations has been handled by the finance department and not by the data warehouse team. If the allocation process is too controversial or too complicated, the data warehouse team may be distracted and delayed. Also, in many companies, the need to rationally allocate costs has been recognized already, and this function is completely independent of the data warehouse team—there may be a task force creating "activity-based costing" measures, for example. This is just another name for allocating.

In the event that allocating facts down to the lowest level is impossible, the designer has no choice but to present the higher level facts in separate fact tables. It is correct to think of these higher-level facts as existing within an aggregation or at the same level as an aggregation. A reasonable example of this situation would be high-level plans or fore-

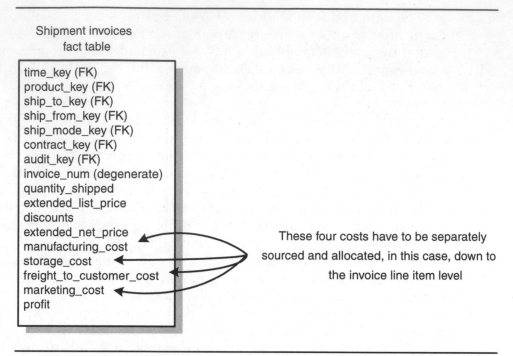

Shipment invoices
fact table

time_key (FK)
product_key (FK)
ship_to_key (FK)
ship_from_key (FK)
ship_mode_key (FK)
contract_key (FK)
audit_key (FK)
invoice_num (degenerate)
quantity_shipped
extended_list_price
discounts
extended_net_price
manufacturing_cost
storage_cost
freight_to_customer_cost
marketing_cost
profit

These four costs have to be separately
sourced and allocated, in this case, down to
the invoice line item level

FIGURE 6.12   A shipment invoices fact table showing how a full view of profitability can be expressed at the invoice line item level by allocating costs to the lowest level.

casts. The management team may meet periodically to create high-level revenue and cost plans. These usually exist only at relatively rarefied aggregation levels, and it makes no sense to try allocate such plans down to an individual invoice line item. In this case, a requesting query or report that tries to match actuals to plans needs to roll up the actuals to the right levels implied by the plans. Hopefully, for performance reasons, the actuals are already being expressed as prestored aggregates. It may be helpful to make sure that the actual aggregates exist at exactly the same level as the plans. If the list of dimensions are identical, as in Figure 6.13, then the two tables could even be merged into a single table, simplifying the querying process even further.

However, one or both of the tables may have additional dimensions, making this merger impossible. For example, the plans fact table could have a plan version dimension that would need to be constrained to a particular value (e.g., Preliminary, Final, Approved) before running the

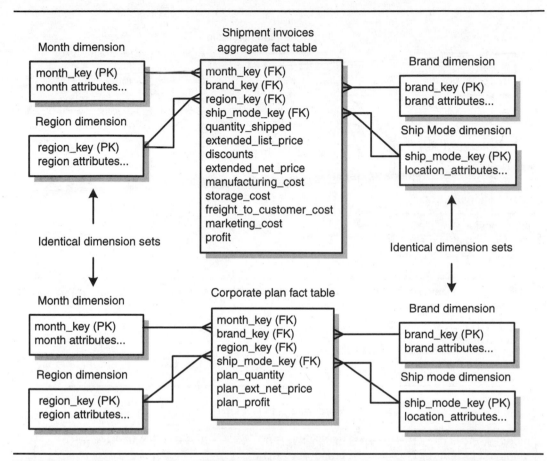

FIGURE 6.13 **When an aggregate table and a plan table share exactly the same dimensions, it may be reasonable to combine them into a single physical table.**

report. In this case, the plan table would remain separate as shown in Figure 6.14.

A design mistake is sometimes made in the design of individual fact table records in an effort to improve performance or to reduce query complexity. Aggregated facts sometimes sneak into the fact record. In Figure 6.15 we show year-to-date totals and national totals in a record that is expressed at a daily grain. These totals are dangerous because they are not perfectly additive. While a year-to-date total reduces the complexity and runtime of a few specific queries, having it in the daily

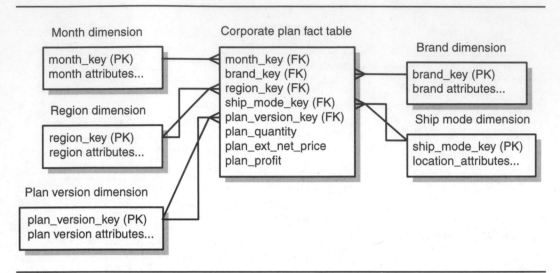

FIGURE 6.14   **A plan table with an extra dimension (plan version) that makes it impossible to combine with an aggregate table.**

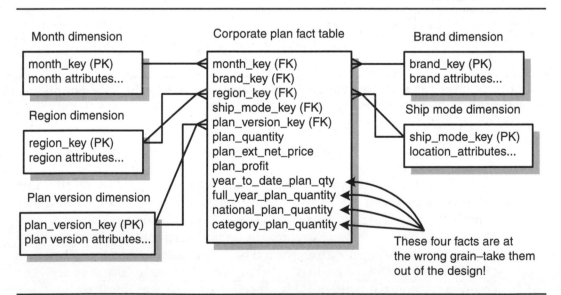

FIGURE 6.15   **A fact table with facts at the wrong grain.**

grain fact table invites a query or report to double count this field if more than one day is ever included in a query. Similarly, the national market total will double count if the query ever includes more than one location. It is very important that once the grain of a fact table is chosen, all of the additive facts are presented at this uniform grain.

Time of Day

Fine-scale tracking of individual transactions may introduce a meaningful date and time stamp into the data that is accurate to the minute or even the second. In this case, we do not create a time dimension with one record for every minute or second in the entire epoch! Usually, the notions of day are quite distinct from the notions of time within the day, and we separate these into two entries in the fact table as in Figure 6.16. The day measure is virtually always expressed as a surrogate key to a full-fledged day dimension table that contains calendar information. But the time-of-day measure may be best expressed as a simple numerical fact rather than as a dimension, unless there are textual descriptions of certain periods within the day that are meaningful, like Lunch Hour or Graveyard Shift. The time of day should be expressed as a number of minutes or number of seconds since midnight.

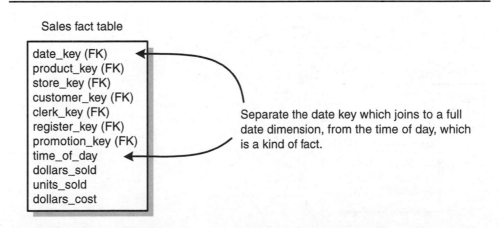

FIGURE 6.16   A sales fact table with transaction time recorded to the minute and split off from the transaction date.

Break the time of day off from the calendar date, and make it a simple numeric fact.

In applications that span multiple time zones, both the date and time of day may need to be expressed both in local time and Greenwich Mean Time (GMT). This must be done with separate date dimensions for local and GMT and separate time-of-day facts as well, as in Figure 6.17. Merely providing for offsets in either the time dimension table or the fact table doesn't work because of the number of possible time zones and the complexities of switching to and from daylight savings time. Having two explicit time interpretations can be quite useful. In analyzing call center behavior where there are multiple call centers in different time zones, calling behavior can be aligned in real time by using the GMT interpretation and aligned on similar local times (but not real time) by using the local time interpretation. Finally, if it is easier for the users to understand, the GMT interpretation can be something more familiar, like Eastern Standard Time in the United States.

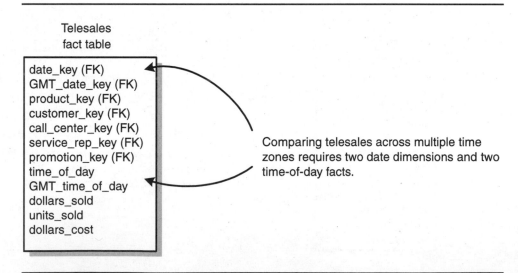

FIGURE 6.17   A sales fact table spanning multiple time zones where comparing comparable telesales across time zones is required.

Multiple Units of Measure

Sometimes, in a value chain involving several business processes monitoring the flow of products through a system or multiple measures of inventory at different points, a conflict arises in presenting the amounts. Everyone may agree that the numbers are correct, but different parties along the chain may wish to see the numbers expressed in different units of measure. For instance, manufacturing managers may wish to see the entire product flow in terms of car loads or pallets. Store managers, on the other hand, may wish to see the amounts in shipping cases, retail cases, scan units (sales packs), or consumer units (individual sticks of gum). Similarly, the same quantity of a product may have several possible economic valuations. We may wish to express the valuation in terms of inventory valuation, in list price, in original selling price, or in final selling price. Finally, this situation may be exacerbated by having many fundamental quantity facts in each fact record.

Consider an example (generalized from *The Data Warehouse Toolkit*) where we have 13 fundamental quantity facts, 5 unit-of-measure interpretations, and 4 valuation schemes. It would be a mistake to present only the 13 quantity facts in the fact table and then leave it up to the user or application developer to seek the correct conversion factors in remote dimension tables, as in Figure 6.18, especially if the user queries the product table at a separate time from the fact table without forcing the join to occur. It would be equally bad to try to present all the combinations of facts expressed in the different units of measure in the main fact table. This would require 13×5 quantity facts plus 13×4 valuation facts or 117 facts in each fact table record! The correct compromise is to build an underlying physical record with 13 quantity facts, 4 unit-of-measure conversion *factors*, and 4 valuation *factors*. We need only 4 unit-of-conversion factors rather than 5 since the base facts are already expressed in one of the units of measure. Our physical design now has $13 + 4 + 4$, or 21, facts as shown in Figure 6.19.

 Packaging all the facts and all the conversion factors together in the same fact table record provides the safest guarantee that these factors will be used correctly.

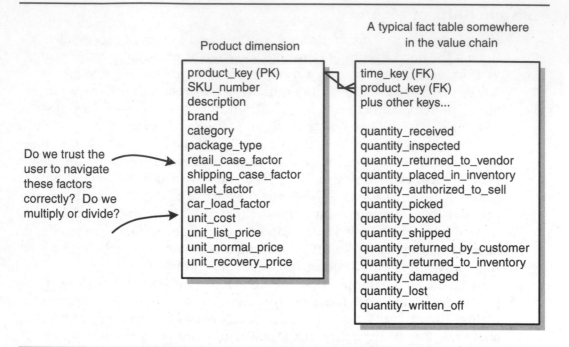

FIGURE 6.18 The wrong design when fact table quantities need to be expressed in several units of measure.

Finally, packaging these factors in the fact table reduces the pressure on the product dimension table to issue new product records to reflect minor changes in these factors, especially the cost and price factors. These items, especially if they routinely evolve over time, are much more like facts than dimension attributes.

We now actually deliver this fact table to the users through one or more views. The most comprehensive view could actually show all 117 combinations of units of measure and valuations, but obviously we could simplify the user interface for any specific user group by only making available the units of measure and valuation factors that the group wanted to see.

Multinational Currency Tracking

In a multinational enterprise we may have transactions expressed in a dozen or more currencies. Although the idea of translating a number of

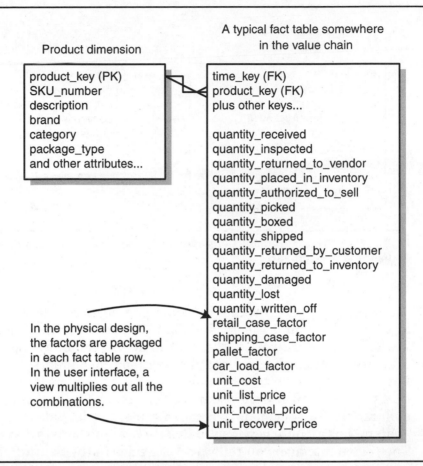

Product dimension

A typical fact table somewhere
in the value chain

product_key (PK)
SKU_number
description
brand
category
package_type
and other attributes...

time_key (FK)
product_key (FK)
plus other keys...

quantity_received
quantity_inspected
quantity_returned_to_vendor
quantity_placed_in_inventory
quantity_authorized_to_sell
quantity_picked
quantity_boxed
quantity_shipped
quantity_returned_by_customer
quantity_returned_to_inventory
quantity_damaged
quantity_lost
quantity_written_off
retail_case_factor
shipping_case_factor
pallet_factor
car_load_factor
unit_cost
unit_list_price
unit_normal_price
unit_recovery_price

In the physical design,
the factors are packaged
in each fact table row.
In the user interface, a
view multiplies out all the
combinations.

FIGURE 6.19 **The recommended design for multiple units of measure places the conversion factors directly in the fact table record to eliminate the possibility of choosing the wrong factors.**

local currencies into a single standard currency is obvious, we wish to make the database more flexible, so that any manager in any country can see summaries of the enterprise in any currency. This flexibility can be accomplished by expressing all currency amounts in primary fact records both in terms of the applicable local currency as well as the international standard currency and by adding a special currency conversion fact table to the design. This design is shown in Figure 6.20.

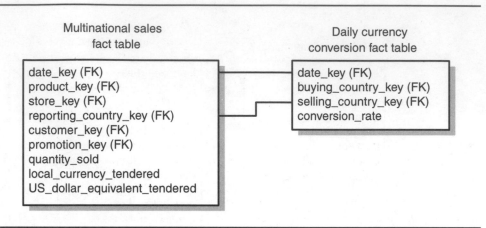

FIGURE 6.20 Tracking transactions in multiple currencies requires a daily currency exchange conversion fact table.

Suppose we are tracking the sales of a large retailer with locations in cities all around the Pacific Rim. Suppose further that the New Zealand stores are part of the South Pacific region, whose regional offices are in Australia. The main operational headquarters are in California, and the executive headquarters are in Switzerland. We assume that the standard currency that is common to all fact table records is US dollars. Now a specific fact record for a sale that takes place in New Zealand has amounts expressed in New Zealand dollars and US dollars. The region manager can roll up all the sales in the South Pacific region in Australian dollars by using the special currency conversion table. Finally, the senior executives in Zurich can roll up the worldwide business in Swiss francs in a similar way.

Within each fact table record, the amount expressed in local currency is always exactly accurate since the sale was conducted in that currency on that day. The equivalent US dollar value would be based on a conversion rate to US dollars for that day. The conversion rate table has all combinations of effective currency exchange rates going in both directions since it is assumed that the symmetric rates between any two countries are not exactly equal. Notice that since the exchange rate table reflects daily rate fluctuations, some moderately sophisticated analyses can be done that take into account delays in actually moving cash in and out of various currencies.

Value Band Reporting

Our final design example involving fact tables occurs when we want to perform value-band reporting on a fact. For instance, suppose that we have a large table of account balances, as shown in Figure 6.21, and we want to run a report of the form:

Balance Range	Number of Accounts	Total of Balances
0–1000	45,678	$10,222,543
1001–2000	36,788	$45,777,216
2001–5000	11,775	$31,553,884
5001–10000	2,566	$22,438,287
10001 and up	477	$ 8,336,728

It is not easy to create this report directly from the fact table. SQL has no generalization of the GROUP BY clause that clumps additive values into ranges. Also note that the ranges are of unequal size and they have textual names like *10001 and up*. The SQL CASE statement provides a rudimentary IF-THEN capability to create these ranges, but it is not easily accessible to end users. Also, one would like to have the flexibility to redefine the bands to have different boundaries or different levels of precision.

The schema design shown in Figure 6.21 allows us to do flexible value-band reporting. The band definition table contains as many sets of different reporting bands as desired. The name of a particular group of bands is stored in the band group field. When the band definition table is joined to the fact table, it is joined by a less-than, greater-than pair of joins to the balance fact. The report uses the band name as the row header and sorts the report on the band sort field.

 Value-band reporting benefits from an index created directly on the affected fact in the fact table.

The performance of a query that constrains or groups on the value of a fact like balance will be improved enormously if the DBMS can efficiently sort and compress an individual fact. Such an approach was pi-

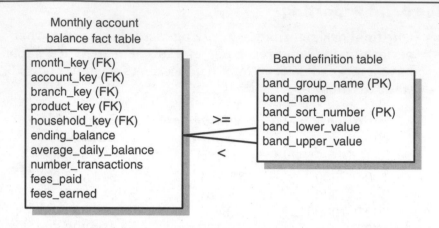

FIGURE 6.21 Arbitrary value band reporting can be done with a band definition table and a pair of nonequijoins.

oneered by the Sybase IQ product in the early 1990s, and it is now becoming a standard indexing option on several of the competing DBMSs that want to provide a high performance solution for this kind of report. Notice that the style of a value-band report encourages a scan of a very large number of accounts because the point of the report is to take a broad perspective across many accounts.

ADVANCED ROLAP QUERYING AND REPORTING

In this section we discuss a number of advanced techniques for querying and reporting that have become important. For a more basic discussion of querying and reporting in a dimensional environment, see Chapters 14, 15, and 16 in *The Data Warehouse Toolkit*.

Drill-Across Queries with Multiple Technologies

Having made the claim that by conforming dimension and conforming facts, we can tie together disparate data marts, we need to take a look at exactly how that is done. Clearly, if we step far enough back and consider data marts implemented on different DBMSs and even remote data marts implemented on various proprietary OLAP platforms, there is no way to launch a single massive SQL-based query to any single machine and get a conformed drill-across–style answer.

To drill across multiple query technologies, we must launch a series of queries against each data mart and bring the separate results sets back to an intermediate platform, where we tie the answers together by performing a sort-merge on the row headers of the answer sets.

A series of drill-across queries that solves this problem can be imagined by visualizing the icon flow in Figure 6.22. At the level of the join operation in the icon flow, it doesn't make any difference what the un-

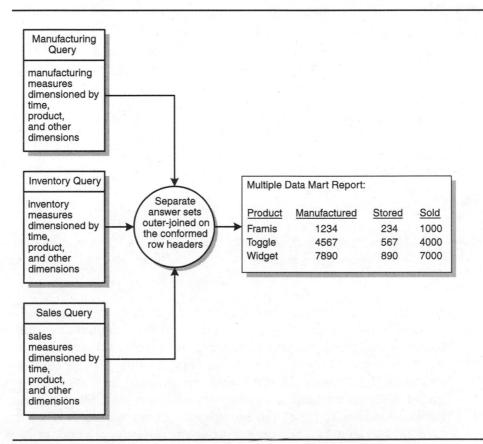

FIGURE 6.22   The query architecture for disparate conformed data sources.

derlying technologies of the query sources happen to be, as long as the dimensions are carefully conformed so that the sorted row header lists in the answer sets can be matched perfectly on a character-by-character basis. Of course, there is always the deeper issue with conformed dimensions that requires the separate copies of the conformed dimensions to be perfectly administered in unison so that the internal relationships among the attributes are synchronized. Keeping such disparate dimensions perfectly synchronized is a matter for the dimension replication function in the data staging area, which is discussed in detail in Chapter 16.

Self Referencing Queries, Behavior Tracking, and Sequential Subsetting

SQL is very seductive. Simple SQL statements seem to read like English-language requests for information from a database. After all, almost everyone can figure out the intent of a simple SQL request like

Select Product_Description, Sum(dollars)	—all the columns in the final output
From Product, Time, Sales	—the tables needed in the query
Where Sales.Product_key = Product.Product_key	—joining the Sales table to the Product table
And Sales.Time_key = Time.Time_key	—joining the Sales table to the Time table
And Time.Month = 'September, 1997'	—the "application" constraint
Group by Product_Description	—the row header in the final output

Here we are asking for the September sales of each of our products.

Unfortunately, almost any more ambitious business request begins to make the SQL complex to write and complex to read. For too long, query tool vendors did not venture very far beyond the safe havens of simple SQL requests like the preceding example. In the early days, most query tools automated the construction of simple SQL requests, sometimes even showing the SQL clauses as they were being built. It has only been in the last two or three years that query tool vendors have seriously tackled how to issue the really complex SQL needed for serious business questions. Some vendors have deepened their tools by allowing the user to construct embedded subqueries. Others have also implemented multipass SQL, in which complex requests are broken into many separate queries whose results are combined after the database has completed processing.

But, are these approaches sufficient? Are we able to pose all the interesting business questions we want? Aren't there some business results that beg to be recognized but are trapped in the database because we just can't "speak" clearly enough? Should the SQL language committee give us more power to ask hard business questions, and could the database vendors implement these language extensions, all before the next millennium?

To get some perspective on these issues, let us propose seven categories of business questions, ordered from the most simple to the most complex, in terms of the logical complexity of isolating exactly the records in the database needed to answer the question. This isn't the only possible taxonomy of business questions or SQL queries, but it is useful as a scale to judge SQL and SQL-producing tools. As you read the following seven categories of queries, try to imagine whether SQL could pose such a query, and try to imagine whether your query tool could produce such SQL. The seven categories of queries are:

1. **Simple constraints.**   Constraints against literal constants, such as "Show the sales of candy products in September 1997."
2. **Simple subqueries.**   Constraints against a global value found in the data, such as "Show the sales of candy products in September 1997 in those stores that had above-average sales of candy products."
3. **Correlated subqueries.**   Constraints against a value defined by each output row, such as "Show the sales of candy products for each month of 1997 in those stores that had above-average sales of candy in that month."
4. **Simple behavioral queries.**   Constraints against values that are the result of an exception report or a complex series of queries that isolates desired behavior, such as "Show the sales of those candy products in September 1997 whose household penetration for our grocery chain in the 12 months prior to September were more than two standard deviations less than the household penetration of the same products across our ten biggest retail competitors." This is a variation of the classic opportunity gap analysis.

5. **Derived behavioral queries.**   Constraints against values found in set operations (union, intersection, and set difference) on more than one complex exception report or series of queries, such as "Show the sales of those candy products identified in example 4 and which also experienced a merchandise return rate more than two standard deviations greater than our ten biggest retail competitors." This is a set intersection of two behavioral queries.

6. **Progressive subsetting queries.**   Constraints against values as in example 4, but also temporally ordered so that membership in an exception report is dependent on membership in a previous exception report, such as "Show the sales of those candy products in example number four that were similarly selected in August 1997 but were not similarly selected in either June or July 1997." An important health care example of a progressive subsetting query would be "Show the oldest 100 patients who initially complained of chest pain, then had either treatment A or treatment B, then subsequently did not have surgery, and are still alive today."

7. **Classification queries.**   Constraints on values that are the results of classifying records against a set of defined clusters using nearest neighbor and fuzzy matching logic, such as "Show the percentage of low-calorie candy sales contained in the 1000 market baskets whose content most closely matches a Young Health-Conscious Family profile."

The business questions in these seven categories grow progressively more interesting as we move down the list. The questions in categories 4–7 lead almost directly to decisions made and actions taken. Decisions made and actions taken are the true outputs of a data warehouse, and in that sense we should be devoting a large part of our creative energy to making these kinds of complex queries possible.

How did you do in comparing these business questions to SQL and to industry-standard tools? Not too well, we assume. Most query tools can really only handle category 1 (simple constraints) easily. Some of the high-end tools can also handle category 2 (simple subqueries), although the user interface commands for doing these subqueries may be cumbersome. A few are aggressively selling their ability to handle category 3 (correlated subqueries).

As far as we know, none of the standard query or reporting products have direct user interfaces for categories 4–7. If you are trying to support queries in these categories, you are faced with an architectural problem: These business questions are too complex to express in a single request. Not only should the user partition these queries into sequential processing steps in order to think clearly about the problem, but the underlying algorithms may be more stable and easier to control if they are doing less in each step. So how do you attack these hard problems in categories 4–7, and can you use your current tools to get you part way or all the way to useful answers?

The key is to use a technique that has been developed for doing behavior tracking applications in relational environments. This approach could be an important step forward for query tools that would extend their reach across categories 4, 5, and 6 (simple and derived behavioral queries and progressive subsetting queries). In some sense, this is a way to turbocharge existing query and reporting tools to perform deeper analyses than they could before. The technique partitions the problem into two steps.

First, run an exception report or series of queries that defines the complex behavior you wish to label. For instance, define the candy products in September 1997 whose household penetration for our grocery chain in the 12 months prior to September were more than 2 standard deviations less than the household penetration of the same products across our 10 biggest retail competitors. Although this is a complex request, most of the good report and analysis systems on the market should be able to handle it, perhaps with several steps. After running the exception report (in this case yielding a list of products), *capture the product keys* of the products identified in the exception report as an actual physical table that consists of a single product key column.

 The secret to building complex behavioral queries and progressive subsetting queries is to capture the keys of the customers or products whose behavior you are tracking. You then use the captured keys to subsequently constrain other fact tables.

Now use the special behavior dimension table of product keys whenever you wish to constrain any analysis on any table to that set of spe-

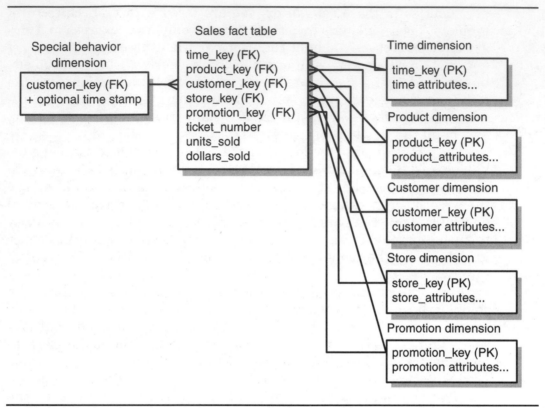

FIGURE 6.23   A special behavior dimension consisting only of keys of some selected dimension can be attached directly to any fact table containing that dimension's keys.

cially defined products. The only requirement is that the target fact table contain a product key as part of its overall composite key.

The use of the special behavior dimension is shown in Figure 6.23.

The special behavior dimension is just attached with an equijoin to the product key component of the fact table's composite key. This can even be done in a view that hides the explicit join to the special behavior dimension. In this way, the star schema looks and behaves like a regular, uncomplicated star. If the special dimension table is hidden under a view, and we call this view Special Product Sales instead of Sales, then virtually every query tool, report writer, and ROLAP tool should be able to smoothly analyze this specially restricted star schema without paying a syntax or user-interface penalty for the complex processing that defined the original exception report.

Like any design decision, this one has certain compromises. First, this approach requires a user interface for capturing, creating, and administering real physical tables in the data warehouse. We can imagine building a simple applet in Visual Basic that sits outside of your favorite query tool or report writer. Whenever a complex exception report has been defined on the screen, you make sure that the appropriate set of keys are displayed and then capture them into the applet with the Cut and Paste commands. This applet then creates the special behavior dimension table.

A second reality is that these tables must live in the same space as the primary fact table because they are going to be joined to the fact table directly. This affects the DBA's responsibilities.

Third, the use of a random set of product keys as in the preceding example will affect aggregate navigation on the product dimension. A sophisticated approach could build custom aggregations on the special behavior set for all the queries that summed over the whole set rather than enumerating the individual members. Aggregate navigation on all the other dimensions should be unaffected.

By storing the keys in the special behavior dimensions in sorted order, set operations of union, intersection, and set difference can be handled in a single pass. This allows us to construct derived behavior dimensions that are the combinations of two or more complex exception reports or series of queries.

Finally, by generalizing the behavior dimension to also include a time key in each record along with the product key (in the preceding example), the time key can be used to constrain out records in the master fact table that occurred *after* the behaviorally defined event. In this way, we can search for behavior that happens in a sequential order.

One complexity arises in this approach if you are also tracking the product using slowly changing dimension technique number 2, where a new record and a new surrogate key for the product table is created whenever a change in the product's profile occurs. In this case, new surrogate keys would occasionally be created representing the same product. Depending on the business rules underlying the desired analysis, a periodic maintenance step is needed for the behavior dimension. If the analysis wants to track the individual product forward in time, allowing changes in the product's description, then subsequent surrogate keys generated for that product would have to be added to the behavior dimension. This could be done in several different ways. If the frequency of updating product profiles is low, then each day, the few updated product profiles could trigger an update of the behavior dimension tables. The behavior dimension tables would be searched for the existence of the old value of a surrogate product key that had changed today. If the old value were found, then the new value would be also added at the end of the behavior dimension. The behavior dimensions should be sorted in order of the keys in any case to facilitate rapid set operations between these tables, like union, intersection, and set difference. This administrative step of updating the behavior dimensions is a little utility that is run as part of the daily extract operations. If any new surrogate product keys are created because of changing product profiles, then the utility must be run.

Market Basket Analysis

Market basket analysis consists of noticing the combinations of products that sell together. Although many market basket analyses are literally the analysis of grocery store market baskets, the concept can easily be extended to other situations. A different but perfectly good example is cable television purchases made within the month following the purchase of a sports viewing package.

Conceptually, the idea of recording market basket correlations is simple, but the sheer combinatorics of the large number of products makes the problem very challenging. For example, in Figure 6.24 we show how a standard retail sales fact table could drive the population of a market basket table that records all possible pairs of products sold together. A useful market basket table represents an aggregation over one or more of the major dimensions such as time or store. If there are N products in the store, and we attempt to build such a table with every possible pair of product keys encountered in real market baskets, we will approach N^2 product combinations (actually $N*(N-1)$ for the mathematicians among you). In modern retail environments, this is ridiculous. Even a small retail store with 10,000 SKUs could generate $10,000^2 = 100,000,000$ pairwise combinations. If we asked for the three-way combinations, we would worry about $10,000^3$ combinations, although in fairness we should point out that many market baskets would never be encountered. At some point in these kinds of arguments, the laws of physics intervene. Nevertheless, we are left with the absurdity of perhaps recording all the possible combinations of products.

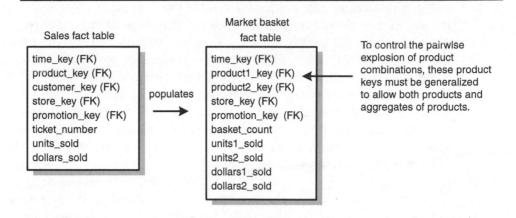

FIGURE 6.24   **A market basket fact table populated from a sales fact table, showing the product keys that must be generalized to handle either base-level products or aggregate-level products, in any mixture.**

    The secret of performing market basket analysis efficiently is to start at the top of the merchandise hierarchy and begin subdividing it, with the goal of always balancing the number of baskets in each group.

By setting a threshold number of records in the market basket fact table, we can control the explosion and stop when we have generated as much detail as we can tolerate. In Figure 6.24 we indicate how the fact table schema for performing this analysis should be generalized.

To populate this schema, we start at the top of the merchandise hierarchy, which we will assume is department. We first calculate the market basket counts for all pairs of departments. If there are 20 departments, we will calculate the counts for up to 400 pairs. We then rank order the results by total market basket counts. The most desirable results of this first iteration are the records near the top of the list, where the dollars or the units from the two departments are reasonably balanced. These records are high-level (department) answers to the original question of what sold together. By the way, one could also ask the reverse question, namely what did *not* sell together. Answering this reverse question would require the additional step of recording baskets from which a department was missing from the basket if this was not already done. Although most baskets are missing many departments, the number of department pairs under consideration is still 400. Again, the department pairs results start to answer the question. We look near the top of the basket count list for pairs of departments that are out of balance. These records would be evidence of many shopping experiences in which the two departments in question either did not occur in the same basket or one department was much more heavily represented. An extreme form of this measurement would find a place in the fact table to record separately the baskets where one of the departments was completely missing. This would require a Type dimension in the market basket fact table to distinguish these baskets from the merely unbalanced baskets.

The key step in market basket analysis, however, is not to be content with the department pairs we have generated already. We must now push down to the next level of detail, which we will assume is category. We start with the high-frequency department pairs generated in the first step. To avoid the combinatorial explosion, we make a decision about descending to the next level depending on whether the department dollars or units are reasonably balanced. If the dollars (or the units) for both departments are reasonably balanced, then we calculate the category pairs for all the categories in both departments. Again, if both departments have 20 categories, we are looking for up to 400 combinations, and we repeat the logic of the preceding paragraph, only at the category level within the selected pair of departments.

If both departments are *not* evenly balanced, we explode only the categories of the more populous department. This is the crucial step in avoiding the pairwise products explosion. Now we are just looking at 20 categories selling with one department. We process this shorter list just as we processed the more balanced lists, by looking for the highest-ranking category-to-department market basket counts and hoping to find some of these that have reasonable balance.

This process continues until enough records have been collected to satisfy the analyst's curiosity. One can imagine automating this process, searching the merchandise hierarchy downward, ignoring the low basket count results, and always striving for balanced dollars and units with the high basket counts. The process could halt when the number of product pairs reached some desired threshold or when the total activity expressed in basket count, dollars, or units reached some lower limit.

A variation on this schema could, of course, start with a specific department, category, brand, or even a specific product. Again, the idea is to combine this specific item first with all the departments, and then work down the tree.

SUMMARY

This collection of design techniques extends the basic dimensional design principles to address complex situations that occur rather frequently in the real world. We discussed advanced modeling situations for dimension tables such as many-valued dimensions, role-playing dimensions, and hierarchical dimensions. We looked at a human resources example where the large employee dimension can be time stamped and associated with every underlying transaction in such a way that precise snapshots can be made of the entire set of employees at any arbitrary point in time. We finished the dimension discussion with a design for a special audit dimension that provides a way to trace the extract lineage of any fact record.

The second part of this chapter described advanced modeling techniques for fact tables, including handling facts of differing granularity, different units of measure, and different international currencies. The last part of the chapter described how to use dimensional models to perform very complex queries such as progressive subsetting and market basket analysis.

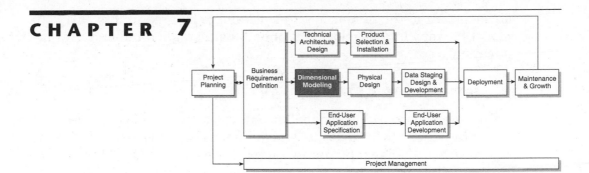

CHAPTER 7

Building Dimensional Models

In Chapter 4 we described how to elicit the business requirements of an organization, and in Chapters 5 and 6 we justified the dimensional modeling approach and learned the skills of dimensional modeling. Now it is time to turn our attention to building dimensional models in real environments. In this chapter, we describe a methodology for scoping the whole modeling job quickly, and then selectively drilling down on the groups of fact tables that comprise each data mart. We will conclude the chapter with a practical discussion of how to organize the modeling team, how to communicate business needs to the team, how to communicate the modeling results to the end users, and how to grow the design iteratively.

This chapter should be read by all of the team members, particularly the data modeler and database administrator, who must understand this phase well enough to be able to lead the effort. The project manager also needs to be able to understand the process to ensure that this critical piece of the project is on track. The business systems analyst must understand dimensional modeling to help the data modeler translate the business requirements into the database design. The other team members must have a basic understanding of this topic to support the development of the dimensional model and to be prepared to carry the model forward into development of both data staging and end user applications.

MATRIX METHOD FOR GETTING STARTED

Taken together, our dimensional models constitute the logical design of the data warehouse. To decide which dimensional models to build, we begin with a top-down planning approach we call the Data Warehouse Bus Architecture matrix. The matrix forces us to name all the data marts we could possibly build and to name all the dimensions implied by those data marts.

Once we have identified all the possible data marts and dimensions, we can get very specific about the design of individual fact tables within these data marts. For each fact table we apply the four-step method described in Chapter 5 to carry out the design. We will review the highlights of the four-step method again in this chapter.

Build the Matrix

It is very useful to think of a data mart as a collection of related facts that need to be used together. For instance, in a retail bank, a data mart might be built from a set of facts related to account activity such as:

- Deposit amount
- Withdrawal amount
- Fee amount
- Number of transactions
- Number of people standing in line

 The best way to get started on the data warehouse design is to build a matrix of data marts and dimensions.

At this stage we don't place severe restrictions on what goes into a data mart or whether all these facts are consistent with each other. Generally the most useful items in a data mart are numerical facts that we "encounter" in the marketplace. Obviously, we are looking for candidate facts to go into fact tables. At this stage we are just collecting a clump of facts that look like they could be used together. We call this clump of facts a *data mart*.

A data mart is a pragmatic collection of related facts, but it does not have to be exhaustive or exclusive. Certainly, a data mart is both a kind of *subject area* and an *application*, but these terms have been used in so many different contexts that we don't find them very useful. A data mart is, more than anything, a collection of numeric facts. That should be the guiding idea in identifying a data mart.

It will be easiest if a data mart is chosen from a single business process, like Account Transactions or Customer Billing. One of the strengths of the matrix approach is that we can always combine simpler, single-source data marts into complex, multiple-source data marts.

A data mart can overlap another data mart. For instance, the single-source data mart defined earlier might be called Account Activity. We might define a multiple source data mart called Account Profitability, which includes facts such as:

- Deposit amount
- Withdrawal amount
- Fee amount
- Processing cost
- Labor cost
- Other infrastructure cost

This data mart overlaps the first data mart, since the first three facts are common to both groups, but the last three facts may need to be derived from three more sources. This is a typical situation when you are listing all the data marts you are interested in.

We advise you to list 10 to 30 data marts for a large organization. In other words, choose the data marts to be fairly high-level business subjects, like Account Activity and Account Profitability. As you may suspect, each of these data marts will later devolve into a cluster of related fact tables that will be used together. If you choose fewer than 10 data marts, you run the risk of making the data mart definitions unreasonably broad. You haven't accomplished anything useful if a data mart has every known business fact and every possible dimension in it. The idea is to divide and conquer.

If you choose more than 30 or 40 data marts, you have probably divided the problem down to too fine a grain. Several of your data marts could probably be usefully combined because they are drawn from the same sources and they will be used together over and over by the requesting reports and applications.

Do the Necessary Homework

Before you can do a good job of defining your data marts, you need to do some homework. You must thoroughly canvass your organization's business needs and thoroughly canvass the data resources. These two homework assignments are absolutely necessary preconditions for proposing the data marts. You must know what kinds of business questions will come from the various user groups, and you must know what facts you can bring to the party. In the long run, achieving the best balance between satisfying the urgent questions of the organization and sourcing the most accessible data in your organization is the art of data warehousing.

List the Data Marts

To start building the matrix, we list a series of single-source data marts. A single-source data mart is deliberately chosen to revolve around a single kind of data source. In a second step, we propose multiple-source data marts that combine the single-source designs into broader views of the business such as profitability. But we want you to reduce your development risk by focusing initially on single sources of data so that you can bring your first deliverables to completion. Don't worry: We are going to avoid stovepipes, even though we are focusing this first step of the design rather narrowly.

Let us imagine that we are a large telephone company and our task is to build the data mart matrix for the overall data warehouse effort in this company. A large telephone company has many interesting sources of data. Here is a possible candidate set of single-source data marts for such a company:

- Customer billing statements (residential and commercial)
- Scheduled service and installation orders
- Trouble reports
- Yellow page advertising orders
- Customer service and billing inquiries
- Marketing promotions and customer communications
- Call detail from the billing perspective
- Call detail from the network switch perspective
- Customer inventory (instruments, Centrex systems, features)

- Network inventory (switches, lines, computers)
- Real estate inventory (poles, rights of way, buildings, street corner box locations, underground locations)
- Labor and payroll
- Computer system job processing and chargeback
- Purchase orders to suppliers
- Deliveries from suppliers

Every one of these single-source data marts could be an interesting data mart all by itself. That is a very important insight. You reduce your development risk and your personal career risk by choosing a doable project. By judiciously choosing one of the aforementioned single-source data marts for your first real deliverable, you may be able to get it into the hands of the end users much more quickly than if you take on something too ambitious. If you also have to deliver a second data mart from the list or if you have to deliver a multiple-source data mart, then at least some of your users will be busy and happy with your first deliverable while you are working on the more difficult projects. Multiple-source data marts drawn from the list might include:

- Combined field operations tracking (service orders, trouble reports, customer/network inventory)
- Customer relationship management (customer billing, customer inquiries, promotion tracking)
- Customer profitability (just about everything on the list if you are analyzing costs in great detail!)

While we love customer profitability as a data mart, we hope you see the danger of starting with this one if you intend to source all the cost drivers in detail. You may inadvertently sign up to extract and clean every data source in your company before you even get started.

 If you really are forced by your users to bring up customer profitability quickly, you should just bring up the revenue pieces like customer billing, and start by providing the costs only as simple rule-of-thumb ratios from the customer activity (i.e., computer processing costs are always one cent per phone call).

In this way, your users will have some results quickly while you slog away building the long list of single-source data marts.

List the Dimensions

The rows of the Data Warehouse Bus Architecture matrix are the data marts and the columns are the dimensions. The lists of data marts and dimensions can be created independently, but it is probably easiest to create the data mart list first and then have a creative session where all the conceivable dimensions for each data mart are listed.

At this stage of the design we don't need to be highly analytic or restrictive in naming dimensions. We simply decide if it is reasonable to list a dimension with a data mart, regardless of whether we have a clear example of a production data source that ties the dimension into the data. For example, in the first data mart, customer billing statements, we might list the following dimensions:

- Time (date of billing)
- Customer (residential or commercial)
- Service
- Rate category (including promotion)
- Local service provider

In this design we are suppressing the call item detail that often appears on a telephone bill. That could appear in a data mart oriented around call detail billing. This call detail billing data mart might include these dimensions plus:

- Calling party
- Called party
- Long-distance provider

Proceeding down the list, we generate an imposing list of dimensions.

Mark the Intersections

With the rows and columns of our matrix defined, we systematically mark all the intersections where a dimension exists for a data mart. For our telephone company example, we might end up with a matrix that looks like Figure 7.1.

	Time	Customer	Service	Rate Category	Local Service Provider	Calling Party	Called Party	Long-Distance Provider	Internal Organization	Employee	Location	Equipment Type	Supplier	Item Supplied	Weather	Account Status
Customer Billing	✓	✓	✓	✓	✓			✓			✓					✓
Service Orders	✓	✓	✓		✓			✓	✓	✓	✓	✓			✓	✓
Trouble Reports	✓	✓	✓		✓	✓		✓	✓	✓	✓	✓	✓	✓	✓	✓
Yellow Page Ads	✓	✓		✓		✓			✓	✓	✓					✓
Customer Inquiries	✓	✓	✓	✓	✓	✓		✓	✓	✓	✓				✓	✓
Promotions & Comm'n	✓	✓	✓	✓	✓	✓		✓	✓	✓	✓	✓	✓	✓		
Billing Call Detail	✓	✓	✓	✓	✓	✓	✓	✓	✓		✓	✓	✓	✓	✓	✓
Network Call Detail	✓	✓	✓	✓	✓	✓	✓	✓	✓		✓	✓	✓	✓	✓	✓
Customer Inventory	✓	✓	✓	✓	✓				✓	✓	✓	✓		✓		✓
Network Inventory	✓		✓						✓	✓	✓	✓	✓	✓		
Real Estate	✓								✓	✓	✓	✓				
Labor & Payroll	✓								✓	✓	✓					
Computer Charges	✓	✓	✓		✓				✓	✓	✓	✓	✓	✓		
Purchase Orders	✓								✓	✓	✓	✓	✓	✓		
Supplier Deliveries	✓								✓	✓	✓	✓	✓	✓		
Combined Field Ops.	✓	✓	✓	✓	✓	✓		✓	✓	✓	✓	✓	✓	✓	✓	✓
Customer Reln. Mgmt.	✓	✓	✓	✓	✓	✓	✓	✓	✓	✓	✓	✓	✓	✓	✓	✓
Customer Profit	✓	✓	✓	✓	✓	✓	✓	✓	✓	✓	✓	✓	✓	✓	✓	✓

FIGURE 7.1   The Data Warehouse Bus Architecture matrix for a telephone company.

Building a matrix such as the one in Figure 7.1 is usually an eye opener. Quite frequently the first reaction is that the matrix is surprisingly dense. A lot of the dimensions appear in a lot of the data marts. Looking across the rows of the matrix reveals the "connectedness" of a given data mart. The average data mart in Figure 7.1 encompasses roughly ten dimensions. Filling in the matrix is often a creative exercise because it forces you to ask whether each candidate dimension might in some way be linked to a given data mart. Often some obscure associations can be found by thinking this way.

Looking down the columns is even more valuable. If a given column representing a dimension has a lot of check marks, that dimension is important and it must be carefully conformed across all the data marts.

 The matrix is a kind of map of the political process that has to be undertaken to get all the groups to agree on the common definition of the dimension. Remember that there is no such thing as a half-way effort when it comes to conforming dimensions.

Not only must all the dimensions be conformed, but each dimension must be conformed correctly across all the data marts it touches.

A real matrix for a real data warehouse design will be larger and more complex than Figure 7.1. Additional smaller data marts and dimensions will be added to the bottom and the right. These additions are likely to give rise to a sparser part of the matrix. For instance, if we add customer payments as a new data mart, we might decide that such payments only intersect the time, customer, and account status dimensions. Similarly, if we add a general ledger budget center dimension, we might decide that this dimension does not intersect very many of the data marts.

Use the Four-Step Method to Design Each Fact Table

When the data marts and their associated dimensions have been identified and their content has been communicated to all concerned parties, the team is ready to start the detailed logical and physical design of individual tables. It is worthwhile to do this even before the first data mart is chosen for implementation, although in many cases the first data mart that must be implemented is obvious from the user demand. We discussed the four-step method in detail in Chapter 5, but we will review the highlights here.

Step 1. Choose the Data Mart

We look down the row headings of our matrix and choose one of the data marts. The first fact table in the design should come from a single source data mart. The choice of the data mart, and hence the source of data, anchors our thinking. As designers, we try to avoid idealized designs that model the way data *should be*, rather than the way it is. This is why we keep returning to actual data sources (single-source data marts) as the starting point.

Step 2. Declare the Grain

We emphasized in Chapter 5 that the dimensional design of a fact table could not happen unless the grain of that fact table was declared by the design team at the beginning. Declaring the grain is equivalent to saying what is an individual fact table record. If an individual fact table record represents the daily item sales total in a retail store, then that is the grain. If an individual fact table record is a line item on an order, then that is the grain. If the individual fact table record is a customer transaction at an ATM, then that is the grain. Every decision made in Steps 3 and 4 depend on correctly visualizing the grain.

 Most arguments and misunderstandings in the design of dimensional databases result from not paying close enough attention to the grain declaration.

Having made such a high-contrast requirement for carefully declaring the grain, it is reasonable for the design team to change their minds about the grain of a particular fact table at some point in the design. For instance, if the grain has been declared to be the daily inventory level of individual stock items in a distribution center, then the design team might decide that it would be possible to instead track lot numbers that roll up to stock items because it was discovered that the legacy systems were correctly tracking lot numbers. Adding the extra detail of lot numbers might have a significant effect on the choice of dimensions and facts in Steps 3 and 4. The only point of this story is that at any point in time, the design team must visualize very clearly what the declared grain of the target fact table is.

Step 3. Choose the Dimensions

A good clear declaration of the grain often makes it easy to choose the dimensions for the particular fact table. Frequently, the grain is stated in terms of primary dimensions. "Daily inventory levels of individual stock items in a distribution center" clearly specifies the time dimension, the stock item dimension, and perhaps the location dimension. Other dimensions can quickly be tested against the grain to see if they make sense.

 If a dimension doesn't match the grain, the design team has two main choices: drop the dimension from consideration or change the grain declaration. Multivalued dimensions as discussed in the advanced modeling sections of Chapter 6 only rarely make sense.

In the customer billing example from the telephone company, we might choose the grain to be the individual line item on each monthly customer bill. This grain clearly specifies a time dimension, a customer dimension, a service (line item) dimension, and perhaps a rate or promotion dimension.

The design team should be quite creative in this step. All of the dimensions in the master "portfolio" of possible dimensions should be tested against the grain to see if they fit. Any dimension that takes on a single value in the presence of the grain is a viable candidate. For instance, a retail database might have the obvious dimensions of time, product, and store, but the design team could decide that a weather dimension be added to the data. It helps, of course, for the design team to have a weather data source in mind. It is up to the business users to decide if such a coarse dimension is useful.

Note that billing month is not the same as calendar month and separate fact tables using these two interpretations of time must label them as distinct dimensions. This is one of the lessons of conformed dimensions. When things are the same, they should be exactly the same and have the same names. When things are different, they must have different names.

Once a dimension is chosen, there may be a large number of descriptive attributes, which can be used to populate the dimension. These descriptive attributes may come from several sources. At this point in the four-step process it is helpful to make a long linear list of all the known descriptive attributes available to describe an item in the dimension (a product, a service, a customer, a location, or a day). The goal at this stage of the design is to be comprehensive and verbose. The details of data sourcing and data quality will be resolved during the detailed design of the implementation phase.

Step 4. Choose the Facts

The last step is to add as many facts as possible within the context of the declared grain. As we said in Chapter 5, it is very important to resist the urge to add facts from the wrong grain.

Using our telephone customer billing example, if the grain is the individual line item on an individual customer bill, we might have a dozen or more line items that represent services, such as toll charges, recurring charges, installation fees, and various taxes. With this line item grain definition, assuming we have a service dimension to distinguish each type of charge, we generate a simple list of facts:

- Line item amount
- Line item quantity

Note other possible facts having to do with the entire bill summary are excluded from this table because they do not fit the fact table grain. These might include:

- Total recurring charges
- Total late charges
- Number of days since last statement

At this stage of the design, it is important not to get hung up on details of key administration. The leader of the design process should simply defer the key discussion. The answer, of course, is that we recommend

DETAILED DESIGN TIPS

In this section we list a number of miscellaneous design tips that have been useful when working with a team of designers to progress through the four steps:

- The labels that are used to identify the data marts, dimensions, attributes, and facts will probably be the standard business names that will be displayed to the end users. Choose these labels carefully.
- An attribute can live in one and only one dimension, whereas a fact can be repeated in multiple fact tables.
- If a single dimension, such as business entity, appears to reside in more than one place, several roles are probably being played. Name the roles uniquely and treat them as separate dimensions. This is called a role model, and it is discussed in Chapter 6.
- A single field in the underlying source data can have one or more logical columns associated with it. For example, the product attribute field may translate to product code, product short description, and product long description.
- Every fact should have a default aggregation rule (sum, min, max, latest, semiadditive, special algorithm, and not aggregatable). Not every query tool or report writer will be able to invoke the complete list of aggregation techniques, but this will serve as a requirements list when evaluating query tools and report writers.

using surrogate keys for all the dimensions, but trying to discuss the details of this approach with all the DBAs in the room at this stage of the design is a mistake. The objective of this exercise is to correctly identify the dimensions and the facts and to complete that process.

MANAGING THE DIMENSIONAL MODELING PROJECT

In the first part of this chapter we described the sequence of steps of building a real set of dimensional models for a large organization. Like any procedural description, this one is somewhat idealized. The rest of this chapter takes a more descriptive approach to dealing with the realities of an actual design.

Much of the process of managing a dimensional modeling project is communicating the design back and forth between people. Visualization is absolutely essential to making the communication work. We recommend four graphical tools to facilitate the project:

1. Data Warehouse Bus Architecture matrix
2. Fact table diagram
3. Fact table detail
4. Dimension table detail

The diagrams should be combined with descriptive information to provide a comprehensive design document. This design document should include a brief introduction of dimensional modeling concepts and terminology.

Data Warehouse Bus Architecture Matrix

The matrix developed by the design team in their internal meetings can be cleaned up and used as a presentation aid for meetings with other designers, administrators, and end users. The matrix is very useful as a high-level introduction to the design. It gives each audience a view of what the eventual scope of the data warehouse will become. The matrix shown in Figure 7.1 is a reasonable example.

Fact Table Diagram

After preparing the Bus Architecture matrix, it is very worthwhile to prepare a logical diagram of each completed fact table. The fact table diagram for the telephone billing line item example is shown in Figure 7.2.

The fact table diagram not only shows the specifics of a given fact table but the context of the fact table in the overall data mart. The fact table diagram names the fact table, clearly states its grain, and shows all the dimensions to which it is connected. The fact table diagram includes an overview of all of the dimensions that have been identified for the business. This serves as an introduction to the overall model. The supporting information for the diagram includes the name of each dimension and a description of that dimension.

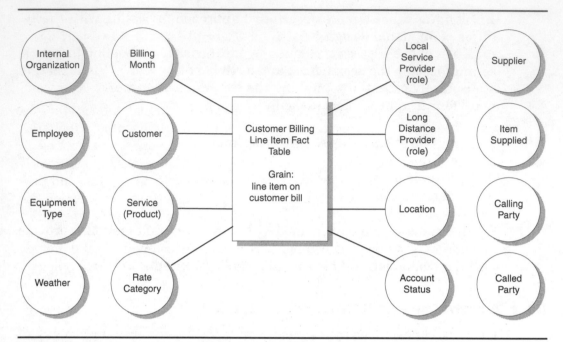

FIGURE 7.2   **The telephone billing fact table diagram. Disconnected dimensions are shown on both sides of the diagram.**

For each of the dimensions, a brief description should also be provided. If possible, the descriptions should appear directly with the diagram to enhance the usefulness of the model. Too often, all the pieces of a dimension model are developed, documented separately, and cross-referenced in detail. All the parts are there, but when attempting to actually use this information, you need to flip back and forth between documents or sections of documents. This is not easy to do and the process of searching for the pieces can be extremely frustrating, even for experienced data modelers. Keep your descriptions and diagrams together.

The fact table diagram also shows all the other dimensions proposed for the data mart *without connections*. These disconnected dimensions can serve as creative additional dimensions that could be goals for connecting to the specific fact table or as warnings of dimensions that cannot be provided for the specific fact table.

The fact table diagram also serves multiple communications purposes including:

- **Link between IS and users.**   The development of the fact table diagram allows close partnering between IS and the users. The fact table diagram builds ownership of the business users in the project. The document can also be used for formal acceptance of the design by the business.

- **Help with data access tool selection.**   A scaled-back version of the fact table diagram can be submitted to data access tool vendors with a few key business questions. The vendors are asked to evaluate if and how they could address the business questions. If you have narrowed down the list of possible vendors, you could provide sample data and have the vendors develop their solution for your evaluation. More details about how to do this can be found in Chapter 13.

- **End user training.**   The fact table diagram has been proven to be a successful training tool because it provides an introduction to the data that is understandable by the users.

To aid in the understanding of the model, it is important to retain consistency in the fact table diagrams. Think about the order that you place the dimensions around the hub. We recommend that you put the time dimension at the top and work your way around the fact table in order of importance of the dimension. Once you have selected an order of the dimensions, make sure all diagrams are arranged in the same order. As you work with the model, the users will remember the location of the dimension visually. If you change the location of a dimension from one fact table diagram to the next, they will get confused (and you probably will, too).

Also, some organizations prefer to eliminate a dimension completely when it does not apply to a specific fact table. If this is the case, leave that space blank while retaining the visual location of the other dimensions.

 The emphasis on a business perspective in the design stage of a data warehouse is often missing. The fact table diagram should be the start of such a perspective.

Fact Table Detail

The fact table detail provides a complete list of all the facts available through the fact table. See Figure 7.3. This list includes actual facts in the physical table, derived facts presented though DBMS views, and other facts that are possible to calculate from the first two groups. Aggregation rules should be provided with each fact to warn the reviewer that some facts may be semiadditive or nonadditive across certain dimensions. For instance, account balances are always semiadditive because they must be averaged across time, but they may be additive across other dimensions, such as customer. Other facts, such as temperatures, are completely nonadditive across all dimensions, but they can be averaged.

The list of facts in a given fact table can reflect data that is not currently available but is desired by the business as long as these hypothetical facts are clearly labeled as such. The users can see that their requirements have been heard and understood, even if they cannot be addressed with the initial release of the data warehouse. The future el-

---

Customer Billing Line Item Fact
Table:

Billing_Month_key
Customer_key
Service_key
Rate_Category_key
Account_Status_key
Local_Service_Provider_key
Long_Distance_Provider_key
Location_key

line_item_amount
line_item_quantity
average_line_item_price*
line_item_rate_category_discount*

FIGURE 7.3   Fact table detail diagram showing dimension keys, basic facts, and derived facts (with asterisks).

ements may not be captured anywhere today, or they may come from a data source that is not within the scope of this project. These elements provide the roadmap for the future.

Dimension Table Detail

The second type of detail diagram is the dimension table detail diagram, as shown in Figure 7.4. This shows the individual attributes within a single dimension. Each dimension will have a separate diagram. The diagram shows the explicit grain of each dimension. The dimension table detail shows the approximate cardinality of each dimension attribute and allows the users to quickly see the multiple hierarchies and relationships between the attributes. The relationships between the attributes define the default drill paths. The detailed dimension diagram also

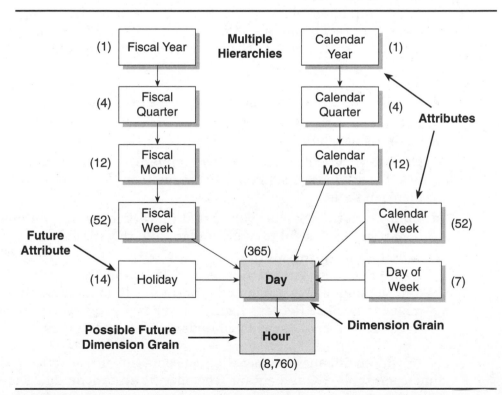

FIGURE 7.4 Dimension table detail diagram (relative cardinalities shown in parentheses).

provides the ability to include attributes that are desired by the users but are not available or are not within the scope of the initial project. This allows you to clearly communicate with the business. Users see that you have not forgotten some of their requirements, but they can also see some will not be available initially. This provides a tool to help you manage expectations. The supporting information required for this diagram includes: attribute name, attribute description, and sample values. Use of existing data element names and descriptions is fine as long as they are indeed the same thing and are written in business terms.

Consider the visual location of the attributes as you create the diagrams. It may be helpful to place "anchor" attributes (those with the highest cardinality) at the bottom, with no other attributes below them. Place the primary hierarchies in the middle of the diagram. The purpose is to be able to quickly distinguish between the primary hierarchies and the other attributes.

Again, full descriptive information must be provided to support the diagram. Figure 7.5 shows a sample of what should be documented for each dimension attribute. Each dimension attribute should have the following:

- **Attribute name.**   The official business attribute name.
- **Attribute definition.**   A brief but meaningful description of the business attribute.
- **Cardinality.**   The best intuitive estimate of how many distinct values this attribute has relative to the number of rows in the whole dimension table.
- **Sample data.**   Sample values that this attribute will contain. This is particularly useful to really understand the attributes.
- **Slowly changing policy.**   Type 1 (overwritten), Type 2 (new record created when a change is detected), and Type 3 (an old and a new version of this attribute is continuously maintained in the dimension record). Perhaps there is a Type 0 as well, where the value in the record is never updated under any circumstances.

Advanced dimensional modeling concepts can also be reflected in the dimension table detail diagram. The specific situations that should be reflected in the model include many-to-many relationships, slowly changing dimensions, and artificial attributes.

Attribute Name	Attribute Description	Cardinality	Slowly Changing Dimension Policy	Sample Values
Day	Represents the specific date.	365	Not Updated	01/14/1998
Holiday	Represents calendar holidays.	14	Overwritten	Easter, Thanksgiving
Day of Week	Name of the day in the week.	7	Not Updated	Thursday
Calendar Week	Represents the week ending Saturdays.	53	Not Updated	WE 01/17/1998
Calendar Month	Represents the calendar month	12	Not Updated	1998/01, 1998/02
Calendar Quarter	Represents the calendar quarter.	4	Not Updated	1998 Q1, 1998 Q2
Calendar Year	Calendar Year	1	Not Updated	1998
Fiscal Week	Collection of days by week ending Sundays, as defined by the corporate calendar.	53	Not Updated	F 01/18/1998, F 01/25/1998
Fiscal Month	Collection of fiscal weeks rolled up to fiscal months as defined by the corporate calendar. Follows a 4-4-5 pattern.	12	Not Updated	F 1998/01, F 1998/02
Fiscal Quarter	The collection of three fiscal months that are reported as corporate quarters.	4	Not Updated	F 1998 Q1, F 1998 Q2
Fiscal Year	The collection of fiscal quarters that are reported as the corporate year.	1	Not Updated	F 1998

FIGURE 7.5 Dimension attribute detail descriptions.

- **Many-to-many relationships.** The many-to-many relationships should be identified. Recall the examples in Figures 6.2 and 6.3. The level of detail should be reviewed to determine if there truly is a many-to-many relationship. Note this when interviewing the users, then resolve the relationship within the design team. Quite often, many-to-many relationships are identified in the initial sessions, but further research into the true data yields only one or two that remain. These can be resolved in the logical database design. In most cases, they can be represented as a separate bridge table that gracefully represents the many-to-many relationship. See Figure 7.6 and the in-depth discussion of this technique in Chapter 6.

- **Slowly changing dimensions.** Each attribute that is known to be slowly changing should be designated on the diagram. See Figure 7.6.

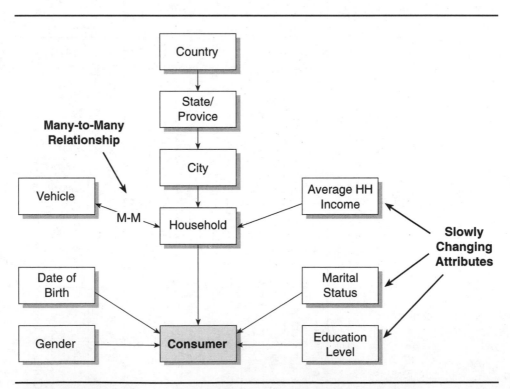

FIGURE 7.6 Many-to-many and slowly changing dimension attributes.

- **Artificial attributes.** Often, when struggling with a dimension, there may be a need to create an attribute that does not exist within the business today. In these cases there may not be a need for users to constrain or view this attribute, but it is needed at the lowest level of detail to support the other rollups within that dimension. In other cases, when combining similar dimensions into a single dimension, there may be a need to create an attribute to represent the existence of the Cartesian product of the branches of the new combined dimension. For example, a set of invoices may have both discount codes and allowance codes. We may decide to create a single dimension that covers both discounts and allowances. Perhaps discounts and allowances are not especially well correlated. The design would then benefit from an artificial attribute that described the combination of discount and allowance. Figure 7.7 shows an example of an artificial attribute.

Steps for the Dimensional Modeling Team

As with any data modeling, the development of the dimensional model is an iterative process. You will work back and forth between business user requirements and selected source file details. Always be willing to change the model as you learn more. You may identify another dimen-

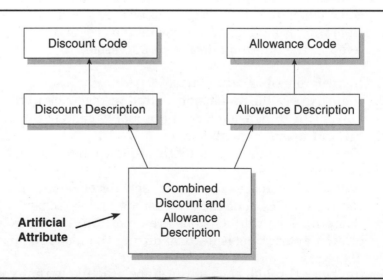

FIGURE 7.7 A dimension with a correlated attribute.

sion or discover that two dimensions are really just one. Changes to the grain are also common.

Highly experienced data warehouse designers can develop the initial dimensional model and then present it to the team for review. While this can be done, it does not allow the whole project team to truly observe the process and to learn how to develop a model themselves. It is important to keep in mind the dual objective of most data warehouse project tasks: to get the work done and to teach the team to become self-sufficient. The approach that we have found to be the most successful over the years to meet both of these goals is to work as a team to develop the model.

Create the Initial Draft

The initial modeling should be done with a core data modeling team consisting of the data modelers and database administrators and source system experts, along with the business system analysts. A dimensional modeling team of between three and six people tends to be a good size to get the work done in a timely manner. The larger the group, the longer it takes to complete the first draft.

The most effective method to develop the initial model is using flip charts. As you work through the model, you will wallpaper the conference room. Keep in mind that much of the initial modeling includes a great deal of brainstorming. Try to capture the ideas, but don't get bogged down with a specific question. Until the entire model is sketched out, it is very difficult to address what may seem like simple request. We have found the following flow to be successful:

1. Identify possible data marts.
2. Identify possible dimensions, often in response to the proposed data marts (the dimension list will probably change several times).
3. Fill in the matrix with these proposals.
4. For each data mart, identify the dimensions that apply and the grain for each one.
5. Identify specific base business facts for each data mart.
6. Refine and flesh out the dimensions as needed through the process. Sometimes new dimensions are identified, others may be combined or split apart. This is natural during the modeling process.

As you work through each of the steps, it is likely that you will think of additional things that should be added to parts of the model you have already started on. Take the time to go back and add the new information to the model (so it is helpful to have the charts hanging on the walls around you). You may find yourselves moving back and forth between all of these steps. This is common. A completed model can later be presented in a clean step-by-step manner.

 To minimize detailed design debate, capture questions and move on. These questions should be included in an issue log.

When you review the log after several weeks, you will probably see some questions that seem absurd in light of what you now know, but when you are just getting started it is hard to tell which questions are trivial and which ones are important.

One person should document the first draft while others begin researching questions. The core team should meet again, after the first draft has been cleaned up and made into a presentable form, to review and revise the model based upon clear thought and results of research. You must walk away for a day or two. Some of the best ideas will pop into your mind while you are in the shower or while brushing your teeth.

Track Base Facts and Derived Facts

The fields in your fact tables are *not* just source data columns. There may be many more columns that the business wants to analyze such as year-to-date sales, percentage difference in claims paid vs. prior year, and gross profit. You need to keep track of the derived facts as well as the base facts.

There are two kinds of derived facts. Derived facts that are additive and that can be calculated entirely from the other facts in the same fact table record can be shown in a user view as if they existed in the real data. The user will never know the difference. The multiple units of measure discussion in Chapter 6 was an example of providing such a virtual extension of the fact table.

The second kind of derived fact is a nonadditive calculation, such as a ratio, or a cumulative fact that is expressed at a different grain than the base facts themselves. A cumulative fact might be a year-to-date fact. In any case, these kinds of derived facts cannot be presented in a simple view at the DBMS level. They need to be calculated at query time by the query tool or report writer.

Defining the full range of facts is a delicate political process. You may be defining the numbers and calculations that determine a large part of the senior management financial incentive plan. These executives usually have strong opinions about this. Also, the broader the audience, the more opinions need to be considered, and the greater divergence among them. The data warehouse project will strain under this burden.

Many data access tools today offer a library capability that you can use to develop and maintain derived facts. This is where the official formulas and calculations are defined and then used by everyone.

 Too often, the basic database design is completed and then no thought is put into the derived facts until the team is ready to begin developing the end user applications. This is too late in the process because often hundreds of business calculations are needed, and you must gain user consensus for the exact formulas. This takes time!

While the derived facts do not need to be complete prior to moving forward with the development of the data staging process, it is important to ensure that all the base facts are accounted for. If there is a specific derived fact that is required for the initial phase, but one part of the calculation is not reflected in the model, then action must be taken. The source for the missing data must be identified.

When the business users have specific ideas about what they want and need, the derived facts can be identified with a small session. In some cases, the users may not have concrete ideas, but you still need to develop a starting set of derived facts. Keep in mind that the initial list of facts is not definitive—once the users get their hands on the system, they will want more. You will need to decide who has the authority to add new derived facts to the library.

On one project the authors worked on, the data was coming from a proprietary system via standard reports. It was unclear which columns of information were the actual facts and which columns were derived facts. The following process was used not only to identify the derived facts but to define the base facts as well. The steps included:

- **Candidate facts.**   Identify all possible base and derived facts. Collect all reports submitted via the interview process. Compile a spreadsheet to contain all of the facts that were listed on reports or requested in the interviews. Capture the fact name, where it was identified (report name or interview), and who provided it (name of person interviewed or who gave the report). In one case more than 500 facts were identified initially.

- **Remove duplicate facts.**   Sort through all of the facts to eliminate duplicates. You may need to group the possible duplicates together and work with the key business users to make sure. Identify base facts vs. derived facts. This is just the first pass. Identify the obvious ones, and research the others.

- **Discover and document the underlying calculations.**   Identify the ones that are the same derived fact with different criteria. For example, Total US Sales Dollars and Western Region Sales Dollars may be the same calculation, but they are constrained to different values in the organization dimension. In our project, we reduced the original 500 facts to 150 distinct facts.

- **Cross reference base facts.**   Ensure that all base facts that are needed for calculations are included, even if they are not displayed on any reports. We found that only six base facts were needed to derive the 150 derived facts.

- **Final derived fact approval.**   Now that the basics are captured, you can move forward to have the derived facts approved by the business users and management. You need to gain consensus on the names of the facts and the exact calculations.

The derived fact worksheet, shown in Figure 7.8, is helpful when working through this process and documenting the final results.

The derived fact worksheet contains the following columns:

- **Change flag.**   Indicates a row that has changed since the last release of the document. This is particularly helpful when dealing with dozens of calculations. The reviewer can quickly focus on the items that have changed rather than wade through the entire document again.

Chg Flag	Fact Group	Measure Name	Measure Description	Type	Agg Rule	Formula	Constraints	Transformations
	POS	$ Sales	The dollar amount of the goods sold through the retail channel	Col	Sum	sum(Dollar Sales)	None	None
	POS	Total US $ Sales	The dollar amount sold for the total US geography.	Cnstr	Sum	sum(Dollar Sales)	Geography= Total US	None
	POS	% of Total US $	Dollar sales as a percentage of total US geography.	Calc	Recalc	($ Sales/Total US $ Sales) * 100	NA	NA
	POS	Prev. $ Sales	The dollar amount of the goods sold through the retail channel during the previous period.	Txfm	Sum	sum(Dollar Sales)	None	Previous Period
	POS	Prev. Tot US $ Sales	The dollar amount sold for the total US during the previous period.	Txfm Cnstr	Sum	sum(Dollar Sales)	Geography= Total US	Previous Period
	POS	Prev. % of Total US $	The previous period dollars as a percentage of the previous period total US dollars.	Calc	Recalc	(Prev $ Sales/Prev Tot US $ Sales) * 100	NA	NA
	POS	$ Chg vs. Prev	The actual change in dollars from previous period.	Calc	Sum	$ Sales—Prev $ Sales	NA	NA
	POS	Units	The number of consumer units sold.	Col	Sum	sum(Units)	None	None
	POS	Avg Retail Price	The average price at the register.	Calc	Recalc	$ Sales/Units	None	None
	POS	Inventory $	The dollar value of units in inventory.	Col w/Lim	Sum w/Limit	sum(inv Units) except across time, then take value from max date.		
	Fcast	Forecast $	The dollar amount of the expected sales through the retail sales channel.	Col	Sum	sum(Forecast Dollars)	None	None
	Multi Group	% Var to Forecast $	The percentage difference between actual and forecast sales dollars	Calc	Recalc	(sum(Dollar Sales) – sum(Forecast Dollars))/ sum(Dollar Sales)	None	None

FIGURE 7.8 Derived fact worksheet.

- **Data mart.**   The name of the data mart where the base facts reside. If the fact is a calculation, this would be a list of all the data marts that are needed.

- **Fact name.**   The name of the derived fact as to be seen through data access tools and on reports.

- **Fact description.**   A brief description of the fact.

- **Type.**   Indicates what kind of fact from the following:

  - *Column.* An actual base fact. Pulling basic information directly from a column in a fact table.

  - *Constraints.* A base fact with a predefined constraint. These are often created as building blocks for other calculations. For example, Total US Sales Units (sales units constrained on geography to be the total US) is needed to create the final derived fact of the percentage of Total US Sales Units. Other query constraints would be applied at the time of the query.

  - *Transformation.* A pre-defined process to translate a specific value within a dimension to another value within that same dimension. When this is supported via a data access tool, this eliminates the need for a user to specify (at the time of query) both the specific value and the transformed value. For example, allow the end user to specify only the current time period for the report and automatically transform that date to be able to identify the appropriate year ago date.

  - *Calculation.* A straightforward calculation based upon one or more previously defined facts.

  - *Column with limits.* Semiadditive fact, one that is not aggregatable across all dimensions. This requires you to specify what the specific limits are for this fact.

- **Aggregation rule.**   Determines the default aggregation rule for this fact. Sometimes the result of a calculation can be summed, but in other cases, the components must be aggregated separately and the final derived fact recalculated.

- **Formula.**   Specific mathematical formula to create this fact.

- **Constraints.**   Indicates constraints that must be applied to the data in order to create this fact.

- **Transformations.**   Indicates specific translations that must be calculated when creating this fact. For example, the query specifies a reporting time period. A calculation may reflect prior period comparisons. This prior period must be based off the specified reporting period. In some cases, the user may be required to also enter the prior period specifically to apply to this fact. In other cases the data access tool may automatically determine the prior period based upon the business metadata.

The derived facts can also be used as part of the end user tool selection process. You should not ask any vendor to develop all of these. Rather, select a representative sample (one of each mathematical type) to see how the software supports the calculation.

Once the list of derived facts is completed, it can be used to build the metadata for the data access tool when you get to that point in the project.

Get IS Team Input

After several iterations of the overall data mart design with the core design team, it is time to get more input. Resist the urge to try to perfect the design. To facilitate communication in the meeting, the best approach is to use overhead foils and provide handouts for participants. This allows everyone to see changes to the model as you work.

Presenting the model to the rest of the IS team serves several purposes. First, it forces you to practice presenting the model in preparation for the end users. Second, it brings the rest of the IS project team up to speed with the modeling process. Third, the other team members may have knowledge that can resolve open issues or point you in the right direction to get answers.

Once the initial design is drafted, the sessions to review the model with others are facilitated design sessions. The information is presented, and discussion is encouraged to explore the model's support for the business.

Work with Core Business Users

Now you are ready to present to select business users. Do not present initially to a large group of users. Instead, choose one or two key users. These should be people who are actively working on the project and who have the responsibility to assist in answering questions and resolving business questions, such as the business project lead.

From the core design team, two primary roles need to be filled for these meetings. The first is the presenter/facilitator. This person is responsible for keeping the meeting going, focusing on one thing at a time, and for actually presenting the model. The second role is that of scribe. This person needs to make sure that any open issues are captured to be added to the issue log. Also, the scribe needs to assist the presenter to ask specific questions that are on the issue log.

Begin the session with a high-level introduction to dimensional modeling concepts so they will better grasp the materials being presented. As you introduce the group to the model, ask them to be patient. You may not answer their questions immediately since many of their questions will be answered as you walk through the entire model. Introduce all of the dimensions that have been identified for your business. Next, walk through an example business question to assist the users in grasping how the dimensional model works.

Now you are ready to dive into the details. Review each dimension in detail. Make corrections to relationships and add dimension attributes as suggested by the users. When adding a new dimension attribute, note where it could be sourced if you know, but don't worry about it if you don't know at this time.

Ask the users to think of all the ways that they would want to report on the data. Also ask them to consider what would help them to navigate through a large dimension—you can't (and don't want to) scroll through 10,000 products searching for the one you are interested in. What would help you get to the one you are interested in?

As new issues are identified and existing issues remain open, these core end users should take responsibility for resolving any business-related issues. These users are also expected to assist in naming dimensions, attributes, and facts and ensuring that the descriptions are accurate and meaningful.

Present to Business Users

When most of the issues have been resolved, it is time to move beyond the core users and confirm the design with a broader set of users. This group can include all of the people who were interviewed, except senior management. The same process used to present to the core users should be followed. Most of the discussion should be about the support of business questions. If many questions about the structure of the model are raised, you may need to back up and include additional users from different functions to refine the model.

You will find that the model makes sense to the users, once they understand how to interpret the diagrams. There are usually only minor adjustments to the model once you get to this point. After working so hard to develop the model, the users may not show what you consider to be appropriate enthusiasm. They may not ooh and aah. The model seems obvious to the users and makes sense (after all it is a reflection of their business). Do not be disappointed—that means you have done your job well! The oohs and aahs will come when the users see the real data for the first time.

Managing Issues in the Modeling Process

The core design team will meet between the facilitated sessions. The flow of these meetings will change from overall design discussions to very focused discussion of the remaining open issues. The team should review each open issue and determine what needs to be done to get closure. Do not be afraid to solicit additional assistance from the project manager. In many cases, the primary obstacle to getting closure is freeing up enough time to work on the issues. The project manager may need to work with both IS and business management to get the required time allocated. Make sure that management understands what is at stake—if the modeling process is delayed, the entire project will be delayed!

As you work through the modeling process, maintain an issue log as discussed in Chapter 3. Most of these issues simply require additional research. It is very common to log 75 or 100 issues that need to be addressed. Typical issues that are logged during the modeling process include:

- **Do Regions report to Zones or the other way around?** The actual hierarchical order of an organization structure often generates discussion. This is usually easily resolved by a quick conversation with the business users.

- **What is the Claims City attribute?** You may get many attributes suggested during interactive modeling sessions that you may not know details about. Rather than stopping the flow of the session, just note it as a question and follow up later.

- **Confirm that the Transaction Edit Flag is not used for analysis.** First review the content with the operational system owner, who may be able to identify the field as processing information. If not, review the field and its contents with the key users. *Never* ask directly, "Do you need this field?" Rather, ask, "How would you use this for analysis?"

- **Evaluate the options of representing customer and field organization as one or two dimensions. Walk through business scenarios.** Sketch out what the model would look like both ways. Review the types of uses for this information. Try to determine what you could not do for each scenario. Explore additional capability with each scenario. At this point, if one alternative is not clearly better, consider several overall factors. How many dimensions do you have? What are the size ramifications of an additional dimension (as this will increase the size of the primary key of the fact table)?

- **What does the Primary Units column contain? How does it differ from Shipped Units?** Understand each possible data element. Do not duplicate an element, and do not let different elements share the same name.

- **Users want to see average prices and the actual price as on the invoice. Ensure that the model supports this.** After the model is completely fleshed out, review examples of what users expect to be able to do. Make sure that the required information can indeed be supported by the model.

- **Customer invoice data reflects the expected sales amount but does not include refunds or actual amounts paid.** Use the issue log to document specific details that you do not want to lose throughout the process. This is not really an issue, but it is important that the users understand the data content. This may be included in the end user training. This type of issue is often opened and closed on the same day.

- **Document each candidate data source and the reasoning behind the final source selection.** Too often the actual data sources, the rationale for selection, and other sources that were considered is not written down. This is critical to assist in managing expectations and managing project scope.

- **Review each data source to ensure all columns/fields are accounted for.** Although this is talked about, it is important for everyone to understand that once the modeling process is done, each incoming data source needs to be reviewed once more, field by field, to ensure completeness. This issue should be listed specifically for every source. Often, a different person is responsible for each source.

Identifying the Sources for Each Fact Table and Dimension Table

Data analysis is the homework that you must complete in order to develop your dimensional model. Two levels of analysis must occur. First, you must understand what data has been requested by the business. This helps you select your data sources. Second, you must gain an in-depth understanding of each of the data sources that are to be included in this iteration of the data warehouse. While developing the dimensional model, you bring together what the users have requested with a large dose of the realities of the data that exists today.

The user requirements process we discussed in Chapter 4 identifies both formal and informal data sources. The formal sources are supported by IS, and some rigor is associated with the maintenance and integrity of the data. Informal data comes directly from the business and is used in the decision making process. Although the informal data is not stored in the corporate data vaults, the information is collected and used by the business today. Someone is responsible for collecting and distributing the information on a regular basis.

 Users want and need to use informal data in conjunction with the formal data sources.

Informal data sources are often included in the data warehouse through the development of a new process for IS to capture this data. In some cases this is simply importing data from a personal database or through the development of screens for the users to enter this data. In both cases, the input data needs to be treated as another data source. This means the data must be cleaned and manipulated as you would any other data source. *Do not* simply allow users to input data directly into the data warehouse. While including informal data sources may not be in the initial project scope, seriously assess the impact of leaving it out. If the data is central to the users' business, it must be treated seriously.

Understanding Candidate Data Sources

By understanding the data requested by the end users, we do not mean that as the very first step you must perform a detailed analysis of each data source requested. There are often more than 20 sources mentioned throughout the interviewing process. You do need to understand at a high level what each of these sources are, what their availability is, and who is responsible for them. You eventually need to research in great detail the sources that are to be the basis of this project. It is worthwhile to have the greatest in-depth understanding of the sources that are closely related to the primary sources and those that have been identified as the next sources to implement.

In many cases, your data warehouse project is defined and based upon making data from a specific data source available to the business such as customer billings or trouble report transactions. When this is the basis for your project, selecting the data source is much more straightforward. However, some decisions need to be made. Often, the supporting dimensional information such as the detailed customer descriptions will come from a different source. This is almost always true in a conformed dimension environment.

You will also need to decide at which point in the processing the data should be extracted for the warehouse. If your project is not bounded by a specific data source, then there is more work to be done to determine where to start.

Candidate data sources are those listed in the user requirements document and others that may be needed to support them. Typically the users will state that they need sales, inventory, and financial data. Rarely do users also specify that they need the customer master reference data as well as the corporate product database. These supporting data sources are implied when users request basic performance data by customer, region, and line of business.

Additional candidate sources can be identified by the veterans in the IS shop. They are familiar with the data that exists in the nooks and crannies of the organization. They also know much of the history of these sources and other decision support or analysis initiatives. Today, many organizations already have some sort of decision support capability in place or have design information about failed attempts. It is useful to know about these prior successes and failures. Understanding them can provide insight into what works and what does not in your organization.

While it may seem very basic to pull together a list of candidate sources with descriptive information about each, such a list does not exist in a single place for most organizations today. Each individual source may or may not have a general description, and there is rarely a consolidated list of them all. Figure 7.9 shows a sample data source definition.

In your data source definitions, make sure that you include the following information:

- **Source.** The name of the source system.
- **Business owner.** The name of the primary contact within the business who is responsible for this data.
- **IS owner.** The name of the person who is responsible for this source system.
- **Platform.** The operating environment where this system runs.
- **Location.** The actual location of the system. The name of the city and the specific machine where this system runs. For distributed applications, include the number of locations, too.
- **Description.** A brief description of what this system does.

Source	Business Owner	IS Owner	Platform	Location	Description
Gemini	Tom Owens	Alison Jones	Unix	HQ - Chicago	Distribution center inventory
Billings	Craig Bennet	Steve Dill	MVS	MF - Dallas	Customer Billings
Plant	Sylvia York	Bob Mitchell	Unix	6 Plants across country	Plant shipments
Sales Forecast	Sandra Phillips	None	Win95	HQ - Sales Dept.	Spreadsheet-based consolidated sales forecast.
Competitor Sales	Sandra Phillips	None	Win95	HQ - Sales Dept.	FoxPro database containing data from external supplier.

FIGURE 7.9 Data source definitions.

Source Data Ownership

Establishing responsibility for data quality and integrity can be extremely difficult in the data warehousing environment. Most operational systems effectively capture key operational data. A line in the order entry system will typically identify a valid customer, product, and quantity. Other optional fields that may be captured at that point, such as end user name or customer SIC code, are not usually validated, if they get filled in at all. Operational system owners are not measured on how accurate or complete these fields are. They are measured on whether or not the orders get taken, filled, and billed.

Source data owners need to be identified from two different groups for each data source: the business and IS. If you are purchasing external data, one person is responsible for that data and for monitoring its quality and tracking down issues related to the data. Treat your internal data the same way from a business standpoint.

Data Providers

Operational system owners need to feel a responsibility to provide data to the warehouse as a regular part of their operational processes. The closer they are to the warehouse, the more likely the warehouse will know ahead of time before a major change in the source system is implemented.

Data providers include external-source data vendors, external sources from other divisions of the organization, as well as people who are responsible for a system and need to provide an extract file to the data warehouse team.

Detailed Criteria for Selecting the Data Sources

After the conformed dimensions have been identified, the individual data sources can be identified. A small number of actual data sources must be identified as the primary focus for the first phase project. It is not recommended to tackle too many at once. Successful projects generally begin with one or two primary data sources. Additional sources may be used for dimension construction, especially when the definition of the conformed dimension suggests multiple sources, but the facts are usually retrieved only from a single source system. The selection of the primary data source is often driven by the business.

The biggest business pain that can be solved with a concrete set of data is usually the recommended place to start. In some cases the data could be extracted from multiple places. The decision must be made about where the data will be extracted from. The criteria to consider include:

- **Data accessibility.** If two possible feeds exist for the data, one is stored in binary files maintained by a set of programs written before the youngest project team member was born and the other is from a system that already reads the binary files and provides additional processing, then the decision is obvious. Use the second option for your source data.

- **Longevity of the feed.** Often, data for the warehouse could be intercepted at many places throughout a processing stream. If the data coming out of Step 5 is the cleanest, but that step is scheduled to be phased out in the next six months, then consider extracting from Step 4. Understand the additional processing that is done in Step 5 that may clean the data. Include this type of processing in the data staging process.

- **Data accuracy.** As data is passed from system to system, many modifications are made. Sometimes data elements from other systems are added, and sometimes existing elements are processed to create new elements and other elements are dropped. Each system performs its own function well. However, it may become difficult or impossible to recognize the original data. In some cases, the data no longer represents what the business wants for analysis. If you provide the data from these downstream systems, the users may question the accuracy. In this case, it may be better to go back to the original source to ensure accuracy. Keep in mind that pulling data from downstream systems is not always bad. Consider the use of electronic data interchange (EDI) data. If you take in raw EDI feeds, you will be responsible for providing cleansing and editing of these transactions. It is much better to capture the data after the editing has happened. This will also ensure that the data is synchronized with the other sources that use this same data.

- **Project scheduling.** In many organizations the data warehouse project begins as part of a rewrite of an existing OLTP system. As the new system development project begins to unfold, it is often the case that the business users who are now firmly convinced of the value of a data warehouse begin to insist that the data warehouse be implemented sooner rather than later. In order to provide historical data, you need to include the data from the existing system in your data warehouse. If the rewrite of the old system is delayed, the data warehouse can continue using the existing system. Once the new system is released for production, the data feeds can be switched to it. In many cases it is possible to deliver the data warehouse before the new operational system can be completed.

You will want to document any sources that were considered and not selected. This documentation will be extremely helpful months later when questions may arise about the source of the data.

Some dimensional information usually comes with the transaction or fact data, but it is usually minimal and often only in the form of codes. The additional attributes that the users may want and need are often fed from other systems or corporate master files. In many instances there can be multiple master files, especially for the customer dimension. There are often separate files that are used across an organization. Sales, Marketing and Finance may have their own customer master files. There are two difficult issues when this happens. First, the customers who are included in these files may differ, and the attributes about each customer may differ. To an extent, this is good, because it provides richer information. Second, the common information may not match. If you have unlimited time and money you can pull rich information from all sources and then merge it into a single comprehensive view of customers. In most cases, there is not enough time or money to do that all at once. In these cases, it is recommended that the users prioritize the information, and you start with what you can and expand in the future.

Detailed data analysis should be done for every data source that is to be included in this iteration of the data warehouse. The goal is to gain a realistic understanding of the content of the data sources. Information can be gleaned from existing data models, file layouts, and corporate metadata. The information that you will need about each data source includes:

- Business owner
- IS owner

- System platform (UNIX, MVS)
- File structure (flat files, Oracle, DB2, FoxPro)
- Physical system location (HQ production mainframe, manufacturing plant A)
- Data volumes (number of transactions per day, average transactions per week)
- Primary and foreign key identification
- Physical field characteristics (data type, length, precision)
- Data integrity (real and perceived)
- Integration experiences (Has the data been successfully integrated in the past? Why or why not?)
- Future direction of the source (Is it being replaced by a new system? If so when?)

The detailed review sessions should be conducted with the data modeler and/or the programmer analyst responsible for that system. One of the most effective sessions we have seen was when one of the programmer/analysts responsible for the system came with copies of the programs in hand. When we had a question, she simply looked it up right then. This eliminated the need to compile an extensive list of questions to be researched later. Another technique that helps in collecting this information is to have sample data from the source. If it is extremely time consuming to pull sample data, try working where you can easily access the system on-line to see what is contained in the fields.

Customer Matching and Householding

Combining data about customers from disparate data sources is a classic data warehousing problem. It may go under the names of *de-duplicating* or *customer matching*, where the same customer is represented in two customer records because it hasn't been recognized that they are the same customer. This problem may also go under the name of *householding*, where multiple individuals who are members of the same economic unit need to be recognized and matched. The science of customer matching is more sophisticated than it might appear. It is generally not worthwhile to build an in-house customer matching or householding system. The fuzzy matching logic is simply too complicated.

Although these commercial systems are expensive and complex, we recommend that it is worthwhile to make such an investment if customer matching is a significant activity in your organization.

 A competent IS programmer, starting from scratch, with a few months of programming, might be able to match 75 percent of the customers who in reality are the same customer or belong to the same household. However, commercially available systems from software vendors who specialize in customer matching and householding can probably achieve better than a 90 percent customer matching score.

Browsing the Data Content

To better understand actual data content, a study can be performed against current source system data. This can be done with a data exploration prototype, which is a relatively new concept in data warehousing. In recent years, many companies have put more standard infrastructure in place as they move to client/server–based operational systems. As part of this shift, operations data stores have migrated to relational platforms. This more open systems environment makes it much easier to set up a small system that extracts data from the desired sources and dumps it into a temporary exploration environment. The data exploration prototype gives you the opportunity to browse through the source data and learn its idiosyncrasies first hand.

This browsing process helps you understand the contents of the source files and get a sense for the cleanliness of the data. Essentially, the process involves building a set of data audit and data cleanliness queries much like the ones that will eventually be part of the data staging process as described in Chapter 16. This includes queries that count the number of rows with each value of a given attribute, like gender, or size, or status. Or, bringing back all the distinct values of an attribute, such as the customer name, and sorting them to see what they contain such as how many duplicates or similar spellings exist for the same customer.

The target database for the data exploration prototype should be the most readily available platform. If it is the same platform as the ultimate warehouse, so much the better, but it is not critical. Speed and ease of implementation are more important. Of course, if you can, use the same database as the one you expect to use for the production warehouse database, even if you use a desktop version for the exploration. It is always good to get some practice.

Don't spend a lot of time on design work for the target. In fact, it is probably easiest to simply duplicate the source system directly.

 The goal of setting up a browser for source data is to explore the source and get an understanding of the size and magnitude of the extraction effort, not to test a warehouse design.

If the source systems are already in relational tables, it may be possible to point the ad hoc query tool directly at the source and query away. Of course, be careful of this. You don't want to be the one who submitted the query that brought the order entry system to its knees for three hours. Work with the source system owners to do your queries and extracts according to their schedule.

The primary deliverable for the data exploration prototype is a report on the data issues that were uncovered. Often, this report will have several audiences. Many of the problems are of interest to the source system owners. Others will need to be addressed in the data staging process. Still others are education issues for the user community.

Mapping Data from Source to Target

The source-to-target data map is the foundation for the development of the data staging process. The primary purpose is to document specifically where the data can be located. It can also ensure that all of the source data has been analyzed. The complete map includes data elements that are in the source but are not to be included in the data warehouse. Figure 7.10 shows a sample source-to-target data map.

This is just one sample of what could be used to collect this information. Additional information may be useful to fully leverage data transformation tools. Each individual vendor should be able to help you determine what will be needed. Keep in mind that the full data transformation business rules will be developed in future project tasks. This is simply capturing information that is known at this time. The columns that are included are:

- **Table name.**   The name of the logical table in the data warehouse.
- **Column name.**   The name of the logical column in the data warehouse.
- **Data type.**   The data type of the logical column in the data warehouse (char, number, date).
- **Length.**   The length of the field of the logical column.
- **Target column description.**   A description of the logical column.
- **Source system.**   The name of the source system where data feeds the target logical column. There may be more than one source system for a single logical column.
- **Source table/file.**   The name of the specific table or file where data feeds the target logical column. There may be more than one source system for a single logical column.
- **Source column/field.**   The name of the specific column or field where data feeds the target logical column. There may be more than one source system for a single logical column.
- **Data transform.**   Notes about any transformations that are required to translate the source information into the format required by the target column. This is not intended to be a complete list of the specific business rules but a place to note any anomalies or issues that are known at this time.
- **Dimension/data mart.**   The name of the dimension or data mart that this column represents.
- **Attribute/fact.**   The name of the specific attribute within a dimension table or fact table.

The map also serves to identify differences between the source and target. Often these differences are easy to resolve. For example, incoming

Table Name	ColumnName	Data Type	Len	Target Column Description	Source System	Source Table/File	Source Column/Field	Data Txform
Period Dimension	PERIOD_KEY	Date	—	The unique primary key for the period dimension table.	New	New	New	Create
Product Dimension	PROD_KEY	Num	8	The unique primary key for the product dimension table.	MIDAS	PROD_MSTR	X_P_ID, X_CAT_ID	Concat X_CAT_ID + X_P_ID
Product Dimension	prod_desc	Char	40	The unique description for the product.	MIDAS	PROD_MSTR	X_P_CH	Direct
Inventory Facts	PERIOD_KEY	Date	—	See primary key table.	POS	TRANS	TXN_DTE	Direct
Inventory Facts	PROD_KEY	Num	8	See primary key table.	POS	TRANS	X_P_ID, X_CAT_ID	Concat X_CAT_ID + X_P_ID
Inventory Facts	units_sold	Num	9	The number of units sold.	POS	TRANS	REG_UNITS	Direct
Inventory Facts	dollars_sold	Num	9,2	The dollar amount for the purchase.	POS	TRANS	REG_AMT	Direct
Inventory Facts	inventory	Num	9	The number of consumer units in stock.	POS	TRANS	UNITS_RMN	Direct
Ship Facts	PERIOD_KEY	Date	—	See primary key table.	DCS	ORDERS	SHIP_DTE	Direct
Ship Facts	PROD_KEY	Num	8	See primary key table.	DCS	ORDERS	PROD_NUM	Translate to master product codes
Ship Facts	dollars_ship	Num	9,2	The dollar value of the shipment.	DCS	ORDERS	INV_AMT	Direct
Ship Facts	cases_ship	Num	5	The number of cases shipped.	DCS	ORDERS	INV_UNITS	Direct
Ship Facts	consmr_units_ship	Num	9	The number of consumer units shipped.	DCS	CASE_MSTR	NO_UNITS INV_UNITS	NO_UNITS

FIGURE 7.10 Sample source-to-target data map.

data may contain only codes but no descriptions. Using the codes to look up the proper descriptive data is straightforward. Other common differences are in the length of the field. Using several sources, the physical format of the data may vary.

Complex transformations may need to be performed. Initially, the need for additional transformations can be noted. Later the actual transformation based upon business rules must be developed. Development of detailed specifications is typically done during the design of the data staging process, discussed in Chapter 16.

Data elements that do not exist in the selected source are also identified. In some cases, the data may not be captured anywhere. In other cases, the data does exist, but the current scope of the project does not include that source.

When the source-to-target data map has been completed, it is important to revise the fact table designs to reflect what will actually be included. You will often find that some attributes must be flagged as future and some you thought were future can be included, and you may have also uncovered new attributes that must be added to the fact table design.

When Are You Done?

You can consider yourself finished when you have exhausted the issues list or the project team, whichever comes first. Realistically, the project team will be exhausted long before the dimensional model is complete. As with other data modeling, you could spend years trying to track down every single issue. It is simply not feasible to take that much time. Over the years it has been proven that the last several issues can take as much time to resolve as the first 50 or 60, and the final result has minimal actual business impact. Once most of the issues have been addressed, the remaining should be prioritized. The major categories are:

- **Critical data issues.** Identifies issues that must be resolved in order to move forward at all or are required to meet the intended business goal. These issues relate to the data itself and may require business assistance to resolve.
- **Critical business policy issues.** Identifies issues that must be resolved in order to move forward at all or are required to meet the intended business goal. These issues are not simply data issues.

There is a need for a business decision on how to handle a situation or changes may be needed to existing business policies in order to support the data warehouse.

- **Future/Out of Scope.** Identifies items that would be nice to have, but are not worth delaying initial implementation to address. Often these are attributes that would come from data sources that are not to be included with the first iteration.

As time goes on, you will find that more and more of the issues are either resolved or determined to be future enhancements. If you are waiting on input from other people to continue, then you must escalate this to the project manager. The entire project schedule can be delayed by waiting for people to answer questions.

The final fact table diagram, plus an issues log providing the history, justification and decisions made during the modeling process, are the final deliverables. The user sponsor can be asked to formally sign off on the design. This is a commitment that if the team delivers what has been designed that it will meet their business needs within the scope of the project.

Preparing for the Future

In most cases, the funding and justification for the data warehouse hinges on setting the foundation for growth. Often, the next critical data sources have been identified and are slated to be included in the warehouse once the first set of data is loaded. There are two approaches to take to ensure that the initial design can indeed be expanded.

First, the additional data sources can be analyzed in detail and included in the dimensional model. While this does indeed ensure that these sources will fit into the design, it can expand the data modeling efforts by weeks or months. This type of delay is usually not acceptable.

Second, the additional sources can be analyzed at a high level to assess how they will fit into the newly developed model. The overall review should take half a day. There will be some areas where the sharing of dimensions will be obvious, and they will fit exactly. Other areas, the conformed dimension may apply, but the exact level of detail and integratability may not be clear. Document any issues and concerns for the future. Share the document with both IS and business management. Depending upon the severity of the concerns, management may decide to move forward as originally planned or to step back and perform additional analysis, which will impact the project schedule.

Using a Data Modeling Tool

You should use a data modeling tool to develop the physical data model, preferably one that stores your model's structure in a relational database. As the data staging tools mature, information will flow more naturally from the popular data modeling tools, through the transformation engine, and into the metadata that users will access to learn about the data in the warehouse.

The advantages of a data modeling tool include:

- Integrates the data warehouse model with other corporate data models.
- Helps assure consistency in naming.
- Creates good documentation in a variety of useful formats.
- Generates physical object DDL (data definition language) for most popular RDBMSs.
- Provides a reasonably intuitive user interface for entering comments about objects (tables and columns). Many data modeling tools support two types of object comments. In a data warehouse, it works best to reserve one comment field for:
  - *Technical documentation.* Notes about the data transformation requirements or other pertinent tidbits. For example "From T58.CUSTNAME, converting to title case and changing NULL to 'N/A'."
  - *Link to the dimension table designs.* Tie the logical columns to a dimension and attribute.
  - *Business users documentation.* Information about the content of the column such as "Customer name as Last, First, e.g. 'Smith, Joe'."

Retaining the relationship between the logical table design and the business dimensional model is important to ensure that the final data does indeed tie back to the original business requirements. This capability is just beginning to appear within data modeling tools.

Estimating the Number of Rows

The first inclination to determine the database size is to take the number of rows for each dimension, multiply them all together to determine how many rows will exist in the fact table. Then, determine the overall size requirement based upon the length of the fact row. Anyone who has tried this approach knows that these numbers are enormous! When you work this out, your first instinct is that you typed the numbers in wrong or that you have an error in your spreadsheet. So, you check everything and then look once again at the bottom line. Your thoughts run out of control—this is just an estimate of raw data storage, not even including indexes or work space. You begin to review in your mind how many zeros are in *mega-*, *giga-*, and *tera-*. By now, you are hoping that no one else is looking your way because they might feel the need to call for medical help. The good news is that you have just determined the largest theoretical size for your raw data, not how big your data warehouse is likely to be.

You need to step back and consider specific characteristics of your business. You probably do not sell every product to every customer every day from every sales region. Taking these basic business assumptions into consideration you will find that you have much more reasonable estimates. Keep in mind, the sizing is based upon business assumptions—your estimate will only be as accurate as the input.

Another, more accurate method to estimate the number of rows is through actual analysis of the source data. This can be gathered from the data exploration prototype described earlier. If a full data exploration prototype was not developed and your data mart table is at the transaction grain, volumes may be very easy to estimate. For example, you should be able to get a rough estimate of the number of invoice lines shipped or customer service calls answered last year without having to estimate how sparse it is.

The sparsity of the data is the key factor for correctly estimating the final size of the database. In most cases it is far more effective to measure the sparsity with a sample of real data than it is to estimate the sparsity. You will need to estimate the number of rows in each table as input to the database size estimation process as described in Chapter 15.

Designing for Aggregation

All data warehouses will contain pre-stored aggregates. Once you have determined your overall design approach, you need to consider the strategy you will use to design your aggregate fact and dimension tables. For an in-depth discussion of aggregation, please study the material in Chapter 14. The design points that require consideration now are listed next. The other design points come into play during implementation of the design.

- Aggregates must be stored in their own fact tables, separate from the base-level data. In addition, each distinct aggregation level must occupy its own unique fact table.
- The dimension tables attached to the aggregate fact tables must, whenever possible, be shrunken versions of the dimension tables associated with the base fact table.

Again, use these as guidelines, but ensure that your approach will work well with your data access tool.

Deciding What to Aggregate

Before you get too concerned about deciding which aggregates to build, keep in mind that these will change. You will add and take away aggregates periodically. Remember, aggregates are a performance-tuning vehicle. You need to build some aggregates, conduct some performance tests, and then revise the aggregates you will use in production. From there, you need to monitor aggregate use over time and make adjustments accordingly. Relax, changing your stored aggregates is not complicated as long as your users are isolated from changes with an aggregate navigator.

You need to consider two different areas when selecting which aggregates to build. First, you need to consider common business requests, and then you need to consider the statistical distribution of your data. We recommend that you develop document candidate aggregates when you have just finished data modeling. At this time, the user's requirements are still fresh in your mind. By the time you have loaded detail data into the warehouse, you may have forgotten what the user's common requests are.

First, determine what might be useful. Review the requirements document looking for mention of higher-level reporting needs. When working with your business users, you will get a sense of the primary reporting levels that are in place today. Often these are by major geographic groupings, major product lines, and regular reporting time periods (weeks or months). Review each dimension to determine attributes that are commonly reported on. Next, review the combinations of these attributes to determine which ones are used together. The more dimensions you have, the more careful you need to be. If each dimension has 3 attributes that are candidates for aggregation and you have 4 dimensions, then you could build 256 different aggregates. However, if you have 8 dimensions (and each one has 3 candidate attributes), the number of possible aggregates jumps to 65,536! Not all combinations of these candidate attributes will be commonly used together.

Second, you need to assess the statistical distribution of the data itself. Refer to the data exploration prototype, the database design information, and possibly to the data itself, looking for counts at each level of the hierarchy in each dimension.

As you move past these design guidelines to the detailed planning of your aggregates, please consult Chapter 14.

SUMMARY

In this chapter we reviewed the process used to apply dimensional modeling techniques to your project. First we introduced the Bus Architecture matrix to lay out your data marts and dimensions. Next, we reviewed the four-step method to design a single data mart. We also introduced diagramming techniques to use during the modeling process. A proven process was presented to assist you in developing and refining the dimensional model. Also, data sourcing and mapping processes were reviewed. Before you move on, don't forget to consult the project plan tasks spreadsheet at the end of this chapter for a summary of the tasks and responsibilities for building the dimensional model (Figure 7.11).

In this section of the book we have focused on the data. In the next chapters, we want to step back and follow a different path of the lifecycle—the technical architecture.

KEYS ROLES

Key roles for building the dimensional model include:

- The data modeler and database administrator step forward to lead the dimensional modeling efforts.
- The dimensional model must be reviewed by the business users and the core project team. This can lead to modifications of project scope.
- The data staging team gets involved to identify the data sources needed to populate the dimensional model.
- The database and data access tool vendors should also be involved to provide principles for database design to optimize their products.

ESTIMATING CONSIDERATIONS

It can take from 2 weeks to 12 months to build a model, depending upon the complexity of the data, the industry, and the willingness and access to key business personnel to make decisions. The scope of the project is also a factor. If you're designing a single-source data mart, expect the following elapsed times:

- Four-step logical database design: 3–8 weeks
- Source-to-target data map: 2–4 weeks
- Define business facts: 2–4 weeks

TEMPLATES

The following templates for building the dimensional model can be found on the CD:

- Template 7.1 Data Mart Matrix
- Template 7.2 Dimensional Model Document
- Template 7.3 Derived Fact Worksheet
- Template 7.4 Logical Table Design
- Template 7.5 Data Source Definition Document
- Template 7.6 Source to Target Data Map

Project Task	Fans: Business End Users	Front Office: Business Sponsor	IS Sponsor	Business Driver	Coaches: Bus. Project Lead	Project Manager	Regular Line-Up: Bus. Sys. Analyst	Data Modeler	DW DBA	Data Staging Designer	DW Educator	E/U Appl Devel	Special Teams: Tech/Security Architect	Tech. Sppt Specialists	Data Staging Programmer	Data Steward	DW QA Analyst
DIMENSIONAL MODELING																	
1 Build Matrix					○	○	○	●	○	▲							
2 Choose Data Mart		○	○	○	●	●	▶	▶									
3 Declare Grain					○	○	○	●	▲								
4 Choose Dimensions							○	●	▲								
5 Develop Fact Table Diagram							○	●	▲								
6 Document Fact Table Detail							○	●	▲								
7 Design Dimension Detail							○	●	▲								
8 Develop Derived Fact Worksheet	○			▶	○	○	●	○	▲			○					
9 User Review & Acceptance	○	□	□	○	●	○	○	○	▲								
10 Review DB Design Recommendations for E/U Tool								○	●	○		○			○		
11 Review DB Design Recommendations for DBMS								○	●								
12 Complete Logical Database Design								○	●								
13 Identify Candidate Prestored Aggregates	▶			▶	○		○	●	○								
14 Develop Aggregation Table Design Strategy								○	●								
15 Review Logical Database Design w/Team						○	○	○	●	○	▲	○			○		
16 Certify DB Design with DSS Tool Vendor									●								
17 User Acceptance/Project Review	○	□	□	○	●	○	○	○	○	○	▲	○	▲	▲	▲	▲	▲
ANALYZE DATA SOURCES																	
1 Identify Candidate Data Sources							▲	○	○	●					▲		
2 Browse Data Content							▲	○	○	●					▲		
3 Develop Source to Target Data Map								○	○	●					●		
4 Estimate Number of Rows					▶	▶	▶	○	●	○							
5 User Acceptance/Project Review	○	□	□	□	●	○	○	○	○	○	▲	○	▲	▲	○	▲	▲

LEGEND:

Primary Responsibility for the Task =	●
Involved in the Task =	○
Provides Input to the Task =	▶
Informed Task Results =	□
Optional Involvement in the Task =	▲

FIGURE 7.11 Project plan tasks for building the dimensional model.

SECTION 3

Architecture

CHAPTER **8**

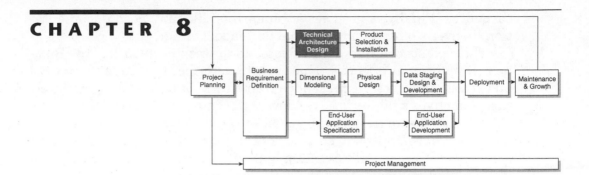

Introducing Data Warehouse Architecture

ost of us wouldn't think of building a $150,000 house without a set of blueprints. Yet, it's quite common for people to dive right into a data warehouse project costing 10 times as much without any clear idea of what they're actually building. The most common example we see is the data warehouse project that starts out with an RDBMS running on a leftover server from some other project's recent upgrade. It's like saying, "Hey, I've got some wood and some concrete, let's build a house!" The point is, you have to have a plan before you get started.

The analogy of architectural blueprints for a house is helpful to show the purpose and value of an IS architecture. First, the blueprints help the architect and the customer communicate about the desired results and the nature of the construction effort. Next, before the first shovel digs into the dirt, a good contractor can examine the blueprints and determine the resources required, dependencies, timing, and costs of the project. Next, the subcontractors can also work from the blueprints to understand their roles in the project—one worries about the plumbing, another about the electrical systems, and another about the finished carpentry. Finally, a good set of blueprints, like any good documentation, helps us later when it is time to remodel or add on.

The next six chapters are dedicated to the technical track of the Business Dimensional Lifecycle. This chapter describes the value of creating an explicit architecture, presents a framework for approaching architecture, and gives a high-level overview of the data warehouse technical architecture. Most of the following chapters are descriptive in nature. They describe what happens in each part of the architecture and list specific examples of the capabilities that might be needed in each section. Specifically, Chapter 9 zooms in on the data acquisition side of the architecture, called the back room. Chapter 10 concentrates on the data access half of the technical architecture, called the front room. Chapter 11 describes the underpinnings of the architecture: infrastructure and metadata. Chapter 12 presents a special graduate course on the Internet and security relative to the data warehouse. Finally, Chapter 13 presents the practical steps for creating an architecture and selecting products.

Chapters 8, 9, and 10 are targeted primarily for the technical architects and specialists. These people need to have an in-depth understanding of this material in order to create a data warehouse architecture. The team members who are responsible for back-room tasks, the data staging team and database administrator, should read these chapters to understand the major components they will be working with and how they fit together. The project manager must become familiar enough with this material to be able to identify landmines and steer the team around them. These chapters are optional reading for nontechnical team members.

THE VALUE OF ARCHITECTURE

In the information systems world, an architecture adds value in much the same way blueprints for a construction project do: better communication and planning. Beyond that, an effective architecture will increase the flexibility of the system, facilitate learning, and improve productivity.

- **Communication.** The architecture plan is an excellent communications tool at several levels. It helps communicate up, providing a way to help management understand the magnitude and complexity of the project. Imagine trying to sell senior management on a $2 million server investment without a clear understanding of what the load processing demands will be, what the query load will be, how it fits with other pieces of the solution, and so on.

An architecture functions as a communications tool within the team and with other IS groups, providing participants with a sense for where they fit in the process and what they need to accomplish. This kind of communication and coordination is particularly important when other IS groups are also working on a data warehouse or data mart project.

- **Planning.**   The architecture provides a cross-check for the project plan. Many architectural details end up scattered throughout and buried in the depths of the project plan. The architecture brings them all out in one place and prescribes how they will fit together. The architecture plan also typically uncovers technical requirements and dependencies that do not come out as part of the planning process for a specific project. For example, suddenly realizing the data access tool you picked requires a separate NT server while you are attempting to load the software can be distressing. Unexpectedly having to ask for more money (or time) is never fun.

- **Flexibility and maintenance.**   Creating an architecture is really about anticipating as many of the issues as possible and building a system that can handle those issues as a matter of course, rather than after they become problems. The architecture described in this chapter relies heavily on models, tools, and metadata. This adds what we call a *semantic* layer to the warehouse. This layer both describes the warehouse contents and processes and is used in those processes to create, navigate, and maintain the warehouse. Practically speaking, this means the data warehouse is more flexible and easier to maintain. For example, we can use these tools and metadata to quickly add new data sources.

  The data models and metadata allow us to analyze the impact of a major change, like the conversion to a new transaction system, and, potentially, a single point of change to support that conversion.

 The architecture's interface standards, especially the Bus Architecture developed in this book, allow the plug and play of new tools as they improve.

- **Learning.** The architecture plays an important role as documentation for the system. It can help new members of the team get up to speed more quickly on the components, contents, and connections. The alternative is to turn new people loose to build their own mental maps through trial, error, and folklore. The accuracy of these kinds of self-built maps is suspect at best. A certain close family member of one of the authors still believes, after 12 years of using a personal computer, that the only way to copy a file is to start up the application, open the file, and do a "Save As" to save the copy of the file to the new location. The point is, people working from their own mental maps are not going to be as productive as they would be if they had accurate, professional documentation. You don't want people building your data warehouse based on myths and folklore.

- **Productivity and reuse.** The architecture we describe takes advantage of tools and metadata as the primary enablers of productivity and reuse. Productivity is improved because the architecture helps us choose tools to automate parts of the warehouse process, rather than build layers and layers of custom code by hand. Because we can understand the warehouse processes and database contents more quickly, it becomes easier for a developer to reuse existing processes than to build from scratch. If it is necessary to build, the ability to search the metadata makes it possible to find and borrow code from similar processes and models. Building a new data mart or adding a new data source is easier if you can use generic load utilities and work from existing examples.

AN ARCHITECTURAL FRAMEWORK AND APPROACH

There are many different approaches to defining and developing a systems architecture. We've taken the same basic framework John A. Zachman of Zachman International uses for IS architecture and adapted it to data warehousing. We've simplified it significantly because the data warehouse doesn't (or shouldn't) own the responsibility for the entire systems architecture. For example, the warehouse shouldn't have to worry about transaction processing infrastructure. In Figure 8.1 we show the complete architecture framework. Please study the major column headings and row headings. The column headings show the major architecture areas: data, technical, and infrastructure. These column

ARCHITECTURE AREA

| LEVEL OF DETAIL | Data (What) | Technical (How) | | Infrastructure (Where) |
		Back Room	Front Room	
Business Requirements and Audit	What information do we need to make better business decisions? How do the available data assets tie into the Bus Architecture matrix?	How will we get at the data, transform it, and make it available to our users? How is this done today?	What are the major business issues we face? How will we measure these issues? How do we want to analyze the data?	What hardware and system level capabilities do we need to be successful? What do we currently have in place?
Architecture Models and Documents	**The Dimensional Model:** What are the major entities (the facts and dimensions) that make up this information, and how do they relate to each other? How should these entities be structured?	What are the specific capabilities we will need to get the data into a usable form in the desired locations at the appropriate times? What are the major data stores, and where should they be located?	What will users need to get the information out in a usable form? What major classes of analysis and reporting do we need to provide, and what are the priorities?	Where is the data coming from and going to? Do we have enough calculation and storage capacity? What are the specific capabilities we are counting on? Do they exist? Who is responsible for them?
Detailed Models and Specs	**The Logical and Physical Models:** What are the individual elements, their definitions, domains, and rules for derivation? What are the sources, and how do they map to the targets?	What standards and products provide the needed capabilities? How will we hook them together? What are our development standards for code management, naming, etc.?	What are the specifics for the report templates, including the rows, columns, sections, headers, filters, etc.? Who needs them? How often? How do we distribute them?	How do we interact with these capabilities? What are the system utilities, calls, APIs, etc.?
Implementation	Create the databases, indexes, backup, etc. Document.	Write the extracts and loads. Automate the process. Document.	Implement the reporting and analysis environment, build the initial report set, and train the users. Document.	Install and test new infrastructure components. Connect the sources to the targets to the desktop. Document.

FIGURE 8.1   The data warehouse architecture framework.

headings are intersected by the rows which represent increasing levels of detail: business requirements, architecture models, detailed models, and implementation.

The art of developing your data warehouse architecture is traversing this framework in the right sequence. We generally believe in a top-down approach. For each of the architecture areas (the columns of the framework) you should expect to gradually work downward as you approach the actual implementation.

 Start with the big picture and break the architecture down into smaller and smaller pieces until you reach a point where the pieces can actually be implemented.

The columns, of course, are not independent. But it is helpful to compartmentalize tasks to make progress. In Chapter 13, we show how these columns interact and when you need to consider more than one "Zachman step." As you are developing the big picture, you need to have a clear understanding of what is available and possible in the real world today. Reconciling the vision of what it should be with the reality of what it can be is what makes architecture so difficult.

Now that you have had a chance to study the framework, let us be a little more precise about the architectural areas, the columns, and the levels of detail, the rows.

Defining the Columns

Each column defines an area of the architecture. Each area starts with a subset of the business requirements gathering process described in Chapter 4.

The Data Architecture Area

The contents of the data warehouse are data—the objects we work with, the physical pieces we shuffle around, add together, graph, and examine. Data is the "what" that the data warehouse is all about. The data area of the architecture includes the contents of the warehouse—the list of data that is important to the business, the data stores that make up the overall warehouse environment and the sources that feed it. It also includes the design of the logical and physical data models, aggregations, hierarchies, and so on, again, all based on business needs. The data architecture also defines the granularity, volume, and timing of the data at various points in the warehouse. This becomes an important parameter for the technical architecture and infrastructure. This column should seem familiar because Chapters 5, 6, and 7 were dedicated to data architecture.

Technical Architecture Area

Technical architecture covers the processes and tools we apply to the data. This area answers the question "how"—how do we get at this data at its source, put it in a form that meets the business requirements, and move it to a place that's accessible? The technical architecture is made up of the tools, utilities, code, and so on that bring the warehouse to life. They are the pumps and valves that keep the data flowing to the right places at the right times. The places where data is moved from and to are also part of the technical architecture.

Two main subsets of the technical architecture area have different enough requirements to warrant independent consideration. We've labeled these two areas the *back room* and the *front room*. The back room is the part of the warehouse responsible for gathering and preparing the data. Another common term for the back room is *data acquisition*. The front room is the part responsible for delivering data to the user community. Another common term for the front room is *data access*. The front room and back room have their own services and data store components.

The technical architecture for most warehouses is a combination of custom code, home grown utilities, and off-the-shelf tools.

 The balance of the technical architecture is definitely shifting toward off-the-shelf tools as they become more capable of handling a broader range of complex warehouse requirements.

The second half of Chapter 8 and all of Chapters 9 and 10 concentrate on the technical architecture.

Infrastructure Architecture Area

Infrastructure is about the platforms that host the data and processes. The infrastructure is the physical plant of the data warehouse—the pipes and platforms that hold and transport the data and support the applications. This is the hardware and operating-level software. Much of the infrastructure for the data warehouse already exists as part of the overall IS infrastructure. For most of us, IS infrastructure is so much a part of daily life that we don't think about it. On the other hand, there are some parts of the infrastructure upon which the warehouse may place an unexpected burden. We need to carefully examine the IS infrastructure to make sure any special warehouse needs are addressed and to make sure we don't assume something is there when it really isn't. The lines between the infrastructure and technical architecture areas can be a bit blurry. For example, in many cases, the DBMS is a given for the data warehouse and is essentially part of the infrastructure. Chapter 11 dives into the depths of infrastructure and metadata. Chapter 12 deals with the security components of infrastructure.

Defining the Levels of Detail (the Rows)

Now we turn to the rows of the framework, starting at the highest level of detail. Part of this architectural thinking process involves creating lots of drawings and documents at various levels of detail with greater or lesser ties to reality. We call these *models*. Models are the communications medium of architecture. They are the blueprints for the warehouse. We use higher-level *architecture models* to give us a structure for understanding and managing the lower levels of detail. Without a map of the forest, we'd constantly get lost among the trees. We use detailed models to capture the details of the architecture as we define it and shape it to meet the business needs we've identified.

Business Requirements Level

The business requirements level is explicitly non-technical. The systems planner must be disciplined to not seek technical solutions at this level, but rather to understand the major business forces and boundary conditions that affect the data warehouse project. In this book, Chapter 4 is aimed directly at establishing the business requirements. In scanning across the first row of the framework in Figure 8.1, it should be apparent that the business requirements are a comprehensive mixture of end-user business needs, source data realities, state-of-the-art technology, and budget realities. We strongly recommend a realistic and down to earth perspective for stating the business realities. We are not very impressed with idealistic plans for source data or for analysis capabilities, if the means to achieve these goals are not already on the table.

A very useful technique for uncovering the technical underpinnings of the business requirements is the data discovery or audit process described in Chapter 4. This audit, along with the requirements findings, provides a comprehensive, high-level enumeration within each of the columns of Figure 8.1. In this context, an audit is a long list of requirements, or realities, that does not descend to the levels of detail described in the next three sections.

Architecture Models Level

Architecture models are the first level of serious response to the requirements. An architecture model proposes the major components of the architecture that must be available to address the requirements. All of the types of technology must be named specifically, and an argument must be made that these technologies will fit together into a system. At this level, the system perspective addresses whether the various technical components can communicate with each other, whether the administrative assumptions surrounding the use of the technologies are reasonable, and whether the organization has the resources to support the technologies. The data matrix described in Chapter 7 is the high-level data architecture model. The technical architecture model is described in general terms in this chapter and detailed in Chapters 9 and 10.

Detailed Models Level

Detailed models are the functional specifications of each of the architectural components, at a significant level of detail. The detailed models must include enough information to serve as a reliable implementation guide for the team member or contractor. The detailed models also must be complete enough to create a legal contract so that when the work is done, it can be held up to the functional specification to see whether the implementation is complete and conforms to the specification. It really doesn't matter if the work is being done by an employee or by an outside contractor; this level of detail is extremely helpful for setting expectations and for communicating the intent. As we remarked at the beginning of the chapter, the detailed models are especially valuable for communicating with and educating everyone on the team. The dimensional models and physical models for each fact table are the detailed models for the data area. The technical architecture plan document serves as the detailed model for the technical architecture area.

Implementation Level

The implementation is the response to the detailed models. For a software deliverable, it is the code itself. For the data area, it's the data definition language used to build the database, and in some ways, the data itself. For many of the technical components, the implementation is expressed in metadata, whether it is a job schedule, an extract specification, or a set of query tool parameters. An implementation must, above all, be documented.

Logical Models and Physical Models

We use models across all three columns of the framework. We have data models, technical architecture models, network models, and so on. Frequently, models are referred to as either logical or physical. As you develop a model, the first thing you might have to determine is whether it will be a logical or physical model.

The distinction between logical models and physical models is sometimes confusing. When most people talk about logical models vs. physical models, they are really talking about the ideological vs. the actual. The logical model is often the vision of what the warehouse should be—the ideal we'd like to attain—it's simple, understandable, and it solves the problem. Logical models are found in the top rows of the framework.

Next, we have to face the real world. For example, some of our business requirements might rely on data that does not even exist or might not be usable. Or we can't get machines big enough to load all the detail or provide answers quickly enough. Or the tools we need to implement our vision don't exist, are too expensive, or don't run on our platforms. So, we make changes to the logical model to get it to work in the real world. This doesn't mean the logical model was wrong or that it didn't do its job. It's just that its job is to guide us in the right direction. The physical models are created in the bottom rows of the framework.

If the models are clearly labeled as logical or physical, they both serve a useful purpose. You should be aware that the authors are very real-world oriented. As a result, the models discussed in this book stick very close to the physical (i.e., real) interpretation. Thus, our logical data models are usually meant to be implemented literally as the table diagrams imply.

Framework Summary

The data warehouse architecture framework helps break the architecture task into manageable pieces. The three columns—data, technical, and infrastructure—address separate but related areas. Within each column, we can proceed in a rational fashion, from the business requirements down through the models and specifications to the implementation details.

In a way, this framework is a functional twist on the Lifecycle's process flow. Most of the steps in the Lifecycle deliver an element that fits into the architecture framework. In fact, we've already worked through the top three rows of the first column of Figure 8.1, the data architecture, in Chapters 5–7. The dimensional models that define the Data Warehouse Bus are the overall *data* blueprint for the warehouse. They are the cornerstone for data integration among data marts. Without the dimensional models and the bus architecture, we risk building a set of stovepipe data marts that may solve a narrow range of problems but are not usable from an enterprise point of view.

In Chapter 5 we described how the Data Warehouse Bus acts as the skeleton, which is fleshed out through the dimensional models and physical database designs. Finally, we described the various data stores where all this data might exist at various stages in the process. We also touched on the implications and risks of some of these data stores. At this point, you should be an expert at gathering the requirements from the business community and interpreting those requirements as a series of dimensional models. The rest of this chapter provides an overview of the middle column of the framework—the technical architecture.

TECHNICAL ARCHITECTURE OVERVIEW

Now that we've identified the data, how do we get it into a useful form? We must now turn our attention to the middle columns of Figure 8.1, the technical architecture. We have to get the data out of its source systems, transform and transport it to the presentation servers, and then make it available to use in an effective manner by the ultimate end user clients of the data warehouse.

The framework described earlier starts with business requirements. While every business faces a different set of challenges, the high-level data warehouse functions and processes tend to be similar from a systems point of view. The real deliverable from the technical architecture effort is the set of technical models and detailed models specifically designed to meet your business requirements.

What we describe here is meant to be a starting point for your own customized technical architecture based on your organization's requirements and resources. Your mileage may vary.

 Remember that the business requirements are your primary guide to what should be in your architecture and what the priorities are.

The technical architecture breaks into two big pieces that are reflected in Figure 8.1, the back room and the front room. In spite of this compartmentalization, both applications interact in very significant ways, as shown in Figure 8.2.

Whereas the requirements answer the question "What do we need to do?" the technical architecture answers the question "How will we do it?" The technical architecture is the overall plan for what we want the warehouse to be when it matures. It describes the flow of data from the source systems to the decision makers and the transformations that data goes through along the way. It also specifies the tools and techniques we will need to make it happen. This is where the technology proves itself. These are the tools and utilities that make our jobs easier.

This area is changing rapidly, both in the overall context of client/server computing and even more so within the confines of the data warehousing market. Major product upgrades and entirely new tools are constantly surfacing. Even entire tool categories are being created on a regular basis.

Figure 8.2 provides the high-level elements of the technical architecture. In this section, we discuss a natural separation between the internal workings of the warehouse—the back room—and its public face—the front room. This separation provides a useful organizing device for many of the concepts because different roles, and often different

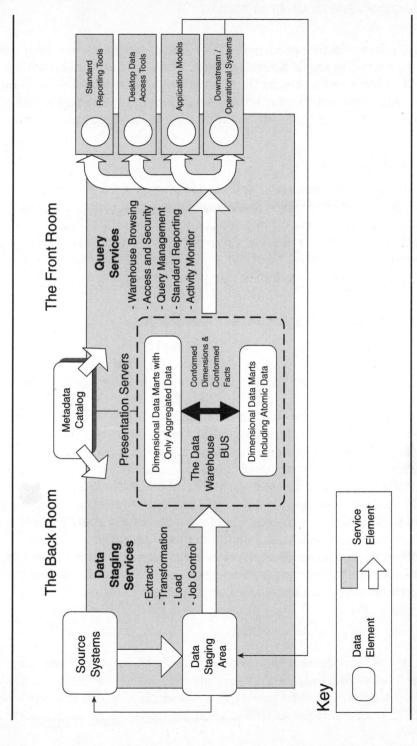

Figure 8.2 High-level technical architecture model.

329

people, focus on these two areas. We'll also examine the concept of metadata and the metadata catalog and its role in the warehouse.

It is important to note that Figure 8.2 is a logical model. The actual physical representation will probably be very different depending on many factors, including the maturity of the warehouse, its size, and nature.

Services and Data Stores

The technical architecture depicted in Figure 8.2 has two major types of components: services and data stores. Services are the functions needed to accomplish the required tasks of the warehouse. For example, copying a table from one place to another is a basic data movement service. If services are the verbs of the warehouse, data stores are the nouns. Data stores are the temporary or permanent landing places for data.

Flow from Source System to User Desktop

From a high-level view, data moves from the source systems to the staging area using the applications provided as part of the data staging services layer. This flow is driven by metadata kept in the metadata catalog: data that describes the locations and definitions of the sources and targets, data transformations, timings, and dependencies. Once the data is combined and aligned in the staging area, the same set of data staging services are used to select, aggregate, and restructure the data into data sets as defined in Chapter 7. These data sets are loaded onto the presentation server platforms and tied together via the conformed dimension and conformed facts that are the specifications of the Data Warehouse Bus. Remember that all data that is accessed in any way by an end user, a query tool, a report writer, or a software model is defined by us to belong to a data mart. Some data marts will therefore have very granular data, and other data marts will have only aggregated data. In any case, it is essential to separate the issues of data staging from data presentation.

 The data staging area does not provide query services. Only the presentation servers provide query services, and they rely on storing and presenting the data in a dimensional format.

The flow from source system to user desktop is supported by metadata from the metadata catalog.

Finally, users gain access to the data through desktop data access tools, which are usually a combination of off-the-shelf tools and custom front-ends created with programming products. These tools should take advantage of query support services to help manage the logon, locate the appropriate data, and collect information about the usage and performance of the system. Some front-end tools come with their own query support services. What we are calling query support services can take on many forms ranging from custom code to vendor-supplied data warehouse application products.

We have been describing logical data flows and haven't yet dealt with which piece is actually running on which machine. Certainly, the presentation server is the first place where logical and physical tend to get mixed up. From the user's point of view, there should only be one place to go for information. The dotted line around the presentation server represents this single logical view of the world; it is a simplifying layer that makes all data marts accessible to the user community. This simplifying layer can be created in many ways, the most common being physically locating the data together. If that isn't possible, other approaches like middleware, application servers, gateways, metadata, physical tables, or some combination can provide this simplifying layer to the users.

Key Technical Architecture Features

Several features of the technical architecture apply across the board. These are the basic design principles that underlie all of the tools, processes, and components of the service layers.

Metadata Driven

The fact that metadata drives the warehouse is the literal truth. If you think you won't use metadata, you are mistaken.

Metadata provides flexibility by buffering the various components of the system from each other. For example, when a source migrates to a new operational system, substituting in the new data source is relatively easy. Because the metadata catalog holds the mapping information from source to target, the warehouse manager can map the new source to the existing target in the warehouse. People will continue to access the old target without necessarily realizing the source has changed. To the extent that the new source collects additional data, the warehouse manager can add that data as needed.

 The metadata catalog plays such a critical role in the architecture that it makes sense to describe the architecture as being *metadata driven*. The metadata catalog provides parameters and information that allow the applications to perform their tasks—a set of control information about the warehouse, its contents, the source systems, and its load processes.

The metadata catalog itself is really only a logical concept at this point. The holy grail of data warehousing is to have a single source for metadata. In that case, a single change made in the metadata catalog would be reflected throughout the architecture—it would be available to all services at once. In most cases, it's not practical to bring all the information into a single place. Metadata lives in the various tools, programs, and utilities that make the data warehouse work. You will be well served if you are aware of what metadata you keep, centralize it where possible, track it carefully, and keep it up to date.

Flexible Services Layers

The data staging services and data query services are application layers that also provide a level of indirection that add to the flexibility of the architecture. For example, when a user issues a query, it is submitted to a query service which in turn uses a part of the metadata catalog to resolve the location and nature of the request. This might be particularly important when a database is moved from one system to another. In a metadata-driven environment, the desktop tools are not hard coded to point to a particular IP address. Instead, a change is made in the domain name server (DNS) metadata to indicate its new location. The next user that requests information from that database will automatically be routed to the new location. On the back end, such a database move might involve switching from one database vendor to another. In this case, some of the warehouse management utilities will help migrate the database based on a combination of the descriptive metadata, and the tool's ability to generate vendor-specific data definition language (DDL). Both of the service layers work with the metadata catalog to insulate the user from the constant changes of the systems world, to automate processes, and to provide information and documentation about the warehouse.

Caveats

Not all tools and services on the market currently support the concept of an open metadata catalog or query services indirection. As a result, we recommend a phased approach to implementing the architecture. Set up the basic structure first, and add components as the warehouse grows and resources permit. This allows you to transition to tools that support your architecture as they become available. The rapid development of software products in this area means you should set expectations that major parts of your architecture will be transitioning to new approaches in one-and-a-half to three years.

Evolution of Your Data Warehouse Architecture

The architectural plan evolves continuously. Business requirements change, new data becomes available, and new technologies sprout up in the marketplace. In fact, the warehouse itself causes many of these changes. You will know you are successful if the business users are pressuring you to make significant changes. Your initial implementation of the warehouse will cover only a small section of your possible architecture. As products, platforms, and designs improve over time, the physical implementation you choose will evolve to more closely resemble the logical model. The architecture will also evolve over time as you learn more about the business and technology from your own experience and the experiences of others (typically a much cheaper and less painful way to learn).

Many of the techniques we teach in this book are intended to be robust in the face of a changing architecture. For instance, we always are more comfortable with granular data expressed at the lowest possible level. Premature aggregation of data is one of the biggest enemies of a flexible architecture. Granular data is highly resilient in the face of changing business requirements and the availability of more powerful technology. Perhaps the other important perspective we teach in this book that insulates against architectural changes is the dimensional modeling approach. As we argued at the beginning of Chapter 5, the dimensional modeling approach is so symmetric that every user request, even ones we have never seen before, follows the same pattern and is not surprising. That is what we mean when we say we are resilient when faced with changes in the architecture of the data warehouse. Once you have defined your bus architecture, you can be assured that your dimensional data marts will connect together.

SUMMARY

In an effort to convince you to invest in an architecture effort, this chapter started out by listing the major benefits of architecture. Then we described a framework for approaching architecture, with data, technical and infrastructure areas. Finally, we gave a high-level summary of the middle columns of the framework, the technical architecture area, which is the focus of the next two chapters.

CHAPTER 9

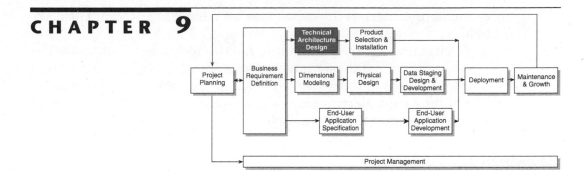

Back Room Technical Architecture

The back room is where the data staging process takes place. It is the engine room of the data warehouse. The primary concern of DBAs and system administrators in the back room is with solving the specific problem of getting the right data from point A to point B with the appropriate transformations, at the appropriate time. Another common term for the back room and the data staging process is *data acquisition.*

The data staging process began as a manually coded development effort, like shoveling coal into the boiler of a steam engine. Fortunately, the industry has developed some tools and techniques to support the back room, so it is becoming more like running a diesel generator. It can be automated to some degree, but it is still a complex, temperamental piece of technology.

This chapter examines the components and services of the technical architecture for the back room. We start out by cataloging the primary data stores in the back room. Then we get a sense for the services that tie the data stores together, and help move data from one store to another. Finally, we describe a set of asset management services that help maintain and protect the back room. The goal of this chapter is to communicate the range of elements you will find in the back room architecture, and help you determine what your back room architecture needs to include.

This chapter is required reading for the technical architects. The data staging and database administrator must also understand the specifics of back room architecture. Again, the project manager must have a high-level understanding of each component in the Lifecycle to properly orchestrate the entire project.

BACK ROOM DATA STORES

Data stores are the temporary or permanent landing places for data along the way. What data gets physically stored has obvious implications for the warehouse infrastructure—you need a place to put it. Most of the primary data stores are found in the back room of the warehouse, especially in small- and medium-sized projects. The data stores described here are based on the technical architecture shown in Figure 9.1. The actual data stores you will need depend on your business requirements and the complexity of your extract and transformation process.

Source Systems

The transaction systems are the obvious sources of interesting business information. Usually, the initial, crying business need is for access to the core operational systems of the business, including order entry, production, shipping, customer service, and the accounting systems. Other high-value sources may be external to the business, like demographic customer information, target customer lists, customer business segments (standard industry classifications or SIC codes), and competitive sales data. The data staging process is iterative in nature, so the source for a particular load process may also be another data warehouse or the target data warehouse itself.

Source system data storage types are dictated by the source system. Many older legacy systems are standard mainframe data storage facilities. IMS, IDMS, VSAM, flat files, and DB2 are all common in this environment. In some cases, the desired data source is actually a standard batch report that everyone gets, and it has been the agreed-on source for years. If you can't reverse-engineer the data transformations that take place in creating this report, then the report image itself becomes the source. The flat file is one of the standard sources for the warehouse.

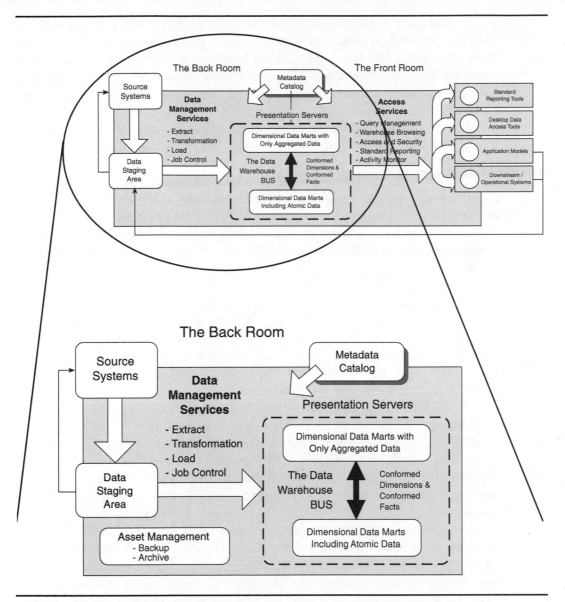

FIGURE 9.1   Back room technical architecture.

It is usually easier to convince the source systems group to generate flat files for the warehouse as part of their regular processing than to convince them to give you direct access to the source system. Often, these files are already generated as part of the daily processing and are used for operational reporting. Note that just because they are flat doesn't mean they are simple.

Source system data models cover the gamut of alternatives—hierarchical, fully denormalized flat file, and third normal form as dictated by the source system.

Understanding the nature of the source systems is critical to creating the back room architecture. The tools, connections, and services all depend in part on where the data is coming from and what form it will be in. A few specific source systems bear additional discussion. These include client/server ERP systems, the reporting instance, and the ODS.

Client/Server ERP Systems

A few major companies have won the battle to provide the client/server generation of operational systems. These systems, called *Enterprise Resource Planning* (ERP) systems, are typically made of up several modules that cover major functional areas of the business, such as Human Resources, Manufacturing, and so on. These systems have been created to address the stovepipe problem.

We pay two major penalties for this wonderful integration from the data warehouse point of view. First, there are often literally thousands of tables in these ERP source systems, and in some cases, they may be named in a different language from yours (such as German). Figuring out which tables hold the interesting data for the warehouse and how they interconnect can be a nightmare. Second, these systems typically cannot support decision support. This should come as no surprise since it has long been known that systems designed for transaction processing have trouble with decision support—that is the whole reasoning behind the data warehouse and OLAP. Also, these systems have to manage a much more complex distributed process. They rarely have the cycles left for decision support.

The ERP vendors and many other third parties have recognized this gap and are working to include data warehouse capabilities in their products. These range from extract systems to help pull the appropriate data out of the ERP to complete canned data warehouse schema designs. If you need to extract from a client/server ERP system, contact your vendor to see what tools and services they provide that might help.

Note that using a vendor-supplied, canned data warehouse does not mean you can forget about business requirements, design, and architecture. You must make sure the ERP warehouse product can address the business requirements and will most likely still need the standard warehouse tools and processes to load data kept in systems other than the ERP.

A canned data warehouse from an ERP vendor will probably not give you enough flexibility to store all of your data sources or use your preferred client tools.

Reporting Instance

Many of our customers with client/server based transaction systems or resource-constrained legacy systems end up creating a separate copy of the operational database to serve as the reporting environment for the operational systems. This comes about because the operational systems do not have enough horsepower to support both transaction processing and standard reporting, let alone ad hoc decision support queries. For some reason, one of the fundamental tenets of data warehousing ends up surprising a lot of transaction system implementers—that a database design and implementation optimized for transactions will not effectively handle decision support.

Don't get distracted by the idea that the reporting instance is really just another part of the data warehouse.

A reporting instance should be managed as a core component of the operational system with appropriate service levels, monitoring, tuning, and planning. It is another data source from the warehouse point of view.

Operational Data Store

The operational data store (ODS) is a part of the data warehouse environment many managers have ambivalent or confused feelings about. We are often asked "Should I build an ODS?" We have decided that the real underlying question is "What is an ODS, anyway?"

In *Building the Operational Data Store* (Wiley 1996), Bill Inmon, Claudia Imhoff, and Greg Battas describe an ODS as a "subject oriented, integrated, volatile, current valued data store containing only corporate detailed data." As we stated in Chapter 1, there are two primary interpretations of the ODS that serve fundamentally different purposes.

In the first case, the ODS serves as a point of integration for operational systems. It is a truly operational, real-time source for balances, histories, and other detailed lookups. In many cases, these ODSs are implemented to better support one-to-one customer relationships in the order entry or customer service function. Since this type of ODS supports constant operational access and updates, it should be housed outside the warehouse. It's impossible to structure a single system to meet both operational and decision support needs and performance requirements.

The second interpretation of the ODS is to supply current, detailed data for decision support. As our data warehouses have matured, there is a growing thirst for analyzing ever more detailed customer behavior and ever more specific operational texture. In most cases, the analysis must be done on the most granular and detailed data possible. The emergence of data mining has also demanded that we crawl through reams of the lowest-level data, looking for correlations and patterns.

In our view, the first interpretation of the ODS is a valuable component of the operational environment and the second is simply a part of the data warehouse.

Bringing the ODS into the Data Warehouse

Until now, the decision support oriented ODS was often thought to be a different system from the main data warehouse because it was based on "operational" data, meaning detailed, transaction-level data. Conventional wisdom used to say that the data warehouse was almost always somewhat summarized. Since the warehouse was a complete historical record, we didn't dare store this operational, transaction data as a complete history—we couldn't afford to.

However, the hardware and software technology that supports warehousing has matured, and we are now able to store and query more data. We have also figured out how to extract and clean data rapidly, and how to model it for user comprehension and extreme query performance. We are no longer willing to accept the original ODS assumption that you cannot store the individual transactions of a large business in a historical time series.

If our regular data warehouses can now embrace the lowest-level transaction data as a multiyear historical time series, and we are using high-performance data extracting and cleaning tools to pull this data out of the legacy systems at almost any desired frequency each day, then why is the ODS a separate system?

Let us take this opportunity to tighten and restrict the definition of the ODS. We view the decision support–oriented ODS simply as the "front edge" of the data warehouse, no longer warranting a separate designation or environment. Thus, the only free-standing ODS we should expect to encounter is supporting operational systems with integrated transaction data.

 The ODS should be a subject-oriented, integrated, frequently updated store of detailed data to support transaction systems with integrated data. Any detailed data used for decision support should simply be viewed as the lowest atomic level of the data warehouse.

Thus, the atomic level of detailed, operational data in the warehouse is characterized by the following:

- **Subject oriented.** The atomic level, like the rest of the data warehouse, is organized around specific business processes such as customer orders, claims, or shipments.
- **Integrated.** The atomic level gracefully bridges between subjects and presents an overarching view of the business rather than an incompatible stovepipe view of the business.
- **Frequently augmented.** The atomic level data is constantly being added to. This requirement is a significant departure from the original ODS statement, which said the ODS was *volatile*; that is, the ODS was constantly being overwritten, and its data structures were constantly changing. This new requirement of frequently augmenting the data also invalidates the original statement that the ODS contains only *current valued data*. We aren't afraid to store the

transaction history at the atomic level. In fact, that has now become our mission.

- **Sits within the full data warehouse framework of historical and summarized data.** In a data warehouse containing a monthly summarized view of data, in addition to the transaction detail, the input flow of atomic data also contributes to a special "current rolling month." In many cases, when the last day of the month is reached, the current rolling month becomes the most recent member of the standard months in the time series and a new current rolling month is created.

- **Naturally supports a collective view of data.** We now see how the atomic level presents a collective view to the business user. The user can immediately and gracefully link to last month's collective view of the customer (via the time series) and to the surrounding class of customers (via the data warehouse aggregations).

- **Organized for rapid updating directly from the legacy system.** The data extraction and cleaning industry has come a long way in the last few years. We can pipeline the data from the legacy systems through data cleaning and integrating steps and drop it into the atomic level of the data warehouse. The original distinctions of Class I (near real-time upload), Class II (upload every few hours), and Class III (upload perhaps once per day) described in *Building the Operational Data Store* are still valid, but the architectural differences in the extract pipeline are far less interesting than they used to be. The ability to upload data very frequently will probably be based more on waiting for remote operational systems to deliver necessary data than for computing or bandwidth restrictions in the data pipeline.

- **Should be organized around a star join schema design.** Inmon, Imhoff and Battas recommend the star join data model as "the most fundamental description of the design of the data found in the operational data store." We wholeheartedly agree. The star join, or dimensional model, is the basic preferred data model for achieving user understandability and predictable high performance, for both atomic and aggregated data.

- **Contains all of the text and numbers required to describe low-level transactions.** However, it may additionally contain back references to the legacy system that would allow real-time links to be opened to the legacy systems through terminal or transaction based interfaces. This is an interesting aspect of the original definition of the ODS, and it is somewhat straightforward if the low-level transactions are streamed out of the legacy system and into the atomic level portion of the data warehouse. Technically what this means is that operational keys, like the invoice number and line number, are kept in the data flow all the way into the atomic level, so that an application can pick up these keys and link successfully back to the legacy system interface. Note that if this link is meant to support real-time transaction loads, you are back to the original definition of the ODS in an operational, transaction-oriented environment.

- **Supported by extensive metadata.**   Metadata is needed to explain and present the meaning of the data to end users through query and reporting tools, as well as describe an extract "audit" of the data warehouse contents.

If you already have something that you believe is an ODS, examine it carefully to determine its purpose. If it is meant to play an operational, real-time role, then it is truly an operational data store and should have its own place in your systems environment. On the other hand, if it is meant to provide reporting or decision support capabilities, it should be integrated into the warehouse at the atomic level, conforming with the Data Warehouse Bus Architecture.

Bringing the decision support–oriented ODS into the existing data warehouse framework solves a number of problems. We can now focus on building a single data extract pipeline. We don't need to have a split personality where we are willing to have a volatile, changing structure of data with no history or support for performance enhancing aggregations. And, we can go back to a single definition for the ODS.

 We now understand how to take a flow of atomic level transactions, put them into a dimensional framework, and simultaneously build a detailed transaction history with no compromised details.

Finally, if you have been saying to yourself that your organization doesn't need to store all that transaction detail because your management only looks at high-level summaries, then you need to broaden your perspective and listen to what is going on in the world. We are in a major move to one-on-one marketing where organizations are seeking to understand and respond to detailed and individual customer behavior. Banks need to know exactly who is at that ATM between 5 and 6 P.M., what transactions they are performing, and how that pattern has evolved this year in response to various bank incentive programs. Catalina Marketing, a leading provider of in-store electronic scanner-activated consumer promotions, is ready to print coupons at your grocery store register that respond to what is in your market basket and what you have bought on recent trips to the store. To do this, these organizations need all the gory transaction details, both current and historical.

Data Staging Area

The data staging area is the construction site for the warehouse. We will decompose the activities of the data staging area in detail in Chapter 16, but suffice it to say that this is where much of the data transformation takes place and where much of the added value of the data warehouse is created. Since many of these transformations, like the conversion to surrogate keys, are useful across the enterprise, it makes sense to do them only once. Actually, in the case of key mapping, you need to have a single, official place where the mapping takes place. This central role for the staging area means that in many cases it evolves to become the "source system of record" for all downstream DSS and reporting environments and less-than-real-time interfaces between systems.

 Investment in a solid data staging area that services a broad range of transformation requirements will avoid requiring each business process to invest in deciphering the source systems and performing the same calculations.

Data Staging Storage Types

The major storage types we've seen include flat files, relational tables, and proprietary structures used by data staging tools. The choice depends on the data quantities and the timeframes involved. Fast processing of large volumes may require compiled COBOL or C code running against flat files. Utilities like Syncsort work better with some file types than others. Staging the data in a relational database is common, and although it has many advantages, it is not all that efficient. The relational system imposes a lot of overhead to load, index, sort, and otherwise manipulate the data. The programming languages built into RDBMSs are relatively slow as well. On the other hand, one big advantage of a relational platform is its broad accessibility. Many of the data staging tools are designed to work with relational databases. Also, you can choose from a wide range of query tools to examine the contents of the data staging area at any point in time.

The data staging area will archive and store data for a number of purposes. Conformed dimensions are created in the data staging area and are replicated out to all the requesting data marts. These conformed dimensions must be permanently housed in the data staging area as flat files ready for export. The data staging area may be the best place to hold data for emergency recovery operations, especially if the data mart machines are remote affairs under the control of user departments. The data staging area must also be the source of the most atomic transactional data, especially if the client data marts do not use all of that data at any given point in time. This atomic data then becomes available for further extraction. Again, this archival data may well be stored as flat files available for export or processing by a variety of tools.

 The data staging area is really an assembly plant and is not intended to be seen by users.

Data Staging Data Models

The data models can be designed for performance and ease of development. This means they are likely to match a combination of source structures on the incoming side and dimensional warehouse structures on the "finished goods" side, with the transformation process managing the conversion. Third normal form or E/R models often appear in the data staging area because the source systems are duplicated (like the reporting instance or ODS), and become the starting point for the process, or they are built in the staging area to help tease apart the real nature of the sources.

The Presentation Servers

As we described in Chapter 1, presentation servers are the target platforms where the data is stored for direct querying by end users, reporting systems and other applications. Early data warehouses were built in a monolithic structure with detail and aggregates in a single location. This single instance proved frustrating for business process areas that had to wait their turn and led to the development of independent data marts. The idea of the Data Warehouse Bus allows parallel development of business process data marts with the ability to integrate these data marts ensured by their use of conformed dimensions. Moving forward, we believe the approach that makes the most sense involves loading detail and aggregate data into data marts segmented by business process. The conformed dimensions used in these data marts will allow query management software to combine data across data marts for fully integrated enterprise analysis and reporting.

We show two kinds of data marts in Figures 8.2 and 9.1: data marts with atomic data and those containing only aggregated data. There is no significant difference in our minds between these two types, since in all cases the data must be presented to the query services in a dimensional format. We show the two examples to reinforce the point that atomic data belongs in a data mart framework. It is also helpful to show the two types because they are often kept in different DBMSs on different platforms. Depending on your business requirements, the size of your warehouse, and the tools you select, you may or may not need both types.

The Data Warehouse Bus matrix from Chapter 7 provides the elements of a descriptive metaphor that helps us organize data in the presentation layer. In a way, the matrix is like the system bus in your computer. Each dimension is like a connector, or wire, on the bus. It carries a standard (i.e., conformed) "signal," like product or customer. Each business process is an expansion card that plugs into the data connectors as appropriate. Figure 9.2 gives a conceptual example of how the bus might work for two business processes: manufacturing production and order entry. They both plug into the same bus, but they only over-

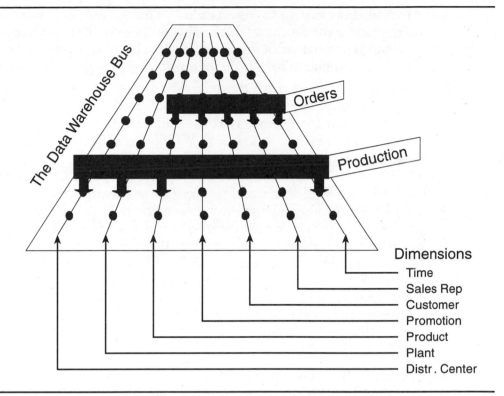

FIGURE 9.2   Two processes plugging into the Data Warehouse Bus Architecture.

lap in two areas, time and product. As new business process data sets are added, they are able to plug into the existing data bus.

Atomic Data Marts

Atomic data marts hold data at the lowest-common-denominator level, that is, at the lowest level of detail necessary to meet most of the high-value business requirements.

Aggregate tables might be considered part of the business process data mart or part of the atomic data mart. Part of this decision is logical in nature. In other words, where you draw the line doesn't have a big impact on what you actually do. So, the atomic data mart may contain a range of aggregates designed to improve performance. The choice of aggregates will change over time based on analysis of actual warehouse usage.

- **Atomic data mart storage types.** The atomic data mart should be relational rather than OLAP. This is because of the extreme level of detail, the number of dimensions, the size of the dimensions, and the broad accessibility relational databases provide.

- **Atomic data mart data model.** We recommend that atomic data marts be built around the dimensional model, not an E/R model. Whenever someone insists that the atomic data mart should be kept in third normal form, it is usually a problem of how something is defined, not a true difference of opinion. Ask two questions to clarify the issue: (1) What is the preferred model to support user access and (2) will users need or want to access the detail? Almost everyone we've talked to agrees that the dimensional model is the best user access model. Everyone also agrees that users will want to access the detail at some point, either via a drill-through process or directly. Since the atomic data mart contains the lowest level of detail and users will want to access it, it should be kept in the same dimensional model. It makes no sense to carry the overhead of some kind of complex mapping layer to give users the simplified, dimensional view of the business they need but from an E/R source.

Aggregated Business Process Data Marts

Each core business process, like taking customer orders, generates data that is of interest to multiple business functions. The business function called Marketing might like to analyze that data to get a sense for promotional effectiveness. Sales might like to examine that data to understand regional, district, and individual sales performance. Customer service might like to analyze that data to understand the relationship between orders and service calls by product. The list goes on. We call the data related to each core business process a *business process data mart*. Business process data marts simplify the view of the world by bringing together relevant sets of data from the atomic data mart and presenting it in a dimensional form that is meaningful to the business users.

Often, the first data warehouse project in a company is a single business process data mart. That is, the atomic data mart and the business process data mart are essentially indistinguishable. In fact, there is often only one presentation server involved rather than two. As the company adds data marts, the atomic data mart and the staging area must expand to accommodate the additional data and transformation processes. Note that this expansion has organizational implications for the warehouse team. During the first development effort, the atomic data mart and the business process data mart are typically created by a single team. As more data marts are created, the atomic data mart must become an enterprise resource, while the business process data mart is more effective if it can focus on the needs surrounding the business process it is derived from. A central warehouse team evolves that is responsible for the master conformed dimension tables, warehouse tools, and data mart integration.

As the data warehouse expands, individual data mart projects will likely be built and managed independently by other IS teams that are dedicated to each major business process or even by power users with desktop database tools. One problem we see with many data mart projects is that organizations have no idea how much effort is required to successfully extract and transform data. There is often a temptation to avoid the central warehouse team because "they'll only slow us down." The central warehouse team inadvertently fosters this impression because they sound like the harbingers of doom when they describe how difficult the project will be. From an enterprise point of view, the goal is to encourage all data mart projects to leverage the work that has already been done and to source their internal data through the atomic data mart, and occasionally directly from the staging area (in the case of external data, for example). The warehouse team can accomplish this by making the value added in the data staging process so great that alternative sources aren't even considered. This will cause future data marts to be based on the same standard sources and to use the same dimensions. As a result, they will be consistent with each other. They will also be able to take advantage of the data management and access services tools to speed development and improve maintenance.

- **Business process data mart storage.**   In our experience, business process data marts are usually either relational or proprietary multidimensional OLAP databases. Some projects house their data marts in a proprietary 4GL tool, many of which have added on data warehouse–style functions.

- **Business process data mart model.**   The data loaded into these data marts should follow the same dimensional structure of the data in the atomic data mart. The basic dimensionality of the data is the same, but its presentation may use different business rules and con-

> ### METADATA CATALOG
>
> One of the data stores, called the *metadata catalog,* is really an integral part of the overall architecture. We discuss the metadata catalog separately because it represents the set of information that describes the warehouse and plays an active role in its creation, use, and maintenance. A major part of Chapter 11 is dedicated to exploring the topic of metadata in detail.

tain different derived facts (e.g., gross sales versus net sales). Some of the dimensions may be trimmed or omitted altogether as you ascend to higher levels of summarization. Additionally, information of interest only to a particular business process may be appended to the dimension tables during the load process. These differences are based on the different views of the world Marketing, Finance, Sales, Manufacturing, and so on all have. For example, Finance may be concerned with revenue and have a very strict definition of what gets counted as revenue. The sales organization may be more interested in analyzing sales, which has a different (and somewhat less strict) definition in terms of timing, allocations to sales reps, and so on.

BACK ROOM SERVICES

Back room services, or data staging services, are the tools and techniques employed in the data staging process. (Of course, you recall the back room is where the data staging process takes place; it is the engine room of the data warehouse.) Our focus in this section is to describe the major services we've seen to be valuable in various warehouse environments. Your warehouse will probably not need all of these services, at least not all at once.

We define a service as an elemental function or task. It might be as simple as to creating a table in a database. An application is a software product that provides one or more services. An application may be code created by the warehouse team, an in-house utility, a vendor utility, or a full-scale vendor product designed for data warehousing. It depends on the business requirements, resources, and priorities. Again, our goal here is to describe the nature and range of service functionality your warehouse might require. Additional detail about many of the services we describe here, along with examples, can be found in Chapter 16, which covers data staging, and Chapter 13, which covers tool selection.

The data-staging process involves three major operations: extracting the data from the sources, running it through a set of transformation processes, and loading it into the target systems. These operations tend to overlap. For example, in many cases, it makes sense to include some of the data transformations in the extract process. It is easy to apply certain calculations and aggregations as the data is pulled out. Also, there may be cycles available on the source system platform to help speed the extract process. Finally, it may just be easier for the programmer.

General Data Staging Requirements

Before we start listing detailed data staging capabilities, it is helpful to consider a set of overall requirements for the data staging system. These cluster around the areas of productivity and usability.

- **Productivity support.** Any system you decide to implement needs to provide basic development environment capabilities like code library management check in/check out, version control, and production and development system builds. Initially, and for smaller projects, these can be implemented through a standards document, a process description, and a set of standard directories. In the long run, and for larger projects, your data staging services will need to include these capabilities.

- **Usability.** The data staging system also must be as usable as possible, given the underlying complexity of the task. In the last few years, this has translated into a graphical user interface. A good interface can reduce learning time, speed development, and be self-documenting (to a degree). Of course, a bad GUI can reduce productivity instead of improve it.

  System documentation is another part of usability. The data staging system needs to provide a way for developers to easily capture information about the processes that they are creating. This metadata should go into the information catalog and be easily accessible to the team and the users as necessary.

- **Metadata driven.** One of the most important characteristics of the services that support the data staging process is that they should be metadata driven. By this, we mean they should draw from a database of information about the tables, columns, jobs, and so on needed to create and maintain the warehouse rather than embed this information in COBOL or SQL code, where it is almost impossible to find and change. It is becoming less common for the back room processes to use hard-coded data management services. Today most warehouses take advantage of tools that automate the warehouse development process in some way, even if it means using daemons, scripts, and CRONTAB to schedule the nightly loads. This move toward metadata-based processes is driven, at least in part, by the overall push toward nightly (or more frequent) loads. When the load cycle happened only once a month, someone could marshal it through by hand. Not so when the load has to happen every night—at least not reliably. Note that this push for more frequent loads is really a business-driven requirement.

EXAMPLE METADATA-DRIVEN DATA STAGING UTILITIES

Metadata can play an active or passive role in the data warehouse; it can serve as documentation for the contents and processes of the warehouse, and it can directly serve as the instruction set for those processes. The documentation role is valuable because it is the most effective way to educate someone on the contents of the warehouse and how it works. This is important both for new members of the team and for new users of the warehouse.

Documentation is always the neglected step-child of the information systems project. However, if metadata is an active part of the process itself, it must be created and captured; otherwise, the process won't work. This example shows how metadata can drive the data staging process. We are not encouraging you to build a set of utilities, although many early data warehouse teams have done so. At this point, smaller projects can take advantage of data staging utilities that are now being built into the current generation of DBMS products. Larger systems should rely on full-featured, market-tested commercial products. View this example as a good vehicle for understanding the value a data staging tool provides.

Basically, these data staging utilities are wrapper programs that tie some of the core data manipulation statements to a metadata structure. Let us use the CREATE TABLE command as an example.

Dropping and creating tables is common in the load process as dimension tables are refreshed, tables are copied from test to production, and so on. A simple version of the syntax for the SQL CREATE TABLE command looks something like this:

```
CREATE TABLE employee
(
    emp_id          INTEGER,
    fname           CHAR(20)        NOT NULL,
    minitial        CHAR(1)         NULL,
    lname           VARCHAR(30)     NOT NULL,
    hire_date       DATE            NOT NULL,
    job_id          SMALLINT        NOT NULL
)
```

The metadata-driven version would rely on two metadata tables and a procedure. One table has information about tables in it—one row per table. The second table has information about columns in it—one row per column. It ties back to the Tables table through a common Table_Name column. Rough pseudocode for the procedure would go something like this:

```
Proc Create_Tab(TabName, DatabaseName, HostName, UserName,
Password, DropFlag)
Declare Command_String, Length_String as string
Command_String = "CREATE TABLE " & TabName & " ("
' Create a results set with an SQL call
Connect MetadataHost, UserName/Password
Select column_name, data_type, length, Null_value from
Columns_Table where Columns_Table.TableName = TabName

' Loop through the results set to build the SQL command by
appending to Command_String
For Each Record 'Loop until end of results set
    IF length = NULL THEN
        Length_String = ""
    ELSE
```

```
        Length_String = "(" & length & ")"
    END IF
    Command_String = Command_String & column_name & " " &
data_type & Length_String & " " and Null_value & ","
Next Record 'End Loop

' Finish the command (get rid of the last comma, add a close
parenthesis)
Command_String = Substring(Command_String, 1,
Length(Command_String) -1)
Command_String = Command_String & ")"

' Submit the final command string to the database
Connect HostName UserName/Password
Use DatabaseName
IF table_exists THEN
IF DropFlag = TRUE THEN
Drop Table TabName
Command_String
ELSE LogWrite( "Table already exists")
ELSE
Command_String
End IF
LogWrite(TabName & " created on " & HostName & " / " &
DatabaseName & " at " & NOW)
End Proc
```

Now, instead of needing 8 lines of code (or 60!) to create a table, we can do it in one statement:

```
Create_Tab(Employee, DataWH, DWTest, system, manager, TRUE).
```

Once this kind of procedure becomes part of the data staging process, the programs become more independent of the data. For example, in the old way, if the number of columns or data types changed in the Employee table, we would have to change every reference to it. In the metadata model, all we need to do is change the metadata, and the procedure buffers the data staging programs from this change.

In fact, you can store metadata from one of the open modeling tools on the server and use it as the source for your metadata tables.

Note that deciphering the database structure of many of these tools can require days of effort. Once you figure out the mapping, you have an off-the-shelf metadata management tool as well. This is exactly the kind of metadata exchange many of the vendors are trying to accomplish automatically.

Basic Procedures and Tables:

Procedures:
Create table
Create index
Drop table
Drop index
Copy table
Add user
Drop user
Run SQL Script
Run DBMS Table Loader

Metadata tables
Table_Defs
Column_Defs
Index_Defs
User_Security
Activity_Log

These tables will be very similar to existing data definition tables found in the DBMS. The major difference is that the contents of these tables are persistent. If you delete a table from the database, its definition is removed from the DBMS data dictionary. These metadata tables give the definition a permanent home so you can recreate it as needed. Look at your DBMS and front-end tool data dictionaries for examples of what kinds of information these tables should contain. Note that it is also possible to draw this information from the underlying relational tables of one of the open data modeling tools. In this case, you don't have to create the tables, just the SQL to extract the information you need. You may need multiple tables for several of the following tables to track repeating items like physical storage, constraints, keys, and so on.

Build versus Buy

Most of the services we describe in this section are available in the form of off-the-shelf tools specifically designed for data warehousing. They are constantly improving and are becoming less expensive as the data warehouse market matures. These tools can improve productivity immensely but don't expect to see the payback on day one. In our experience, these tools do not improve productivity *in the first round* of a data warehouse. In most cases, it takes as much time to set them up and learn how to use them as they save in the first round. After that, as new data areas are added and the initial database is improved, the productivity gains become clear (and significant). In a production data warehouse with a typical legacy environment, programmers can be as much as three times more productive with these tools. Or, if programming folks are all tied up on Year 2000 projects, a tool can help the warehouse team succeed with fewer programming resources.

 Data extraction tools are complex and expensive and often do not improve productivity in the first round of a data warehouse. But they become quite cost effective for the second and subsequent iterations of the extraction programming.

It may make sense to implement the first-round effort by hand, especially if you have time and resources for a separate prototype phase. This will give you the opportunity to understand the challenges and complexities of implementing a warehouse first hand. It will also help you define the services you need in your environment and better understand the strengths and weaknesses of the tool alternatives.

However, you should plan to invest time and money on data staging tools. If you do build the first round by hand, make sure you include time and resources to convert it. We wouldn't want to build a serious warehouse without a tool. Separate data staging tools may not be cost effective for a small warehouse effort. These projects should start with whatever tools come bundled with the DBMS and add on any missing functionality needed to meet their requirements. At the other end of the spectrum, very large volume data warehouse projects with lots of custom-coding requirements may have to go outside the tool too often to get the data loaded in a reasonable timeframe, but for most projects, it makes sense to get a tool.

 Graphical flat-file transformation systems running on destination data warehouse platforms such as NT and UNIX are cheaper and provide better productivity gains in the first round of a data warehouse. Such systems usually require that the data is extracted first from the mainframe and presented to the target system as a flat file.

That said, let us take a look at the data staging process.

Extract Services

Pulling the data from the source systems is probably the largest single effort in the data warehouse project, especially if the source systems are decades-old, mainframe-based, mystery-house–style systems.

 As a rule of thumb, about 60 percent of the warehouse development hours are spent on the extract process. If you are building a new extract system, count on at least two months elapsed time. Six work-months of total development time on each separate legacy source is a reasonable first estimate.

Most often, the challenge is determining what data to extract and what kinds of filters to apply. We all have stories about fields that have multiple uses, values that can't possibly exist, payments being made from accounts that haven't been created, and so on. From an architecture point of view, we need to understand the requirements of the extract process so we can determine what kinds of services will be needed.

Most extract processes generate temporary load files that become the input data for the next activity downstream. This is true even for the standalone extract tools, although their intermediate files may be buried inside their extract and transformation system. Most extracts we see are based on the host platform and are designed to get the data out of the source and into a simplified and easily accessible form. The following represent the major classes of requirements we've come across and, therefore, a potential list of what your code and tools will need to deal with.

These are the kinds of capabilities your extract system will need to provide, whether you code it all yourself or buy a $300,000 package.

Multiple Sources

It is a rare data warehouse, especially at the enterprise level, that does not pull data from multiple sources. In most cases, data must be pulled from multiple systems built with multiple data stores hosted on multiple platforms. Even the lucky folks who are extracting data from one of the integrated client/server packages may still need to deal with multiple platforms and versions (not to mention the thousands of source tables to choose from, possibly named in a foreign language).

Code Generation

In some cases, code generation means generating actual code that runs in the source system to create the extract files (like COBOL on the mainframe). Or, for many tools, this means internal code that is executed by the extract engine, which in turn will issue commands against the source system. In either case, some kind of executable code needs to be created to get the data out. These code-generation tools are somewhat limited in the source data formats they can work with and the platforms they can pull from. Make sure the tools you are interested in work with your key source systems, or that you are willing and able to generate the extract code needed to get the data into a neutral format (like a flat file).

Multiple Extract Types

Several common types of extracts serve different purposes in building the warehouse:

- **Incremental loads.** Most data warehouses use incremental loads. Even tables that involve snapshots, like a monthly account balance table, usually extract the balance only at the end of the current month. In many cases, the warehouse has grown too large to completely replace the central facts tables in a single load window.

  This is typically based on a transaction date or some kind of indicator flag in the source system. The date of the last load is a nice little piece of metadata to keep handy for the load process.

It is much more efficient to incrementally load only the records that have changed or been added since the previous load.

- **Transaction events.** The extract must be able to identify several different kinds of transactions because the transformation and load processes will have to treat them differently. Since the previous load occurred, we may want to see all new transactions, updated records, and potentially deleted records (since this may indicate a cancelled state). In some cases, the source system does not have a reliable date stamp, so we don't know if something occurred after the previous load. Then it becomes necessary to use some other technique to identify changed records. In some cases, the transaction log file can be pressed into service. It is possible, but it isn't pretty.

- **Full refresh.** Sometimes it is necessary to pull certain tables in their entirety rather than worry about figuring out what has changed. We've seen data sources where history could be changed by the transaction system without leaving any identifying marks. When the facts begin to drift like this, you may have to pull the whole table over on a regular basis. Obviously, there are size limits to this strategy, but even in the case of a large data source, it may make sense to resynchronize it once a quarter. Smaller dimension tables will probably be pulled in their entirety. In many cases, you need to identify changed records yourself as part of managing the dimensions, but that usually takes place in the staging area.

Replication

Replication has several meanings depending on the database vendor or product involved. In a warehouse context, it may be used to continuously update a table in the staging database during the day, so it is up-to-date and available to support the data staging process overnight. Replication is especially valuable in enterprise warehouse situations where multiple load processes depend on access to updated versions of the conformed dimension tables. Bulk replication can mirror or copy the dimensions to multiple data staging areas.

Compression/Decompression

Data compression can be an important capability in the extract stream if you plan to transfer large amounts of data over a significant distance. In this case, the communications link is often the bottleneck. If most of the elapsed time is spent transmitting the data, compression can reduce the transmission time by a third to a half or more, depending on the nature of the original data file.

Data Transformation Services

Once the data is extracted from the source system, a range of unnatural acts are performed on it to convert it into something presentable to the users and valuable to the business. In one recent example, we had to run a customer service data set through more than 20 transformation steps to get it into a usable state. This involved steps like remapping the old activity codes into the new codes, cleaning up some of the free-form entry fields, and filling in a dummy customer ID for pre-sales inquiries. The following list is representative of the kinds of transformations you will probably need to include in your warehouse. Many of these are illustrated with more detailed examples elsewhere in the book.

- **Integration.**   Integration involves generating surrogate keys, mapping keys from one system to another, and mapping codes into full descriptions. There is also an implied responsibility to maintain a master key lookup table behind this transformation.

- **Slowly changing dimension maintenance.**   Identifying changed values and creating surrogate keys is a tricky process, but it is not space-warp mathematics. If you buy a data staging tool, it should have the algorithms for managing slowly changing dimensions built in. If not, ask your vendor when they are going to provide this and hold them to it.

- **Referential integrity checking.**   Referential integrity (RI) means the data in one table matches the corresponding data in another table. If you have a sale in the fact table for product number 323442, you need to have a product in the Product dimension table with the same number or you won't know what you've sold. Indeed, if there is no record in the dimension table with that product number, a user can easily construct a query that will omit this sale without even realizing it. RI can be managed at the database level rather than as part of the transformation process, but it will reduce your flexibility and it doesn't fix the problem. It just won't let you load the data.

- **Denormalization and renormalization.**   Denormalizing a hierarchy of separate tables into a dimension is a standard warehouse transformation process. Some of the data staging tools offer a star schema feature that automatically performs this function. In addition, some denormalization takes place in the fact table process. For example, a financial schema may have a dimension that is the amount type, with the values Actual, Budget, or Forecast. Depending on the level of detail these records contain, it may make a lot of sense to pivot this column out into a single row with three columns of dollar amounts, one for each amount type.

  In other cases, a source comes in as a fully denormalized flat file, and you need to normalize parts of the record. Keeping data in monthly "buckets" is a common example from legacy systems. The source may keep a rolling 12 months of data in 12 columns, or buckets. In that case, we need to create a month column and convert the original record into 12 records, one for each of the 12 monthly buckets.

- **Cleansing, deduping, merge/purge.**   This is a big problem for many data warehouses, especially those concerned with external entities like customers, businesses, doctors, and patients. It is a complex process, but several vendors offer tools and services specifically for this problem. We discuss this process in more detail in Chapters 6 and 16.

- **Data type conversion.**   This involves lower-level transformations converting one data type or format to another. This ranges from converting IBM's mainframe character set EBCDIC to ASCII, to converting date, numeric, and character representations from one database to another.

- **Calculation, derivation, allocation.**   These are transformations to apply the business rules you identified during the requirements process. Make sure the tool you choose has a full set of functions available, including string manipulation, date and time arithmetic, conditional statements, and basic math. User extensibility for these functions is very valuable. One tool we worked with let us add a simple Nice_Name function that took a user-entered name field (first and last) and cleaned it up so it looked nice. *Nice* in this case means we capitalized the first and last name, changing the all-caps entries to title case. It was no big deal, but it made the reports much more readable and appealing to the user community.

- **Aggregation.** Aggregation can be handled in any part of the load process, depending on which resources are available at which stage. If we calculate aggregations as part of the extract or transformation process, it is possible to apply tools like Syncsort directly to the flat files. These utilities are optimized for sorting and summarizing and are extremely good at it. On the other hand, some database products provide the ability to create aggregates as part of the load process. In some cases, it is worth pulling data out of the database, running it through a utility, and loading the results back in. We've dedicated Chapter 14 to a detailed discussion of the creation and maintenance of aggregations.

- **Data content audit.** The transformation process should spin off check sums, row counts, and tests of reasonableness as a matter of course. These are then compared to figures generated by the source system and alerts generated when they don't match. We saw a problem that took days to resolve and required a significant reload effort when a new employee in Japan converted sales figures from yen to dollars before the data was entered into the transaction system. Unfortunately, the system also did the conversion, so the sales were about 130 times greater than normal. You can't check everything, but a few solid tests can save a lot of painful recovery time.

- **Data lineage audit.** The extract and transformation process can create logs of the specific runs that created specific dimension records and fact records. In Chapter 6 we described a technique for associating these data lineage audit results with each record in a fact table or a dimension table.

- **Tool- or analysis-specific transformation.** Some tools require specific data elements to be marked or updated as part of every load process. For example, a tool may rely on a "current date" flag in the calendar table. Data mining is particularly sensitive to the nature and content of the data. It is common to have to flag abnormal facts or changed status, or to normalize facts so they range between 0 and 1. This prepares the data for the statistical analysis tools that are the heart of data mining systems. Chapter 16 on data staging describes several of these transformations in more detail.

- **Null values.**   Nulls can be a problem because many legacy systems didn't have a means to represent nulls. To handle nulls, programmers chose a particularly unlikely value (like 9/9/99 for the date, or –1 for the product number). Since all the interaction with the data was moderated through a program, it was easy to apply the appropriate interpretation for the null. No one ever saw the unlikely value. Now, if you pull the data directly from the source, those null-substitute values look like legitimate values. Analyses will go wrong, and people will get hurt. You need to identify these null-substitute values and develop rules for handling them in the database. Again, Chapter 16 has more discussion on handling nulls.

- **Pre- and post-step exits.**   This actually applies across the data staging processes. Every step you define in the process should have a way to make an external function call as a part of the step, both before and after the step is run. This can be critical when you need to do something outside the capabilities of the tool or utility. For example, it may make sense to run the data set through a sort routine before the load process. Or, it may be necessary to call a proprietary function that scores a record based on a predetermined formula.

Data Loading Services

The capabilities you need during the data loading process are, in large part, a function of the target platform. Some of the capabilities you will likely need during the loading process are:

- **Support for multiple targets.**   The atomic data mart may be on one DBMS, and the business process data marts may be on another. Each target will probably have its own syntax and idiosyncrasies, and your load process should know about these differences and use or avoid them as appropriate.

- **Load optimization.**   Most DBMSs have a bulk loading capability that includes a range of features and can be scripted or invoked by your data staging tool through an API. Every database product has a set of techniques and tricks that optimize its load performance.

These include steps like avoiding logging during loads and taking advantage of bulk loader capabilities like creating indexes and aggregates during the load.

- **Entire load process support.**   The loading services also need to support requirements before and after the actual load, like dropping and re-creating indexes and physical partitioning of table and indexes.

Data Staging Job Control Services

The entire data staging job stream should be managed, to the extent possible, through a single, metadata-driven job control environment. The job control process also captures metadata regarding the progress and statistics of the daily job itself. The infrastructure to manage this can be as basic (and labor-intensive) as a set of SQL stored procedures, or the process could implement a tool designed to help manage and orchestrate multi-platform data extract and loading processes. In any case, you need to set up an environment for creating, managing, and monitoring the data staging job stream. It is essential to facilitate maintenance and to develop a cohesive set of extract statistics metadata.

The job control services needed include:

- **Job definition.**   The first step in creating an operations process is to have some way to define a series of steps as a job and to specify some relationship among jobs. This is where the flow of the data warehouse is written. In many cases, if the load of a given table fails, it will impact your ability to load tables that depend on it. For example, if the customer table is not properly updated, loading sales facts for new customers that did not make it into the customer table is risky. In some databases, it is impossible.

- **Job scheduling.**   At a minimum, the operations environment needs to provide standard capabilities, like time- and event-based scheduling. Warehouse loads are almost always based on some upstream system event, like the successful completion of the general ledger close or the successful application of sales adjustments to yesterday's sales figures. This includes the ability to monitor database flags, check for the existence of files, compare creation dates, and so on.

- **Monitoring.**   No self-respecting systems person would tolerate a black box scheduling system. The folks responsible for running the loads want to know as much as possible about what is going on. The system needs to provide information about what step the load is on, what time it started, how long it took, and so on. In the handcrafted warehouse, this can be accomplished by having each step write to a log file or table as described next. A store-bought system should provide a more visual means of keeping you informed about what is happening. If you are sharing computing resources, the more sophisticated systems will also tell you what else was running on the system during the data staging process, give you comparison reports with average times for each process, and so on.

- **Logging.**   This means collecting information about the entire load process, not just what is happening at the moment. Log information supports the recovery and restarting of a process in case of errors during the job execution. Logging to text files is the minimum acceptable level. We prefer a system that logs to a database. The structure makes it much easier to create graphs and reports. It also makes it possible to create time series studies to help analyze and optimize the load process.

- **Exception handling.**   Some systems have better data than others. At some point, the load process will hit a record with an incorrect data type, or it will fail a referential integrity check. The system needs a place to put rejected rows, a limit on how many errors are acceptable, and a way to exit gracefully. You also need a process to handle rows that are rejected during the load process. This can be as simple as manually inspecting and correcting the file, and rerunning the process. Where possible, data that was rejected due to basic data content errors, like a character in a numeric field, should be routed directly to the source system owner for correction. Try to get the data owners involved—they are usually eager to correct problems but have no way of knowing these problems exist. They'd rather hear about the problem from you than from the CEO.

  Historically, the primary focus in IS has been on getting transactions done as fast as possible. The after-the-fact analysis of this data has been a much lower priority (hence the frustration of many senior business executives with IS). It is as if your auto mechanic decided he was only going to work on the engine and accelerator. The brakes, headlights, and so on are your problem. Clearly, this front-end focus is a bit short-sighted. As data warehouses have proven their value, IS organizations are shifting toward a broader understanding of the importance of information and of their responsibility for providing more than just transaction processing. In the short term, this will mean a greater degree of cooperation on issues like data quality. In the long run, it means a more active role in providing data to the warehouse.

 This issue of handling rejected records is really just a symptom of a larger problem: determining who is responsible for providing business information, and holding him or her accountable for data quality.

- **Error handling.** You must plan for unrecoverable errors during the load because they will happen. Your system should anticipate this and provide crash recovery, stop, and restart capability. First, look for tools and design your extracts to minimize the impact of a crash. For example, a load process should commit relatively small sets of records at a time and keep track of what has been committed. The size of the set should be adjustable, since the transaction size has performance implications on different DBMSs. One of our customers based a central extract on technology that loaded a large table from one database to another over the network. Unfortunately, it wrapped the entire load into a single commit statement. This would work most days, but every so often, the network would take a hit in the middle of a load and the whole process would have to back out and be restarted. The reload would take most of the next working day.

- **Notification.** The importance of this capability correlates closely with the number of users and their reliance on the warehouse. If you don't have a lot of users and if they haven't grown to count on the warehouse being available when they need it, you might be able to wait until morning to find out the load failed and restart it.

    This is a luxury you will likely have to give up at some point. Types of notification range from sending a message to the system console, an e-mail, or a page (preferably taken from the on-duty list according to the current date and time).

 Somebody needs to know if anything happened during the load, especially if a response is critical to continuing the process.

BACK ROOM ASSET MANAGEMENT

The data warehouse is subject to the same risks as any other computer system. Disk drives will fail, power supplies will go out, and sprinkler systems will turn on accidentally. In addition to these risks, the warehouse also has a need to keep more data for longer periods of time than operational systems. The backup and recovery process is designed to allow the warehouse to get back to work after taking a hit. The archive and retrieval process is designed to allow business users access to older data that has been moved out of the main warehouse onto a less costly, usually lower-performing media, like tape or optical storage.

Backup and Recovery

Even if you have a fully redundant system with a universal power supply, fully RAIDed disks, parallel processors with failover, and the whole works, some system crisis will eventually visit. Even with perfect hardware, someone can always drop the wrong table (or database). At the risk of stating the obvious, it is better to prepare for this than to handle it on the fly. A full scale backup and recovery system needs to provide the following capabilities:

- **High performance.** The backup needs to fit into the allotted timeframe. This may include on-line backups that don't impact performance significantly.
- **Simple administration.** The administration interface should provide tools that easily allow you to identify objects to back up (including tables, table spaces, redo logs, etc.), create schedules, and maintain backup verification and logs for subsequent restore.

 The physical backup restores much faster than a logical backup because the pages can be read directly to the file system, indexes and all. It is usually easier to restore as well, as long as the target database has not changed in size or segmentation. This speed and ease of recovery can be critical during a crisis situation.

- **Automated, lights-out operations.** The backup and recovery facility must provide storage management services, automated scheduling, media and device handling, reporting, and notification.

The backup done for the warehouse is usually a physical backup. This is an image of the database at a certain point in time, including indexes and physical layout information.

Archive and Retrieval

Deciding what to move out of the warehouse is a cost-benefit analysis. It costs money to keep the data around—it takes up disk space and slows the load and query times. On the other hand, the business users just might need this data to do some critical historical analyses. The solution is not to throw the data away, but to put it some place that costs less, but is still accessible. Archiving is the data security blanket for the warehouse.

How long it takes the data to get stale depends on the industry, the business, and the particular data in question. In some cases, it is fairly obvious when older data has little value. For example, in an industry with rapid evolution of new products and competitors, history doesn't necessarily help you understand today or predict tomorrow. This is particularly true in high-tech where large successful companies can become has-beens almost overnight.

As Chapter 16 describes, the transformation and load steps are a natural place to save a snapshot of the data. We can identify a coherent point-in-time set of data that includes facts and their corresponding dimensions along with additional metadata about the database itself. With this information, we can recreate the environment so the data can be loaded. When it is time to archive from the warehouse, we don't have to redetermine what needs to be archived. We simply delete what we no longer need on-line.

 The assumption about archiving is that it takes place when it is time to move the data off the system. However, it actually makes more sense to archive during the load process.

Some archival systems can be configured to look like part of the database. If you query an archived table, it will automatically be loaded from tape or CD-ROM and included like a regular query object.

Archiving is typically a logical backup of a table or tables in the database. It includes the SQL that created the tables and the data itself. This gives the archive greater portability and flexibility. On the other hand, it is slower because the indexes will need to be rebuilt.

Backup and Archive Planning

The first level of preparation is creating and implementing a backup plan. Start by listing all the tables by category in the warehouse and the staging area. Then, go through and estimate the effort and time it would take to re-create these tables. This exercise often provides enough motivation to start a backup program immediately. Frequently, this process uncovers tables that contain history that essentially could not be re-created. If you crash, you would need to start collecting those sources over again from scratch.

- **Determine an appropriate backup process.** Make a list of what gets backed up, how often, and how long it will take. Work with professionals on this. Backup and recovery is a detail-driven process.
- **Implement the process.** The operations folks who manage the rest of the servers will likely do this.
- **Practice.** Go through the drill of recovering the database at least once. Take extensive notes about what information you need to have and where to find it. Database recovery is like public speaking— most people hate it, but if you have to do it, you will be able to handle the real thing much better if you practice it first.

Extract and Load Security Issues

Security is not as big an issue in the back room as it is in the front room. This is mainly because the back room is an application development activity, and standard system security rules usually suffice. One issue to be careful of is the bulk data movement process. If you are moving data across the network, even if it is within the company firewall, it pays to be careful. Make sure you use a file transfer utility that uses a secure transfer protocol.

Another back room security issue we see has to do with who has administrator access to the production warehouse server and software. We've seen situations where no one on the team had security privileges; in other cases, eveyone had access to everything. Obviously, many members of the team should have privileged access to the development environment, but the production warehouse should be fairly strictly controlled. On the other hand, someone from the warehouse team needs to be able to reset the warehouse machine if something goes wrong. We were recently involved with a project that had no root privileges on the warehouse machine. One day, when the DBAs were not available, the network took a hit and the warehouse connectivity software got confused. The warehouse team was paralyzed, and the users were not happy. Finally, the warehouse team ended up running around to individual users and installing a different connectivity package. In general, it is worth figuring out how to give system administrator privileges to someone on the warehouse team. If the warehouse server is dedicated to the warehouse, it should be pretty straightforward.

Finally, in Chapter 12 we urge you to guard your backup media. The backup media should have as much security surrounding them as the on-line systems.

Future Staging Services

Several major forces are driving the rapid evolution of data warehouse services. The underlying megatrend is that the client/server world is developing real, robust application infrastructures that will become relatively interchangeable. Much of this development is object-based and is driven by a few major efforts like the Object Management Group's Common Object Request Broker Architecture (CORBA) and Microsoft's Distributed Common Object Model (DCOM). In the next few years, these efforts will add value to the warehouse in the following ways.

Transaction Processing Support

Transactional data center operations are supported by a robust, full-featured monitoring system (for scheduling and monitoring jobs). Although most of these capabilities exist in the data warehouse's computing environment, they are not integrated or accessible. All too often, we end up cobbling together a set of standalone utilities to get the job done. Although many data staging tools provide some form of job control, it is usually proprietary. When we have to step outside the tool to get something accomplished, we must use some other means to manage the process.

Active Source System Participation

Although not really a service, one trend that will have a major impact on the warehouse is the shift in ownership of data provision back to the source systems. Several factors, including the growth of data warehouses and the proliferation of ERP systems, are causing IS to realize that the source system must be responsible for providing data to other systems and for coordinating the impact of changes to the source systems. Companies that are reaching this conclusion come to it through a succession of events. First, the data warehouse requests access to the source system. This access is reluctantly granted, with strict rules about the nature of the access (only between 1:30 A.M. and 3:00 A.M.). The source system owner grants this access with the understanding that they would benefit by not having to create as many reports as before. Now the users will create reports for themselves!

Then a few more groups require access, and then a few more, until it begins to overwhelm the nightly maintenance cycle. At this point, the source system owner's inclination will be to cut off all access—clearly not a viable option. IS management (and perhaps business management) will then be called in to solve the problem.

 We have come to recognize that the source systems have traded the burden of writing thousands of individual reports for the responsibility of providing a robust feeding mechanism for the systems that have taken over the reporting task.

Data Push

Push technology is a likely direction source system owners will take as they begin to fully understand their role in providing business information to the company. One approach to managing data push is to use the publish and subscribe paradigm. In this case, when the customer table is ready, it is automatically made available (published) to all systems that have registered an interest in it (subscribed). The publish and subscribe analogy was popularized by Digital Equipment Corporation and Apple Computer in the 1980s and early 1990s with their VITAL architecture effort. Another approach to distributing source system data uses a data bus concept (not to be confused with the Data Warehouse Bus we discuss throughout this book). In this case, systems all share a communications channel, like the system bus on a computer. All the peripherals plug into the bus and use its command set and standards to exchange information with each other as needed. In this scenario, the warehouse could request a data set directly from the source system along with specifications for business rules, formats, delivery times, and dependencies.

Object-Oriented Systems

Objects are gradually working their way into the systems development mainstream. Objects can be made available to the warehouse in several ways. First, the warehouse can ask for an object like the customer table through an object request broker. It is the object broker's job to figure out where the data object is, submit the request, and return the results. These data objects are designed to insulate the destination from changes in the source. For example, intelligence about how the data should be structured and filtered can be built into a special method in the object called warehouse_extract. In fact, the parameters for the method could be pulled from the metadata, and that big investment in metadata will finally pay off.

SUMMARY

Data staging is a conceptually straightforward process, even if the details and complexities of building a data staging system can be overwhelming. We return to this topic in Chapter 16 for a step-by-step description of the data staging process. The list of data staging services in this chapter should be enough to get you started on your own list. In the next chapter, let us move out to the front room and take a look at the major data stores and services employed there.

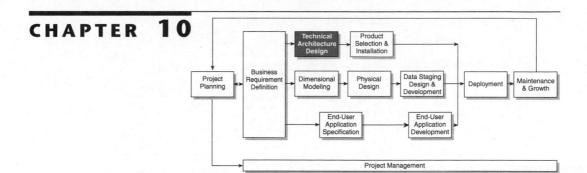

CHAPTER **10**

Architecture for the Front Room

The front room is the public face of the warehouse. It's what the business users see and work with day-to-day. In fact, for most folks, the user interface is the data warehouse. They don't know (or care) about all the time, energy, and resources behind it—they just want answers. Unfortunately, the data they want to access is complex. The dimensional model helps reduce the complexity, but businesses are rife with rules and exceptions that must be included in the warehouse so we can analyze and understand them. This complexity only gets worse when we reach the implementation phase and add more elements to the design to achieve better performance (like aggregate tables).

The primary goal of the warehouse should be to make information as accessible as possible—to help people get the information they need. To accomplish this, we need to build a layer between the users and the information that will hide some of the complexities and help them find what they are looking for. That is the primary purpose of the data access services layer. Figure 10.1 shows the major stores and services to be found in the front room.

This chapter is laid out much like Chapter 9 was. First, we review the data stores that support the front room. Next, we discuss the types

373

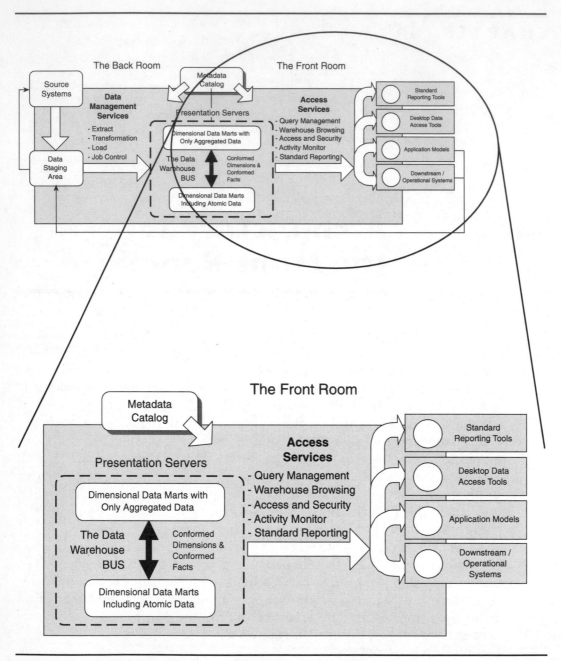

FIGURE 10.1   Front room technical architecture.

of services that are needed in the front room to deliver information to the end users and manage the environment. We describe the general characteristics of data access tools, followed by a discussion about data mining. Finally, we take a moment to discuss the impact of the Internet on the front room architecture.

This chapter is required reading for the technical architects and end-user application developers. The other project team members may find this material interesting at a high level when evaluating products in the data access marketplace. As usual, the project manager needs to spend some time reviewing this chapter to be able to interact effectively with tool vendors and manage expectations of the business community.

FRONT ROOM DATA STORES

Once the answer set to a specific data request leaves the presentation server, it usually ends up on the user's desktop. Alternatively, the result set can be fed into a local data mart or a special-purpose downstream system. This section looks at the architecture issues around front-end tools and other data stores downstream from the warehouse.

Access Tool Data Stores

As data moves into the front room and closer to the user, it becomes more diffused. Users can generate hundreds of ad hoc queries and reports in a day. These are typically centered on a specific question, investigation of an anomaly, or tracking the impact of a program or event. Most individual queries yield result sets with less than 10,000 rows—a large percentage have less than 1,000 rows. These result sets are stored in the data access tool, at least temporarily. Much of the time, the results are actually transferred into a spreadsheet and analyzed further.

Some data access tools work with their own intermediate application server. In some cases, this server provides an additional data store to cache the results of user queries and standard reports. This cache provides much faster response time when it receives a request for a previously retrieved result set.

Standard Reporting Data Stores

As more transaction systems migrate to client/server packages, the tasks performed by the old mainframe reporting systems are being left undone or are being done poorly. As a result, client/server–based standard reporting environments are beginning to pop up in the marketplace. These applications usually take advantage of the data warehouse as a primary data source. They may use multiple data stores, including a separate reporting database that draws from the warehouse and the operational systems. They may also have a report library or cache of some sort that holds a preexecuted set of reports to provide lightning-fast response time.

Personal Data Marts

The idea of a personal data mart seems like a whole new market if you listen to vendors who have recently released tools positioned specifically for this purpose. Actually, the idea is as old as the personal computer and dBase. People have been downloading data into dBase, Access, FoxPro, and even Excel for years. What is new is that industrial-strength database tools have made it to the desktop. The merchant database vendors all have desktop versions that are essentially full-strength, no-compromise relational databases. There are also new products on the market that take advantage of data compression and indexing techniques to give amazing capacity and performance on a desktop computer.

 Be careful with personal data marts. The temptation to solve a problem by throwing data at it is strong, and it is made more seductive by the ease with which we can use new local database tools. But we are essentially talking about the difference between a prototype and a production system. It's easy to populate the database the first time, but you need to be able to keep it updated, in synch, and secure. Otherwise, you'll end up with another stovepipe data mart and a maintenance headache you didn't plan for.

Personal data marts are going to spread. You should plan for this component and make it easy to take advantage of standard warehouse tools and processes (like metadata, job scheduling, event notification, etc.). Personal data marts may require a replication framework to ensure they are always in synch with the data warehouse.

The personal data mart is also the home turf of many of the MOLAP products. These products were born in the PC/NT environment and were created to target individual power users or departments with specific reporting needs, like the financial reporting group. They will continue to play an important role in this personal segment of the marketplace.

Disposable Data Marts

The disposable data mart is a set of data created to support a specific short-lived business situation. It is similar to the personal data mart, but it is intended to have a limited life span. For example, a company may be launching a significant promotion or new product or service (e.g., acquisition analysis or product recall) and want to set up a special launch control room.

Theoretically, the business needs of the disposable data mart can be met from the rest of the data warehouse. In practice, it may make sense to create a separate data mart. There may be temporary external data sources to feed in or internal sources that are not yet in the warehouse. There may be security reasons for creating a separate environment, as when a company is evaluating a merger or acquisition candidate. The disposable data mart also allows the data to be designed specifically for the event, applying business rules and filters to create a simple sandbox for the analysts to play in.

Application Models

Data mining is the primary example of an application model. Data mining is a confusing area mainly because it isn't one entity. It's a collection of powerful analysis techniques for making sense out of very large data sets. From a data store point of view, each of these analytical processes usually sit on a separate machine (or at least a separate process) and works with its own data drawn from the data warehouse. Often, it makes sense to feed the results of a data mining process back into the warehouse to use as an attribute in one of the dimensions. Credit rating and churn scores are good examples of data mining output that would be valuable in the context of the rest of the data in the warehouse. We'll return to data mining later in this chapter.

Downstream Systems

As the data warehouse becomes the authoritative data source for analysis and reporting, other systems are drawn to it as the data source of choice. The basic purpose of these systems is still reporting, but they tend to fall closer to the operational edge of the spectrum.

While these systems are typically transaction oriented, they gain significant value by including some of the history in the warehouse. Good examples are budgeting systems that pull some of their input from the warehouse (e.g., monthly average phone charges by office last year) and forecasting systems that draw on as many years of history as possible and whatever causal data might be available. Another interesting application that has been growing in popularity is the use of warehouse data to support customer interactions. Many sales force automation systems are pulling in as much information as they can about a company's relationship with its customers. The same is true on the customer support side. When the phone rings in the call center, it can be extremely helpful to have access to the customer's order history, aligned with payments, credits, and open orders—all on the same screen. These applications draw from data in the data warehouse, but are enabled in separate environments.

FRONT ROOM SERVICES FOR DATA ACCESS

There isn't much in the way of standalone data access services in most data warehouses today. Most of what exists is hard-wired into the front-end tools—the primary data stores and service providers of the front room. Two major forces are dragging the data access services out of the front-end tools and moving it into the applications layer. First, the buying power of the data warehouse market is putting pressure on database vendors to improve their products specifically for data warehousing. Second, the demand for Web-based tools is causing tool vendors to slim down their desktop clients and move some of the shared functionality to an application server. In the best of all possible data warehouses, the data access services would be independent of specific tools, available to all, and add as much value to the data access process as the data management services do in the back room.

Data access services cover five major types of activities in the data warehouse: warehouse or metadata browsing; access and security; activity monitoring; query management; and standard reporting. As you gather architectural requirements, keep an eye out for the following kinds of functionality that would reside in the data access services layer.

Warehouse Browsing

Warehouse browsing takes advantage of the metadata catalog to support the users in their efforts to find and access the information they need. Ideally, a user who needs business information should be able to start with some type of browsing tool and peruse the data warehouse to look for the appropriate subject area.

 The warehouse browser should be dynamically linked to the metadata catalog to display currently available subject areas and the data elements within those subjects. It should be able to pull in the definitions and derivations of the various data elements and show a set of standard reports that include those elements. Once the user finds the item of interest, the browser should provide a link to the appropriate resource: a canned report, a tool, or a report scheduler.

This sounds like a lot of work, but the payback is a self-sufficient user community. We've seen home-grown systems that provide much of this functionality. Historically, these browsers were built on the Web or use tools like Visual Basic, Microsoft Access, and even desktop help systems. Moving forward, companies that are rolling their own are mostly using Web-based tools to provide some portion of this service.

Providing warehouse browsing services has not been the main focus of most data warehouses. In general, the front-end tool has been the beginning and end of the navigation process. A user opens the tool, and whatever they see is what they can get to. Fortunately, front ends have grown more sophisticated and now use metadata to define subsets of the database to simplify the user's view. They also provide ways to hook into the descriptive metadata to provide column names and comments.

Recently, several tools specifically designed to provide this kind of browsing capability have come on the market. One interesting twist is that a data modeling tool company has released a warehouse metadata browsing tool. This makes perfect sense in that the data modeling tool is one of the most likely places to capture the descriptive metadata about the model.

Access and Security Services

Access and security services facilitate a user's connection to the database. This can be a major design and management challenge. We've dedicated Chapter 12 to a graduate-level discussion of access and security. Our goal in this section is merely to present an overview of how access and security fit into the architecture.

Access and security rely on authorization and authentication services where the user is identified and access rights are determined or access is refused. For our purposes, *authentication* means some method of verifying that you are who you say you are. There are several levels of authentication, and how far you go depends on how sensitive the data is. A simple, constant password is the first level, followed by a system-enforced password pattern and periodically required changes. Beyond the password, it is also possible to require some physical evidence of identity, like a magnetic card. There are hardware- and network-based schemes that work from a preassigned IP address, particularly on dial-in connections. Authentication is really one of those infrastructure services that the warehouse should be able to count on.

On the database side, we strongly encourage assignment of a unique ID to each user. Although it means more work maintaining IDs, it helps in tracking warehouse usage and in identifying individuals who need help.

Once we've identified someone to our satisfaction, we need to determine what they are authorized to see. Some of this depends on the corporate culture. In some companies, management wants people to see only a limited range of information. For example, regional managers can only see sales and expense information for their regions. We believe the value of a data warehouse is correlated with the richness and breadth of the data sources provided. Therefore, we encourage our clients to make the warehouse as broadly available as possible.

Authorization is a much more complex problem in the warehouse than authentication, because limiting access can have significant maintenance and computational overhead, especially in a relational environment.

Activity Monitoring Services

Activity monitoring involves capturing information about the use of the data warehouse. There are several excellent reasons to include resources in your project plan to create an activity monitoring capability centered around four areas: performance, user support, marketing, and planning.

- **Performance.** Gather information about usage, and apply that information to tune the warehouse more effectively. The DBA can use the data to see which tables and columns are most often joined, selected, aggregated, and filtered. In many cases, this can lead to changes in the aggregate tables, the indexes, and fundamental changes in the schema design.
- **User support.** The data warehouse team should monitor newly trained users to ensure they have successful experiences with the data warehouse in the weeks following training. Also, the team should be in the habit of monitoring query text occasionally throughout the day. This will help the team understand what users are doing, and it can also help them intervene to assist users in constructing more efficient queries.
- **Marketing.** Publish simple usage statistics to inform management of how their investment is being used. A nice growth curve is a wonderful marketing tool, and a flat or decreasing curve might be motivating for the warehouse team.
- **Planning.** Monitor usage growth, average query time, concurrent user counts, database sizes, and load times to quantify the need and timing for capacity increases. This information also could support a mainframe-style charge-back system, if necessary.

Like many of the services we've discussed, you can build a rudimentary version of an activity monitor yourself or buy a more full-featured package. Chapter 15, which focuses on physical design, has additional information on activity monitoring. There are packages on the market specifically designed to monitor data warehouse user activity. Many of the query management tools also offer some level of query monitoring as a natural byproduct of managing the query process. Some of the front-end tools offer rudimentary activity monitoring support as well.

Query Management Services

Query management services are the set of capabilities that manage the exchange between the query formulation, the execution of the query on the database, and the return of the result set to the desktop. These services arguably have the broadest impact on user interactions with the database. The following paragraphs describe the major query management services you will likely want to include in your architecture. Each of the items in the list has a corresponding business requirement. For example, many of the query formulation services are driven by a need to create certain kinds of reports that are difficult for simple SQL generators to do. We'll explore some of these capabilities further in the tool selection section in Chapter 13. Note that many of these services are metadata driven.

- **Content simplification.** These techniques attempt to shield the user from the complexities of the data and the query language before any specific queries are formulated. This includes limiting the user's view to subsets of the tables and columns, predefined join rules (including columns, types, and path preferences), and standard filters.

  Content simplification metadata is usually specific to the front-end tool rather than a generally available service. The simplification rules are usually hidden in the front-end tool's metadata repository.

 Content simplification metadata is usually created by the tool administrator during the tool implementation. Today, there are no standards at all for this type of information.

- **Query reformulation.** As we saw in Chapter 6, query formulation can be extremely complex if you want to solve real-world business problems. Tool developers have been struggling with this problem for decades, and have come up with a range of solutions, with varying degrees of success. The basic problem is that most interesting business questions require a lot of data manipulation. Even simple-sounding questions like "How much did we grow last year" or "Which accounts grew by more than 100 percent?" can be a challenge to the tool. The query reformulation service needs to parse an incoming query and figure out how it can best be resolved. Query retargeting, as described in the next section, is the simplest form of reformulation. Beyond that, a query reformulation service should be able to generate complex SQL, including subqueries and unions. Many of these queries require multipass SQL, where the results of the first query are part of the formulation of the second query. Since data access tools provide most of the original query formulation capabilities, we discuss this further in the data access tools section later in this chapter.

- **Query retargeting and multipass SQL.**   The query retargeting service parses the incoming query, looks up the elements in the metadata to see where they actually exist, and then redirects the query or its components as appropriate. This includes simple redirects, heterogeneous joins, and set functions such as union and minus. This simple-sounding function is actually what makes it possible to host separate fact tables on separate hardware platforms. It allows us to query data from two fact tables, like manufacturing costs and customer sales, on two different servers, and seamlessly integrate the results into a customer contribution report.

- **Aggregate awareness.**   Aggregate awareness is a special case of query retargeting where the service recognizes that a query can be satisfied by an available aggregate table rather than summing up detail records on the fly. For example, if someone asks for sales by month from the daily table, the service would reformulate the query to run against the monthly fact table. The user gets better performance and doesn't need to know there are additional fact tables out there.

  The aggregate navigator is the component that provides this aggregate awareness. In the same way that indexes are automatically chosen by the database software, the aggregate navigator facility automatically chooses aggregates. The aggregate navigator sits above the DBMS and intercepts the SQL sent by the requesting client, as illustrated in Figure 10.2. The best aggregate navigators are independent of the end user tools and provide the aggregate navigation benefit for all clients sending SQL to the DBMS. An aggregate navigator that is embedded in the end user tool is isolated to that specific tool and creates a problem for the DBA who must support multiple tools in a complex environment.

  A good aggregate navigator maintains statistics on all incoming SQL and not only reports on the usage levels of existing aggregates but suggests additional aggregates that should be built by the DBA.

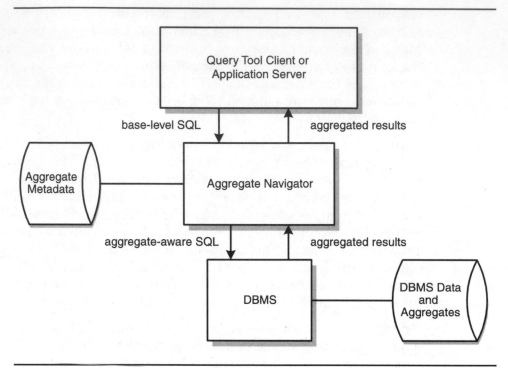

FIGURE 10.2   The aggregate navigator.

- **Date awareness.**   The date awareness service allows the user to ask for items like current year-to-date and prior year-to-date sales without having to figure out the specific date ranges. This usually involves maintaining attributes in the Periods dimension table to identify the appropriate dates.

- **Query governing.**   Unfortunately, it's relatively easy to create a query that can bring the data warehouse to its knees, especially a large database. Almost every warehouse has a list of queries from hell. These are usually poorly formed and often incorrect queries that lead to a nested loop of full table scans on the largest table in the database. Obviously, you'd like to stop these before they happen. After good design and good training, the next line of defense against these runaway queries is a query governing service.

    Query governing is still in its nascent stages. With many tools, you can place a simple limit on the number of minutes a query can run or the number of rows it can return. The problem with these limits is that they are imposed after the fact. If you let a query run for an hour before you kill it, an hour of processing time is lost. Besides, the user who submitted it probably suspects it would have finished in the next minute or two if you hadn't killed it. To govern queries effectively, the service needs to be able to estimate the effort of executing a query before it is actually run. This can be accomplished in some cases by getting the query plan from the database optimizer and using its estimate. A sophisticated query manager could also keep records of similar queries and use previous performance as an indicator of cost. It can then check to see if the user has permission to run such a long query, ask if the user wants to schedule it for later execution, or just tell the user to reformulate it.

Query Service Locations

There are three major options for where query services can be located in the architecture: on the desktop, on an application server, or in the database. Today, most of these services are delivered as part of the front-end toolset and reside on the desktop. In fact, all of the major front-end tool providers have had to develop many of these services over the years. The problem is that everything they've developed is locked inside their tools. The tools have become large and costly, and other tools are unable to take advantage of the query management infrastructure already in place for the first tool. This is a good strategy from the vendor's point of view because it locks their customers into a major dollar and time investment. However, it's not so good for the business when multiple tools are needed or demanded to meet multiple business requirements.

Some front-end tool vendors have created their own three-tier architecture and located many of these services on an application server between the desktop front-end and the database. Architecturally, this works well because it allows any client to take advantage of a shared resource. The client can concentrate on presenting the query formulation and report creation environment and need not carry the additional burden of query management. It also allows the query to be directed to multiple databases, potentially in multiple database platforms on multiple systems. The application server can own the task of combining the results sets as appropriate. Unfortunately, few standards for these application servers exist yet, so they are relatively proprietary.

There are also stand-alone middleware products that provide many of the data access services described above. Unfortunately, the major alternatives in this group are also proprietary, limited to a specific hardware or database platform.

Database vendors are moving to include some of these services in the core database engine. This is significantly better than having them trapped in the front end tool because all front end tools can then take advantage of the service. On the other hand, it is a little more limiting than the application-server approach because it makes it difficult to support cross-machine or cross-database awareness.

As you gain experience with these services, you'll see how many of them would be much more valuable if they were based either in a common application layer or in the database platform itself rather than in the desktop tool. We encourage you to explore the marketplace and communicate your requirements for these kinds of services to your tool and database vendors.

Standard Reporting Services

Standard reporting provides the ability to create production style fixed-format reports that have limited user interaction, a broad audience, and regular execution schedules. The application templates described in Chapter 17 are essentially a casual kind of standard report. At the formal end of the spectrum, large standard reporting systems tend to surface when the ERP system cannot handle the workload of operational transactions and reporting. Be careful not to take this on as a side effort of the data warehouse. Full-scale standard reporting is a big job that involves its own set of requirements and services. In this case, there should be a standard reporting project solely responsible for managing this effort.

Of course, the data warehouse needs to support standard reports regardless of whether there is a large-scale standard reporting environment. In fact, most of the query activity on many warehouses today comes from what could be considered standard reporting. In some ways, this idea of running production reports in an end user environment seems inappropriate, but it is actually a natural evolution. Often, analyses that are developed in an ad hoc fashion become standard reports. The ability to put these into a managed reporting environment is an obvious requirement. They will need to be run on a regular basis and made available to a broad base of consumers either on a push or pull basis (e.g., e-mail or Web posting). Most of the front-end tool developers include some form of this reporting capability in their products. Requirements for standard reporting tools include:

- **Report development environment.** This should include most of the ad hoc tool functionality and usability.
- **Report execution server.** The report execution server offloads running the reports and stages them for delivery, either as finished reports in a file system or in a custom report cache.
- **Parameter- or variable-driven capabilities.** For example, you can change the Region name in one parameter and have an entire set of reports run based on that new parameter value.
- **Time- and event-based scheduling of report execution.** A report can be scheduled to run at a particular time of day or after a value in some database table has been updated.
- **Iterative execution.** For example, provide a list of regions and create the same report for each region. Each report could then be a separate file e-mailed to each regional manager. This is similar to the concept of a report section or page break, where every time a new value of a given column is encountered, the report starts over on a new page with new subtotals, except it generates separate files.
- **Flexible report definitions.** These should include compound document layout (graphs and tables on the same page) and full pivot capabilities for tables.
- **Flexible report delivery:**
  - Via multiple delivery methods (e-mail, Web, network directory, desktop directory and automatic fax).
  - In the form of multiple result types (data access tool file, database table, spreadsheet).
- **User accessible publish and subscribe.** Users should be able to make reports they've created available to their departments or to the whole company. Likewise, they should be able to subscribe to reports others have made and receive copies or notification whenever the report is refreshed or improved.
- **Report linking.** This is a simple method for providing drill-down. If you have pre-run reports for all the departments in a division, you

should be able to click on a department name in the division summary report and have the department detail report show up.

- **Report library with browsing capability.**   This is a kind of metadata reference that describes each report in the library, when it was run, and what its content is. A user interface is provided that allows the user to search the library using different criteria.

- **Mass distribution.**   Simple, cheap access tools for mass distribution (Web-based).

- **Report environment administration tools.**   The administrator should be able to schedule, monitor, and troubleshoot report problems from the administrator's module. This also includes the ability to monitor usage and weed out unused reports.

Future Access Services

It's worth taking a few moments to speculate on the direction of access services so we can anticipate where future services might fit into our architecture.

- **Authentication and authorization.**   Logging on to the network once will be enough to identify you to any system you want to work with. If you need to go into the financial system to check on an order status or go to the data warehouse to see a customer's entire history, one logon should give you access to both. Beyond that, a common security mechanism will tell the warehouse which security groups you belong to and which permissions you have. In Chapter 12 we describe the state of the market for "directory servers" that will fulfill this single logon function.

- **Push toward centralized services.**   Data access services soon will migrate either to the application server or back to the database. Three forces are driving this change. The first is the leverage the warehouse team gets by implementing one set of access services (and associated metadata) and making it available to a range of front-end tools. The second is the push that tools are getting from the Web. To function on the Web, vendors have to slim down the desktop footprint. One obvious way to do this is to move the access services to an application server. The third is the competition among database vendors to grab a piece of the data warehouse market. Once one vendor implements a service like aggregate awareness, the rest have to follow.

- **Vendor consolidation.**   There are too many front-end tool vendors for the market to support in the long run. The Web push will cause some of them to slip. Once a few clear leaders emerge, the rest will begin falling quickly.

 The implication for architecture is that unless you get lucky and pick a winner, you should expect a tool migration within three years.

- **Web-based customer access.**   Another implication of Web access to the warehouse is that businesses might view the Web as a means of providing customers with direct access to their information, similar to the lookup services provided by express package delivery companies today. For example, a credit card company might provide significant value to its corporate customers by allowing them to analyze their employees' spending patterns directly, without having to stage the data in-house. Or, any manufacturer or service provider might be able to provide customers with monthly summaries of their purchases, sliced in various interesting ways. The security, maintenance, and infrastructure issues are significant, but the business value might be significant as well.

Desktop Services

Only a few services actually live on the desktop, but they are arguably the most important services in the warehouse. These services are found in the front-end tools that provide users with access to the data in the warehouse. Much of the quality of the user's overall experience with the warehouse will be determined by how well these tools meet their needs. To them, the rest of the warehouse is plumbing—they just want it to work (and things get messy if it doesn't). This section first looks at the different types of users and kinds of information needs that typically exist in a business. Next, it reviews the categories of tools available to meet those needs. Then, it examines each category for the specific capabilities a tool in that category should provide. Your architecture will draw from this list of capabilities and augment it with needs that are specific to your business. This list of capabilities will then be the primary guide for the front-end tool technology evaluation described in Chapter 13.

Multiple Consumer Types

Folks in the IS organization often forget this, but people vary significantly in terms of the depth and quality of their technological capabilities. We often have been surprised by how difficult it is for many people in the business community to understand what we thought was simple technology. The warehouse needs to support a range of technical skill levels and degrees of analytical sophistication. Figure 10.3 shows where these users fall across a technical skill level spectrum and what kinds of tools are appropriate to support their needs.

This profile is changing as computers become more prevalent in the education process and the computer literate generation grows up. But it's a slow change coming.

Usage Area	User Type			
	Paper User	*Push-Button*	*Simple Ad Hoc*	*Power User*
General computer use	None	E-mail, some word processing	Word processing, spreadsheets, presentations	Macros, utilities, Web publishing
Data warehouse	Rely on others to navigate	Standard reports, default parameters, EIS	Create simple queries, modify existing queries, browse/change parameters, navigate hierarchies	Build full queries from scratch, direct database access

FIGURE 10.3   Technology styles.

Multiple Information Needs

Figure 10.4 lists four major categories of information needs and several corresponding attributes for each need. Although we've listed user roles in each category, it's common for the same person to have needs across several categories. Although individuals play one role most of the time, roles do change from moment to moment, especially in today's business environment. Downsizing, increased competition, and empowerment mean that managers may have to know the details of a specific order or

Information Needs Category	User Roles	Data Access Category	Common Tools	Audience Size
High level monitoring—key metrics, flags	Senior management	Push-button—"dash board"	EIS-style interface; some query tool environments can support this, as well as MS Access or Visual Basic	Small
Business tracking—markets, products, customers, etc. ; drill down to detail	Midmanagement, field sales, marketing managers, business managers, customer service reps, etc.	Standard Reports—parameter driven	Reporting tools; OLAP-style front end tools with built-in report scheduling; managed query environments	Large
Investigating—exceptions; new problems or opportunities; business case development	Same as above plus business analysts	Ad hoc analysis	OLAP-style tools; managed query environments; high-end analysis tools	Medium
Complex analysis—composite querying, statistical analysis, model development	Business analysts and analytical experts	Data mining—advanced analysis	High-end analysis tools; statistical tools; data mining tools	Small

FIGURE 10.4   Information needs and attributes.

that someone on the production line may need to know total revenues (and profits) by customer in order to allocate a scarce product. Note that the size of the audience isn't necessarily directly correlated with its potential impact on the business or its importance to the warehouse.

Data Access Tool Capabilities

It's possible to avoid much of the frustration of the front end tool selection process if you do your architecture homework now. The basic steps are:

- Understand who your primary consumers are and the information needs you are trying to meet. Study the requirements documents, the user interview notes, the dimensional model, and the application specs. We are sorry to be so repetitive, but this is important.
- Identify the capabilities required to meet those needs. List these in detail as you spot them during the requirements gathering phase. Collect a set of representative examples you can use for testing later.

Four main data access categories are identified in Figure 10.4: push-button, standard reports, ad hoc, and data mining. Push button applications generally provide a push-button interface to a limited set of key reports, targeted at a specific user community. Standard reports are the approved, official view of information. They are typically fixed-format, regularly scheduled reports that are delivered to a broad set of users. Ad hoc tools provide users with the ability to create their own reports from scratch. Data mining tools provide complex statistical analysis routines that can be applied to data from the warehouse. Each of these categories provides certain capabilities that meet specific business requirements. Some of the more common capabilities are described next.

Push-Button Access

The term *executive information system* (EIS) has fallen out of favor in recent years, most likely because the data warehouse has effectively replaced the concept of an EIS. Early EIS systems had to do all the cleaning and integration the warehouse does but without the tool support. Also, the systems could not contain much data, so true analysis was difficult. It was often possible to identify a potential problem, but not the explanation. Nevertheless, the need for an executive front-end still exists. In many companies, push-button access can be supplied through the standard reporting system. In others, some requirements call for a separate delivery system that is extremely graphical in nature and simple to navigate. It includes the following kinds of functionality:

- Easy generation of sophisticated, interactive, engaging front-end screens.
- Simple navigation controls.
- Automatic replacement or on-the-fly creation of underlying report contents.
- User interface controls for conceptual representations like stoplights (high, medium, low), gauges, and sophisticated charts.
- Geographical charts with links to underlying reports.
- "Alerters," or controls that monitor specified values, ranges, or differences and notify the user when they exceed target levels. See Norton Utilities for a good example of this capability.
- Ability to define and interact with multiple simultaneous connections to multiple data sources.

Over time, we expect these capabilities to be provided as a matter of course on the Web. However, the category may continue to exist because the audience (senior executives) often has a distinct set of requirements.

The EIS concept has been continually reborn. Robert Kaplan and David Norton described an EIS-like concept in their book, *The Balanced Scorecard: Translating Strategy into Action* (Harvard Business School Press 1996). In the February 17, 1997 issue of *Fortune,* Joel Kurtzman wrote, "In essence, the corporate scorecard is a sophisticated business model that helps a company understand what's really driving its success. It acts a bit like the control panel on a spaceship—the business equivalent of a flight speedometer, odometer, and temperature gauge all rolled into one." Whatever form the EIS takes, it is likely to be a major consumer of data from the warehouse.

Standard Reports

Since the bulk of the standard reporting environment is server based, we covered the major capabilities these systems need in the standard reporting services section. On the front end, standard reports need to provide the same formatting capabilities and user interface controls as the push-button access systems we just described. In many cases, the ad hoc tool providers have incorporated a subset of these capabilities into their tools. Check the functionality these vendors provide against your list of requirements. You may find that you don't need a full-blown reporting environment.

Ad Hoc

Ad hoc query tools are the mainstays of data access in the warehouse. These tools support direct, interactive exploration of the data. It's fairly easy to build a tool that can generate straightforward select statements and return a set of rows and columns. Unfortunately, a tool that provides only this limited functionality will not survive more than 30 minutes in the real world. Part of the problem is that SQL was not meant to be a report writer language. In Chapter 6, we list several examples of SQL's deficiency in formulating analytical queries. These tools must overcome the underlying deficiency of the language.

As a result, these tools can be challenging to use for anything beyond the simplest query. They demo well, but the real world is usually not as pretty. Their use is typically limited to business analysts and power users because they require a fairly significant investment in learning, not just for the tool but for the data as well.

In general, ad hoc query tools should include the following kinds of functionality. This list is not meant to be exhaustive; we left out many basic ad hoc capabilities.

Query Formulation

As its name suggests, the query tool's chief task is to formulate queries. This is a challenging task made more difficult by the evolution of SQL standards that allow the creation of increasingly complex queries. The kinds of query formulation capabilities you may need include:

- **Multipass SQL.** To calculate comparisons or to correctly calculate nonadditive measures in report break rows, the query tool must break the report down into a number of simple queries that are processed separately by the DBMS. The query tool then automatically combines the results of the separate queries in an intelligent way. Multipass SQL also allows drilling across to different fact tables in several conformed data marts, potentially in different databases. For example, sales and costs might be in different databases, but as long as they share the same dimensions, like Organization and Period, we can create a simple contribution report by querying the two sources and combining the results in the query tool. The processing of a single galactic SQL statement would otherwise be impossible. Finally, multipass SQL gives the aggregate navigator a chance to speed up the report, because each atomic SQL request is simple and easily analyzed by the aggregate navigator.

- **Highlighting.**   Highlighting is the interactive form of alerts. As data volumes blow through the roof, the query tool needs to help the user identify records that stand out from the others, like "show me districts that had a sales drop or increase of more than 10 percent over last month." An automatic All Other value is extremely helpful on this type of report. It lets the user put in a line that automatically aggregates all the remaining records. This means the report can show the exceptions along with the totals for the whole company. In a sense, highlighting is a rudimentary form of data mining.

- **Successive constraints.**   The results of one query are used as a limit or filter on subsequent queries. This is a particularly important capability for behavioral studies when you identify a cohort and examine its behavior as a unit. This happens almost any time information on individual people is involved. For example, doctors and researchers might be interested in identifying a group of patients with specific characteristics and then tracking their progress over time. They might want to identify the heavy smokers in a clinical trial group and see if the drug being tested reduces the risk of getting lung cancer. Any database with customer information will need successive constraints at some point. The value of this capability is not limited to people, however. A semiconductor company may want to identify a set of silicon chip wafers and follow them through the production process to examine failure rates. These constraint lists may be too large to store in the tool and thus may need to be passed back to the database so the join can be performed remotely. (It's also possible to generate these lists by creating temporary tables or view definitions in the database, although talk of writing lists or views to the database will make the DBAs nervous.)

- **Semiadditive summations.**   There is an important class of numeric measures in common business fact tables that are not completely additive. Anything that is a measure of intensity is usually not additive, especially across the Time dimension. For example, inventory levels and account balances are not additive across time.

These are called semiadditive facts. Everyone is familiar with the idea of taking one of these semiadditive facts, such as a bank balance, and creating a useful summary at the end of the month by averaging across time. Unfortunately, you cannot use the basic SQL AVG function to calculate this kind of average across time. AVG averages across all of the dimensions, not just time. If you fetch five accounts and four time periods from the DBMS, AVG will divide the total account balance by 20 (five times four) rather than doing what you want, which is to divide by four. It isn't difficult to divide by four, but it is a distraction for the end user or the application developer, who must stop and store the number four in the application explicitly. What is needed is a generalization of the SUM operator to become AVGTIMESUM. This function automatically performs a sum, but it also automatically divides by the cardinality of the time constraint in the surrounding query. This feature makes all applications involving inventory levels, account balances, and other measures of intensity significantly simpler.

- **ANSI SQL 92 support.** Lots of interesting SQL92 capabilities, such as UNIONs, MINUS, and nested SELECTS in various locations of a SELECT statement (including the FROM clause!), are not supported by many tool vendors. Nested selects offer another alternative to the successive constraint problem without having to write to the database.

- **Direct SQL entry.** As a last resort, you will need to be able to view and alter the SQL generated by the tool. This includes creating complex queries and adding optimizer hints. If you find yourself doing this very often, something is wrong with your tool or your design.

Analysis and Presentation Capabilities

It is no longer enough to get the data and bring it back to the desktop in a tabular form. The tool must support the business requirements for manipulating data and putting it into a presentation quality format.

- **Basic calculations on the results set.** This should include a range of math, statistical, string, sequential processing, conditional, and reporting functions. These calculations are often used to overcome other deficiencies in the tool. For example, it is possible to create a computed column using an IF or CASE statement that copies the Description column if the rank ≤ 25 or the value All Other if it's greater. This new column can then be used as the description in the pivot step to show a top 25 report that includes the total for the company, and it can even calculate the percentage of total for each of the top 25. How much of your business do your top 25 customers represent, anyway?

- **Pivot the results.**   Pivoting is the basis of multidimensional analysis. The row-based results set that SQL generates almost always end up being presented in a format with one or more dimensions displayed across the top of the report and one or more down the side. The report title usually gives it away (e.g., monthly sales report by region, or monthly sales by sales rep by product).

- **Column calculations on pivot results.**   These calculations create a computed column that is a function of two or more of the pivoted columns. For example, if a query returned two months of data, say, July 1998 and August 1998, you should be able to calculate a change or percentage change between the two columns. Single-column calculations, like percentage of column, cumulative, and n-tiles, fall into this category as well.

- **Column and row calculations.**   Some calculations, like showing one row value as a percentage of another row value are useful. Share calculations and ratios rely on this capability.

- **Sorting.**   Sorting, especially by a nondisplaying element, is important. For example, a financial report might show line items in a particular order that has nothing to do with the information displayed. It is not alphabetical, it may not even be in order by line item number. In such a case, a sort order column in the dimension specifies the appropriate display order. You don't necessarily want to see that element on the report, but you do want to use it in the sort.

- **Complex formatting.**   The tool should be able to create multisection reports, each with a different format such as compound documents with mixed tabular reports, pivots, and charts. Formatting is often more important than it probably should be. Whatever productivity gains we may have reaped from the personal computer have been diluted by the print-tweak-repeat cycle. Of course, formatting can be critical, especially if senior management is the audience. You need to have a full range of graphic design tools like lines, boxes, shading, fonts, sizes, and so on.

- **Charting and graphs.** These elements are the sizzle of the analytical steak. Almost every report ends up as a graph, if only to do some eyeball correlation analysis or forecasting. If the data has to leave the tool to go elsewhere for this capability, the transfer had better be truly seamless. It should be push-button simple, and the data source query should be linked to the charting tool to make it possible to automatically update the chart the next time the query is run.

- **User-changeable variables.** User-changeable variables can be included anywhere in the query document, from the query filter to the report headings. For example, if you limit a sales rep report to a single region, you'd like that region name to be accessible to the report header in the final report: Sales by rep for the last 12 months for the Southeast Region. Variables should also be used to prompt users for input. When this happens, they should have access to the appropriate pick lists. Finally, the tool should be able to iteratively set variables based on a list or query result set. The region sales report above could be run for a list of regions dynamically created by a query stored in the region name variable.

User Experience

The road to success in high technology is littered with the remains of superior technology. This applies to front-end tools as well. It doesn't matter that the tool meets all of your technical requirements if the users can't use it. The following capabilities help improve the user's experience of the analytical process:

- **Ease of use.** The tool should feel natural and have an intuitive interface. This is a matter of opinion. Often it means the tool works like a Microsoft tool. You must involve your users in assessing this area. Let them participate in the evaluation of any tool and get a sense of how they rate the usability of the tool.

- **Metadata access.** The tool should provide the user with context-sensitive help, not only about the tool, but about the data as well. This means the tool must provide a flexible way to draw from the descriptive data in the metadata catalog.

- **Pick lists.** The tool should provide a way to look up the list of values that can be used as constraints or filters in a query. Ideally, this list should be done in a way that supports the cross-browsing of dimension attributes. For larger dimensions, a simple SELECT DISTINCT isn't helpful if thousands of rows (or more) are returned. In one case we worked on recently, the largest dimension table had more than 75 million rows, each with a unique description. A direct pick list request against the column can never return to the desktop, but there is a hierarchy in the dimension that allows the user to constrain the query at a higher level, thus limiting the results of subsequent pick lists. It's possible to get down to a short list pretty quickly. A smart tool will allow you to protect the user from asking for a SELECT DISTINCT on 75 million rows.

- **Seamless integration with other applications.** At minimum, this includes cut and paste with full maintenance of display attributes (font, style, size). Better integration includes Object Linking and Embedding (OLE) of the report or chart pages.

- **Export to multiple file types, including HTML.** Ideally, this includes a full publishing capability of the final report and/or chart to a file directory, e-mail, or directly to the Web.

- **Embedded queries.** Users should be able to initiate queries from other applications. It should be possible, for example, to call a query from a spreadsheet and have it return rows into a specific region, which then feeds a complex financial model.

Technical Features

The following technical issues are not sexy demo features, and the need for them may not be immediately obvious. Some, like the ability to multitask and cancel queries are so fundamental to the tool's usability that your users will get angry if they are missing.

- **Multitasking.** Users must be able to run other programs and create and run other queries while a query is running.

- **Cancel query.** Users should be able to kill a single query in process without killing all of them. This cancel should manage a clean break from the database server, and it should not require rebooting the desktop machine.

- **Scripting.** A scripting language is critical for automating report execution.

- **Connectivity.** Make sure you can get to all the database platforms desired. We began a recent project thinking that we would only be querying one database platform, but found ourselves querying data in four different database platforms within a few weeks. Connectivity includes connecting to other data sources—text and spreadsheet files and other database products (OLAP engines).

- **Scheduling.** The tool needs to provide or take advantage of some kind of scheduling system. Users will want to defer queries for overnight processing or set them up for processing on a regular basis. This does not have to be the robust, enterprise structure described in the Standard Reporting section, but it does have to work.

- **Metadata driven.** The administrator should be able to define simple subsets of the warehouse, including predefined join paths, business descriptions, calculated columns, pick list sources, and so on. This setup process should be simple and fast.

- **Software administration.** This may be a disappearing problem with the adoption of the Web as an application platform. Until the transition is complete, make sure the vendor includes administration utilities that allow you to update any software, data models, local pick lists, connectivity software, and so on from a central location.

- **Security.** Ideally, the tool will participate in whatever user authentication system is available. Tool-based security is not that valuable in the warehouse environment unless it participates with the network system and the database.

- **Querying.** Direct querying of the database should be supported without an administrative layer or with minimal work (i.e., initial setup of less than 10 minutes). This is especially valuable for the warehouse team because they are constantly examining new data sources, often on different platforms.

Modeling Applications and Data Mining

In our architecture, modeling applications includes several types of model-based analysis. This could include financial models, customer scoring systems, process optimization, and forecasting along with the hard-core data mining activities described next. Although it's not necessarily a desktop tool, data mining can be one of the major data access methods to the warehouse. Since data mining is the most common example of a modeling application, we will devote most of this section to it.

Origins of Data Mining

Although the marketplace for data mining currently features a host of new products and companies, the underlying subject matter has a rich tradition of research and practice that goes back at least 30 years. The first name for data mining, beginning in the 1960s, was *statistical analysis*. The pioneers of statistical analysis, in our opinion, were SAS, SPSS, and IBM. All three of these companies are very active in the data mining field today and have very credible product offerings based on their years of experience. Originally, statistical analysis consisted of classical statistical routines such as correlation, regression, chi-square, and cross-tabulation. SAS and SPSS, in particular, still offer these classical approaches, but they and most other data mining vendors have moved beyond these statistical measures to more insightful approaches that try to explain or predict what is going on in the data.

In the late 1980s, classical statistical analysis was augmented with a more eclectic set of techniques, including fuzzy logic, heuristic reasoning, and neural networks. This was the heyday of AI, or artificial intelligence. Although perhaps a harsh indictment, we should admit that AI was a failure as packaged and sold in the 1980s. Far too much was promised. The successes of AI turned out to be limited to special problem domains, and often required a very complicated investment to encode a human expert's knowledge into the system. Perhaps most seriously, AI forever remained a black box that most of us normal IS people couldn't relate to. Try selling the CEO on an expensive package that performs fuzzy logic.

Now in the late 1990s, we have learned how to package the best approaches from classical statistical analysis, neural networks, decision trees, market basket analysis, and other powerful techniques and present them in a much more compelling and effective way. Additionally, we believe that the arrival of serious data warehouse systems was the necessary ingredient that has made data mining real and actionable.

Data mining is a complete topic by itself, and not one we can do justice to in this book. If you plan to do data mining at some point down the road, the following list will help you think about the kinds of functionality your organization might need, and you might therefore need to provide. Data mining breaks out into four major categories: clustering, classifying, estimating and predicting, and affinity grouping.

Clustering

Clustering is a pure example of undirected data mining, where the user has no specific agenda and hopes that the data mining tool will reveal some meaningful structure. An example of clustering is looking through a large number of initially undifferentiated customers and trying to see if they fall into natural groupings. The input records to this clustering exercise ideally should be high-quality verbose descriptions of each customer with both demographic and behavioral indicators attached to each record. Clustering algorithms work well with all kinds of data, including categorical, numerical, and textual data. It is not even necessary to identify inputs and outputs at the start of the job run. Usually the only decision the user must make is to ask for a specific number of candidate clusters. The clustering algorithm will find the best partitioning of all the customer records (in our example) and will provide descriptions of the *centroid* of each cluster in terms of the user's original data. In many cases, these clusters have an obvious interpretation that provides insight into the customer base. Specific techniques that can be used for clustering include statistics, memory-based reasoning, neural networks, and decision trees.

Classifying

An example of classifying is to examine a candidate customer and assign that customer to a predetermined cluster or classification. Another example of classifying is medical diagnosis. In both cases, a verbose description of the customer or patient is fed into the classification algorithm. The classifier determines to which cluster centroid the candidate customer or patient is nearest or most similar. Viewed in this way, we see that clustering may well be a natural first step that is followed by classifying. Classifying in the most general sense is immensely useful in many data warehouse environments. A classification is a decision. We may be classifying customers as credit worthy or credit unworthy, or we may be classifying patients as either needing or not needing treatment.

Techniques that can be used for classifying include standard statistics, memory-based reasoning, genetic algorithms, link analysis, decision trees, and neural networks.

Estimating and Predicting

Estimating and predicting are two similar activities that normally yield a numerical measure as the result. For example, we may find a set of existing customers who have the same profile as a candidate customer. From the set of existing customers we may estimate the overall indebtedness of the candidate customer. Prediction is the same as estimation except that we are trying to determine a result that will occur in the future. Estimation and prediction can also drive classification. For instance, we may decide that all customers with more than $100,000 of indebtedness are to be classified as poor credit risks. Numerical estimates have the additional advantage that the candidates can be rank-ordered. We may have enough money in an advertising budget to send promotion offers to the top 10,000 customers ranked by an estimate of their future value to the company. In this case, an estimate is more useful than a simple binary classification.

Specific techniques that can be used for estimating and predicting include standard statistics and neural networks for numerical variables, as well as all the techniques described for classifying when predicting only a discrete outcome.

Affinity Grouping

Affinity grouping is a special kind of clustering that identifies events or transactions that occur simultaneously. A well-known example of affinity grouping is market basket analysis. Market basket analysis attempts to understand what items are sold together at the same time. This is a hard problem from a data processing point of view because in a typical retail environment there are thousands of different products. It is pointless to enumerate all the combinations of items sold together because the list quickly reaches astronomical proportions. The art of market basket analysis is to find the meaningful combinations of different levels in the item hierarchy that are sold together. For instance, it may be meaningful to discover that the individual item Super Cola 12 oz. is very frequently sold with the category of Frozen Pasta Dinners.

Specific techniques that can be used for affinity grouping include standard statistics, memory-based reasoning, link analysis, and special-purpose market basket analysis tools.

Data mining, like standard reporting, is typically a separate system (or systems) with separate tools designed to apply various forms of statistical analysis. It is also like another client to the warehouse, but without the daily demands a reporting system might have. The services a data mining application might need from the warehouse are more like the data staging services a data mart would need, including:

- Support for periodic pulls of large files.
- Transformation services as described in the data staging section.
- Update access to the staging area to return the result of scoring or forecasting runs.

In an interesting twist, the data mining tools might also be called on to act as service providers themselves. That is, they could be considered an application layer between the front-end tools and the database. In this scenario, a front-end tool would use the APIs of the data mining tool to pass it a set of parameters and instructions. The front-end tool might then incorporate the results directly into a report or model. This scenario becomes more likely given that the database vendors are working to incorporate data mining capabilities directly into the database engine (while at the same time, front-end tool vendors are trying to add their own data mining capabilities).

 Successful data mining is not easy. It involves a complex set of tools and requires a solid understanding of statistical analysis. It also requires an additional set of data transformations, which are described in Chapter 16.

If data mining is critical to your organization and will be a part of your next data warehouse project, we encourage you to get a copy of Michael Berry and Gordon Linoff's book, *Data Mining Techniques for Marketing, Sales, and Customer Support* (Wiley 1997). The categorization described in this chapter comes from this book; it will give you a wealth of information about specific tools and techniques.

Web Implications for Data Access

Web access is a requirement for the vast majority of data warehouses today, and it is a requirement with architectural implications. First, on the practical side, your architecture will need to include access services for a Web server that supports access to your database. At the low end of the spectrum, many tools can create HTML documents. These static documents could be put in a directory and made available to the business community through a series of standard links on a Web page. On the other hand, most of the dynamic, Web-based data access alternatives work in connection with an existing Web server. See Chapter 11, which covers infrastructure, for more details.

Second, and longer term, the Web is having a significant impact on the data access tools market. Web-based tools are extremely attractive from an IS point of view. In theory, they are platform independent, zero maintenance, and low cost. As a result, IS organizations are voicing an overwhelming demand for Web-based tools. Unfortunately, their legacy code base hinders many of the front-end tool vendors. They have created a monolithic desktop product by incorporating data access services into their tools, which has slowed their transition to Web-based tools. At the same time, new companies are rushing to fill the need with recently developed Web products. Unfortunately, these companies don't have the experience or resources to develop a full set of query and reporting capabilities. What this means is that there will be a period of radical change on the data access tool side until the winners surface. Plan on significant front-end tool upgrades every 6 to 12 months, with at least one tool switch over the next 3 years.

TAKE ADVANTAGE OF THE WEB

The Web will be extremely important as we move forward. It has a great potential for generating major benefits. The Web is an ideal distribution channel for standard reports and simple ad hoc access. It has low maintenance costs in terms of distributing the software itself and broad availability in terms of the number of people in an organization who have access to a browser. If your metadata catalog is stored in an open DBMS, the Web will be a good mechanism for providing access to the business metadata. The users should be able to access dynamic Web pages that query the metadata catalog and allow them to browse its contents.

Desktop Tool Architecture Approaches

Different vendors have chosen to implement different subsets of the data access functions described earlier, and they have implemented them in different ways. Figures 10.5 through 10.7 will help prepare you for this. These three alternatives represent the major approaches the market has taken to providing data access functionality.

Direct Connect (Two Tier)

As illustrated in Figure 10.5, the desktop tool is designed to connect directly to the database. You may insert a query management layer, but it is not required for the tool to work. This is a common place to start because it is easy to install and relatively simple to manage. However, it does not scale well, so expect to migrate to a new tool if you have significant growth plans. Also watch out for quick-fix software designed to provide functionality at the checklist level but maybe not at the real-world level. A common example of this is the report server that is essentially a workstation with an automated query scheduler. It provides

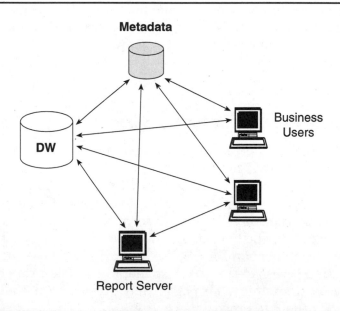

FIGURE 10.5   Direct access.

no added value in terms of managing reports, managing the queries, caching results, and so on.

The simplicity of a two-tier desktop tool is both its greatest advantage and its greatest drawback. These tools typically are very easy to install and administer, but that very simplicity implies a sparser metadata store and less functionality than the other front room architectures described next.

ROLAP Application Layer (Three Tier)

The second approach, shown in Figure 10.6, is to separate most of the query management functions from the desktop front-end and centralize them on an application server. This method is becoming more common as front-end tools migrate to the Web. The shared query management function lightens the footprint of the desktop front end. This architecture is also called relational OLAP (ROLAP) since the server presents the database to the client as a multidimensional environment.

The ROLAP tools make extensive use of metadata. The metadata resides in relational tables and describes the facts, dimensions, dimensional attributes, hierarchical relationships, business metrics, aggregate navigation, and user profiles. Any change to data structures, aggregates, metrics, relationships, and user profiles can be centrally managed.

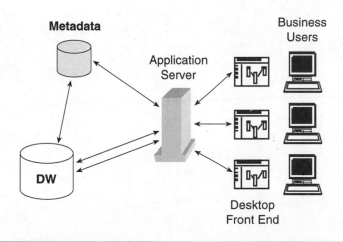

FIGURE 10.6   ROLAP application layer.

MOLAP Application Layer (Three+ Tier)

The third example is similar to the ROLAP strategy in that it incorporates a middle tier between the relational data warehouse and the user. However, in this case, the middle tier includes its own database structure, called a *multidimensional database cube*. This cube is essentially a preaggregated rollup of the database. User queries are managed by the OLAP server, which either sends it to the OLAP cube or passes it through to the base level warehouse if the answer cannot be generated from the data in the cube. Recently, database vendors have been moving to incorporate OLAP cubes into the relational database engine. In fact, this hybrid architecture is similar to the MOLAP architecture in Figure 10.7, except that the data warehouse and the cube occupy the same address space. The database vendors should be able to create tighter links and easier drill through to detail since they are responsible for both sides of the solution. We shall see.

Each vendor in this class has developed its own multidimensional cube technology. The end user metadata layer in this class of tool is typically embedded within the cube, although it may exist additionally in the database. The metadata tends to be as rich as, and very similar to, metadata for ROLAP (application layer) tools.

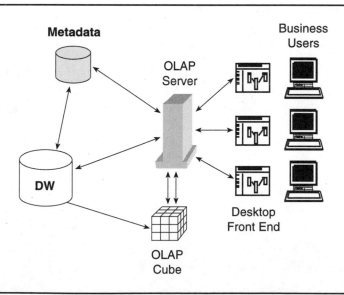

FIGURE 10.7   MOLAP application layer.

Since the MOLAP tools were built for decision support, they tend to have much stronger analytical functions built into the engine. Some of the MOLAP tools allow both reads and writes to the data, which makes them very important for applications like forecasting and budgeting.

SUMMARY

The front room is, in some ways, the easiest part of the architecture to develop. It is certainly the richest part of the warehouse as far as the variety of available tools is concerned. In fact, this very wealth of choices makes tool selection difficult, as discussed in Chapter 13.

The front room is vital, because it's the part of the warehouse that your business users see and use. Most users don't care about the database or the difficulties of architecture and implementation and equate the warehouse with the tool on their desktops.

As we discussed in this chapter, your warehouse will serve a broad user community with diverse needs, and you must architect the front room to support that variety. The first step is to understand the types of front room data stores your implementation will use. All data warehouses will use access tool data stores and may additionally use standard reporting data stores and personal or disposable data marts. They may also feed data to data mining or other downstream systems.

The front room services consist of browsing, security, monitoring, reporting, administration, and—by far most important—querying and other desktop services. It is in the desktop services that the wide variety of business user requirements will most affect your architecture. This chapter describes many features that are commonly required of query, reporting, and analysis tools. As of yet, no one tool provides all these features. You need to understand and document the types of users your system will serve, the kinds of problems they need to solve, and which of the features described in this chapter are going to be most valuable.

CHAPTER 11

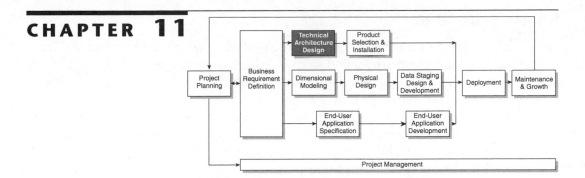

Infrastructure and Metadata

Infrastructure and metadata provide the foundation for all of the architectural elements we described in Chapters 8, 9, and 10. Infrastructure for the data warehouse includes the hardware, network, and lower-level functions, such as security, that the higher-level components take for granted. Metadata is a bit more ethereal than infrastructure, but it provides the same kind of supporting base layer for the back room and front room tool sets. This chapter identifies and defines the major infrastructure and metadata components of a data warehouse.

In the first part of this chapter, we will look at the general factors that must be considered when looking at back room infrastructure. Then we will review specific considerations for hardware, operating systems, and DBMS platforms, including some basic definitions. Next, we will take a similar look at the front room. Then, to tie these all together, we'll take a quick look at connectivity and networking.

The second part of this chapter focuses on all the different flavors of metadata. We will close this chapter with an example of active metadata usage and considerations for metadata maintenance. Although this chapter has a strong technical focus, it is intended to assist all team members in understanding these essential foundation pieces.

INFRASTRUCTURE

Many factors combine to determine the appropriate infrastructure for a given implementation, and many of them are not necessarily technical. Let's be clear right up front about the fact that we are not infrastructure experts. Our strategy has always been to work closely with our client's infrastructure experts (i.e., your coworkers) to help them clearly understand the warehouse's infrastructure requirements. Our goal in this section is to identify and define the major infrastructure components involved in a typical data warehouse.

Drivers of Infrastructure

Even in the deepest technical layers of the warehouse, business requirements are still the primary determinant of what we need to provide. At the infrastructure level, business requirements are represented through measures that are more technical. For example, the business should determine the appropriate level of detail the warehouse needs to carry and across what time spans. This tells us how much data the infrastructure needs to manage. Other business requirements determine things like how often we need to load data and how complex the business rules are that we need to apply during the transformation process. These in turn help us estimate how much computing horsepower we will need to make it all happen.

Technical and systems issues often drive infrastructure choices. In some cases, the performance drain of the extract process on the operational systems is too great. It can actually necessitate an investment in a separate mirrored hardware environment. Another common determining factor has to do with the specific skills and experience of the data warehouse implementers. Back room teams with mostly mainframe experience tend to develop mainframe-based warehouses and vice versa. The same holds true for the database platform. If the DBAs have invested significant time and energy learning a specific DBMS, getting them to switch will be nontrivial.

Policy and other organizational issues also play a role in determining infrastructure. Often, there are "temporary" limits on capital spending, which means you will need to secure infrastructure through more creative means. Also, information systems policies often dictate certain platform decisions. Standardizing on a single platform allows a company to negotiate significant discounts, develop a core expertise, and ultimately, develop applications that are relatively easy to move from one system to another as the application grows.

The Evolution of Infrastructure

Hardware infrastructure for the data warehouse includes the hardware platforms for each of the data stores, for any application servers, and for the desktop.

 The basic tenet when considering hardware platforms is to remember that the warehouse will grow quickly in the first 18 months, in terms of both data and usage.

The first step in determining platforms is to decide which platforms will actually be required. That is, what data stores are you going to implement, and how many of them need to have separate hardware platforms? Figure 11.1 shows some typical hardware platform configurations for various sized warehouse initiatives.

Each box in the figure represents a machine, or a physical box, in the warehouse. At one end of the spectrum, a small or initial warehouse can be successfully implemented in a two-tier environment. However, even the smallest systems should expect to have an application server to support Web-based data access. Larger, more mature warehouses tend to split out the staging area from the warehouse or mart. Many companies start out at this level because they plan to grow and want to avoid the effort of migrating to a three-tier architecture. Moving down the figure, a large, enterprise-level warehouse is often implemented across several separate servers. Obviously, there is plenty of room for variation, but the message is that the number of servers can grow significantly.

Back Room Infrastructure Factors

The first step in any platform selection process is to understand the requirements. Simply understanding what a platform should do and how it should perform from a technical perspective is not sufficient. It is crit-

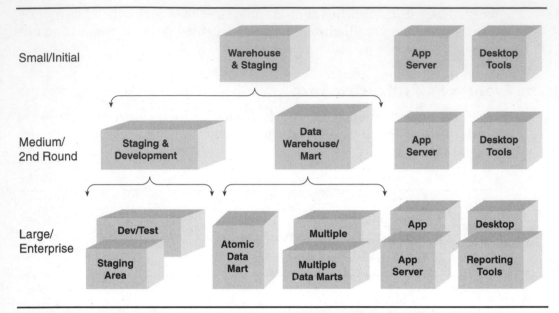

FIGURE 11.1 Hardware platforms by data warehouse size and maturity.

ical to consider the business requirements, too. The requirements then help narrow down the alternatives to those that meet the needs, and then we can compare costs and other factors to find the best alternative. The database server is the biggest hardware platform decision most data warehouse projects take on. The major factors in determining requirements for the server platform include the following:

■ **Data size.** How much data you need is determined by the business problems you are trying to solve. If the business goal is to develop one-to-one customer relationships, you will need customer-level transaction detail. Most data warehouse/data mart projects tend to start out with no more than 200 GB. In fact, they tend to start much smaller and grow as history accumulates, aggregates are created, and new data sources are added. Anything less than 200 GB is well within the bounds of manageability. We'll designate data warehouses of less than 100 GB as small, those from 100 to 500 GB as typical, and those with more than 500 GB to be large. These break points will continue to climb with the advance of hardware and database platform capabilities.

- **Volatility.**   Volatility measures the dynamic nature of the database. It includes areas like how often the database will be updated, how much data changes or is replaced each time, and how long the load window is. Again, look to the business requirements for clues to the volatility of the warehouse. Daily data is obviously more volatile than weekly or monthly data. Customer churn rates can tell you how much your customer dimension will change over time. The answers to these questions have a direct impact on the size and speed of the hardware platform. Data warehouses bear the full brunt of both the business and technology curves. That is, business and technology are changing rapidly, and the data warehouse has to adjust to both.

- **Number of users.**   Obviously, the number of users, how active they are, how many are active concurrently, and any periodic peaks in their activity (e.g., month end) are all important factors in selecting a platform. For a Fortune 1000–sized organization, the initial data warehouse/data mart efforts we work with usually start out with 25 to 50 active users. Within 18 months or so, this number grows to between 100 and 200, and in 3 years, there can be thousands of users, especially if the warehouse is used for both ad hoc purposes and to create standard or push-button reports in a large organization. The geographical distribution of users is also important. If you have users around the world, 24-hour availability might be a requirement. This has implications for hardware. In this case, if the operational systems are centralized, the warehouse would probably be centralized, too, but the hardware would need to support parallel or trickle load processes that allow it to be constantly available. If the operational systems are decentralized, it may make sense to have decentralized data marts as well.

- **Number of business processes.**   The number of distinct business processes supported in the warehouse increases the complexity significantly. If the user population is large enough or the business justification strong enough, it makes sense to have separate hardware platforms for each business process. Note that you may still need a large, centralized server if consolidated data is critical to senior management, and middleware methods of providing virtual consolidation are not effective in your case.

- **Nature of use.** The nature of usage and the front-end tool choices also have implications on platform selection. A few active ad hoc users can put a significant strain on a data warehouse. It is difficult to optimize for this kind of use because good analysts are all over the map, looking for opportunities. On the other hand, a system that mostly generates push-button–style standard reports can be optimized around those reports. (Note that if you are providing only structured access to the data through standard reports with limited flexibility, you will probably not get full value out of your data warehouse investment.) Many of the reporting tools on the market provide for the scheduling of canned reports so they run in the early morning hours, after the load is complete but before people arrive for work. This helps balance the load by shifting many of the standard reports into the off-peak hours. Larger-scale data mining also puts a massive demand on the hardware platform, both in terms of data size and I/O scalability. These beasts need to suck in huge amounts of data, comb through it with the teeth of a good mining tool, and stream the results back out to support further analysis and downstream business uses. It is important to understand the types of queries coming in because ad hoc use, reporting, and data mining all have different query profiles and may do better on different platforms.

- **Technical readiness.** From an administrative perspective, the server environment is similar to the mainframe environment at a conceptual level, but it is very different at the implementation level. Do not think you can simply install a UNIX server or even a large NT system without benefit of an experienced, professional system support resource as part of the warehouse team. Servers have a range of support requirements, from basic hardware and system software administration, to connectivity (both out to the desktop and back to the source systems), DBA experience, backup and recovery, and so on. We're not quite at the point where we can just plug them in and forget them—at least not yet. The quantity, quality, and experience of the IS support resources you are able to muster may have a significant impact on your platform decision.

- **Software availability.** Often, the requirements analysis will indicate a need for a certain capability, like a geographic information system that allows you to display warehouse data on a map. The software selection process may reveal that the best geographic mapping software for your particular requirements only runs on a certain high-end, graphics-based platform. Obviously, your decision is easy in a case like this. The business requirement simplifies the platform decision significantly.

- **Financial resources.** The amount of money spent on a project is usually a function of the project's expected value. With data warehouses, this is usually a chicken-and-egg problem. As we discussed in the section on cost justification in Chapter 3, it's tough to identify and communicate the value of a data warehouse before you have one in place. In terms of hardware, the bottom line is get the biggest server you can.

Considerations for Hardware and Operating System Platforms

Since the machine won't work without an operating system (OS), hardware and operating systems come as a package. In the mainframe environment, there is really only one operating system option. In the open systems world, every hardware manufacturer has its own flavor of UNIX. Even NT has different flavors that do not all offer native support for much of the Intel/NT software base. The major hardware platform and OS platform options fall into the following categories:

- **Mainframes.** Lately, there has been a spate of articles about applications returning to the mainframe after failing in the client/server environment. The data warehouse is probably the one application to which this does not apply. In general, the mainframe is not the first-choice platform for data warehousing. Although there are many successful mainframe-based data warehouses, most of them have either been on the mainframe for several years and would be costly to migrate, or they are taking advantage of excess capacity, so the marginal cost is relatively low. The mainframe is not necessarily cost effective for data warehousing. Administrative, hardware, and programming costs are typically higher than on open system platforms, in part because the mainframe environment includes a robust transaction-processing infrastructure that is not critical to data warehousing.

  Also, because the mainframe is designed primarily to support transaction requirements, it is relatively inflexible from a programming point of view. Although the tools and techniques are robust, they are also difficult to use. Adding new data sources to the warehouse, or simply maintaining existing extracts can be an onerous task.

Also, mainframe capacity is limited in many companies, and investment in additional capacity for new applications is unlikely. Clearly, if you have room, use it. However, if a new investment has to be made, the best choice is often a server environment.

- **Open system servers.**   Open system, or UNIX, servers are the primary platform for most medium-sized or larger data warehouses today. UNIX is generally robust enough to support production applications, and it was adapted for parallel processing more than a decade ago. The UNIX server market is fairly commoditized. From a process point of view, UNIX can be a fairly cryptic and foreign environment for mainframe experts or PC programmers to adapt to. Many of the standard mainframe tools and utilities are not standard in UNIX. If you choose a UNIX server as your platform, the warehouse team will need to include the resources and experience to set up and manage a UNIX environment. This is usually accomplished through a close, participatory relationship with the server management group. If the data warehouse is based on a UNIX environment, the warehouse team will also need to know basic UNIX commands and utilities to be able to develop and manage the warehouse. Make sure people get training if they need it. Keep in mind that UNIX is not a standard. Each manufacturer has its own flavor of UNIX, and each one has its own idiosyncrasies.

- **NT servers.**   Although NT is by far the fastest growing operating system in the server market, it has only recently attained the ability to support a medium-sized warehouse. Viable large-scale hardware platforms for NT are just becoming available. Parallel processing capabilities have been limited to single-digit processor counts, and NT server clustering is only now becoming an operational reality. Given Microsoft's history, NT will certainly evolve into a powerful operating system platform, but it is not the best choice for medium-to-large warehouses at this point. However, NT is certainly a cost-effective platform for smaller warehouses or data marts that might be populated from the atomic data mart.

Parallel Processing Architectures

The hardware industry pioneered the creative use of acronyms, and they continue to turn out new ones at a rapid pace. There are three basic parallel processing hardware architectures in the server market: symmetric multiprocessing (SMP), massively parallel processing (MPP), and non-uniform memory architecture (NUMA), as shown in Figure 11.2. These architectures differ in the way the processors work with disk, memory, and each other. Over time, the defining edges of these architectures are getting fuzzy as manufacturers improve their offerings. The following sections summarize how they apply to data warehousing.

Symmetric Multiprocessing (SMP)

The SMP architecture is a single machine with multiple processors, all managed by one operating system and all accessing the same disk and memory area. An SMP machine with 8 to 32 processors, a parallel database, large memory (two or more gigabytes), good disk, and a good de-

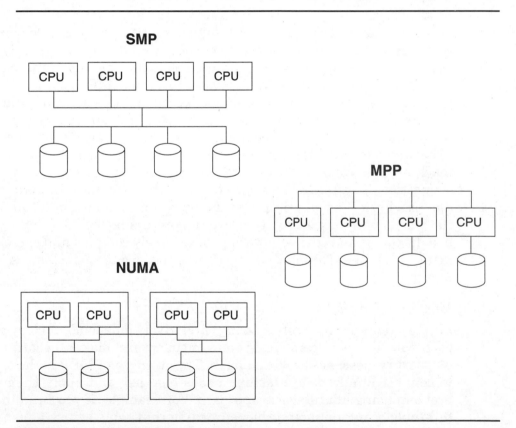

FIGURE 11.2 **Basic hardware architectures.**

sign should perform well with a medium-sized warehouse. To take advantage of multiple processors, the database needs to be able to run its processes in parallel, and the data warehouse processes need to be designed to take advantage of parallel capabilities.

 The "shared everything" architecture means SMP machines are well suited for ad hoc queries. In an ad hoc query environment, the access paths are not known ahead of time. The shared, centralized nature of the SMP architecture gives the system the ability to allocate processing power across the entire database.

SMP's "shared everything" strength is also its weakness. The processors can access shared resources (memory and disk) very quickly, but the access path they use to get at those resources, the backplane, can become a bottleneck as the system scales. Since the SMP machine is a single entity, it also has the weakness of being a single point of failure in the warehouse. In an effort to overcome these problems, hardware companies have come up with techniques that allow several SMP machines to be linked to each other, or clustered. In a cluster, each node is an SMP machine that runs its own operating system, but the cluster includes connections and control software to allow the machines to share disks and provide fail-over backup. In this case, if one machine fails, others in the cluster can temporarily take over its processing load. Of course, this benefit comes at a cost—clustering is extremely complex and can be difficult to manage. The database technology needed to span clusters is improving.

Massively Parallel Processing (MPP)

MPP systems are basically a string of relatively independent computers, each with its own operating system, memory and disk, all coordinated by passing messages back and forth. The strength of MPP is the ability to connect hundreds of machine nodes together and apply them to a problem using a brute-force approach. For example, if you need to do a full-table scan of a large table, spreading that table across a 100-node MPP system and letting each node scan its 1/100th of the table should be relatively fast. It's the computer equivalent of "many hands make light work." The challenge comes when the problem is difficult to split into clean, well-segmented pieces. For example, joining two large tables together, if both are spread across the 100 nodes, can be a problem. Any given record in one table may have matching records in the other table that are located on any (or all!) of the other 99 nodes. In this case, the coordination task among nodes can get overloaded. Of course, developers of MPP-based systems have designed workarounds for this and other parallelization issues.

MPP systems are typically found in larger scale (i.e., over one terabyte) data warehouses and data-intensive applications (e.g., data mining). They can be configured for high availability by mirroring data on multiple nodes. MPP machines work best when the data access paths are predefined and the data can be spread across nodes and disks accordingly.

 MPP systems tend to support canned query or standard reporting environments, or else they play the role of the atomic data mart feeder system. MPP is considered to be more expensive and more difficult to tune and manage. Again, the database needs to be designed to take advantage of this hardware structure—the physical design for MPP can be significantly different than for SMP.

Non-Uniform Memory Architecture (NUMA)

NUMA is essentially a combination of SMP and MPP in an attempt to combine the shared disk flexibility of SMP with the parallel speed of MPP. This architecture is a relatively recent innovation, and it may prove viable for data warehousing in the long run. NUMA is conceptually similar to the idea of clustering SMP machines, but with tighter connections, more bandwidth, and greater coordination among nodes. If you can segment your warehouse into relatively independent usage groups and place each group on its own node, the NUMA architecture may be effective for you.

Considerations Common to All Parallel Architectures

As with all platforms, it pays to ask specific questions about software availability and system administration complexities. In particular, consider the following:

- **What type and version of the operating system does it run?** Remember that UNIX is not a standard.

- **What other applications are available on this version of the operating system?** If the vendor of the software you want has not ported its package to your operating system, it just won't work. In particular, you want to know if it runs the most current version of your RDBMS, data warehouse utilities, application servers, and so on.

Hardware Performance Boosters

Disk speed and memory are especially important for data warehouses because the queries can be data intensive. A transaction system request typically retrieves a single record from a table optimized to already have that record in cache. A data warehouse query may require aggregation of thousands of records from across several tables.

Disk Issues

Disk drives can have a major impact on the performance, flexibility, and scalability of the warehouse platform. The price range for server disks goes from about $0.10 to $2.00 per megabyte. At the high end, the drives are essentially built into a standalone computer or disk subsystem that manages disk access. These drive systems are fast, easily expandable (especially important for growth) and portable (they can be moved across servers and operating systems). They can also be set up with redundant storage for data protection (RAID 1 or 5) to give the warehouse greater availability. Note that databases tend to need large temporary storage spaces where sorts, joins, and aggregations are performed. This space needs to be on high-performance drives and controllers, but it does not need to be mirrored—a cost savings. These drive systems can be configured to be hot swappable to minimize downtime when there is a problem. Redundancy and hot swapping are important because disk drives are the most likely components to fail. Disk drive subsystems are more expensive but represent a good value over time. Start with enough disk for the next year or two, and expand as needed and as prices drop.

Memory

When it comes to memory, more is better for data warehousing. Again, this is another difference between decision support and transaction processing. Transaction requests are small and typically don't need much memory. Decision support queries are much larger and often involve several passes through large tables. If the table can fit in memory, performance can theoretically improve by one to two orders of magnitude, or 10 to 100 times. This is one of the big advantages of 64-bit platforms. For example, 32-bit systems are limited to 2 GB (4 in some cases), but 64-bit chips can address a much larger memory space. (Note that, for a 64-bit chip to be effective, the machine, operating system, and database all must be based on 64-bit code.)

The idea of preferring memory to disk has been around for decades—the speed difference is irresistable. In round numbers, the access time for a disk drive is about 10 milliseconds compared to about 0.1 millisecond for memory, making memory about 100 times faster than disk. Of course, the effective improvement of doing database processing with data already in memory instead of on disk is less than 100 times due to lots of intervening factors (like disk read-aheads and memory cache on the controller or in the operating system). Nonetheless, we've seen improvements in data warehouse performance of 10 to 30 times simply by adding a lot more memory to the database configuration.

Service Level Agreements

The type and amount of hardware you need should take into consideration the level of availability you will need to provide. If the requirement is to provide worldwide access, parallel machines and significant component redundancy may be necessary (when do we have downtime to load and maintain the database?). Availability of the atomic data mart is critical since it is the repository for the lowest level of detail and will probably be linked to all of the data marts in a drill-through fashion. Processing power is also key since the atomic data mart is a central part of the load process, and it must be able to move new data out to the data marts in a small time window.

Secondary Storage

Make sure your configuration includes resources to support backup and archiving. If at all possible, try to get a backup system that is fast enough to do the job during the load window. Although it is possible to back up a warehouse while it is on-line, doing so can add significant overhead, which will compete with the business users' queries for CPU cycles.

Additional Factors for the Hardware Platform

The UNIX and NT server environments are the platforms of choice for most data warehouses at this point, with UNIX being the primary option for medium-to-large warehouses. Some of the advantages of servers over mainframes are:

- **More tool options.** Most of the new tools and utilities for data warehouses are being developed for server platforms first (and exclusively, in many cases).

- **Database vendor development focus.** Most database vendors develop on an operating system of choice. It's usually the first platform the company supported, and it's usually the one on which the product runs best. Once the core product is developed, it is ported to other operating systems and other versions of UNIX. Of course, waiting for a release can be a benefit; the early adopters will be your test team.

 The further your platform choice is from the core product platform, the longer you will wait for the next release and the less support you will get for platform specific capabilities.

- **Application servers require UNIX- or NT-based platforms.** Some data access products come with an application server component that needs to run on a server platform. If the warehouse is already server based, any application server can share the platform initially rather than forcing an additional hardware purchase. This probably isn't a good idea in the long run, but it can make the start-up process easier. Additional considerations for application servers follow in the front room section of this chaper.

- **Flexibility.**   The server environment is less tightly controlled than the mainframe, especially if the server is dedicated to the data warehouse. This will provide the local team with direct access to the warehouse and the ability to test new scenarios, build new tables, and so on, without relying on remote resources.

Considerations for the Database Platform

In the data warehouse world, the choice of database platform is as incendiary as religion or politics. There are over a dozen alternative database platforms, each with examples of successful data warehouse implementations and each with its own pack of supporting (and opposing) zealots. Aside from the major relational database products, most of the major fourth-generation language (4GL) companies have data warehouse offerings. Some data warehouses are implemented in mainframe-based database products. Others are implemented using specialized multidimensional database products called *multidimensional on-line analytical processing* (MOLAP) engines. Many of the factors that drive the hardware platform decision also apply to the database decision. In our experience, what's right for you depends on considerations specific to your situation. One of the biggest considerations is the choice between relational and multidimensional databases.

Relational versus Multidimensional Databases

In terms of sheer numbers, the biggest debate is between relational databases and multidimensional databases, with relational leading the pack. A heated debate has echoed through the decision support industry over the last few years about the benefits of selecting one of these approaches for analytical processing. Unfortunately, the debate is mostly heat and very little light.

The basic issue is more clearly understood when you examine it from a business requirements perspective. Multidimensional databases, also known as MOLAP engines, came about in response to three main user requirements: simple data access, cross-tab–style reports, and fast response time. Specialized databases were developed when standard relational databases and their predecessors were unable to meet these requirements. Many of these MOLAP products have been around for more than a decade. The following sections highlight some of the pros and cons of the two alternatives.

Characteristics of Relational Engines

Most major relational database vendors have invested in data warehouse–specific improvements over the last few years and now provide reasonably good performance. The major RDBMS vendors have added capabilities like dimensional model support, star joins, bit-mapped indexes, and improved cost-based optimizers. These advances and the advent of technologies like aggregate awareness have narrowed the performance gap significantly. Relational databases have the advantage of being able to hold much more data at a detailed level. Of course, systems that are designed to solve specific problems must have advantages over general-purpose systems in order to survive in the marketplace.

 If you're building your warehouse on a relational platform, it makes little sense to consider anything other than the mainstream RDBMS alternatives for most small-to-medium efforts.

In any case, it is extremely valuable to get references from similar warehouse implementations, and do some testing first. Identify a set of challenging reports, especially multitable joins among large tables and see how they perform. This is especially true for some of the more recent releases that include warehouse specific features. Generally, the vendors will provide resources to help with the testing process. You also may be able to take advantage of internal experience with a product from other IS projects.

 Some relational databases are specifically designed to handle data warehouse–type database designs and queries. They are typically faster than the mainstream RDBMS products and work well—in fact, are almost mandatory—for high-end data warehouses.

Characteristics of MOLAP Engines

MOLAP engines, also known as multidimensional database management systems, are proprietary database management systems that are designed to provide highly specialized support for analysis. MOLAP engines can make an excellent data mart platform for business requirements that can be met by a fairly simple star schema—that is, relatively few dimensions, each with relatively few rows. The MOLAP engine adds a layer of complexity to the load and management processes.

 Assuming there is a atomic data mart on an RDBMS platform, implementing a MOLAP engine means you will have a separate environment to administer and tune, and it will probably need its own server.

The most significant benefits of using a MOLAP engine is the end user query performance. Facts are prestored at all valid combinations of the dimensions. This delivers incredible end user response time. On the other hand, storing all of these aggregates tends to expand the quantity of data. Historically, there were limitations on the amount of data that could be stored in the multidimensional database. The typical multidimensional database size limitation has been less than 10 GB. The industry is investing resources to address these physical storage limitations. However, a practical limit based upon the amount of time required to load new data or refresh the database still exists. Many business end users today require both detailed data and summarized information. To meet this need, the capability to drill through the MOLAP engine directly into a relational database has been added to most of the MOLAP engines. Another significant strength of many MOLAP engines is their ability to handle edits, complex calculations, and roll-ups. This makes them perfect candidates for budgeting and forecasting systems.

The evaluation of multidimensional engines cannot be uncoupled from the end user data access tool evaluation, described in detail in Chapter 13. Some MOLAP products offer a full-scale end user data access tool and the database environment. Other MOLAP products provide the engine and a development environment. In this case, you must either develop your own end user application or acquire the end user application from a third-party supplier.

As of the time of writing this book, the drill-through capabilities from MOLAP- to SQL-based RDBMSs are rudimentary at best. Note that the need for links from the MOLAP engine into the relational environment is exactly why we believe the detail-level data also needs to be stored in a dimensional model. If the two levels have radically different designs, the ability to provide seamless access to the supporting detail is limited.

You must test candidate MOLAP products carefully with clear user requirements, understanding of architecture, and remote usage tests before making any major commitment. Lightweight desktop-based solutions could be attractive in the short term, but they will likely end up creating more work than value. The warehouse team needs to assess the product's size limitations and functionality carefully. Scalability will always be a challenge.

 As of the writing of this book, the most serious scalability issues for MOLAP systems are the total size of the input data for the main fact table and the number or rows in the largest possible dimension. In early 1998, the typical working limits for MOLAP systems are 5 GB of input data and 300,000 rows in the largest dimension.

The whole multivendor/multiproduct issue may just disappear as the RDBMS vendors incorporate MOLAP capabilities into their products. All of the major vendors are moving toward hybrid implementations that include both relational and MOLAP functionality. Note that just because the products come from the same vendor doesn't mean it will be cheaper—the MOLAP vs. RDBMS decision may still exist depending on your budget.

Front Room Infrastructure Factors

Infrastructure requirements for the front room are more diverse because they are much more business and tool dependent and there are many more alternatives to chose from. Let's look at some of the high-level considerations that affect the front room.

Application Server Considerations

Servers are proliferating in the front room like mad. There are servers to handle data access from the Web, query management, standard reporting, authentication, metadata databases, and more. It's difficult to give any meaningful information or advice on these devices since there are so many and they are so different. The best tactic you can take is to ask the vendor for detailed configuration information well in advance. In particular, ask about the following:

- **Memory.**   How much memory does the system require? How much does it take to perform well?
- **Disk.**   What determines disk usage? How much do you typically need? How fast does it usually grow?
- **Platform sharing.**   Is it okay to run multiple services on the same hardware platform? What are the performance impacts? What are the trade-offs? Are there any products that have poor compatibility?
- **Bottlenecks.**   What creates hot spots in the system? What slows it down? Is it truly multithreaded? Can it spawn independent processes and let them run to completion? What difference will multiple processors make? How many simultaneous users can it handle?

Desktop Considerations

The size of the desktop machine depends on the nature of the user and the associated tool requirements. A casual user whose information needs are met by HTML reports through a Web browser needs only as much power as it takes to run the Web browser. On the other hand, a power user who builds complex queries and analyses from scratch will probably need a much more powerful machine. Here are some of the main desktop-related challenges to watch out for.

Cross-Platform Support

Some organizations still have Macintosh hold-outs in the marketing organization, and many companies use UNIX workstations in engineering and manufacturing. Supporting multiple desktop platforms means much more work for the front-end team. Installation and support issues vary from platform to platform, requiring the team to have expertise in all platforms. And the problems don't end once the software is successfully installed. Often reports will need to be created on each platform, potentially doubling the development and maintenance effort. Few front-end vendors still support platforms other than Windows/Intel. The good news is that a requirement to support multiple desktop platforms will simplify the data access tool selection process.

Desktop OS

Even if everyone is on the same desktop hardware platform, they still may not be able to support the client software because they are not on the right version of the desktop operating system. Find out which OS version your tools require and take a survey to make sure it matches reality.

 In the Windows world, if your users are not on Windows 95 or higher or NT 4.0 or higher, expect trouble.

Software Distribution

This is an insidious problem for the data warehouse because it can sneak up slowly and quietly, and then hit you smack in the face. It's easy to install the first few sets of users. You typically know who they are, because they've been involved in some of the design sessions. They're eager to get the software and to get going. Then a few more folks need it, and then some people out in the regions, and then, the next thing you know, you've got a couple hundred copies out on random desktops around the company. Of course, this is when your tool vendor releases the big new version that gives you everything everyone wants—oh, but it's not really backward compatible. You have to somehow upgrade everyone at once —by yourself. The point here, from an architecture view, is to make sure you understand what your company is going to do about this problem (because it's not one the data warehouse invented) and make sure you are prepared to take advantage of your resources.

Web-Based Tools

A main attraction of the Web and related technologies is that they provide the possibility of platform independence and seamless distribution. This is only true in principle and only at the simple report access level. True ad hoc analysis tends to require a significant desktop presence. Not that this isn't possible based on a large applet—in fact, we were building complex applications based on a true diskless network computer at Metaphor back in 1984. The problem is that the tool providers have spent years developing a large code base and do not have the resources to port it (nor is the development infrastructure as robust yet). The new Web-based tool companies don't have the legacy to drag with them, but they also haven't had the time or experience to develop a powerful tool yet. They will need to go through several iterations, just like the generation before them.

Memory

It should come as no surprise that memory can make a big difference in performance on the desktop machine. One company we worked with spent a lot of time and energy researching network issues only to find out that the performance bottleneck was caused by the fact that the machines in question did not have enough memory. They were spending most of their time paging data and programs in and out of virtual memory.

Desktop Summary

Our recommendation is to chose a standard platform and determine the minimum configuration that will support your tool set in a responsive way. Make it big enough to be effective. Consider a separate, more powerful, recommended configuration especially for power users, since these folks are few in number but large in impact. It's best not to artificially limit their impact on the company (and thereby the value of the data warehouse) by saving a few thousand dollars on computers.

Also, although it's not as common a problem as computer prices drop, we strongly recommend one desktop computer per user. The idea of shared workstations doesn't work very well because it raises the perceived cost of using the warehouse for the analyst. If the analyst has to get up and go to the shared DSS workstation, perform some queries there, then somehow get the results back to the primary desktop computer, it tends to not happen. It's easier to just stay put and do it the old way.

Connectivity and Networking Factors

Connectivity and networking provide the links between the back room and front room. In general, connectivity is a straightforward portion of the infrastructure. Since this is a prerequisite to implementing any kind of client/server application, the groundwork is usually already in place. Most organizations have established a LAN or set of LANs connected together, along with a group dedicated to keeping it working. If this isn't the case for your organization, push to have an infrastructure task force set up immediately and figure out what needs to be done. Other connectivity issues that are likely to come up include:

Bandwidth

Often, it helps to isolate the database and application servers on a dedicated high-speed LAN (100 MBPS Ethernet or FDDI). This provides the needed bandwidth to transfer large blocks of data as quickly as possible.

Remote Access

If you have users in remote locations, they will obviously need to have access to the warehouse in much the same fashion as local users. This means you need a reliable, high-bandwidth connection between their LAN and the LAN where the database and application servers are located.

Bandwidth is becoming more important because the front-end tools are changing their approach. Many tools are now providing the ability to specify an interesting analytical set of the data, retrieve it and slice and dice it locally. This means a fairly large chunk of data is coming down the pipe. Once you have a sense of what the reporting requirements are, work with the networking folks who can help you determine if the connection has enough bandwidth (and when it's available).

If your remote users are not connected to a LAN, you will need to provide dial-up access. Test this carefully for performance and be sure to read Chapter 12 on security.

Gateways

Most database vendors have gateway products that provide connectivity to databases from other vendors and legacy data sources. Bringing up these gateways can be handy for accessing data located in other databases from the warehouse. Third-party middleware products provide this connectivity as well and include the ability to combine data from multiple sources—this is called a heterogeneous join. These gateways can have some limitations in terms of speed, and they tend to be best used for batch imports and small table lookups. Test them at full volume to make sure they don't break.

File Transfer

There are many file transfer protocols out there, along with programs that implement them. Certainly chief among them is File Transfer Protocol (FTP), which is a universal data transfer utility. FTP has been around as long as the Internet, and it provides file transfer services among the various and sundry computers on the Internet. It provides a base-level capability for establishing connectivity between two machines and moving flat files across that connection. One of the newer protocols, Secured Sockets Layer (SSL), comes from Netscape. It has the advantage of providing encryption built into the process so someone tapping into your network won't get the senior executive sales summary before the senior executives do. SSL is widely implemented in the UNIX server world because it is used to conduct secure transactions between Web browsers and servers. SSL has been submitted to the Internet Engineering Task Force for approval as a standard protocol.

Database Connectivity

Database connectivity is typically provided by the front-end tool providers. Most vendors provide a range of connection alternatives, including the proprietary protocol embedded in most database products. There are also some standards for database connectivity, including Open Database Connectivity (ODBC), originally developed by Microsoft, and Java Database Connectivity (JDBC), originally developed by JavaSoft. ODBC's goal is to provide a standard database access method to access any data from any application. ODBC accomplishes this by inserting a layer that translates the queries from the application into commands the database can handle. ODBC has historically been the second-choice connectivity driver because many specific implementations have not performed as well as the native database drivers. More robust drivers are now available, and ODBC is becoming a more popular alternative for database connectivity. JDBC has benefited from the ODBC evolution, and it is getting more use.

Meanwhile, the market moves forward. Microsoft has created a whole new superset of connectivity standards called OLE DB that promise to make database connectivity even better.

Directory Services

Your networking infrastructure needs to provide some form of host naming and address independence. At the simplest level, the Internet/intranet provides a Domain Name Service (DNS) that will look up a name in a list and return its corresponding Internet protocol (IP) address. This allows you to assign a name to the IP address of your database server and configure the front-end tools to ask for that name. The name is then translated dynamically to the IP address of the machine where the database lives. If you move the database to a new machine, all you need to do is change the entry in the DNS list. You see this name translation every time you use a Web browser to go to a particular site. When you type in *www.site_name.com,* that name is converted to an IP address by a DNS server before the request for a page is sent to the actual site itself.

Other, more complex directory services exist in the form of X.500 or Lightweight Directory Access Protocol (LDAP) directories. These directories contain much richer information than simple IP addresses. They can incorporate many types of directories, including: name and address, e-mail addresses, telephone lists, and hardware directories (like printers, computers, etc.)—just about anything you might want to look up. These directories can be used to list the locations of servers, user directories for data delivery, e-mail lists for distribution standard reports, and so on. In Chapter 12, we argue strongly that you should plan for an LDAP directory server as a single point of logon and as a single point of administration.

Infrastructure Summary

As we've seen, there are a lot of components in the warehouse infrastructure covering hardware platforms, connectivity and networking, and the desktop. For each of these major areas, we need to understand the business requirements we have to meet and the pivotal decision points. Fortunately, the responsibility for infrastructure extends well beyond the data warehouse. New client/server operational systems have very similar infrastructure requirements, so in most cases, the data warehouse can simply rely on existing infrastructure. However, infrastructure is like a snake in the grass—it will rise up and bite you if you are not careful, and you won't realize you've been bitten until it's too late.

METADATA AND THE METADATA CATALOG

Metadata is a big terminology battleground. In this section we offer up a descriptive definition of metadata (to help you know it when you see it). Then we take a look at an example of the supporting role metadata plays in the warehouse. Finally, we describe the concept of the metadata catalog and offer some suggestions on tracking your metadata.

Metadata: What Is It?

Metadata is an amazing topic in the data warehouse world. Considering that we don't know exactly what it is or where it is, we spend more time talking about it, more time worrying about it, and more time feeling guilty we aren't doing anything about it than any other topic. Several years ago we decided that metadata is any data about data. This wasn't very helpful because it didn't paint a clear picture in our minds as to what exactly this darn stuff was. This fuzzy view gradually clarified and recently we have been talking more confidently about the "back room metadata" and "front room metadata." The back room metadata is process related, and it guides the extraction, cleaning, and loading processes. The front room metadata is more descriptive, and it helps query tools and report writers function smoothly. Of course, process and descriptive metadata overlap, but it is useful to think about them separately.

The back room metadata presumably helps the DBA bring the data into the warehouse, and it is probably also of interest to business users when they ask where the data comes from. The front room metadata is mostly for the benefit of the end user, and its definition has been expanded to not only be the oil that makes our tools function smoothly but to be a kind of dictionary of business content represented by all the data elements.

Even these definitions, as helpful as they may be, fail to give data warehouse managers much of a feeling for what they are supposed to do. But one can apply a traditional information technology perspective to metadata. At the very least we should do the following:

- Make a nice annotated list of all of the metadata.
- Decide just how important each part is.
- Take responsibility for it or assign that responsibility to someone else.
- Decide what constitutes a consistent and working set of it.
- Decide whether to make or buy the tools to manage the metadata.

- Store it somewhere for backup and recovery.
- Make it available to the people who need it.
- Quality assure it and make it complete and up-to-date.
- Control it from one place.
- Document all of these responsibilities well enough to hand this job off (soon).

The only trouble is, we haven't really said what *it* is yet. We do notice that the last item in the preceding list really isn't metadata—it's data about metadata. With a sinking feeling, we realize we probably need meta meta data data. To understand this better, let's try to make a complete list of all possible types of metadata. We surely won't succeed in our first try, but we will learn a lot.

Source System Metadata

First, let's go to the source systems, which could be mainframes, separate nonmainframe servers, users' desktops, third-party data providers, or even on-line sources. We will assume that all we do here is read the source data and extract it to a data staging area that could be on the mainframe or could be a downstream machine.

Source Specifications
- Repositories
- Source schemas
- Copy books
- Proprietary or third-party source schemas
- Print spool file sources
- Old formats for archived mainframe data
- Relational source system tables and DDL
- Spreadsheet sources
- Lotus Notes databases
- Presentation graphics (e.g., PowerPoint)
- Universal resource locator (URL) source specifications

Source Descriptive Information
- Ownership descriptions of each source
- Business descriptions of each source
- Update frequencies of original sources

- Legal limitations on the use of each source
- Access methods, access rights, privileges, and passwords for source access

Process Information

- Mainframe or source system job schedules
- COBOL/JCL, C, Basic, or other code to implement extraction
- The automated extract tool settings, if we use such a tool
- Results of specific extract jobs, including exact times, content, and completeness

Data Staging Metadata

Now let's list all the metadata needed to get the data into a data staging area and prepare it for loading into one or more data marts. We may do this on the mainframe with hand-coded COBOL or use an automated extract tool. We may also bring the flat file extracts more or less untouched into a separate data staging area on a different machine. In any case, we have to be concerned about metadata, especially as it pertains to the following sections.

Data Acquisition Information

- Data transmission scheduling and results of specific transmissions
- File usage in the data staging area including duration, volatility, and ownership

Dimension Table Management

- Definitions of conformed dimensions and conformed facts
- Job specifications for joining sources, stripping out fields, and looking up attributes
- Slowly changing dimension policies for each incoming descriptive attribute (e.g., overwrite, create new record, or create new field)
- Current surrogate key assignments for each production key, including a fast lookup table to perform this mapping in memory
- Yesterday's copy of production dimensions to use as the basis for DIFF COMPARE

Transformation and Aggregation

- Data cleaning specifications
- Data enhancement and mapping transformations (e.g., expand abbreviations and provide more detail)

- Transformations required for data mining (e.g., interpret nulls and scale numerics)
- Target schema designs, source-to-target data flows, and target data ownership
- DBMS load scripts
- Aggregate definitions
- Aggregate usage statistics, base table usage statistics, and potential aggregates
- Aggregate modification logs

Audit, Job Logs, and Documentation

- Data lineage and audit records (where *exactly* did this record come from and when?)
- Data transform run time logs, success summaries, and time stamps
- Data transform software version numbers
- Business descriptions of extract processing
- Security settings for extract files, extract software, and extract metadata
- Security settings for data transmission (e.g., passwords, certificates)
- Data staging area archive logs and recovery procedures
- Data staging archive security settings

DBMS Metadata

Once we have finally transferred the data to the data warehouse or data mart DBMS, another set of metadata comes into play, including:

- DBMS system table contents
- Partition settings
- Indexes
- Disk striping specifications
- Processing hints
- DBMS-level security privileges and grants
- View definitions
- Stored procedures and SQL administrative scripts
- DBMS backup status, backup procedures, and backup security

Front Room Metadata

In the front room we have metadata extending to the horizon, including:

- Business names and descriptions for columns, tables, and groupings
- Canned query and report definitions
- Join specification tool settings
- Pretty print tool specifications (for relabeling fields in readable ways)
- End-user documentation and training aids (both vendor supplied and IT supplied)
- Network security user privilege profiles
- Network security authentication certificates
- Network security usage statistics, including logon attempts, access attempts, and user ID by location reports
- Individual user profiles, with link to Human Resources to track promotions, transfers, and resignations that affect access rights
- Link to contractor and partner tracking, where access rights are affected
- Usage and access maps for data elements, tables, views, and reports
- Resource charge-back statistics
- Favorite Web sites (as a paradigm for all data warehouse access)

Now we can see why we didn't know exactly what this metadata was all about. It is everything! Except for the data itself. All of a sudden, the data seems like the simplest part. In a sense, metadata is the DNA of the data warehouse. It defines what all the elements are and how they work together.

While this list helps give us a descriptive feel for metadata, another approach to understanding it is to see it in action.

An Active Metadata Example

Gathering and maintaining metadata because we are supposed to isn't enough motivation in the long run. Metadata is like traditional systems documentation (in fact, it is documentation), and at some point, the resources needed to create and maintain it will be diverted to other "more urgent" projects. Active metadata helps solve this problem. Active metadata is metadata that drives a process rather than documents it. The fact that it documents the process as well is a fortuitous side effect.

Let's see how this works by stepping through a simple metadata flow chart. First, you need a data model of the data warehouse. This process is technically straightforward using one of the popular modeling tools. Most of these tools will reverse- and forward-engineer, so you can use them to extract metadata from existing databases. You need to create both logical and physical models, including the logical, or business, column names, the physical column names, associated business terms and descriptions, example values, and query tips. Once each model is built, you save it out to the tool's own open storage model in a relational database. Step 1 in Figure 11.3 shows this process.

Next, we'll add a little data staging metadata to the flow. The data warehouse models created in Step 1 provide the information we need to know about the targets for the staging process. The data staging tool also needs to know about the sources. So, Step 2 is to capture the source definitions. As we described earlier, these can be anything from flat files to mainframe databases. The data staging tool usually provides a way to capture this information since it relies on it so heavily. Next, in Step 3, we use the staging tool to pull down the table definitions and define the mapping relationships among the sources and targets. Step 3 also involves capturing information about any transformations that might take place during the staging process. If we have a good staging tool, it leverages the metadata we've already created about the target tables in

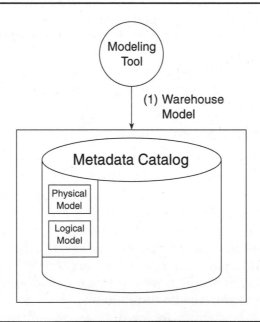

FIGURE 11.3   Step 1: Capturing the warehouse data models.

Step 1. Finally, in Step 4, we save all this out into the data staging tool's relational-based open storage model. This might look like Figure 11.4.

Note that the process of creating these mappings in Step 3 is mostly just defining a relationship between two already existing metadata entries. We did most of the work when we built the data model. Now we can create as many mappings as we like and store them in the metadata catalog.

Once we have completed all these definitions, we finally get some data loaded, as shown in Figure 11.5. To do this, the data staging tool queries the metadata in Step 5 to find out everything it needs to know

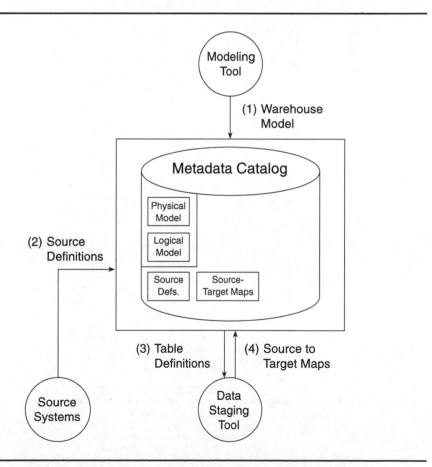

FIGURE 11.4 Steps 2–4: Capturing source defintions and target mapping.

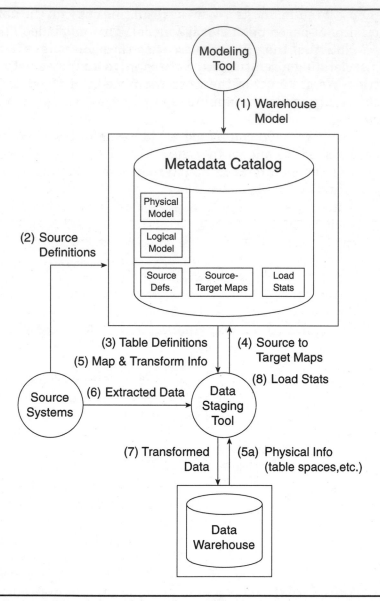

FIGURE 11.5 Steps 5–8: Extract, transform, and load.

about the source data types and locations, the target data types and locations, and the mappings between the two. It may also query the target database in Step 5a for current information on the physical state of the system, like how much disk space is available. In Step 6, we actually extract the raw source data, and in Step 7, we load the transformed data into the warehouse. Step 8 captures some statistics and audit information about the load and saves it back to the metadata catalog.

Now that we've finally loaded some data, the users are probably itching to get at it, but they need something to tell them what information can be found where. Fortunately, we have most of that in the data model already. The table and column names, descriptions and examples of the contents, and so on are all there. Before we open the front doors, we need to provide a little more business structure to the warehouse. An alphabetical listing of tables and columns isn't going to be helpful because people tend to think in terms of business groupings, not alphabetical listings. These groups would probably be the fact tables we described in the modeling chapters. The front-end tool or application server usually provides a way to create this metadata.

Once this business metadata is available, Step 9 shows how it might be helpful to provide a simple Web-based front end to the metadata. Users could browse the business groupings, drill down to see which tables are in the groupings, and drill further to see which columns are in the tables. Alternatively, they could use a simple search tool to look for columns or table descriptions that have, for example, the words *sales* or *revenue* in them.

Once they've found the right data, the users can formulate a query and submit it to the database in Step 10. Note that the query also relies on physical table and column definitions retrieved in Step 9 to formulate the correct query syntax. The results are returned to the user in Step 11, and a good query tool writes out some usage information in Step 12.

This progression shows the central role the metadata catalog plays in a simple warehouse example. Notice that only 3 of the 12 interactions actually involve data—the rest is metadata. Note also that portions of the same metadata are used in many different places. For example, the model we created in Step 1 contains the original physical table definitions. The data staging tool needs those before it can do the source-to-

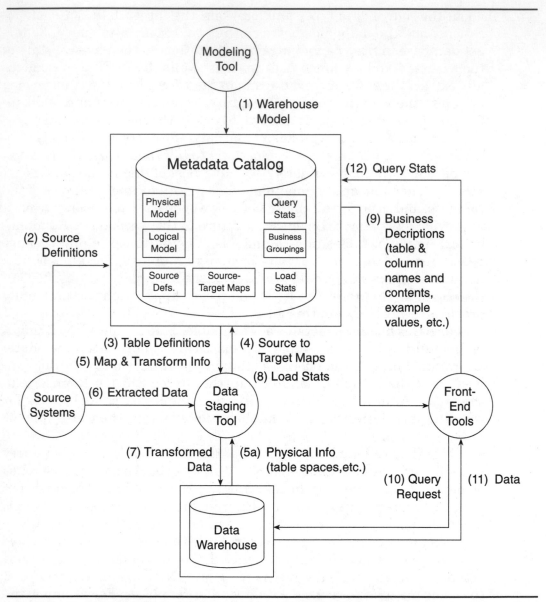

FIGURE 11.6   The role of metadata in driving front-end tools.

target mapping and again when it's time to actually transform and load the data. Finally, the query tool (or application server) needs to know the physical table definitions to formulate the correct queries.

Hopefully, the metadata list and the flow example have given you some perspective on metadata. But with this perspective, do we really need to keep track of all this? Yes, in our opinion. This list of metadata is the essential framework of your data warehouse. Just listing it as we have done seems quite helpful. It's a long list, but we can go down through it finding each of these kinds of metadata, identifying what it is used for, and where it is stored.

There are some sobering realizations, however. Much of this metadata needs to reside on the machines close to where the work occurs. Programs, settings, and specifications that drive processes have to be in certain destination locations and in certain very specific formats. That isn't likely to change very soon.

Metadata Catalog Maintenance

Terms like *information library, repository,* and *metadatabase,* among others, have all been used to describe this data store. We've chosen the term *metadata catalog* as a generic descriptor for the overall set of metadata used in the warehouse. In the best of all possible worlds, the metadata catalog would be the single, common storage point for information that drives the entire warehouse process. Every step in the warehouse, from the initial model through the recurring extract and load process to the navigation and access from the user's desktop would use the metadata catalog. We don't expect this single common storage point to actually exist anytime soon, so in the meantime we'll treat the metadata catalog as a logical construct that actually exists in many different physical locations.

 You need a tool for cataloging all of this metadata and keeping track of it. The tool probably can't read and write all the metadata directly, but it should at least help you manage the metadata that is stored in so many locations.

Fortunately, there is a category of tools, loosely called *metadata catalog tools,* dedicated to this very purpose. A good listing of these tools can be found on Larry Greenfield's Web site at http://pwp.starnetinc.com/larryg/catalog.html.

The warehouse team also needs to provide basic maintenance tools to manage any metadata in the metadata catalog that is not created and managed by one of the tools or services. For example, user-entered comments, custom hierarchies, or specifications for a custom-ordered personal data mart might not be supported by existing products and would need a separate service.

Other functionality around the metadata catalog may involve creating remote procedure calls (RPCs) to provide direct access to metadata for source systems and navigation tools.

Finally, data staging and data access services need to be able to work with security-related metadata in the metadata catalog. That metadata will need to be developed and maintained by a tool or function. This includes adding and deleting new users and groups, assigning access rights to users and groups, and so on. This metadata also needs to be integrated with database platform security tables (more metadata!).

The list of functions and services required in the metadata catalog maintenance area includes the following:

- Information catalog integration/merge (e.g., from the data model to the database to the front-end tool)
- Metadata management (e.g., remove old, unused entries)
- Capture existing metadata (e.g., DDL from mainframe or other sources)
- Manage and display graphical and tabular representations of the metadata catalog contents (the metadata browser)
- Maintain user profiles for application and security use
- Security for the metadata catalog
- Local or centralized metadata catalog support

Once we have taken the first step of getting our metadata corralled and under control, can we hope for even more powerful tools that will pull all the metadata together in one place and be able to read it and write it as well? With such a tool, not only would we have a uniform user interface for all this disparate metadata, but we would be able to consistently snapshot all the metadata at once, back it up, secure it, and restore it if we ever lost it.

In our opinion, this will not happen soon. This is a very hard problem, and to encompass all forms of metadata will require a kind of systems integration we don't have today. We believe the Metadata Coalition (a group of vendors trying seriously to solve the metadata problem) will make some reasonable progress in defining common syntax and semantics for metadata, but this effort started in mid-1995. Unfortunately, Oracle and Microsoft, two of the biggest DBMS players, chose not to participate in this effort and have promised to release their own proprietary metadata standards. One would need to see significant and compelling business advantages offered by these vendors as a magnet for other vendors to write to their specifications if the metadata problem is going to be solved in a deep sense.

Metadata Summary

Metadata is the data warehouse's Gordian knot, and Alexander and his sword are nowhere in sight. So, what can we do to cope with it in the meantime? Here are a few steps you can take to loosen the knot a little.

- Insist, in a loud voice, that the vendors you select support some form of open metadata exchange capability.
- Fill in the gaps with simple utilities to help you copy metadata from its primary source to other places where it is needed and manage the most repetitive metadata tasks.
- Manage the rest by hand. Catalog the metadata you have so you can maintain it properly and migrate it to the integrated metadata catalog when it shows up. Remind your vendors of their commitment to open metadata exchange.

SUMMARY

Infrastructure and metadata provide the foundation upon which we build the warehouse. Either under-powered or insufficient infrastructure or limited, poorly maintained metadata can weaken the entire warehouse. It makes no difference how clean or complete the data is if you can't get it to the user's desktop in a reliable, understandable, and predictable form.

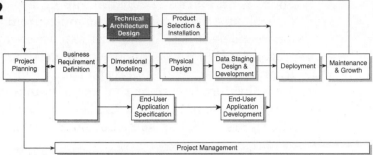

CHAPTER 12

A Graduate Course on the Internet and Security

One of the ironies of the job of data warehouse manager is the tension between the publishing responsibility and the protection responsibility. On the one hand, the data warehouse manager is judged by how easily an end user can access all the data in the data warehouse. On the other hand, the data warehouse manager is blamed if sensitive data gets into the wrong hands or if data is lost. The data warehouse manager has been entrusted with the crown jewels of the organization (the data) but may be held responsible if the crown jewels are lost, or stolen, or forcibly taken away.

 The loss of data warehouse data to hostile parties can have extremely serious legal, financial, and competitive impacts on an organization.

There is an alarming cultural gap in most IS shops separating the data warehouse publishing responsibility from the data warehouse protection responsibility. As we will explore in more detail later in this chapter, most IS data warehouse managers believe that someone else in the IS organization will take responsibility for security. Yet, upon a moment's reflection, it is clear that security in a data warehouse environment is largely about recognizing legitimate users and giving them very specific rights to look at some but not all of the data.

 No one in the organization is better equipped to qualify users and grant them data warehouse rights than the data warehouse manager.

Data warehouse managers must immediately step up to their professional responsibility: They must actively manage data warehouse security. This means that data warehouse managers must have a fairly good understanding of security issues, so they can hire and supervise security experts who are dedicated to the data warehouse effort. Overseeing security in a large data warehouse environment is a full-time job for at least one person.

As if the basic security issues of the data warehouse weren't enough, the growth of the Internet has been an express train that has run over IS shops in general and data warehouse installations in particular. As data warehouse configurations were moving slowly from two-tier configurations (with a fat client talking directly to the DBMS machine) to three-tier configurations with an application server between the client and the DBMS, along came the Internet with several more layers. Every data warehouse manager now had the added burden of dealing with a Web server, a directory server, and several layers of firewalls and packet filters.

The modern data warehouse manager must understand the Internet because almost every component of the data warehouse is being retrofitted to work in a Web environment, even when networks are not connected to the real Internet. Thus not only has the technical complexity of the warehouse environment increased by a quantum leap, the risks to the data warehouse have increased just as much. It is as if we have set up our business on a street corner, instead of in the privacy of offices in our own building. Data warehouse owners cannot ignore the impact of the Internet on their mission and their own jobs. Data warehouse owners must educate themselves about the risks, the technologies, and the new administrative perspectives brought about by the Internet. This chapter aims to provide an introduction to the Internet from a data warehouse manager's perspective. Although it is somewhat technical, we feel that these topics must be understood by every data warehouse manager at the level of detail presented in this chapter.

A reasonable, basic view of the architecture in between the user and the data may look like Figure 12.1. This chapter will discuss each of the

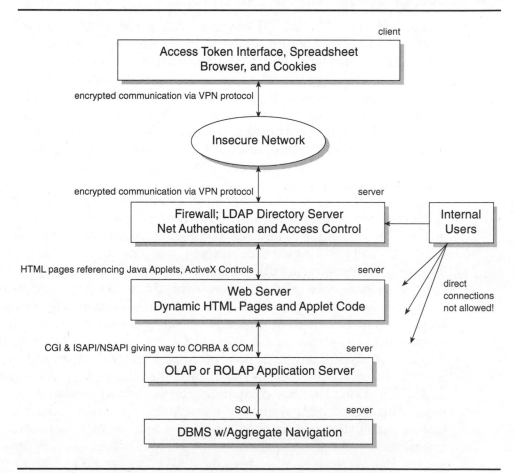

FIGURE 12.1   A typical modern data warehouse server architecture.

components of Figure 12.1 in just enough detail to educate the data warehouse manager about what is important.

We start our discussion of security with a short overview of component software architecture. Just what are all these machines doing, anyway? We then try to list all the kinds of risks and exposures that the data warehouse manager needs to be aware of. We then take a fairly quick tour of the technologies that are ready to help deal with our security and communications issues, and finally we present a checklist for immediate action.

COMPONENT SOFTWARE ARCHITECTURE

The period from 1995 to 1997 saw a number of significant advances in the way we think about building distributed systems. A profound architectural advance has been quietly brewing both inside and outside of the Microsoft camp. This profound advance is called *component software*. Some time ago, the software industry realized that the task of producing large software systems has grown too complex to continue using a monolithic approach. In the monolithic approach, each new large software system is coded from the ground up, and all the interfaces between the software routines are defined as the project proceeds. Not only does this approach fail to capitalize on previously built software, but the sheer size of modern software makes a monolithic development effort impossible to manage. A recent release of Microsoft Windows 95 reportedly was based on 14 million lines of source code. Such a large body of software requires the efforts of literally thousands of developers over a number of years. The only hope of building systems this complicated, and of meeting ever more aggressive release schedules, is to base everything on component software.

By the end of 1997, two significant competing systems for component software had emerged. Microsoft's system is based on an architecture known as the Distributed Component Object Model (DCOM). Although the DCOM specification is now no longer controlled directly by Microsoft, the company remains the dominant supplier. Its suite of services and applications that use component software is known as Active Platform. The components themselves are ActiveX controls, and the application shells that are invoked on clients and servers to launch these components are a generalization of HTML pages known as Active Server Pages. ActiveX controls and Active Server Page scripts can be written in a number of languages, including Visual Basic and C.

The competing component software approach is sponsored by the non-Microsoft camp, including Sun Microsystems, Netscape, and Oracle. This system is based on the Common Object Request Broker Architecture (CORBA). This suite of services uses component software known as Enterprise Java. The components themselves are JavaBeans. JavaBeans can be called from HTML pages, and are meant to be written in the Java language.

From 1998 onward, the data warehouse marketplace will see most systems building on one or both of these architectural approaches. However, the impact of componentized software on data warehousing is much more significant than simply understanding how professional software developers put their products together. The very nature of software has changed in fundamental ways:

- Software can be sold and released in a much more modular fashion. An upgrade or a service pack need only consist of selected software components.
- Many more vendors and software development teams can add functionality to a system by producing standalone software components that obey disciplined component interfaces. We are already quite familiar with software plug-ins for graphics packages.
- IS shops will undoubtedly buy major systems from large software vendors, but they will have many opportunities to develop their own custom components to fit into this scheme. To add custom components, the IS shop will obviously have to invest in modern, robust, component software–based architectures like DCOM and CORBA. Very soon it will not make sense to buy new software that does not conform to one of these architectures.
- Software components have very specific protocols for communicating among themselves. These communications protocols allow software modules to find each other in different parts of memory, in different locations on the local hard drive, and on remote machines, all transparently from the user's point of view. Software components also are usually written to be multithreaded so that a single component can be used by many applications simultaneously.
- Software components encourage distributed applications, in which the various interacting components reside on different machines. We are well past the point where a networked computer can be viewed as a standalone bastion of hardware and software with well-defined

boundaries. As Scott McNealy, the chairman of Sun Microsystems said, "The network is the computer."

■ Our reliance on distributed systems has made the issues of security enormously more difficult to understand and control. Our little software components are busy talking to each other all around the net and very few of us understand the implications. In order to not be distracted by this huge issue, we will complete our discussion of component software architecture in this section and we will forestall the discussion of security until the next section.

The Impact of the Internet on Architecture

The Internet has encouraged and accelerated the use of software components and put tremendous pressure on vendors to solve a number of compatibility, performance, and security problems. Suddenly the client paradigm has changed. All clients are becoming HTML browsers. Some of the browsers reside on the local network and some are connecting through the Internet or a dial-up phone line. In many cases, the same users switch on a daily basis between all three modes of access with their browsers. These users expect the same software to work no matter how they access the data warehouse.

At the same time, the original monolithic database engine is fragmenting into multiple processes running on multiple machines. There may be an aggregate navigator intercepting SQL intended for the relational DBMS and directing the SQL to a number of separate machines. There may be an application server whose task it is to assemble a complex report or analysis by separately querying multiple data sources. How do we sort all of this out?

In Figure 12.2, we show how a Web client (an HTTP-based browser) interacts with a Web server to establish a session with a database application. We show the connection between the client and server as either being over the Internet or a protected intranet to emphasize that the two architectures are identical. We will postpone adding the security layers until the next section so that we can discuss the flow of control mandated by the component software approach without being distracted.

Referring to Figure 12.2 we follow the Steps 1 through 8 to understand how a user session is handled. In Step 1, the user at the client browser specifies an HTTP-based URL located on a remote Web server.

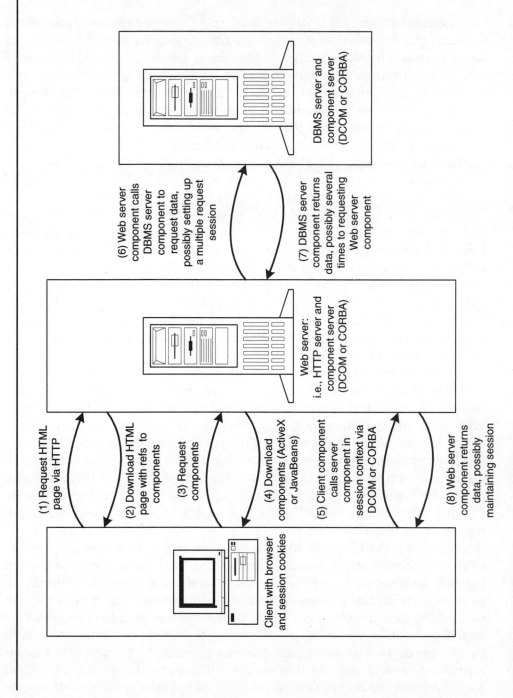

FIGURE 12.2 The browser-server HTTP session.

The diagram shows three stacked components. The bottom component is labeled "Client with browser and session cookies." The middle component is labeled "Web server: i.e., HTTP server and component server (DCOM or CORBA)." The top component is labeled "DBMS server and component server (DCOM or CORBA)."

The following interactions are shown:

(1) Request HTML page via HTTP

(2) Download HTML page with refs to components

(3) Request components

(4) Download components (ActiveX or JavaBeans)

(5) Client component calls server component in session context via DCOM or CORBA

(6) Web server component calls DBMS server component to request data, possibly setting up a multiple request session

(7) DBMS server component returns data, possibly several times to requesting Web server component

(8) Web server component returns data, possibly maintaining session

455

We assume the client browser and the Web server are connected through the Internet or an intranet. Step 2 causes an HTML page to be sent from the Web server to the client browser. The HTML page contains references to downloadable software components or more comprehensive applications that consist of software components. In the Microsoft world, these downloadable components are ActiveX controls, and in the non-Microsoft world they are JavaBeans, or more generally, Java applets that may be composed of JavaBeans.

In Steps 3 and 4, the client browser downloads the requested software components and loads them into memory. The key new capability these components have is that they can communicate directly with other components, either elsewhere in the client browser or on the Web server. They do not need to launch a new HTTP request or open a new Web page. All of the various software components communicate directly via CORBA or DCOM. Thus in Step 5, a client software component calls a server software component. The server software component can be an arbitrary program, with the ability to make further calls to other machines, including database engines, as in Step 6. In Step 7, the database engine returns data to the server software component, and in Step 8, the data is transferred to the client browser.

These steps can be repeated at the request of the end user as many times as desired in the context of the original HTML page. The user doesn't think of the screen as an HTML page, but rather as a single graphical user interface that is controlling a coherent session. This ability to have a single page act as a comprehensive user interface with many possible responses to the user and to have the single page mediate the complete user session is a huge leap forward in interactivity using the Web browser model. The original static page-oriented model for Web browsing prior to CORBA and DCOM could not support the notion of an interactive session.

The basic HTTP protocol remains as a stateless protocol. In other words, HTTP by itself does not provide support for a user session. To provide for a continuous coherent session, the Web server must rely on session information provided by the client browser each time a request is made between machines. Each Web server application requires its own information to maintain a coherent session, and thus the Web server requires that the client browser assemble and keep this information so that it can be revealed every time the client and the server communicate. This piece of information is called a *cookie*. Cookies are small text files containing information of interest to the Web server that are stored in special cookie folders on the client machine. Cookies are controversial because they can potentially reveal information to a requesting Web server that the user may feel uncomfortable divulging. These security issues are discussed in the next section.

As the marketplace develops more useful solutions based on component software architectures, the data warehouse team must navigate through a confusing array of new products and conflicting terminology. To be safe, we recommend, for any new software acquisitions, that you avoid products based on static HTML generation or those that use the Common Gateway Interface (CGI) or its derivatives, ISAPI and NSAPI. CGI, in particular, is the first-generation approach to providing interactive Web pages, and it has severe problems. CGI, like HTTP itself, is stateless. Each request sent from a client browser screen to a CGI application, causes CGI to load and execute a fresh instance of the application. This is a performance showstopper for the Web server in a large data warehouse environment.

SECURITY: VULNERABILITIES

The transformation of our enterprise computer environments to fully distributed, networked client/server systems together with the intrusion of the Internet has, within the space of one or two years, changed the game dramatically for the owners of data warehouses. As an industry we are sitting on a time bomb. Our data is grossly exposed and at risk. We face significant legal and professional challenges in understanding our vulnerabilities and responding to them effectively. Certainly, as of the time of this writing, data warehouse managers were generally not paying close attention to security issues. In this section we try to frame the security problem, and in the next section we suggest how to understand and manage security in a data warehouse environment.

This section may be somewhat painful reading. Although we are not trying to be alarmist, we feel that the data warehouse community has sidestepped the main issues of security up until now. Most data warehouse managers have something of a positive marketing attitude, which can make them blind to security issues. The data warehouse represents an opportunity to learn new things about the enterprise and its customers. Most data warehouse managers spend a significant amount of energy talking about these opportunities and selling the benefits of the data warehouse. It is difficult for most of us to turn our thinking away from the benefits and look at risks and at the downside.

The total size of the security problem is surprising and underappreciated. As early as October 1996, Ernst and Young stated in *Information Week* that "78% of Information Security Chiefs, Information Security Officers and other higher-level executives [reported that their companies had] lost money from security breaches [related to information technology]. More than 25% reported losses greater than twenty-five thousand dollars, and inside hackers were at fault for nearly 32% [of the losses]." In 1997, the Aberdeen Group, using slightly different measures, reported that the typical causes of "compromised information" included:

- 35 percent: human error
- 25 percent: human omission
- 15 percent: disgruntled employees
- 10 percent: external people
- 7 percent: fire
- 5 percent: flood
- 3 percent: other natural disasters

These findings suggest that the sources of vulnerability are very diverse, and that there is a very significant level of threat from internal sources, not just "hackers on the Internet." Charles Pfleeger, in his seminal book, *Security in Computing* (Prentice-Hall 1989) divides the disgruntled employees and external people listed earlier into three categories:

- **Amateurs.**   Normal people who exploit a flaw in a security system that allows them access to information, cash, or other valuables. This also includes disgruntled employees who are motivated to attack a system to settle a grudge.
- **Crackers.**   Often juveniles or isolated individuals for whom breaking through a system's security is a challenge and a thrill. Some crackers simply try to penetrate a system as if to keep score, while others attack for personal gain or to deliberately cause chaos, loss, or harm.
- **Career criminals.**   Computer professionals who engage in computer crime, including organized crime and international groups

with political or terrorist agendas. Additionally, a growing group of electronic spies and information brokers have begun to trade in companies' or individuals' secrets.

For the rest of this section, please try to think like a good security analyst instead of a data warehouse manager. Without offering any good news, we will systematically analyze all the vulnerabilities we can think of in a modern networked data warehouse. We will be suspicious of everything and everyone. We will assume that we are under attack. Obviously, a draconian solution is to not let anyone have access to the data warehouse, but we must keep in mind that we have a job to publish and disseminate enterprise information. Later in this chapter, we will try to resolve this conflict, but for now we will just examine our vulnerabilities. For each type of vulnerability we invite the reader to imagine how the activities of a data warehouse could be specifically impacted if the vulnerability were exploited and how a responsible data warehouse manager could act to reduce or eliminate the vulnerability.

Physical Assets

Our physical assets are the obvious ones, including mainframes and servers, desktop PCs, and laptops. Physical assets also include communications equipment, wires and fiber optics, buildings, file drawers, and off-line media. The main vulnerabilities of physical assets are shown in Figure 12.3.

Information Assets: Data, Financial Assets, and Reputation

Data and information assets include nearly everything of value that isn't a physical asset and isn't software that we obtain from outsiders. These assets include all of the metadata categories listed earlier in the previous chapter, as well as all of our "real" data in documents, spreadsheets, e-mail, graphics systems, and databases of all kinds. Our data and information assets also include all *derivative* forms of electronic information, including printouts, photocopies, and the information carried in people's heads.

Although in most respects our financial assets seem to take the form of information, such assets have an obvious and special significance be-

Vulnerability	Basic Description	How the Data Warehouse Could Be Involved
Theft	The loss of a physical asset because someone simply takes it off premises.	A PC may contain data warehouse information results; a PC may contain logon privileges or built-in passwords to data warehouse; a PC may contain data warehouse encryption passwords not stored elsewhere; a PC may contain private key used for authentication of user to data warehouse or certification of data warehouse results as being trustworthy; an asset may contain metadata needed for data warehouse operations. Loss by theft raises the possibility that the content of the information has fallen into hostile hands, requiring changing of access methods, procedures, and personnel.
Intentional Destruction	A deliberate attack on a physical asset. There are endless ways in which a physical asset can be destroyed by a determined individual, including smashing with a heavy instrument, setting on fire, dousing with liquid, prying open with a screw driver, dropping out a window, and many others.	Loss of data warehouse data; loss of passwords; loss of metadata supporting data warehouse operations; loss of backups; resultant inability to recover information; loss may target specific information resource to cause maximum disruption or to disguise other fraud.
Fire	Accidental fire or deliberate arson, affecting the information system specifically or as part of a larger fire. This category includes smoke damage and water damage from fire fighting.	Same as intentional destruction; may be more widespread, simultaneously affecting primary and backup systems.
Moisture	Degradation of a physical asset because it is stored improperly.	Inability to recover old versions of data; loss likely to go unnoticed until it is far too late to provide protection.
Water	Destruction of an asset because of flooding, being doused with water, or being dropped in water.	Many high-tech portable devices, such as portable PCs, become instantly worthless when they are dropped in water. Less damaging than outright theft because the information is merely lost rather than compromised.
Dirt	Destruction of an asset because of improper storage or handling. Dirt infiltrates fragile computer systems. Circuits short out and disk heads crash.	Same issues as moisture, plus likelihood of wasted time and money trying to use and repair damaged systems.

FIGURE 12.3 Vulnerabilities of physical assets.

Vulnerability	Basic Description	How the Data Warehouse Could Be Involved
Aging	Destruction of an asset because it wears out, becomes fragile, or gradually is altered chemically. Maybe it has been left in the sun. Maybe it has been roughly handled.	Same issues as moisture.
Electrical Discharge and Electrical Interference	Destruction of an asset because the asset is not protected against power circuit surges, spikes, or brownouts. Also includes the effects of lightning as well as equipment such as airport security systems.	Loss of a current on-line data warehouse asset such as a client machine or a server, and perhaps an asset that is on-line or possesses volatile data that has not been backed up.
Magnetic Disturbance	Destruction of an asset by exposing it to a magnetic field, such as a powerful sound speaker or a security system.	Disk drives and other magnetic media that are compromised by a destructive magnetic field are usually complete losses and cannot be recovered.
Loss Through Oversight	An asset is rendered useless because "the keys to it are lost."	No one can remember what the significance of the tapes are, or no one can remember what the password or the encryption key to the tapes is. No one can remember what happened to the special cable that connects the two boxes together. It is likely that anyone who does remember the intended use of the tapes or the special devices will not be able to find them because they have not been tracked or described in inventory.
Loss Through Technological Obsolescence	An asset is rendered useless because there is no card punch reader, paper tape reader, or 8-inch floppy device left anywhere that still works. Technological obsolescence can take place anywhere in the system: hardware, software, or procedures. Technological obsolescence can take place because there are no more replacement parts to fix an asset.	Even storage media that have been properly cared for and properly inventoried can be lost if the hardware systems, software systems, and procedures surrounding their use have not been kept current. This kind of loss is a gigantic risk to the data warehouse owner. Old data assumed to be available is not available, and today's data has a much shorter shelf life than the plan calls for.
Hijacked Assets	An intruder takes control over all or part of a physical machine. This can be viewed as a loss of control or	A data warehouse can be attacked or compromised through a hijacked asset in many ways. A hijacked control may

FIGURE 12.3   *Continued*

Vulnerability	Basic Description	How the Data Warehouse Could Be Involved
Hijacked Assets (*cont.*)	compromised trust. Perhaps the intruder exploits the physical access to replace a trusted software component with a rogue component. For example, a trusted Web browser could be replaced with a Web browser that would silently reveal information the user did not want disclosed. Or perhaps the intruder places a tap on the local intranet. If no one in your organization has ever lifted the ceiling tiles to look for unauthorized taps on the network cable, then you are not paranoid enough.	reveal security codes to give the intruder unintended access. A physical tap on the network can accomplish the same purpose. Both of these attack modes can of course send real data results to the intruder, not just security codes. A hijacked asset destroys trust in the data warehouse system.

FIGURE 12.3 *Continued*

cause they are often liquid and many times they are anonymous. Financial assets can be thought of as information assets that can be physically removed from us, not just copied.

Finally, there is a special kind of information asset that has a qualitative aspect to it: our reputation. Our reputation is what people think of us, what people believe they know about us, and how much goodwill we have. In the deepest sense our reputation is our identity. Our reputation can be destroyed, damaged, and even stolen from us just like other forms of assets.

There are many vulnerabilities to these kinds of assets, which for brevity we will call *information assets* in all of the following. First, let us discuss the general vulnerability to information theft, summarized in Figure 12.4.

There are many ways to accomplish theft in our open, distributed information systems. Several modes of theft are illustrated in Figure 12.5.

In many cases, the goal of a security breach is not to steal information but to modify it. Deliberate modification of information assets include the kinds of information modification shown in Figure 12.6.

Vulnerability	Basic Description	How the Data Warehouse Could Be Involved
Confidential Disclosure of Plans	Disclosure of your confidential plans or tentative decisions.	The data warehouse is a known location for confidential plans such as budgets, projections, and other what-if analyses, and therefore, it will be the target of anyone trying to find these plans. The data warehouse may signal the presence of confidential information in many ways. Detail data is obvious because it may be explicitly labeled, but summary data such as a yearly projection or a statistic attributed to a group of people can be just as revealing.
Disclosure of Codes	Disclosure of your own codes or account numbers or passwords that can lead to further theft or disruptive actions.	There are many places in the data warehouse where security and access codes are either entered or stored. Many forms of metadata are stored in the data warehouse and may contain explicit codes. Many data warehouse primary data tables contain sensitive information about individuals such as bank card numbers or mothers' maiden names, which are kinds of codes.
Disclosure of Information Held in Trust	Disclosure of confidential information you hold in trust for a third party, such as credit card numbers, social security numbers, health information, or business private data belonging to a third party.	This class of information exposure is especially bad not only because the owner of the information may be directly damaged, but you as the trusted holder of the information are probably liable for the loss and perhaps for additional damages. You also are likely to lose the relationship you have with the third party. If this isn't enough, if you are the responsible employee who is held at fault for allowing this information to be stolen, you will probably lose your job.
Disclosure of Sensitive Information	Disclosure of politically sensitive, ethically sensitive, or legally sensitive information, that you may hold, whether or not it is factually true. Also the use of this information for blackmail.	The data warehouse may be in an awkward position of storing data that really should not be stored or should not be kept any longer. If the data warehouse contains politically, ethically, or legally sensitive data, it may be the target of legal actions such as subpoenas. Such data would also be a primary target of intruders. Data warehouses tracking the behavior of individuals have a set of very serious exposures ranging from simple privacy objections, to legally protected privacy requirements, to blackmail.

FIGURE 12.4 **Vulnerabilities of information assets.**

Vulnerability	Basic Description	How the Data Warehouse Could Be Involved
Removal of Protection or Time Advantage	Removal, in a financial sense, of a time advantage you may have with product plans, investment plans, or knowledge of other future events. Also, in the same vein, disclosure of a trade secret that is not otherwise protected by patent.	Many what-if analyses take the form of trial forecasts or trial budgets, or other future time series. These time series may naturally be stored in the data warehouse environment, and therefore will be the target of intruders seeking this information.
Theft of Financial Assets	Direct theft of financial assets by transferring funds to other accounts and by being able to invoke meaningful financial transactions using your authority.	The direct theft of financial assets would probably be the result of compromising account numbers, access codes, or other tokens such as maiden names through the data warehouse.
Theft of Service Assets	Direct theft of service assets by revealing authorization codes for telephone service, for instance.	Telephone numbers and their access codes are a very obvious exposure, if the data warehouse contains such information. Other unlisted telephone numbers can cause problems, if they lead an intruder to a system that can be easily cracked.
Theft of Information to Leverage Violence or Terrorism	The theft of information, such as travel plans, that places individuals in danger of kidnapping or terrorism.	The more transaction-level information we record in our data warehouses about the behavior of individuals, the more risk we have that this information can be used to leverage violence or terrorism. Credit card transactions, for instance, would be very revealing.
Theft of Identity	Theft of identity in such a way that your authority or your credit or your goodwill is used by someone else against your wishes. This kind of theft for individuals often turns out to be a real loss like the loss of a physical or financial asset because it is surprisingly difficult to persuade the world that the previous use of your identity was fraudulent and that your really are who you say you are.	Identity theft may only require a few pieces of information from the data warehouse. Chief among these are account numbers, and security tokens such as, once again, your mother's maiden name.
Theft of Privacy	Theft of privacy so that your personal life details, beliefs, and activities are revealed against your wishes.	As an industry, we have a huge challenge to balance the desires of our marketing and sales departments to store customer behavioral data in the data warehouse, with the opposite desire to preserve our customers' anonymity, dignity, and safety.

FIGURE 12.4   *Continued*

Mode of Theft	Basic Description	How the Data Warehouse Could Let Down Its Guard
Opportunistic Snatching	The information is unprotected by any real security system. Perhaps the information is in an obscure location. The thief may chance upon the information without a focused prior intention to steal it, or the thief may be looking just for such unprotected information.	Many aspects of our data warehouses have no real security protection at all. Temporary tables or derived aggregate tables may have no security protection. Perhaps the membership of the primary user access groups is not maintained effectively. Perhaps contractors, outsiders, and ex-employees are also members of such groups. Perhaps the backup media have no security and are stored in less-than-secure environments.
Inadvertent Broadcasting	The information is accidentally left in the open. Perhaps someone forgets to encrypt the file or to set its access permissions. Perhaps the information is inadvertently sent in an e-mail.	This case is similar to opportunistic snatching, but the proximate cause is likely to be a breakdown in procedure. Perhaps an employee is careless or does not understand how to use a system. Probably no one has checked to see if the shared files contain sensitive information, or who exactly has accessed the sensitive files. These lapses are typically simple procedural gaffes caused by users and managers not thinking about security.
Eavesdropping	The thief mounts a deliberate attack on the information system and is able to intercept communications intended for others. Eavesdropping includes electronic eavesdropping on the Internet or the local intranet, as well as electromagnetic eavesdropping with sophisticated equipment capable of picking up emanations from wires, screens, and keyboards. Eavesdropping also includes listening to verbal conversations, and watching over someone's shoulder as they use a computer. Eavesdropping on a local intranet can be accomplished easily by equipping a normal PC with a "promiscuous packet sniffer" that can analyze all packets flowing by on the Ethernet. Commonly available adminis-	Eavesdropping attacks can involve the data warehouse in many obvious ways, including the direct compromising of passwords and information results. Since eavesdropping can take many forms, there is no one solution. Sensitization of employees and managers is an important first step. Encryption techniques can reduce many of the eavesdropping risks.

FIGURE 12.5   **Modes of theft.**

Mode of Theft	Basic Description	How the Data Warehouse Could Let Down Its Guard
Eavesdropping (*cont.*)	trative tools that otherwise have many legitimate uses can be used by anyone to eavesdrop on e-mail messages, login sessions, and Web surfing sessions from all remote users connected to that particular intranet.	
Physical Theft as a Means to Theft of Information	The thief physically takes the computer, the laptop, or the backup tapes off-site in order to use them to gain information. The information may reside on the physical asset taken, or the physical asset may include the authentication means to gain access elsewhere.	The data warehouse manager should be concerned about the physical security of laptops owned by employees with significant access to the data warehouse. Increasingly, laptops are being targeted for theft because of what they contain, not because of the underlying hardware.
Hijacked Session	The thief eavesdrops on a user session until after the security is established, and then forcibly breaks the connection between the user and the server and takes over the remainder of the session, with the thief thus being fully authenticated and authorized.	The data warehouse manager can protect against some forms of hijacked sessions by controlling eavesdropping but should consider systems such Kerberos-protected systems to provide more effective protection against hijacked sessions.
Impersonation	The thief pretends to be someone else, and is thereby authenticated by the system. The thief can accomplish this by acquiring the security tokens. If these tokens are simply the text name and text password of the user, then impersonation may be ridiculously easy. Passwords are notorious for not providing effective security in the real world. Passwords are often divulged. Passwords can be guessed in many cases, especially if they consist of English words or simple numbers or they are short. Impersonation is also called *spoofing*, and in a networked environment may not require a user name and password but may only require impersonating a machine address such as an IP address in the TCP/IP protocol used between machines on the Internet.	The data warehouse manager must not ignore the serious issues of authentication and access control. Even standard password-based systems can be pretty secure if management and employees use their password system correctly. But since most organizations lack the will to enforce strong password administration and use, the data warehouse manager should look to replacing conventional passwords with access tokens such as smart cards or biometric feedback systems.

FIGURE 12.5   *Continued*

Mode of Theft	Basic Description	How the Data Warehouse Could Let Down Its Guard
Trapdoor	The thief prepares or plants software that leaves a trapdoor available. The trapdoor is a undocumented means of access into a system.	The data warehouse manager must take responsibility for the security of the complete access chain from the user's desktop to the disk of the relational database engine. Typically, no one besides the data warehouse manager has this perspective. To guard against trapdoors, all software in this pipeline must be certified as reliable by a trusted and knowledgeable authority.
Bribery, Robbery, and Extortion	All of these techniques are direct manipulation of a trusted person or employee who then grants the thief access or passes information or steals something.	The data warehouse may be able to diagnose or intercept unusual access modes into the data warehouse system. Mostly what is needed is a monitoring system that reports unusual patterns, and accounts for all accesses to certain data.

FIGURE 12.5   *Continued*

Software Assets

Your software assets are vulnerable. We distinguish these vulnerabilities from physical asset and information asset vulnerabilities, although clearly they overlap and combine with each other. Software vulnerabilities include the ones listed in Figure 12.7.

The Ability to Conduct Your Business

In other cases, the attack is meant to affect your ability to provide a service or conduct your business mission, including the vulnerabilities shown in Figure 12.8.

Network Threats

The popularity of the Internet has driven nearly all of us to support the Internet's communication scheme as the way we implement wide area networks. The good news is that the Internet has become a common high-

Kinds of Modification	Basic Description	How the Data Warehouse Could Be Involved
Misdelivery	The information being delivered to an intended party is copied or diverted to other parties. The goal may be to reveal sensitive information or to keep the original recipient from receiving the information.	Data warehouse results are often e-mailed. Users with this kind of data access need to use a reliable and secure e-mail protocol.
Misrepresentation	The information is delivered under false pretenses or with a false origin address. This kind of security breach is very damaging because it is hard to reach everyone who may have received the original fraudulent message, and it is hard to erase the original impressions created. A serious form of misrepresentation includes the destruction of someone's reputation.	Misrepresentation is easy in an open e-mail environment, whether it is inside an intranet or across the Web. The data warehouse manager should work with IS to implement public key encryption on all business e-mail so that the recipients can be sure the sender is who they claim to be.
False Repudiation	A person or a business attempts to claim that they never engaged in a communication or invoked a transaction, when in fact they did.	False repudiation is a huge issue in transaction processing systems, and a relatively minor one in data warehouse systems. The main concern is making sure that someone who invokes a change in the data warehouse can be held responsible for that change. If users can update budgets or forecasts or plans, then the issue of repudiation is somewhat important. Individuals with database administrator privileges or responsibilities may need to pass the false repudiation test if they are dealing with very sensitive data.

FIGURE 12.6   Kinds of information modification.

way that connects all of us together, but the bad news is that the Internet was never designed to protect privacy or commerce. The Internet is a largely UNIX-oriented system that was designed in the 1960s as a way for universities and researchers to communicate informally. The Internet uses the Transmission Control Protocol/Internet Protocol (TCP/IP). This communications protocol is actually two schemes that work together, as

Vulnerabilities	Basic Description	How the Data Warehouse Could Be Affected
Theft of Object Code	The thief copies your software in order to use it or sell it elsewhere. The thief's use, if discovered, may create a liability for you to the original software developer.	The data warehouse environment often has a serious set of software license responsibilities. Query tools, reporting tools, modeling tools, and other licensed software must be controlled.
Theft of Source Code	The thief uses the source code to build derivative software or to disclose your trade secrets against your wishes.	The data warehouse may have a lot of custom software, from serious system code to spreadsheet cell formulas. Source code can reveal proprietary analysis techniques, and mistakes in source code, if revealed, can lead to lawsuits or damaging publicity.
Hijacked Control	The thief inserts unwanted code into a software component that is otherwise trusted.	If this happens, then many other forms of data warehouse security breaches become possible, depending on how much control the software has of the target machine. A Trojan horse is a variant of a hijacked control in which a seemingly innocuous or normal piece of software has a hidden function that appears later or can be turned on by the thief remotely. The hidden function can wake up and disclose data warehouse information against your wishes or can cause damage to your information.
Compromised Certification	The thief gains access to a private encryption key that is used to certify software or certify the identity of a user or a server. Until this is discovered, the thief can then plant hijacked controls in all those machines that otherwise would trust the software.	Compromised certification is a nightmare not only because of the damage that is directly caused by the intruder but because of the cost to restore the trust and issue new certificates.
Virus	An unwanted piece of software that enters your system and either replicates itself, draws attention to itself, or causes damage to your information. Viruses can be attached to programs or data.	Virus threats are fairly well understood by data warehouse managers compared to many of the other security threats. Most viruses that invade data warehouse environments cause an interruption of service rather than direct compromising of data warehouse information.

FIGURE 12.7   Vulnerabilities to software theft.

Vulnerabilities	Basic Description	How the Data Warehouse Is Involved
Denial of Service Attack	Your information system is compromised specifically for the purpose of halting or bottlenecking one or more critical components. For example, your servers may be deluged with thousands or millions of false requests. A well-known denial of service attack (the SYN flood) involves sending TCP/IP connection requests to a server without completing all of the necessary machine acknowledgments. Another similar denial of service attack is the FRAG attack, in which TCP/IP packets are sent with confusing or missing sequence numbers.	Denial of service is very possible almost anywhere in the data warehouse delivery pipeline. Outside attacks from the Web are more likely to affect the firewall and the Web server. If the firewall is brought down, legitimate outside users will not be able to access the data warehouse. If the Web server is brought down, all data warehouse users, both inside and outside the firewall, may be denied service due to our increasing reliance on browser-enabled user interfaces. A DBMS can be a direct target of a denial of service attack in the form of many huge queries, or certain queries that are known to cause the DBMS to hang. Users with direct SQL access to the DBMS can hang the DBMS fairly easily if that is their express purpose.
Inability to Reconstruct Consistent Software Snapshot	Through deliberate sabotage, accidental loss, or simple oversight, you may not be able to reconstruct a consistent snapshot of your systems.	The loss of a consistent snapshot of your data warehouse business data has many serious financial and legal consequences. The loss of a consistent snapshot of your metadata may mean that you cannot restore a data pipeline or that you lose business rules you have been applying to data transformations.
Terrorism	A very serious kind of denial of service attack is one intended to cause major public infrastructure to fail. For example an area's 911 emergency call service might be bottlenecked or hung. One might imagine a public utility such as a telephone company or a power utility subject to a denial of service attack through an information systems security breach. This is not far-fetched. Is it possible that such utilities have remote diagnostic and control interfaces that have real power? This form of terrorism could only be a password away.	Normally a true data warehouse is not put in the position of being a critical link in an operational system. However, some kinds of data warehouses are very close to the operational line. For instance, if a data warehouse provides background information on the identity of a caller, and this information is linked into a 911 or emergency response system, then this system has ceased to be a data warehouse and needs to be a nonstop fault tolerant operational system. A data warehouse manager needs to judge whether their system is gravitating in this direction.

FIGURE 12.8 **Vulnerabilities to conducting your business.**

the abbreviations suggest. TCP governs how two machines establish and maintain a connection. TCP forces the communicating machines to engage in a three-way handshake. For instance, the first machine will tell the second machine how to synchronize the segments of an upcoming message. This is called *sending the SYN bit*. The second machine is then supposed to acknowledge (ACK) the SYN bit. Finally, the original machine sends a FIN bit to finish the communication. It is this three-way handshake that is at the root of a notorious denial of service attack. If the first machine floods the second machine with SYN bit requests but never sends the final FIN bits, the receiving machine can become clogged with incomplete sessions that must slowly time out before being dropped. This is called a *SYN Flood* denial of service attack. Due to the open nature of all machines connected to the Internet, there is no way to stop a SYN Flood from arriving at the front door. The receiving machine must somehow recognize and ignore a SYN Flood without being disabled by it. This is not simple. Remember that very busy machines connected to the Internet may receive millions of connection requests per day.

The IP portion of the protocol governs how machines on the Internet find each other. It can be thought of as the envelope, the intended address, and the return address, but not the enclosed greeting or the enclosed message. Like the envelope/address metaphor, IP is in some sense unreliable. In other words, IP by itself does not guarantee that a message is delivered or that the message is in any way legitimate. IP simply provides the addresses and the envelope. As a result of the logical separation of the IP addressing scheme from all other issues, and from the open nature of the IP addresses themselves, messages on the Internet are subject to abuse. Like a real envelope, they have to be viewed with a certain level of suspicion. An IP source address can be "spoofed" by anyone with a physical connection to the Internet backbone. In other words, you have no real guarantee that a communication is from a known host just by looking at the IP source address. Similarly, a communication packet from a legitimate source can be diverted to any destination by copying the packet and replacing the destination IP address. Although this all sounds horrifying, it is important not to get side tracked by the weaknesses of IP. (We can achieve all the reliability and security we need using TCP/IP, but we do it by protecting the *contents* of the envelope, not by tinkering with the addresses on the outside. Read on.)

Inside our organizations, on our intranets, we use the TCP/IP protocol extensively. Our intranets are usually configured in one of two different modes. Our internal machines can be configured with IP addresses that make sense to the outside world and are actively connected to the outside world, or they can be configured with IP addresses that are not compatible with the rest of the world. If the internal machines have private IP addresses, they cannot communicate with the Internet unless the internal machines are connected through a gateway or firewall that provides the internal machines with an "outside" identity. Such a gateway or firewall is an excellent place to impose some security and control over Internet communications.

Before discussing gateways and firewalls, we must reveal some dirty laundry. Almost all of our internal networks, such as Ethernet-based systems, are so-called CS/MA/CD networks. This imposing abbreviation stands for Carrier Sense/Multiple Access/Collision Detection. This means that the little cable strung around in the ceiling is carrying everyone's communications at once. All the computers connected to the network are capable of seeing all the communications. It is just politeness that keeps any one of them from listening to everything. And there is no real incentive to be polite.

In a CS/MA/CD network like Ethernet, every computer on the network looks at every packet to see if packets are being addressed to it. If so, the packets are stored by the intended computer and eventually assembled (thanks to TCP) into complete messages or files. There is no reason why an impolite computer cannot listen to everyone's messages. Later in this chapter we describe how such a promiscuous packet sniffer could compromise security.

 If we really need to protect our communications, then we must protect the contents, not the addressing scheme. If we continue to insist on sending everything via postcards, with the messages in effect being written for everyone to see, then we get what we deserve.

SECURITY: SOLUTIONS

The last section was probably overwhelming for most readers. There are so many vulnerabilities that one person cannot think of them all simultaneously. The problems seem so pervasive and complex that it is difficult

BLINDNESS TO SECURITY

Perhaps the biggest reason the data warehouse team does not address security is the feeling that "it's not our problem." Variations on this theme include "security is handled by central IS," or "security is handled by the firewall," or "I don't handle facilities," or "I am not responsible for contractors," or "I am not responsible for personnel," or "I don't understand it," or "it's not in my job description," or "anything up to $50 is their problem" (with regard to credit cards). We go to great lengths to avoid confronting security issues. If we think someone else is responsible for a security issue, we stop worrying. "We do have a modem policy, but it will be okay just this once." Yet, we the data warehouse managers are exactly the people our organizations expect to own, understand, publish, and protect the corporate data asset. The data warehouse team uniquely understands who needs to access the data and what they do with the data. Only we can make judgments about appropriate access or appropriate use. Whether we like it or not, we are in the driver's seat.

Another reason for not paying enough attention to security is that in spite of our many years of experience, networked computers are still an unfamiliar medium. In many important situations we just have the wrong instincts. Many times we have an inappropriate illusion of security. We seem to be alone in our offices. We are typing quietly. We cannot directly see other users. We easily imagine that we are not being noticed. We imagine that we are anonymous. But all of this may be false. It is possible that our keystrokes and actions are being monitored by multiple individuals in multiple locations. We are often not aware when our software is exchanging information with other entities. We discount the active nature of a threat because we don't experience it in normal ways.

Our lack of experience and our lack of tangible feedback with the networked computer medium can lead to naïve recklessness. We log in to remote services and decide to reveal sensitive information in the clear because we think that no one is watching. We are probably right—most of the time. We use FTP from our laptops over a conventional modem. We use the same password for the remote service that we use to secure our local machines. We don't stop to think that FTP on the Internet sends such passwords in the clear. When we for-

> get that the networked computer medium is truly a different medium, we allow our emotions to affect our communications, especially with e-mail. Humor rarely succeeds in e-mail and often comes across as dumb or insulting. Attempts at sarcasm are a disaster. Only the biting "under message" comes across. Anger is even worse. Anger comes across as anger very effectively. But after we cool off, we die a thousand deaths as we realize what we have written cannot be retracted. Most of us have had the experience, after sending a message, of sending a second message an hour or two later asking everyone on the distribution list to ignore the first message.

to know where to start. Security is a fundamentally negative topic, and it doesn't have an "up side" like most other topics in data warehousing. But it is just this kind of reaction that causes paralysis. Before we finally put all the pieces together and dig ourselves out of this mess, please read the "Blindness to Security" sidebar to examine the sources of our avoidance and why we don't want to dwell seriously on security issues.

In this section we describe the security technologies you need to know about. We deliberately take a manager's perspective here, rather than a technologist's perspective. There are many good books on security, like Charles Pfleeger's *Security in Computing,* that go into great detail about the technology, but the preoccupation with the technology is part of the problem with the emerging security solutions industry. It is time for us to step back from this technology and instead focus on understanding how to deploy it. The technology is almost ready, but we the marketplace are not nearly as ready.

Routers and Firewalls

Every place one network connects to another we must have a device called a *router* that transmits packets between the two networks. The router listens to every TCP/IP packet on each net and looks at the destination addresses. If a packet on one network is addressed to a computer on the other network, then the job of the router is to pass that packet through. If nothing else, routers do a useful job of isolating the "local" traffic on each network. If this didn't happen, there would be far too much unnecessary noise on remote networks. Routers also know what to do if they see a packet addressed to a "faraway" network. Even if they don't know where the faraway network is, they know where a higher visibility router is located, and they pass the packet on through, on the assumption that eventually some router a few hops away will know exactly how to deliver the packet. Routers are very smart. They communicate with each other frequently, and they adapt when a new router is attached to the network. The "community" of routers is very good at seeking the shortest path to a destination. This adaptive routing is a source of significant security problems. If an employee in a company connects his or her internally networked PC to the Internet through a dial-up telephone connection, it is quite possible that the community of routers will discover this connection and start transmitting communications from the employee's PC across the Internet to another location, even within the same company, if the number of hops over the Internet connection is less than the number of hops through the company's secured intranet connections. This is one of the reasons why dial-up modem connections from within a secure intranet environment should be prohibited.

Obviously, since a router looks at every destination address in every packet, it can also look at the source address. In this way, a router can serve as a *packet filter*. See Figure 12.9. Although we have already seen that source addresses cannot be entirely trusted, packet filtering is very important and should be used in multiple places in every network system. A packet-filtering router, also called a packet-filtering firewall, can provide the following useful functions:

- **Rejecting connection attempts from unknown hosts.** The packet-filtering firewall only lets known IP source addresses through. Although this doesn't stop professional spoofing, it stops every other unauthorized host. The data warehouse manager may set up a packet filter to accept special dynamically created IP addresses that represent legitimate remote users. The use of dynamic addresses may defeat most attempts for outsiders to spoof as legitimate users.

- **Rejecting attempts from the outside that are spoofing as insiders.** The packet-filtering firewall in Figure 12.9 is the unique position of being able to recognize an outside intruder who is trying to spoof as an insider, because the outside intruder cannot legiti-

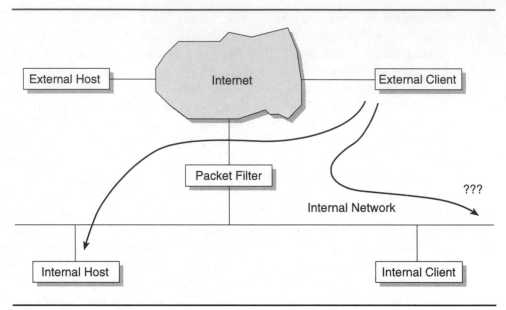

FIGURE 12.9   A packet filtering firewall.

mately be arriving with an inside IP address. If the firewall were to let this outsider through, then the outsider might have special status on the protected network. This is another form of protection against outsiders trying to break in to the data warehouse.

- **Isolating all traffic to come from a single machine.**   A packet-filtering firewall can serve as a kind of guardian to a small number of protected machines such as database servers, which are allowed to be accessed only through a specific applications server on a surrounding less secure network. This is a key recommended configuration for the data warehouse. It is shown specifically in Figure 12.10.

- **Halting pollution and sniffing.**   The packet-filtering firewall can keep an insecure or unstable network from interfering with the more secure intranets by restricting outbound traffic originating from the insecure or unstable network. Additionally, the presence of the packet-filtering firewall defeats an attempt to sniff the packets on the more secure networks from the public network. The data warehouse manager may wish to set up certain terminals and certain database systems on isolated networks so that contractors, consul-

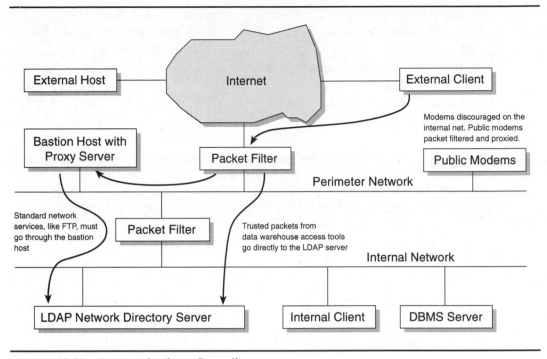

FIGURE 12.10   Screened subnet firewall.

tants, and industrial partners can get their work done, but they cannot access, sniff, or otherwise detect network activity elsewhere in the organization.

 Packet-filtering firewalls are one of the basic elements of security. The data warehouse architect should develop a specific plan for isolating and protecting key pieces of the technical architecture.

A good overall security configuration for a data warehouse environment is the so-called screened subnet firewall configuration shown in Figure 12.10. The screened subnet firewall actually has two packet filters. The first filter acts as a primary firewall and sends nearly all incoming network traffic to a special internal host called the *bastion server*. The bastion server is as a powerful, controlling bottleneck for all communications coming to the organization from the outside. Except for certain specially qualified outsiders, all communications must go through "proxy" applications running on the bastion server. A proxy application is what it sounds like. It is not the real application, but rather a kind of fake application that shakes hands correctly with the remote requester, takes the requester's commands one at a time, and then, if the commands are safe and legitimate, passes the commands on through to the real application inside the organization. A common example of a proxy application is FTP. A remote user wants to download a file, but does not get to talk directly to the FTP application of an internal host. Only by being accepted by the proxy FTP server on the bastion host can an outsider gain the desired FTP services.

The idea of proxy servers is wonderful, but the limitation is that only rather simple applications like FTP and Gopher have fully implemented proxies. Modern query tools and report writers usually cannot engage a proxy because none is available.

However, the packet-filtering firewall can carefully allow selected external hosts to bypass the bastion server and directly access other internal servers. These "trusted packets" do not need a proxy server. They are allowed to talk to the real server. If this configuration is coupled with a powerful authentication and encryption system (which is discussed later in this chapter), then an organization can get the best of both worlds. Powerful high-tech remote applications from trusted and authenticated clients can get full access to internal resources, whereas ordinary, low-tech access attempts have to run the gantlet of the bastion server.

A proxy application running on the bastion server can also mediate outbound traffic. Users wishing to make a Web browser or FTP connection to the outside world have to go through the proxy server in order to make a connection. A proxy server for Web page browsing can serve several useful functions in this configuration, depending upon your point of view.

- **Monitoring and auditing Web page access patterns.**   The Web access bottleneck created by the firewall allows all Web access usage to be monitored and recorded.

- **Restricting Web access.**   Certain prohibited sites, such as pornographic sites, could be impossible to reach from the inside network. As of this writing, it is unclear whether the censors or the pornographers are winning the race. The number of sites that must be filtered out now number in the thousands, and many of these lists of sites are only partially implemented. At the very least the site list would have to updated every few days, much as virus signatures are.

- **Caching Web pages for more efficient access.**   A Web server proxy can cache Web pages to make access more efficient. This proxy server function may become obsolete, however, as Web sites become larger, more continuously dynamic, and more personalized. The news service Internet sites are being changed every few minutes as news breaks. Also, some of the sites have become too big to cache. The main Microsoft site (www.microsoft.com) in mid-1998 consisted of more than 150,000 Web pages.

Notice that in the screened subnet firewall configuration shown in Figure 12.10, we have isolated the internal network with a second packet filter. This extra level of screening allows protection against a breached bastion server and gives this configuration the name *screened subnet*. If the bastion server is compromised by an intruder and taken over, the bastion server is sitting on an "uninteresting" network. The perimeter network is like a public waiting room. The intruder may be inside the door, but is not in a position to listen to sensitive traffic or probe other internal machines. No internal traffic passes over the perimeter network.

 On any corporate network environment, the main data warehouse application servers should be protected at a minimum by a screened subnet firewall.

The Directory Server

In Figure 12.10, the incoming access requests are shown as arriving at the Lightweight Directory Access Protocol (LDAP) network directory server. Although the world may still not be organized as ideally as this by the time you read these pages, we believe that all large organizations will have to gravitate to this kind of model to control their distributed networks and distributed applications.

The directory server is a kind of data warehouse of resources available on the associated network. Resources include database machines, individual databases, document repositories, transaction systems, file storage areas, printers, and people. The people descriptions include names and addresses, organization roles, e-mail addresses, and more. The directory server reveals selected items of information to legitimate, authenticated requesters. It is meant to be the useful, centralized, controlling resource for finding out how to communicate on the associated network.

Many vendors have agreed on the LDAP standard for communicating with a directory server, and, thus, implicitly for implementing a directory server. The term *lightweight* (the "L" in the acronym) is a reaction to a more comprehensive directory standard previously proposed, known as X.500, that was regarded as too complicated and cumbersome to implement fully. LDAP is a derivative of X.500.

The directory server is very important to the data warehouse manager. It must be the single, central point for authenticating and authorizing all users of the data warehouse, regardless of whether they are connected to the internal network or are coming in from the Internet.

The directory server has the following characteristics:

- **Single point of access.**   All access comes through a single point of control. Consistent and complete administration and auditing are possible with this approach. The single point of access allows a single metadata description of security privileges and security use.
- **Single point of authorization.**   Everyone must run the same authorization gantlet regardless of how they connect to a data warehouse resource.

- **Single console.**   Perhaps most important, the directory server is a single administrative console where access policies are defined and enforced just once. Lacking such an approach, the DBA may try to race from machine to machine, setting up low-level SQL GRANTS and REVOKES to implement security. This approach invites disaster and defeats flexibility.

Encryption

In the preceding sections we have tried to whittle down the security nightmare somewhat by erecting multiple layer firewalls and concentrating all data warehouse access attempts onto a single directory server. So far, so good. But all along we have been warning that the real protection has to apply to the contents of the communications, not just the mechanisms for delivering the communications.

Fortunately, we have a powerful technology that, if used correctly, can largely deliver the protection we want for the contents of our communications. This technology is encryption.

Encryption in the broadest sense is altering a message with a secret code so that it can be read only by people who know the code. In a sense, that is all the data warehouse manager has to know about encryption. There is an unfortunate tendency for encryption enthusiasts to describe the mathematical underpinning of the coding schemes. The mathematics of encryption, as appealing as it is to us techies, is basically irrelevant to the issue of using encryption, so we will refer the interested reader to more detailed books, such as Pfleeger's, if that is what you want. Data warehouse managers need to understand the *uses* of a half dozen forms of encryption. No one encryption scheme will solve every security problem. Encryption schemes range from being automatic and anonymous and of almost no concern to the data warehouse manager to being highly visible to all users of the data warehouse and potentially an onerous burden if implemented incorrectly.

Symmetric Key Encryption

The simplest form of encryption is *symmetric key encryption*. This kind of encryption is also called private key encryption. With symmetric key encryption, a single secret key can both lock the data and unlock the data. Symmetric key encryption is mainly interesting in two situations:

- **Private encryption of data.** The user encrypts data with a private key that the user does not reveal to anyone else. If the key is a good one, it is essentially impossible for anyone else to decrypt the data. Obviously, in this situation if the user forgets the key or dies, the data is lost forever. Private encryption of data would have many uses in the data warehouse. Any data that is especially sensitive could be so encrypted. Private key encryption would work best for numeric fact table data that was not being constrained upon. Encrypted fact table data would need to be decrypted by the database engine as the numbers arrived in the answer set to be summed.

- **Shared secret encryption of data.** If two parties already know the secret key and no one else knows the key, then the two parties have a virtually bullet proof means of communicating securely. This kind of shared secret is the basis of many forms of secure communication. The big issue, of course, is how the two parties decide on the key and communicate it with each other without giving anyone else a chance to intercept the key. Symmetric key encryption is the basis for many secure communication schemes between data warehouse clients and servers and between users.

The main symmetric encryption technique that is relevant to data warehouse managers is the Data Encryption Standard (DES) algorithm. The DES algorithm has been officially sanctioned by the U.S. government and by the International Standards Organization (ISO). The main thing data warehouse managers need to know is that the strength of the DES approach is based on the length of the key that a user chooses for encryption.

The National Security Agency (NSA) in the United States has a conflict of interest in recommending and allowing encryption standards. The NSA believes that it has the right to decrypt any message it deems to be a threat to national security, and the NSA has tried to limit the power of the keys used with the DES approach. In 1976, when the DES algorithm was first adopted, a 40-bit key was thought to be sufficient to balance the difficulty of decrypting with the NSA's desire to override encrypted communications. From the perspective of 1998, a 40-bit key is ridiculous. A message or file encrypted with a 40-bit DES key can be decrypted with a modern personal computer in a few hours today. The NSA is now trying to mandate a 56-bit key. However, in a widely publicized test, a team of researchers using a brute-force approach recently was able to decrypt a message encrypted with a 56-bit key. Although this brute force decryption was a tour de force of parallel computing that would not be practical or fast to duplicate, nevertheless, it showed that 56 bits will soon be a meaningless limit. Keys of 80 bits or more in length are quite feasible to implement, but they are currently illegal to export outside the United States. They are classified by the government as munitions. It is conceivable that Congress will pass laws at some point that will make 80-bit DES encryption illegal anywhere. High-tech industries have a fairly poor record of influencing Congress. Other countries have already passed such laws. Encryption of any sort is illegal in France as of this writing.

This situation leaves the data warehouse manager in the position of needing to protect data from standard eavesdropping and amateur attacks while realizing that completely bullet proof symmetric key protection of data will probably not be allowed.

Nevertheless, symmetric key encryption remains a primary encryption technique we must all use. We will use symmetric key encryption to encrypt personal files, and we will use symmetric key encryption as a fleeting, temporary way to encrypt many forms of digital communications. If two parties can agree on an encryption key, even if it is the equivalent of a 56-bit DES key, then if they use the key for only 60 seconds (literally), their session can be thought of as highly secure during those 60 seconds. If the parties can agree on a different key for the subsequent 60 seconds and keep repeating this process, then a long, highly secure communication session can be established. If this approach is coupled with careful time stamp monitoring by both parties, then even a delayed decryption of the communication may be of no use to the intruder.

Symmetric key encryption has the advantage that coding and decoding a message with the intended key is extremely fast. Even if a communication has been set up with the more powerful public key encryption technique we are about to describe, most of a communication episode will usually be handled by a symmetric key approach because of its speed.

Public Key Encryption

Symmetric key encryption has the major problem of how to securely distribute the keys. A different set of encryption schemes has been developed to handle the problem of two remote parties setting up a secure communications link, even over the Internet. These encryption schemes are called *public key encryption.*

With public key encryption, there are two keys. One key encrypts the data and the other key decrypts the data. The keys can be used in either order. In this scheme, one of the keys is designated as the *private key* and the other is the *public key*. As the names imply, the private key is held in secret by the owner of the data and the public key is broadcast freely and widely to everyone in the world. Lists of public keys can be published anywhere. It would be reasonable to know the public key of the President of the United States.

Now, if an individual possesses a private key and has published the corresponding public key, two important scenarios are possible:

- **Secure delivery to the individual.** Any other person in the world can encrypt a message with the individual's public key and deliver it to the individual. Since only the individual has the private key, the message cannot be read by anyone except that person. The message in our example could be a download of sensitive data from a data warehouse server to a client, perhaps on a batch basis. See Figure 12.11.

- **Guaranteed authenticity from the individual.** If the individual encrypts a message with a private key, then everyone in the world can verify that the message is genuine, because the only way to decrypt the message is with the person's unique public key. If a user needs to upload planning numbers or budget numbers to the data warehouse, this scheme could be used to guarantee that the numbers indeed came from the designated individual. See Figure 12.12.

If two different individuals (A and B) have public and private keys, then they can engage in secure communications:

- **Secure communications between parties.** Person A encrypts the outgoing message with B's public key. However, inside the message, person A appends his or her signature encrypted with A's private key. B receives the message and successfully decrypts the body of the message with B's private key. B then verifies the authenticity of A's signature by decrypting the signature with A's public key. See Figure 12.13. This scheme is the basis of most secure communications over insecure media like the Internet or a public telephone line. Since it is computationally expensive, this scheme is often used to securely exchange a higher-performance symmetric key that both par-

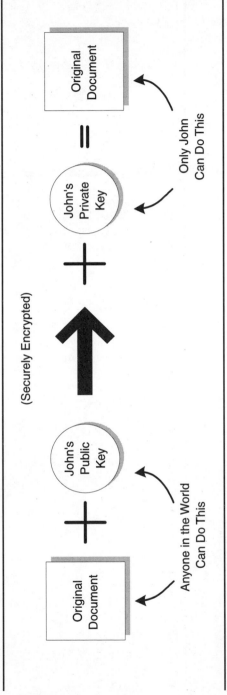

FIGURE 12.11 Secure delivery to the individual named John.

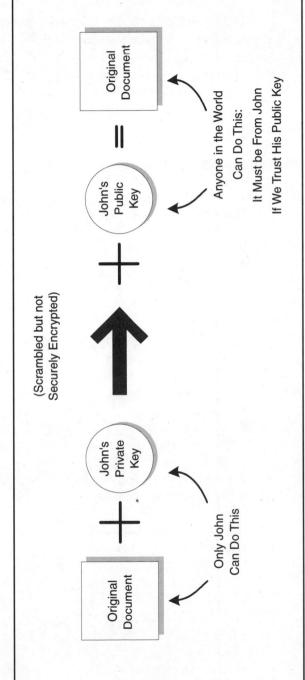

FIGURE 12.12 Guaranteed authenticity from the individual named John.

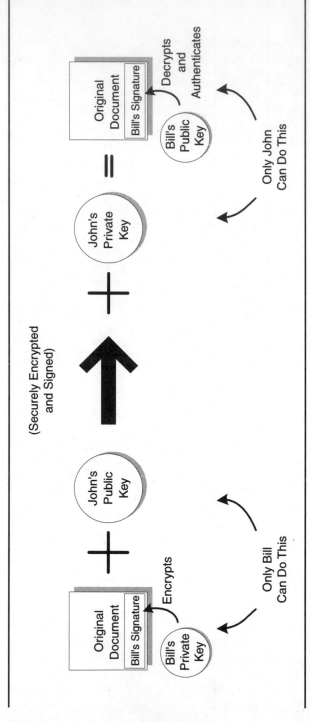

FIGURE 12.13 Secure communications between parties.

ties can use temporarily to rapidly exchange large amounts of data. This is how the Secure Sockets Layer (SSL) works. SSL is discussed later in this section.

The alert reader who has been following all of this may have a nagging concern. All of this sounds good, but how does anyone know that the public key for anyone really is the public key for that person? If the public key we are depending on for a remote party is falsified, then the whole house of cards comes crashing down.

Trusted Certificate Authorities

The answer to the public key problem is a *trusted certificate authority* (CA). Imagine that there is an impeccable public authority that we "know in our hearts" is ethical and secure. We also understand and trust the authority's mechanisms for collecting public keys. If they claim to have Bill Clinton's public key, then we trust that it really is the public key for Bill Clinton and not someone else. Finally, we have been given a CD-ROM or some other physical medium that contains the CA's public key. We decide to trust the public key given to us on the CD-ROM completely. Now we are ready to do business.

- **Secure retrieval of a person's or company's public key.** We connect to the CA's Web server and request the public key for the desired individual or company. We receive the CA's response, encrypted by their private key. We decrypt the message with the CA's public key, verifying that indeed the message came from the CA. Inside the message is the public key for the desired individual or company. See Figure 12.14. This is how people get public keys that they can trust. This is how a remote user gets your public key. This is how a remote user may get the public key of his or her own company. This is how the remote user gets the public key of a software vendor so that the user can verify a software download legitimately originates with that vendor.

Although this system for dealing with private and public keys is pretty air tight, there are real-life situations that have to be dealt with. The most serious is:

- **Revocation of a public key.** A public key may have to be revoked because either the corresponding private key has been compromised

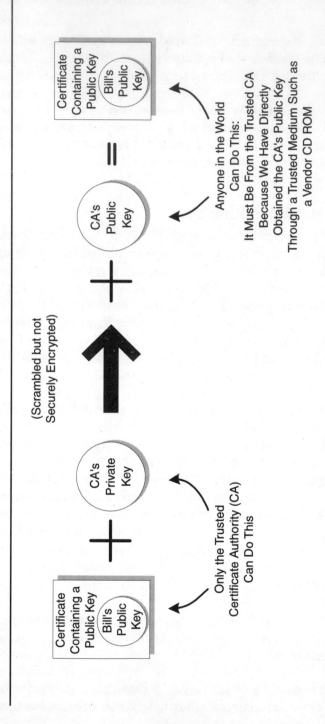

FIGURE 12.14 Secure retrieval of a person's or company's public key.

or the basis for trust in the individual or company is no longer valid. Perhaps the person lied about his or her identity. Perhaps the person is no longer entitled to the authority granted by the ownership of the private key. Revocation of a public key is a tricky issue because in effect the CA has to communicate with every possible user of the invalidated public key. If a certificate has been revoked, in many cases there will be a window of vulnerability before all affected parties can be alerted to the revocation.

Signed Software Certificates

The public key encryption scheme can be used to validate and trust software. Basically, any given software component comes with a signed certificate.

- **Receiving a trusted software component.**   The software component is accompanied by a message identifying the creator of the software that is encrypted using the software creator's private key. As the consumer, you accept the software component if, and only if, you possess the software creator's public key. If you don't have this public key, you can request it from (guess who) the trusted certificate authority. After you verify that the software component is indeed from a particular software vendor, you can decide if you want to let it run on your system.

Signed software certificates are, like other forms of public keys, pretty airtight, but there are still a couple of tricky situations. You may successfully verify that a software component has arrived at your computer doorstep from Ralph Kimball Software in some unknown city. If you have never heard of Ralph Kimball Software, you may not know whether to trust this vendor. The CA cannot provide this level of trust. All the CA tells you is that Ralph Kimball registered successfully with them as a commercial software developer and that his certificate has not been revoked. Maybe the CA tries to qualify software developers to a degree, but realistically we cannot expect the CA to do too much in this regard. So you are left with a personal decision whether to accept the software component.

Another tricky situation arises when a disgruntled employee plants a Trojan horse or a virus inside an otherwise legitimate software component. It will not be feasible to revoke the software certificate of a major software vendor if this happens. The software vendor will have to deal with this problem the way it deals with the same problem in physically distributed media, namely by recalling the infected media and perhaps offering on-line software patches.

Sandbox Software

The bulk of this section describes security through various forms of encryption. An important aspect of security is the trust we need to have in downloaded software components that we receive from various sources. The signed certificate model of software deployment says nothing about the software itself, but it places the burden entirely on the trust we confer on the authenticated vendor. The Java development model, in its pure form, is based on a very different model. The Java language is defined to operate with the Java Virtual Machine, which is technically known as a *sandbox*. Within the Java sandbox, a Java program gains its security by being drastically limited in its function. A pure Java program cannot read or write files on the surrounding machine, access other hardware devices, or access memory directly. Although this approach is intellectually appealing, it is proving difficult for Java developers to stay so disciplined and so confined. As of this writing, there is significant pressure on the Java community to relax the strong sandbox discipline and adopt some parts of the encryption-based signed certificate model.

Secure Sockets Layer (SSL)

In 1995, Netscape proposed Secure Sockets Layer (SSL) as an industry standard protocol for secure communication between a client and a server. This standard is now widely used on the Internet and all the major commercial browsers support it. SSL uses a combination of public key encryption and symmetric key encryption. Public key encryption is used, most typically, for the user at the client machine to verify that indeed a connection has been established with the intended server machine. Optionally, the server can also demand verification of the client's identity. This initial secure handshake is used as the basis for the two machines to agree in secret upon a shared symmetric encryption key. The symmetric encryption key is used as a "bulk" encryption key for the actual high-speed communications dialogue that follows. The symmetric encryption key can be changed by the two machines every few seconds, as desired, in order to maintain the highest degree of confidence in the security.

Virtual Private Networks

Once a client and a host establish a secure symmetric encryption key, sometimes called a session key, the client can be trusted by the host as if the client were physically local to the host. This is the basis for a virtual private network (VPN) connection, also called an encrypted tunnel. The original Microsoft Point-to-Point Tunneling Protocol (PPTP) and the competing Cisco Layer 2 Forwarding (L2F) scheme have been merged to create a new standard called Layer 2 Tunneling Protocol (L2TP). It is likely that L2TP will be the basis for most virtual private network implementations in the future.

 Virtual private networks will dominate the market for remote data warehouse access. The data warehouse manager needs to follow the development of this technology and work with his or her security manager to implement a flexible, scalable solution that does not impose an unreasonable administrative overhead or performance overhead.

It is technically important to choose a tunneling technology that performs data compression before performing data encryption, rather than the other way around. Data encryption largely defeats the ability to compress, and thus if these steps are done in the wrong order, you will pay a huge and unnecessary performance penalty. In particular, modern high-speed modems rely on the ability to compress most data. If this is your only data compression step, it will not work if the data is encrypted before it arrives at the modem.

Kerberos Authentication

Kerberos authentication is a relatively strong and secure authentication and access-granting system that was originally developed at MIT. It is specifically designed to provide secure authentication and access privilege granting in an insecure networked environment. It is intended to withstand eavesdropping attacks, hijacked session attacks, and replay attacks. As of this writing, Kerberos authentication is planned as an intrinsic facility in Microsoft NT Server 5.0.

Kerberos authentication depends on three different sever entities, as shown in Figure 12.15. To use an application, the user first opens a con-

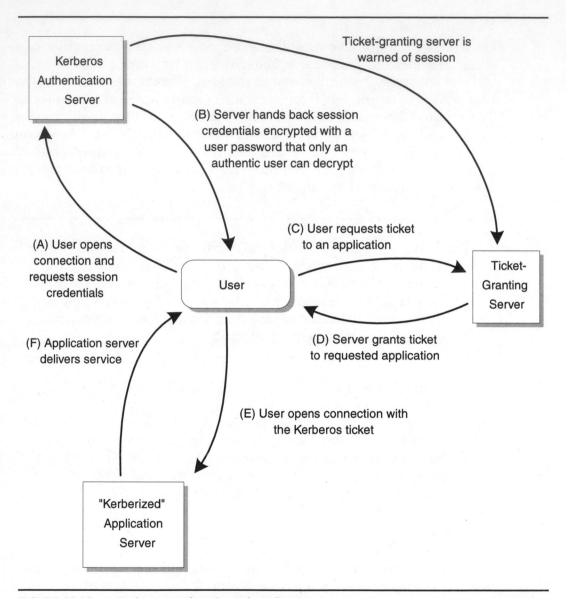

FIGURE 12.15 A Kerberos authenticated application.

nection (Step A) to the Kerberos authentication server and requests credentials. The authentication server issues credentials encrypted with the user's password and passes them back to the client (Step B). The client cannot proceed unless the client is legitimate, because only the client knows his or her own password. Although this scheme avoids passing any form of the user's password over the network, it is still dependent on a password, and it is only as secure as the user's password may be.

When the user has received and decrypted the credentials, the user possesses a "ticket" and a temporary session encryption key to access the second server, the ticket-granting server. Meanwhile, the authentication server has passed the session encryption key to the ticket-granting server over a securely encrypted communications session.

The user now opens a connection to the ticket-granting server (Step C) and requests another ticket to the final application. The ticket-granting server passes this ticket back to the user through the secure session (Step D).

Finally, the user opens the intended application connection with the Kerberos application server using the session key originally provided (Step E). The application server authenticates the user and allows the actual usage that started the whole process (Step F).

In most Kerberos implementations, the session ticket given to the user has a specific time stamp and a short time out fuse that limits the ticket's validity. This is intended to thwart replay attacks and to defeat attempts to override the encryption schemes.

Obviously, this scheme is intricate and powerful. Kerberos systems have been criticized on three grounds:

- **Password vulnerability.** A user's security is only as strong as the password or other security token the user employs at the client workstation. If the password or security token is compromised, then the security vanishes.

- **Need to "Kerberize" each application.** The final target applications must be specifically modified to support the Kerberos scheme. It is not possible to take an arbitrary client/server application and embed it in a Kerberos environment. However, because of the increasing adoption of the Kerberos system, it is expected that software vendors will widely provide support for Kerberos.

- **Alleged difficulty in scaling.** Security experts have criticized Kerberos for not scaling easily past a single security domain. In other words, the administrative concerns grow significantly when an organization has two or more separate Kerberos environments that must work with each other. It is beyond the scope of this chapter to analyze the prospects for Kerberos scalability, but this is an issue in 1998 that data warehouse designers should be aware of.

Authentication Tokens

Plain text passwords typed by the user into computer keyboards are one of the glaring weaknesses in network security. Passwords can be guessed, either by knowing something about the end user or by mounting a "dictionary attack" that systematically tries millions of combinations. Passwords are notorious for being compromised, given to other users voluntarily, being displayed in plain text on pieces of paper, and being reused. Let's face it, no one likes hard to remember passwords.

 Every data warehouse manager should consider upgrading their security authentication to use tokens or perhaps to use biometric approaches if that technology improves enough.

There a number of promising alternatives to typed-in passwords that are worth considering:

- **Smart cards.** Similar to an ATM card, these cards are possessed by the end user and are presented at login time to a card slot or a card swipe device. Also, like an ATM card, the user may be required to enter a personal identification number (PIN) to thwart simple theft of the smart card. Many smart cards contain sophisticated electronics that may be able to generate session encryption keys every minute or two. This approach provides automatic protection against replay attacks and after-the-fact decryption of a session key. It seems likely that an inexpensive peripheral for swiping the smart card could be developed that accompanies each personal computer in a large organization.

- **Thumbprint biometric scanning.** In this case, the user presses his or her thumb against a sensor at login time. Although this alternative does not provide the fancy generation-of-session encryption keys that smart cards can provide, biometric scanning has the singular advantage of requiring the actual human being to be physically present in order to be authenticated. Hopefully, you can't steal a thumb. Thumbprints are highly individualistic and there are almost no false positive identifications. However, something like 3 percent of the population have very rough or very smooth prints that cannot be recognized reliably by the biometric scanners. One can expect this percentage to be improved somewhat as biometric scanning technology improves, but there will always need to be an alternative means of authentication for some individuals.

- **Retinal pattern biometric scanning.** The human retinal pattern has many of the strong uniqueness characteristics of fingerprints. Retinal scanners can be made to work fairly well at a terminal like an ATM, even when the users are wearing eyeglasses or contacts. However, it seems less likely that retinal scanning technology could be made cost effective for individual personal computers.

Cookies

In the previous section on component software, we described cookies as special text files written by the client into the client's file system, which are divulged to the remote server whenever a client/sever session is established. Cookies in some form are required in the stateless HTTP world to provide session identifiers between clients and servers. Although cookies have gotten a bad name for alleged security and privacy abuses, as an architectural component they are going to have to be tolerated if we want to have interactive HTTP-based sessions on the Internet. The answer to the cookies issue is not to ban cookies, but to filter them so that they don't reveal information we don't want disclosed and to discriminate against vendors that allow their cookies to contain too much information about the client environment. Going back to the initial discussion in this chapter on software components, a fully enabled software component like an ActiveX component can in theory write anything into a cookie.

MANAGING SECURITY IN A DATA WAREHOUSE ENVIRONMENT

Now that we have analyzed the many vulnerabilities of our networked computer systems and taken a tour of the new technologies we have to enforce our security, what do we actually do? What is the role of the data warehouse manager?

This book takes the strong view that the data warehouse manager has the central responsibility for data warehouse security and that no one else is going to do the job. As we remarked earlier, that data warehouse manager uniquely understands the data, uniquely understand what uses can be made of it, and uniquely understands who should access the data and who should not.

An effective security program is a *continuous cultural emphasis*, not a one-time technological solution. The challenges of security are too multifaceted and too dynamic to snapshot any one fixed solution and expect it to work. The data warehouse manager should protect his or her information assets with a security program comprised of the following elements:

- **Awareness.** The need for security must be continuously reinforced through a constant education process. Just like safety, the main ideas of security need to be visible on posters, in briefings, and on the screen.

- **Executive support.** Executive management must be educated about the importance of security and the main elements of security. Executives should work hard to create a healthy respect for the security measures in place and to set good examples.

- **Policies.** Security must be implemented through a comprehensive set of well-thought-out policies that are visible, actionable, and fair. Computer and network security policies should be provided along with the employee reference manual, and the human resources staff should be aware and appreciative of the need for security.

- **Vigilance.** Effective security involves continuous vigilance. Security must be checked and renewed constantly.

- **Suspicion.** Someone on the data warehouse team must adopt a continuously suspicious attitude. Such a person should be reviewing login attempt records, lifting ceiling tiles, and asking *why* people need to see the data. Although this suspicious attitude cannot dominate the security management, it is absolutely necessary to have this attitude available to act as a counterweight to all the people who want to overlook security or not examine it closely.

- **Continuous renewal.** Security must be a dynamic, continuously evolving quest. If it becomes static, it will be compromised. Every few months, the state of the local networks and the state of the industry as a whole must be reviewed, with the potential of upgrading security measures. It should be expected that the technology available both to the data warehouse manager as well as to the intruder will change, adapt, and become more powerful.

WHAT TO DO NOW ABOUT SECURITY

We conclude our long discussion of security with a set of very specific recommendations. You will perhaps be stunned by this list. It pulls no punches. We believe in strong security. Our job as data warehouse managers is to professionally publish and protect our information assets.

The first measures are tactical things that should be done immediately. The second group is more strategic, although perhaps there is no hard boundary between the two.

Immediate Tactical Measures

- Install virus checking software everywhere. Install virus checkers especially on end user PCs, but also on all servers. Renew the virus signature files on a frequent basis. Make sure that new sources of viruses such as macro viruses are handled by your virus checkers. Keep up-to-date on virus alerts and changes in virus technology.
- Remove floppy disks drives from your environment. If a user needs to read a floppy disk, the user must take the disk to the local system administrator, who will check it manually for viruses and for trusted software and then will mount it on a server with a floppy drive for remote access.
- Remove local modems from your environment. Prohibit the use of dial-out modems inside your corporate facilities from any end user PC, portable or fixed. It is possible to allow packet-filtered, proxy-supported modems on the perimeter network (refer to Figure 12.10) that are relatively safe, and they can be used by internal users for dialing out.
- Control all software installed on internal machines. Inspect and qualify all executables. Install a runtime program that reports all executables on all machines to a centralized database for analysis.
- Assign your users passwords that they must memorize and use. These passwords should be robust and well-constructed meaningless combinations of upper- and lower-case letters and numbers. (In the strategic section following, plan on replacing all text passwords with more sophisticated and effective security tokens. Hopefully, the era of onerous passwords will be short and sweet.)
- Funnel all Internet access through an Internet proxy server. Monitor and control access to remote sites. Provide clear written guidelines for appropriate Internet use.
- Install a packet-filtering firewall to restrict access from the outside world to known IP addresses. Install a bastion server to intercept all

service requests from the outside world except known service requests from known IP addresses, which you regard as trusted. Isolate the bastion server from the true internal network with a second packet-filtering firewall.

- Remove all unnecessary services from the bastion server so that if it is breached, there is very little the intruder can do. Follow modern security practices for trimming and isolating the functions available on the bastion server.

- Implement a program for security education and security appreciation. Systematically educate executives.

- Implement a program for auditing threats to security, such as break-in attempts, failed login attempts, and inappropriate use.

- Implement a security tracking program that regularly reviews the security privileges of all employees (what information they can see) as well as the security exposures of all information resources (who has access to the data). Make sure that both on-line and backup media are covered by this analysis.

- Physically secure all servers and all backup media. Inspect and secure all communications facilities and cable vaults. Apply an electrical sweep of all networks and account for all taps and connections.

Strategic Measures

The following measures are strategic steps that in many cases require both technology and a change in behavior within the organization:

- Commit to an access token approach to replace all use of typed passwords (e.g., smart cards or biometric scanning) both internally and in the field. Include all contractors and all industrial partners.

- Assign a public/private key combination to every end user to use as the basis for secure authentication. This pair of keys is probably coupled to the access token specified in the preceding paragraph.

- Commit to a secure tunneling approach for remote access by trusted individuals.

- Centralize all authentication and access control through a directory server based on the LDAP protocol. Require all users to funnel through the directory server whether they are internal or external users. Administer all security from this one central point. Do not allow direct access to a database or application server by anyone.

- Require all software downloads to be based on signed certificates. Actively administer the list of trusted software vendors whose software you will accept.

SUMMARY

In this chapter we have raised the understanding of why security is so important to the data warehouse. Then we provided a technical primer on the basics of modern systems security. Finally, we provided a set of action items that you can immediately act upon as well as guidance for developing your strategic security plan. The project tasks are listed in Figure 12.16 and at the end of Chapter 13, so anyone who skimmed this graduate-level chapter will still see the recommended tasks.

KEY ROLES

Key roles for implementing security are:

- The project manager must take a lead role in the battle for a secure environment. The project manager or a dedicated security specialist must start by educating the organization to be sensitive about security issues, and then must ensure that proper measures such as those described in this chapter are implemented and maintained. Although the project manager will not, in most cases, be the one to actually implement these measures, the project manager must feel the responsibility; otherwise security will slip through the cracks.
- Specific technical specialists will need to actually implement any changes to the environment, based upon the tactical and strategic plans.

ESTIMATING CONSIDERATIONS

There are too many cultural factors to estimate how long it will take to establish a secure environment. Building awareness may take many months. The actual implementation of these security measures may also take an extended period of time. More optimistically, little additional effort may be required of the data warehouse team if your organization is already tackling these issues.

Project Task	Fans	Front Office			Coaches		Regular Line-Up						Special Teams				
	Business End Users	Business Sponsor	IS Sponsor	Business Driver	Bus. Project Lead	Project Manager	Bus. Sys. Analyst	Data Modeler	DW DBA	Data Staging Designer	DW Educator	E/U Appl Devel	Tech/Security Architect	Tech. Sppt Specialists	Data Staging Programmer	Data Steward	DW QA Analyst
IMPLEMENT TACTICAL SECURITY MEASURES																	
1 Develop Tactical Security Plan					○	○							●	○			
2 Secure Physical Environment						○							○	●			
3 Install Virus Checking Software						○							○	●			
4 Secure Access into Environment						○							●	○			
5 Secure Access out of Environment						○							●	○			
6 Implement Rigorous Password Scheme						○							●	○			
7 Implement Controls for Software Installation						○							○	●			
8 Audit Security Violations					○	○							●	○			
9 Monitor Security Privileges by Individual					○	●							○	○			
10 User Acceptance/Project Review	□	□	□	□	○	●	□	□	□	□	□	□	○	○	□	□	□
DEVELOP STRATEGIC SECURITY PLAN																	
1 Design Security Architecture						●							●	○			
2 Implement Access Tokens (Elim. Passwords)						○							●	○			
3 Implement Public/Private Keys for Authentication						○							●	○			
4 Implement Secure Tunneling for Remote Access						○							●	○			
5 Centralize Authentication & Access Control						○							●	○			
6 Implement Signed Certificates for Software Downloads						○							●	○			
7 User Acceptance/Project Review	□	□	□	□	○	●	□	□	□	□	□	□	○	○	□	□	□

LEGEND:
Primary Responsibility for the Task = ●
Involved in the Task = ○
Provides Input to the Task = ◗
Informed Task Results = □
Optional Involvement in the Task = ▲

FIGURE 12.16 Project plan tasks and responsibilities for implementing security.

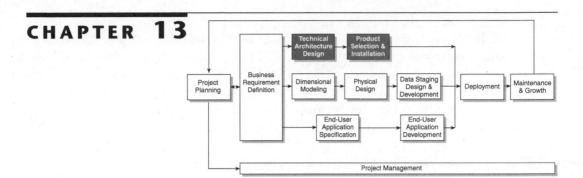

CHAPTER 13

Creating the Architecture Plan and Selecting Products

In this chapter, we switch from the theoretical details of architectural components and services to the practical matters of how to actually design your architecture and then select products to support it. The first part of this chapter concentrates on the process of designing the architecture. The architecture plan is the technical translation of the business requirements. It says "these are the capabilities we need to meet the information needs of the business." The second half discusses product selection—the process of comparing the architecture to the real world to see who shines and who fades.

Your job in the architecture phase is to identify the capabilities that are most important to your organization. Once you have this list, you can work on identifying the vendors who provide these capabilities, and determine which is the best fit for your situation. You may not find a single tool that meets the needs of the entire range of users. Start with the highest priority requirements and make a decision. You will learn a lot from the first set of experiences that you can apply to the second round. Also, remember that having multiple tools is not necessarily a bad thing. After all, you are addressing multiple problems. However, using multiple tools does have implications for software investment, training, and ongoing support.

While the primary audience for this chapter is the technical architects, other project team members should review it as well, since they often participate in the product selection process. The entire team must be familiar with your architecture design and the role they play in bringing it to life.

CREATING THE ARCHITECTURE

As we described in Chapter 8, there are many approaches to developing a systems architecture, especially a data warehouse architecture. One standalone methodology comes from John A. Zachman of the Zachman International. The Zachman Framework was developed based on Zachman's experience developing systems in the aerospace and construction industries. He reasoned that if it was possible to build something as complex as an airplane or a large building on time and on budget, you ought to be able to do the same for an information system. He and others took the tools and techniques that enabled an aerospace company to produce an airplane and transferred them to systems development. Zachman first formalized these concepts in a 1987 article in *IBM Systems Journal* titled "A Framework for Information Systems Architecture." He and others have extended the concepts in several articles and books since then.

As you might guess, the Zachman Framework is a rigorous, comprehensive approach to architecture development. From a warehouse point of view, many sections of the Zachman Framework deal with overall IS issues, and thus fall outside of the warehouse span of control. Although a straight application of the Zachman Framework is probably more than you need for all but the largest data warehouse projects, it's worth examining to make sure you haven't missed any major issues.

The approach we use to develop an architecture is definitely based on the 80–20 rule; that is, we spend 20 percent of the effort to get 80 percent of the benefit. This is not to say that more wouldn't be better, but in our experience, most organizations can barely muster the resources for this 20 percent. Of course, this approach is an iterative process, much like the warehouse overall. Get the big picture in place, determine the priorities, and split the implementation into phases. As you move forward, you will uncover new information that will cause you to revise significant parts of the architecture. Celebrate these changes—they mean your map of the world is getting more accurate (and your chances of falling off the edge are decreasing).

Architecture Development Process

Figure 13.1 depicts the process flow for creating a data warehouse architecture. The flow diagram actually covers the entire lifecycle of the warehouse, because the architecture both defines and draws from the other parts of the Lifecycle. In the beginning, the requirements set the boundaries and baselines for the architecture. At the other end, the implementation is the realization of the architecture.

Although it is tempting to compartmentalize the three architectural threads we saw back in Figure 8.1, we know that they interact significantly. Figure 13.1 shows the way we think these architecture projects

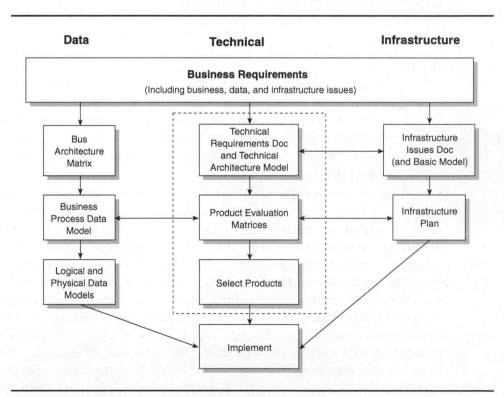

FIGURE 13.1 Architecture development process flow chart.

interact as we work our way down from the business requirements to the ultimate implementation.

The layer enclosed in the dashed-line box near the top of Figure 13.1 is what we tend to think of as architecture; essentially, this is the technical architecture. This section outlines a process for creating the technical architecture. While we will discuss the data and infrastructure efforts, we will focus primarily on the data staging and end user application architectures.

You will create two major deliverables from the technical architecture development process: the technical architecture plan and the infrastructure plan. The technical architecture plan seems daunting—it is usually 50 to 70 pages long, and it describes your vision for the future structure of the warehouse. As always, begin the document with a review of the driving business requirements. Just as we have structured the architecture section of this book (Chapter 8–12), discuss source systems and back room requirements, front room architecture, your plans for using metadata, and security.

 Remember that the warehouse architecture document will get fairly wide distribution within your company, among people who may know relatively little about data warehousing. A significant portion of the document should be devoted to explanations detailed enough to ensure that most readers understand the context.

Sometimes we include the infrastructure plan within the technical architecture plan, but we prefer to create it as a standalone document, which the architecture plan refers to. The infrastructure plan describes the nuts and bolts of the warehouse: the servers, network, and desktop. We use it primarily to communicate with the IS Operations folks who will help support the warehouse, to provide a clear and early warning of what the data warehouse will require of their groups. We have found that it's easy to forget about Ops, and simply assume they will support the warehouse as they would any system. Generally they are quite willing to do so, but they do need to be told what the requirements are and don't like to be surprised.

Create the Technical Architecture Plan

If your warehouse architect has not been through a data warehouse project before, it's a good idea to hold off on the architecture development until after the requirements have been identified and the initial dimensional models created. This deferment is valuable because it is difficult to create an architecture for a warehouse without having already seen one up close. Of course, postponing the architecture development will extend the duration of the project, so if you cannot afford to extend the project an extra month or two, plan to bring in an experienced data warehouse architecture person early on. Whenever you are ready to get started, the following outline will be useful for creating the application architecture:

- **Form an architecture task force.** The task force is an ad hoc group brought together specifically to create the warehouse architecture. The task force is led by the technical architect, and most of the members should come from the warehouse team, with representatives from both the back room and the front room. It is also valuable to include a representative from the broader IS community. In particular, look for someone who is creative and flexible and who has significant experience in the company. The size of the task force depends on the magnitude of the project. In general, a small group of two to four people is better than a larger group. Even for a small warehouse project, where one person might create the architecture (in her spare time), it helps to include another participant to provide an additional viewpoint. Identify the team early on so they know they will be responsible for the architecture and can keep it in mind during the early stages.

- **Gather architecture-related requirements.** During the requirements gathering process, it's a good idea to discuss the question sets with the lead interviewer ahead of time to make sure some of the questions address architectural topics. Attend the user interviews and listen carefully for architecture-related issues. Make sure you don't sidetrack the process. If you need to, conduct additional interviews. In particular, there are probably some IS development and infrastructure folks who didn't make the business interview list. Figure 13.2 shows a set of sample questions targeted at IS people. While you're talking to the technical folks, keep an eye out for existing architectural "stakes" and directions.

EXAMPLE QUESTIONS FOR ADDITIONAL ARCHITECTURE AND INFRASTRUCTURE INTERVIEWS

IS Business Role

1. How important is business or data analysis in support of management decision making at the company?
2. What role does IS play in the management decision making process?
3. Is this changing (due to the competitive environment, organizational restructuring, etc.)?

Technology Direction

4. What is the company's general approach to information technology over the next few years (e.g., aggressive client/server development, Web-based apps, ERP)?
5. Is there a general direction or plan to address the related software infrastructure requirements (DCOM, CORBA, object orientation, etc.)?
6. What are your plans and priorities for the foreseeable future?
7. What infrastructure initiatives or plans will have an impact on information access (data movement, task scheduling, name servers, security, software distribution, etc.)?
8. Is there a specific role for metadata? How will it be managed?
9. What are the company's standard products today? What platforms, system software, DBMS, client software, and utilities do you think are going to be strategic over the next few years?
10. What are the biggest bottlenecks or issues in the infrastructure area?
11. Is there a group responsible for architecture, or are any documents or guidelines available?

Infrastructure Process

12. What groups are involved in acquiring, installing, and supporting new infrastructure (e.g., servers, utility software, connectivity)? What is the process for securing required infrastructure?
13. Is there a centralized data and systems security function in the organization? How do they work with other groups?
14. What kinds of timeframes are typically involved in these activities?

Figure 13.2 Example architecture-related interview questions.

- **Create a draft architectural requirements document.** Review and summarize interview documentation and other materials from an architectural view. Look for requirements that set boundaries and baselines or that indicate a need for some capability or service. One useful focusing technique, as soft as it sounds, is to develop the overall vision of the warehouse, sort of a technical mission statement. Think about the major business issues you can address from an architecture point of view. For example, if lack of integrated data is a major stumbling block for the company, providing an integrated data source should be a key goal. If multiple conflicting data sources is a problem, providing the authoritative source should be a key goal (this implies good understanding of the source systems, strong data checking, and excellent documentation of what the differences are and why they occur). The vision thing can help. It's like John Chattergee said, "If you don't know where you're going, any road will take you there."

- **Review the draft** with key players from both the IS and business user areas.
- **Incorporate feedback** into a "final" architecture requirements document.
- **Create the technical architecture model** and supporting descriptions based on requirements. The easiest way to do this is to get the architecture task force in a conference room with a couple of big white boards for two days and hash it out. Work from the architecture requirements document to make sure you include all the necessary components and capabilities.
- **Determine the architecture implementation phases.** First, determine the priorities for the major components of the architecture and the estimated resources (people and money) needed to implement them. Look for logical boundaries in the architecture that deliver business value, are cost effective, and can be accomplished in a reasonable timeframe.
- **Identify clear deliverables for each phase of the architecture.**
- **Review the final architecture with key players (management and key technical resources).**
- **Create a Technical Architecture Plan document.** Take the results from the aforementioned activities and roll it all into a master plan document.

Technical Architecture Plan Sample

The sample model in Figure 13.3 is for a fairly large retail grocery chain that has decided to implement a Club Card program for its frequent shoppers. The Club Card program is the high-value business issue that will serve as the primary focus for the initial data warehouse effort. The warehouse will draw from two primary source systems: the legacy sales tracking system and a new client/server system built to track and man-

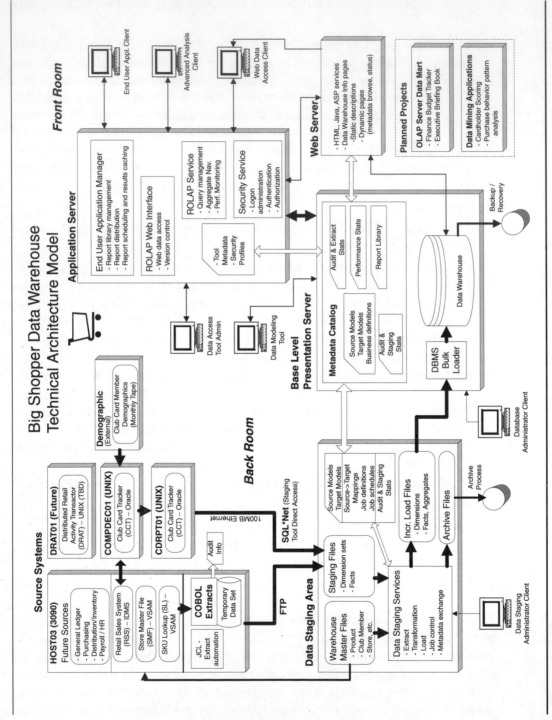

Big Shopper Data Warehouse
Technical Architecture Model

Front Room

Application Server

End User Application Manager
- Report library management
- Report distribution
- Report scheduling and results caching

ROLAP Web Interface
- Web data access
- Version control

ROLAP Service
- Query management
- Aggregate Nav.
- Perf. Monitoring

Security Service
- Logon administration
- Authentication
- Authorization

- Tool Metadata
- Security Profiles

End User Appl. Client

Advanced Analysis Client

Web Data Access Client

Web Server
- HTML, Java, ASP services
- Data Warehouse Info pages
  - Static descriptions
  - Dynamic pages (metadata browse, status)

Planned Projects

OLAP Server Data Mart
- Finance Budget Tracker
- Executive Briefing Book

Data Mining Applications
- Cardholder Scoring
- Purchase behavior pattern analysis

Data Access Tool Admin

Data Modeling Tool

Base Level Presentation Server

Metadata Catalog
Source Models
Target Models
Business definitions

Audit & Staging Stats

Audit & Extract Stats

Performance Stats

Report Library

Data Warehouse

Backup / Recovery

Source Systems

Demographic (External)
Club Card Member Demographics (Monthly Tape)

DRAT01 (Future)
Distributed Retail Activity Transactor (DRAT) – UNIX (TBD)

COMPDEC01 (UNIX)
Club Card Tracker (CCT) – Oracle

CDRPT01 (UNIX)
Club Card Tracker (CCT) – Oracle

HOST03 (3090)
Future Sources
- General Ledger
- Purchasing
- Distribution/Inventory
- Payroll / HR

Retail Sales System (RSS) – IDMS
Store Master File (SMF) – VSAM
SKU Lookup (SL) – VSAM

Back Room

100MB Ethernet

SQL*Net (Staging Tool Direct Access)

COBOL Extracts

Temporary Data Set

JCL – Extract automation

Audit Info

FTP

Data Staging Area

Staging Files
- Dimension sets
- Facts

Warehouse Master Files
- Product
- Club Member
- Store, etc.

Data Staging Services
- Extract
- Transformation
- Load
- Job control
- Metadata exchange

Source Models
Target Models
Source->Target Mappings
Job definitions
Job schedules
Audit & Staging Stats

Incr. Load Files
- Dimensions
- Facts, Aggregates

Archive Files

DBMS Bulk Loader

Archive Process

Database Administrator Client

Data Staging Administrator Client

FIGURE 13.3 Technical architecture model sample.

508

age the Club Card member information. Fortunately, the Club Card system has to integrate the demographic information to provide the point-of-sale (POS) system with coupons and discounts.

Figure 13.3 includes some data sources and data access systems that are not part of the initial effort. Listing them helps you keep them in mind so you don't make implementation decisions that will limit your ability to include these new elements down the road. It also shows that you are aware of the business need for these elements. To manage expectations, make sure you identify them as *future* phases—you might even consider graying them out on the model.

This sample model is based on a combination of our experiences, and it does not represent any specific projects we have worked with. Remember that this model is only an example—one possible approach to a single situation—not the answer. Your model will be very different. Also, what you see here is only the tip of the iceberg with respect to the data warehouse architecture for a mid-sized warehouse. This graphical representation would typically be accompanied by an architecture plan with 50 or more pages of detailed description of the required components and functions, business rules, and definitions where appropriate, and priorities, resources, and implementation timeframes. A sample table of contents for the plan is included in Figure 13.4.

Even though it has been simplified to fit on one page, don't let the model intimidate you. It is appropriate for a mid-sized data warehouse project. Most smaller projects will have simpler architectures. If you start from the business requirements and take it step by step, the model and the plan will fall neatly into place.

The technical architecture plan describes a high-level map for what you plan to do and where you plan to go with your data warehouse. Write the document with the expectation that a wide variety of people in your IS organization will read it, and do not assume the readers have any significant knowledge of data warehousing.

Begin with a summary of the warehouse's business requirements, focusing on how those requirements affect the architecture. Describe the types of users and different access requirements. Discuss significant data issues. For example, if you must develop a service to identify unique individuals from across multiple systems, you should introduce that concept here. Describe the business requirements for shared data and the need for aligned corporate reporting. Outline organizational issues for supporting a successful warehouse, including education and training.

Big Shopper Data Warehouse (BSDW)
Technical Architecture Document

FIGURE 13.4 Technical architecture plan document sample table of contents.

In describing the architectural elements, remember throughout that you are describing your vision for the future. Describe required services, such as data staging and data access, in enough detail that this document can help guide the product selection process.

 The architecture plan itself should be detached from products. In fact, you will find that products do not yet exist to fill all your requirements. It's particularly important to have an architecture plan so you can build the components modularly and plan for new products and services to "snap into" the existing infrastructure.

Create the Infrastructure Plan

As we described at the beginning of this chapter, the purpose of the infrastructure plan is to communicate infrastructure requirements to your operations group. Without spending some time to think about infrastructure—and to communicate those thoughts to the people chartered with delivering that infrastructure—you run a high risk of delaying the project for a Really Stupid Reason. For example, the machine room does not have enough floor space (electricity, air conditioning, etc.) to host the warehouse server; there's not enough network bandwidth between the machine room and users' desktops; user desktop computers are underpowered; or a security shell does not permit data transfer between operational systems and the warehouse server. All of these problems are easy enough to solve, but they all require time, money, and management attention.

Since the goal of the infrastructure plan is to communicate requirements to the operational groups in IS, it's best to structure the plan so that each group's requirements are in a separate section. Work with the operational groups to finalize the plan. There are three main areas to cover in the infrastructure plan: server hardware, network, and desktop.

- **Server hardware.** At this point in the project, you should be putting your first stakes in the ground for your hardware requirements. Decide what your main warehouse platform (hardware and OS) will be, based on business requirements and initial sizing estimates. Decide whether your staging area will live on the source system, on its own server, or be co-hosted with the warehouse, and what its size requirements are. It's harder to specify the number of smaller application servers you will need until the end user tools have been chosen, but you can give the server group a heads-up on the kinds of requirements you will have and when you expect them.

- **Network.** There are two parts of the network to consider. You need a big pipe between the source systems, staging area, and warehouse and good throughput between the warehouse and user desktops. Broadly specify the volumes and frequencies that data will be moving between different systems. Document how the security systems will affect data flow, and outline the solution for moving data through different security protocols.

- **Desktop.** Decide what kind of user access applications the warehouse will support. Does your organization have an intranet that can support Web access to warehouse data? Most active warehouse users have a client application on their desktops. Even if you haven't yet chosen that software, you can specify the general parameters for the desktop PC. Generally, these tools require a fairly powerful PC to run well. Specify the desktop operating systems the project will support. Specify the connectivity software that will be required. Is ODBC alone sufficient, or will you also need to install native database drivers?

You should plan to continue to keep the infrastructure document reasonably up-to-date as the warehouse evolves over time. What starts as a description of hardware, operating systems, and software expected from the operations group will turn into documentation for an increasingly complex system. Figure 13.5 illustrates an infrastructure model for a mature warehouse. Your model may not start out as complex as this one, but it probably won't take long.

Additional Information Resources

If you want more detailed guidance after reading this, there are plenty of places to look. Most of the major consulting organizations have data warehouse practice groups, and several of the major vendors in the data warehouse market have architecture subsections as part of their warehouse development methodologies. If you already have a relationship

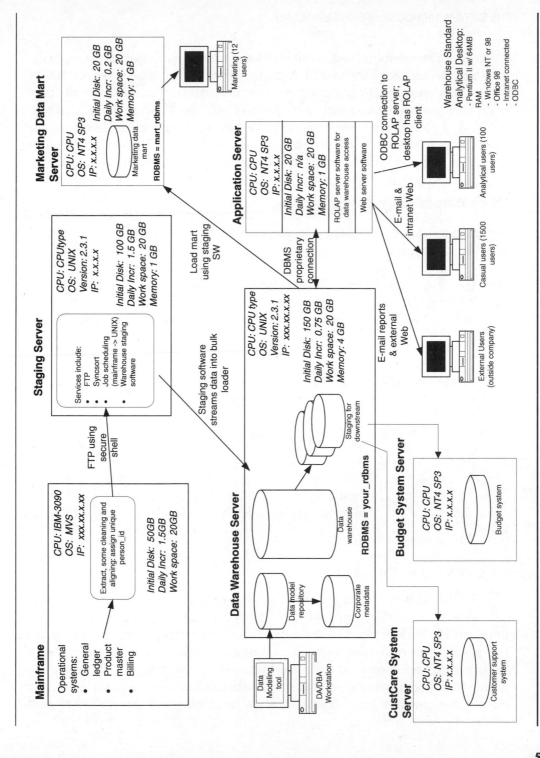

Mainframe

CPU: IBM-3090
OS: MVS
IP: xxx.xx.x.xx

Operational systems:
• General ledger
• Product master
• Billing

Extract, some cleaning and aligning; assign unique person_id

Initial Disk: 50GB
Daily Incr: 1.5GB
Work space: 20GB

FTP using secure shell

Staging Server

CPU: CPUtype
OS: UNIX
Version: 2.3.1
IP: x.x.x.x

Initial Disk: 100 GB
Daily Incr: 1.5 GB
Work space: 20 GB
Memory: 1 GB

Services include:
• FTP
• Syncsort
• Job scheduling (mainframe -> UNIX)
• Warehouse staging software

Staging software streams data into bulk loader

Data Warehouse Server

CPU: CPU type
OS: UNIX
Version: 2.3.1
IP: xxx.xx.x.xx

Initial Disk: 150 GB
Daily Incr: 0.75 GB
Work space: 20 GB
Memory: 4 GB

Data warehouse

Staging for downstream

Data model repository

Corporate metadata

RDBMS = your_rdbms

Data Modeling tool

DA/DBA Workstation

Budget System Server

CPU: CPU
OS: NT4 SP3
IP: x.x.x.x

Budget system

CustCare System Server

CPU: CPU
OS: NT4 SP3
IP: x.x.x.x

Customer support system

Marketing Data Mart Server

CPU: CPU
OS: NT4 SP3
IP: x.x.x.x

Initial Disk: 20 GB
Daily Incr: 0.2 GB
Work space: 20 GB
Memory: 1 GB

Marketing data mart

RDBMS = mart_rdbms

Marketing (12 users)

Load mart using staging SW

Application Server

CPU: CPU
OS: NT4 SP3
IP: x.x.x.x

Initial Disk: 20 GB
Daily Incr: n/a
Work space: 20 GB
Memory: 1 GB

ROLAP server software for data warehouse access

Web server software

DBMS proprietary connection

E-mail reports & external Web

E-mail & intranet Web

ODBC connection to ROLAP server; desktop has ROLAP client

Analytical users (100 users)

Casual users (1500 users)

External Users (outside company)

Warehouse Standard Analytical Desktop:
- Pentium II w/ 64MB RAM
- Windows NT or 98
- Office 98
- Intranet connected
- ODBC

FIGURE 13.5   Sample mature warehouse infrastructure model.

513

with any of these folks, ask them what they have and what they are willing to make available to you. A number of books have also been written about data warehouse architecture. Get information and examples from a few different sources, and read them carefully. Then just get started.

Trying to build a warehouse without an architecture is like using a 14th century map of the world to plan a trip. Once you step outside the narrowly defined known world, the terrain is gray and uncharted. Without an accurate map, we are doomed to wander aimlessly around the systems landscape. If we're lucky, we'll discover the new world. More likely, we'll sail off the edge of the earth or get eaten by dragons. In our experience, there are plenty of dragons in the data warehouse implementation process.

This concludes our discussion on the process of designing the architecture. More detailed project plan tasks and estimating considerations associated with creating the architecture are located at the end of this chapter.

SELECTING THE PRODUCTS

Now you can turn your efforts to selecting specific products that can bring your architecture to life. Once the data warehouse architecture is in place, you have in hand the two key components that drive the selection of products: business and technical requirements.

In this section we discuss the major areas where product evaluations are typically focused. Next, we walk through a process that can be used for each area. This process includes an optional prototype project. Finally, we review details that are specific to a single area.

Keeping a Business Focus

This is our standard liturgy: How can you make a rational, effective tool selection if you don't know what you need to do with that tool? At this point in the Lifecycle it may seem absurd to you to even consider attempting to select a tool without having the slightest idea of your users' requirements. Unfortunately, we have seen this happen. The project plan, the architecture, and the requirements documents are your guides. One of the early comments we hear all too often is "we're just getting started, but we have the database and hardware up and running." The timing of the technical evaluation is key. If you do it too early, you won't have a real understanding of the requirements, and you will end up testing product features in a vacuum. If you do it too late, you won't have enough information about the platform and product-driven requirements in the physical database design process. You will end up redesigning and rebuilding to support these requirements.

Major Warehouse Evaluation Areas

There are four major purchase areas for the typical warehouse, and each can include multiple tools to consider in a technical evaluation process:

- **Hardware platform(s).** There may be multiple hardware platforms in the data warehouse, including different servers/platforms for the staging area, data marts, and application server/engine. Most hardware testing is about scale, throughput, and capacity.
- **DBMS platform.** In most medium-sized warehouses, the base-level warehouse DBMS is a relational engine—not that that makes the evaluation any easier. In most cases, we find that the DBMS choice is a corporate standard, and any deviation requires a serious justification effort. The DBMS evaluation is tightly linked to the hardware platform.
- **Data staging tool.** This can be a major cost for the warehouse. It is also such a rapidly changing area that an evaluation is almost mandatory.
- **Data access tools.** Most warehouses end up with more than one tool to support different kinds of requirements. The sheer quantity of tool options and lack of a clear market leader in many categories makes this evaluation process a particularly difficult one.

This list of evaluation areas is a little daunting. The good news is that, at least at the hardware and database platform level, the choices are relatively equal. That is, for most of the small-to-medium–sized warehouses, the mainstream open systems vendors and database vendors all have reasonable platforms. On the other hand, if you expect your warehouse to be large, you must evaluate all the areas very carefully.

Evaluation Process

There are several basic steps that are common to the evaluation process for each of the areas described earlier. This section outlines those steps, and the following sections describe the twists, additions, and deletions specific to each of the areas.

A critical step to ensure a meaningful and thorough product evaluation process is to make sure that resources are assigned to this effort. Even if much of the hands-on "prove it" work is done by the vendors, someone from your team has to deal with the vendors directly and absorb the feedback.

The timeline for evaluating and selecting products must be reasonable. You need to allow enough time for the vendors to properly respond to your request. The rate that technology is changing today is almost alarming. If you take too long to complete your technical evaluation, your information may be obsolete. Players eliminated from consideration early in the process may have actually caught up or, more likely, have leapfrogged other competitors.

Be warned that no matter how good a job you do on product evaluation, even if you do a thorough prototype, it's never good enough. You just cannot know about all the quirks of a product until you are deep in to the details, at which point it's often too late. Our advice, which the vendor community will hate, is to follow a thorough evaluation process, make your best choice, and tell your vendor that you want a 90-day trial period. Implement the product as best you can, and at the end of the 90 days you will have a list of significant issues to discuss with the vendor (we promise, you will!). You will be in a very good position—before the contract has been signed—to negotiate resolution of these issues. Or you may have found problems that are deep enough that you need to back down from your first choice and try an alternative product.

Develop the Product Evaluation Matrix

At this point in the project the business requirements have been collected following the guidelines given in Chapter 4. The technical requirements have been defined by the technical architecture, as detailed in Chapters 8–12. It is also critical for you to gather information about the product vendors themselves. Vendor evaluation criteria are described in a moment. The combined business, technical, and vendor criteria become the yard (or meter) stick by which you can evaluate different products.

All of the requirements, both business and technical, should be prioritized. At a minimum, the requirements should be flagged as "must have" or "nice to have." Prioritization allows you to apply different weighting factors to different requirements. Assign a numeric value, typically between 1 and 5, to how each requirement is handled for each product. These values can then be analyzed. We have seen multiple products end up with relatively equal scores. In these cases, simply reassessing priorities can often break a tie.

Any evaluation matrix we include here will be misleading for two reasons. First, the market is different today than it was when we wrote this book. Second, your situation and requirements are different from any generic situation we could imagine. On the other hand, there is value in seeing how someone else approached a problem. Figure 13.6 shows a simplified version of an evaluation matrix for data staging tools. Remember that yours will not be like this one.

Vendor Evaluation Criteria

The tool you buy is not a standalone product. It is an extension of the vendor who created it. You will have a relationship with this vendor for as long as you own the tool, so part of determining capabilities for the tool involves determining required capabilities for the vendor as well. Most of these have to do with the nature and extent of support you can expect from the vendor and the technical community. This is where market share counts. The larger the installed base of the tool, the more likely it is that you will be able to find someone who can help when problems surface.

- **Vendor Support.** What kind of resources do they have to help you be successful? In particular, look for the following:
  - *Documentation.* You should expect a range of well-written materials targeted at specific readers: business users, power users, developers, and the administrator. The materials should be available on-line in a form that's easy to search and browse.
  - *Training.* Local training facilities are useful if you will not be setting up your own training facility. Training materials need to be extremely hands-on. Classes should be set up with one student per computer. The company should offer customized training and on-line materials you can customize yourself.
  - *Technical support.* This one is hard to gauge in advance. Ask the references about their experience with the vendor's technical sup-

Feature	Feature Weight	Product 1	Product 2	Product 3	. . .
Basic Staging Capabilities					
Supports source extract from multiple legacy and warehouse platforms, including RDBMS, IDMS, WKS, DB2, VSAM	85				
Can determine net change from source log/journal	50				
Provides fast copy, replication	85				
Provides data compression/ decompression	50				
Supports transformation functions validate, translate, integrate, check integrity, calculate, derive, aggregate allocate	85				
Provides loading of target via replace, append, update functions on target RDBMS	85				
Job Control and Scheduling					
Supports job scheduling (time/event-based)	75				
Supports monitoring, reporting, re-covery from unsuccessful completion	75				
Supports archive/restore	25				
Supports security via access and encryption checks	25				
Provides online synchronization of updates	25				
Metadata and Standards					
Driven by open repository	100				
Supports metadata exchange with other key products	85				
Supports messaging standards, including COM, DCE, CORBA	25				
Supports transport levels, including TCP/IP, FTP	25				
Vendor Items					
Cost	85				
Tech support	85				
Documentation	50				
Training availability/quality	25				
Consulting availability/quality	50				
TOTAL SCORE (based on 1–5 rating scale)	5975	0	0	0	
Ranking					

FIGURE 13.6 Sample data staging tool product evaluation matrix.

port services. In addition to pure technical expertise, you want the technical support organization to have the right attitude: a real willingness to help figure out solutions to the inevitable problems.

- *Consulting.* The company should have an organization of consultants who are experts in the tool. They should also have a list of consulting organizations in the area that have been trained and are experienced with the tool.

- **External support.**   Beyond what the company can give you, look for external support structures as well. These include an active technical support forum on-line and a local user group for the product

- **Vendor relationship.**   How will this company be to work with? The representatives should be reasonable, rational people. The company should offer flexible pricing and a fair upgrade policy. It should be financially stable with a good growth record. In particular, check into these areas:

  - *Company background.* How long has the company been in business? How many developers are on staff? Ask about the firm's revenue, profitability, growth, and product release history.

  - *References.* Check references. It's not that difficult, and you usually find a wealth of information.

Conduct Market Research

The goal of this market research is for you to become an informed consumer. We find that the variety and selection of data warehouse related products can be overwhelming, especially since many products profess to solve all of your problems. Basic information about products can be collected using the following techniques:

- Search the Web.
- Read trade publications.
- Seek opinions from industry analysts. Most IS organizations have contracts with one or more major information technology consulting firms. Ask your corporate library or IT research folks.
- Attend data warehouse conferences and seminars.
- Collect marketing literature from the vendors.

This kind of basic research can help you identify candidate products. As you begin to collect and distill this information, use your product evaluation matrix.

Narrow Your Options to the Short List

While the task of narrowing the list of products to evaluate seems overwhelming at first, we find that the results of your market research can quickly narrow down the list of products that meet your combined business and technical criteria. You should select no more than five products that you believe may be able to meet your requirements. In many cases, only two or three products need to be scrutinized in more detail.

The most important thing to consider when selecting candidates for the short list is to seek comparable products. Too often, we see organizations attempting to compare apples and snow shovels. If you do not feel that you are equipped to make these decisions, get more help. There are sessions on selecting technologies at most of the trade shows. Seek the advice of other professionals, with one caveat: Make sure that you

---

WHY REQUESTS FOR INFORMATION DON'T WORK

An age-old practice to assist product selection is to create a formal Request for Information (RFI) or Request for Proposal (RFP). It requires a lot of time to put together a comprehensive request. This is a compilation of the questions you think are important. Each of the vendors that respond will do what they can to respond positively to each of your questions. They are vying for the opportunity to compete. In our experience, the responses don't really tell you much more than who has a better marketing or proposal generating organization. You don't really learn more about the product's functionality or what is required to deliver that functionality.

A few high-quality vendors do not routinely respond to RFIs because they recognize the beauty-contest nature of the process.

If your organization's standard mode of operations requires an RFI, provide each vendor on the short list with the same business case study to solve. This case study should be small, but it should contain well-defined examples of your key requirements. Ask each vendor to respond with a working demonstration that solves the business problem. You will often find several vendors graciously bowing out of the competition. Of those who remain, you have a first-hand view of what the solution looks like.

understand clearly the formal and informal relationships between your advisor and any vendors.

Evaluate the Options

Now is the time to begin working directly with the vendors. Set up meetings with each candidate. Provide each vendor with the same information about what you are trying to accomplish:

- Listen to each vendor's pitch. Allow them to highlight their strengths.
- Ask pointed questions that address your requirements.
- Ask each competitor to discuss *how* they would deliver key functionality.
- Present a business case study that emphasizes your key requirements (this can be provided in advance or introduced during the meeting).
- Use the evaluation matrix as a guide during these sessions. Fill it in as you get answers to each issue.

You may want to have more than one meeting with the different vendors. This allows you the opportunity to pursue issues you have learned from meeting with their competitors. It is also helpful to include the representatives from the target user group to participate in these sessions.

CHECK REFERENCES

This is incredibly important, as it's only from other customers that you will get reliable information about how the product works in the real world. Ideally, you'll want to talk to a customer that is "just like you," which practically speaking means that you'll need to talk to a handful of references and synthesize the results. Just because the product works with a "3-terabyte warehouse" doesn't mean their implementation is anything like yours. Make sure that one or more references have implemented a dimensional warehouse. Talk to them without the vendor present. You are more likely to get the full story.

As a result of these sessions, decide which product you believe is most likely to meet your requirements. Before making a final commitment, you may want to develop a prototype to make sure that everything works as advertised. If you have narrowed the selection to two vendors, but are unable to see a clear decision, it can be helpful to develop a prototype for each.

Optional: Develop a Prototype

In some cases, the product choice is clear from research, including reference checks. If it isn't, multiple products need to be evaluated more closely. In this case, the goal is to be able to compare and contrast a set of similar products to see which one best meets your needs. We call this a "bake off." All candidates are given the same problem to solve and the same amount of time to develop the solution. It is important that you provide each vendor with the flexibility to solve the problem the best way they can. Do not impose artificial limitations upon the competing vendors. By allowing them to take the same input and produce the required result, you are able to see what it takes to make each solution work. In these situations, you should not ask many vendors to participate. This only wastes their resources and yours. Once you understand your requirements, you should research the marketplace to select the primary candidates. We suggest that you limit the development of a technical evaluation prototype to two or three vendors.

 The primary purpose of developing a prototype is to confirm that the design and the technologies will meet the business requirements before you invest significant time and money developing the full data transformation system.

The most common prototyping process is to install the product at your location for hands-on testing. This allows the team to learn the technology and discover issues first hand. A second type of prototype involves testing in a controlled environment, like your corporate software laboratory. This is often a strict requirement within large organizations before allowing the technology to be approved for use within the company. The purpose is not to determine if it will meet any business need but to prove that it would not disrupt existing applications if it were implemented within the company. The testing group will also determine if the product works with the supported versions of other software. A corporate architecture group is often responsible for this technology evaluation. Evaluation of the overall functional capabilities of the product is left to the individual project teams.

Prototype Scale

Often, prototypes are built using data that is convenient for IS and not usually selected to prove any specific business value. Consequently, you may not gain any insight into how this technology can solve business issues.

We suggest that you carefully select a small yet representative subset of data to use for prototyping. If you are evaluating hardware and/or database platforms, this small subset can be exploded out to high volumes yet retain realistic distribution of your data. A small subset can be effectively used to evaluate data staging and access tools. The key here is to select data that is a meaningful business set of data, not just whatever is easiest to get your hands on.

On the other hand, if your project is dealing with significant amounts of data, and the data staging window is likely to be a problem from day 1 of operations, you really need to test with a lot of data. A lot of performance-related issues will not arise until you're dealing with large volumes of data. Although building a prototype on a huge dataset is not easy, you may need to step up to it. We advocate building a smaller prototype, as discussed next, and then scaling it up to test large volumes only on the points that are most problematic. The scaled-up data doesn't need to be real. We usually duplicate a small set over and over, adjusting the keys if necessary to assure uniqueness.

One common mistake when developing a prototype is to ignore performance tuning. To understand how a design will work, some time must be spent in tuning. If you cannot get small sample data to work quickly, how will the system perform at full volume?

On one project, we assisted in the data modeling process, and the team went on to use the model to develop a proof of design prototype. We were called back later with a request for additional data modeling assistance. The team was very concerned because as far as they could tell, the initial data model did not work—performance was completely unacceptable. Basic queries took between 10 and 20 minutes, and some of the more complex queries ran for hours. The project team, which had a solid data design background, concluded that the design must be wrong. A little probing revealed that no tuning had been done at all! In our experience one or two well-placed indexes can take queries that run for hours down to less than a minute, even on small volumes of data. Rather than jumping into a complete revision of the data model, the team spent several days tuning the prototype. It turned out that the data model was just fine. The prototype must include a tuning step. This is especially important because there have been instances where people who don't understand dimensional star schema design will pounce on a poorly performing prototype as proof that star schemas don't work.

Develop a Meaningful Test Suite

A typical test suite for a technology evaluation strives to test the components across a range of requirements. Typically, these include the following areas:

- **Simple/complex functionality.** Technical evaluations need to explore the full range of functions that will be needed. Too often the focus is on only one extreme. Some explore only simple requirements. In other instances the most difficult case that anyone could dream up is provided as the base criteria. You need to take a balanced approach. If the most complex report has never been developed using any tool, it is probably not the only thing to use in an evaluation. This does not mean you should ignore it, but you also need to gain an understanding of the basic and middle complexity requirements.

- **Low/high data volume.** For many technologies, testing with low volume alone is sufficient if paired with solid reference checking. In some cases, high-volume testing may be wise, such as selection of RDBMS software, especially for a large warehouse.

- **Single/multiuser.** Single user testing can provide insight into how the functions work. Multiuser testing provides insight into performance implications of multiple users. The multiuser tests should reflect a combination of short browsing queries and multitable join queries. Again, reference checking can be used to learn about broadscale usage characteristics.

Define Completion Criteria

A prototype is really a microproject. All the steps in the Lifecycle must be done, but in a scaled-back fashion. The biggest problem with prototyping is that a prototype is often started without clear completion criteria.

Depending upon the product under evaluation, you may need to define and develop a data model, extract and transform the data, and develop queries and reports. Like the full data warehouse project, the prototype must have a well-defined scope. Things to consider include:

- What are you trying to accomplish?
- How will you know when you are done?
- What are your decision criteria?
- What must be accomplished for the prototype to be considered a success?

Never Move a Prototype into Production

One large organization we've worked with was doing a technical evaluation of multiple data access tools. The data model developed for this evaluation was used for the production data warehouse as well without further analysis. Rather than simply being an evaluation, the prototype was viewed as a quick way to get the data warehouse up and running. The biggest problem with this approach was that the user requirements were not adequately gathered, and a few days of modeling was not sufficient to fully develop the data model. The evaluation of the technologies became tied up with massive revisions of the data model based upon actual data content and user input. Consequently, the evaluation dragged on, and the data model was still not production ready. The entire process ended up taking several months.

It may take longer to work through a runaway prototype than it would if complete requirements were gathered and full data modeling had occurred. To put it another way, prototype development in no way diminishes the need for true requirements analysis and robust data modeling.

Other Lessons to Learn

For many companies, the development of a prototype provides the team with its first full dose of hands-on data warehouse experience. We find it useful to keep a list of what you learned during the process. In addition to product evaluation input, you should also learn about:

■ **Design issues.**   The prototype will highlight your current design's strengths and weaknesses. Expect several major issues to fall out of the prototype. The good news is this gives you a chance to figure out solutions to issues before they become big, public problems.

■ **Data challenges.**   The prototype gives you another opportunity to understand what is really in the data (as opposed to what everyone thought was in the data). Tracking everything that was corrected, unusual, or wrong in the data is important. These irregularities are typically manually corrected or simply thrown out during prototype development. Every quick fix applied during the prototype must have a corresponding function in the production data transformation process. In some cases the actual data content may drive modifications to the data model itself.

■ **Usability.**   By working with the front-end tool in the context of the proof of design, the application developers can gain a realistic understanding of what will be required to build applications. The end users can look at the prototype to validate the data model and tool capabilities. This is more of a guided process than hands-on training for the users. It doesn't make sense to train them at this point because they won't be able to do real queries for a while. By the time they actually get the tool, they will have forgotten the training. Instead, it is much more effective to sit with the users in a controlled setting to review what they need to be able to do. The users can pose questions, while a member of the core project team constructs the required analyses. In some cases, the users may want to build the analyses themselves. In these cases, the core project team member should guide them through one step at a time. This provides the feedback you need with minimal time required from the business.

■ **Analytical power.**   Once the data is loaded, you can build samples of the types of analyses needed by the business. If you did a technical evaluation of the front-end tool, there should be few surprises here. If you chose a tool through some other means (e.g., management fiat), the proof of design is especially important to verify that the tool provides the needed functionality. Although you reviewed your requirements during the sales cycle with the vendors, this gives you a hands-on opportunity to not only prove that it can be done but to see what is required to do so. Usually, when you ask a vendor if they provide a certain capability, the answer will be yes. Remember that we are dealing with computers and software here—you can probably figure out a way to do anything with any given tool. What you really need to know, is *how*. Then you need to ensure that this is acceptable to your organization.

Speed of Prototype Development

The development of a prototype is often completed in about 4 to 6 weeks. Since this is very resource intensive, some vendors charge for this service. While it is great to be able to see results so quickly, do not let the speed of development cause expectations to rise to unattainable heights.

 Many people, within both IS and the business community, think that if a prototype can be developed in 2 weeks, the production system should be ready in a month. This is not possible!

Several reasons why prototypes can be developed so quickly include:

- **Scope modifications.**   To meet the short deadline, the scope of the data is often modified (i.e., simplified) during development. For example, if an attribute is unclear, it may be eliminated from the model.
- **Manual data correction.**   In most cases, the data is not auditable. No business decisions should be made from these prototypes. If errors are discovered in the data, such as two products with the same product code, one may simply be dropped. If a description is unclear about what additional attributes apply, an educated guess is made. While these modifications can be made manually to get the prototype working quickly, they will change the meaning of the data. The real warehouse development process includes additional research to determine the correct handling of data errors.
- **No update mechanism.**   The method used to create the prototype database is usually either manual or quickly coded programs. These are not designed to be efficient or repeatable, and they typically don't perform error checking. They are created simply to move the data quickly.

- **Vendor consultant time.** Once the sample data is delivered to a vendor, you do not know the real effort that went into the development. Consultants working on these prototypes often work extremely long hours and over the weekends to get them completed—we can vouch for this from first-hand experience.

- **Data warehouse experience.** The vendor consultants already have a good understanding of data warehouse concepts and design. They know the technology extremely well and have direct access to their own gurus.

Recommend a Product

This product recommendation should be presented in the form of a report summarizing what was learned and rationale for the team's recommendations. The recommendation typically must be approved by a variety of people or committees. Once the recommendation has been accepted, the contract negotiation can begin. Different vendors price based on different measures, such as concurrent users, named users, number of connections, site, enterprise, and so on. Watch out for maintenance, services, support, and other add-on costs.

Whatever product choices you make, keep in mind that the data warehouse market is changing rapidly, especially in the front-end and data staging tool areas. You should expect to reevaluate your choices in two or three years and migrate to new tools if the benefits support it.

Evaluation Shortcuts

It is rare for a warehouse project to go through detailed evaluations for all four of the major areas listed earlier. Usually, one of several factors intervenes to make the evaluation process irrelevant. Some of these factors include:

- **Existing IS product standards.** In other words, "we only buy our servers from (fill in the blank for your organization)."

- **Existing resources.** This usually means spare boxes or software licenses. Typically, these are cast-offs as a result of upgrades done to save troubled client/server transaction systems. Site licenses are a part of this factor. If your company has a site license for a certain database product, it will take some strong evidence to justify additional spending.

PROTOTYPING GUIDELINES

There are several basic guidelines to follow when building a data warehouse prototype, whether it is being done as a proof of concept (described in Chapter 3), to select a product, or to simply prove the design. Regardless of the type of prototype you are building, the following guidelines apply:

- Ensure you define your prototype scope, including completion criteria.
- Avoid tackling too much at once.
- Use a meaningful but small subset of data.
- Provide only a quick and dirty data load process. A manual manipulation process helps you avoid the urge to run those programs to load data that would turn your prototype into a weak, unstable production system.
- Learn as much as possible about source system data problems during prototype development.
- Learn as much as possible about hardware and software capabilities during prototype development.
- Learn as much as possible about support requirements during prototype development.
- Get end user feedback. Don't just put the tool on their desk and ask them what they think after a week or two. Work side by side with them for several short sessions.
- Get references and call them. You'll be amazed at what you learn, and you may end up with another resource to call on when you need some experienced guidance.
- Do not allow a prototype to be put into production!
- Keep a close handle on expectations. Do not allow them to spiral out of control.

Most of all, be honest about what you see and learn while developing a prototype. Celebrate the positives and explore the negatives to determine what can be done to resolve or minimize the impact on the project. An objective analysis here can save a lot of time and money down the road.

- **Team experience or relationships.**   Often, if someone on the team has had a successful experience with a data warehouse product, that product becomes the leading candidate. This internal experience with a known quantity is extremely valuable to the team.

Note that product selection by decree doesn't necessarily mean failure, but it does mean you need to review your requirements against the imposed system and immediately report any reduction in scope or capability caused by this decision. For example, you may not be able to update all the data every night, or the system might not be physically able to store the level of detail or amount of history desired. This trade-off should be a business decision. Present the alternatives to business management and work with them to reach a decision.

Evaluations for the Back Room

While following the general process described earlier, there are characteristics that are unique to each specific area of evaluation. The next several sections provide a high-level summary of back room evaluation areas.

Hardware Platform Evaluation

A full hardware selection is relatively rare for a small first data warehouse project due to the effort involved. If your needs fall within a certain range, a full test probably isn't necessary. Work with a vendor to identify references with similar warehouse projects. If you do an actual test, take advantage of vendor facilities and resources as much as possible. The test suites should include both front room and back room activities, along with multiuser stress tests. A hardware test is useful if you will be using a cast-off server. In this case, you want to verify that it has the capacity to handle your needs.

1. Determine configuration based on architecture, requirements, and database testing. Key factors include:
   - *Memory*. Data warehouses are memory hogs, and performance is often greatly improved by having a lot of memory. The 64-bit architecture allows very large memory configurations (i.e., more than 2 GB RAM).
   - *CPUs*. Start with at least two, even for small implementations.

- *Disk.* See the discussion in Chapter 15 about RAID configurations.
- *Database optimizer.* Verify the specific features of your database across different hardware platforms (e.g., versions, platform-specific improvements).

2. Design and implement routines to collect test results.
3. Design the physical database (disk, indexes, etc.).
4. Load test data.
5. Code and implement the test suite and results collection process.
6. Run baseline tests.
7. Tune.
8. Run final tests.

DBMS Platform Evaluation

The database evaluation is similar to the hardware evaluation because in a sense, they are two sides of the same coin. You need database operations to test the hardware performance, and the hardware platform will have a major impact on the database performance. The same test suite should apply to both evaluation processes. Database evaluations are especially important with large warehouses—make sure you can load the data within the load window and that queries return in a reasonable amount of time.

1. Design and implement routines to collect test results.
2. Design the physical database, including disk layout, indexes, and striping.
3. Load test data.
4. Code and implement test suite, including staging and query scenarios, and results collection process.
5. Run baseline tests.
6. Tune.
7. Run final tests.

Data Staging Tool Evaluation

If you don't have data warehouse experience, you'll find that data staging tools are unlike any other software products. You will typically have to learn how to use the product from scratch before you can test it. Count on one to three weeks of training before you can start testing.

1. Test across a range of load and transformation scenarios—more than the initial warehouse set.
2. Test key load processes, like dimension management and fact table updates.
   - Can they generate surrogate keys and do key look-ups?
   - How do they handle slowly changing dimensions?
   - Can they create aggregations?

Other tools that your data warehousing project may use include scheduling, code maintenance, bug tracking, FTP, telnet, and Web server software. Typically, these tool choices have already been made for you. This is fine, since the warehouse project's requirements for these tools are very similar to other projects' requirements.

Evaluations for the Front Room

The most critical area requiring evaluation in the front room is for a data access tool. Hardware must be selected here, too, but it is often an easy choice based upon the end user tool and the data warehouse hardware platform. Hardware platform evaluation considerations are discussed in the preceding section and are not repeated here.

Data Access Tool Evaluation

The data access tool market space has become one of most complex and confusing segments in the industry. Ten years ago there were approximately five vendors selling data access tools. Today there are more than 75 vendors selling data access tools or components of tools. The problem is that most of these vendors will claim they can solve all of your business and technical problems. Common sense tells us it isn't possible for every tool vendor to solve all of our problems. If each of them could, why are there so many of them? All of the vendors give beautiful demonstrations of their solutions. It then becomes your job to sort out fact from fiction and begin to understand how the different tools work from both a functional and an architectural perspective. In fairness, most of the vendors can actually perform the functions that are in their demos.

Selecting a front-end tool is an exasperating process. There are so many alternatives, they all have different strengths and weaknesses, and none of them ever seems to solve the problem completely. As we described in Chapter 10, this is because there is more than one problem to

CHOOSING A DATA MODELING TOOL

Although affordable tools to support the modeling process are fairly well developed at this point, they still tend to lack an enterprise focus and need to improve their openness in terms of exchanging metadata. In general, the following list describes the desired functionality needed to support the model creation and maintenance process:

- The tool must be based on an open metadata model. That is, it must be able to read and write to standard RDBMSs so it can store its own metadata on the data warehouse platform.
- Reverse-engineering capability (source access, standard format).
- Generate formal data definitions (DDL) for a range of database targets.
- Allow specification of both sources and targets.
- Support both logical and physical models.
- Capture business descriptions, textual info, example values, and help.
- Capture business rules and transformation definitions.
- Specific data warehouse capabilities (e.g., star schema modeling support).
- Enterprise-oriented with multiuser, multisite availability of models. This includes:
  - Model coordination and synchronization
  - Development capabilities (project support)
  - Version control
  - Library (check in, check out)
- Provide a range of standard reports and flexible report customization.
- Ease of use. Present the model in a readable, controllable graphical representation, with the ability to identify subsections of the model.
- Import/export the model to and from other modeling tools.
- Generate DDL for only those elements that have changed (instead of an entire new version).
- Support for database capabilities (e.g., triggers, stored procedures).
- Support for existing development tools.

We feel obliged to note that we've been able to build many successful warehouses with data modeling tools no more sophisticated than Microsoft Excel and PowerPoint.

solve. Tool selection is tough when we don't understand that there is a range of needs, and that one tool might not meet all of them. We actually want all of the capabilities from all the categories in a single, excellent tool. For example, once we build a query and validate it in the ad hoc environment, it may make sense to schedule that query and have it run as a standard report from then on. Next, we'll want to use the same query in a push-button EIS system. This all-in-one desire has only made the tool choice problem more difficult. Most of the tool vendors have their roots in one category, but they've been pushed to include some or all of the remaining categories. They all can safely say they provide many of the functions described next. Your challenge will be to see which ones can actually meet your requirements.

 The real question for data access tool evaluation is not only *how* they perform the functions, but how well do the tools scale, how much administration do the tools require, and what is the payoff for that level of administration.

The data access tool evaluation is probably the one evaluation area almost every warehouse project goes through at some point. It is different because it includes significant user participation. The first and critical step is to revisit the requirements and architecture. Although these steps follow the general evaluation process described earlier in this chapter, the nuances of the data access tool warrant additional clarification. The following recommendations should help clearly define what a tool needs to provide:

- Be very specific about the requirements. Compile a comprehensive list of the types of calculations that the tool will need to support (this year/last year, regression, time period comparisons, share, etc.). Include other critical functionality, like Web publishing, complex formatting, report scheduling, and so on.
- Educate yourself and the evaluation team on the basics so that the vendors cannot pull the wool over your eyes. Conduct literature searches for product information. Obtain industry analyst reports on tool comparison. Contact anyone you know who may have some direct experience.

- Review the data access tool features that we discussed in Chapter 10, to make sure you haven't forgotten to list important features.
- Identify product candidates and rank based on priorities.
- Develop a business case that represents a reasonable scenario. Don't ask for the monster report that no one has been able to produce to date, but rather a realistic instance. Include business measures that mathematically represent the range that will be required overall. This, tied with a scaled-down dimensional model, will be very helpful. You'll get the information you need, and the vendors get a request that is in terms they can understand. (We still feel compassion for those presales consultants.)
- Install and test top candidates.
- Conduct user review sessions. User involvement is invaluable for two reasons: to get their perspective and to get their support for the final choice.
- Heavy use of references is also important. You are looking for sites with similar business problems, similar technical environments, and similar data/user volumes. Of course, all these characteristics will probably never be shared by the same reference, so you need to talk to or visit several sites.
- Collect and organize test results and user feedback.
- Expect to be surprised when you actually select and install the tool and get it working for real in your own environment. No matter how good your tool selection process, there will always be surprises.

INSTALLATION

Installation issues are very different among software products, and obviously different between software and hardware. Your best bet to ensure successful installation is to pay close attention and take careful notes during the prototype process. In most cases, you should have an expert in the product involved in the installation. Certain configuration parameters set during installation can have a major impact on the performance of the warehouse. The following major steps should help you ask the right questions:

- **Site preparation.** Make sure you have a place to put the component, whether it is hardware or software. There's more to installing a large server than just plugging it in. You need a controlled environment with clean power and space. Servers have proliferated over the last few years, and in many cases, space is at a premium. Make sure you work with the operations folks to find out where the box is going before it shows up on the loading dock.

- **Training.** Hopefully, the operations group has experience with the components you are bringing in. The team will need to know how it works as well, so include appropriate training in your install plan. This includes hardware and operating system administration training. There is nothing more frustrating than for an uninitiated team member to be stumbling around in UNIX, trying to figure out what is going on by trial and error.
- **Installation, checkout and test.** Bring it in and get it going.
- **Acceptance criteria.** Especially for a large warehouse, it's a good idea to negotiate acceptance criteria based on minimum performance levels determined during the evaluation process.

SUMMARY

In this chapter we have reviewed the processes used to create and implement the architecture required to support the data warehouse. First we reviewed creation of your architecture, focusing on the two main deliverables from the architecture process: the architecture plan and the infrastructure plan. Then we described how to select products to make your architecture real. Finally, we briefly reviewed general considerations for installing those products. Be sure to consult the project plan spreadsheet at the end of this chapter for a summary of the tasks and responsibilities for creating the architecture plan and selecting products (Figure 13.8).

KEY ROLES

Keys roles for creating the architecture plan and selecting products are highlighted below. Tasks to address short- and long-term security issues are included here too, although the concepts and tasks are detailed in Chapter 12. Since Chapter 12 is a graduate course, we want to ensure that all readers note the need for tasks devoted to security:

KEY ROLES (*Continued*)

- The special teams play a driving role in creating the technical architecture. The data warehouse architecture must be an extension of the existing corporate architecture, thus requiring participation from mainframe, client/server, networking, and security specialists.
- The project manager must take a lead role in the battle for a secure environment, starting with educating the organization through ensuring that proper measures are implemented and maintained. While the project manager will not be the one to implement these measures in most cases, he or she does need to be held responsible, otherwise it will slip through the cracks.
- Specific technical specialists need to implement any changes to the environment, based upon the tactical and strategic plans.
- The product selection process requires involvement from the technical specialists as well as from the key team members who are the primary users of that component. For example, the data staging team plays a critical role in selection of extract, cleansing, and transformation products.
- Installation again requires joint effort between the core data warehouse team and the technical specialists who have the necessary skills to install each component properly.

ESTIMATING CONSIDERATIONS FOR CREATING THE ARCHITECTURE PLAN

 You must have an initial architecture plan in place early in the process. This initial plan can be at a high level and incomplete, but it should allow the team to identify their parts and begin working on them in parallel. Additional architectural details will fall into place over time, as you gather real world experience working with the data, the platforms, the tools, and the users.

There is a spectrum of approaches to creating an architecture, ranging from a few scribbles on the back of an envelope, to a full-blown, multiperson, multiyear struggle. In general, where your project falls on the spectrum depends on the overall size and scope of the

ESTIMATING CONSIDERATIONS FOR CREATING THE ARCHITECTURE PLAN (*Continued*)

warehouse and on the level of detail desired. The approach we advocate is somewhere in the middle, requiring a month or two of elapsed time, concurrent with other activities as illustrated on the lifecycle diagram, and resulting in a practical, usable blueprint for the warehouse. Figure 13.7 shows a matrix of the major drivers of an architecture effort.

The closer you can get to the lower-left quadrant, the better. The upper-right quadrant ends up being an enterprise architecture project and usually gets tangled up in a complex web of organizational and technical issues.

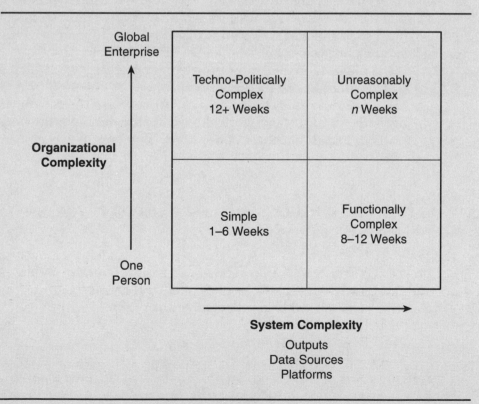

FIGURE 13.7   Architecture development effort.

ESTIMATING CONSIDERATIONS FOR SELECTING PRODUCTS

 Often hardware and/or software vendors provide (sometimes at minimal or no cost) resources to develop a prototype. You will want to actively participate, too. Since development is occurring at your own facility, you should absolutely use this opportunity to begin to learn the technology. This also allows you to discover any installation challenges first hand. If you go through a full-blown product selection process, count on two person-months of effort for each major area.

TEMPLATES

 The following templates for creating the architecture plan and selecting products are included on the CD-ROM:

- Template 13.1 Technical Architecture Plan Document
- Template 13.2 Product Evaluation Matrix
- Template 13.3 Product Evaluation Matrix Example

Project Task	Business End Users	Business Sponsor	IS Sponsor	Business Driver	Bus. Project Lead	Project Manager	Bus. Sys. Analyst	Data Modeler	DW DBA	Data Staging Designer	DW Educator	E/U Appl Devel	Tech/Security Architect	Tech. Sppt Specialists	Data Staging Programmer	Data Steward	DW QA Analyst
	Fans	Front Office			Coaches		Regular Line-Up						Special Teams				
TECHNICAL ARCHITECTURE DESIGN																	
1 Create Architecture Task Force					○	○							●	○			
2 Gather & Document Technical Requirements						▸	▸	▸	▸	▸	▸	▸	●	○			
3 Review Current Technical Environment					▸	○	○	○	○	○		○	●	○			
4 Create Architecture Plan						▸	▸	▸	▸	▸		▸	●	○			
5 Determine Phased Implementation Approach					○	○							●	○			
7 Create Infrastructure Plan													●	○			
8 Develop Configuration Recommendations													●	○			
9 User Acceptance/Project Review	□	□	□	□	○	●	□	□	□	□	□	□	○	○	□	□	□
PRODUCT SELECTION																	
(Repeat for each selection area)																	
1 Develop Evaluation Matrix					●	●	○	○					●	○			
2 Research Candidate Products						○	○	○	○	○		○	●	○			
3 Develop Product Short List						○	○	○	○	○		○	●				
4 Evaluate Product Options	▸					○	○	○	○	○		○	●				
5 Optional Prototype (May repeat for different products)																	
Select Business Process/Data for Evaluation					●	●	○	○									
Define Completion Criteria					●	●							○				
Acquire Resources (Internal/Vendor)					○	●											
Determine Test Configuration						○			○	○		○	●	○			
Install Evaluation Prerequisities & Components							○	○	○	○		○	○	●			
Train the Evaluation Team	○				○	●	○	○	○	○	○	○	○	○			
Develop & Tune Prototype						○	○	●	●	●		●	○	●			
Conduct Tests	▸				▸	▸	▸	▸	●	●	▸	●	▸	●			
Analyze & Document Results	▸				○	●	▸	▸	▸	▸		▸	●	○			
6 Determine Product Recommendation		□	□	□	●	●	○	○	○	○		○	●	○			
7 Present Findings/Results to Management		□	□	□	●	●	▸	▸	▸	▸		▸	▸	▸			
8 Negotiate Contract						●											
9 User Acceptance/Project Review	□	□	□	□	●	●	○	○	○	○	○	○	○	○	▲	▲	▲
PRODUCT INSTALLATION																	
(Repeat for each product)																	
1 Installation Planning													●	○			
2 Meet Prerequisites													○	●			
3 Install Hardware/Software													○	●			
4 Test Hardware/Software													○	●			
5 User Acceptance/Project Review	▲	□	□	□	○	●	○	○	○	○	▲	○	○	○	▲	▲	▲

LEGEND:

Primary Responsibility for the Task =	●
Involved in the Task =	○
Provides Input to the Task =	▸
Informed Task Results =	□
Optional Involvement in the Task =	▲

FIGURE 13.8 Project plan tasks and responsibilities for creating the architecture plan and selecting products.

SECTION 4

Implementation

CHAPTER 14

A Graduate Course on Aggregates

The single most dramatic way to affect performance in a large data warehouse is to provide a proper set of aggregate (summary) records that coexist with the primary base records.

Aggregates can have a very significant effect on performance, in some cases speeding queries by a factor of 100 or even 1000. No other means exist to harvest such spectacular gains. Certainly, the IS owners of a data warehouse should exhaust the potential for using aggregates before investing in new hardware.

The benefits of a comprehensive aggregate building program can be realized with almost every data warehouse hardware and software configuration, including all of the popular relational DBMSs such as Oracle, Red Brick, Informix, Sybase, and DB2, as well as uniprocessor, SMP, and MPP architectures. We describe how to structure a data warehouse to maximize the benefits of aggregates, and how to build and use those aggregates without requiring complex accompanying metadata.

The basics of aggregate navigation have been summarized earlier in the book. The main points are:

- In a properly designed data warehouse environment, multiple sets of aggregates are built, representing common grouping levels within the key dimensions of the data warehouse.
- An aggregate navigator is a piece of middleware that sits between the requesting client and the DBMS as shown in Figure 10.2. An aggregate navigator intercepts the client's SQL and, wherever possible, transforms base-level SQL into aggregate-aware SQL. An aggregate navigator understands how to transform base-level SQL into aggregate-aware SQL, because it uses special metadata that describes the data warehouse aggregate portfolio.

While this chapter does contain advanced content, it is also useful for anyone who wants to understand what aggregates are and the basic principles of their design. Data modelers and DBAs should study this chapter to understand how aggregate structures should be designed. The data staging team also needs to study this chapter to understand how to create and maintain aggregates.

AGGREGATION GOALS AND RISKS

The goal of an aggregate strategy in a large data warehouse must be more than just improving performance. A good aggregate strategy should also do the following:

- Provide dramatic performance gains for as many categories of user queries as possible.
- Add only a reasonable amount of extra data storage to the warehouse. What is reasonable is up to the DBA, but many data warehouse DBAs strive to increase the overall disk storage for the data warehouse by a factor of two or less.
- Be completely transparent to end users and to application designers except for the obvious performance benefits; in other words, no end-user application SQL should reference the aggregates.
- Directly benefit all users of the data warehouse, regardless of which query tool they use.
- Impact the cost of the data extract system as little as possible. Inevitably, a lot of aggregates must be built every time data is loaded, but their specification should be as automated as possible.

- Impact the DBA's administrative responsibilities as little as possible. The metadata that supports aggregates should be very limited and easy to maintain.

A well-designed aggregate environment can achieve all of these objectives. A poorly designed aggregate environment can fail all of the objectives. We begin by helping you decide what to aggregate, and then we will provide four design goals that, if followed, will achieve all of your desired objectives.

DECIDING WHAT TO AGGREGATE

First, all data warehouses will contain prestored aggregates. If you are developing a data warehouse that will not have any history loaded initially, you may think that you do not need to build any aggregates. However, depending upon the size of your data, you may still need to consider building some aggregates. Two different areas need attention when you are designing aggregates: the structure of storing them and which ones to build. Details about aggregate structures can be found later in this chapter. Here, we will review the process you can use to determine which aggregates you need to build.

Before you get too concerned about deciding which aggregates to build, keep in mind that these will change. You will add and take away aggregates periodically. They should be considered a performance-tuning vehicle. You need to build some aggregates, conduct some performance tests, and then revise which aggregates you will use in production. From there, you need to monitor aggregate use over time and make adjustments accordingly. Relax, changing your prestored aggregates is not a complicated thing as long as your users are isolated from changes with an aggregate navigator. Decide on a set of aggregates to start with, and then make adjustments as needed.

Two different areas need to be considered when selecting which aggregates to build. First, you need to consider common business requests. Second, you need to consider statistical distribution of your data. When working with your business users, you will get a sense of the primary reporting levels that are in place already. Often these are categorized by major geographic groupings, major product lines, and regular reporting time periods (weeks or months). Review each dimension to determine which attributes are commonly used for grouping. Next, review the combinations of these attributes to determine which ones are used together.

Pay careful attention to this if you have a lot of dimensions. If each dimension has 3 attributes that are candidates for aggregation, and you have 4 dimensions, you could build 256 different aggregates. This is perhaps possible, although likely unnecessary. However, if you have 8 dimensions (each having 3 candidate attributes), then the possible aggregates jumps to 65,536! Not all combinations of these candidate attributes will be commonly used together.

Another thing to consider is the number of values for attributes that are candidates for aggregation. For example, suppose that you have 1,000,000 values for the lowest level product package. There is a need to report at the product level, which is the next level of detail, and it has 500,000 values. Prestoring a product level would not provide a significant improvement since you are dealing with almost the same number of rows. However, if the product level has only 75,000 values, it would be a very strong candidate for a prestored aggregate.

This statistical view can also be used to identify possible aggregates that would provide a significant reduction in the number of rows processed, even if it is not a common business request. For example, you are tracking inventory for 300,000 parts. The most common reporting attribute in the part hierarchy is part class that only has 100 values. You may want to consider aggregating to part type, which is not commonly used by the business today but has 500 values. Another thing that would support this decision is if there are additional attributes that relate to part type that are of interest to the business, even though they are not commonly used today.

Another possibility is to create a composite aggregate, one that contains more than one attribute from a dimension. For example, suppose that you have 10,000,000 consumers in your data warehouse. You know that many requests are needed for state/province reporting, which has less than 100 values. The users are unable to clearly identify other specific attributes that will be used frequently. In order to support these other common requests, consider building an age/gender/income range aggregate. Business users may not ask questions that pull data directly from this aggregate table, but this aggregate may be used to create additional aggregates on the fly. Before implementing a composite aggregate, consult with your data access or aggregate navigation software vendor to find out if they can use this type of aggregate.

We recommend that you develop a list of initial aggregates that you would like to build right after you finish data modeling, when the users' requirements are still fresh in your mind. By the time you have loaded data into the database, you may have forgotten what the common requests are.

DEVELOP THE AGGREGATE TABLE PLAN

In many ways, the creation and use of aggregates parallels the creation and use of indexes. Like an index, an aggregate is a data structure that facilitates performance and requires the attention of the database administrator. Chapter 16 on data staging describes the creation and administration of aggregates in detail.

Note that what you do with aggregates depends in a large part on what tools you have available. Specifically, you need to have an aggregate navigator to help your users take advantage of aggregate tables without having to learn to navigate them manually. If your aggregate navigator is built into the front-end tool, you may also need to collect usage information for aggregates, both the aggregate tables and all queries with aggregate functions, out of your usage monitoring tables. This is important because the initial aggregates you choose are not likely to be the ones people use most.

Still, your initial plan can come close if you do a little research. First, determine what might be useful. Review the requirements document and application plan, looking for mention of higher-level grouping needs. Next, determine what might make an impact. Go back through the data audit and database design information (and potentially the data itself), looking for counts at each level of the hierarchy in each dimension. An easy example of this is the Period dimension table. If we had a Period table that covered five years, the information would look like this:

Level	Count
Day	1,826
Month	60
Quarter	20
Year	5
Total	1

A simple Product dimension table might look like this:

Level	Count
SKU	2,023
Product	723
Brand	44
Category	15
Total	1

Next, you need to get a sense for the sparsity of the data. In our case, we need to know what percentage of products are sold on a given day. Once you have all this information, a little spreadsheet work will help you calculate the number of aggregate rows you would have at each level of aggregation. In the extreme case, where there is no sparsity, every SKU is sold every day, which results in almost 3.7 million rows at the detail level. Figure 14.1 shows the row counts for the zero sparsity case, in thousands, for every intersection of the two dimensions. Figure 14.2 shows the row counts for the 50-percent sparsity case (half the SKUs are sold on a given day).

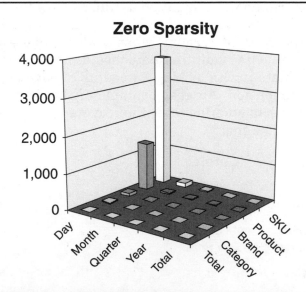

FIGURE 14.1   Aggregate counts with zero sparsity.

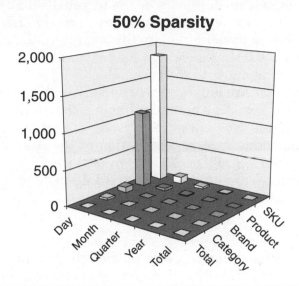

50% Sparsity

FIGURE 14.2 Aggregate counts with 50 percent sparsity.

Finally, look for places where there are both value and impact. In our example, an aggregate by Month and one by Brand are two places to start. At the risk of stating the obvious, the Month aggregate alone cuts the data to 1/30 of the detail size. The Brand aggregate cuts it again to about 1/50 of the detail size. That means if someone asks for brand totals by month in the zero sparsity case, we need only select 2,640 rows from the aggregate table rather than summing 3,693,998 rows from the detail table. This has to be faster, regardless of the platform.

A Product aggregate may be useful if a lot of reporting is done at the product level. Note that a product aggregate has less impact if the detail data is somewhat sparse. Our two-dimensional example is much simpler than the real world. Determining the interactions among multiple dimensions can be mind bending. This is another argument for getting a tool to help.

PROCESSING AGGREGATES

How do we actually create aggregates? The only absolute requirement is that aggregates are fed from the underlying atomic base data. There are several variations on the theme of building aggregates:

1. Aggregates are built outside the target DBMS by sorting the granular input data and calculating break rows. The break rows are the aggregates, by definition. In this approach, the aggregates exist outside the DBMS before the load step, and they can be separately archived along with the base data.
2. Aggregates are built over a period of time by adding the current load records to existing accumulating buckets in the DBMS.
3. Aggregates are built automatically as part of the load process. This can be thought of as a variation of the first two techniques, but where the aggregates do not physically exist outside the DBMS.
4. Aggregates are built inside the DBMS using SQL after the granular data has been loaded.

Generally, we do not recommend the last option. Aggregate building involves two steps that may be inefficient inside the DBMS. First, aggregate building is necessarily a sorting operation. Sorting may be much faster outside the DBMS with a dedicated sort package than inside the DBMS using the ORDER BY clause in SQL. Second, a crucial step in aggregate creation is looking up the appropriate surrogate key value for the aggregate or possibly even assigning a new surrogate key if the aggregate has never been encountered in the data before. The logic for doing these operations is simple enough, but this is sequential processing, not relational processing.

 The surest sign that aggregate creation is based on the wrong technology is the existence of a long programming script with embedded SQL SELECT, INSERT, UPDATE, and DELETE statements. Most aggregate creation should be done outside the DBMS with dedicated sorting packages and flat file programming logic. This process is not relational.

The creation of aggregates is equivalent to the creation of break rows in a report. If aggregates representing product category totals are needed, then the incoming data must be sorted by product. Actually, several passes may be required to produce all the category aggregates. For example, if the base fact table data has a granularity of product by store by day, we might want to produce the following aggregates:

- Category by store by day
- Category by region by day
- Category by store by month and
- Category by region by month

If we are loading data every day, then for each day the first two aggregates can be created entirely from the daily load. Two sorts of the data are required: The first is store/product with products rolling up to categories within each store. The second is region/product with products rolling up to categories within each region. If stores roll into regions, we could create the aggregates with a single sort.

The first sort can also be used to augment the category by store by month aggregate by replacing the day surrogate key with the proper month surrogate key and presenting this record to the category by store by month fact table. When we say *augment,* we mean that the records generated each day either cause an insert or an update. We can't tell whether an insert or an update is required until we present the new aggregate record to the fact table. If a record with the same key is already present, we do an update, adding the appropriate facts to those already in the target record. If the record with the same key is not in the fact table, we perform an insert. It is a good idea to have a DBMS loader that can perform these augmenting loads in a bulk mode. If a sequential program has to check the database record by record to decide whether to perform an update or an insert, the load process will run far more slowly.

Every time we encounter a new aggregate that we have never seen before, we need to generate a new surrogate key for it. For instance, if we encounter a new product category, we must create a new key.

Keys for aggregates are by definition surrogate keys. To put it another way, there is no bar code for the Candy category. To maintain the needed flexibility for the data warehouse, the DBA should assign aggregate keys during the aggregate creation process. For the same reason we do not use production keys at the granular product level in our data warehouse, we do not want to use production keys for aggregate entities like category or sales district. Sooner or later, the requirements for the production keys will diverge from the requirements for the data warehouse keys. It is much better for the data warehouse to assign its own keys for everything at the outset.

Each load of new fact records requires that aggregates be calculated or augmented. It is very important to keep the aggregates synchronized with the base data at every instant in time.

If the base data is updated and placed on-line, but a delay ensues before the aggregates are updated, then the old aggregates must be taken off-line until the new ones are ready. Otherwise, the aggregates will not correctly mirror the base data. In this situation, the DBA has to choose between delaying the publishing of the data until both the base data and the aggregates are ready or releasing the revised base data in a performance-degraded mode while the aggregates are being updated off-line.

ADMINISTERING THE AGGREGATES

Over the course of time, the DBA will create and drop aggregates. The beauty of the aggregate navigator architecture is that the aggregates behave very much like indexes. They are used if they are present, but the system runs if they are not present. End users and application developers do not have to explicitly code their applications for the presence of aggregates.

Aggregates are a dynamic resource in the data warehouse environment. The DBA needs to study the aggregate statistics fairly frequently. Aggregates that are not being used can be dropped. This will free up disk space and will simplify the extract and load process. Hopefully, the statistics will also give a clear picture of which new aggregates should be built and what the trade-offs will be. The DBA needs to estimate how big the new aggregates will be and how long it will take to build or augment them during each extract and load cycle. Ideally, the DBA should estimate how much query time will be saved, but this may have to wait to be measured directly.

 As a general rule of thumb, it is reasonable to plan on a 100 percent storage overhead for aggregates as a target for the overall data warehouse.

In other words, the sum of all the aggregate tables should be approximately equal in storage to the sum of the lowest-level base tables. If the sum of the aggregate tables is 25 percent or less of the base tables, then almost certainly the users are paying performance penalties that should be addressed. Similarly if the sum of the aggregate tables is several times that of the base tables, too many aggregates have been built. Some are not being used, and the biggest aggregate tables probably have been built too close to the base level. There is a detailed discussion of a phenomenon known as *sparsity failure* in *The Data Warehouse Toolkit*, where we explained how the size of the aggregate tables can overwhelm a data warehouse.

It is also possible to build aggregates that are too close to each other. If only five subcategories roll up to a category, it probably isn't worthwhile to build aggregates at both levels. Try taking the category aggregate off-line. The subcategory aggregate will then be chosen for all category queries, and this may yield satisfactory performance. Conversely, perhaps no one is asking for subcategories. In that case, keep the category aggregates instead.

The underlying physical sort order of the database often provides a kind of wild card that reduces the need for aggregates in at least one dimension. For instance, if we have retail sales data physically sorted by time by product by store, then all the records for today may be in a set of sequentially assigned disk blocks. Within each of these blocks will be a large number of records, all for a given single product. The individual adjacent records will represent each store. See Figure 14.3. A query that

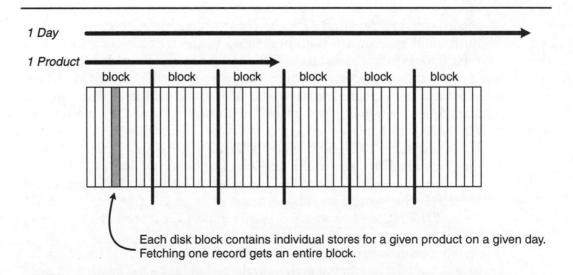

Each disk block contains individual stores for a given product on a given day. Fetching one record gets an entire block.

FIGURE 14.3   Sort order wild card.

looks at a single product on a single day will automatically access many store records with each disk block fetch. Thus a one-way Region aggregate on the store dimension would probably not result in improved performance. The store aggregate should be left out of the aggregate plan if the physical sort order is time by product by store.

The DBA should take advantage of the flexibility afforded by the aggregate navigator and should feel free to take aggregates off-line and put them on-line at any time. Doing so allows aggregate processing to take place after the primary loading.

The DBMS loader should support the natural activities of building and maintaining aggregates. If the DBMS loader does not support the creation of aggregates as part of the primary data load, the aggregates will have to be loaded by passing the data through the loader multiple times. Individual sales transaction records, for instance, may be loaded initially into a transaction grain fact table one by one. These same records may then be loaded into one or more monthly accumulating buckets. There are two main scenarios for loading this monthly data:

1. The incoming data is saved until the end of the month when it is totaled correctly outside the DBMS and loaded in that form. The monthly records simply are stored in a fresh monthly bucket when this load event takes place.

2. The incoming data is loaded incrementally each day into an accumulating monthly bucket. In this case, the timestamp on each incoming record must be replaced with the correct monthly surrogate key. The individual records are then presented to the DBMS loader. As each record arrives in the monthly file, the loader must decide whether to create a new record or whether to augment an existing record. A new record will be created whenever a product is sold in a store for the first time in a month. Otherwise, the incoming record must augment one with the same set of keys. It is very desirable for the DBMS loader to support high-speed bulk loading with this option of augmenting existing records. If the DBA builds a SQL script that tests for the existence of a record and branches to either an UPDATE or an INSERT, the resulting load operation will run 100 times more slowly than if the DBMS loader has native support for augmenting.

It is fairly common to change the boundaries of aggregates. The Sales department may decide that aspirin should no longer be in Cough and Cold but should be in Over the Counter. Once such a decision is made, Sales usually wants past history to reflect the change, not just the history from this point in time forward. In *The Data Warehouse Toolkit,* we discussed a so-called Type 3 change that allows the sales department to carry both categorizations for a period of time. The DBA has a couple of interesting choices in this situation. If the Type 3 change has been implemented with Over the Counter as the value of the Category attribute, and Cough and Cold as the value of the Old Category attribute, then aggregates can be built on both Category and Old Category. The aggregate navigator will transparently provide the performance benefit for both choices. If, however, the change is made permanent and the Cough and Cold designation is discarded, the DBA should just build the new aggregate.

When aspirin is transferred out of Cough and Cold, the DBA probably should not rebuild the entire set of Cough and Cold aggregates from scratch. The aspirin time series can merely be decremented from Cough and Cold, by using the augmentation feature of the loader described earlier. Then the aspirin time series must be added to the Over the Counter aggregates by reversing the procedure.

In organizations with category managers, such as packaged goods manufacturing, distribution, or retail, this kind of category boundary adjustment happens continually. It would be worthwhile for the IS department to build an application specifically for automating this aggregation maintenance process.

Finally, aggregates play an important role during system recovery. If a data mart must be rebuilt either because of system failure or an administrative blunder, and no current disk-level backups are available, then the daily load scenario may have to be replayed forward from some point in time. Generally, this is easier if this scenario is mostly loading and very little administering. By storing the aggregates for safekeeping during the extract process, the DBA may be able to add them to the bulk loading process rather than running slower in-DBMS processes.

DESIGN GOALS FOR AN AGGREGATE NAVIGATION SYSTEM

The remainder of this chapter describes a specific architecture for building aggregates in your data marts and surrounding those aggregates with a minimal amount of easily maintained metadata. This architecture is simple enough that you could consider building it yourself, if you can provide some system programming between your query and reporting tools and your database server. If you are not inclined to develop your own aggregate navigation tools, this section can be used as a guideline for judging the complexity of various vendors' aggregate navigation approaches.

Keep in mind as you read this next section that your choice of front-end tools will also have an impact on aggregate design.

Design Goal 1

 Aggregates must be stored in their own fact tables, separate from the base atomic data. In addition, each distinct aggregation level must occupy its own unique fact table.

The separation of aggregates into their own fact tables is very important. First, the aggregate navigation scheme we describe is simpler when the aggregates occupy their own tables, because the aggregate navigator can learn almost everything it needs from the DBMS's ordinary system catalog, rather than requiring additional metadata.

Second, an end user is less likely to double-count additive fact totals accidentally when the aggregates are in separate tables because every query against a given fact table will by definition go against data of a uniform granularity. Double-counting is a significant risk when the aggregates are placed in the same fact table as the base data.

Third, the small number of giant numerical entries representing, for instance, national sales totals for the entire year do not have to be shoe-horned into the base table. Often, the presence of these few giant numbers forces the database designer to increase the field widths of all entries in the database, thereby wasting disk storage. Because the base table is a huge table that can occupy as much as half of the entire database, it is very helpful to keep its field widths as tight as possible.

Fourth, the dimension record that represents the aggregated item (say, a category record in a low-level product table) will be much simpler if it is represented in a shrunken version of the dimension table that is separate from the expanded, original version of the dimension table. If the aggregate dimension entry is stored in the low-level table, it is represented at the wrong grain and must contain many null or "not applicable" field entries. For instance, a category record in a typical 50-attribute product dimension table might contain 45 nulls, because attributes like flavor and package size do not make sense at the category level. All of these null entries cause hiccups in user interfaces and queries.

Fifth, the administration of aggregates is more modular and segmented when the aggregates occupy separate tables. Aggregates can be built at separate times, and using an aggregate navigator, individual aggregates can be taken off-line and placed back on-line throughout the day without impacting other data.

Design Goal 2

 The dimension tables attached to the aggregate fact tables must, wherever possible, be shrunken versions of the dimension tables associated with the base fact table.

We assume a typical star join schema structure exists in which a large central fact table is surrounded by a single level of independent dimension tables. This schema is illustrated in Figure 14.4.

In other words, using the base-level fact table in Figure 14.4, you might wish to build category-level aggregates that represent the product dimension rolled up from the individual product to the category. See Figure 14.5.

Notice that in this example you have not requested aggregates in either the Time dimension or the Store dimension. The central Sales fact table in Figure 14.5 represents how much of a category of product was sold in each store each day. Your design requirement tells you that the original Product table must now be augmented with a shrunken Product table, called Category. A simple way to look at this shrunken Product table is to think of it as containing only those fields that survive the aggregation from individual product up to the category level. Only a few fields will still be uniquely defined. For example, both the category description and the department description would be well defined at the category level, and they must have the same field names they have in the base product dimension table. However, the individual SKU number, the package type, and the size would not exist at this level and must not appear in the category table. This addresses the fourth point in the preceding section.

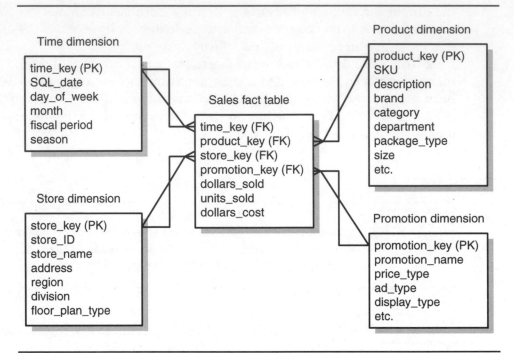

FIGURE 14.4   A typical unaggregated set of fact and dimension tables.

Shrunken dimension tables are extremely important for aggregate navigation because the scope of any particular aggregation level can be determined by looking in the system catalog description of the shrunken table. In other words, when you look in the Category table, all you find is category description and department description. If a query asks for product flavor, you know immediately that this aggregation level cannot satisfy the query, and thus the aggregate navigator must look elsewhere.

Shrunken dimension tables are also attractive because they let you avoid filling the original dimension tables with null or "not applicable" values for all of the dimension attributes that are not applicable at the higher levels of aggregation. Because you don't have package type and size in the category table, you don't have to dream up null values for these fields, and you don't have to encode user applications with tests for these null values.

Although we have focused on shrunken dimension tables, it is possible that the fact table will also shrink as you build ever-higher levels of aggregation. Most of the basic additive facts, such as dollar sales, unit

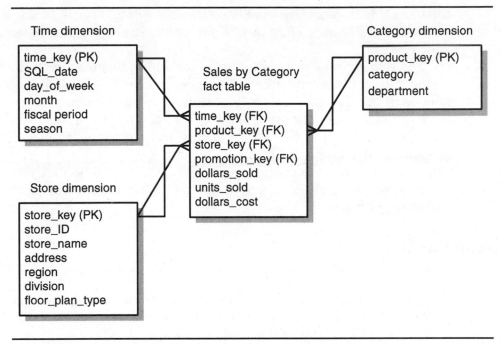

FIGURE 14.5   The one-way category aggregate schema.

sales, and dollar cost, will survive at all levels of aggregation, but some dimensions, such as promotion, and some facts, such as promotion cost, may make sense only at the base level and may need to be dropped in the aggregate fact tables.

Design Goal 3

The base atomic fact table and all of its related aggregate fact tables must be associated together as a "family of schemas" so that the aggregate navigator knows which tables are related to one another.

Any single schema in the family consists of a fact table and its associated dimension tables. There is always exactly one base atomic schema that is the unaggregated data, and there will be one or more aggregate schemas, which represent computed summary data. Figure 14.4 is a base schema and Figure 14.5 is one of perhaps many aggregate schemas in your family.

The registration of this family of fact tables, together with the associated full-size and shrunken dimension tables, is the sole metadata needed in this design. Obviously, this design is a guide for you. You may have a specific query or reporting tool that departs from this level of detail. However, one of the points of this section argues that aggregate navigation can be fairly simple. If a candidate query or reporting tool imposes a much more complex aggregate administration on your data warehouse than is described here, you may want to continue looking for something simpler.

Design Goal 4

 Force all SQL created by any end user data access tool or application to refer exclusively to the base fact table and its associated full-size dimension tables.

This design requirement pervades all user interfaces and end-user applications. When users examine a graphical depiction of the database, they should only see the equivalent of Figure 14.4. They should not be aware that aggregate tables even exist. Similarly, all hand-coded SQL embedded in report writers or other complex applications should reference only the base fact table and its associated full-size dimension tables. In environments in which ad hoc query tools let the end users see every table in the system, it is a good idea to place the aggregate tables in a separate database to hide them from end users. Because the aggregate navigator maintains its own connections to the DBMS, this should not present a technical problem.

AGGREGATE NAVIGATION ALGORITHM

Assuming that you built your dimensional data warehouse according to these four design requirements, you are now in a position to understand how aggregate navigation works.

The aggregate navigation algorithm is very simple. It consists of only three steps:

1. Sort the schemas from smallest to largest based on row count. For any given SQL statement presented to the DBMS, find the smallest fact table. Choose the smallest schema and proceed to Step 2.
2. Compare the table fields in the SQL statement to the table fields in the particular fact and dimension tables being examined. This is a series of lookups in the DBMS system catalog. If all of the fields in the SQL statement can be found in the fact and dimension tables being examined, alter the original SQL by simply substituting destination table names for original table names. No field names need to be changed. If any field in the SQL statement cannot be found in the current fact and dimension tables, go back to Step 1 and find the next larger fact table. This process is guaranteed to terminate successfully because eventually you arrive at the base schema, which is always guaranteed to satisfy the query.
3. Run the altered SQL. It is guaranteed to return the correct answer because all of the fields in the SQL statement are present in the chosen schema.

The beauty of this algorithm is that almost no metadata is required to support general navigation. The metadata amounts to only one row for each fact table and dimension table in the aggregate schemas. The maintenance of the metadata does not require complex logical modeling. Only the existence of the shrunken fact and dimension tables must be recorded.

In actually implementing this algorithm, several points are worth noting. In Step 2, only the shrunken dimension tables and the fact table must be examined. If a given schema uses a base-level dimension table, then its fields do not need to be searched because a match is guaranteed. For example, in the aggregate schema shown in Figure 14.5, the time and store dimension tables are not shrunken. Any SQL reference to a field in one of these tables does not need to be checked. Only references to fields in the product table and the fact table itself must be checked. In the case of Figure 14.5, the check will be successful only if the references to the product table are restricted to the category description, the department description, or both. In a successful match, the final SQL differs from the original SQL only by the substitution of Category for the table name Product and sales_fact_ agg_by_category for the table name sales_fact.

For example, if our original SQL is:

```
select p.category, sum(f.dollar_sales), sum(f.dollar.cost)
from sales_fact f, product p, time t, store s
where f.product_key = p.product_key
  and f.time_key = t.time_key
  and f.store_key = s.store_key
  and p.category = 'Candy'
  and t.day_of_week = 'Saturday'
  and s.floor_plan_type = 'Super Market'
group by p.category
```

we are asking for the total dollar sales and total dollar cost of all candy sold in supermarket stores on Saturdays. The aggregate navigator scans this SQL and first looks at the aggregate tables in Figure 14.6 because that aggregate is the smallest, having only 200 fact table rows. However, this aggregate fails because the constraints on time (day_of_week)

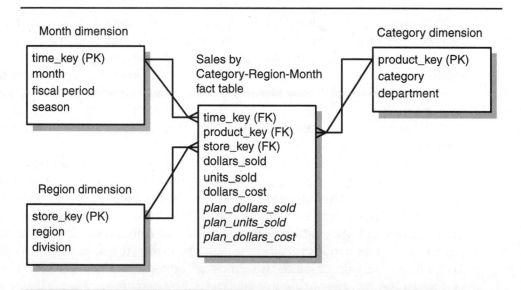

FIGURE 14.6   The three-way category-month-region aggregate schema.

and store (floorplan_type) both violate this schema. Day_ of_week cannot be found in the Month aggregate dimension table, and floor-plan_type cannot be found in the Region aggregate dimension table.

Then the aggregate navigator tries the next larger schema, shown in Figure 14.5. This time it is successful. All of the fields in the SQL query match. In particular, the product references to Category are found in the shrunken product table named Category. Now the aggregate navigator replaces the table references and produces the following SQL. Only the items set in bold are different:

```
select p.category, sum(f.dollar_sales), sum(f.dollar.cost)
from sales_fact_agg_by_category f, category p, time t, store s
where f.product_key = p.product_key
  and f.time_key = t.time_key
  and f.store_key = s.store_key
  and p.category = 'Candy'
  and t.day_of_week = 'Saturday'
  and s.floor_plan_type = 'Super Market'group by p.category
```

The most straightforward implementation of the aggregate navigation algorithm would decompose the SQL query and look up each field name in Step 2 of the algorithm. Each such lookup would be a SQL call to the DBMS's system tables. This is not a crazy approach because such calls are quite efficient and should run in a few hundred milliseconds each. However, in a large and complex data warehouse environment, a practical consideration arises. Calls to the DBMS system tables may take several seconds each, rather than several hundred milliseconds. If six or eight layers of aggregate tables exist, the aggregate navigator may take 20 seconds to determine the correct choice. This is an example of snatching defeat from the jaws of victory.

A better approach is to cache the system tables in the aggregate navigator so that the lookup of prospective field names does not require a SQL call to the DBMS. This approach is wonderful from a performance point of view, but it makes the aggregate navigator somewhat more difficult to design. First, the navigator must be able to read and store complicated system table configurations including, in the worst case, those with potentially thousands of fields scattered across hundreds of tables. Of course, you restrict your readout of the system tables to only those fields named in your aggregate navigator metadata table. Second, the navigator must have some idea of when to return to the real DBMS system tables to refresh its representation.

The aggregate navigation algorithm has certain limitations. Note that we are assuming a kind of data warehouse law that no star join query will ever mention more than one fact table in the from clause. The basis of this law is the presumption that any DBMS that attempts to join multiple huge fact tables together in a single query will lose control of performance. Fortunately, few, if any, end-user query tools let users easily combine multiple fact tables. In the vast majority of cases, the query is a simple set of joins between a single fact table and a suite of dimension tables. So this is not a serious restriction.

A second limitation is that each aggregation is "complete." For example, our category aggregate table in Figure 14.5 contains summaries for every possible aggregate. The aggregate tables are not restricted to a subset of values. Suppose the complete list of categories had 10 names. Our category table must always contain entries for all 10. You could not build a category table for just the categories Snacks and Candy. It would be difficult to generalize the algorithm to handle a subset of values because there is no obvious representation of a subset of values that could be quickly stored and that it could be compared against. For example, with Snacks and Candy, do you store the text names of the categories, their underlying key values, or a more complex criterion such as in the Convenience department, but not including Hardware? And how would you handle very long lists with hundreds or even thousands of entries?

Intersecting Planning Data

Our design approach has one major and unexpected benefit. As you ascend the various dimension hierarchies, you are likely to intersect the natural levels at which corporate planning and budgeting occur. For instance, in Figure 14.6, we show an aggregate fact table that could easily arise from the aggregate construction process. This table shows sales at the category by region by month level. In Figure 14.6, all three of the dimensions are shrunken. Although this is a small table physically, it may be accessed frequently for high-level analyses. For completely coincidental reasons, it is likely that the corporate planning (or budgeting) process is producing plans at the same level, namely category by region by month.

A goal of most data warehouses is to compare plans to actuals. This is very efficient if these comparisons are intrarecord computations. When you notice the serendipitous correspondence between your aggregate fact table at the category by region by month level and the planning table at the same level, take the opportunity to combine these two tables. You should add the italicized fields in Figure 14.6. At a certain high level of the aggregate hierarchy, planning (or budgeting) data "snaps in" and resides in the same table.

The addition of planning or budgeting data at high levels of aggregation requires generalizing your algorithm somewhat. You now have fields that don't exist at the base level. The search for tables that match all of the fields in the query becomes more complicated. The end user's interfaces now must know about planning (or budgeting) fields. However, these fields can only be used successfully in the example at the category by region by month level and above. The aggregate navigator must now be able to detect when its search for fields in successively lower-level fact tables fails. For instance, if a user tries to compare planned and actual results at the level of product flavor, the system will deny the request because planning is not performed at the flavor level.

Handling MIN, MAX, COUNT, and AVG

An optional extension of this design allows the SQL functions of MIN, MAX, COUNT, and AVG to be handled in addition to SUM. This extension of the design may be of some value, although these additional functions are used far less than SUM in most applications.

Once an aggregate fact table has been created, it is not possible to correctly determine these other functions unless they have been prestored at the time the aggregate table was derived from the base data. For example, the minimum value of an additive fact could be separately stored in the aggregate fact table. If the base fact name is dollars_sold, then the special value for the minimum function could be min_dollars_sold. The aggregate navigator would have to look for this special fact if a request of the form SELECT MIN(DOLLARS_SOLD) was made by the user. The maximum and count functions could be handled the same way. The average function does not need to be stored if the SUM and the COUNT are available.

Interestingly, these special facts can be updated incrementally along with the normal summed values if the aggregate fact table is administered that way. Any incoming fact would be added to the SUM value, and tested against the MIN and MAX values. The COUNT total would be incremented by 1.

Finally note that constructions such as COUNT(DISTINCT fact) cannot be supported using this scheme.

Aggregates for Everyone

The aggregate architecture described in this chapter allows for a very flexible administration. Aggregates are always behind the scenes. Neither the users nor the application developers need ever be aware that specific aggregations have been built. Aggregates can be added or removed by the DBA, even on an hourly basis. A good aggregate navigator should be accompanied by query usage statistics that guide the DBA in building new aggregates. If a group of queries is observed to be running slowly and all of them are requesting sales summaries by calendar quarter, the DBA should be alerted to this pattern and begin thinking about building quarterly aggregates. Note that quarterly aggregates would almost never be needed if a "close by" aggregate, such as month aggregates, already exists. There would be little advantage in providing a new level of aggregate that only represents a rollup of a factor of three from an existing aggregate. A quarterly aggregate would make much more sense if the next lower time aggregate was by week, in which case the quarterly aggregate would offer a 13-fold (52 weeks/4 quarters) advantage.

 It is very important that the aggregate navigator capability is available to all clients of the data warehouse. It is not acceptable to have aggregate navigation built into only a single client tool because then only some of the end users would experience the benefits of navigation.

Because it is practically impossible to restrict a large corporate environment to using one end-user tool, an embedded navigator approach would be an administrative headache. The worst scenario would involve two or more incompatible navigator schemes, potentially with different aggregate table structures and different metadata. The aggregate navigator must be a corporate network resource, and it must be a uniform DBMS front-end for all query clients.

This chapter describes a simple but powerful architecture for aggregate navigation. If DBAs would adhere to the design requirements we've outlined, and if one or more DBMS or middleware vendors would market an aggregate navigator similar to the one we describe, your database query performance would improve, your DBAs would spend their time on activities other than fighting with aggregates, and your metadata maintenance responsibilities would drop drastically.

SUMMARY

In this chapter we discussed the principles that guide the design of aggregate structures and determine which aggregates to build. The process to create and maintain aggregates was also presented. Overall, remember that aggregates are as important as indexes for providing acceptable query response time.

CHAPTER 15

Completing the Physical Design

This chapter outlines the steps required to turn a logical design into a physical database. Because the details of implementation vary widely by platform and project and because software, hardware, and tools are evolving rapidly, this chapter can at best offer only a broad introduction to the subject. Our goal is to provide the warehouse project manager with a sufficient understanding of the topic to be able to make informed decisions about staff and resources and to develop a sound project plan. We also hope to provide a few technical pointers that might not be obvious.

The details of the physical data model and database implementation are, of course, highly dependent on the individual factors of a project: the logical data model, the warehouse RDBMS, data volumes, usage patterns, and access tools. Nonetheless, some overarching themes and guidelines appear:

- Make a plan, even during a prototype. Tie this physical implementation plan to the overall project plan.
- Don't succumb to the temptation to do something the easy (but wrong) way. It's very likely to stay that way.

- Develop standards and follow them.
- Use tools where available.

Figure 15.1 shows a high-level model of the physical design process. The basic sequence of events is to start out with a little planning—develop naming and database standards, and a security strategy. Next, build the physical model, including a cut at the preliminary database size and growth rates. The aggregate plan is a key part of the physical model for which you need to develop an initial plan. Once you know what all the tables are, you can take a cut at the preliminary index strategy. At this point, you can actually begin to get physical. You now have enough information about what is going into the database and when, and you can design and build the database instance. Finally, plan out the physical details like partitioning, tablespaces, and disk layout.

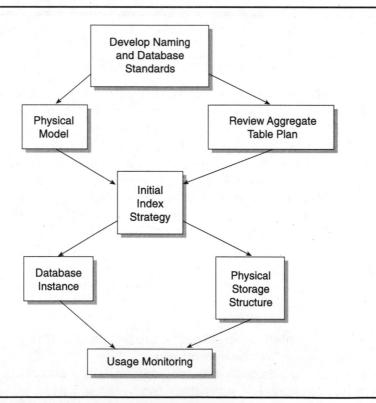

FIGURE 15.1 The high-level physical design process.

DEVELOP STANDARDS

It is more important to have standards and follow them than they be perfect. Remember, it's only a *foolish* consistency that's the hobgoblin of little minds. A reasonable consistency is a fine and desirable thing. If your company's IS department has standards, you should use them. However, existing standards were probably developed for OLTP systems, and they may need to be modified for your purposes. For data warehousing, there are two important sets of standards: those for database object names and those for physical file names and locations.

Database Object Naming Standards

Essentially, there are three basic components of any database object name: prime words, class words, and qualifiers. Data element definitions, logical data element names, and physical data element names are all composed of these three basic components:

- **Prime words.**   A prime word describes the data element's subject area—*what is this object?* Some examples of prime words include: *customer*, *product*, *account*, *city*, *state*, *postal code*, and *region*. Each prime word should have a clear, unambiguous definition that goes right into the information catalog.

- **Class words.**   A class word describes the major classification of data associated with a data element—*what type of object is this?* Some examples of class words are: *average*, *total*, *count*, *code*, *date*, *flag*, *ID*, *name*, *description*, *amount*, and *number*.

- **Qualifiers.**   Qualifiers are optional elements that can further define or describe the prime and class words. Some examples of qualifiers are: *start*, *end*, *primary*, and *secondary*.

Database object naming usually follows a prescribed syntax that goes something like Prime_Qualifier_Class, as in account_start_date. You may need a qualifier first to help describe the column, like primary_customer_id. We've included an example taxonomy on the companion CD-ROM, but the highlights of our recommendations follow:

- Decide whether objects will have the same name for their physical representation—for internal programming use—and the more descriptive logical or business name.

Programmers often argue the other side, in their desire to minimize typing and to retain names that are similar to those used in the source systems. Since our entire methodology focuses on the business rather than the data, it should come as little surprise that we recommend that object names do the same. Programmers are increasingly using productivity tools that reduce the typing they must do, further weakening the other argument.

- List all your prime words and work with the user community to define them.
- To the extent that you need to abbreviate, develop a reasonable list of abbreviations that would be obvious to a new employee the first day on the job. For example, *descr* obviously means *description*, but *spo* is not an intuitive abbreviation for *sponsored projects office*.
- Use class words. List them and define them. We prefer to suffix all column names with a class word.
- Most RDBMSs support a structure such as "database" or "schema" that permits at least one level of object grouping. You should create a schema or database for development and/or test and one for production, naming objects identically within the schema. Similarly, you should create development and production stage schemas to hold the staging tables associated with the development and production processes. You will almost certainly end up moving the development schemas onto their own machine, but usually most or all of the staging tables are in the same instance or server as the end-user tables they support.
- Name staging tables in a way that ties them to the process or purpose they serve. Good examples are *usage_facts_daily_stage* or *newly_encountered_page_keys*.
- Find a good balance between being incredibly specific (*my_company_billingDW_customer_id*) and far too vague (*description*). Remember that column names are often seen out of the table's context and that they become default report headers in many query and reporting tools. It can be helpful to include a table or subject reference as part of the column name for standard class names, since these will often appear in the same query. For example, if you had the product description and store description in the same query, it helps to have names like *product_descr* and *store_descr* when someone comes along to decipher your query later on. On the other hand, everyone knows

what company—and probably what subject area—the warehouse or data mart is for.

- The data steward is responsible for resolving name disputes. This is a business-oriented task; don't go off in the corner and come up with names that make sense to you. Pull together a representative group of business folks and go through the process of gathering suggestions, making choices, and getting buy-in.

- Use underscores rather than spaces or capital letters to delineate separate words in an object's name. Underscores work just about everywhere. (Except at one site where the IS team had written a utility to substitute spaces for underscores in their DNS load utility. They substituted a dash for an underscore in our server name, thinking that must be what we meant. It took a while to figure out why we couldn't find our server on the network.)

- Be very careful with capitalization. Some databases have a case-sensitive mode, which leads to more legible scripts. However, it means every script, query, and so on must have the correct case for all database objects (tables, columns, etc.). This case-sensitive (or binary) mode can also impact performance for better or worse, depending on the database. You may have to reinstall (i.e., unload the database, drop it, and re-create it) to change it.

- Document your naming standards, especially any choices provoking controversy within the team.

- Plan for the naming standards to be a living document. Follow the standards, but be willing to modify them as real needs arise.

 In general we recommend that logical and physical names be identical and as descriptive as possible.

 It may be best to assume case sensitivity from the start, even if you don't turn the feature on. That way, you don't have to go back and redo everything if you migrate to a database that is case sensitive.

Use Synonyms for All Tables That Users Access

As an exception to the rule that both business users and programmers use the same names, we recommend that access to all tables be granted through synonyms, which most RDBMSs support. A *synonym* is simply another name for a table, analogous to an alias or shortcut to a file on your PC. This sounds like an arbitrary rule, but we have never regretted following it and have always regretted not doing so. The reason this rule is worth following is that the time will come when the data warehouse team needs to physically restructure a large table. It is much easier to change the synonym to point to the new version than it is to change the maintenance and access applications, or retrain the users. Trust us now; you'll thank us someday.

An alternative or complementary approach is to provide access through views. A view appears to users of the database like a table, but it can be a complex, multitable query. Through views, you can create a more user-friendly interface atop a physically normalized structure. For example, if the physical design calls for a snowflaked dimension—typically because of access tool requirements—we usually create a denormalized "collapsed" star dimension view for those few users who occasionally must access the data more directly. We cautiously evaluate the performance consequences of using any view—even a single-table view—before incorporating it into the data warehouse. In theory, there should be no noticeable performance degradation for access through a view, but experience tells us otherwise.

 We recommend only limited—and carefully planned and justified—use of multitable views in the data warehouse.

Although it is tempting to think that you can create your warehouse by defining simplifying views over a normalized data structure, it works only for the tiniest data stores. If your users have more than a very occasional need for data to be structured dimensionally you really should structure it dimensionally.

Physical File Locations

It is very important to develop and use standards for the locations of source code, scripts, binaries (if any), and database files. Even if there is only one or a few developers during the initial phase, a successful warehouse will require teamwork—in series if not in parallel.

- Ideally, the data warehouse project should use a code maintenance system that manages code with capabilities like checkout, check-in, and merge. Realistically, a prototype warehouse is unlikely to receive approval for such a purchase if the tool is not already in-house, so you will probably need to develop internal procedures for code management.
- Whether using a tool or going it alone, the warehouse team needs to decide how to structure the code libraries. There is always some code, even with the best tool. One approach is to have the major branches of your code tree based on subject area or table, like Billing, Customer, and Product. Figure 15.2 shows an example table-oriented data warehouse code tree. Another approach is to have the top branches based on similar functions, such as DDL, initial loads, and daily loads.
- Develop standards for where to locate application documents, such as data models and documents required by your chosen extract/transformation/load application.
- Place database files outside the directory structure of the RDBMS and the application code tree.

DEVELOP THE PHYSICAL DATA MODEL

The starting point for the physical data model is the logical model. The physical model should mirror the logical model as much as possible, although some changes in the structure of tables and columns will be necessary to accommodate the idiosyncrasies of your chosen RDBMS and access tools. In addition, your physical model will include staging and other maintenance tables that are usually not included in the logical model.

The major difference between the physical and logical models, though, is the thorough and detailed specification of the physical database characteristics, starting with the data types and flowing through to table segmentation, table storage parameters, and disk striping.

This book is not intended to be a reference guide for physical database design, nor is it intended to replace a skilled DBA on the project team. Rather, the following discussion will focus on how database ad-

Drive A 4 GB RAID1 **(fully mirrored)**	
RDBMS	**Directory contains RDBMS executables**
STAGE_TOOL	**Directory contains data staging tool executables**
LOG	**Directory contains RDBMS log files**
logfile1.dbf	RDBMS log file 1
logfile2.dbf	RDBMS log file 2
SCRIPT_PROD	**Directory contains all production SQL scripts**
metadata	*Scripts for managing metadata store*
customer	*For dimension table customer*
crt_customer.sql	DDL for creating customer table
crt_cust_stage.sql	DDL for creating the staging table for customer
crx_customer.sql	DDL for creating customer table indexes
drx_customer.sql	DDL for dropping customer table indexes
customer_stage.ctl	Control script for bulk-loading the customer staging table
upd_customer.sql	SQL script for updating customer from customer_stage
readme	Describes everything in the directory
calendar	*For dimension table calendar*
crt_calendar.sql	DDL for creating period table, including indexes
calendar.ctl	Control script for bulk-loading the period table (dumped from Excel)
calendar.xls	Excel spreadsheet in which period table was developed
period_calendar_upd.sql	Stored procedure script to update "current_day_ind" every night
readme	Describes everything in the directory
product	*For dimension table product*
sales_detail_fact	*For fact table*
store_market	*For dimension table store*
SCRIPT_DEV	**Directory contains all SQL scripts in development**
	Directory structure should match script_prod
DRIVE B RAID5	
DATABASE	**Directory contains all database files**
dims.dbf	
dims_inx.dbf	
fact1.dbf	
fact1_inx.dbf	
fact2.dbf	
fact2_inx.dbf	
DRIVE C NO RAID	
DATASTAGE	**Directory contains data (flat) files**
customer_hist.dat	
customer_upd.dat	
period.dat	
TEMPDATA	**Directory contains database temp space**
JOBLOGS	**Directory contains all script/job output and logs**

FIGURE 15.2   Example code tree directory structure.

ministration for a data warehouse is different than for an OLTP system, and where, in our experience, the greatest pitfalls lie.

The Beverage Store Sales Case Study

To assist our explanation of the physical design tasks, we have developed a set of examples around the case of a fictitious national chain of beverage stores, which has recently implemented a point-of-sale "RewardCard" program. Although the program is relatively new, with RewardCard sales accounting for less than 5 percent of overall sales nationwide, management is very interested in understanding customer-level sales and marketing, and in learning whether their RewardCard customers' purchases differ from anonymous customers' patterns. We have identified the logical model illustrated in Figure 15.3 as meeting the broad spectrum of analytical requirements.

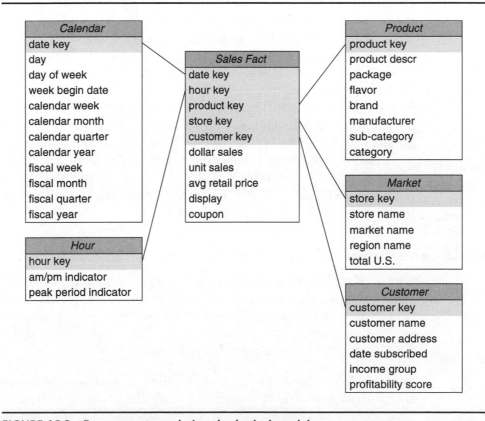

FIGURE 15.3   Beverage store chain sales logical model.

Use a Data Modeling Tool

As discussed in Chapter 7, you should use a data modeling tool, preferably one that stores your model's structure in a relational database, to develop the physical data model. As the data staging tools mature, information will flow more naturally from the popular data modeling tools, through the transformation engine, and into the metadata that users will access to learn about the data in the warehouse.

The advantages of using a data modeling tool include:

- It integrates the data warehouse model with other corporate data models.
- It helps assure consistency in naming and definition. A data modeling tool is not a magic bullet, but most tools have features that let the team create a pool of commonly used column names, or permit one column to inherit the characteristics of another, and even to change characteristics when the parent column's definition changes. To take greatest advantage of your data modeling tool, the team must develop and follow a set of standards for its use in your environment.
- It creates good documentation in a variety of useful formats.
- It generates physical object DDL (data definition language) for most popular RDBMSs.
- It provides a reasonably intuitive user interface for entering comments about objects (tables and columns). Many data modeling tools support at least two types of object comments. In a data warehouse, it works best to reserve one comment field for technical documentation, such as "From T58.CUSTNAME, converting to title case and changing NULL to 'N/A'," and one for business users "Customer name as Last, First, e.g., 'Smith, Joe'."

Design the Physical Data Structure

Keep it as simple and as much like the logical model, as possible. Differences between the physical and logical models are inevitable, however. They can be necessary to support the specific requirements of your access tool, to improve query performance, and even to keep the maintenance cycle within an acceptable window.

- Start with the logical model. If you have not already done so, enter the logical model into your data modeling tool, ignoring physical characteristics. Save a copy of the logical model at this point.

- Alter object names to conform to your naming standards.
- Determine which columns will have data types that differ from their representation in the source systems. Much of this determination can be rules-based, and it may flow directly from the naming conventions. For example, the zip code may be stored as an integer in the source system and as CHAR within the warehouse.
- Document, usually in the technical comments field in the data modeling tool, an overview of the transformation rule. For example "Source ADDRESS_ZIPCODE converted from integer to character."
- Determine the data types for your key columns. For good performance in querying, it's important that key columns be the most efficient data type for joining. This characteristic varies among databases, but it's usually an integer. At least one major database stores all numbers, integer or float, in the same format, so for relatively low-cardinality keys, a fixed-length CHAR may be more efficient. Your DBAs need to understand the storage characteristics of your RDBMS.
- Date keys should also be reduced to efficient surrogate keys, despite the temptation to leave them as dates. Almost all warehouse queries involve a condition on time, so it's especially important that the join to the period table be efficient. A surrogate key for date also allows the existence of non-date entries, like "not applicable" rather than null, or 12/31/2099.
- Determine and specify columns that permit nulls. To save space in the table's storage, all not-null columns should be physically ordered before columns that permit nulls. Remember, you should be able to change the display order for your users in the front-end tool. If you can't, you probably want to know before you've installed the tool on 25 desktops.

 We advise instituting a general rule against nullable columns because they pose difficulties for business users in ad hoc querying. Even if your database allows you to define a nullable column as part of the primary key, you should never do so.

- Specify primary and foreign key relationships in the data model.
- Decide whether to explicitly declare primary/foreign keys in the database. You may choose to not enforce referential integrity within the database, if your loading process is clean and careful, as those

constraints create additional burden on the database. On the other hand, some RDBMSs' query optimizers develop better query plans if the primary and foreign key relationships are declared.

- Be sure to model all permanent tables and views, including staging tables. Generally, staging and aggregate tables are placed on a separate "page," or submodel, of the data model document.

- Plan to represent all table indexes in the physical data model. Model the basic structure of the primary and foreign key indexes without worrying about storage parameters at this point.

- If your main user access tool has already been chosen, modify the schema to address its requirements. Some tools require that dimension tables be normalized into a snowflake, but others are more flexible. If the tool requires a snowflake yet hides that complexity from the end user, it's perfectly acceptable to deviate from the logical model. Some tools require additional columns in the dimensions that are typically not part of the logical model. An example of these additional columns is a level indicator for hierarchies within dimensions. Another example is a current period indicator in the period table. Keep the dimensions in a denormalized star structure unless you have an excellent reason for snowflaking. The OLTP design guide that says "normalization=good" is not an excellent reason in this case.

- If the main user access tool requires a snowflake design, consider keeping a denormalized star version of the data accessible for users of other tools. Sometimes it is acceptable to present a "star version" as a database view joining physical snowflakes or to present a snowflake as a view on a physical star. More often, though, the cost of replicating the data in the form most efficient for multiple tools is amply repaid by improved usability and performance. In the case of very large dimensions, though, you usually want to store only a single version, and you must decide where to compromise.

- If your data warehouse faces maintenance problems—if you have trouble loading data within an acceptable window—think creatively about the transformation process, as discussed in more detail in Chapter 16. Very often, a difficult maintenance application problem is solved by breaking a complex step into multiple staging tables or by timestamping or otherwise annotating data.

- The physical specification for the user tables in our case study is illustrated in Figure 15.4. Note that we have identified two potential aggregate tables and have modeled them as well. This information

Table/column name	Data type	Permit nulls?	Prim. Key	Comment
calendar				**Calendar or period dimension table**
date_key	integer	n	1	Surrogate key
day_date	date	n		Date, can be used for date arithmetic
day_of_week_name	varchar(9)	n		Weekday, e.g., "Monday"
week_begin_date_key	integer	n		Key of this week's Monday
week_begin_date	date	n		Date of this week's Monday
calendar_week_num	smallint	n		Takes values 1..53. Week 1 begins first Mon in year
calendar_month_num	smallint	n		Takes values 1..12
calendar_month_name	varchar(9)	n		Month, e.g., "January"
calendar_quarter_num	smallint	n		Takes values 1..4.
calendar_year_num	integer	n		Calendar year carried as a number
year_month_num	integer	n		Year and month, carried as a number, e.g., 199801
fiscal_week_num	integer	n		Takes values 1..53. Week 1 begins first Monday in fiscal year
fiscal_month_num	integer	n		Takes values 1..12
fiscal_quarter_num	integer	n		Takes values 1..4.
fiscal_year_num	integer	n		Fiscal year carried as a number
weekday_ind	char(8)	n		Takes values "weekday" or "weekend"
hour				**Hour dimension**
hour_key	integer	n	1	Integer, 0..23, corresponds to hour in which purchase occurred
hour_time	time	n		Corresponding time, can be used for time arithmetic
am_pm_ind	char(2)	n		Takes values am/pm
peak_period_ind	char(8)	n		Takes values peak/off-peak. "peak" when hour btwn 15-20 (3p-8p)
product				**Product dimension**
product_key	integer	n	1	Surrogate key
brand_key	integer	n		Surrogate key, may be used for building aggregates
manufacturer_key	integer	n		Surrogate key, may be used for building aggregates
sub_category_key	integer	n		Surrogate key, may be used for building aggregates
category_key	integer	n		Surrogate key, may be used for building aggregates
product_name	varchar(15)	n		Short product name, use as column headings
brand_name	varchar(15)	n		Brand name, aggregates to manufacturer and sub-category
manufacturer_name	varchar(20)	n		Manufacturer name
sub_category_name	varchar(25)	n		Sub-category, aggregates to category
category_name	varchar(25)	n		Product category name
product_descr	varchar(125)	n		Long product name
package_size_amt	number(11,2)	y		Package size as a number
pkg_size_unit_name	varchar(15)	y		Units of package size, e.g., "ounce" or "quart"
package_size_group	varchar(15)	y		Package group, e.g., "family"
flavor_name	varchar(25)	y		Flavor, e.g., "chocolate"
store_market				**Store/market dimension**
store_key	integer	n	1	Surrogate key
market_key	integer	n		Key for markets, may be used to build aggregate tables

FIGURE 15.4   Beverage chain case study physical model.

Table/column name	Data type	Permit nulls?	Prim. Key	Comment
region_key	integer	n		Key for regions, may be used to build aggregate tables
country_key	integer	n		Key for countries, may be used in aggregate tables
store_name	varchar(50)	n		Store name, aggregates to market
store_zip5_code	char(5)	n		5-digit zip code of store
market_name	varchar(50)	n		Market name, aggregates to region
region_name	varchar(50)	n		Region name, aggregates to country
country_name	varchar(50)	n		Currently takes one value: "Total U.S."
customer				**Customer dimension. Tracks our RewardCard customers and "all other"**
customer key	integer	n	1	Surrogate key; Most transactions occur with customer_key=0 (no RewardCard)
customer_acctnum	char(20)	n		Customer RewardCard account number
customer_state_code	char(2)	n		U.S. state for customer's billing address
customer_zip5_code	char(5)	n		5-digit zip code
customer_area_code	char(3)	n		Telephone area code
phone_prefix_code	char(3)	n		First 3 characters of phone number
subscribe_date	date	n		Date customer subscribed to RewardCard service
customer_ssn	char(11)	n		Social Security number, '000-00-0000' if unknown; limited user access
customer_city_name	varchar(50)	n		City in customer's billing address
income_group_num	integer	n		Takes value 0..9. Data are purchased, updated quarterly
profitability_score_num	integer	n		Takes value 0..9. Data come from offline customer scoring process, updated monthly.
customer_last_name	varchar(50)	n		Customer last name; limited user access
customer_first_name	varchar(50)	n		Customer first name; limited user access
customer_billing_address	varchar(250)	n		Street address (excluding City/State/Zip); limited user access
sales_detail_fact				**Fact table, with sales by store, day, hour, customer (if known), and product**
date_key	integer	n	1	Foreign key to period.date_key
customer_key	integer	n	2	Foreign key to customer.customer_key
product_key	integer	n	3	Foreign key to product.product_key
store_key	integer	n	4	Foreign key to market.store_key
hour_key	integer	n	5	Foreign key to hour.hour_key
dollar_sales_amt	number(11,2)	n		Dollar amount sold of item
unit_sales_amt	integer	n		Quantity sold
retail_price	number(11,2)	n		Price per item
transaction_dollar_ sales_amt	number(11,2)	n		Total transaction dollar value (all items in transaction)
coupon_cnt	integer	n		Takes value 1 if customer used a coupon on this item
row_batch_key	integer	n		Foreign key to meta_load_batch table (not modeled here)

FIGURE 15.4 *Continued*

Table/column name	Data type	Permit nulls?	Prim. Key	Comment
Aggregate Tables				
sales_week_prod_ store_fact				**Aggregate table, sum over customer & hour, retaining product, store, aggregate day to week**
week_begin_date_key	integer	n	1	Foreign key to period.date_key (We'll probably need to instantiate a week_period table)
product_key	integer	n	2	Foreign key to product.product_key
store_key	integer	n	3	Foreign key to market.store_key
dollar_sales_amt	number(11,2)	n		Dollar amount sold of item (aggregated from detail)
unit_sales_amt	integer	n		Quantity sold (aggregated from detail)
avg_retail_price	number(11,2)	n		Average price per item (computed from detail)
transaction_cnt	integer	n		Count of transactions within date/store for this product (computed from detail)
transaction_avg_amt	number(11,2)	n		Average transaction size that included this item (computed from detail)
coupon_cnt	integer	n		Count of these transactions that used a coupon (computed from detail)
sales_day_prod_ mkt_fact				**Aggregate table, sum over customer & hour, retaining day, product, aggregate store to market**
date_key	integer	n	1	Foreign key to period.date_key
product_key	integer	n	2	Foreign key to product.product_key
market_key	integer	n	3	Foreign key to market.market_key
dollar_sales_amt	number(11,2)	n		Dollar amount sold of item
unit_sales_amt	integer	n		Quantity sold
retail_price	number(11,2)	n		Price per item
transaction_dollar_ sales_amt	number(11,2)	n		Total transaction dollar value (all items in transaction)
coupon_cnt	integer	n		Takes value 1 if customer used a coupon on this item

FIGURE 15.4   *Continued*

is carried within a data modeling tool differently, and it is laid out here in tabular form for illustrative purposes.

Develop Initial Sizing Estimates

In the early stages of the physical design, the data warehouse team is often pressured to estimate the warehouse's size. Whether you need to support platform decisions, order disks, or simply satisfy management's curiosity, it's useful at this point to develop a quick ballpark estimate of storage requirements of the entire warehouse. Your team's DBA will develop a much more accurate estimate of short- and long-term space requirements when designing the database's physical storage.

Although in theory we would prefer to use the modeling tool to develop sizing estimates, those tools have not been convenient for this stage of the project. We usually use annotations on the data models' printouts combined with a simple spreadsheet to store the calculations as the rather inadequate "tools of choice" here. See what your data modeling tool can do for you first.

Tasks to develop the preliminary sizing estimates include:

- Estimate row lengths, taking into account that VARCHAR and nullable columns are typically much smaller than their maximum length. (We usually sample 1000 or so rows from the source to get a reasonable estimate.)
- For each table, estimate the number of rows for the initial prototype, for the full historical load (by year of history if the size of the historical load is still under debate), and for incremental rows per load when in production.
- For a standard RDBMS, count on indexes to take up as much room as the base data. You'll do a more precise estimate later, after you develop the initial indexing plan.
- For temp/sort space, you typically need about twice as much temp space as an index to build that index. You should also think about what kinds of sorting and grouping operations you expect your users to execute or that you need to build aggregations. If someone will be doing a grouping operation on the entirety of your largest table, your temp space must be at least as large as your largest table. By using partitioned tables, as discussed shortly, you may be able to reduce the temp space requirements.
- Reserve 20 MB for metadata tables. That should be more than enough. Don't waste time on more precise computations.
- Aggregate tables can take up considerable space, depending on the degree of aggregates stored in the database, the sparsity of the data, and the depths of the hierarchies. There are more thorough discussions of aggregates in Chapters 9 and 14, but on average, aggregates and their indexes take up as much room as the base-level fact tables. This is a very general rule of thumb, and it should be smothered with caveats if you need to use it.

- In sum, a very general rule of thumb is that the entire data warehouse typically takes up three or four times as much space as the data in your atomic star schema.

Figure 15.5 includes sample calculations for computing the database size for our case study. As is usually the case, the dimension tables' size pales in comparison with the fact tables. In fact, we didn't even bother to compute the index sizes for the dimension tables for this initial sizing. If the RewardCard program is extremely successful, and we have 50 million identified customers in the customer dimension, the dimension table will, of course, be large enough to appear on our radar screen.

 In almost all data warehouses, the size of the dimension tables is insignificant compared to the size of the fact tables. The second biggest thing in the environment is the size of the indexes on the fact tables.

For our case study schema, most of the fact table's size is taken up by data outside our area of direct interest—the sales to "anonymous" customers. For a prototype, we would probably choose to aggregate this data at least past the hourly level (reducing data volume ten-fold) or possibly eliminate the anonymous customer data from the prototype.

At this point we have not specified our indexes, but we do know what types of indexes we will have, and we can consider their space requirements when ordering disk. In this situation, considering the expected growth of the data over the coming six months, we would probably order 450 GB of disk. This estimate does not include space required for development, staging, test, and so on.

DEVELOP THE INITIAL INDEX PLAN

Get into the habit of thinking of the index plan that you develop at this stage in the project as the *initial* index plan. Plan to adjust indexes over the life of the warehouse, as you better understand usage patterns and as usage patterns change. Use an expert for the initial plan if one is available, but you absolutely must develop expertise in-house. Learn how to generate and read the query plans generated by your RDBMS.

Table Name	Initial Rowcount	Avg Row Length	Grows with	Expected Monthly Growth	Initial Table Size (rounded)	Table Size 6 mo (rounded)	Comment
Calendar	1,825	111	static	0	0.2 MB	0.2 MB	
Hour	24	20	static	0	—	—	
Product	5,000	180	new products	2%	1 MB	1 MB	
Market	2,500	108	new stores	1%	0.3 MB	0.3 MB	
Customer	200,000	157	subscriptions	15%	32 MB	75 MB	Customer growth expected to level off in 3Q1999
sales_detail_fact consists of:	1,104,000,000	66	all dimensions		73 GB	90 GB	Plan to keep detail data for 3 months only
(unknown customer)	1,092,000,000	66	products, stores	3%	72 GB	87 GB	Most of the data are sales for "unknown" customers
(RewardCard customer)	12,000,000	66	customer, prod, store	18%	1 GB	3 GB	
sales_week_prod_store_fact	50,000,000	58	products, stores, time	3%	3 GB	9 GB	Plan to keep one year of history
sales_day_prod_mkt_fact	35,000,000	54	products, stores, time	3%	2 GB	6 GB	Plan to keep one year of history
All tables					*78 GB*	*180 GB*	

Fact Table Indexes	Key Indexes				Initial Table Size (rounded)	Table Size 6 mo (rounded)	
Sales_detail_fact_pkey	5 keys				45 GB	54 GB	
Sales_detail_fact_inx2	3 keys				27 GB	33 GB	
Sales_detail_fact_inx3	3 keys				27 GB	33 GB	
Sales_week_prod_store_pkey	3 keys				1.5 GB	4.5 GB	
Sales_week_prod_store_inx2	2 keys				2 GB	6 GB	
Sales_day_prod_mkt_pkey	3 keys				1 GB	3 GB	
Sales_day_prod_mkt_inx2	2 keys				0.75 GB	2 GB	
All fact table indexes					*105 GB*	*135 GB*	
Temp space					*73 GB*	*90 GB*	
Total space required					**256 GB**	**405 GB**	

FIGURE 15.5 Beverage chain initial database sizing.

When hiring or contracting with an expert for indexing, it is particularly important to verify expertise and experience with *star schema* warehouses. Do not pay a premium for a consultant—however skilled—whose experience is limited to OLTP and normalized databases.

This section briefly examines the different types of indexes and query strategies that are used by the major RDBMSs, and then discusses in greater detail the indexing strategies for fact and dimension tables.

Overview of Indexes and Query Strategies

To develop a useful index plan, it's important to understand how your RDBMS's query optimizer and indexes work and how warehouse requirements differ from OLTP requirements. Remember that most RDBMSs were developed first to support OLTP systems, and only relatively recently have been modified to support the fundamentally different requirements of data warehousing. The following discussion is necessarily general and incomplete, and it is not intended to substitute for expertise in your RDBMS.

The B-Tree Index

The first kind of index that RDBMSs developed is the classic B-tree, which is particularly valuable for high-cardinality columns like product_key or customer_key. The B-tree index builds a tree of possible values with a list of row IDs that have the leaf value. Finding the rows that contain a given value involves moving up the tree, comparing the value at each branch with the given value. If the given value is higher, you go up one branch, if it is lower, you go down the other branch. If it is the same, you have found your match, and you return the list of row IDs associated with that node or leaf. B-tree indexes may be built on multiple columns. Although some RDBMSs have developed alternative indexing techniques that are useful to data warehousing, others use only B-trees. The B-tree is the default index type for most databases.

Most RDBMSs automatically build a unique B-tree index on the declared primary key of a table; it is through this index that the primary key constraint is enforced.

Traditionally, RDBMSs would use only one index during each step of a query. As of this writing, the latest version of most RDBMSs have query optimizers that use multiple indexes. As discussed in the next few sections, this change makes indexing much easier than in the past.

The Bitmapped Index

Some RDBMSs support bitmapped indexes, which are the "opposite" of B-tree indexes in that they are more appropriate for columns of low cardinality. The classic examples are indexes on gender codes or yes/no indicators. The bitmapped index is essentially a string of bits for each possible value of the column. Each bit string has one bit for each row. Each bit is set to 1 if the row has the value the bit string represents, or 0 if it doesn't. In the case of a 50,000 row customer table with a gender column, there might be three bit strings in the bitmapped index, one for the "M" values, one for the "F" values and one for the "?" values. Each of these bit strings will be 50,000 bits long (or 6,250 bytes—about 6 KB). Therefore, the bitmapped index will be about 18 KB compared with about 300 KB for a typical B-tree index on the same column. Computers are particularly good at the vector manipulations involved in comparing these bit strings. It's fairly easy to combine bitmapped indexes.

Usually, bitmapped indexes can be built only on a single column, although the database optimizer can use more than one bitmapped index in a query. Thus while a single bitmapped index on gender provides little benefit, if a query's condition includes limits on gender, age, and income and those three columns are bitmapped, a relatively small subset of rows can be targeted using the bitmapped indexes together. Bitmapped indexes are commonly used on the attributes and hierarchies of dimension tables and are used today by several RDBMSs for the fact tables.

> Bitmapped indexes are a major advance in indexing that benefit data warehouse applications. Bitmap indexes are used both with dimension tables and with fact tables, where the constraint on the table results in a low cardinality match with the table.

The Hash Index

A few RDBMSs support hash indexes, which use a hashing algorithm to represent a composite in a succinct (but unreadable by human eyes) form. A hashing algorithm is used to assign a set of characters to represent a text string such as a composite of keys or partial keys, and compresses the underlying data enormously. Consider, for example, that a 12-character hash key can represent the full range of possible URLs with infinitesimal chance of repetition.

A hash index, because it so tersely represents the underlying data, can very efficiently be used to locate data rows. The downside is that hash indexes take longer to build and are supported by relatively few RDBMSs.

Other Index Types

Some RDBMSs use additional index structures or optimization strategies that are usually proprietary. Many of these are particularly useful to data warehouse applications, as we discuss in greater detail later in this chapter. You should carefully evaluate the index technologies available within your chosen RDBMS. Indeed, the indexing and query optimization technologies available and their applicability to data warehousing applications should be among the most important factors in your RDBMS decision making process.

Columnar RDBMSs

A few RDBMSs designed for data warehousing store data in columns rather than rows. These databases store data as (R1C1, R2C1, R3C1 . . .) rather than the more familiar (R1C1, R1C2, R1C3 . . .) format. These databases and their optimizers apply a wide range of index structures, depending on the column's cardinality.

Columnar databases offer significant data compression, which is valuable in data warehousing. These databases differ in their implementation details, but typically you index, as a single-column index, each column potentially used in a join or condition. Some databases force you to index all columns; some databases allow the DBA to specify what type of the many index structures to apply to each column, while others determine the appropriate structure automatically from the cardinality of the data.

Since you index most or all columns, and the optimizer will use multiple indexes in a query regardless of index type, indexing is generally much easier for columnar databases than for the standard RDBMSs.

Star Schema Optimization

Some relational databases attack the n-way join problem inherent in a star query by providing star schema optimization. We have seen performance improvement of up to *60 times* from using star schema optimization rather than classic sequential joins on systems that are otherwise configured identically.

You want standard queries against a dimensional star schema to start at the dimension tables that have conditions on them, and then assemble a list of composite dimension key combinations that meet those conditions. Typically, this is a relatively small list compared to the total number of keys in the fact table. Next, the optimizer should use this list of partial or complete fact table keys to extract the appropriate rows from the fact table, using an index on the fact table keys.

The reason that many RDBMSs do not include star schema optimization is that the strategy effectively requires a Cartesian product between the unrelated dimension tables. In theory, a Cartesian product is a very bad thing, but in the case of star schema queries, it is far more efficient than joining the dimension tables through the fact table one by one.

Some RDBMSs that support star schema optimization require special indexes for that optimization to work. Other RDBMSs determine if a star strategy is appropriate from the structure of the query.

Indexing Fact Tables

The first fact table index will be a B-tree on the primary key. When you declare a primary key constraint on a table, a unique index is built on those columns in the order they were declared. Some optimizers are strongly drawn to the primary key index, especially if the table's data are sorted in the same order as the index. Thus, we strongly recommend that the primary key, and hence its primary key index, be carefully constructed to be of greatest use in querying. Most data warehouse queries are constrained by date, and the date_key should be in the first position in the primary key index. Having the date_key in first position also speeds the warehouse maintenance process, in which incremental loads are keyed by date.

The determination of other fact table indexes, outside of the primary key index, is very dependent on the index types and optimization strategies available within your RDBMS. As of this writing, the latest releases of the major RDBMSs permit more than one index on a table to be used at the same time in resolving the query. As discussed next, in the old days we had to define multiple composite indexes on the fact table keys to cover the likely query paths. Now, it is much more common simply to create a single-column index on *each* fact table key and let the optimizer combine those indexes as appropriate to resolve the queries.

If your chosen RDBMS does not permit multiple indexes in a query, then almost certainly you did not choose that RDBMS but rather had the choice thrust upon you. You must create multiple composite indexes on the fact table columns. Typically, we do not include all of the key columns in all of the composite indexes, and we alternate the order of columns in a useful way. As the complexity of the schema increases, so does the number of fact table key indexes. A four-dimension schema may have two- or three-key indexes, including the obligatory primary key index; an eight-dimension schema may have six or more.

The initial index plan often includes no fact table indexes other than the key indexes. If the business requirements indicate that users will frequently be filtering on fact column values, for example, looking for transactions greater than $1,000,000, the initial index plan will also include an index on those fact columns. Typically, non-key fact table indexes are single-column indexes, are relatively rare, and are usually less useful than key indexes.

Indexing Dimension Tables

Dimension tables should have a single-column primary key and hence one unique index on that key. If bitmapped indexes are available in your RDBMS, add single-column bitmapped indexes to the nonselective dimension attributes that are most commonly used for applying filters or for row headers.

Small dimension tables seldom benefit from additional indexing. Large dimension tables, such as a customer dimension, are often very useful for queries in their own right. They often support useful questions like "How many customers meet a specific profile?" If your business requirements indicate that these queries will be executed frequently and the dimension table is large, then it will be valuable to develop a set of multicolumn indexes on the dimension attributes that are most frequently used together in filters.

As with the fact tables, columnar RDBMSs with a wide range of index types have simpler index rules: index individually every column likely to be used as a join condition, filter, or group by.

Indexing for Loads

Most of the time, we think about indexes' utility for users' queries. However, most successful warehouses are under pressure to keep the system's load and maintenance period as brief as possible. Be sure to analyze any queries used in the maintenance process and build indexes to make those important and time-consuming steps as efficient as possible.

If a load adds more than 10 to 20 percent to the size of a table, it is often more time-effective to drop indexes before insertion, add the data, and then rebuild all the indexes.

Analyze Tables and Indexes after the Load

The multipurpose RDBMSs such as DB2, Informix, Sybase, and Oracle do not automatically recompute statistics on tables and indexes after each load process, nor even after a complete index rebuild. This is a very important step to postpend to any load or index creation process, as the query optimizer must have accurate information on the size of tables and indexes, to develop effective query plans.

Case Study Indexes

Figure 15.6 documents the initial index plan for our beverage chain case study schema. Notice that the justifications for indexes are driven most often by business user requirements and occasionally for requirements of the maintenance application. As the warehouse evolves, it is very important to keep an up-to-date list of the indexes (existing, removed, and planned) and the reasons and results obtained from them.

DESIGN AND BUILD THE DATABASE INSTANCE

Your data warehouse or data mart should exist in its own instance of the RDBMS on its own hardware server so that system-wide parameters, such as memory, can be optimized to your warehouse's requirements. Although the specific settings vary by RDBMS and by project, a few parameters are absolutely vital to data warehouse database performance. As usual, document exactly what you are setting each parameter to, why, and which parameters are most likely to require adjustment as the database grows and evolves.

Sales_detail_fact

Index name	Index type	Unique	Columns	Location	Justification
sales_detail_pkey	B-tree	Y	Date_key, product_key, store_key, customer_key, hour_key	Segmented in TS pkey_inx	Primary key index.
sales_detail_date	Bitmapped	N	Date_key	Segmented in TS pkey_inx	Used in most star-join user queries
sales_detail_customer	B-tree	N	Customer_key	TS sales_indexes	Used in most star-join user queries
sales_detail_product	B-tree	N	Product_key	TS sales_indexes	Used in most star-join user queries
sales_detail_store	Bitmapped	N	Store_key	TS sales_indexes	Used in most star-join user queries
sales_detail_hour	Bitmapped	N	Hour_key	TS sales_indexes	Used in most star-join user queries
sales_detail_prod_display	Bitmapped	N	Product_display_name	TS sales_indexes	Speed many queries by the marketing group. See p.27 of the business reqts document.
sales_detail_batch	Bitmapped	N	Row_batch_key	TS sales_indexes	For rapid extraction of data to downstream data mart

Calendar

Index name	Index type	Unique	Columns	Location	Justification
calendar_pkey	B-tree	Y	date_key	TS dim_indexes	Primary key index
calendar_week_name	Bitmapped	N	day_of_week_name	TS dim_indexes	Sales analysis often performed by day of week
calendar_week_date	Bitmapped	N	week_begin_date_key	TS dim_indexes	Helps drive the application to compute the aggregate table sales_week_prod_store_fact.
calendar_month	Bitmapped	N	calendar_month_name	TS dim_indexes	Used in group-by clause
calendar_year	Bitmapped	N	calendar_year_num	TS dim_indexes	dimension browsing, filtering, and group-by in many queries
calendar_year_month	Bitmapped	N	year_month_num	TS dim_indexes	Often used in browsing to limit date_key

Hour

Index name	Index type	Unique	Columns	Location	Justification
hour_pkey	B-tree	Y	Hour_key	TS dim_indexes	Primary key index

Product

Index name	Index type	Unique	Columns	Location	Justification
prod_pkey	B-tree	Y	product_key	TS dim_indexes	Primary key index
prod_product	B-tree	N	product_name	TS dim_indexes	dimension browsing, filtering, and group-by
prod_brand	Bitmapped	N	brand_name	TS dim_indexes	dimension browsing, filtering, and group-by
prod_sub_category	Bitmapped	N	sub_category_name	TS dim_indexes	dimension browsing, filtering, and group-by
prod_category	Bitmapped	N	category_name	TS dim_indexes	dimension browsing, filtering, and group-by
prod_package_size	Bitmapped	N	package_size_group	TS dim_indexes	dimension browsing, filtering, and group-by

FIGURE 15.6 Case study index plan.

continues

Index name	Index type	Unique	Columns	Location	Justification
Store/market					
store_pkey	B-tree	Y	store_key	TS dim_indexes	Primary key index
store_name	B-tree	N	store_name	TS dim_indexes	dimension browsing, filtering, and group-by
store_zip5_code	B-tree	N	store_zip5_code	TS dim_indexes	dimension browsing, filtering, and group-by
store_market	Bitmapped	N	market_name	TS dim_indexes	dimension browsing, filtering, and group-by
store_region	Bitmapped	N	region_name	TS dim_indexes	dimension browsing, filtering, and group-by
store_country	Bitmapped	N	country_name	TS dim_indexes	dimension browsing, filtering, and group-by
Customer					
cust_pkey	B-tree	Y	customer_key	TS cust_indexes	Primary key index
cust_acctnum	B-tree		customer_acctnum	TS cust_indexes	Customer-care single-person queries. See p.31 of Business reqts document
cust_subscribe_date	B-tree	N	subscribe_date	TS cust_indexes	Common filter condition
cust_state	Bitmapped	N	customer_state_code	TS cust_indexes	Dimension browsing, filtering, and group-by
cust_zip5	B-tree	N	customer_zip5_code	TS cust_indexes	Dimension group-by; also join to DMA data
cust_income	Bitmapped	N	income_group_num	TS cust_indexes	Dimension filtering and group-by
cust_profitability	Bitmapped	N	profitability_score_num	TS cust_indexes	Dimension filtering and group-by

FIGURE 15.6 *Continued*

Memory

Data warehouse query performance benefits from significant memory, because most queries involve multistep processing. If the results of the first step of a complex query can be held in memory, the subsequent processing is much faster than if the temporary results must be written to disk.

Some warehouse applications are able to keep a working set of data in memory, to be accessed at memory speeds by multiple users. Even very large warehouses tend to use a subset of data most often, perhaps dimension tables or corporate data from the most recent week. If most users of the system are querying the same data and that data set is small enough to fit in memory, the queries will benefit from the memory cache. The benefits can be significant, with performance improvements of up to 30 times resulting from accessing data in memory rather than from disk.

Blocksize

Most RDBMSs support only a fixed block size as the amount of information brought into memory on a single read. Some RDBMSs permit the DBA to select the database's block size, typically ranging from 2 K to 32 K. Many data warehouse operations are performed much faster in a database with large blocks: data loads and table scans are examples. Other operations, notably queries that retrieve data scattered throughout the fact table, are less efficient with large blocks. This may seem counterintuitive, but remember that any read operation will bring the entire block into memory. This is great if the target data is contiguous, but if they are not, then relatively little of the result set will fit in cache, because each block consists mostly of data that is of little interest.

The answer then, as with so many data warehouse configuration problems, depends on the unique circumstances of your system. If your load window is a real problem or you know the key query access patterns and can efficiently sort the data accordingly, you should choose large blocks and structure the data so that frequently accessed data are contiguous. If loading is less of a problem and access patterns are unpredictable, small blocks are a better bet.

Disk Access Example

Let us examine a simple query and get a sense for the impact of different indexes and block size. Often, the marketing organization is interested in identifying subsets of the customer table. This segmentation is usually based on constraining several columns in the customer table to specific values and counting the results set. For example, the marketing group for the beverage retailer described earlier has decided to create a Platinum Shopper card for its best customers, and wants to test-market the idea in one state before rolling it out nationwide. The initial question is "How many customers having a high profitability score and high income live in state X?" Our customer table is 157 bytes wide. If we use 8K blocks, each block would hold about 52 rows, so the whole table would take up about 3,846 blocks. The worst case would be a full table scan where we have to retrieve all 3,846 blocks.

Let's see how standard RDBMS B-tree indexes help speed this up. The B-tree index is based on a tree structure where the leaves contain row IDs (or lists of row IDs). The B-tree index on a single column usually takes less than 10 bytes per row. Most RDBMSs can only select from one B-tree index before they go to the underlying table. In our case, we chose the most selective index, use the resulting row ID list to get the matching rows, and then checked each row for the remaining constraints. The state constraint is the most selective if we assume the target state is average size:

Column	Selectivity
Income group	1/10
Profitablility score	1/10
State	1/50

This sounds like a significant advantage—we should only have to examine 1/50 of the customer records for their income and profitability values, or about 4,000 rows. We pay a small price in that we have to read in the index to find the row IDs for the target 4,000 rows first, but that should be trivial, right? The B-tree index typically takes less than 10 bytes per row, or about 2 MB for the State index, which is about 244 8-K pages. Once we have the row IDs, we can go look them up in the table. Here is where the trouble starts. If the rows are distributed relatively evenly, it could mean that every 50th row comes from the target state. Since there are 52 rows in a block, we end up bringing back every block anyway. Note that a larger block size almost guarantees that we bring back every block. The disk access kills the advantage we gained by using the index.

You can improve this significantly with multicolumn indexes, but the order of the columns in the index matters, and the indexes are bigger.

Bitmapped indexes help significantly in this case because they can be combined and counted without having to go to the base table. Since all our constraints are set to equal a single value, we only need one bitmap vector for each constraint. Each vector is one bit wide by the number of rows in the table: 200,000 rows × 1 bit = about 24 K, or three-disk blocks. We can get the answer using a bitmapped index by reading only 9 blocks, (one set for each of the three columns). The RDBMS can AND the results and count the successful matches. This gives us a more than 400 times improvement over the full table scan.

Of course, this is a simple example for a single table, but it shows how bitmapped indexes can be used on dimension tables in conjunction with other indexes on the facts table to dramatically speed query performance.

Save the Database Build Scripts and Parameter Files

Most RDBMSs permit the DBA to configure and build the database using a point-and-click GUI. Although such GUIs are convenient, they typically do not self-document well. We recommend the use of such an interface only if the DBA uses a process or tool to capture the resulting information. At the minimum, you should have a script scheduled to run every night against the data dictionary tables to generate and archive the DDL from the actual schema.

Any team member who changes the layout of a physical table should model that change first in the data modeling tool and preferably generate the changes from the tool rather than by retyping (or pointing and clicking) at the database console. However, we have found that data modeling tools do not always generate the complete DDL in the way it needs to be run, especially when the change is to an existing table. (You typically do not want to drop and re-create a very large table in order to add a new column.) In this case, start with the data model, generate the DDL from the model, and edit and save the DDL according to your group's code management standards.

Once again we want to emphasize the benefits of using a code management tool for the data warehouse. We have seldom had the luxury of using such a tool, but when it has been available we have really appreciated the benefits. The best tools ease the coordination problems associated with large teams working on the same code base. You can generate reports (easily posted as Web pages) of the changed code, and permit reverting to earlier code should you—unlikely as it sounds—mess things up.

DEVELOP THE PHYSICAL STORAGE STRUCTURE

There is a level to the physical model that lies below the data structures we've already discussed: the storage structures of blocks, files, disks, partitions, and table spaces or databases. Your warehouse project will greatly benefit from the services of a physical DBA who has extensive experience with your hardware and RDBMS platform and, just as important, is knowledgeable about the requirements of data warehouses. If such a resource is not available within your company, consider bringing in a consultant either to do the work outlined next or perhaps to conduct a review of the physical design.

Compute Table and Index Sizes

As discussed earlier in this chapter, we recommend that a rough estimate of disk requirements be made at the beginning of the physical design process. The main goal of the preliminary sizing estimates was to support platform decision making.

Now that the logical design has been finalized, it's time actually to put data to disk. Accurate computations are necessary: Use an expert for this process. If you really need to go it alone, thoroughly read and follow the documentation provided by your RDBMS vendor, and use vendor-supplied sizing tools where available.

Determine the timeframe for which you are planning your storage requirements, but document and understand the growth requirements beyond that timeframe. Typically, we plan for an initial data load of fixed size, plus at least six months of growth during ongoing loads. Plan for success, and understand how and when to add new drives should your team be pressured to move swiftly into production or to add more historical data.

Develop the Partitioning Plan

If your RDBMS supports partitioning tables, you should plan to take advantage of it if possible. The best way to partition tables is by date, with data segmented by month, quarter, or year into separate storage partitions. Typically, only fact tables and very large dimension tables and their indexes are partitioned. The partitioned table looks like a single table, but it is managed in separate pieces.

The advantages of partitioning are two-fold: A query will access only the partitions necessary to resolve the query, and an entire partition can easily and quickly be added or dropped from the table. This can greatly reduce the maintenance burden for a warehouse that keeps only recent data directly active and accessible. It also helps if you need to restructure or restate data in a fact table.

To take full advantage of table partitioning, you typically have to declare the criteria that uniquely determine into which partition a row will be placed and similarly partition your indexes. The second condition can certainly be eased, but at the cost of some performance both during queries and maintenance.

 Partitioning can significantly improve your warehouse's performance and maintainability, and implementing partitions from the outset adds no cost to your project. If your RDBMS supports partitioning, use it.

Set up RAID

RAID stands for redundant array of inexpensive disks. We strongly recommend the use of RAID storage for your data warehouse. The minimum RAID configuration, RAID0, will stripe the data for you. By *striping the data*, we mean that it will spread the storage for a file across multiple physical drives. You should choose RAID technology that uses an external RAID controller rather than have the RDBMS CPU double as the RAID manager. Disk subsystems can cost significantly more than your hardware vendor's standard disk drives, but we have found them to be worth the price. A disk subsystem provides its own controllers and cache. They are also relatively machine- and operating system–independent, and they can be moved from one machine to another fairly quickly.

Fault Tolerance

If your budget is flexible, RAID5 is an extremely valuable configuration. RAID5, like RAID0, spreads data across multiple disks, with the valuable additional feature of redundancy across a set of disks. You typically lose 20 percent of storage capacity, so a RAID5 drive defined over 100 GB of physical disk will hold 80 GB of data. With RAID5, if a disk fails, your data warehouse will continue to function seamlessly (albeit a bit more slowly). Recovery is automatic as well, upon insertion of a new disk, especially if your RAID technology supports "hot swapping" of disks. This redundancy is important because the disk drives are the most likely point of failure across the hardware platform.

If money is no object, RAID1 is the ideal configuration: it offers 100 percent mirroring of the data and index disks. Full mirroring gives you full and instant recovery from a disk failure with no degradation in performance.

Remember, however, that no RAID configuration is a substitute for regular backups. Even with a fully mirrored configuration, someone could login under the system account and delete a fact table or inadvertently corrupt data by running the wrong script.

Configuration of Volumes and Drives

The easiest configuration to manage, regardless of the level of fault tolerance, is one that defines a single array volume to hold all the database's tables and indexes. The RAID controller balances the application's I/O by performing low-level data striping of files across all the disks in the volume, without further intervention required by the DBA. This configuration delivers very good query performance and is easy to manage. It is appropriate for small data warehouses.

If you are not using RAID technology, the DBA and system administrator need to understand access patterns well enough to predict which tables and indexes will be accessed simultaneously and segment the data so each drive receives approximately the same number of data requests. This is particularly difficult to do in a data warehousing environment where usage patterns are constantly evolving.

When the amount of data and indexes exceeds the capacity of a single controller, you will have a multiple-volume system. When your warehouse is managing a medium-to-large amount of data, requiring multiple volumes, the length of the load window is often a significant problem. A good way to segment data on a multiple volume system is to do it in such a way as to improve load performance. If you are loading from a flat file into the database, you want the source data on one volume, the tables and indexes on a second and third, and the transaction log (if you have one) segmented on a fourth volume.

Be careful to avoid creating a bottleneck for querying. For best query performance, you should segment storage so that data accessed together, such as the customer dimension and the fact table, are on different disks. Although large warehouses are more difficult to manage, at least they use enough disk that you can usually segment data so that it meets *both* the easier-to-load and the faster-to-query requirements.

 Remember that the best way to avoid I/O bottlenecks is to have as many disk controllers as possible. You are better off with many smaller drives controlled by multiple controllers, than a few large drives and a few controllers. Clearly, the large-drives-and-few-controllers option is more cost-effective. You need to find the best balance between cost and performance for your system.

With a multiple volume system, you may choose to implement multiple levels of fault tolerance. Operating system files, database executables, database system tables, and transaction logs coexist well on a volume with some fault tolerance (RAID1 or RAID5). Depending on the project's budget and requirements for data availability, we often recommend less fault tolerance (RAID5 or RAID0) for the data table and index volumes.

If an unprotected drive fails, the database instance will crash, and the database must be restored from backups. If a protected drive fails, by contrast, the database typically remains up and available for use while repairs are under way, although performance does slow down.

Temp Database

The exception to the RAID rule is the temp database. If your database can handle a crash in the temp space, then it does not need to be RAIDed. Temp space disk should be as fast as possible. Consider using silicon disk for your temp space if it fits within your budget.

IMPLEMENT USAGE MONITORING

As discussed in Chapter 10, you should build or implement a usage monitoring system for your data warehouse as early in the project as possible. Especially during the very early days of the project, you must be able to monitor the system's response to loads and queries. You will want to capture and present information on what processes are running, what resources they're using, who submitted them, and how long they took. This information is particularly vital during the development of the warehouse database and maintenance systems.

Activity monitoring captures information about the use of the data warehouse. There are several excellent reasons to include resources in your project plan to create an activity monitoring capability. These mainly center around four areas: performance, user support, marketing, and planning.

Performance

Collecting information about usage over time allows the DBA to tune the warehouse more effectively. The DBA can use the data to see what tables and columns are most often joined, selected, aggregated, and filtered. In many cases, this can lead to changes in the aggregate tables, the indexes, and the schema design.

We typically build a set of queries early on that point at the system tables so we can get a quick sense of what's going on. These queries are especially helpful if they include the user name and the actual SQL being processed. These queries actually become a critical part of the database management toolset for large data warehouses. Often, the way someone formulates a query can mean the difference between getting an answer in seconds and not getting an answer at all. The DBA can spot these runaway queries (through an investigation usually sparked by the fact that the warehouse has slowed to a crawl), and contact the user to help them understand how to reformulate the query and get them to kill the existing one.

User Support

We encourage our clients to watch for activity from users who recently went through training. People who use the warehouse right away often need help formulating effective queries, and people who wait too long will probably need help with the basics. If someone doesn't log on at all within a few weeks, it's worth a call to at least find out why. Often they either haven't come across a real business need yet, or they tried to use the warehouse and couldn't connect to the database. Most people will solve a problem with a predictable approach rather than risk spending a significant amount of time and not get any results. If they aren't successful the first time, they are unlikely to try again without some encouragement.

The next step beyond monitoring current activity is to keep a history of query activity. Ideally, this should include the resources used (CPU seconds, cache hits, disk reads), elapsed time, completion status, query source, and possibly the query SQL. We have often developed a basic usage history system simply by snapshotting the appropriate system monitor tables at midnight, storing the day's activity in a history table, and resetting the monitored values to zero. This information will allow the DBA to gain an understanding of how the warehouse is used over time: where it needs to be tuned, where aggregate tables should be added or dropped, and so on.

Marketing

Marketing is an extremely valuable side benefit of activity monitoring. Publishing simple usage statistics over time will let management know that their investment is being used. A nice growth curve is a wonderful marketing tool. On the other hand, a flat or decreasing curve might provide motivation for the warehouse team.

We've also seen this information create a significant rise in demand for the data warehouse. A simple report that shows who is creating the most queries (along with their department), can really get peoples' competitive juices flowing. In one case, a few months after the initial rollout of a warehouse at a large finance institution, a manager's meeting came to a halt when they all gathered around to see a user activity report the warehouse manager happened to have in his briefcase and wasn't even planning to show.

Planning

Monitoring usage growth, average query time, concurrent user counts, database sizes, load times, and so on will provide data needed to help quantify capacity increases and timing. This information also could support a mainframe-style chargeback system. We don't encourage this return to the glass-house mentality, especially in the early days of the warehouse. If everyone is concerned about how much a query will cost, they won't do the experimentation they need to do to learn the tools and the data or the exploration they need to find the real business value.

Tools

Like most of the services we've discussed, you can build a rudimentary version yourself or buy a full-featured package. There are packages on the market specifically designed to monitor user activity. Many of the query management tools also offer query monitoring as a natural byproduct of managing the query process, as do some of the front-end application toolsets.

Most RDBMSs provide basic monitoring tools, which usually are turned off by default at RDBMS installation because they use significant system resources. The most expensive kind of usage to monitor is the capture of the SQL used in queries. You should develop a plan for how much, when, and how to monitor and store query text, and filter out system-issued queries such as those run in the maintenance application. As tempting as it sounds to save a copy of all the SQL issued in the database, without a tool to parse and make sense of those queries you end up with far more data than information.

Few tools do more than capture the SQL and resource statistics while they are monitoring the system. You may be faced with the task of monitoring a large and complex data warehouse, with little or no a priori knowledge of the database structure or usage patterns. With little information about how the database is used, you will have little choice but to capture all SQL for a week or two. To make sense of the resulting data, you can write a custom application to parse the SQL text, looking particularly for tables that are used together and columns that are used in join conditions, filters, and group-bys. Be sure to sort the results by user group (e.g., Marketing, Planning). This is an unpleasant task, but the results are usually extremely valuable. In one instance we learned that 85 percent of all queries issued against a schema with 6,000 data elements were resolved by a mere 200 data elements. This knowledge helped make a gargantuan task (redesigning a huge enterprise-wide schema) much more reasonable.

For a new data warehouse that is designed and built from user requirements, we expect that the data warehouse team would remain close enough to the users that such draconian measures would not be necessary. The standard tools that monitor CPU usage, cache hits, and the count of queries executed per user usually suffice.

SUMMARY

The details of physical implementation vary dramatically from project to project. The data volumes of the project are one of the key drivers, as it is significantly harder to complete the physical design for a terabyte warehouse as it is for a 50 GB mart, although their business requirements and logical designs may be identical.

The hardware, software, and tools available to the team can make the implementation tasks much easier or much more difficult than they need to be. With the help of good tools, the team can spend less time managing file layouts, partitions, and indexes, and more time designing new implementations and meeting the users' data access requirements in a successful data warehouse. Be sure to consult the project plan spreadsheet at the end of this chapter for a summary of the tasks and responsibilities for completing the physical design (Figure 15.7).

KEY ROLES

Key roles for completing the physical design include:

- The database administrator needs to be the primary driver for all of these tasks.
- The business systems analyst, data modeler, project manager, and business project lead need to support the database administrator to answer any questions that may arise.

ESTIMATING CONSIDERATIONS

The physical design process effort can vary significantly. At one end of the spectrum, it could be a two-week effort in the case where a DBA is implementing a well-designed logical model for a single, relatively small data mart. At the other end of the spectrum, the physical design effort can take months.

continued

ESTIMATING CONSIDERATIONS (*Continued*)

Planning for physical design can be a time-consuming process if naming conventions aren't already in place. An even greater degree of uncertainty stems from a lack of clarity around the logical or business names for the data elements. Vague, conflicting definitions at this point are a sure sign of trouble. These problems have to be resolved at this point, or they will haunt the warehouse for a very long time.

The size of the database and the complexity of the warehouse technical environment have a major impact on the effort. The process is multiplicative rather than additive as complexity increases. Multiple platforms and multiple instances bring the added difficulty of inter-operation.

The level of DBA skill and experience with the target platform can also extend the timeline significantly. An inexperienced DBA can more than double the length of the physical design process, and in most cases, will produce an inferior implementation.

TEMPLATES

The following templates for completing the physical design can be found on the CD-ROM:

- Template 15.1 DBMS Server Code Tree
- Template 15.2 Physical Database Design
- Template 15.3 Index Plan

	Fans	Front Office			Coaches		Regular Line-Up						Special Teams				
Project Task	Business End Users	Business Sponsor	IS Sponsor	Business Driver	Bus. Project Lead	Project Manager	Bus. Sys. Analyst	Data Modeler	DW DBA	Data Staging Designer	DW Educator	E/U Appl Devel	Tech/Security Architect	Tech. Sppt Specialists	Data Staging Programmer	Data Steward	DW QA Analyst
PHYSICAL DATABASE DESIGN																	
1 Define Standards									●								
2 Design Physical tables & Columns								▶	●								
3 Estimate Database Size						▶	▶	▶	●	▶							
4 Develop Initial Index Plan							▶	▶	●			▶					
5 Develop Initial Aggregation Plan							○	○	●								
6 Develop Initial Partitioning Plan									●								
7 User Acceptance/Project Review	□	□	□	□		●	○	○	○	○	▲	○	▲	▲	○	▲	▲
PHYSICAL DATABASE IMPLEMENTATION																	
1 Determine DBMS Fixed Parameters									●								
2 Install DBMS									●				○	○			
3 Optimize DBMS Changeable Parameters									●								
4 Build Physical Storage Structure									●								
5 Setup RAID									●				○	○			
6 Complete Table and Index Sizing								▶	●								
7 Create Tables and Indexes									●								
8 User Acceptance/Project Review	□	□	□	□		●	○	○	○	○	▲	○	▲	▲	▲	▲	▲

LEGEND:
Primary Responsibility for the Task = ●
Involved in the Task = ○
Provides Input to the Task = ▶
Informed Task Results = □
Optional Involvement in the Task = ▲

FIGURE 15.7 Project plan tasks and responsibilities for completing the physical design.

CHAPTER 16

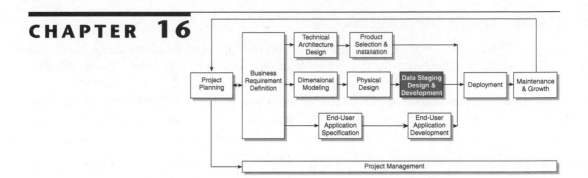

Data Staging

The data staging process is the iceberg of the data warehouse project. So many challenges are buried in the data sources and the systems they run on that this part of the process invariably takes much more time than you expect. This chapter is structured as a ten-step plan for creating the data staging application for a data mart. It lays out the ten steps in detail, then reviews data quality and cleansing issues. Some additional administrative issues are covered at the end of the chapter. The concepts and approach described in this chapter apply to both hand-coded staging systems and data staging tools. Most of the examples are code-based, since that represents a lowest-common-denominator approach.

This chapter should be read in detail by each member of the data staging team. The data modelers and DBAs should also be familiar with the techniques described in this chapter. The project manager should use this chapter as the foundation for educating the rest of the organization about why data staging development is so complex and time consuming. The rest of the project team can simply skim the chapter to become familiar with the basic steps. These other team members do not need to have in-depth knowledge of these concepts.

DATA STAGING OVERVIEW

How do you think we will advise you to begin the process of building the data staging application? For once we will skip our primary mantra of *focus on the business requirements* and present our second-favorite aphorism: *Make a plan.* It's rare to see a data staging process that is planned in a concrete and documented way. This is understandable, for so much of the work to this point has been planning and designing; now everyone is anxious to see some real data.

Nonetheless, you really need a plan. Like anything else, if you don't have a plan, you cannot explain to others where you are going or how you expect to get there.

This chapter uses the following structure to describe the data staging planning and implementation process.

Plan:

1. Create a very high-level, one-page schematic of the source-to-target flow.
2. Test, choose, and implement a data staging tool.
3. Drill down by target table, graphically sketching any complex data restructuring or transformations. Graphically illustrate the surrogate-key generation process. Develop preliminary job sequencing.

Dimension loads:

4. Build and test a static dimension table load. The primary goal of this step is to work out the infrastructure kinks, including connectivity, file transfer, and security problems.
5. Build and test the slowly changing process for one dimension.
6. Build and test remaining dimension loads.

Fact tables and automation:

7. Build and test the historical fact table loads (base tables only), including surrogate key lookup and substitution.
8. Build and test the incremental load process.
9. Build and test aggregate table loads and/or MOLAP loads.
10. Design, build, and test the staging application automation.

DO THE PRELIMINARY WORK

Before you begin the data staging application design for a set of fact tables, you should have completed the logical design, drafted your high-level architecture plan, and completed (or nearly so) the source-to-target mapping for all data elements. The physical design and implementation work should be well under way.

The data staging system design process is critical. Gather all the relevant information, including the processing burden your extracts will be allowed to place on the transaction systems. Test some of the key alternatives. Does it make sense to host the transformation process on the source system, the target system, or its own platform? What tools are available on each, and how effective are they? Set up the development environment, including directories, naming conventions (Development, Test, Production, etc.). If you end up writing code from scratch, take advantage of code management systems that might be available. Again, what you actually need to do depends on the scope of your project and the tools available to you.

Importance of Good System Development Practices

Data warehouse development may follow an iterative, interactive process, but the fundamentals of good systems development still apply. The data warehouse team should always:

- Set up a header format and comment fields for your code.
- Hold structured design reviews early enough to allow changes.
- Write clean, well-commented code.
- Stick to the naming standards.
- Use the code library and management system.
- Test everything—both unit testing and system testing.
- Document everything—hopefully in the information catalog.

PLAN EFFECTIVELY

The planning phase starts out with the high-level plan, which is independent of the specific approach. However, it's a good idea to decide on a data staging tool before you do any detailed planning. This will save you some redesign and rework later in the process.

Step 1. High-Level Plan

Start the design process with a very simple schematic of the pieces of the plan that you know: the sources and targets. Keep it very high-level, a one-pager that highlights where data are coming from, and annotate the major challenges that you already know about. Figure 16.1 illustrates what we mean. This schematic is for a fictitious utility company's data warehouse, which is primarily sourced from a 30-year-old COBOL system. (Note: Utility company schemas are usually far more complex than this.) In this example, additional attribute information comes from the customer and geography masters in an RDBMS, a departmental system in Microsoft Access, and an as-yet-unidentified source for the period table. Put in a placeholder box in your model to represent data element sources that are as yet unmapped, to highlight the lack. It will feel great when you finally do get to fill in these empty boxes.

If most or all of the data come from a modern relational OLTP system, the boxes often represent a logical grouping of tables in the transaction system model (the billing group, the customer group, etc.).

This one-pager is a good way to communicate some of the project's complexity to management. It's probably as deep as they—indeed, most people—will want to delve into the staging application.

Data staging applications perform three major steps: they *extract* data from a source, *transform* it, and *load* it into the warehouse. You can see those three steps in the high-level schematic: getting data out of sources, transforming it and loading it into the targets.

There is quite a bit of overlap among the steps—only the end points are discrete. Although most of the standard transformations take place in the staging area, transformations can occur in any of the three steps, and in any of the three data stores.

Step 2. Data Staging Tools

The extracts are typically written in source system code (e.g., COBOL, PL/SQL, etc.) since this is what the source environment is set up to support. Historically, data staging tools were source system code generators. These products are effectively CASE tools that have been customized to support data warehousing. Most of them have been upgraded to create code based on a graphical representation of the extract process. This code is stored and managed in a repository that drives the product's execution module.

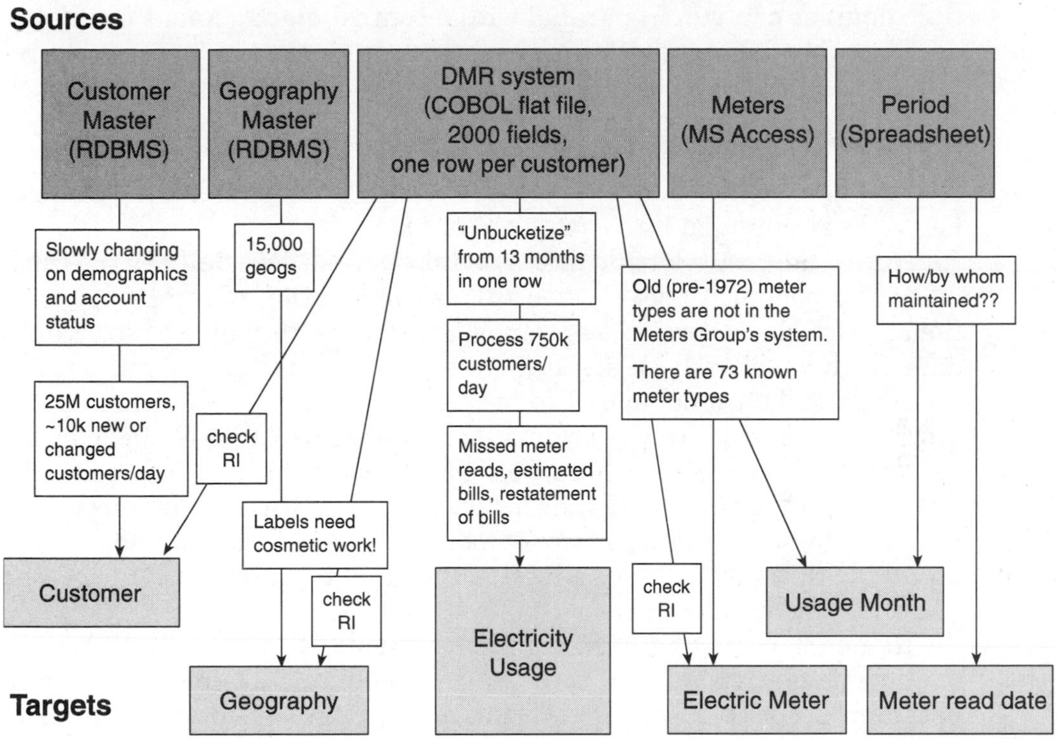

Sources

FIGURE 16.1   Basic high-level data staging plan schematic.

The decision to use a data staging tool instead of hand-coding the extracts is becoming easier as data warehousing becomes a mainstream market. Although a few high-end mainframe-based vendors have been around for years, a second generation of tools began to emerge in this area beginning around 1995. By the end of 1997, these second-generation vendors had reasonable customer bases and were quickly learning the full range of extract and transformation requirements. Their new releases are now showing a significant increase in functionality and usability. Many of these new tools have a different architecture from the first generation. They are based around a transformation engine that is designed to perform the kinds of transformations common to data warehousing. The transformation engine improves scalability because multiple engines can run in parallel with a central management facility.

The new tools are also improving the transformation process by creating reusable transformation modules, or objects, that build in business rules. If the rules change, a single change to the base module will cause all the instances of it to also update. The first-generation tools tended to generate standalone code for each extract process. Any changes had to be recompiled into each piece of code.

New vendors are forcing prices to drop as well, especially as the capability and popularity of NT grows. This combination of improving functionality and lower prices is so compelling that we recommend selecting a data staging tool early on and using it right from the start—for the prototype if possible. Do not expect to recoup the investment in a staging tool during your first prototype or data mart project: Because of the learning curve, it seldom saves much time or money compared with developing the initial staging by hand. Significant benefits from the staging tools come from turning the prototype into a production system that can be updated nightly with minimal human intervention and from building the second and subsequent data marts.

Remember, though, this decision must be based on the nature of your systems environment. If you have a complex, custom source system based on proprietary databases, the tool options are more limited and more costly. Also, if the first effort is a proof of concept that has not really been approved by management, and is not intended to become production, the extra cost and time of including a data staging tool may not be worth it. In a production system, however, the long-term improvements in manageability, productivity, and training are significant.

If it is possible to defer the decision whether to purchase a staging tool (and which one) until this point in the design process, you will be able to make a well-informed decision. You can present alternative vendors with your high-level schematic and a 5- to 30-page detailed plan and expect clear responses to your well-educated and specific questions.

Throughout this chapter we will use the lowest common denominator of a code-based approach to describe the data staging process. If you are using a data staging tool, it will need to provide the functionality described.

Whether you are hand-coding or choosing a tool, an important functionality across the data staging process is pre- and post-step exits. Every step you define in the process should have a way to make an external function call as a part of the step, both before and after the step is run. This can be critical when you need to do something outside the capabilities of the tool or utility. For example, it may make sense to run the data set through a sort routine before the load process. Or, it may be necessary to call a proprietary function that scores a record based on a predetermined formula.

Step 3. Detailed Plan

The next step, not surprisingly, is to drill down on each of the flows. Start planning which tables to work on, in which order, and for sequencing the transformations within each data set. Graphically diagram the complex restructurings. Where the high-level plan fits a set of fact tables onto a single page (more or less), the detailed plan graphics can devote a page or more to each complex target table. Sometimes it makes more sense to structure the diagrams around the source tables instead of the target tables. The schematic is backed up with a few pages of pseudocode detailing complex transformations. Figure 16.2 illustrates the first pass on the detailed plan schematic for the main utility fact table.

All of the dimension tables must be processed before the key lookup steps for the fact table. The dimension tables are usually fairly independent from each other—that's why they are dimensions, after all.

Organizing the Data Staging Area

The data staging area is the data warehouse workbench. It is the place where raw data is loaded, cleaned, combined, archived, and quickly exported to one or more presentation server platforms. The overriding goal of the data staging area is to get the data ready to be loaded into a presentation server (a relational DBMS or an OLAP engine). We assume that the data staging area is not a query service. In other words, any database that is used for querying is assumed to be physically downstream from the data staging area.

If the raw data is naturally available in a relational database and the load window is large enough, it may make sense to perform all the processing steps within the relational framework, especially if the source relational database and the eventual target data mart database are from the same vendor. This makes even more sense when there is a high-speed link between the source and target databases.

However, there are many variations on this theme, and in many cases it may not make sense to load the source data into a relational database for transformation. In the detailed descriptions of the processing steps, we

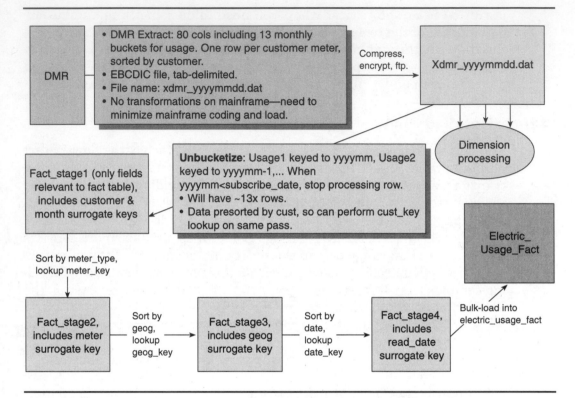

FIGURE 16.2 First draft of historical load schematic for the fact table.

will see that almost all the processing is sorting, followed by a single sequential pass through one or two tables. This simple processing paradigm does not need the power or overhead of a relational DBMS. In some cases, it may be a serious mistake to load the data into a relational database when what is needed is sequential flat file processing.

 If the raw data is not in a normalized entity-relation format, it often does not pay to convert it. The most important data integrity steps involving the enforcement of one-to-one and one-to-many relationships can be performed with simple sorting and sequential processing.

If you build your application with a staging tool, that tool's requirements will drive your physical infrastructure implementation. We describe the underlying processes here so you can implement them directly or understand what your data staging tool is up to.

DIMENSION TABLE STAGING

Start building the data staging application with the simplest dimension table. Usually, at least one dimension table is static; that is, it is not a slowly changing dimension. The primary goal of this step is to work out the infrastructure kinks, including connectivity, security, and file transfer problems (which always seem to exist). If all of your dimension tables are complex, we recommend that you do a static load of the simplest one, to get started. Later you can loop back and build the change logic.

Once you have successfully built your first dimension table, tackle the slowly changing dimension problem. Typically, the techniques or code that you develop for one slowly changing dimension are reusable for all. Your second and subsequent slowly changing dimensions will be much easier than your first, even if they are larger tables.

You also need to build those dimension tables that are largely or entirely "made up." A common example is the period table, which we usually build from spreadsheets. The Period table is so easy that we like to leave it as a treat for some day when we're feeling downhearted about the whole project.

Step 4. Populate a Simple Dimension Table

The primary reason to start with a static dimension table is that it is the simplest sort of table to populate. We will take the opportunity in this section to present information about the data staging process that is relevant to all types of target tables.

Static Dimension Extract

The extract process for a static dimension table is usually straightforward. The primary source is often a lookup table or file that can be pulled in its entirety to the staging area. Work closely with the data owners and source system team so that you understand the characteristics of the source. Is the file you have been directed to the authoritative source for the dimension information? How is it updated? Is there a time of day when you should not access it? When are transactions against it complete for the target load period? Is there a reliable time-stamp for changed records?

Sometimes the file, although logically simple, is stored in an inaccessible way. The source system owners can most efficiently convert the file into a useful structure. More often than not, they will use their standard reporting tools to generate an extract "report." A report, as long as it is correctly defined and can be scheduled, is a perfectly acceptable extract mechanism.

Creating and Moving the Result Set

There are two primary methods for getting data from a source system: as a file or as a stream. If the source is an aging mainframe system, it is often much easier to extract into files and then move those files to the staging server.

If you are using a staging tool and your data are in a database (not necessarily an RDBMS), you may be able to set up the extract as a stream. Note that we're not necessarily talking about an ongoing "trickle" stream, but rather that the extract can be constructed so that data flow out of the source system, through the transformation engine, and into the staging database as a single process. An extract to file approach, by contrast, consists of three or four discrete steps: extract to file, move file to staging server, transform file contents, and load transformed data into the staging database.

Although the stream extract is more appealing, extracts to file do have some advantages. They are easy to restart at various points. As long as you save the extract file, you can rerun the load. You can easily encrypt and compress the data before transferring across the network. Finally, it is easy to verify that all data has moved correctly by comparing file row counts before and after the transfer. Generally, we use a data transfer utility such as FTP to move the extracted file.

Data compression is important if you need to transfer large amounts of data over a significant distance or through a public network. In this case, the communications link is often the bottleneck. If too much time is spent transmitting the data, compression can reduce the transmission time by 30 to 50 percent or more, depending on the nature of the original data file.

Data encryption is important if you are transferring data through a public network, or even internally in some situations. If this is the case, it is best to send everything through an encrypted link and not worry about what needs to be secure and what doesn't. Remember to compress before encrypting as described in Chapter 12.

Static Dimension Transformation

Even the simplest dimension table may require substantial data cleanup, and it will certainly require surrogate key assignment. Data cleanup is a huge topic, tackled in a separate section at the end of this chapter.

Simple Data Transformations

The most common, and easiest, form of data transformation is data type conversion. At the most basic level, data that comes from a mainframe has to be converted from the EBCDIC character set to ASCII. In addition, your logical and physical models often specify that values be stored in a different data type than the source: date, number, or character. All databases and file-based toolsets have rich functions for data type conversion. This task can be tedious, but it is seldom onerous.

For dimension tables, another common and easy transformation is to "pretty up" the dimension labels. Make sure your tools offer a full set of functions, including string manipulation and conditional statements. User extensibility to these functions is very valuable. One tool we've used let us add a simple Nice_Name function that took a user-entered name field (first and last) and cleaned it up so it looked nice. *Nice* in this case means we capitalized the first and last name, and changed the all caps entries to title case. No big deal, but it made the reports much more readable and appealing to the user community.

Surrogate Key Assignment

Once you are confident that you have a version of your dimension table with one row for each true unique dimension value, you can assign the surrogate keys. Although other staging tables may be deleted after the dimension processing is complete, you need to maintain a table in the staging area matching production keys to surrogate keys. This key map will be used later during fact table processing.

Surrogate keys are typically assigned as integers, increasing by one for each new key. If your staging area is in an RDBMS, surrogate key assignment is elegantly accomplished by creating a sequence. Although syntax varies among the RDBMS, the process looks like this:

- One-time creation of the sequence:

```
create sequence dim1_seq cache=1000; — choose appropriate cache
level
```

- Populate the key map table:

```
insert into dim1_key_map (production_key_id, dim1_key)
select production_key_id, dim1_seq.NEXT
from dim1_extract_table;
```

If your staging area is file-based, your surrogate key assignment logic should be equally straightforward. If you do not use a database sequence, you need to save the current (or next) surrogate key to be assigned in the metadata to avoid performing a max(surrogate_key)+1 operation every time you need to assign a new key.

Combining from Separate Sources

Often dimensions are derived from several sources. Customer information may need to be merged from several lines of business and from outside sources. There is seldom a universal key that makes this merge operation easy. The raw data and the existing dimension table data may need to be sorted at different times on different fields to attempt a match. Sometimes a match may be based on fuzzy criteria. Names and addresses may match except for minor spelling differences. In these cases, a sequential processing paradigm is more natural than a relational equijoin. As we described in Chapter 9, there are tools and companies who can help with this process.

Once a pair of records is determined to be a match, place an entry in a mapping table with the warehouse surrogate key, and the matching keys from all the various source systems.

A common merging task in data preparation is looking up text equivalents for production codes. In many cases, the text equivalents are sourced informally from a nonproduction source. Again, the task of adding the text equivalents can be done in a single pass by first sorting the raw data and the text lookup table by the production code.

Validating One-to-One and One-to-Many Relationships

If two attributes in a dimension are supposed to have a one-to-one relationship, for example, key-to-label, this can be checked easily by sorting the dimension records on one of the attributes. A sequential scan of the data will show whether there are any violations. Each attribute value in the sorted column must have exactly one value in the other column. Reverse the check by sorting on the second column and repeating.

A many-to-one relationship, such as zip code-to-state, can similarly be verified by sorting on the "many" attribute and verifying that each value has a unique value on the "one" attribute.

Load

Once the data is properly prepared, the load process is fairly straightforward. This is particularly true for the process we've described since the transformations have been performed in the staging area. All we have to do now is load the prepared data into the target tables. Even though the first dimension table is usually small, you should load it using your database's bulk loader program.

 The bulk loader is a utility built to get data into the database as quickly as possible, and every mainstream database has one. The bulk loader is the most efficient way to load data, and you should take this opportunity to become familiar with its capabilities.

Even if your staging area is in the same RDBMS and server as the target warehouse, you should plan to use the bulk loader. Although anyone can write the SQL to SELECT FROM the staging table and INSERT INTO the target table, this approach is inefficient, slow, and often fails because of insufficient log or rollback space. Remember, most of the RDBMSs will log transactions, and it's not feasible to keep sufficient log space to support a large table load. Equally important, INSERT INTO is extremely slow. The requirement to use the bulk loader is nearly universal; we have worked with only one RDBMS that does efficient discrete INSERTs.

Bulk Loader

The bulk load utilities tend to be script driven and come with a range of parameters and transformation capabilities. If you are using a data staging tool, make sure it works directly with your database's bulk loader and takes advantage of its features. Some of the primary suggestions for using these utilities are:

- **Turn off logging.** Transaction-oriented databases keep track of all changes to the database in a log file. Logging allows the database to recover its current state if it runs into a fatal error. It is vital for a transaction database. However, the log adds significant overhead and is not valuable when loading data warehouse tables. If something goes wrong, you still have the load file in the staging area.

- **Pre-sort the file.** Sorting the file in the order of the primary index speeds up the indexing process significantly. In some cases, this is a parameter in the bulk loader or in the index command.

- **Transform with caution.** In some cases, the loader will let you do data conversions, calculations, string and date/time manipulation, and so on. Use these features carefully, and test performance. In some cases, these transformations cause the loader to switch out of high-speed mode into a line-by-line evaluation of the load file. If you are doing transformations that involve lookups on other tables, (e.g., RI checking), make sure the lookup tables are indexed to support it.

- **Aggregations.** If your bulk loader supports the creation of aggregations as part of the loading process, definitely take advantage of it. In some cases, this can speed the load process significantly.

- **Use the bulk loader to perform "within-database" inserts.** As discussed earlier, even if your staging area is simply a different schema within the target RDBMS, you should use the bulk loader to move data from staging table to target. Write a query that extracts from the staging table (typically "select * from stage_table"), and stream the results into the bulk loader. If you are writing this code by hand, this is a one-line shell script, where "QueryProgram" is the program (like isql, sqlplus, or risql) that executes SQL, and "LoaderProgram" is the bulk loader (bcp, sqlload, tmu):

```
QueryProgram &username &password <extract_query.sql | \
LoaderProgram load_script.ctl &username &password
```

The loader control file (load_script.ctl) notifies the bulk loader that the data is coming in as a stream rather than from a file as is more common. This approach is elegant and does not require extra disk space to store the result set out in the file system.

Truncate Target Table before Full Refresh

Most RDBMSs have a "truncate table" command that is logically equivalent to a delete all rows command. Physically, a truncate table is much more efficient, because it does not log the deletions and frees up all table space without needing to reorganize or restructure the table. Be warned, however, that there is often no way to undo a truncate table command.

Index Management

Recall from Chapter 15 on physical design, that indexes are costly during the load process. Each record added to the table also has to be added to every index. Several indexes on a table can cause the load time to balloon. Adding rows to an index can also throw the index structure out of balance and adversely affect queries. You basically have two choices during the load: drop and re-create the indexes or add rows with the indexes in place.

- **Drop and reindex.** Take this approach if you are loading a significant portion of the table each time. As a rule of thumb, if you are adding more than 10 to 15 percent of the total rows, you are probably better off dropping and rebuilding the indexes, especially if your RDBMS supports partitioned indexes.
- **Keep indexes in place.** With this approach, it is important to understand how data will be added to the various indexes so you can create them with appropriate fill factors and with room to grow. It's also a good idea to rebuild the indexes every so often so they don't get too fragmented.

The right cutoff will vary depending on the database, the hardware configuration (especially memory), and how many indexes you have. Test these options out in your environment. It doesn't take long to try it a few different ways and see what works best.

Maintaining Dimension Tables

The dimension tables in the warehouse almost always end up with additional attributes that are important to business analysis, but not to the transaction systems. Many of the data cleansing steps, like name and address processing, geo-coding, scoring, or householding, end up creating these attributes. Other attributes, like the entire Period table, are created manually. Wherever they come from, these attributes must be kept up to date. When a hierarchy changes, or new rows come into the dimension table, the corresponding additional attribute values must be added. This can happen in two places:

Warehouse-Managed Maintenance

Most often, the warehouse ends up with stewardship responsibility for these new "master" dimension tables. The best-case scenario here is to have the appropriate user department agree to own the maintenance of these attributes. The warehouse team needs to provide a user interface for this maintenance. Typically this takes the form of a simple application built using the company's standard visual programming tool. The data staging process should add default attribute values for new rows, and the user-owner needs to update them. If these rows are loaded into the warehouse before they are changed, they still appear in reports with whatever default description is supplied.

 The warehouse staging process should create a unique default-dimension attribute description that shows that someone hasn't done their data stewardship job yet. We favor a label that concatenates the phrase "Not yet assigned" with the surrogate key value: "Not yet assigned 157." That way, multiple "Not yet assigned" values do not inadvertently get lumped together in reports and aggregate tables. This also helps identify the row when someone wants to correct it.

Source System–Managed Maintenance

The ideal situation, at least from the warehouse point of view, is to have the source system take on the ownership of these analytic attributes, just like the other attributes of the dimension. The source system owners are better equipped to create the maintenance applications, and the new attributes will then be available in the source system for operational reporting that matches the warehouse. The warehouse can then simply extract the full dimension.

Step 5. Implement Dimension Change Logic

Recall that every data warehouse key should be a surrogate key because the data warehouse DBA must have the flexibility to respond to changing descriptions and abnormal conditions in the raw data. If the physical join key between dimension and fact tables is a direct derivation of a production key, the data warehouse DBA eventually will face an impossible situation. Production keys can be reused or reformatted, or the dimension value itself might be unknown. The most common need for a generalized key is when the data warehouse wants to track a revised dimensional description, and the production key has not been changed.

Almost every warehouse project we have worked with has immediately or eventually required at least one slowly changing dimension. In this chapter, we focus on the Type 2 slowly changing dimension, wherein a new dimension row is created for a substantive change in the dimension attributes. The Type 2 logic is the most complicated, but it also serves as the primary slowly changing dimension technique.

Dimension Table Extracts

In many cases, there is a customer master file or product master file that can serve as the single source for a dimension. In other cases, the raw data is a mixture of dimensional and fact data. For example, customer orders may include customer information, product information, and numeric facts from the detailed line items of the order.

Often, it's easiest to pull the current snapshots of the dimension tables in their entirety and let the transformation step deal with determining what has changed and how to handle it.

If the dimension tables are large, you must use the fact table technique, described later in this chapter, for identifying the changed record set. It can take a long time to look up each entry in a large dimension table, even if it hasn't changed from the existing entry.

There is often a paradox having to do with deleted items. Sometimes, an operational system will remove something from an active status by simply deleting it. Unfortunately, if there is no record there, we cannot pull it out in the extract. We may want to know about this deletion in the warehouse, so we can handle it appropriately, typically by marking it as inactive. It's rare to delete from the warehouse because we keep so much more history than operational systems do. Even if a product is not available today, we presumably sold some when it was available, and we need to be able to report that. Also, management will invariably want to know how many products have we deleted in the past five years. If they're not there, how will we know?

If possible, construct the extract to pull only rows that have changed. This is particularly easy and valuable if the source system maintains an indicator of the type of change. With such an indicator we can put new records in one file to be added to the dimension table without lookups. Updated records are placed in a second file that will undergo the slowly changing dimension process. If we don't know the change type, the entire results set of changed records goes through the slowly changing dimension process.

Processing Slowly Changing Dimensions

The data staging application must contain business rules to determine how to handle an attribute value that has changed from the value already stored in the data warehouse. If the revised description is determined to be a legitimate and reliable update to previous information, then the techniques of slowly changing dimensions must be used.

The first step in preparing a dimension record is to decide if we already have that record. The raw data will usually have a production key value, which must be matched to the same field in the "current" dimension record. Remember, the production key in the data warehouse dimension is an ordinary dimensional attribute and is not the dimension's surrogate key. If all the incoming dimensional information matches what we already have, then no further action is required. If the dimensional information has changed, we apply a Type 1, Type 2, or Type 3 change to the dimension. Recall the meaning of the types:

- **Type 1: Overwrite.**   We take the revised description in the raw data and overwrite the dimension table contents. For instance, we may receive a corrected customer address. In this case, overwriting is the right choice. Note that if the dimension table includes Type 2 change tracking, we should overwrite all existing records for that particular customer.

- **Type 2: Create a new dimension record.**   We copy the previous version of the dimension record and create a new dimension record with a new surrogate key. If there is not a previous version of the dimension record, we create a new one from scratch. We then update this record with the fields that have changed and add any other fields that are needed. For instance, we may receive a record of a transaction that changes a customer's marital state. If we believe this is an actual change rather than a correction, we should use this method. This is the main workhorse technique for handling occasional changes in a dimension record.

- **Type 3: Push down the changed value into an "old" attribute field.**   In this case we have anticipated that an attribute may experience "soft" changes that require a user to refer either to the old value of the attribute or the new value. For example, if a sales team is assigned to a newly named sales region, there may be a need to track the team both in the old region assignment as well as the new one.

Each dimension table will use one, two, or all three of these techniques to manage data changes. The most useful and most difficult to manage is Type 2. This is because you must create a new dimension row and a new surrogate key every time you encounter a changed dimension record. The only attributes in the new record that differ from the original record are the surrogate key and whichever fields triggered the changed description.

The lookup and key assignment logic for handling a changed dimension record during the extract process is shown in Figures 16.3 and 16.4. In Figure 16.3, an upstream process has identified the record as changed, so all we need to do is generate a new surrogate key from the key sequence and update the surrogate key lookup table.

In Figure 16.4, we have today's version of the entire dimension table, and must first determine which records have changed. Once we have the

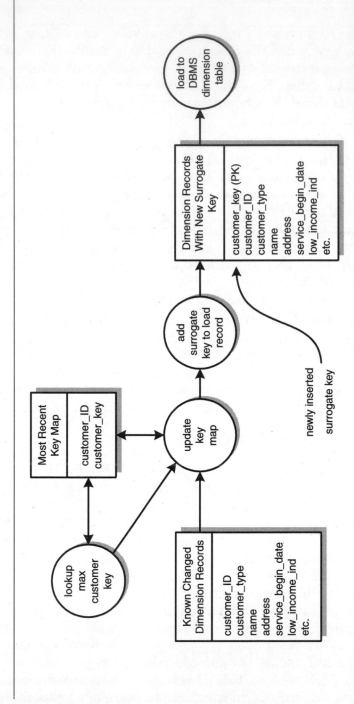

FIGURE 16.3 The lookup and key assignment logic for handling a changed dimension record when we know that the input represents only changed records.

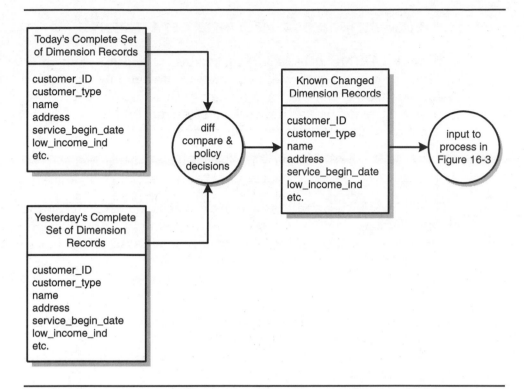

FIGURE 16.4   The logic for determining if an input dimension record has been changed.

changed records, the logic for handling the surrogate key is the same as the first scenario.

Slowly Changing Dimension Table Transformation and Load

Other than the slowly changing dimension processing, these dimensions are subject to the same transformations and loading techniques as other dimension tables. Very large dimensions share some characteristics with fact tables. You should examine the section on fact tables before finalizing the data staging design for a very large dimension.

Step 6. Populate Remaining Dimensions

At this point in the process, you should be able to populate the remaining dimensions with relative ease, unless there are major data quality

IMPLEMENTING YOUR OWN INSERT STATEMENTS

If your RDBMS does not support direct loading from an ODBC client, you can generate the "insert" statements directly in the spreadsheet. After you have set up all the dimension columns, construct a string using the worksheet string functions. The spreadsheet formula will look something like:

```
="insert into period (key, day_name, month_name)
values ('"&A1&"', '"&B1&"', '"&C1&"');"
```

This ugly thing will resolve to an executable INSERT statement, and you can copy and paste the entire table into the database in a few moments. The multiple quotes seem overwhelming, but you get the hang of it very quickly.

issues. Follow the logical steps outlined earlier for simple and slowly changing dimensions, as appropriate.

The Period table, which appears in virtually all data warehouses, is usually created "by hand." Because the Period table is so small—3,650 rows for a ten-year daily table—it is very easy to generate in a spreadsheet. An example Period table spreadsheet is included on the book's CD-ROM. Other dimensions that, like the Period table, are updated infrequently, may also be developed and maintained by hand, although a system as described in Step 4 is greatly preferable.

FACT TABLE LOADS AND WAREHOUSE OPERATIONS

Most warehouses grow too large to completely replace their central fact tables in a single load window, and even some of the dimension tables are too large to pull in all at once.

 It is much more efficient to incrementally load only the records that have been added or updated since the previous load. This is especially true in a journal-style system where history is never changed and only adjustments in the current period are allowed.

Some systems do not limit changes to the current period. Sales compensation systems, for example, can have significant changes to history (you may have seen some of those battles about who should get credit for which sale). You need to be able to identify those changed records and pull them out into the staging table.

Even with warehouses that start off with incremental loads, typically we begin with an initial population of some historical data.

Step 7. Historical Load of Atomic-Level Facts

Historic Fact Table Extracts

As you are identifying records that fall within the basic parameters of your extract, you need to make sure these records are useful for the data warehouse. Many transaction systems keep operational information in the source system that may not be interesting from a business point of view. These include entries to track intercompany transactions, accounting adjustments, amortized transactions, set up a new order, and so on. The business rules created during the design phase will help determine how each of these events is to be represented in the warehouse and which filters and sums should be applied during the extract as a result.

Determining and validating these rules can get unpleasant. Your extract has little chance of being right the first time. Business rules that were overlooked or forgotten during data analysis surface during the extract process. Tracking down these subtle differences requires skillful detective work and endless patience.

It's also a good idea to accumulate audit statistics during this step. As the extract creates the results set, it is often possible to capture various subtotals, totals, and row counts.

Audit Statistics

If the statistics haven't been captured yet, this step will make a pass through the data, resorting it if needed, and calculate the various numbers that were identified as useful for comparison. These numbers should tie backward to operational reports and forward to the results of the load process in the warehouse. They should be stored in the metadata catalog in a table or file created for this information.

The tie back to the operational system is important because it is what establishes the credibility of the warehouse. Pick a report from the operational system that is agreed on as the official definition of what is right: the authoritative source. If the results set doesn't tie back to the source, it's likely that something has changed in the business rules that has not been reflected in the extract. It is better to stop the process and check it out now. This is a good argument for including the extract as part of the source system's responsibilities. If they make substantive changes in the source, they may forget to pass that information on. On the other hand, if they own the extract process, they are more likely to roll any changes all the way through.

  The issue of having the warehouse tie back to the source system is controversial. In many cases, the data warehouse extract includes many business rules that have not been applied to the source systems. Also, differences in timing make it even more difficult to cross-foot the data. If it's not possible to tie the data back exactly, you need to be able to explain the differences. As a general rule, you should not agree to make your data warehouse automatically tie to the general ledger.

Fact Table Processing

Every data staging process must include a step for replacing the production IDs in the incoming fact table record with the data warehouse surrogate keys, for each dimension in the fact table. Other processing, computation, and restructuring may also be necessary.

Fact Table Surrogate Key Lookup

In the warehouse, Referential integrity (RI) means that for each foreign key in the fact table, an entry exists in the corresponding dimension table. Recall from Chapter 9, if you have a sale in the fact table for product number 323442, you need to have a product in the Product dimension table with the same number, or you won't know what you've sold. You have a sale for what appears to be a nonexistent product. Even worse, without the product number in the dimension, a user can easily construct a query that will omit this sale, without even realizing it. The disciplined and consistent use of surrogate keys means that your extract logic always does two kinds of surrogate key lookups. First, you must create a new surrogate key every time you encounter a changed dimension record and you wish to use slowly changing dimension technique Type 2. Recall that this is the main workhorse technique for handling occasional changes in a dimension record. You must create a new dimension record for the changed item and assign it a brand new surrogate key. The only attributes in this new record that are different from the original record are the surrogate key and whichever field or fields that triggered the changed description.

The second kind of surrogate key lookup occurs when the fact table records are being processed. Remember that to preserve referential integrity, we always complete our updating of the dimension records first. In that way, the dimension tables are always the legitimate source of primary keys. In this second kind of surrogate key lookup, we must replace the production keys in the fact table record with the proper current values of the surrogate keys. This processing is depicted in Figure 16.5.

In this case we could always use the actual dimension table as the source for the most current value of the surrogate key to use with each production key. Each time we need the current surrogate key, we would look up all the records with the production key equal to the desired value and then take the maximum value of the all the surrogate keys found. While this is logically correct, this approach is clearly inefficient. It is much faster to maintain a surrogate key lookup table that has exactly one record for each production key. These records contain the single current value of the surrogate key to use with the production key. If the fact records are sorted by the particular production key, then this lookup between the incoming fact record and the surrogate key lookup table can be accomplished with a single pass sort merge operation.

When all the fact table production keys have been replaced with surrogate keys, the fact record is ready to load. The keys in the fact table record have been chosen to be proper foreign keys to the respective dimension tables, and the fact table is guaranteed to have referential integrity with respect to the dimension tables. It is worthwhile, however, to be paranoid in this situation. All of the fancy administration we have described in this section sets up referential integrity prior to actual database loading. It is still very possible to destroy referential integrity by failing to load one or more of the dimension tables or by making other administrative mistakes, like deleting dimensional records when there are still fact records depending on the dimension key values.

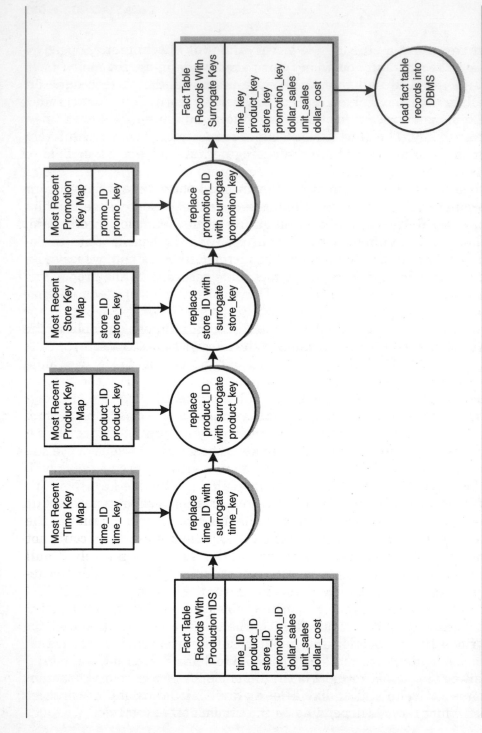

FIGURE 16.5 The processing of a fact table record showing how the production IDs are replaced with data warehouse surrogate keys.

An alternative approach, which works well when the staging application uses relational technology, is to maintain a current indicator in the dimension table and join between the fact staging table and the dimension table where the current indicator is "yes." A bitmapped index on the current indicator column really helps out here.

Note that you will need a separate process to perform surrogate key lookups if you ever need to reload history because you don't want to map the most current value to a historical event. In this case, you need to create logic to find the surrogate key that applied at the time the fact record was generated. This means finding the surrogate key where the fact transaction date is between the key's effective start date and end date.

When the fact table production keys have been replaced with surrogate keys, the fact record is ready to load. The keys in the fact table record have been chosen to be proper foreign keys, and the fact table is guaranteed to have referential integrity with respect to the dimension tables. Strictly speaking, it is not necessary to declare referential integrity between facts and dimensions, but we recommend doing so because every database otherwise develops integrity problems.

Null Fact Table Values

All major RDBMSs support a null value explicitly. In many source systems, however, the null value is represented by a special value of what should be a legitimate fact. Perhaps the special value of −1 is understood to represent null. Null dates are often represented by some agreed-upon date like January 1, 1900. (We hope you haven't been using January 1, 2000.)

Null values in data are tricky because philosophically there are at least two kinds of nulls. A null value in the data may mean that at the time of the measurement, the value literally did not exist and could not exist. In other words, any data value at all is wrong. Conversely, a null value in the data may mean that the measurement process failed to deliver the data, but the value certainly existed at some point. In this second case, you might argue that to use an estimate value would be better than to disqualify the fact record from analysis. As discussed shortly, this distinction is particularly important in data mining applications.

If you have ignored our repeated advice about surrogate keys and have designed a fact table that uses dates as foreign keys to the date dimension table, null dates will present a particular problem. There is not a good way to represent null dates in your fact table record. You cannot use a null-valued foreign key in the fact table because null in SQL is never equal to itself. In other words, you cannot use a null value in a join between a fact table and a dimension table. You should implement the join with an anonymous integer key and then have a special record in the dimension table to represent the null date.

Improving Fact Table Content

As we discussed in Chapter 5, all of the facts in the final fact table record must be expressed in the same grain. This means that there must be no facts representing totals for the year in a daily fact table or totals for some geography larger than the fact table grain. If your extract includes an interleaving of facts at different grains, the transformation process must eliminate these aggregations, or move them into the appropriate aggregate tables.

The fact record may contain derived facts, although in many cases it is more efficient to calculate derived facts in a view rather than in the physical table. For instance, a fact record that contains revenues and costs may want a fact representing net profit. It is very important that the net profit value be calculated correctly every time a user accesses it. If the data warehouse forces all users to access the data through a view, it would be fine to calculate the net profit in that view. If users are allowed to see the physical table, or if they often filter on net profit and thus you'd want to index it, precomputing it and storing it physically is preferable.

Similarly, if some facts need to be presented simultaneously with multiple units of measure, the same logic applies. If users access the data through a view, then the various versions of the facts can efficiently be calculated at access time. As we remarked in Chapter 6, this approach is nearly mandatory when we have several facts and several units of measure.

Data Restructuring

Improving the content of the data isn't the only fact table transformation that takes place in the staging area. Sometimes the structure also needs work: either denormalizing or renormalizing the database. In some cases, we denormalize to make the database more useful from a business point of view. A common example is a financial schema that has an amount type field in the source for the fact table, indicating whether the associated number is a budget, actual, or forecast amount.

In the warehouse, it usually is better to pivot those entries into separate columns, simplifying the calculation of variances. Although each database has a different syntax, the following SQL gives an example of how to accomplish this pivot on the RDBMS:

```
select account_num,
     sum(case when amt_type='actual' then trxn_amt else 0) as actual_amt,
     sum(case when amt_type='budget' then trxn_amt else 0) as budget_amt
from source_trxn_table
group by account_num;
```

Normalization is also common in the transformation process. In many legacy systems, the main data source is a large flat file that is used for report generation. These numbers are the "right" numbers, so this is the source to draw from. However, the file is usually completely denormalized, and a long history is usually the biggest casualty. Data get distributed across the row in buckets—there is one for each month the source system reports on. The transformation task here is to take that information and "unpivot" it from a single row into a period column and the associated amounts, with a row for each period.

Data Mining Transformations

Data mining has its own set of requirements beyond the business requirements you've gathered from the user community. Many of these are driven by the technical, statistical nature of the data mining process. For a full discussion of data mining, we encourage you to consult *Data Mining Techniques for Marketing, Sales, and Customer Support,* a wonderful book by Michael Berry and Gordon Linoff (Wiley 1997). Most of the techniques we discuss next are useful for a general data warehouse and imperative for data mining applications. If you know that data mining is in your future, even if it is not a Phase 1 application, you should consider making the investment now to develop these flags. Usually, the flags are hidden from the business user applications.

- **Flag normal, abnormal, out of bounds, or impossible facts.** Marking measured facts with special flags may be extremely helpful. Some measured facts may be correct but highly unusual. Perhaps these facts are based on a small sample or a special circumstance. Other facts may be present in the data but must be regarded as impossible or inexplicable. For each of these circumstances, it is better to mark the data with a status flag so that it can be constrained into or out of the analysis, rather than to delete the unusual value from the table. A good way to handle these cases is to create a special data status dimension for the fact record. You can use this dimension as a constraint and to describe the status of each fact.

- **Recognize random or noise values from context and mask out.** A special case of the preceding transformation is to recognize when the legacy system has supplied a random number rather than a real fact. This can happen when no value is meant to be delivered by the legacy system, but a number left over in a buffer has been passed down to the data warehouse. When this case can be recognized, the random number should be replaced with a null value. See the next transformation.

- **Apply a uniform treatment to null values.** As discussed earlier, data mining tools are sensitive to the distinction between "cannot exist" and "exists but is unknown." Some data mining professionals assign a most probable or median value in the second case, so that the rest of the fact table record can participate in the analysis. This could be done either in the original data by overwriting the null value with the estimated value, or it could be handled by a sophisticated data mining tool that knows how to process null data with various analysis options.

- **Flag fact records with changed status.** A helpful data transformation is to add a special status indicator to a fact table record to show that the status of that account (or customer or product or location) has just changed or is about to change. The status indicator is implemented as a status dimension in the star join design. This status can be combined with the status dimension that we illustrated in Figure 5.13. Useful statuses include New Customer, Customer Defaulted, Customer About to Cancel, or Changed Order. The Customer About to Cancel status is especially valuable because without this flag the only evidence that the customer canceled may be the absence of account records beginning the next billing period. Finding such an absence by noticing that records don't exist is impractical in most database applications.

- **Classify an individual record by one of its aggregates.** In some cases it may be desirable to identify the sale of a very specific product, such as a garment in a particular color and size combination or by one of the garment's aggregates, such as its brand. Using the detailed color or size description in this case might generate so much output in the market basket report that the correlation of the clothing brand with say, a shoe style, would be hard to see. One of the goals of using an aggregate label in this way is to produce reporting buckets that are statistically significant.

Beyond these general transformations for data mining, many of the tools and approaches require additional transformation steps before they can do their thing.

- **Divide data into training, test, and evaluation sets.** Almost all data mining applications require that the raw input data be separated into three groups. For example, the data could be separated randomly into three control groups, or it could be separated by time. The first data group is used for training the data mining tool. A clustering tool, a neural network tool, or a decision tree tool absorbs this first data set and establishes parameters from which future classifications and predictions can be made. The second data set is then used to test these parameters to see how well the model performs. Michael Berry and Gordon Linoff discuss an interesting problem in their book *Data Mining Techniques for Marketing, Sales, and Customer Support* (Wiley 1997) that occurs when the data mining tool has been trained too intensively on the first set. In this case the data is said to be "over-fitted" because it predicts results from the first data set too well and does poorly on the test data set. This is the reason to have a fresh second set of data for testing. When the data mining tool has been properly tuned on the first and second data sets, it is then applied to the third evaluation data set, where the clusters, classifications, and predictions coming from the tool are to be trusted and used.

- **Add computed fields as inputs or targets.** A data mining exercise can be greatly leveraged by letting the data mining tool operate on computed values as well as on base data. For instance, a computed field such as profit or customer satisfaction that represents the value of a set of customer transactions may be required as a target for the data mining tool to pick out the best customers, or to pick out behavior that you want to encourage. You may not have to modify your base schemas with these computed values if you can present the data mining tool with a view that contains these computed values. In other cases where the added information is too complicated to compute at query time in a view, you have to add the values to the base data itself before you can perform data mining.

- **Map continuous values into ranges.**   Some data mining tools, such as decision trees, encourage you to "band" continuous values into discrete ranges. You may be able to do this by joining your fact table to a little band values dimension table, but this may be an expensive join against millions or billions of unindexed numeric facts. In such a case, you may have to add a textual bucket fact or even a bucket dimension to your fact table if the fact in question is important enough to be used as a frequent data mining target.

- **Normalize values between 0 and 1.**   Neural network data mining tools usually require that all numeric values be mapped into a range of zero to one. Berry and Linoff warn that you should make your data range a little larger than the observed data for this normalization calculation so that you can accommodate new values that fall outside the actual data you have on hand in your training set.

- **Convert from textual to numeric or numeral category.**   Some data mining tools may only operate on numeric input. In these cases, discrete text values need to be assigned codes. You should do this only when the data mining tool is smart enough to treat such information categorically, and it does not infer an ordering or a magnitude to these numbers that is unwarranted. For instance, you can convert most locations in the United States into a zip code, but you cannot compute on the zip codes.

- **Emphasize the unusual case abnormally to drive recognition.**   Often a data mining tool is used to describe and recognize unusual cases. Perhaps you are looking for fraud in a series of sales transactions. The problem is that your training set data may not contain enough instances of the target fraud behavior to extract meaningful predictive indicators. In this case you may have to artificially replicate, or seed, the training data with the desired target patterns to make the data mining tool create a useful set of parameters.

Step 8. Incremental Fact Table Staging

Many fact tables become so large they simply cannot be loaded all at once. One of the most common techniques for reducing the length of the staging process is to load only data that is new or has changed.

Incremental Fact Table Extracts

In the ongoing extract process, you generally want to pull the new transactions that occurred since the last extract run. Figuring out what has occurred can be difficult. Transactions are represented in many different ways, and many systems have no need to keep the history of a transaction. Your challenge will be figuring out how the transaction process works and making sure you can get the information you need from it. The problem is, there are actually several types of transactions that occur, and each one has different implications for the warehouse.

- **New transactions.**   When a new order for six devices comes in on Day 1, it is entered into the transaction file with an order date of Day 1. This record will show up when our extract pulls all the records with an order date greater than 12:00 midnight from the night before and less than 12:00 midnight last night. What happens when the order gets changed tomorrow?

- **Updated transactions.**   On Day 2, the customer calls back and increases the order quantity from six to nine. Since our goal is to represent the business events as closely as possible (without making the system unusable), we want to reflect the fact that the customer ordered six devices on Day 1 and three on Day 2. Many legacy systems are *ledger-driven* and will generate a journal entry to reverse the original order of six and add a new order for nine, but keep the original order date. Rows in this source file are never updated; corrections or modifications are accomplished through reversal entries. Other systems generate a net change to the order of +3. In any case, we need to be able to define an extract that can pull what we want.

  A ledger-driven system allows us to develop an extract based on simple row-selection techniques using the transaction table. We select every row from the source system that has been added during the prior day (using the timestamp present in each row), and then extract associated rows from additional tables based on keys present in the transaction detail rows.

- **Database logs.**   In some cases, fields in the source system like update_date or order_date are not reliable or do not exist. In that case, you may need to turn to the database log files to identify what records actually changed during the target time period. Tools that generate database extracts using "change data capture" or "log traversal" techniques are sometimes necessary when no ledgered source system is available to support the business requirements. The log captures every change that occurs to a record. For example, during the span of an initial order entry, the order record can change dozens of times, and all those changes are logged. The first step after the changed records are identified is to collapse the logs into the net change for the day. In one case we know of, collapsing the log yields about a 15-to-1 reduction in the number of rows to be processed downstream. Most projects will collapse the logs on the source system to reduce the network load as the rows are moved to the staging area.

   It is possible to create a specialized log for the warehouse that records only changes of interest to the warehouse. This can be accomplished by adding a trigger to the transaction table of interest. Of course, this adds overhead to the source system, which is generally frowned upon.

   Extracts based on log techniques are more complex to develop and difficult to maintain. Log-based extract products are also highly specific to the version of the source DBMS. If the DBMS version is upgraded, there is no guarantee that the log-based extract tool will be available for the new version in time to meet the source system upgrade schedules. You definitely don't want your extracts to be the reason the operational systems can't upgrade.

- **Replication.**   Replication has several meanings depending on the database vendor or product involved. In a warehouse context, it may be used to create a copy of a table or of changed rows in the staging database during the day. This copy is then available to support the data staging process overnight.

   Replication is also very important when conformed dimensions that support multiple data marts have been created. When a new version of a conformed dimension has been prepared, it should be replicated nearly simultaneously to all the affected data marts. Increasingly, data warehouses are taking advantage of end-user query and reporting tools that can open connections to multiple database servers in the course of building a complex result. If such a tool manages to request data from data mart A with one version of the customer dimension and then requests data from data mart B with an incompatible version of the customer dimension, the result is likely to be wrong. Tracing the problem would be very difficult. The best way to avoid this situation is to replicate the conformed dimensions to all affected data marts simultaneously.

Incremental Fact Table Load

The physical process of loading the incremental fact table rows is the same as we have previously discussed. However, the successful data warehouse will inevitably face pressure to complete more processing in a smaller window. For smaller warehouses, it may take months or years to hit this wall, but for larger warehouses, it may happen before the first deployment.

Speeding Up the Load Cycle

Processing only changed increments is one way to speed up the data staging cycle. This section lists several additional techniques you may find valuable.

More Frequent Loading

Although it is a huge leap to move from a monthly or weekly process to a nightly one, it is an effective way to shorten the load window. Every nightly process involves 1/30 the data volume of a monthly one. Most data warehouses that we've worked with recently are on a nightly refresh process.

Partitioned Files and Indexes

As discussed in Chapter 15, high-end relational databases support partitioned files and partitioned indexes. Useful file partitioning allows a logical and physical segment of the file to be taken off-line and later restored. This should allow the DBA to split off an old segment of a fact table and place it on slower media, or even take it off-line for optional reloading if the data is requested.

Useful index partitioning is similar, and allows the DBA to drop an index on a portion of a large fact table so that bulk loading can occur at a very high rate. When the loading is done, the dropped portion of the index can be recomputed. This is usually far more efficient than dropping the index on the whole table or loading with the index intact.

Using partitions can greatly speed the data staging process, although it does require somewhat more intervention on the part of the DBA and a more complex data staging application.

Parallel Processing

One way to shorten the load time is to parallelize the data staging process. This can happen in two ways: multiple steps running in parallel and a single step running in parallel.

 There are good ways and bad ways to break processing into parallel steps. One very simple way to parallelize is to FTP all source files together, then load and transform the dimensions, and then check referential integrity between the fact table and all dimensions simultaneously. Unfortunately, such an approach is likely to be no faster—and possibly much slower— than the even simpler sequential approach, since each step launches parallel processes that compete for the same system resources such as network bandwidth, I/O, and memory. To structure parallel jobs well, then, you need to account not just for logically sequential steps but for system resources.

- **Multiple load steps.**   Divide the data staging job stream into several independent jobs submitted together. Think carefully about what goes into each job. The primary goal is to create jobs that are independent. If one load requires the results of another load before it can run successfully, the two loads should be sequential in the same job. An obvious example is the referential integrity check from the fact table to the dimensions: Obviously, the dimension processing must complete first.

    On the plus side, parallel processing can be very elegant and efficient. We know of a system that, for a few months before a larger server was purchased, spent 28 hours loading a day's worth of data. The staging process could manage such a feat and still keep up to date only because of very clever parallelization.

- **Parallel execution.** The database itself can also identify certain tasks it can execute in parallel. For example, creating an index can typically be parallelized across as many processors as are available on the machine. Each processor works on a chunk of the data, and the results are merged together at the end. Parallel indexing is especially easy if the table and index are partitioned. In this case, each index is independent of the others; no merging is required. This capability is a standard part of most mainstream databases today. Make sure your database can parallelize activities and that this feature is enabled. Monitor your jobs and see what happens.

Parallel Databases

Although it's expensive, you can use RAID1 to set up a three-way mirror configuration on two servers to maintain a continuous load data warehouse, with one server managing the loads and the second handling the queries. The maintenance window is reduced to a few minutes daily to swap the disks attached to each server.

Duplicate Tables

If your warehouse is small and you must provide nearly 24-hour availability, you can use the parallel tables technique, in which you keep two versions of the database available: one for loading and one for querying. At the end of a load cycle, the switch is nearly instantaneous.

This technique doesn't stretch the load window so much as make it less obvious that the load takes so long. It also has the benefit of buffering users from the load process so the warehouse operations team has time to review and verify the load before it is released to the public. The costs of this approach are retaining three copies of the tables at any given time and running loads and queries on the same server, potentially at the same time. With some middleware to provide indirection between user access tools and the database, it is not too difficult to modify the process described next and illustrated in Figure 16.6 so they run on two servers.

- **Step 0.** The active_fact1 table is active and queried by users.
- **Step 1.** The load_fact1 table starts off being identical to active_fact1. Load the incremental facts into the load_fact1 table. At the end of this step, load_fact1 table is the most up-to-date version of the fact1 table, but users do not yet access it.

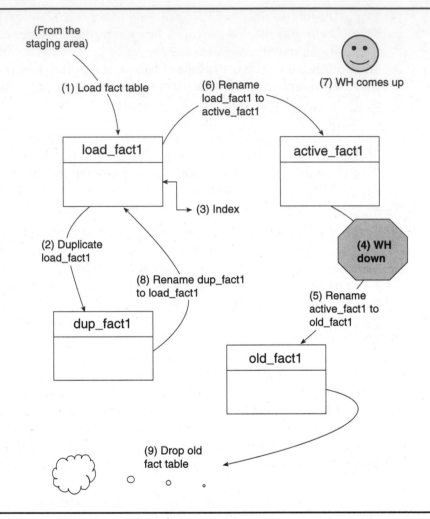

FIGURE 16.6   Duplicate table loading technique.

- **Step 2.** Prepare for the next load by duplicating load_fact1 into dup_fact1. You now have three copies of the fact table, which is the main reason this method is appropriate only for smaller warehouses. You need this third copy of the fact table only if your loads are incremental. Tomorrow's load will need a current version of the load_fact1 table to load into, so we make a copy of the table *after* this just-completed load. If your fact table is loaded via a complete re-fresh, you can skip Steps 2 and 9. You also need less disk space by the size of one copy of the table.

- **Step 3.** Index the load_fact1 table according to the final index list.
- **Step 4.** "Bring down" the warehouse, forbidding user access.
- **Step 5.** Rename the active_fact1 table to old_fact1. (Not every RDBMS can rename tables.) User applications should not be affected by this change. The rename may also be accomplished with synonyms.
- **Step 6.** Rename the load_fact1 table to active_fact1.
- **Step 7.** Open the warehouse to user activity. Total downtime: seconds!
- **Step 8.** Rename the dup_fact1 table to load_fact1. This step prepares the database for the next load cycle.
- **Step 9.** Drop the old_fact1 table.

We have seen this technique used with zero warehouse downtime by eliminating Steps 4 and 7. In this case, the DBMS allows existing queries against the old table to complete, while any new queries are directed to the new table. It should work—it does work—without forbidding access to the warehouse during the switch. However, we don't trust the database to handle this properly and, therefore, are too paranoid to recommend it unless absolutely necessary.

Step 9. Aggregate Table and MOLAP Loads

An aggregate table is *logically* easy to build. It's simply the results of a really big aggregate query, stored as a table. Not surprisingly, it's usually more difficult than that, but luckily, aggregate tables are often fairly easy to maintain.

The problem with building aggregate tables from a query on the fact table, of course, occurs when the fact table is just too big to process within the load window. Thus we see aggregate tables facing the same incremental versus full refresh choice as the base tables, for the same reason. Luckily, the incremental load file for the fact table is a good source for the aggregate table incremental load. An aggregate table that still includes daily data can easily be appended to, if the incremental fact load includes only the latest day's data.

Often, the aggregation is made over time, to the weekly or monthly level. There are two general cases:

- The aggregate table does not include the most recent month until the month has finished. In this case, define a monthly process that recomputes the latest month from the base fact table when the full month of data is in.
- The aggregate table keeps the current month as "month-to-date." In this case, define a nightly process that updates existing rows in the aggregate table for this month where they already exist and appends new rows where the key combination does not exist. Alternatively, you can delete the rows for the current month and recompute the month-to-date each night.

Matters start to get tricky when the incremental fact load includes reversals of earlier data. Sometimes these reversals come about because of a major change, such as sales region restructuring. In this case, you are probably best off rebuilding the aggregate table.

More troublesome are aggregate tables that see frequent, but smaller, reversals of data. These may result from the date key on the aggregate table being "out of synch" with the data as they flow into the warehouse. Consider, for example, an aggregate table that computes net sales as original sales minus returns, where returns can occur up to 90 days after the original sale.

The first point is that maybe you should redesign the aggregate table so that you don't have to solve this nasty problem. There may be a different aggregate table that delivers similar performance results but is much easier to maintain. If this aggregate table is a firm requirement, you will need to define an UPDATE/APPEND operation that backs out the reversals from the historical aggregate data.

Computation and Loading Techniques

Although it is very tempting to use the database, as described, to perform the aggregate computations, that approach can lead to difficulties. Those problems are related to our nemesis, running out of log or rollback space, discussed earlier. If you use the database to compute the aggregates, use the bulk load technique already presented.

A file utility like Syncsort can aggregate data rapidly. Additionally, some database products provide an ability to create aggregates within the bulk loader.

You will run into operational difficulties with complex aggregate tables that require UPDATEs or DELETEs unless your aggregate table is small. Yes, you will run out of log or rollback space. You should segment the table, isolating the current month in its own segment. Figure out a way to perform the appends and updates without logging. This will be either in the file system or by creating a staging table within the database using a "create table as select unrecoverable" operation that does not log. Drop the old segment (no logging!), and bulk-load the new one in. Doesn't that sound unpleasant? We can't sugarcoat it; it really is pretty ghastly. If you are faced with such a problem, you should be pressing staging tool vendors about their capabilities.

MOLAP Engines

We described the multidimensional OLAP (MOLAP) server and the multidimensional database systems in Chapter 10. These database engines are essentially aggregate processors that are based on dimensional design concepts. Individual vendors tend to change the terminology somewhat, but the underlying principles are the same regardless of whether the physical implementation is relational or MOLAP. Recall that our recommendation is to load the atomic level data, the lowest level of detail, into the data warehouse in a relational form. Any MOLAP-based data marts can be built from this atomic-level data warehouse. Drawing from this common source ensures consistent definitions and derivations.

The MOLAP cube design should match the atomic level warehouse data model. That is, the dimensions in the MOLAP cube should be built directly from the dimension tables in the base-level warehouse. This will make the data mart extract development easier and facilitate easier drill-through from the MOLAP data mart back to the atomic-level detail.

MOLAP engines typically compute their own aggregates. As a result, the loading process of the MOLAP cube can be time consuming. Many MOLAP engine providers are getting smarter about the aggregates they create, and they do not necessarily recompute the entire cube every night or create aggregates for every level in the hierarchy. If you plan to allow access to the atomic level only through a MOLAP drill-through link, it may not be necessary to keep aggregates in the base-level data warehouse. On the other hand, it may be possible to build the MOLAP cubes from the aggregate data, speeding the loading process significantly.

Step 10. Warehouse Operation and Automation

The ultimate warehouse operation would run the regular load processes in a lights-out manner, that is, completely unattended. While this is a difficult outcome to attain, it is possible to get close. Of course, you identified the operational functions you need for your warehouse in your architecture plans, didn't you? As a reminder, we'll list the typical operational functions again here, then offer a brief description of a few approaches to implementing them.

A good data staging tool should be able to perform these ongoing functions in an automated or semiautomated way.

Typical Operational Functions

The following list of operational functions comes from the technical architecture section in Chapter 9:

- Job definition—flows and dependencies
- Job scheduling—time and event based
- Monitoring
- Logging
- Exception handling
- Error handling
- Notification

For the warehouse to truly be a production system, you need to provide these capabilities in some form. They can be rudimentary at first, but you should plan to retrofit with more robust tools fairly soon. Nothing slows down warehouse progress faster than a creaky, failure-prone production process. The whole team can end up being diverted to monitor and patch the process, so new data sources are put on hold. Also, management begins to lose confidence because the problems are fairly public—they usually cause the data to be unavailable at the least opportune time.

Job Control Approaches

The options available to provide job control capabilities depends on the basic infrastructure of the warehouse, the experience base of the team, the complexity of the data staging process, and the funds available. Some sites we've worked with were built on mainframes by mainframe programmers, and rely on mainframe job scheduling tools. These are generally fairly cryptic to use, but they are robust and reliable. Other sites are UNIX oriented, and use UNIX-based tools ranging from CRONTAB to TP monitoring systems. Most of the data staging tools include a reasonable level of scheduling capability. Some even integrate with popular TP monitors so you can take advantage of the full range of capabilities. If you choose to patch together your own system, be sure you understand what it will take to make it scale. Think through how difficult it will be to maintain the system, make changes, and add new data sources. Make sure you have the resources to manage it.

Extract Metadata

Once the extract step has completed, the process needs to record several pieces of metadata. These items fall into the categories of managing or measuring the process.

Process Management

To keep the process moving, the extract step needs to notify the next process to start. The next step could be either the associated transformation process or another extract process that is dependent on the completion of the current process. We've seen a lot of creative ways to accomplish this, all involving some kind of monitoring process.

- **File existence.** In this case, the extract process doesn't need to do anything extra. Simply moving the file to the appropriate directory is enough to set the wheels in motion. A data staging monitor periodically checks the directory where the extract results set is deposited. Once the file appears, the data staging monitor fires up the transformation process, and off we go.
- **Flag set.** In this case, the extract process sets a flag (or writes a record) in the metadata catalog that indicates completion of the extract. A data staging process periodically checks the table for a record or checks the value of the flag. When it is correct, the data staging monitor fires up the transformation process, and off we go.
- **Built in.** If you are using a data staging tool, process management should be built in to the product.

Process Measurement

The extract step should also write out metadata about the extract itself. A simple version will write out the job name, batch ID, userid, start time, stop time, elapsed time (in minutes—calculating it once now saves the trouble of figuring out the formula every time you query the table), row count, success indicator, and, if available, CPU seconds, disk reads, disk writes, and cache hits. This information can also be recorded in an audit dimension attached to the fact table.

Operations Metadata

Metadata should play an active role in the warehouse operations. Any tool you buy should be metadata based, and any process you create yourself will be more flexible if you use metadata from the metadata catalog rather than hard-coding the process.

Typical Job Schedule

The following outline is the high-level job flow for a nightly load process. Each of these steps represents a load for potentially several tables:

- Extract dimensions and write out metadata
- Extract facts and write out metadata
- Process dimensions
    - Surrogate key/slowly changing processing/key lookup, etc.
    - Data quality checks—write out metadata
- Process facts
    - Surrogate key lookup—RI check—write out failed records
    - Process failed records
    - Data transformations
- Process aggregates
- Load dimensions before the fact table to enforce referential integrity
- Load facts
- Load aggregates
- Review load process—validate load against metadata
- Change pointers or switch instance for high uptime (24 × 7) or parallel load warehouses
- Extract, load and notify downstream data marts (and other systems)
- Update metadata as needed
- Write job metadata
- Review job logs, verify successful load cycle

DATA QUALITY AND CLEANSING

Data quality depends on a chain of events, many of which are outside the control of the warehouse team. To get quality data in the warehouse, the data gathering process must be well designed, and the resources— usually people—who enter that data must be committed to delivering quality information. These data gathering processes, however, are typically far removed from the warehouse team. As well, the warehouse project often begins with a load of historical data, which requires cleansing and quality control.

In an ongoing warehouse, clean data comes from two processes: entering clean data and cleaning up problems once the data are entered. As we discuss next, once the value of the data warehouse is established, it is easier to apply leverage to the source systems to modify their data entry processes to deliver better data.

It is unrealistic to expect any system to contain perfect data. Each implementation must define its own standards of acceptable data quality. In defining those standards, it's useful to understand the characteristics of quality data:

- **Accurate.** The data in the warehouse matches with the system of record. Insofar as the numbers are different, and sometimes they must be, you have a documented audit trail that explains the differences.

- **Complete.** The data in the warehouse represents the entire set of relevant data, and the users are notified of the scope. For example, a data element called Total Corporate Income should include the Medical division. If you don't have that division's data, rename the data element.

- **Consistent.** The data in the warehouse is free from contradiction. For example, aggregates are in synch with underlying detail.

- **Unique.** If two elements are the same, they should be called the same thing and given the same key value. For example, I.B.M. and IBM are the same company.

- **Timely.** Data must be updated on a schedule that is useful to the business users; that schedule must be published and adhered to. Any deviations must be posted.

In sum, quality data is "the truth, the whole truth, and nothing but the truth." Come as close as you can with the resources available and commit to full disclosure of uncertainties and deviations.

Data Improvement

The actual content of the data presents a substantial challenge to the warehouse. The data coming out of the operational systems is often surprisingly messy. Problems like the following are common:

- **Inconsistent or incorrect use of codes and special characters.** The Gender field might contain values like "M," "F," "m," "f," "y," "n," "u," and blank. It is common to find values that can't be right when you begin to explore the data.

- **A single field is used for unofficial or undocumented purposes.** Comment fields and extra address lines often contain information gold, but it's usually free-form entry and needs to be cleaned up.

- **Overloaded codes.** Many systems, especially older ones built in the days when saving bits was important, use a single code for multiple purposes. For example, "when the catalog is mailed to one of our existing customers, the code refers to their computed likelihood-to-purchase score; when the catalog is mailed to someone on a purchased list, the code refers to which vendor sold us the list." We're not making this up.

- **Evolving data.** Systems that have evolved over time may have old data and new data that use the same fields for different purposes or where the meaning of the codes have changed over time.

- **Missing, incorrect, or duplicate values.** Names and addresses are the classic example of this problem. Transaction systems do not need to collect information that is useful for business analysis to send out the invoices. In other words, the exact name of a customer isn't necessary, as long as the customer is not offended (it could be IBM or I.B.M., or Tom Jones or Thomas Jones). But they can end up looking like two different customers in the warehouse.

The historical responsibilities and incentive structures around the operational systems are at the root of this confusion. These systems were created to accomplish specific tasks, like take orders, ship products, and send out invoices. The name of the customer doesn't have to be exactly the same for them to successfully receive the product—the ABC company will still receive shipment with any of the spellings given previously. (This is not to say that correct spelling isn't important. There is another rumor in our little industry about a well-known actress who closed her sizable investment account when they couldn't spell her name right—Barbra with two *a*s.) If the orders are shipped and the invoices are sent out on time, nothing else matters—until the data warehouse project comes along.

Adding the data validation checks in the entry system can add unacceptable overhead to the transaction. In a job function where transactions per second is the sole measure of success, you have to be pretty persuasive to add to the transaction time. As we discuss next, fixing the source systems so they deliver accurate information is the right thing to do, but we advise you to choose your battles carefully and muster strong steering committee support for these initiatives.

Processing Names and Addresses

The customer name and address problem described earlier is a specific case of tracking identity information. We find the same problems when tracking physician and patient information, business customers, and even descriptive information about retail locations. The customer name and address example is representative.

Incoming name and address fields often are packed into a small number of generic fields like Address1, Address2, and Address3. Often, these fields are free form entry. They may have different spellings for the same entity (like ABC, A.B.C. Applied Bus. Concepts, etc.), or they may be omitted altogether. They could have the full name on one line, or two names, or the name and the first line of the address. We've done hundreds of queries that count transactions by customer name that show 10 to 20 alternative spellings on average. One of the data cleaning companies claims there are more than 120 different elements in the name and address area. In Chapter 5 we described a recommended verbose encoding of names and addresses. If you plan to use your customer information to drive your business, incoming names and addresses must be parsed, broken down into the elements, corrected, and completed. This specialized processing logic is available from a number of data extract tool providers. We provide a sample name and address parsing scheme in Chapter 5.

Once names and addresses have been cleaned and put into standardized formats, duplications are easier to eliminate. What appear to be two customers at first may turn out to be one. Perhaps one entry has a PO box address and the other has a street address, but the rest of the data clearly indicates that it is the same customer. In this case, the two records should be combined under a single surrogate key. (The trick here is to know which address to pick. That's where the data experts come in.) Any fact records that may exist with an invalidated key will have to be corrected to maintain referential integrity. A database system where referential integrity is enforced will not allow a dimension key to be deleted without first addressing the fact records.

At this point, the data should be fed back into the source systems to ensure consistency and reduce the company's error rate in its customer communications.

A more powerful form of eliminating duplication is householding. In this case, an *economic unit* consisting of several customers is linked under a single household identifier. The most common case would be husband and wife who have various single and joint accounts with various slight differences in name spellings and addresses. There are a number of vendors that specialize in householding tools.

Data cleaning may also check the spelling of an attribute or membership in a list. Once again, this is best accomplished by sorting the raw data and the permissible target values and processing them in a single comparison pass.

An Approach to Improving the Data

The following steps will help you deal with data cleaning issues:

- Where there are alternatives, identify the highest quality source system: the organization's system of record.
- Examine the source to see how bad it is. Our favorite, and rather low-tech, approach is to perform a frequency count on each attribute:

```
select my_attribute, count(*) from source_table
group by my_attribute order by 1;
```

- Upon scanning this list, you will immediately find minor variations in spelling. The attributes with low frequencies can be checked, by hand, if necessary, and corrected. Beyond that, tools exist to help comb through the data to derive the implicit business rules and identify problems.
- Raise problems with the steering committee. Data quality is a business problem, but the warehouse will suffer if the users believe the data is bad. They don't understand the difference between the warehouse and the source systems. All they know is the data in the warehouse is wrong. Clarify the magnitude of the problem and its source, but take care not to blindside the source systems folks in the process. Work with them to identify the causes and potential solutions, and include them in the presentation to the steering committee. They don't want to provide bad data—it just hasn't been their job to improve the data the business users are most interested in.
- Fix problems at the source if at all possible. The ideal solution is to work with source system groups to correct the causes of data problems. Fixing the data downstream does not solve the problem in the long run. You will create a complex set of rules that need to be watched and maintained to account for new oddities in the data. In fact, some problems should not be fixed in the warehouse. If the source system is assigning incorrect state codes, it needs to be fixed. Usually, the source systems group does not have the resources available immediately, so we agree to fix the data in the data staging process until the next release of the source system. Don't count on support from the source system folks. As we've said before, it's just not their job to provide this kind of information (yet).
- Fix some problems during data staging. For the problems you agree to fix, work with your business users to determine the appropriate business rules to clean these up in the transformation process. Often, there is a single pass during the initial load to clean up and align history with current data. Codes, descriptions, and IDs change when the business changes (or when the system runs out of new product numbers).
- Don't fix all the problems. Some problems will simply need to pass through the warehouse and out to the business users. This can help management understand the breadth and severity of the issue when they see spurious entries appearing on their reports. It can also shoot you in the foot. Make sure they understand the nature and source of these problems.

- Use data cleansing tools against the data, and use trusted sources for correct values like address.
- Work with the source system owners to help them institute regular examination and cleansing of the source systems.
- If it's politically feasible, make the source system team responsible for a clean extract. If they are on the hook for an extract of clean data, they may be more eager to revise the transaction system to fix the data problems.

Data Quality Assurance

Now that we have the data prepared and ready to load, let's stop and ask an interesting question. Is the data you are about to load correct? The basic data staging audit information tells us we have the right number of rows, and referential integrity checking tells us everything matches up. But how do we know if the contents are right?

Cross-Footing

To the extent that the data comes from a known source, it is possible to run several queries against the source system at different levels and compare the results with queries against the load set. This process can even be automated to save a log of the results of every run and set a "proceed" flag when the data matches or send an e-mail when the numbers are off by a certain amount.

If you are building a financial warehouse, make sure that assets = liabilities + equity and revenue – expense = profit. Accounting users are really fussy about that.

Manual Examination

In some cases, the data cannot be traced back to a single source system. It may be consolidated from several systems (or thousands in the case of a retail data warehouse). The only alternative here is to do some reasonableness checks. This involves looking for numbers that fall outside of acceptable ranges. Share changes or sales changes greater than ± 5 percent are likely to be data errors. Work with your business users and the source systems owners to create a solid set of data checks. In this case, the data may not be released to the users until the checks are complete.

Process Validation

The whole issue of how close is close enough is a slippery one. This is especially problematic during the initial transition to the warehouse. People are still getting information from two sources, and they want to know why they are different. The old numbers are considered to be the right numbers, mainly because they were there first. For the Finance group, the answer to the question of how close is clear—it usually has to be pretty close. For Marketing, exact figures usually aren't critical. For Sales, the numbers can be off, but only if they are high. In large companies, there are always exceptions and timing differences that cause the warehouse to be slightly different from the source systems at any given point in time. It is worth the effort to work with the Finance group to validate the extract process and the data in the data warehouse.

MISCELLANEOUS ISSUES

Several other items have big consequences for the reliability of the data staging process. This section describes a few we see on a regular basis.

Archiving in the Data Staging Area

An important function of the data staging area is to archive the data both in its most granular form as well as in all of its aggregated forms. This archived data serves a number of purposes. The data may be more granular or more complete than any of the downstream data marts. If this is true, then none of the data marts could logically maintain a complete archive. The end user groups may wish to return to the archive to access more data elements, or to process the final extract differently. Sometimes data is transformed for the purposes of data mining, and the data staging area may be the place to archive untransformed data.

The central data staging archive should also be able to help a data mart recover from data loss. This can relieve the data marts of much of its backup overhead.

Source System Rollback Segments

When extracting from a relational source, extracts that take a long time can be problematic. If an extract asks for all records updated in the last

24 hours, the system must locate the appropriate set of records. This means no other users can change the updated_date field while your request is being processed. As transactions flow in during your query, they are queued up in a separate place called a *rollback segment,* to be applied once your request is finished. If your query takes too long, this queue gets too large and runs out of space. The system then kills your job and processes the transactions that have been queued up. In general, the folks responsible for the transaction system don't like this kind of behavior.

Disk Space Management

One of the most common problems in the data staging process is running out of physical storage space in the middle of a staging cycle. This can happen at any time during the staging process and for several major reasons, only one of which is the availability of raw disk space. Most databases manage their own use of disk space because a database can span several disks. When a table is created, it is usually assigned to a certain logical space, usually called a *tablespace* or *segment*. It is also assigned parameters that determine the size of each growth increment, and the total number of increments it is allowed to have. So, a table can run out of space in the table space or use up its allotment of growth increments. It is important for the DBA to pay close attention to how much space is available, how much is used, what the typical increments are for the major tables, and so on. This should be a daily task. It is fairly straightforward to build reports against the system tables that will highlight potential trouble spots.

It is also possible to automate this process through clever use of the metadata in the database system tables. One of our customers has built an automated data staging environment that is entirely metadata driven. It builds the extracts, checks for room on the target system (and creates it if necessary), and loads the data, all based on about two dozen metadata tables. As a result, the size is always set up appropriately, and the reliability of the data staging process has improved significantly.

SUMMARY

The data staging application is one of the most difficult pieces of the data warehouse project. We have found that no matter how thorough our interviewing and analysis, there is nothing like working with real data to uncover data quality problems—some of which may be bad enough to force a redesign of the schema.

The extract logic is a challenging step. You need to work closely with the source system programmers to develop an extract process that generates quality data, does not place an unbearable burden on the transaction system, and can be incorporated into the flow of your automated data staging application.

Data transformation may sound mysterious, but hopefully at this point you realize that it's really fairly straightforward. We have tried to demystify the jargon around implementing dimensional designs, emphasizing the importance of using surrogate keys and describing in detail how to implement key assignment.

Data loading at its heart is quite simple: Always use the bulk loader. But, as with all aspects of data warehousing, there are many tricks and techniques that help minimize the load window.

Finally, we hope that the many ideas presented in this chapter have sparked your creativity for designing your data staging application. More than anything else, we want to leave you with the notion that there are very many ways to solve any problem. The most difficult problems require patience and perseverance—a willingness to keep bashing your head against the wall—but an elegant and efficient solution is its own reward. Be sure to consult the project plan spreadsheet at the end of this chapter for a summary of the tasks and responsibilities for data staging development (Figure 16.7).

KEY ROLES

Key roles for data staging development include the following:

- The data staging team is on the front line for this entire part of the project. The staging team must communicate clearly and often to the rest of the team. This not only keeps them informed about progress but makes it easy to solicit assistance when appropriate.
- The project manager must take a proactive role to partner closely with the data staging team. Often, the data staging team gets overwhelmed and buried in the details. The project manager must keep an eye on the big picture and intercede on their behalf.
- The quality assurance analysts and data stewards begin to take an active role during data staging development. The quality assurance processes need to be designed with their guidance. Also, as the data is loaded, it must be validated.
- The database administrator continues active involvement by setting up appropriate backup, recovery, and archival processes.

ESTIMATING CONSIDERATIONS

Much of the estimating for designing the data staging area has already been included in the physical design, which was the subject of the previous chapter. However, it is worth pointing out that the overall estimate of the effort of the data staging area is the single largest source of uncertainty and risk in planning a data warehouse. It is impossible to know how complex the data staging area needs to be until the programmer faces the actual data sources in microscopic detail. If a single data field is discovered that has been used for two purposes, the complexity of the data extract routines can double. An off-the-shelf tool may need to be augmented with custom hand-written code. Although many people tend to wince at the following guideline, we have found over the years that allocating six months of programming labor for each dimensional model turns out in the long run to be wise.

If the project is going to take nine months to finish, you are much better off estimating twelve months and beating the schedule by three months, than estimating six months and slipping by three months.

FIGURE 16.7 Project plan tasks and responsibilities for data staging development.

Column groups: Fans = Business End Users · Front Office = Business Sponsor, IS Sponsor, Business Driver · Coaches = Bus. Project Lead, Project Manager · Regular Line-Up = Bus. Sys. Analyst, Data Modeler, DW DBA, Data Staging Designer, DW Educator, E/U Appl. Devel. · Special Teams = Tech./Security Architect, Tech. Sppt. Specialists, Data Staging Programmer, Data Steward, DW QA Analyst

Project Task	Bus. End Users	Bus. Sponsor	IS Sponsor	Bus. Driver	Bus. Project Lead	Project Manager	Bus. Sys. Analyst	Data Modeler	DW DBA	Data Staging Designer	DW Educator	E/U Appl. Devel.	Tech./Security Architect	Tech. Sppt. Specialists	Data Staging Programmer	Data Steward	DW QA Analyst
DATA STAGING DESIGN & DEVELOPMENT																	
1 Design High-Level Staging Process										●					○		
2 Develop Detailed Staging Plan by Table										●					○		
3 Set Up Development Environment									●	○			○	○	○		
4 Define & Implement Staging Metadata								▸	▸	●					●		
5 Develop 1st Static Dimension Table Process (Extract, Transformation & Load)								▸	▸	○					●		
6 Develop 1st Dimension Maintenance Process								▸	▸	○					●		
7 Develop Remaining Dimension Table Processes								▸	▸	○					●		
8 Develop Fact Table Process (Extract, Transformation & Load)								▸	▸	○					●		
9 Develop Incremental Fact Table Process								▸	▸	○					●		
10 Design & Implement Data Cleansing							▸	▸	▸	●					●	○	○
11 Design and Develop Aggregation Process						▸	▸	▸	▸	●		▸			●		
12 Automate Entire Process						○				○					●		
13 Develop Data Quality Assurance Processes						○	○	○	○	○					○	○	●
14 Implement DB Administration (Archive, Backup & Recovery)						○			●	▸					▸		○
15 User Acceptance/Project Review	□	□	□		○	●	○	○	○	○	○	○	▲	▲	○	○	○
POPULATE & VALIDATE DATABASE																	
1 Set Up Production Environment									●				○	○			
2 Load Initial Test Data										○					●		
3 Initial Data Validation/Quality Assurance					○	○				○					○	○	●
4 Load Historical Data										○					●		
5 Perform Data Validation/Quality Assurance					○	○				○					○	○	●
6 User Acceptance/Project Review	□	□	○		●	○	○	○	○	○	○	○	▲	▲	○	○	○
PERFORMANCE TUNING																	
1 Set Up Benchmark Queries					○	○	○	○	●			●	○	○			
2 Review Indexing & Aggregation					○	○	○	○	●			○					
3 Review Tool Specific Tuning					○	○			○			●					
4 Conduct Ongoing Database Monitoring					□	□			●								
5 User Acceptance/Project Review	□	□	□		○	●	▲	▲	○	○	▲	○	▲	▲	▲	▲	▲

LEGEND:
- Primary Responsibility for the Task = ●
- Involved in the Task = ○
- Provides Input to the Task = ▸
- Informed Task Results = □
- Optional Involvement in the Task = ▲

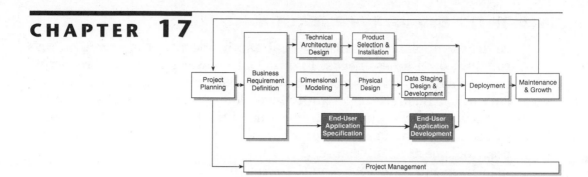

CHAPTER 17

Building End User Applications

At this point in our explanation of the Lifecycle, we climb out of the detailed back room issues of architecture and database design and development and move into the front room. The main front room development activity involves creating the starter set of canned reports we call *end user application templates*. This chapter is about the process of creating these application templates. It starts by defining the concept of the end user application and its role in providing access to business information. The bulk of the chapter provides a description of the process of creating these applications, divided in two major phases: specification and development. This is a very exciting point in the process because we finally get to see the business impact of all the design and development efforts that have occurred thus far.

This chapter is a must-read for the entire team. Because technical details are specific to individual products, this chapter is not technical in nature. It does provide the basics so that the whole team can communicate effectively. The task of relating the general end user application approach to a specific technology is the responsibility of the end user application developer.

ROLE OF THE END USER APPLICATION

End user applications fill a critical gap in meeting the organization's range of data access needs. Figure 17.1 shows the range of reporting needs from operational to strategic. Strategic reporting and analysis occurs at the business opportunity level: longer term in focus and ad hoc in nature. Operational reporting occurs at the tactical level; it has short-term impact, and is usually predefined. As we described in the data access tools section in Chapter 10, a large percentage of the warehouse user base will fall in between these two points.

To most business professionals, *ad hoc* is simply the ability to change the parameters on a report to create their own personalized version of that report. This need shows itself through statements like "I want this report, but by month rather than quarter," or "Can we see this report at the district level instead of region?" For many users, this is as ad hoc as they ever want to get. The end user applications provide the primary access tool for most of these business users.

Figure 17.1 also shows the value provided by end user applications. For power users, these canned reports provide a set of reporting and analysis examples. They can use these reports as a learning vehicle and take them apart to understand how to achieve certain results. Or, they can use the reports as a starting point and make incremental modifications rather than starting from scratch. These reports also serve as a quality-assured reference point for various measures of the business. If an ad hoc user can tie query results back to results from the end user applications, they can be reasonably certain that they are using the appropriate query logic. The value to the push-button user is a little different. To this group, the end user applications represent a low-cost (i.e., easy to use, short learning curve) means to get at the information in the data warehouse. The applications are typically more flexible and more current, in terms of how they view the business, than other alternatives. The organization overall gets value from the applications as well, because they provide an early delivery of information from the warehouse.

Another valuable aspect of end user applications is the role they play in helping to define an organization's official standard reports. Once the

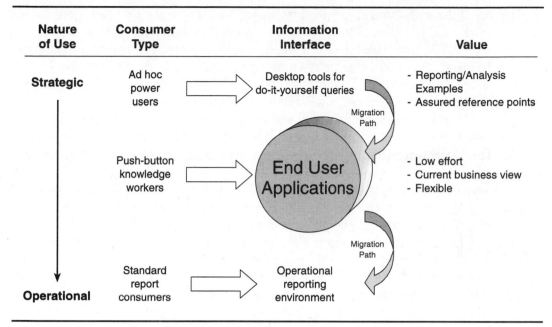

Nature of Use	Consumer Type	Information Interface	Value
Strategic	Ad hoc power users	Desktop tools for do-it-yourself queries	- Reporting/Analysis Examples - Assured reference points
	Push-button knowledge workers	End User Applications	- Low effort - Current business view - Flexible
Operational	Standard report consumers	Operational reporting environment	

FIGURE 17.1   The role of end user applications.

data warehouse is in place, reports usually begin as part of an ad hoc exploration process—business analysts use the warehouse to determine a new way of looking at the business. The most valuable, enlightening alternatives become end user applications, almost in a Darwinian fashion. Over time, this new way of looking at the world trickles down to the operational reporting systems so the business has a consistent way of measuring the business. The end user applications are development and test area for which reports will be useful to the business.

What Is an End User Application Template?

Now that we have told you why end user applications are so valuable, you are probably wondering just what these things are. An end user application template provides the layout and structure of a report that is driven by a set of parameters. The user sets the parameters from pick lists, or by accepting the defaults when they run the template. This parameter-driven approach allows users to generate dozens or potentially hundreds of similarly structured reports from a single template.

This may sound familiar to you. This is simply the new generation of the old 4GL-based menu-driven reporting systems that were built in the 1970s and 1980s. The differences: these modern reports are easier to build, the user interface is more graphical, and you do not have to deal with all the data management issues since the data warehouse is your starting point. Figure 17.2 shows a sample report template.

The user parameter for the geography dimension is a combination of constraints that will be used to select the desired geographic areas and then combine them for the purposes of this report. For example, this template could produce reports at the level of the Total Company, Eastern Region, Southeast District, and Southern Florida Zone—from the top of the hierarchy all the way down to the lowest level of detail. These different reports can be produced simply by changing the constraints on the geography dimension, with no changes to the structure of the template. Likewise, this could be a daily, monthly, or quarterly report based upon the constraints on the period dimension. A user can also flexibly define the previous period, perhaps as year ago or yesterday. This template produces a report by product line. Some constraints may be applied to limit the product lines to be included.

Through the use of drill-down capabilities, a user could produce reports on other product attributes. This action results in changing the actual template structure. Many data access tools provide this functionality transparently. By leveraging this functionality, a single template can produce even more reports.

\<Geography Name\>
Topline Performance Report

\<Period\> Compared to \<Previous Period\>

Product Line	Sales Units	YA Sales Units	Sales Index	Market Share	% Var Prev Share
XXXXXXXXXX	XXX,XXX	XXX,XXX	XX.X	XX.XX	X.X
XXXXXXXXXX	XXX,XXX	XXX,XXX	XX.X	XX.XX	X.X
XXXXXXXXXX	XXX,XXX	XXX,XXX	XX.X	XX.XX	X.X
XXXXXXXXXX	XXX,XXX	XXX,XXX	XX.X	XX.XX	X.X
XXXXXXXXXX	XXX,XXX	XXX,XXX	XX.X	XX.XX	X.X

FIGURE 17.2   Sample template for topline report.

APPLICATION MODELS: PLANNING, BUDGETING, FORECASTING, AND WHAT-IF

There is a separate class of application that requires both read and write access. These applications include planning, budgeting, forecasting, and what-if modeling. The data to start these applications is often fed from the data warehouse. The current sales information is used to begin the forecasting process. Projections are then developed to predict future sales. This can be as simple as taking prior sales increased by 3 percent, or it may involve intense statistical modeling. Once a forecast is developed, it needs to be stored somewhere. Often multiple versions are desired. These forecast versions can be included in the data warehouse. Separate fact tables must be set up to contain forecast information. After the forecast is stored back in the warehouse, the versions can be compared. When a final forecast is developed, that version is commonly compared with actual performance.

By storing this information in the data warehouse, we introduce a new capability: The users now are writing to the warehouse. This introduces the need for managed database updating of this process, including security and some kind of transaction monitoring. However, keep in mind that the volume of activity is generally much lower than most production operational systems.

Due to the read-and-write nature of this type of application, multiple technologies will be needed for development. Most data access tools provide only half of the functionality (read) and do not support write capabilities. Your data access functionality needs to be closely tied to another application to provide write capabilities. MOLAP tools excel in this area.

Lifecycle Timing

This chapter is a bit discontinuous because the end user application process actually occurs in two places in the Lifecycle. The templates should be specified just after the requirements are completed. Even with a great requirements findings document, a lot of information related to applications is stored only in the brains of the interview participants. It is important to capture this information immediately so that it is not lost. If you wait until you are ready to develop end user applications, the people who were involved in the requirements gathering process may be off on another project. Even if the same team is in place, a several month time lag between the completion of the requirements and application specification will mean a significant rediscovery effort.

Once the specifications are captured, you do not need to return to the application development process until much later in the Lifecycle. It does not make sense, and in fact, it is not really even possible, to begin end user application development until after the data access tool is selected, the initial database design is in place, and some of the initial data loads have been run.

Because of this difference in timing, we have split this chapter into specification and development sections.

APPLICATION SPECIFICATION

There are four major steps in the specification process: determine the initial template set, develop the navigation strategy, determine template standards, and develop detailed template specifications. You should at least get to the second step of determining the report set within a week or two of finishing the requirements phase.

Of course, the mandatory Step 0 is getting user involvement. Creating end user applications is a true software product development effort. You must get your customers involved in the specification process if you want to help solve their business problems. If you go off in the corner and design it by yourself, well, that would be like a software vendor designing their products without talking to their customers. Perhaps that's a bad example, but you know what we mean. Get users involved in reviewing the report list, setting priorities, and evaluating different navigation strategies. If people don't get it, if they don't think the reports are useful, or they can't find the one they want, they will not use it.

Determine the Initial Template Set

The first step in the specification process is to develop the target list of report templates. The goal is to end up with a small set (between 10 and 20) of high-value templates that provide a range of report types. The process to accomplish this involves three tasks: identifying report candidates, consolidating the candidate list, and setting priorities. We will examine each of these tasks in turn.

Identify Report Candidates

The requirement findings document and supporting notes, described in Chapter 4, are the ideal places to start. Each interview write up should have a list of potential reports to draw from. Approach this as a brainstorming process. Use a spreadsheet to make a list of individual report requests, one request per line. Include a name, the type of report, the row data elements, column data elements, and measures. A few additional attributes might help in the consolidation process. For example, list the groups or departments that would be interested in the report. Once you have a first pass of this list, get some users involved in a design session to review it. They should be able to add several more report candidates and help you clarify what you mean by some of the existing candidates.

Consolidate the Candidate List

Once the list is exhausted (or at least long enough), refocus the group on categorizing the list. Categorize according to the items in the spreadsheet—which data elements does each report contain in each section? These categories are the first pass at templates. Sometimes, categories quickly become apparent because of the way the group or the business views the world. It may be helpful to think about the types of analysis businesses typically perform. We have found the following analytical cycle concept to be a useful way to categorize reports.

Typical Analytical Cycle

While the specific issues that are to be addressed by a data warehouse vary widely from company to company, there is a common theme in how analyses are performed. This pattern of analysis is also consistent across many industries:

- **How's business?** The first and primary need for all businesses is to understand current performance. This provides an overall view of key business indicators and their variance over time. Examples include market share, percentage of company sales, required inventory, and minimum assets. The level of detail required depends upon who is asking the question. Senior executives are often interested in total corporate performance, while individual sales managers are concerned with their own sales area's performance. In either case, a single snapshot of performance is often the place to start.

■ **What are the trends?** Given a single-point-in-time view of performance, the next most common question is to determine whether it is an anomaly or a longer-term trend. Providing a look at those same key performance indicators over a period of time allows you to identify short- and long-term trends. The actual elapsed time needed to identify trends varies between industries. For example, phone sales campaigns usually last 30 to 60 days. In these instances, fluctuations that span several days may indicate a trend that requires action. On the other hand, it may take months to identify a trend in credit card payments.

■ **What's unusual?** Quick identification of exceptional situations is important. Identification of both good and bad situations is helpful. Rather than searching and drilling on lots of things to identify these interesting situations, a set of exception reports can be defined. These exception templates can focus on the key performance indicators that vary from the common or expected results. This is *not* data mining. However, data mining could be applied to the data to determine criteria that need to be monitored on an ongoing basis.

■ **What is driving those exceptions?** While it is interesting to identify situations with exceptional performance, it is more interesting to understand what is driving the exception. For example, 15 insurance agents may have opened 150 percent more claims than the highest number of claims they opened during the past 8 months. This is clearly an exception that should be identified. It is also important to note that a severe hail storm in their area caused a higher than normal influx of claims. However, without the causal information, these agents could have been flagged for fraud investigation.

■ **What if . . . ?** Based upon the findings in the data, the next step is to explore a variety of possible situations. What would happen if we increased the price per unit by $0.05? What would the sales dollars be? What is the gap between our products and our competitor's products? If we were left with more products to mark down, how much additional inventory would we have to liquidate? What happens to the overall profit if I can negotiate a 1/100 of a cent decrease in the cost of a major component? As you can see, a simple what-if question can generate many more questions.

- **Make a business decision.**   Now that you have studied the situation, a business decision can be made. Sometimes major decisions, such as restructuring the entire product pricing, are made. In many other cases, smaller decisions are made. A call can be made to a sales representative to compliment their performance or to another sales rep to review poor performance and develop a plan to improve it.

- **Implement the decision.**   One more step is required to complete the cycle: You have to implement the decision. What is required to put the decision into effect? For a pricing decision that impacts 15,000 items, what is required to set these prices in the cash registers across the country? The best situation would be to take the results from the decision support analysis and feed them directly into the operational systems. In the pricing scenario, the new prices could be fed into the current system that sends the prices down to the individual stores/cash registers. This then closes the loop.

This cycle never ends. Now that a decision has been implemented, the next thing is to see the impact of that decision. So, how's business?

Look for this type of pattern in your business as you decide what templates to provide to your users. Do not expect to be able to define templates to support every step in this cycle up front. While this is a common business pattern, in reality it can take months or years to grow your end user application portfolio into a full closed-loop decision-making environment. Today, most organizations provide end user applications that only go up to the point a business decision is made.

Prioritize the Template List

Once you have the list of templates, work with the users to assign a priority to each one. Remember, your goal is to identify a small number of templates that will serve as the starting point. The underlying business goal is to identify a set of templates that will help address the issues that are keeping the executives awake at night. Keep in mind that the initial templates are not intended to provide a total solution for your users. As the business people begin to use the system, they will find that some of the templates they thought they needed are not as useful as expected.

They will also begin to identify new templates that would be useful across the organization. Through use of the data warehouse, the template requirements will change. In fact, if there have been no requests to change the initial templates, it is likely that no one is using the warehouse.

If you can't actually rank them, at least try to split them up into three groups, the As, Bs, and Cs. Limit the A list to 15 or less, keep the B list handy for next iteration, and throw the C list away. The A list is what you plan to implement.

 Do not re-create the past. While it is useful to learn from existing report samples and reporting system structures, avoid the trap of re-creating existing reports if at all possible. This is usually a no-win situation for the warehouse. The new versions rarely match the old versions for reasons we describe later in the chapter, so lots of time and energy is wasted trying to reconcile the two, and users lose confidence in the warehouse. Worse, once you finally get the two sides to reconcile, you have accomplished very little from a business point of view: You have a set of reports that already existed. If you have to convert some reports to get rid of redundant systems, be sure you set expectations that they won't match. Also, do not think you can count this conversion as fulfilling your end user application requirements. We want to see something new and interesting out of the warehouse, not the same old, boring stuff.

Design the Template Navigation Approach

Although you are starting with only 15 or so templates, this will soon change. Over the next 12 months, you will add data from additional business processes with templates to go along with the new data. Also, users will develop new templates that you will want to make available to other users. If users create as many templates as the warehouse team, you will end up with around 100 templates in a year or so. Even with meaningful naming standards, it would be difficult to navigate a list of 100 templates. We need to devise a method for grouping and organizing these objects and templates. Should they be grouped by data content or by who uses them or by the business issue they address? There is no correct answer.

You must develop a strategy that will help your users find what they need quickly. Note that the template metadata can be extremely helpful in supporting this navigation. Make sure you capture it now so you can put it to work in the development process.

At this stage, we are creating a preliminary design for the navigation. Regardless of the tool, this basic business view of the report templates and how they relate to each other should not change. However, since so much of the navigation's implementation depends on the tool set, detailed navigation design will take place during the development phase. Figure 17.3 shows how a simple navigation could be documented.

Determine Template Standards

It makes sense to create a few standards for your templates once you have identified the initial set, but before you dive into the detailed specifications. We spend hours debating the name of each data element and setting up naming standards for the database, but most organizations completely overlook the need to develop standards for the data access environment. These standards cover areas like naming and formatting. They are particularly important in helping users quickly understand the nature of a report—its contents, sources, timing, and so on. Putting

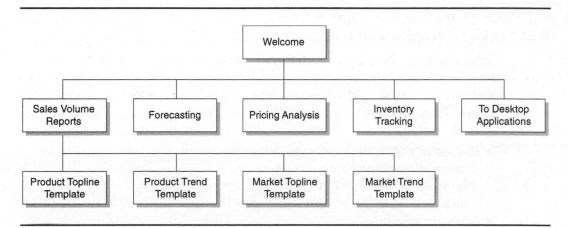

FIGURE 17.3   Template navigation diagram.

some thought into standards now will help you create a consistent set of specifications. These will then be easier to develop and roll out across many user groups. Of course, understand now that your standards will change. The tool you choose may not be able to implement the standards you have defined. (This isn't necessarily bad—there may be a better way to accomplish the same thing.) Be prepared to modify your standards as needed when you get to the development phase.

Naming and Placement of Objects

Naming templates is perhaps the most obvious area for the need for standards. When you name reports, consider including the type of report and type of data in the name. For example, the name Regional Claim Amount Paid Exceptions denotes that the template identifies exceptions based upon paid claim amounts by region. When possible, use your tool's metadata capabilities to provide users with a detailed description of the template from within the tool itself. Depending upon the data access tool, you may need to name multiple kinds of objects such as business measures, filters (constraints), and templates. Develop a consistent naming strategy for each object within the data access environment.

While full names are great, they can become unmanageable within the confined space of a computer screen or sheet of paper, so abbreviations can be helpful. Work with the business users to develop a glossary of acceptable abbreviations. Typical abbreviations include YA for year ago and YTD for year to date.

Output Look and Feel

All output created from the data warehouse is more useful across the organization if it has a common format. Users will quickly learn that the date the report was created can be found in a specific location. Determine now what should be in the report headers and footers. Typical information contained in a header or footer includes:

- Name of the data warehouse/mart
- Name of the template
- Name of the group or division creating the report
- Date and time the report was run
- Page numbers

Additional guidelines should be created for the location and content of report titles. It is also useful to include a list of the constraints that were used to create this report.

Detailed Template Specification

Now that you have determined the template grouping, navigation, and standards, you are ready to define the actual templates. Remember, *do not* define the 100 individual static reports that are to be generated for the users; the goal is to create between 10 and 20 templates for a given user community.

Each organization requires a different level of detail for project documentation. Honestly determine if your project team will formally document the application templates. If the answer is no, you still need to capture the thoughts and ideas generated during the requirements gathering process. Jot down your ideas and file them for future use. Do not completely skip this step even if you are not planning to get user sign-off.

Specification Format

There are two parts of an end user application specification: the definition and the layout. The definition provides basic information about the template, while the layout provides a visual representation of what a report would look like.

The template definition includes the name, description or purpose, frequency, parameters, user input, and default constraints. Unusual processing requirements should also be noted here. Figure 17.4 shows a sample template definition. Only business measures that have been defined as part of the dimensional modeling process should be included on any of the templates. If a new measure is identified for a template, simply add it to the fact table diagram as described in Chapter 7.

The end user application template layout is a sample of what the report would look like with data. The parameters that are provided as input are enclosed in square brackets [ ]. Figure 17.5 shows a sample template layout.

User Review

The template specifications should be compared to the final dimensional model prior to reviewing it with the users. Be sure you do not include elements in the application specifications that are not to be included in the

Template Name:	Product Performance Topline
Description/Purpose:	This template summarizes 4-, 12-, and 52-week unit volume and market share by brand for a specific geography. This provides a snapshot of the volume movement.
Frequency:	Weekly and as needed.
User Inputs:	—Geography: the user is required to select one or more geographies to be included in the report. If more than one geography is selected, the data on the report will be aggregated based upon the rules defined for each business measure. The default is the National total.
	—Current Ending Date: The user is required to select the date that the report will be based on. The default is the most recent date in the data warehouse.
Default Constraints:	This reports defaults to product category for the share calculation.
Calculations:	See Business Measure Worksheet
Notes:	

FIGURE 17.4   Sample end user application template definition.

initial data mart. Now, the template specifications can be reviewed with the users for their approval. These specifications will change when you get to the application development phase of the project, so *make sure* your users know that these specs simply represent a target set of templates to the best of your collective knowledge at this time.

When you review the specifications, be sure to remind the users that these represent a starter set of templates and that each one can generate many reports. They need to also understand that this is not the final and complete list of templates that will be developed. Advanced users will build additional applications and the starter set will be modified and enhanced.

END USER APPLICATION DEVELOPMENT

Now you are ready to begin developing the templates. The steps required for this phase of the Lifecycle are highly dependent upon each organization and the data access tool to be used. This section simply provides ideas about what should be considered. The application development process follows a standard software development flow. We start by selecting an implementation approach, then we do the actual development based on the specs and test, document, and release the product.

Product Performance Topline
4 Weeks Ending [Date]
[Geography]

Product Line	4 Week				12 Week				52 Week			
	Equiv Volume	% Chg YA	Share	+/- YA	Equiv Volume	% Chg YA	Share	+/- YA	Equiv Volume	% Chg YA	Share	+/- YA
Brand 1	xxx,xxx	xx.x	xx.x	x.x	xxx,xxx	xx.x	xx.x	x.x	xxx,xxx	xx.x	xx.x	x.x
Brand 2	xxx,xxx	xx.x	xx.x	x.x	xxx,xxx	xx.x	xx.x	x.x	xxx,xxx	xx.x	xx.x	x.x
Brand 3	xxx,xxx	xx.x	xx.x	x.x	xxx,xxx	xx.x	xx.x	x.x	xxx,xxx	xx.x	xx.x	x.x
Brand 4	xxx,xxx	xx.x	xx.x	x.x	xxx,xxx	xx.x	xx.x	x.x	xxx,xxx	xx.x	xx.x	x.x
Brand 5	xxx,xxx	xx.x	xx.x	x.x	xxx,xxx	xx.x	xx.x	x.x	xxx,xxx	xx.x	xx.x	x.x
Brand 6	xxx,xxx	xx.x	xx.x	x.x	xxx,xxx	xx.x	xx.x	x.x	xxx,xxx	xx.x	xx.x	x.x
Brand 7	xxx,xxx	xx.x	xx.x	x.x	xxx,xxx	xx.x	xx.x	x.x	xxx,xxx	xx.x	xx.x	x.x
etc.	xxx,xxx	xx.x	xx.x	x.x	xxx,xxx	xx.x	xx.x	x.x	xxx,xxx	xx.x	xx.x	x.x

FIGURE 17.5 Sample end user application template layout.

Keep in mind that some time will have passed since the application specification activities described in the last section occurred. The first thing to do at this point is to review the specifications that were developed earlier in the project. Update them to reflect any changes in the data that is going to be available in the data warehouse.

Select an Implementation Approach

The specifications we created earlier in the project were not necessarily based on your data access tool of choice, since that choice may not have been known at the time. The data access tools that are available today provide a wide array of delivery mechanisms. As you develop your end-user applications, you need to revisit the original specifications and the navigation structure. The primary issue at this point is to determine your fundamental approach to implementing these templates. The main alternatives are:

- **Web-based.** We believe this will be the primary delivery vehicle for end user applications. Through their own Web browsers, users can link to these reports via an intranet or the Internet right off the data warehouse home page, among other places. Using the Web has the added benefit of integrating the metadata into the navigation process. If you have stored the report metadata in the metadata catalog, it is possible to set up a few simple queries to allow users to search for reports by category, data element, report type, and so on. Once they find the report they want, the final link will invoke that report. The whole navigation structure is built into the metadata. Reports can easily belong to multiple categories, and changing the navigation structure is simply a matter of editing the metadata. Web-based development tools are taking over all aspects of user interface development. Many of the issues for the data warehouse are virtually the same as general Web site development.

- **Direct tool-based.** Simply develop a set of templates and provide them to the users directly using the standard data access tool interface. If your tool does not have a built-in, shared report repository capability, it is possible to create a simple file structure on the network to match the navigation path. This is not very flexible, but it is fast.

- **Tool-based executive interface.** Provide structured access to the templates via a series of screens. Many data access tools provide some form of EIS-like push-button front-end development capability. This approach uses these extensions to the data access tool to allow the user to easily navigate to their template of choice.

- **Custom-coded interface.** Many data access tools provide an API to allow you to develop your own interface, which then invokes the core tool functionality. This is a typical programming development effort using one of the visual development tools. Again, the interface provides the structured navigation to the appropriate templates.

Application Development

At this point, you know what you want to build, you have a set of standards to follow, and a basic approach. Finally, we can get started with the actual development. It may seem that we spend too much time on up-front planning, but our experience has shown that a little thought up front can save you days, or even weeks, of effort later.

Data Access Tool Metadata Definition

Before we can do anything, we have to get the data access tool set up properly. Most data access tools require that some metadata be defined prior to beginning template development. The richness and complexity of defining the metadata is highly tool dependent. At the low end, definition may simply be selecting tables to be used right out of the DBMS system tables and setting up default joins. At the high end, full business definitions, default drill paths, and common business measures must be predefined.

Once the data access tool metadata has been populated, the basic functions of the data access tool should be working. Test each attribute within each dimension to see if everything has been defined properly. If strange and unusual things happen, it may be because of the metadata definitions, but may also be the result of errors in the data.

Debugging metadata definitions requires a deep understanding of the tool metadata and the ability to look directly at the data in the tables. The data access tools perform many functions on your behalf based upon the metadata and the values in the tables.

Template and Navigation Development

Advances in technology over the past several years may make it possible to construct 10 templates in a day or two. This does not mean that the entire application development effort will be completed in a week!

Some applications are truly complex. Trying to figure out how to build some templates can take a lot of time. There may be additional product features that could accomplish what you need very quickly, but you could spend hours or days searching for them. To develop these advanced applications you may need assistance from the vendor or other resource highly skilled with that technology. It may be well worth the investment to hire a consultant who is highly experienced with this technology to work with you for several weeks. When you hire a consultant, look for someone with expertise using your tool. Check their experience and references. If they check out, request them by name in the contract. Such a consultant will be able to help you learn about real development using your tool that may not be captured in documentation or formal classroom education.

In addition to the templates, the end user navigation must also be developed. Again, this process is tied directly to the software that you are planning to use.

 You must have some test data to adequately develop the templates. The data access tools are driven by the data itself, and it is difficult, if not impossible, to determine if you are on the right track unless you are able to see data.

Prerun Report Selection

Another area that requires consideration is to determine which of the templates should be prerun on a scheduled basis. Templates combined with runtime parameters constitute an end user report. Standard reports can be set up as templates with predefined parameters. If there are five standard reports that all 150 end users look at first thing every morning, it makes sense to run these reports once and allow all the users to view the same result set. These reports may be run at a regularly scheduled time, or they may run as the result of an event such as completion of the data load process. The reports may be stored centrally and retrieved as requested by the users or automatically distributed to specified users.

The specifics of report distribution and management is highly dependent upon the capabilities of your data access tool. Many data access tools support report caching, where users simply retrieve the final report from a report repository. You need to consider the criteria for reports to be included in the scheduler and who is allowed to schedule reports to be run.

This is another area that may not be crystal clear with the initial release of your applications. As the users learn more about what they want and need from a business perspective, you can also learn about what they want and need from a systems perspective.

Testing and Data Verification

As in any successful software development effort, testing is a required step in creating application templates. First, check your logic. Create a simple query and copy the data for a report out into a spreadsheet and recreate the calculations by hand. Verify that your percentages and variances are based on the correct numbers. Change the parameters, and run it again. Run it on another computer, in another building. Enter garbage numbers for the parameters. Once you think it is perfect, have someone else test it.

Once you have confirmed that the tool is working correctly, it is time to take a look at the data itself. It is surprising how quickly data issues can be identified using today's data access tools. Some of the most common issues you are likely to find include:

- **Meaningless descriptions.**   Often the names and descriptions that are supplied by other systems were not designed for browsing and report labels. While it may seem like a good idea to use the existing names, once you see them in a pick list or as row and column headers, you may change your mind.

- **Duplicate dimension information.**   The data staging process should include checks to make sure that there are no duplicate keys. However, two different keys can come from the source data to represent the same thing. This is not obvious in the data staging process, but it will show up when you look at the data via the end user tool.

- **Incorrect dimensional relationships.**   Check to make sure that the correct information is pulled when drilling. Sometimes, the attributes within a dimension are not properly assigned. This causes unusual results when drilling.

- **Data not balancing.** Another data issue that comes up during application development is the inability to balance the data to another existing system. There can be several causes. One could be that the end user application is calculating a business measure differently. Another is that the facts themselves may not represent the same thing as in the legacy system. Finally, the facts should represent the same thing, but the values do not match. While this is often perceived as a data warehouse problem, in many cases we have found the data warehouse to be correct. It means that the existing system is wrong or not as accurate. This can be unsettling to users. Be prepared to conduct detailed sessions to describe why the data warehouse is correct.

The end user application developer must work closely with the data staging team to work through these issues. It is common to continue to identify more issues once the first one or two are corrected. This is simply because the deeper data issues cannot be seen until the initial ones are resolved. It can take several weeks to work through completely.

Document and Roll Out

Beyond the business-level documentation that should already be securely stored in the metadata catalog, it is vital to document the application template infrastructure information as well. This includes the naming standards, information about where the master templates are kept, and who the system owner is. The training materials described in Chapter 18 are also part of this documentation. The rest of the rollout process is described in Chapter 18.

Think Like a Software Development Manager

Throughout application development, testing, documenting, and rollout, it is very helpful to pretend to be a professional software development manager. Actually, it's not pretending. Real software development managers go through the same steps. The best software development managers have also learned some lessons:

- **The project is 25 percent done when your developer gives you the first demo of the working application.** The first demo from a proud developer is an important milestone that you should look forward to, but seasoned software development managers know that the developer has only passed the first *unit test.* The second 25 percent is making the application pass the complete *system test,* where all the units are working. The third 25 percent is validating and debugging the completed system in a *simulated production* environment. The final 25 percent is documenting and *delivering the system* into production.

- **Don't believe developers who say their code is so beautiful that it is self-documenting.**   Every developer must stay on the project long enough to deliver complete, readable, high-quality documentation.

- **Manage against a bug reporting database.**   A bug reporting database should be set up to capture every system crash, every incorrect result, and every suggestion. A manager should scan this database every day, assigning priorities to the new reports. An application cannot be released to the user community if there are any outstanding priority 1 bug reports that have not been fixed.

- **Be proactive if you collect bug reports from users and testers.** Acknowledge receipt of every reported bug, allow the users and testers to see what priority you have assigned to their reports and what the resolution status of their reports is, and then fix all the bugs.

- **Place a very high professional premium on testing and bug reporting.**   Establish bug-finding awards. Have senior management praise these efforts. Make sure that the application developers are patient with end users and testers.

Application Template Maintenance

Over time, you will need to keep the templates up-to-date. This includes the following kinds of activities:

- Adding new templates (from both users and the warehouse team)
- Updating templates to include new data sources or changes to existing sources
- Monitoring template performance
- Removing unused templates (look for a way to capture usage by template name in the database)

SUMMARY

End user application templates play a pivotal role in determining the organization's view of the warehouse. They can help show value quickly, lower the barrier to entry for most of the user community, and help advanced users by giving them examples of how to build more complex reports. It is important to capture the specifications for these reports soon after the completion of the requirement findings document while the information is still fresh in peoples' minds. The development process is fairly standard, except that it is typically based on the data access tool of choice and therefore subject to its idiosyncrasies. For a summary of the project plan tasks and reponsibilities for building end user applications, consult the spreadsheet at the end of the chapter (Figure 17.6).

KEY ROLES

Key roles for building end user applications include the following:

- The end user application developer is the primary driver of these tasks.
- The business systems analyst works closely with the end user application developer when developing the specifications and testing the applications.
- The data warehouse quality assurance analyst should also play a strong role in looking at the data via the applications and verifing the data and application accuracy.

ESTIMATING CONSIDERATIONS

End user application template specification and navigation design can take several weeks. It should start immediately following the requirements and be completed at the same time as the dimensional model.

End user application development may begin as soon as some test data is available in the database structures. In general, you should allow four to six weeks for the development of the templates. This includes time to debug the data staging process. There can be wide vari-

ESTIMATING CONSIDERATIONS (*Continued*)

ations on the development time, depending upon the end user data access tool itself.

Development of the structured navigation paths varies too widely for general guidelines. Work with people who have experience using the software you have selected to develop a realistic timeline for development.

TEMPLATES

The following templates for building end user applications can be found on the CD-ROM:

- Template 17.1 End User Template Definition
- Template 17.2 End User Template Layout

Project Task	Fans	Front Office			Coaches		Regular Line-Up						Special Teams				
	Business End Users	Business Sponsor	IS Sponsor	Business Driver	Bus. Project Lead	Project Manager	Bus. Sys. Analyst	Data Modeler	DW DBA	Data Staging Designer	DW Educator	E/U Appl Devel	Tech/Security Architect	Tech. Sppt Specialists	Data Staging Programmer	Data Steward	DW QA Analyst
END USER (E/U) APPLICATION SPECIFICATION																	
1 Identify & Prioritize Candidate Reports	▶				●	○	○	▶				●					
2 Design Template Navigation Approach					▶	○	▶	▶				●					
3 Develop E/U Application Standards					○	○	▶	▶				●					
4 Document Detailed Template Specifications					▶	○	○	▶				●					
5 Review End User Application Specs w/Users	○			□	●	○	○	○				●					
6 Revise End User Application Specs					▶	○	▶					●					
7 User Acceptance/Project Review	□	□	□	○	●	○	○	○	○	○	▲	○	▲	▲	○	○	▲
END USER (E/U) APPLICATION DEVELOPMENT																	
1 Select Implementation Approach	○				○	○	○	○				●					
2 Review Application Specifications	○				○	○	○	○				●					
3 Review Application Standards					○	○	○					●					
4 Populate E/U Tool Metadata					▶		▶	▶	▶	▶		●			▶	▶	
5 Develop E/U Applications							●	▶				●					
6 Provide Data Accuracy & Cleanliness Feedback					○	○	○			○		○			○	○	●
7 Develop E/U Template Navigation					▶		○					●					
8 Review w/Users	○				○	○	○					●					
9 Document E/U Applications					▶		○				●						
10 Develop E/U Application Maint. Procedures					○	○						●					
11 Develop E/U Application Release Procedures					○	○						●					
12 User Acceptance/Project Review	□	□	□	○	●	○	○	○	○	○	○	○	▲	▲	▲	▲	▲

LEGEND:	
Primary Responsibility for the Task =	●
Involved in the Task =	○
Provides Input to the Task =	▶
Informed Task Results =	□
Optional Involvement in the Task =	▲

FIGURE 17.6 Project plan tasks and responsibilities for building end user applications.

SECTION 5

Deployment and Growth

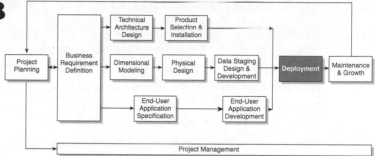

CHAPTER 18

Planning the Deployment

Hopefully, you haven't waited until the completion of your data warehouse development tasks to begin reading this chapter. Data warehouse deployment requires the coordination of numerous variables. You can't wait until two weeks before your promised delivery date to begin getting the puzzle pieces in place. It takes extensive planning. The project team needs to start preparing for the big event months before actual deployment is scheduled to occur.

Deployment is the convergence of technology, data, and applications on the business users' desks, along with the necessary education and user support structure. In this chapter, we'll first discuss deployment issues and considerations, and then provide you with a deployment release framework. Think of this chapter as a recipe for successful deployment, a list of deployment ingredients followed by procedural recommendations.

Project managers and deployment coordinators should read this chapter closely. Team members who will interact directly with the data warehouse users, including desktop administrators, educators, and user support representatives, will also find the material useful. Finally, project sponsors and drivers should be familiar with the overall coordination effort, as well as the deployment readiness checklist.

DETERMINE DESKTOP INSTALLATION READINESS

We discussed the overall technical architecture strategy in Chapter 8. Obviously, many components of your strategy will be implemented prior to deployment. Much of the back room architecture and infrastructure, such as the hardware platform, database management system, metadata catalog, and so on will be established long before deployment as it is needed for development activities.

 The technology that resides on the users' desktops is the last piece that must be put in place prior to deployment. Unfortunately, organizations often underestimate the effort and lead times required to implement the user-oriented components of their technical architecture.

The following checklist outlines the activities that should occur well before deployment to ensure that the appropriate desktop infrastructure is in place for your target business end users:

- Determine client configuration requirements to support end user data access software, including hardware configurations, database connections, intranet and Internet connectivity, and so on.
- Determine LAN addresses for the identified target users if you are not already using dynamically assigned LAN addresses.
- Conduct a physical audit of the technology currently installed on these users' desks and compare it to the stated client configuration requirements.
- Complete the contract and procurement process to acquire any necessary client hardware, software, and upgrades. Depending on the size of your organization, this acquisition process may take an inordinate amount of time. Desktop technology is typically the fiscal responsibility of the user business area, rather than the data warehouse team. Hopefully, the business area has budget funds available to cover any necessary purchases within the project timeframes. Be sure to allow adequate time for the approval and acquisition process because it will probably occur outside your immediate

organization and control. Also, be prepared for unanticipated lead times on client upgrade components.

- Acquire user logons and security approval as necessary for network and database access. Again, depending on your organization, you may be surprised by how much lead-time is required to obtain user logons and security authorizations. You will also need to consider ancillary procedures to comply with your corporate security policies, such as changing your database or UNIX passwords on a regular basis.
- Test installation procedures on a variety of machines. These procedures can be refined via the alpha and beta release processes discussed later in this chapter.
- Schedule the installation with the users to align with their data warehouse education.
- Install the desktop hardware and/or software and complete installation testing. It is important to fully test each installation to verify the user's existing system has not been adversely impacted and to ensure that the appropriate connectivities have been established or retained.

DEVELOP THE END USER EDUCATION STRATEGY

The education for business users differs significantly from the education described in Chapter 3 for the technical project team. Business users will receive less education than their technical counterparts, but their education must be well orchestrated. A robust education strategy for business end users is a prerequisite for data warehouse success. You may have built a very sophisticated architecture and loaded a massive amount of clean, legible data into your warehouse, but it may be for naught without the appropriate user education to leverage your work of art.

Integrate and Tailor Education Content

Education for your business users must address three key aspects of the data warehouse: data content, end user applications, and the data access tool. Business end users don't understand the boundaries between the tool, data, and applications in the warehouse, nor should they be expected to. To users, it's all the data warehouse, not a bunch of discrete components. Your education offering should reflect the same perspective.

Data warehouse teams are too often guilty of interpreting user education to mean end user data access tool training, and forget about the data content and application topics. Tool training is useless unless users understand which data is available, what it means, how to use it, and what to use it for.

As you might expect, sending your business users to generic vendor-provided data access tool training is not very effective, although it's the path of least resistance. Tool training in a classroom environment is definitely preferable to the read-the-manual approach, but it still leaves much room for improvement. Another alternative is to supplement vendor educational offerings with a customized education session on your data and application templates. This is certainly a step in the right direction, but it's still not the most efficient use of time for your business users. The optimal approach is to develop customized education that provides integrated training on the tool, data, and applications. While this is the most effective alternative, it may also be the most costly approach in the short term.

Even if it is tightly integrated, data warehouse education for your business users may be ineffective if it is not correlated to their anticipated type of usage. As you know, users are not homogenous. Each one brings a spectrum of previous experience, skill sets, and interest to bear on the data warehouse. You need to assess their general comfort levels with data, analysis, and technology as these will impact their education needs. At either end of the range, users will have already perhaps stratified into a push-button or advanced ad hoc user profile. Within a user profile class, your education needs to address the average end user.

 Ideally, your data warehouse curriculum should include an advanced techniques course aimed at your more analytical users about two to four months after deployment.

Finally, remember that you will have future opportunities to further educate the business users. You don't need to bombard them with everything they will ever need to know about the data warehouse all at once.

You should let them absorb the basics without overwhelming them with advanced topics initially.

Data Education Content

Data education should provide an overview of the structures, hierarchies, business rules, and definitions. The dimensional modeling techniques, presented in Chapter 7, embody effective graphics for communicating much of this information. A session on the browser for the business metadata in the metadata catalog would also be useful.

As you're making data available to business users, they will naturally compare the data coming from the data warehouse with data on existing reports. There are inevitably going to be situations where the information now available via the data warehouse does not match the information that was previously available to business users. Several factors may cause a discrepancy between data from the data warehouse and previously reported information:

- The data warehouse information is incorrect.
- The data warehouse information has a different or new business definition or meaning.
- The previously reported information was incorrect.

Obviously, the first scenario is to be avoided. Data errors must be corrected before your business users are given access to the warehouse. Data errors will immediately cause a loss of credibility for the data warehouse. The data quality and verification techniques described in Chapter 16 will help ensure that this doesn't happen.

The other two scenarios are very likely to occur with your data warehouse. Before deployment, the data warehouse team needs to identify, document, and communicate these data caveats and inconsistencies to the business users before they stumble across them on their own. Even though it requires some effort, it is much better to be proactive in these situations than to ignore them and hope no one notices.

End User Application Education Content

You will also want to review the prebuilt end user applications during your education offering. The business users should be introduced to the complete inventory of prebuilt end user applications. For each application, you should present the analytic usage or purpose, location or navigation aids and procedures required to initiate the application.

Develop the End User Education

Responsibility for business end user education development needs to be clearly defined up front. Often this responsibility resides within the business community; as described in Chapter 3, sometimes it is shared with the IS team, where IS has responsibility for the tool training and a business representative is responsible for the data and applications training. Figure 18.1 illustrates a sample end user class introductory outline.

The effort required to create an effective education program for the business users is often underestimated. It's also an activity that is frequently squeezed out of a project plan if the team begins to fall behind schedule.

A rule of thumb is that it takes one day to develop one hour of educational material. In other words, it's reasonable to assume that it would take eight days to develop and prepare the materials for a one-day training session, and perhaps even more for the first initiative. Since your ma-

---

End User One-Day Intro Course Outline

A. Introduction to Data Warehousing & Project Background

B. Interacting with the Data Warehouse
   — How to Get Started
   — Hands on Exploration of the Data Warehouse Web Site

C. Data Exploration and Navigation
   — About Your Dimensions
   — Hands on Exploration of Dimensions
   — About Your Facts
   — Hand on Exploration of Facts

D. End User Applications
   — About the Prebuilt Reports
   — How to Access the Report You Want
   — How to Use the Reports for Your Job

E. More Tool Techniques
   — Printing
   — Exporting to Word Processors & Spreadsheets
   — Manipulating Reports—Drilling, Graphing, Surfing, etc.

F. Open Forum
   — Apply What You've Learned to a Real Situation

FIGURE 18.1   Sample end user one-day introductory course outline.

terials are going to cover the available data and application templates, the data and application development efforts must be complete and stable before you can begin to construct education materials. Assuming a one-day training session, your data and application templates should be ready for deployment at least two weeks before the scheduled training date to allow time for course development and preparation. Obviously, the course developer must be knowledgeable about the data, the data access tool, and the prebuilt end user applications prior to creating the class.

 If you intend to educate a large user population, consider building a training database with a subset of the production data warehouse. This approach offers numerous advantages. First, query performance during the education courses will be much more predictable. Likewise, the production environment is isolated from unintentional student errors. Finally, the education exercises will return consistent results, rather than reflecting the latest update to your production data warehouse.

Deliver the End User Education

End user education should occur once all aspects of the deployment are ready to go. Optimally, the business users will return from training with the tools loaded on their desktop ready to access the appropriate data and application templates.

Formal education sessions typically have 10 to 12 business user attendees. This number is often driven by the number of computers available in a single training room. If possible, each student should have their own computer for training.

We suggest you recruit an administrator to handle the details and coordination. Reserving the training rooms, confirming user availability, ordering snacks, and so on is a big job. You will also need to allocate resources to preload the data access software and sample end-user applications and education materials on the training room desktops.

We have already discussed the need to allocate sufficient time to develop the materials once your data and applications are ready for deployment. You should also allocate time to prepare for the course. Teaching in a classroom environment is very much like public speaking.

Granted, the audience will probably be smaller, but the instructor is essentially "on stage" for the entire class. The people who are responsible for delivering education should be strong verbal communicators. They should have a solid understanding of all aspects of the data warehouse, including the tool, data, and applications. They should also be enthusiastic. Education is a key marketing opportunity for the data warehouse. You want users to return to their work environments, motivated to delve into the warehouse, without having unrealistic expectations. It can be challenging to find all these skills and traits in one person. Organizations often use teaching teams, especially in the early stages of the data warehouse. This approach also ensures that students' questions are more quickly answered, given the higher teacher-to-student ratio.

Conduct Education Only If the Warehouse Is Ready

We have worked with some data warehouse teams that intend to install their end user tool early and get the users trained so they have time to play with it. Playing with technology may be viewed as a perk for IS professionals, but most users have little desire to experiment with technology.

It is very important that the users receive their end user tool and education when they can productively use the data warehouse; providing access under any other circumstances is seldom successful and frequently detrimental. If the database still has serious flaws, the applications haven't been built yet, or the technology is not in place so that people can access the data warehouse from their desktops, then you are not ready to train the users yet—even if the training has been on their calendars for weeks. In general, it is better to postpone the training than to continue marching down the path knowing that deployment issues are lurking, although it requires substantial courage to make that tough call.

Establish "No Education—Then No Access" Policy

Inevitably, some users will be unable to attend your training session because of some unexpected business disaster or emergency. You should not let a business user access the data warehouse or associated applications without adequate training. Users' demands for data warehouse support will skyrocket without adequate training. In addition, users' frustration with the data warehouse will also soar. Rather than educating users in a formal class, you'll end up educating the users individually over time with your support staff. We recommend that you establish strict policies up front restricting access without appropriate education.

You should solicit the support of your business sponsor to enforce these policies and to reinforce the importance of education throughout the management ranks.

DEVELOP AN END USER SUPPORT STRATEGY

You will need to establish a strategy for supporting your business end users well in advance of deployment. User support strategies seem to vary by organization and culture, based largely on the expectations of senior business management, coupled with the realities of your data warehouse deliverables. Earlier in the project lifecycle, you conducted meetings with senior business management to better understand their expectations of users' direct interaction with the data warehouse. This feedback served as input for your data access tool and end user application template strategies. It comes into play once again here. If business management expects users to get their hands dirty and muck around in the data, the demands on the data warehouse support staff are reduced. On the other hand, if business management does not expect or want users to perform ad hoc analyses, a larger support staff will be required.

It is critical that you are in sync with business management regarding these expectations because they will drive decisions that impact both the development and deployment of your data warehouse. It is also important to know if there is consensus among your organization's business management regarding these staff expectations. Some business managers have a vision of direct user interaction, while others want data gophers to serve up information to their team. You should acknowledge these differences and plan accordingly.

Finally, it is important to get business management's commitment to reinforce their expectations with their teams. At times, it can be difficult to change the underlying culture regarding information analysis. We saw an organization where a new person at the top wanted to put information on users' desktops, but neglected to inform the users of these expectations. When they said "no thank you" to the data warehouse team, the new business manager backed down from his original course. This organization wasted work-months delivering to a target that moved once they got there. At the other end of the spectrum, we've worked with organizations that modified users' performance evaluation metrics in order to alter their attitude. As you can see, it is critical that the data warehouse team clearly understands the expectations of business management.

Determine the Support Organization Structure

After you deploy the data warehouse, questions from users will run the gamut from tool mechanics to data usage and meaning to application calculations and interpretations. The typical personal computer help desk will not be able to handle the full spectrum of potential user support questions. Some user questions, such as LAN connectivity issues, will fall within the realm of the help desk, but most will be data warehouse-specific.

 Although it is advantageous to have a single support number for users to call regardless of the problem or application, the users will probably tire of a two-step support process where they place a call to the hotline and receive a return call from someone who can really help them.

Typically, we see a tiered user support structure put into place. The first line of defense for user support is a resource that typically resides within the business area. These highly-accessible resources are often the business support analysts who have been involved with the data warehouse from its inception. They already have a good understanding of the data. We typically recommend that the business support analysts attend tool training early and participate in the development of the application templates. The initial data warehouse development efforts serve as further hands-on education for these user support teams. By the time their users attend data warehouse education, the business support analysts are highly proficient in the tool, data, and applications.

Complementing this decentralized team of experts, we typically see a centralized team of support resources. This central team handles the more global data warehouse maintenance responsibilities, as we'll discuss in further detail in Chapter 19. In addition, the centralized team typically serves as a second line of defense and provides a pool of advanced application development resources. There's an opportunity for career advancement and cross-pollination between the centralized and decentralized support teams.

A robust support team is essential for both the initial deployment and long-term viability of your data warehouse. The data warehouse user support resources require a unique set of skills as they must be business-, data-, and technology-savvy. In addition, they must be user-oriented, flexible, patient, and enjoy solving problems for others' benefit. Finally, they have a big impact on user perception and acceptance as they are one of the most visible aspects of the data warehouse.

This extensive skill set requirement makes the support team a difficult resource to both recruit and replace. To further complicate matters, resources in the user support role are often the "forgotten soldiers." Senior management may need to be reminded that the user support team has a huge impact on the organization's ability to use their data warehouse competitively. Your user support teams should be rewarded for their contribution. The organization should also invest in external education as appropriate for these individuals.

It is nearly impossible to provide general staffing guidelines for your centralized and decentralized support organizations because there are just too many variables to consider. It's difficult to even reach agreement regarding the basis for headcount—per user, location, data size, and so on. Any guidelines we could provide would be plus or minus 100 percent, so it is probably best to avoid mentioning any ballpark numbers.

Anticipate Data Reconciliation Support

As we discussed in Chapter 16, data quality verification and reconciliation should occur prior to any user access. However, it is possible that some data errors might slip through the net. As you define your support strategy, it is wise to earmark resources for data reconciliation shortly after deployment.

 Especially when previously reported information is found to be incorrect, it may require some digging to help the users fully comprehend the inaccuracies surrounding information that they had been using for years to run their business.

For example, it's quite possible that historical reporting was based on a series of flags tied to the customer, product, or account file. The logic behind the flag setting has probably become convoluted over time. We've worked on many projects where the historical reporting was incorrect due to error-prone data entry or misinterpretation of the flags within a report-writer module. Over the years, bonuses have been paid, product strategies implemented, and customer retention plans initiated on the basis of this erroneously reported information. It may take some doing to convince your users that they've been using faulty information to support management decision making in the past.

The resources assigned to data reconciliation require a broad set of skills. They will need access to both the data warehouse, as well as to the source systems or production reports. It is also helpful to have a solid understanding of the data transformation process.

Anticipate End User Application Support

The good news about modern data access tools is that end users can get the answers they need, but that does not mean that they generate the most efficient SQL possible to formulate their questions. In fact, users often create queries that are not efficient at all. It may be acceptable to have several inefficient queries developed and executed by individual users. It is unacceptable to allow those inefficient queries to be distributed across the entire user population. Hence, you need to develop a procedure to collect, test, polish, and release end user applications to the general users. It need not be as formal as that required for operational system maintenance, but there should be some guidelines.

The most common application release procedure is for users to submit their personal queries and templates to the support team. The end user application developer, who has been trained to understand the nuances of the technology, can then revise the application as needed to improve performance and ensure that standards, as described in Chapter 17, are followed. Once the end user application developer has polished the application and made it bullet-proof, the application can be released for use by the rest of the business community.

Establish Support Communication and Feedback

It is important to maintain an ongoing dialogue with the data warehouse business users. Communication with your users should, at minimum, consist of general informational and status updates. In addition, success stories can help motivate the more timid or skeptical users.

Inbound communication from your users regarding problems or enhancement requests is even more critical. Processes must be put in place to capture and respond to this user feedback. You need to acknowledge the request and act upon it as soon as possible. The worst thing would be if users stop communicating because they feel like no one is listening.

You should establish a formal tracking system, similar to the one designed for issue tracking that was described in Chapter 3, so that change requests and feedback flowing into multiple support people does not fall between the cracks. Alternatively, you can use the same system as the internal help desk for problem tracking.

Provide Support Documentation

Operational systems are often supported by reams of documentation. In the case of the data warehouse, we recommend that you document the warehouse, such as business definitions and metric calculations, within the warehouse. A data warehouse will evolve quickly. Although the user education materials provide limited system documentation and usage examples, more elaborate and expensive formal documentation will probably be obsolete before it has been distributed. Documentation is nearly worthless if it is not kept current.

At a minimum, we suggest leveraging the documentation capabilities of your end user data access tool by linking into the metadata catalog for detailed attribute descriptions. You should also develop and maintain a listing of your end user applications with a brief description and usage guidelines.

Create a Data Warehouse Web Site

Data warehouse support documentation is often made available via Web pages on your organization's intranet. The Web is an excellent tool for enhanced user communication and support. Figure 18.2 illustrates a sample data warehouse Web site map. This sample site provides both access to the data in the warehouse as well as information about the warehouse. The sample site is organized as follows:

- **Standard Reports and Analysis.** Documentation on the available standard reports and structured navigation to locate and access these reports is included here.
- **Learn About the Warehouse.** This is the central location for reference information about the warehouse. It should include:
  - *Data Warehouse Overview*. Brief overview of the data warehouse project's who, what, when, why, and how.
  - *About the Data*. High-level introduction to the content of the data warehouse. Detailed information is provided through direct links to the metadata catalog.

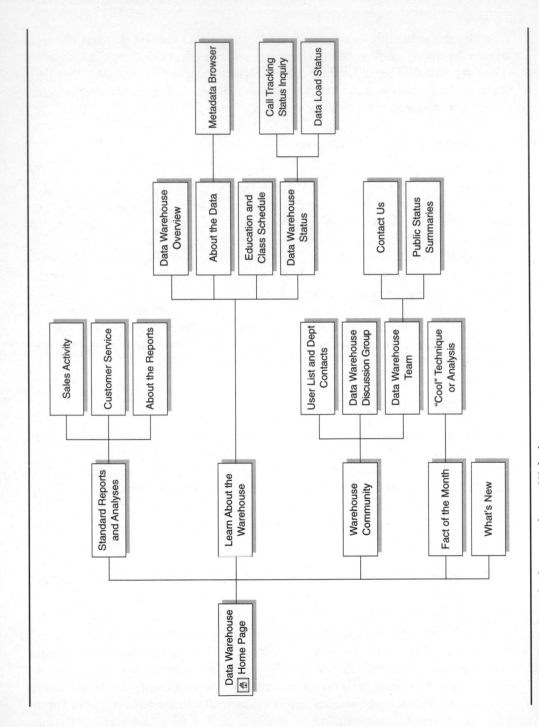

FIGURE 18.2 Sample data warehouse Web site.

- *Education and Class Schedule.* Highlights the data warehouse's education catalog and schedule. On-line registration may also be supported.
- *Data Warehouse Status.* Pertinent details might include the date and status of the most recent data load and number of data feeds included (e.g., number of stores reporting). New dimension records added with the most recent load might be identified. In this site, users can also view the status of any problem or enhancement requests they've submitted.

- **Warehouse Community.**   These pages provide a listing of the data warehouse project team members and their roles so users know who to contact. There may be a similar listing of data warehouse users to encourage collaboration. This site also may include an on-line discussion group.

- **Fact of the Month.**   As success is realized through use of the warehouse, key analyses can be shared here. This page highlights a new, interesting application of the data warehouse each month. The highlighted analyses can then be shared and leveraged across the organization, spawning user creativity and cross-organizational synergy.

- **What's New.**   Quick reference for changes to the data warehouse Web pages.

DEVELOP THE DEPLOYMENT RELEASE FRAMEWORK

Now that we understand the pieces that must converge for a successful deployment, it is helpful to think about deployment within an overall framework. The process used to deploy your data warehouse should be strikingly similar to the process used to deploy a new commercial software package. With a software program, releases are defined for development based on requirements (in theory, at least). The new software release goes through an internal alpha test period, followed by a beta period with a limited number of clients, and then it is finally made generally available.

You can use this same release framework to deploy your data warehouse. Releases are defined for the data warehouse. Every major change to the data warehouse, consisting of new data and/or application content or new groups of users, should be considered a release. As with a new software release, data warehouse releases should go through the same rigors of alpha and beta testing prior to general availability and rollout. Although the initial release of the data warehouse will be the most labor-intensive to deploy, each subsequent release needs to go through the same structured deployment planning process. Let's further define these data warehouse release steps.

Alpha Release

The alpha period is the data warehouse team's first opportunity to conduct an end-to-end system test. Unfortunately, data warehouse teams often interpret their target data warehouse delivery date to mean the first time they deliver data into their data warehouse environment. However, rather than reaching the target goal line, they're really not even ready be at the start of their alpha test period. At this point, the team has probably completed less than half of the work required to deploy this release of the data warehouse.

The goal of the alpha test period is to internally test all the components of the data warehouse developed thus far, including the technical infrastructure, extract and load processes, data quality procedures, performance tuning, application templates, and education materials. Alpha testing is typically an iterative process. The alpha period should not conclude until the team is confident in the quality of the data warehouse, especially concerning the data and application templates. As you define your alpha test period, be sure to allow enough time to correct any problems encountered along the way.

The alpha team typically consists of core data warehouse team members. It may also include specific business representatives, such as business support analysts, if they are tasked with data quality assurance, end user application template development, or education development.

Beta Release

During the beta period, a limited number of business users are given access to the data warehouse. The beta period is sometimes referred to as the *pilot*, but we avoid that terminology given the multitude of definitions. We believe that every major data warehouse release should go through the rigors of a beta period, not just the initial deployment.

The goal of the beta test period is to conduct an end-to-end user test of the variables described earlier in this chapter and to work out any remaining glitches. The beta period should confirm the readiness of the data warehouse release for a more general release to your user population. Variables to be tested include:

- Desktop hardware and software installation
- Data quality and completeness
- End user application quality and business relevance
- End user ad hoc query performance
- Education materials and procedures
- Support infrastructure and user communication and change request procedures
- Ability of the data warehouse to provide meaningful insights into the compelling business requirements

You may need to impose an unnatural structure and discipline during the beta period to ensure that these variables are adequately tested. The data warehouse team should also use the beta period to verify the necessary back-room operational processes before the user population expands, including back-up and archiving procedures, disaster recovery, stress testing, and performance monitoring, as described in Chapter 16.

Beta Team

The beta team consists of key business user representatives who are committed to active participation in this test period with full knowledge of all that can (and probably will) go wrong. We typically limit the beta team to between 10 and 15 users. If you work with fewer beta users, the release may not be tested adequately. If you recruit too many beta users, you've essentially skipped the beta period and gone directly to full availability.

There are several characteristics that you should look for in a beta team candidate, including:

- **Management support.**   The manager of beta team members needs to understand that participating in the beta will consume significant energy. You need management's commitment that the beta will receive a top priority from their perspective.
- **Availability.**   Unfortunately, the star performers are often asked to take on more than should be asked of any one person. Beta team candidates shouldn't already be juggling two jobs and several special

task force assignments. Such candidates are already too overloaded to seriously participate in a data warehouse beta test.

- **Motivation.** Beta users should be excited about the data warehouse initiative in general. Optimally, they're motivated to get their hands on the first cut to make the final deliverable even better.

- **Flexibility.** The beta team must be willing and able to deal with a less than perfect world. They shouldn't object to being guinea pigs.

- **Organizational respect.** Beta users often become the early, informal ambassadors for the data warehouse. The beta team members should be well-respected by the user community. They'll be the first to find valuable business insights in the data to support more effective decision making.

Production Release (a.k.a. Deployment)

The production release, or deployment, of your data warehouse is somewhat analogous to general availability for a software product. As with a software general availability release, your data warehouse must be bug-free and well-supported to be viable in the long term.

General availability is something of a misnomer when applied to the data warehouse. If you hope to deliver a data warehouse content release to 200 people, you can't provide access to all of them at once. We suggest that you identify groups of 10 to 12 users who will be deployed in a single iteration or wave. This is a very manageable number and it approximates the number of people that can be trained at once.

We recommend that you allow several weeks between iterations of a release to various groups of product users. This time lag will allow adequate time for training and initial support for each group of users. It also allows time for the deployment team to learn from the early waves and make any minor course adjustments before the next deployment wave. For this reason, you should allow extra time between the first couple of waves.

Your production users for a given release may come from multiple business areas, locations, etc. In terms of sequencing the rollout to these users, geographic location seems to be the most important variable, although politics runs a close second. Obviously, if your users are in disparate locations, you will want to deploy to all the users in each location at once. You don't want to make multiple trips to a remote office for software installation and user education.

We suggest identifying a team within the data warehouse project team to focus on deployment. These people will operate like a SWAT team that is focused on deployment-related issues. The team will probably consist of the user education resources and several user support representatives. The team should also include someone with technical depth to deal with any desktop infrastructure issues, such as ODBC connection failures.

Assess Deployment Readiness

An optimum deployment might be described as one where the user attends data warehouse education and then returns to their desk the next day with access to accurate data and application templates and readily accessible support if they run into any problems. This convergence of events will not happen by itself.

We encourage you to assess your deployment readiness critically using the following checklist. Deployment of your data warehouse release should be delayed if you are unable to emphatically respond positively to any items on the checklist. It is much wiser to postpone than to attempt deployment when you're not ready. Deployment is somewhat analogous to serving an elaborate holiday meal. Everything should come together as your family is sitting down for dinner—the table must be set, the entree and side dishes ready at the same time, and the dessert prepared and waiting in the kitchen. Your guests would certainly prefer having dinner delayed by a half an hour to being seated on schedule and served food that's only partially cooked.

Deployment Readiness Checklist

Desktop installation:

- Necessary technology in place for business end-user access to data warehouse.
- User logons and security authorizations obtained.

Data quality verification and reconciliation:

- Data quality assurance testing performed (per the guidelines established in Chapter 16).

- Inconsistencies with historically reported data investigated, resolved and documented.
- Beta team business representative signed off on data legibility, completeness, and quality.

End user applications:

- End user applications developed and tested (as recommended in Chapter 17).
- Beta team business representative signed off on application template quality and business relevance.

End user education:

- Introductory business user education materials developed on data content, application templates, and data access tool usage.
- Beta team business representatives signed off on introductory user education offering.
- Education delivery logistics (e.g., venue, projection capabilities, user PCs with necessary data and application access, education materials duplication, etc.) handled.
- Production end users registered for education with appropriate approval from their managers.

End user support:

- Support organization in place and thoroughly trained.
- Support communication, bug report, and change request tracking procedures tested during beta period.

DOCUMENT YOUR DEPLOYMENT STRATEGY

As you plan your deployment, you're putting stakes in the ground regarding each of the variables we have discussed in this chapter. We recommend that you document your strategies as they are being developed within the team and reviewed with your business and IS management and project sponsors. Like any good planning document, the deployment strategy document should have an owner who will facilitate a regular review and update, rather than allowing it to stagnate on someone's book shelf.

SUMMARY

Successful deployment of the data warehouse requires thoughtful planning and coordination prior to the completion of development efforts. Key areas to consider include desktop installation, integrated user education, and support. Most importantly, your deployment readiness should be critically assessed. Deployment must be delayed if your project is not absolutely ready for prime time. For a summary of the project plan tasks and responsibilities for planning the deployment, consult the speadsheet at the end of this chapter (Figure 18.3).

KEY ROLES

Keys roles for planning the deployment include:

- The data warehouse educator responsibilities are front and center now with the development of end user education courses.
- The project manager and business project lead determine the structure and staffing of the end user support organization, based on direction and feedback from management and the project sponsors.
- Special teams' players play a pivotal role during deployment. Hardware and software acquisition, installation, and testing must be accommodated.

ESTIMATING CONSIDERATIONS

Planning for deployment should occur in a relatively short period of time. A core group needs to be convened for working sessions to establish the strategies outlined in this chapter. You should allow time for presentation of these preliminary strategies to the appropriate business and IS management and sponsors, and modification as necessary.

Completing the tasks to then prepare for deployment will vary greatly depending on the strategy you choose to pursue in each area of your deployment plan.

Appropriate lead times for desktop upgrades, installations, and associated security must be considered during deployment planning.

It typically takes one day to develop one hour of educational material. In other words, count on eight days to develop a one-day training session. Course development requires access to complete and stable data and end user applications.

In general, approximately four to eight weeks should be allocated for the combined alpha and beta periods to allow time for iterative testing and correction of any problems identified.

Project Task	Fans	Front Office			Coaches		Regular Line-Up						Special Teams				
	Business End Users	Business Sponsor	IS Sponsor	Business Driver	Bus. Project Lead	Project Manager	Bus. Sys. Analyst	Data Modeler	DW DBA	Data Staging Designer	DW Educator	E/U Appl Devel	Tech/Security Architect	Tech. Sppt Specialists	Data Staging Programmer	Data Steward	DW QA Analyst
DEPLOYMENT PLANNING																	
1 Develop Desktop Infrastructure Checklist						○						▶	●	▶			
2 Develop Initial User Education Strategy	▶		□	●		○	○	○			●	○				○	○
3 Define User Support Strategy			□	●		○					□	○	□				
4 Define Release Plan			○	●		●	▶	▶	▶	▶	▶	▶	▶	▶	▶	▶	▶
5 Review Deployment Strategies & Release Plan	□	□	□	○	●	●	○	○	○	○	○	○	○	○	○	○	○
6 Develop User Course Materials	▶				▶	▶	▶	▶			●	▶					
7 Develop Support Procedures					●	●	○	○	○	○		○				○	
8 User Acceptance/Project Review	□	□	□	□	●	○	○	○	○	○	○	○	▲	▲	○	○	○
COMPLETE SYSTEM TEST																	
1 Run Complete Data Staging Process						○			●	●					●		
2 Perform Standard QA Procedures					○	○			○	○		○			○	○	●
3 Run Core End User Applications					○	○	○					●					
4 Review Overall Process					○	●	○	○	○	○	○	○	○	○	○	○	○
5 User Acceptance/Project Review	□	□	□	○	●	○	○	○	○	○	○	○	○	○	○	○	○
DEPLOYMENT (Alpha, beta & production iterations)																	
1 Assess Deployment Readiness					●	●											
2 Configure & Test Desktop Infrastructure													○		●		
3 Set Up Security Privileges						○			○			○	●	○			
4 Educate Users	○				○	○	○	▲			●	○					
5 User Acceptance/Project Review	□	□	□	○	●	○	○	○	○	○	○	○	○	○	○	○	○

LEGEND:	
Primary Responsibility for the Task =	●
Involved in the Task =	○
Provides Input to the Task =	▶
Informed Task Results =	□
Optional Involvement in the Task =	▲

FIGURE 18.3 Project plan tasks and responsibilities for planning the deployment.

CHAPTER 19

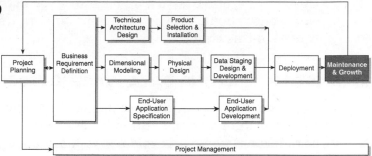

Maintaining and Growing the Data Warehouse

Congratulations, you've successfully deployed your first data warehouse deliverable. However, there's no time for a two-week hiatus yet. Your efforts to date will be an exercise in futility if you don't focus a similar effort on maintaining and growing your data warehouse. The key difference is that business users are now accessing the data warehouse. They're inevitably demanding more from the data warehouse team, while at the same time motivating the team with stories of improved decision making.

We laid the groundwork for this stage of your data warehouse with many of the recommendations of Chapter 18. This chapter expands on those concepts. It is divided into two sections: maintaining your existing data warehouse environment and then preparing for its growth and evolution.

Project managers should read this chapter very closely. Business and IS management and sponsors should also read it to understand the effort required to fully reap the benefits of your data warehouse initiative. Finally, other team members involved in the ongoing support of the warehouse should also become familiar with the recommendations presented in this chapter.

MANAGE THE EXISTING DATA WAREHOUSE ENVIRONMENT

As we enter the maintenance stage, once again the data warehouse requires an approach that differs from traditional operational systems. In a traditional systems development effort, deployment signals a hand-off from the development team to the maintenance organization. However, a data warehouse is never really finished. Ongoing care and feeding of the warehouse simply can't be turned over to a separate maintenance organization while the data warehouse team moves on to tackle the next implementation.

This no-end-in-sight phenomena has a big impact on the investment required to maintain your data warehouse. You need to ensure that there will be adequate funding for dedicated data warehouse maintenance resources beyond the initial construction phase. The maintenance activities described in this chapter are nonnegotiable; they must be performed if you expect a return on your original investment. As a general rule, it takes 50 percent of the development resources to provide ongoing maintenance for a steady-state warehouse, assuming no additional users or data sources. Typically, there is no decline in ongoing needs; therefore, management must be willing to commit to this level of re-

DIAGNOSING THE DYSFUNCTIONAL DATA WAREHOUSE

The reader should be aware that the recommendations presented in this chapter are based on the assumption that your data warehouse is heavily used and warrants the investment in additional resources to maintain it. But what if that's not the case? What do you do if your users aren't jumping on the data warehouse bandwagon? This symptom often points to more serious underlying problems. Take the following data warehouse self-check test. If you're unable to respond affirmatively to these questions, you should refer to the

appropriate project lifecycle chapter and perform resuscitative measures.

- Is the project sponsored by an influential business executive? Does this executive feel strongly about using information to support decision making, or is he or she just jumping on the latest bandwagon? Is this individual still with your organization in a relevant position, or has he or she departed since initially supporting the data warehouse project?
- Does the data warehouse team understand the business user requirements? Do the business users believe the data warehouse team understands what they're trying to accomplish?
- Is the data organized to support business requirements, or is it organized to support operational concerns, like streamlining the extraction process or minimizing disk space requirements? Can business users understand the dimensional model, or are they forced to confront a large number of tables in the initial data mart?
- Were users' analytical requirements given consideration during the data access tool selection process?
- Is the data accurate? Does it match current operational reporting? If not, does the data warehouse team thoroughly understand the data inconsistencies and have they informed the end users?
- Is the data refreshed in a timely manner?
- Is the database properly tuned, or do users typically launch a query and hope it's completed by the time they return from lunch?
- Has the data warehouse team constructed application templates to jump-start the users' analysis?
- Have the business users received basic training on the data, application templates, and data access tools?
- Do the users know what the data means and where it comes from? Do they have access to table and column definitions and what typical values should be?
- Do the business users know who to call if they're having problems with the data warehouse? Does anyone respond to their calls in a timely manner?

sources for the foreseeable future. This represents a drastic change from operational system development projects—don't be surprised if you need to deliver this message to management several times before it sticks.

Focus on Business Users

It's nearly impossible to achieve success with your data warehouse if business users aren't using it. You need to focus attention on the business community first and foremost.

Continue to Support Business Users

The first couple of weeks following users' initial education and deployment are pivotal. You need to maintain the excitement and momentum established during their initial exposure to the data warehouse. With customer service in general, it's more important to maintain an existing customer than it is to recruit a new one. The same could be said of your data warehouse customers. You simply can't afford to have a business user who is dissatisfied with the data warehouse. They'll tell a friend, and before you know it, the data warehouse will have a terrible reputation within the business community.

To avoid this scenario, make sure the support resources described in Chapter 18 are available shortly after the initial training for one-on-one hand-holding. Don't wait for the users to call you—you should go to them before they have a chance to run into a wall of frustration. Also, they will be more likely to admit that they didn't understand something from the formal training sessions if you're working with them independently. These one-on-one sessions can also serve as remedial education for some users.

As we've stressed the importance of the first couple of weeks following deployment, it's also important that the support organization be accessible on an ongoing basis. Users should feel comfortable going to their decentralized expert or business support analyst, as described in Chapter 18, with questions about data, analysis, and tools. This support staff should champion the efforts of the key business drivers within the organization who are likely to have an early breakthrough or business insight from the data warehouse.

One-on-one support sessions with business users, or house calls, should also continue to be provided indefinitely. If you're unable to provide dedicated on-site resources to a team of business users, you might consider setting up a "Doctor Is In" program for user support. Office hours are established so that users know when they can drop in for "urgent care."

The centralized user support organization should be focusing their attention on the decentralized support resources. The decentralized experts or business support analysts are essentially the central data warehouse team's eyes and ears on the street. They'll have keen insight about what's working, what's not, and why. The centralized team should try to make the decentralized tier as productive as possible as this will reflect positively on the data warehouse in general.

Everything we've said so far assumes that your original support strategy continues to make sense given your organizational culture, user skill sets, support resources, and so on. Are the users digging into the data on their own, or are they reluctant to get their hands dirty and want a "data gopher" staff to do the digging for them? We encourage you to reassess your original support strategy about a month or two following deployment. Question whether the original assumptions still make sense or if there needs to be a midcourse adjustment. If the strategy isn't working, design the appropriate changes, get management buy-in, document it in your deployment strategy document, and implement accordingly.

Continue to Educate Business Users

We outlined a basic education strategy for deployment in Chapter 18. When considering longer-term user education, you should think of it as an overall data warehouse curriculum. The following ongoing education options are often neglected:

- **Advanced education.**   There should be an advanced class to satisfy user demands after they have mastered the basics. It should be conducted approximately six to eight weeks following the introductory offering. If you don't offer an advanced class, you'll end up disseminating the advanced concepts to users one at a time through the support organization. A formal advanced class is probably much more efficient and effective.

- **Refresher education.**   Some users may need a refresher course on the data warehouse. They may have attended the introductory class but need a review of the material. The refresher course may offer content similar to the introductory class but at an accelerated pace.

- **New hire education.**   There should be an on-going program to train new hires. Depending on the rate of new hiring, such a training program should be offered at least twice per year.

 You'll need to offer the introductory education program periodically to meet the needs of new hires. We strongly encourage you to continue enforcing a strict access policy: No one is allowed access to the data warehouse unless they have completed introductory training.

- **Regularly scheduled education seminars.**   Some organizations establish a regular forum, perhaps an internal user group meeting and/or quarterly brown bag lunch series, to answer questions, demonstrate new capabilities, present tips and techniques, etc. For example, you could conduct a seminar on strategies for testing your complex ad hoc queries.

  These sessions are typically sponsored by the data warehouse user support or education resources, although you may be able to recruit business users or support analysts who are willing to share tips. Consultants with your end-user tool vendors may welcome the opportunity to present query and application development techniques, although this may not be a free service. The educational material from these sessions should be documented in a data warehouse tip sheet so that it's not missed by those who couldn't attend the session. In addition, the tip sheet provides reference documentation.

- **Newsletter.**   The data warehouse support team often publishes a periodic newsletter that contains project updates, tips and techniques, success stories, and so on.

- **Web site.**   Finally, as we mentioned earlier, many projects have begun using a Web site as a centralized repository for educational materials, tip sheets, frequently asked questions (FAQs), data warehouse load status updates, and on-line tutorials.

Manage Data Warehouse Operations

Gone are the days when you could make multiple attempts to get the data loaded and indexed. In all likelihood, your data warehouse will quickly become a mission-critical application.

Your users will expect the most current information to be rapidly loaded into the data warehouse and accessible to them. Mission-critical status puts a greater burden on the data warehouse operations organization to maintain the technical infrastructure, database management system, and data and metadata management processes. This added burden will also stretch the existing experience and knowledge base of your data warehouse operations team. It's important that you continue to invest in your operations team by providing them with ongoing education and new tools to help them perform their jobs efficiently.

Manage the Technical Infrastructure

The maintenance of your technical infrastructure is one of the few areas where the data warehouse is not that dissimilar from other systems you're familiar with. You can use your tried-and-true techniques to monitor the technical infrastructure. At a minimum, you'll need to monitor network bandwidth, database, and application server disk use and database server fragmentation. Clearly, you should involve the appropriate IS resources to assist with data warehouse technical infrastructure maintenance. For example, your network administration group should play an active role in these activities.

You'll want to capture performance, growth, and usage measures or statistics over time. You can then analyze these trends proactively to identify problems before you're faced with a user revolt. We recommend establishing a core set of application templates that are executed after each load or update to the data warehouse. Tracking the performance of these applications over time will help the data warehouse team monitor and react to performance degradation rather than rely on user feedback to the support organization.

In general, you'll want to go back and review the appropriate chapters of this book to manage your techncial infrastructure. We have provided an abundance of solid advice, much of which will only make sense now that you're ready to think about ongoing maintenance.

Your technical infrastructure will inevitably change, driven by existing data warehouse growth, in addition to vendor-initiated product changes. You will need to continue balancing new and existing technology. We recommend using your organization's standard planning and testing procedures prior to implementing any upgrades to components of your technical infrastructure. At a minimum, you will want to establish separate development and production environments to support the testing of new releases, and so on. This multi-environment strategy will become more important as more people come to rely on the data ware-house and expect it to be there for them.

Tune for Database Performance

The demands on your database platform are bound to change as you load additional information with every update of the data warehouse. These frequent changes warrant ongoing performance monitoring and tuning. Performance tuning should be based on usage and growth char-acteristics—which databases are being accessed frequently, which aggregations are being requested, are the indexes effective, and so on? The predicted usage and growth patterns that you relied on during the initial physical design need to be reevaluated. Also, don't be surprised if you underestimated the growth in data, due in part to additional, dense aggregation tables. We recommend you employ the aggregation, indexing, and partitioning strategies discussed earlier in Chapters 14 and 15 to modify your database tuning strategy as necessary.

Maintain Data and Metadata Management Processes

It's hard for the data warehouse team to complain too loudly about these source system changes. Chances are that the modifications were initiated by the data warehouse team or their users. The deployment of a data warehouse frequently leads to reengineering projects that address data integrity and attribute-sourcing issues in the operating systems.

 Unfortunately, the data extracts from your source systems into the data warehouse will also change all too frequently. These feeder processes are vulnerable to change given the sheer number of source systems they touch. Maintenance re-sources will need to assess the impact and then react to any changes in the source operational systems.

It is frequently more challenging to remain informed of source sys-tem changes than it is to remain informed of user-driven changes. IS management should be cognizant of the implications of source system changes. In many organizations, the data administration function is often aware of underlying system changes. Routine IS change control meetings might be another forum for learning of planned changes. We know of one client where the onus of communicating changes to the data warehouse team was put on the source system maintenance team.

If you elected to defer an investment in a packaged data staging tool, you probably now have a much greater appreciation for its potential value and payback. Of course, the benefit is that you now know the exact capabilities needed. The longer you wait to select and implement a data staging tool, the deeper the data staging maintenance hole you'll have to climb out of.

Finally, the data warehouse often forces organizations to deal with the issues related to data ownership. In many cases, the data warehouse team dealt with data issues during the data warehouse development process because no one else understood the ramifications. It is now time to transfer this ownership and associated responsibilities to the business community working in conjunction with the data steward. Their responsibilities cover a range of data-related issues, from providing consistent high-level data definitions to championing source system changes for improved data capture and quality to ensuring the maintenance of conformed dimension attributes.

Measure and Market Your Data Warehouse Success

It's important that you routinely measure the performance of your data warehouse against agreed-upon success and satisfaction criteria. If the data warehouse is performing well against these criteria, we suggest you market the data warehouse within your organization, and perhaps externally as well. If it's not performing well, we suggest you figure out why.

Monitor Success and Service Metrics

About a month following deployment, we suggest you conduct a thorough post-deployment assessment. Although it would be easier to rely exclusively on input from the data warehouse team, both the business users and team should participate in this assessment. The primary objective is to measure performance against the predetermined success criteria, as well as to gauge the general level of satisfaction with the data warehouse. In addition, you should solicit feedback concerning the business user–oriented education, deployment, and support processes. User input regarding what worked and what didn't is critical for process improvement prior to the next round of development and deployment.

In Chapter 4, we recommended establishing project success criteria following the analysis of business requirements. Agreed-upon success criteria are important for ensuring that the business users and data warehouse team are in sync regarding project goals. It's far too easy to fall into the "moving target" trap unless the criteria for gauging success are established early within the project.

 It's important that you track performance against success and service metrics on a regular basis, not just immediately following the deployment. It is also useful to capture this information over time to support success and service performance trending. Don't assume that no news is good news. No news usually means that no one is using the data warehouse.

Data for many of the metrics can be captured routinely by system utilities, but less operationally-oriented metrics must be gathered directly from the business users. You'll need to talk with your business users to continually assess their satisfaction level and to gauge the fit of the data warehouse with current business requirements. You can't rely on written surveys to gather this type of feedback.

Capture the Decisions Made Using the Data Warehouse

Sometimes a data warehouse is very successful, but no scientific measurements are available to support it. After all, the true valuable output of a data warehouse is the set of business decisions that are made as a result of using the warehouse. The data warehouse manager should be alert to decisions that various business users make and ask their permission to "capture" those decisions as part of the justification for the data warehouse. Once a business decision is marked as coming from the data warehouse, the financial impact of that decision can often be determined without a lot of arguments. The entire data warehouse team should be put on notice to solicit and listen for examples of business improvements attributable to the data warehouse. The support team is a key source for these success stories.

If the impact of such decisions is compared against the cost of the warehouse, a return on investment (ROI) can be computed. A good aspect of this approach is that often some of the big decisions made in a business have a financial impact that is greater than the cost of the warehouse itself. We recommend that in such a case, you take credit only for part of the decision. This is a reasonable stance in any case, and it insulates you from arguments that the data warehouse could not be solely responsible for a major decision.

We strongly advise you to keep a written log of all business impact success stories. You'll want to note who, what, when, how, and how much was associated with each example so you can provide complete details when asked. You'll be surprised by the usefulness of this log, especially if your business sponsor is promoted within (as seems to happen on the majority of data warehouse projects) or leaves the organization and the new person questions whether the ongoing investment is worthwhile.

Proactively Market the Data Warehouse

When you develop a new order-entry system, the system's users don't have much choice about whether they use it or not; if the new system doesn't get used, orders don't get processed. That's typically not the case with the data warehouse; using the data warehouse is often completely optional. Business users have been making decisions without access to information for years, and some will prefer to continue doing so.

Marketing of the data warehouse is important to support both funding for ongoing maintenance as well as growth initiatives. Someone on the team should be assigned responsibility for data warehouse public relations. This individual, often the organization's overall data warehouse coordinator, becomes the internal spokesperson for the data warehouse. A spokesperson is more important for a data warehouse project than for typical systems development projects due to the potential impact it may have on every department within an organization. The data warehouse spokesperson should develop a standard data warehouse presentation—if one isn't already available. This presentation would discuss the data warehouse's mission, accomplishments to date (with examples and dollar impacts), available data, current users and usage trends, and future plans.

Your log of data warehouse business impact examples will be relevant material for your marketing plan. These successes should be broadcast throughout the organization, and the industry, if appropriate. You can employ a variety of media, including data warehouse, IS or corporate newsletters, intranet Web pages, industry publications, and vendor success stories. If possible, you should solicit management's help to broadcast the wins. Users will be motivated to use the data warehouse and perhaps be part of the next success story, if management's support is highly visible.

Communicate Constantly

We've stressed the importance of communication throughout the planning, design, and development stages of your data warehouse project.

 Your maintenance game plan should include an extensive communication strategy as a cornerstone. It is critical to ensuring the continued health of your data warehouse.

The data warehouse team needs to establish a multitiered communication plan to address the information requirements of its many constituencies in both the business and IS communities. This communication plan complements the change request process instituted during the deployment of your data warehouse, as described in Chapter 18.

- **Business sponsors and drivers.**   You can't forget about your business sponsors just because you've deployed the first data warehouse deliverable. You'll need to maintain regular, predictable reporting to sustain their sponsorship. Communication will help address ongoing funding and resource allocation requirements. As we encouraged earlier, you should communicate successes to your business sponsors, as well as issues and your plans for addressing them.

- **Business users.**   The users of the data warehouse need detailed tactical information about the data warehouse. Depending on your organization, you might establish a monthly data warehouse newsletter or maintain an intranet Web site. Some data warehouse teams also communicate with their business users via internal user groups.

  Again, open and honest communication is the key to managing expectations. You should enthusiastically inform the users of successes and of your plans for correcting problems. You can't keep users in the dark regarding data warehouse errors, such as inaccurate data or incorrect application template calculations, in the hope that you'll get them fixed before anyone notices. It's inevitable that someone will notice!

- **General business community.**   You should broadcast general updates to the rest of the business community to keep them informed of current status and future plans. These may take the form of a quarterly one-page update or a column in your corporate newsletter.

- **IS management.** IS management should also receive the general broadcast updates. In addition, you need to make them aware of more detailed plans for the data warehouse to ensure that they're considering implications on their areas of responsibility, such as network capacity planning or operational system application development.
- **Data warehouse team updates.** It's critical that you maintain communication within the data warehouse team. Unfortunately, status meetings are often dropped as the schedule tightens around deployment and then not resumed following deployment. We strongly encourage you to make team communications a priority. Communication is key to making sure that everyone on the team is marching in the same direction, both during the deployment crunch and throughout the ongoing maintenance period.

PREPARE FOR DATA WAREHOUSE GROWTH AND EVOLUTION

If you've taken our advice thus far, your warehouse is bound to evolve and grow. In general, this evolution should be viewed as a sign of success, not failure. It indicates your existing data warehouse business users are asking for more data and application templates. At the same time, they're spreading the news about the data warehouse at the grass roots level, so new users will be clamoring for access to data, and applications.

Operational systems developed 20 years ago still retain many of their original characteristics. Changes to the data warehouse will be more dramatic. Everyone involved with the data warehouse, from both the business and IS communities, should anticipate and appreciate the evolution of the data warehouse.

In addition, the factors that influenced the early design of your data warehouse—including business sponsorship, users and their requirements, technical architecture, and available source data—are evolving rapidly. Your data warehouse will probably change at warp speed compared with more traditional system development efforts. We hope the emphasis we have placed in this Business Dimensional Lifecycle approach in making the data warehouse respond gracefully to change serves you well.

As you've been maintaining the data warehouse, you've been setting the stage for its growth and evolution. We have several additional recommendations to facilitate the ongoing development of your data warehouse.

Establish a Data Warehouse Steering Committee

If your first data warehouse deliverable was successful, other business areas will be knocking down your door to be next in line. We suggest that you avoid the role of data warehouse arbitrator, deciding who's going to be served in what order and at what cost. It's impossible for the data warehouse team to please everyone.

A much safer approach is to form a cross-functional steering committee to establish the overall direction and ground rules for growing the data warehouse. The project end-user steering committee described in Chapter 3 may serve as an initial committee, but you will probably need to expand or modify the roster to ensure broader, corporate-wide perspective. The responsibilities of the data warehouse steering committee typically include the following:

- Establish a process for prioritizing data warehouse initiatives.
- Establish the data warehouse funding procedures based on existing organizational processes and requirements.
- Establish overall infrastructure funding levels.
- Determine ongoing priorities for growth and evolution initiatives.

The data warehouse steering committee should be composed of representatives from both the business area and IS management. By participating in the data warehouse steering committee, the business community becomes part of the solution, rather than merely finding fault with the decisions made by the data warehouse team. The following variables should be considered prior to inviting representatives to participate in the data warehouse steering committee:

- **Organizational level.**   Steering committee representatives are typically "drivers" within their respective organizations rather than senior executives, largely due to their availability and accessibility. However, it's important that the drivers be empowered by their senior executive to represent the area and make decisions.
- **Organizational influence.**   The steering committee members should have influence over their own organizations in addition to commanding cross-organizational authority.

- **Belief in information-based decision making.** It's helpful if the steering committee members have a genuine interest in promoting information-based decision making throughout the organization.
- **Ability to set direction on behalf of the overall organization.** Your steering committee will be totally ineffective if its members are unwilling to look beyond their proprietary worlds. Steering committee members need to be able to put their own personal requirements aside to evaluate initiatives and establish priorities based on the potential benefit to the overall organization.

The data warehouse steering committee typically meets at least once every quarter. More frequent meetings are required during the early formation of the steering committee. In addition, data warehouse steering committees often establish a charter when they are formed. This charter or statement of vision documents their tenets and long-term strategies to ensure that everyone is in sync. The steering committee charter might include bedrock statements such as those illustrated in Figure 19.1.

Prioritize Growth and Evolution Opportunities

One of the data warehouse steering committee's responsibilities is to establish a process for prioritization of data warehouse growth and evolu-

---

Data Warehouse Steering Committee Charter

- All data warehouse initiatives will require a partnership between IS and the business area. Projects will be established as joint business/IS initiatives with joint business/IS project management responsibility. Senior level business management sponsorship is a prerequisite.
- Data warehouse initiatives will be prioritized based on the following criteria:
  - Alignment with overall business objectives
  - Potential business impact/return
  - Cost versus time to implement
  - Strategic importance to overall IS plan (e.g., provides necessary analysis capabilities to complement new ERP operational system)
- Existing technical investments will be leveraged whenever possible.
- The business community will anticipate and embrace change in the data warehouse. Unlike traditional systems development, change will be viewed as a positive sign of success, not failure.

Figure 19.1 Sample steering committee charter.

tion opportunities. The effort required to add another attribute to an existing dimension table differs significantly from that required to add a new fact table to the data warehouse. Typically, we see two processes put into place to handle prioritization of growth and evolution opportunities, one for relatively minor projects and another for major data warehouse initiatives. Both of these processes are described shortly.

Data warehouse errors are typically handled outside the prioritization framework. The error correction may be needed to address inaccurate data transformation, incorrect data definition, or erroneous calculation in an application template. As we've mentioned throughout this book, data warehouse errors cannot be tolerated—they must be addressed as quickly as possible. For this reason, these issues are typically dealt with promptly by the data warehouse maintenance team, rather than burdening the general prioritization processes.

Prioritize Minor Enhancements

A minor enhancement to the data warehouse might consist of additional data elements, additional end user applications based on existing data, changes to existing applications, and so on. The creation of an additional aggregation table would typically also be considered a minor enhancement. There is often a cost estimate limit for minor enhancements, although this cost ceiling varies by organization. Minor enhancements are typically characterized as requiring days or a small number of weeks to complete, rather than measuring the effort in work-months.

Your organization probably already has a process for change service requests in place. The prioritization of minor data warehouse enhancements is typically handled in a similar fashion. The data warehouse support team receives and reviews user feedback, possibly submitted via e-mail to a change request mailbox. The team researches and scopes the effort required to implement the enhancement. The support team then presents a preliminary prioritization recommendation to the steering committee. The goal is to obtain steering committee buy-in without bogging them down with unnecessary tactical details. Also, you don't want the steering committee to become a bottleneck. Depending on their meeting frequency, you may want to deal with minor enhancements by working with general guidelines from the steering committee. Finally, it is paramount that the user who submitted the request receive feedback on its established priority.

Don't fall prey to the simplistic reasoning that because a requested change is small, it is not worth doing. This argument can be extended to not doing anything at all. One of the reasons Japanese cars are such of high quality is the manufacturers' attitude of "1000 little improvements is a strategic advantage."

Prioritize Major Initiatives

A major enhancement to the data warehouse might involve a new fact table derived from a business process that is not yet represented in the data warehouse. Major enhancements typically represent a relatively large investment in incremental design, development, and maintenance resources measured in work-months rather than days of effort.

In these cases, the project's business sponsor typically presents the opportunity to the steering committee. Although a formal requirements analysis, as described in Chapter 4, has probably not yet been done, a feasibility analysis and business case should be completed. Subsequent data warehouse projects should meet the same criteria we described in Chapter 3. Each project should be meaningful to the business (as determined by your prioritization process), manageable (in terms of the number of users, amount of data, and so on), and doable in a reasonable time frame. The steering committee employs their agreed-upon prioritization criteria to establish the sequencing of major initiatives.

Manage Iterative Growth and Evolution Using the Lifecycle

At this point, you're ready to tackle your next data warehouse project. We remind you to remember everything you've read so far in this book. Unfortunately, we've seen organizations that use this business-oriented approach for their first warehouse project fall back into old habits as the next data warehouse project queues up.

As you embark on subsequent projects, you'll be leveraging the foundation already put in place, while preparing for new variables. You may be delivering existing information to new users or new information to existing users. In either case, you should continue to use the Business Dimensional Lifecycle described throughout this book. The knowledge and experience gained during your initial data warehouse project should be leveraged on subsequent projects (without completely abandoning your initial user base).

As illustrated on the overall Business Dimensional Lifecycle diagram, you should now loop back to the beginning of the lifecycle again. The following section reviews each major step of the project lifecycle and highlights changes or extensions as it is applied to subsequent phases.

- **Project planning.**   Each subsequent data warehouse initiative should be established as a defined project. Subsequent initiatives should be clearly scoped, with defined start and stop dates—don't just start tackling a project without a scope document, project workplan, and management techniques as recommended in Chapter 3.

    A project manager should be assigned to each initiative. A project team with roles as described in Chapter 3 needs to be established. Organizations sometimes get greedy as they move beyond their first data warehouse deliverable. They want to satisfy everyone else in the second release, moving from a manageable first project to the "big bang" approach. The reasoning we used to discourage this approach up front still applies as you're expanding your data warehouse. Depending on your resource levels, it is possible to stagger several concurrent initiatives with multiple separate project teams. This approach allows for concurrent design and development, rather than relying on a serial timeline, but it also requires additional coordination and communication.

- **Business requirements definition.**   Users' business requirements should be the driver at all times. The activities described in Chapter 4 are still very applicable as you move forward with your next warehouse project.

- **Technical architecture strategy and infrastructure.**   You'll want to leverage the existing technical architecture, while making adjustments as required. You should be sure to document any changes to the technical architecture strategy.

- **Dimensional modeling.**   As discussed in Chapter 5, embracing the Data Warehouse Bus Architecture concept and conforming your business dimensions is the key to supporting integration within your data warehouse over time.

- **Data staging.**   The data staging processes described in Chapter 16 and constructed for your first data warehouse deliverable should be reused and further built upon.

- **Application design and development.**   You should be able to leverage the application design and development infrastructure, including application development standards, during subsequent warehouse development efforts.

- **Deployment planning, education, and support.**   Once again, you'll want to leverage existing deployment, education, and support processes to the extent possible. User education needs to accompany every release of new data content or application templates to a user population, not just the first deployment. Additional training is also warranted if there are major changes to the end user tool software.

SUMMARY

Congratulations! Your hard work has paid off, and the warehouse is now in full production. In this chapter, we highlighted recommendations to ensure your data warehouse remains a vital and healthy data warehouse, and is poised for growth. Remember to always put the business users first, without sacrificing attention to the back room and technical environment. You should measure, track, and communicate data warehouse successes on an ongoing basis. Be sure to consult Figure 19.2 for a summary of the project plan tasks and responsibilities spreadsheet for maintaining and growing the data warehouse.

Last but not least, remember that success breeds success. Be prepared for the onslaught of requests for more data, reports, and users. You should continue to rely on the Business Dimensional Lifecycle as your data warehouse grows and evolves.

KEY ROLES

Keys roles for maintaining and growing the data warehouse include:

- Superior user support can be achieved only through the coordinated efforts of all team members. Each core team member typically retains responsibility for maintaining their component of the data warehouse.
- The data warehouse steering committee provides direction and establishes priorities for subsequent data warehouse expansion. This group is frequently comprised of business and IS management representatives.

ESTIMATING CONSIDERATIONS

Unlike most systems development projects, the data warehouse is never done. Consequently, there's no end in sight regarding data warehouse maintenance and growth activities and associated timeframes.

As we mentioned earlier, it's not uncommon for the maintenance of your data warehouse to require up to 50 percent of the resources required to develop it. Subsequent projects to address data warehouse growth should be staffed, planned, and managed as described in Chapter 3.

Project Task	Fans	Front Office			Coaches		Regular Line-Up						Special Teams				
	Business End Users	Business Sponsor	IS Sponsor	Business Driver	Bus. Project Lead	Project Manager	Bus. Sys. Analyst	Data Modeler	DW DBA	Data Staging Designer	DW Educator	E/U Appl Devel	Tech/Security Architect	Tech. Sppt Specialists	Data Staging Programmer	Data Steward	DW QA Analyst
DATA WAREHOUSE MAINTENANCE																	
1 Provide Ongoing User Support	○				●	●	○					○		○		○	○
2 Provide Ongoing User Education	○				○	○	▶	▶			●	▶				▶	▶
3 Maintain Technical Infrastructure						○			●				●	●			
4 Monitor End User Query Performance					▶	○	▲		●			●					
5 Monitor Data Staging Performance						○			●	●					●		
6 Monitor Ongoing Success	▶	□	□	▶	●	●	▶	▶	▶	▶	▶	▶	▶	▶	▶	▶	▶
7 Communicate Continuously and Market Success	○	○	○	○	●	●	○	○	○	○	○	○	○	○	○	○	○
8 User Acceptance/Project Review	□	□	□	○	●	○	○	○	○	○	○	○	○	○	○	○	○
DATA WAREHOUSE GROWTH																	
1 Establish Data Warehouse Steering Committee		●	●	●	○	○											
2 Establish Enhancement Prioritization Strategy		●	●	●	○	○											
3 Iteratively Use Business Dimensional Lifecycle	○	○	○	○	●	●	○	○	○	○	○	○	○	○	○	○	○

LEGEND:
Primary Responsibility for the Task = ●
Involved in the Task = ○
Provides Input to the Task = ▶
Informed Task Results = □
Optional Involvement in the Task = ▲

FIGURE 19.2 Project plan tasks and responsibilities for maintaining and growing the data warehouse.

Lifecycle Project Plan

This appendix provides a comprehensive data warehouse lifecycle project plan. The project plan lists all the tasks involved in designing, developing, and deploying a data warehouse, as we have described throughout *The Data Warehouse Lifecycle Toolkit*. This project plan can also be found on the companion CD-ROM.

In addition to listing the project tasks, the lifecycle project plan also identifies the business and IS roles involved in each task. Their level of task responsibility is designated by the following legend:

- ●   *Primary Responsibility for the Task*
- ○   *Involved in the Task*
- ❱   *Provides Input to the Task*
- ❑   *Informed of the Results of the Task*
- ▲   *Optional Involvement in the Task*

PROJECT MANAGEMENT AND REQUIREMENTS

Project Task	Fans	Front Office			Coaches		Regular Line-Up						Special Teams				
	Business End Users	Business Sponsor	IS Sponsor	Business Driver	Bus. Project Lead	Project Manager	Bus. Sys. Analyst	Data Modeler	DW DBA	Data Staging Designer	DW Educator	E/U Appl Devel	Tech/Security Architect	Tech. Sppt Specialists	Data Staging Programmer	Data Steward	DW QA Analyst
PROJECT DEFINITION																	
1 Assess Data Warehousing Readiness		○	○	○	●	●	◗	◗	◗	◗			◗				
2 Develop Preliminary Project Scope		○	○	○	●	●	◗	◗	◗	◗			◗				
3 Build Business Justification	◗	◗	◗	●	●	○	◗										
PROJECT PLANNING & MANAGEMENT																	
1 Establish Project Identity				◗	●	●											
2 Identify Project Resources		○	○	○	●	●											
3 Prepare Draft Project Plan				◗	◗	●	◗	◗	◗	◗	◗	◗	◗	◗	◗	◗	◗
4 Conduct Project Team Kick-Off & Planning		□	□	○	○	●	○	○	○	○	○	○	○	○	○	○	○
5 Revise Project Plan				◗	◗	●	◗	◗	◗	◗	◗	◗	◗	◗	◗	◗	◗
6 Develop Project Communication Plan		◗	◗	◗	○	●	◗	◗	◗	◗	▲	◗	◗	▲	◗	▲	▲
7 Develop Program to Measure Success		○	○	○	●	○											
8 Develop Process to Manage Scope				○	○	●											
9 Ongoing Project Management					○	●											
USER REQUIREMENT DEFINITION																	
1 Identify and Prepare Interview Team						●	○	○									
2 Select Interviewees		◗	◗	◗	●	●											
3 Schedule interviews					○	●											
4 Conduct User Kick-Off & Prepare Interviewees	○	○	○	○	○	●	○	○									
5 Conduct Business User Interviews	○	○		○	○	▲	●	▲				▲					
6 Conduct IS Data Discovery Interviews					▲	●	●	●	○	○		▲			○		
7 Analyze Interview Findings					○	○	●										
8 Document Findings and Review	◗			◗	○	○	●	○				▲					
9 Publish Requirements Deliverables	□	□	□	□	○	○	●	○	□	□	□	□	□	□	□	□	□
10 Prioritize and Revise Project Scope	◗	◗	◗	●	●	●	◗	◗				◗					
11 User Acceptance/Project Review	▲	□	□	○	●	○	○	○	○	○	▲	○	▲	▲	○	▲	▲

FIGURE A.1 The data warehouse lifecycle project plan.

Project Task	Fans	Front Office			Coaches		Regular Line-Up						Special Teams				
	Business End Users	Business Sponsor	IS Sponsor	Business Driver	Bus. Project Lead	Project Manager	Bus. Sys. Analyst	Data Modeler	DW DBA	Data Staging Designer	DW Educator	E/U Appl Devel	Tech/Security Architect	Tech. Sppt Specialists	Data Staging Programmer	Data Steward	DW QA Analyst
DATA DESIGN																	
DIMENSIONAL MODELING																	
1 Build Matrix					○	○	●	●	○	▲							
2 Choose Data Mart		○	○	○	●	●	◗	◗									
3 Declare Grain					○	○	○	●	▲								
4 Choose Dimensions							○	●	▲								
5 Develop Fact Table Diagram							○	●	▲								
6 Document Fact Table Detail							○	●	▲								
7 Design Dimension Detail							○	●	▲								
8 Develop Derived Fact Worksheet	○			◗	○	○	●	○	▲			○					
9 User Review & Acceptance	○	□	□	○	●	○	○	○	▲								
10 Review DB Design Recommendations for E/U Tool								○	●	○		○			○		
11 Review DB Design Recommendations for DBMS								○	●								
12 Complete Logical Database Design								○	●								
13 Identify Candidate Prestored Aggregates	◗				○		○	●	○								
14 Develop Aggregation Table Design Strategy								○	●								
15 Review Logical Database Design w/Team					○	○	○	●	○	▲	○					○	
16 Certify DB Design with DSS Tool Vendor									●								
17 User Acceptance/Project Review	○	□	□	○	●	○	○	○	○	○	○	▲	○	▲	▲	▲	▲
ANALYZE DATA SOURCES																	
1 Identify Candidate Data Sources							▲	○	○	●						▲	
2 Browse Data Content							▲	○	○	●						▲	
3 Develop Source to Target Data Map								○	○	●						●	
4 Estimate Number of Rows					◗	◗	◗	○	●	○							
5 User Acceptance/Project Review	○	□	□	□	●	○	○	○	○	○	▲	○	▲	▲	○	▲	▲

FIGURE A.1 *Continued*

Project Task	Fans	Front Office			Coaches		Regular Line-Up						Special Teams				
	Business End Users	Business Sponsor	IS Sponsor	Business Driver	Bus. Project Lead	Project Manager	Bus. Sys. Analyst	Data Modeler	DW DBA	Data Staging Designer	DW Educator	E/U Appl Devel	Tech/Security Architect	Tech. Sppt Specialists	Data Staging Programmer	Data Steward	DW QA Analyst
ARCHITECTURE																	
TECHNICAL ARCHITECTURE DESIGN																	
1 Create Architecture Task Force					○	○							●	○			
2 Gather & Document Technical Requirements						◗	◗	◗	◗	◗		◗	●	○			
3 Review Current Technical Environment					◗	○	○	○	○	○		○	●	○			
4 Create Architecture Plan						◗	◗	◗	◐	◗		◗	●	○			
5 Determine Phased Implementation Approach					○	○							●	○			
7 Create Infrastructure Plan													●	○			
8 Develop Configuration Recommendations													●	○			
9 User Acceptance/Project Review	☐	☐	☐	☐	○	●	☐	☐	☐	☐	☐	☐	○	○	☐	☐	☐
IMPLEMENT TACTICAL SECURITY MEASURES																	
1 Develop Tactical Security Plan					○	○							●	○			
2 Secure Physical Environment						○							○	●			
3 Install Virus Checking Software						○							○	●			
4 Secure Access into Environment						○							●	○			
5 Secure Access out of Environment						○							●	○			
6 Implement Rigorous Password Scheme						○							●	○			
7 Implement Controls for Software Installation						○							○	●			
8 Audit Security Violations					○	○							●	○			
9 Monitor Security Privileges by Individual					○	●							○	○			
10 User Acceptance/Project Review	☐	☐	☐	☐	○	●	☐	☐	☐	☐	☐	☐	○	○	☐	☐	☐
DEVELOP STRATEGIC SECURITY PLAN																	
1 Design Security Architecture						○							●	○			
2 Implement Access Tokens (Elim. Passwords)						○							●	○			
3 Implement Public/Private Keys for Authentication						○							●	○			
4 Implement Secure Tunneling for Remote Access						○							●	○			

FIGURE A.1 *Continued*

Project Task	Business End Users	Business Sponsor	IS Sponsor	Business Driver	Bus. Project Lead	Project Manager	Bus. Sys. Analyst	Data Modeler	DW DBA	Data Staging Designer	DW Educator	E/U Appl Devel	Tech/Security Architect	Tech. Sppt Specialists	Data Staging Programmer	Data Steward	DW QA Analyst
	Fans	Front Office			Coaches		Regular Line-Up						Special Teams				
5 Centralize Authentication & Access Control						○							●	○			
6 Impl. Signed Certificates for Software Downloads						○							●	○			
7 User Acceptance/Project Review	□	□	□	□	○	●	□	□	□	□	□	□	○	○	□	□	□
PRODUCT SELECTION																	
(Repeat for each selection area)																	
1 Develop Evaluation Matrix					●	●	○	○					●	○			
2 Research Candidate Products						○	○	○	○	○		○	●	○			
3 Develop Product Short List						○	○	○	○	○		○	●				
4 Evaluate Product Options	▶					○	○	○	○	○		○	●				
5 Optional Prototype (May repeat for diff. products)																	
Select Business Process/Data for Evaluation					●	●	○	○									
Define Completion Criteria					●	●							○				
Acquire Resources (Internal/Vendor)					○	●											
Determine Test Configuration						○			○	○		○	●	○			
Install Evaluation Prerequisites & Components							○	○	○	○		○	○	●			
Train the Evaluation Team	○				○	●	○	○	○	○	○	○	○	○			
Develop & Tune Prototype						○	○	●	●	●		●	○	●			
Conduct Tests	▶				▶	▶	▶	▶	●	●	▶	●	▶	●			
Analyze & Document Results	▶				○	●	▶	▶	▶	▶		▶	●	○			
6 Determine Product Recommendation	▶	□	□	□	●	●	○	○	○	○		○	●	○			
7 Present to Findings/Results to Management		□	□	□	●	●	▶	▶	▶	▶		▶	▶	▶			
8 Negotiate Contract						●											
9 User Acceptance/Project Review	▲	□	□	□	●	○	○	○	○	○	○	○	○	○	▲	▲	▲
PRODUCT INSTALLATION																	
(Repeat for each product)																	
1 Installation Planning													●	○			
2 Meet Prerequisites													○	●			
3 Install Hardware/Software													○	●			

FIGURE A.1 *Continued*

Project Task	Business End Users	Business Sponsor	IS Sponsor	Business Driver	Bus. Project Lead	Project Manager	Bus. Sys. Analyst	Data Modeler	DW DBA	Data Staging Designer	DW Educator	E/U Appl Devel	Tech/Security Architect	Tech. Sppt Specialists	Data Staging Programmer	Data Steward	DW QA Analyst
	Fans	Front Office			Coaches		Regular Line-Up						Special Teams				
4 Test Hardware/Software													○	●			
5 User Acceptance/Project Review	▲	□	□	□	○	●	○	○	○	○	▲	○	○	○	▲	▲	▲
IMPLEMENTATION																	
PHYSICAL DATABASE DESIGN																	
1 Define Standards									●								
2 Design Physical Tables & Columns								◗	●								
3 Estimate Database Size						◗	◗	◗	●	◗							
4 Develop Initial Index Plan							◗	◗	●			◗					
5 Develop Initial Aggregation Plan							○	○	●								
6 Develop Initial Partitioning Plan									●								
7 User Acceptance/Project Review		□	□	□	□	●	○	○	○	○	▲	○	▲	▲	○	▲	▲
PHYSICAL DATABASE IMPLEMENTATION																	
1 Determine DBMS Fixed Parameters									●								
2 Install DBMS									●				○	○			
3 Optimize DBMS Changeable Parameters									●								
4 Build Physical Storage Structure									●								
5 Setup RAID									●				○	○			
6 Complete Table and Index Sizing								◗	●								
7 Create Tables and Indexes									●								
8 User Acceptance/Project Review		□	□	□	□	●	○	○	○	○	▲	○	▲	▲	▲	▲	▲
DATA STAGING DESIGN & DEVELOPMENT																	
1 Design High-Level Staging Process										●					○		
2 Develop Detailed Staging Plan by Table										●					○		
3 Set Up Development Environment									●	○			○	○	○		
4 Define & Implement Staging Metadata							◗	◗	●							●	
5 Develop 1st Static Dimension Table Process (Extract, Transformation & Load)							◗	◗	○							●	
6 Develop 1st Dimension Maintenance Process							◗	◗	○							●	

FIGURE A.1 *Continued*

Project Task	Business End Users (Fans)	Business Sponsor (Front Office)	IS Sponsor (Front Office)	Business Driver (Front Office)	Bus. Project Lead (Coaches)	Project Manager (Coaches)	Bus. Sys. Analyst (Regular Line-Up)	Data Modeler	DW DBA	Data Staging Designer	DW Educator	E/U Appl Devel	Tech/Security Architect (Special Teams)	Tech. Sppt Specialists	Data Staging Programmer	Data Steward	DW QA Analyst
7 Develop Remaining Dimension Table Processes								◗	◗	○					●		
8 Develop Fact Table Process (Extract, Transformation & Load)								◗	◗	○					●		
9 Develop Incremental Fact Table Process								◗	◗	○					●		
10 Design & Implement Data Cleansing							◗	◗	◗	●					●	○	○
11 Design and Develop Aggregation Process						◗		◗	◗	◗	●	◗			●		
12 Automate Entire Process						○				○					●		
13 Develop Data Quality Assurance Processes						○	○	○	○	○					○	○	●
14 Implement DB Administration (Archive, Backup & Recovery)						○			●	◗						◗	○
15 User Acceptance/Project Review		□	□	□	○	●	○	○	○	○	○	○	▲	▲	○	○	○
POPULATE & VALIDATE DATABASE																	
1 Set Up Production Environment									●				○	○			
2 Load Initial Test Data										○					●		
3 Initial Data Validation/Quality Assurance					○	○				○					○	○	●
4 Load Historical Data										○					●		
5 Perform Data Validation/Quality Assurance					○	○				○					○	○	●
6 User Acceptance/Project Review		□	□	○	●	○	○	○	○	○	○	○	▲	▲	○	○	○
PERFORMANCE TUNING																	
1 Set Up Benchmark Queries					○	○	○	○	●				○	○	●		
2 Review Indexing & Aggregation					○	○	○	○	●						○		
3 Review Tool Specific Tuning					○	○				○					●		
4 Conduct Ongoing Database Monitoring					□	□			●								
5 User Acceptance/Project Review		□	□	□	○	●	▲	▲	○	○	▲	○	▲	▲	▲	▲	▲
END USER (E/U) APPLICATION SPECIFICATION																	
1 Identify & Prioritize Candidate Reports	◗				●	○	○	◗							●		
2 Design Template Navigation Approach					◗	○	◗	◗							●		

FIGURE A.1 *Continued*

Project Task	Fans	Front Office			Coaches		Regular Line-Up						Special Teams				
	Business End Users	Business Sponsor	IS Sponsor	Business Driver	Bus. Project Lead	Project Manager	Bus. Sys. Analyst	Data Modeler	DW DBA	Data Staging Designer	DW Educator	E/U Appl Devel	Tech/Security Architect	Tech. Sppt Specialists	Data Staging Programmer	Data Steward	DW QA Analyst
3 Develop E/U Application Standards					○	○	◗	◗				●					
4 Document Detailed Template Specifications					◗	○	○	◗				●					
5 Review End User Application Specs w/Users	○			□	●	○	○	○				●					
6 Revise End User Application Specs					◗	○	◗					●					
7 User Acceptance/Project Review	□	□	□	○	●	○	○	○	○	○	▲	○	▲	▲	○	○	▲
END USER (E/U) APPLICATION DEVELOPMENT																	
1 Select Implementation Approach	○				○	○	○	○				●					
2 Review Application Specifications	○				○	○	○	○				●					
3 Review Application Standards					○	○	○					●					
4 Populate E/U Tool Metadata					◗		◗	◗	◗	◗		●			◗	◗	
5 Develop E/U Applications							◗					●					
6 Provide Data Accuracy & Cleanliness Feedback					○	○	○			○		○			○	○	●
7 Develop E/U Template Navigation					◗		◗					●					
8 Review with Users	○				○	○	○					●					
9 Document E/U Applications					◗		◗					●					
10 Develop E/U Application Maint. Procedures						○						●					
11 Develop E/U Application Release Procedures						○						●					
12 User Acceptance/Project Review	○	□	□	○	●	○	○	○	○	○	○	○	▲	▲	▲	▲	▲
DEPLOYMENT AND GROWTH																	
DEPLOYMENT PLANNING																	
1 Develop Desktop Infrastructure Checklist						○							◗	●	◗		
2 Develop Initial User Education Strategy	◗			□	●	●	○	○			●	○				○	○
3 Define User Support Strategy				□	●	●	○				□	○	□				

FIGURE A.1 *Continued*

Project Task	Fans	Front Office			Coaches		Regular Line-Up						Special Teams				
	Business End Users	Business Sponsor	IS Sponsor	Business Driver	Bus. Project Lead	Project Manager	Bus. Sys. Analyst	Data Modeler	DW DBA	Data Staging Designer	DW Educator	E/U Appl Devel	Tech/Security Architect	Tech. Sppt Specialists	Data Staging Programmer	Data Steward	DW QA Analyst
4 Define Release Plan	□			○	●	●	▸	▸	▸	▸	▸	▸	▸	▸	▸	▸	▸
5 Review Deployment Strategies & Release Plan	□	□	□	○	○	●	○	○	○	○	○	○	○	○	○	○	○
6 Develop User Course Materials	▸				▸	▸	▸	▸			●	▸					
7 Develop Support Procedures					●	●	○	○	○	○	○	○			○		
8 User Acceptance/Project Review	□	□	□	□	●	○	○	○	○	○	○	○	▲	▲	○	○	○
COMPLETE SYSTEM TEST																	
1 Run Complete Data Staging Process						○			●	●					●		
2 Perform Standard QA Procedures					○	○			○	○		○			○	○	●
3 Run Core End User Applications					○	○	○					●					
4 Review Overall Process					●	●	○	○	○	○	○	○	○	○	○	○	○
5 User Acceptance/Project Review	□	□	□	○	●	○	○	○	○	○	○	○	○	○	○	○	○
DEPLOYMENT (Alpha, Beta & Production Iterations)																	
1 Assess Deployment Readiness					●	●											
2 Configure & Test Desktop Infrastructure												○		●			
3 Set Up Security Privileges						○			○			○	●	○			
4 Educate Users	○				○	○	○				●	○					
5 User Acceptance/Project Review	□	□	□	○	●	○	○	○	○	○	○	○	○	○	○	○	○
DATA WAREHOUSE MAINTENANCE																	
1 Provide Ongoing User Support	○				○	●	○						○	○		○	○
2 Provide Ongoing User Education	○				○	○	▸	▸			●	▸				▸	▸
3 Maintain Technical Infrastructure						○			●				●	●			
4 Monitor End User Query Performance					▸	○	▲		●			●					
5 Monitor Data Staging Performance						○			●	●					●		
6 Monitor Ongoing Success	▸	□	□	▸	●	●	▸	▸	▸	▸	▸	▸	▸	▸	▸	▸	▸
7 Communicate Continuously and Market Success	○	○	○	○	●	●	○	○	○	○	○	○	○	○	○	○	○
8 User Acceptance/Project Review	□	□	□	○	●	○	○	○	○	○	○	○	○	○	○	○	○

FIGURE A.1 *Continued*

Project Task	Fans	Front Office			Coaches		Regular Line-Up						Special Teams				
	Business End Users	Business Sponsor	IS Sponsor	Business Driver	Bus. Project Lead	Project Manager	Bus. Sys. Analyst	Data Modeler	DW DBA	Data Staging Designer	DW Educator	E/U Appl Devel	Tech/Security Architect	Tech. Sppt Specialists	Data Staging Programmer	Data Steward	DW QA Analyst
DATA WAREHOUSE GROWTH																	
1 Establish Data Warehouse Steering Committee		○	○	●	○	○											
2 Establish Enhancement Prioritization Strategy		●	●	●	○	○											
3 Iteratively Use Business Dimensional Lifecycle	○	○	○	○	●	●	○	○	○	○	○	○	○	○	○	○	○

LEGEND:
Primary Responsibility for the Task = ●
Involved in the Task = ○
Provides Input to the Task = ◗
Informed Task Results = ▢
Optional Involvement in the Task = ▲

FIGURE A.1 *Continued*

APPENDIX B

About the CD-ROM

The companion CD-ROM contains a number of files to support the use of the Business Dimensional Lifecycle approach. This includes a spreadsheet version of the project plan illustrated in Appendix A, an extensive Data Warehouse Bus Architecture design model example (not printed in *The Data Warehouse Lifecycle Toolkit* text), blank digital versions of many of the sample templates, key figures found in the text, and checklists from several chapters.

We hope these templates facilitate your real-world application of the Business Dimensional Lifecycle. This appendix begins with a detailed listing and description of the CD-ROM's contents. Instructions for using the CD-ROM, including guidance on the built-in CD-ROM navigation browser and software requirements, are also provided.

PROJECT PLAN

A high-level project plan that identifies the tasks associated with the complete Business Dimensional Lifecycle and each role's responsibility is included on the CD-ROM. This project plan represents the consolidation of the project plans located at the end of each appropriate chapter.

It is identical to the integrated plan illustrated in Appendix A. You can use this task list as the basis for developing the integrated project plan for your own data warehouse initiative.

This project plan is identified as projplan.xls located in the \chapters\ch03 directory on the CD-ROM.

DATA WAREHOUSE BUS ARCHITECTURE EXAMPLE

The CD-ROM contains a detailed logical design for a telecommunications company, which illustrates the Data Warehouse Bus Architecture. This design starts with the matrix planning step from Chapter 7 and assumes the designer then uses the four-step method to define the process, the grain, the dimensions, and facts for each constituent data mart.

The overall Data Warehouse Bus Architecture matrix is the roadmap for remembering which dimensions are needed with each data mart and for guiding the discussion among data mart teams (also for successfully conforming these dimensions across data marts). The data marts are presented in two levels of detail: first, at a high level, where all the possible dimensions are described, and then at a specific logical level where the dimensions are matched precisely and correctly to the grain of each fact table.

The following Data Warehouse Bus Architecture files are located in the \dwbus-ex directory on the CD-ROM:

- **Data Warehouse Bus Architecture Matrix (1busarch.xls).** The first section of this spreadsheet shows the complete matrix, encompassing all the data marts and all the dimensions for the enterprise. The rows of the matrix represent data marts. By scanning across a row, all the dimensions for that data mart can be seen at a glance. The columns of the matrix represent dimensions. When more than one "X" appears in a column, it is a signal that this dimension needs to be conformed across the affected data marts. The second section of the spreadsheet provides expanded descriptions for each dimension and each data mart.
- **Dimensional Model Document (2model.doc).** This document provides a high-level design for a representative set of dimensions from the overall matrix in the first document. It shows all of the re-

lationships among attributes within each dimension. This document also provides a high-level design for a representative set of fact tables to which these dimensions are attached. At this level of design, we have not chosen the specific fact table granularity or made specific assumptions about which dimension tables can be used in a particular situation.

- **Logical Design Document (3logical.doc).**   This document provides a precise set of designs for a representative set of dimension tables and fact tables drawn from the overall matrix in the first document. The fact tables in this document have been chosen with specific granularities, and therefore the correct set of attached dimensions can be chosen. The six fact tables shown in this document are the central fact tables for the six corresponding data marts with the same names.

TEMPLATES, CHECKLISTS, FIGURES, AND AIDS

The CD-ROM contains an extensive set of templates and checklists used throughout the Business Dimensional Lifecycle. We have also provided several key figures from *The Data Warehouse Lifecycle Toolkit* in digital format to facilitate communication as you design and develop your own data warehouse. In addition, we have included several supplemental aids, such as a sample Period dimension table and naming conventions document.

The templates and checklists are intended to be used in conjunction with the project plan. Your organization may already have methodology and/or documentation standards in place that should supersede these templates—which is fine as long as all of the same appropriate information is captured. Likewise, the checklists are comprehensive. It would be unusual for a single project to accommodate every item on these lists. However, it is important that key elements do not slip through the cracks. Refer to the checklists to make sure you have accounted for every step, even if you have decided to defer the step until a subsequent phase of the data warehouse.

The templates, checklists, figures, and aids are organized by chapter within the \chapters directory on the CD-ROM. The complete listing is provided below, along with each file name and file type in parenthesis.

Chapter 2: Business Dimensional Lifecycle

The following figure, which depicts the overall Business Dimensional Lifecycle, is located in the \chapters\ch02 directory on the CD-ROM:

- Figure 2.1 Business Dimensional Lifecycle Diagram (f-02-01.ppt)

Chapter 3: Project Planning and Management

The following tools for project planning and management are located in the \chapters\ch03 directory:

- Template 3.1 Project Scope Document (t-03-01.doc)
- Template 3.2 User Acceptance Form (t-03-02.doc)
- Template 3.3 Project Kick-Off Meeting Agenda (t-03-03.doc)
- Template 3.4 Status Meeting Agenda (t-03-04.doc)
- Template 3.5 Status Report (t-03-05.doc)
- Template 3.6 Project Issue Log (t-03-06.doc)
- Template 3.7 Change Control Log (t-03-07.doc)
- Template 3.8 Change Request Form (t-03-08.doc)
- Checklist 3.1 Data Warehouse Readiness Litmus Test (c-03-01.doc)
- Checklist 3.2 Project Roles (c-03-02.doc)

Chapter 4: Collecting the Requirements

The following tools for collecting the requirements are located in the \chapters\ch04 directory:

- Template 4.1 User Kick-Off Meeting Agenda (t-04-01.doc)
- Template 4.2 Pre-Interview Letter (t-04-02.doc)
- Template 4.3 Business Executive Questionnaire (t-04-03.doc)
- Template 4.4 Business Manager or Analyst Questionnaire (t-04-04.doc)
- Template 4.5 IS Data Audit Questionnaire (t-04-05.doc)
- Template 4.6 Interview Write-Up (t-04-06.doc)
- Template 4.7 Requirements Findings Document (t-04-07.doc)
- Checklist 4.1 Interview Preparation (c-04-01.doc)

Chapter 7: Building Dimensional Models

The following tools for building the dimensional model are located in the \chapters\ch07 directory:

- Template 7.1 Data Mart Matrix (t-07-01.doc)
- Template 7.2 Dimensional Model Document (t-07-02.doc)
- Template 7.3 Derived Fact Worksheet (t-07-03.doc)
- Template 7.4 Logical Table Design (t-07-04.doc)
- Template 7.5 Data Source Definition Document (t-07-05.doc)
- Template 7.6 Source-to-Target Data Map (t-07-06.doc)
- Checklist 7.1 Dimensional Design Considerations (c-07-01.doc)
- Checklist 7.2 Data Source Checklist (c-07-02.doc)

Chapter 8: Introducing Data Warehouse Architecture

The following tools describing the overall data warehouse architecture are located in the \chapters\ch08 directory:

- Checklist 8.1 Architecture Framework (c-08-01.doc)
- Figure 8.1 Data Warehouse Architecture Framework (f-08-01.ppt)

Chapter 9: Back Room Technical Architecture

The following tools for the back room architecture are located in the \chapters\ch09 directory:

- Checklist 9.1 Back Room Services (c-09-01.doc)
- Figure 9.1 Back Room Technical Architecture (f-09-01.ppt)
- Figure 9.2 The Data Warehouse Bus (f-09-02.ppt)

Chapter 10: Architecture for the Front Room

The following tools for the front room architecture are located in the \chapters\ch10 directory:

- Checklist 10.1 Front Room Services for Data Access (c-10-01.doc)
- Figure 10.1 Front Room Technical Architecture (f-10-01.ppt)

Chapter 11: Infrastructure and Metadata

The following tool for metadata-related considerations is located in the \chapters\ch11 directory:

- Checklist 11.1 Metadata Checklist (c-11-01.doc)

Chapter 12: A Graduate Course on the Internet and Security

The following tool for security-related considerations is located in the \chapters\ch12 directory:

- Checklist 12.1 Security Checklist (c-12-01.doc)

Chapter 13: Creating the Architecture Plan and Selecting Products

The following tools for creating the architecture plan and selecting products are located in the \chapters\ch13 directory:

- Template 13.1 Technical Architecture Plan Document (t-13-01.doc)
- Template 13.2 Product Evaluation Matrix (t-13-02.xls)
- Template 13.3 Product Evaluation Matrix Example (t-13-03.xls)

Chapter 15: Completing the Physical Design

The following tools for completing the physical design are located in the \chapters\ch15 directory:

- Template 15.1 DBMS Server Code Tree (t-15-01.doc)
- Template 15.2 Physical Database Design (t-15-02.doc)
- Template 15.3 Index Plan (t-15-03.doc)
- Aid 15.1 Naming Conventions (numerous files located in the \other\nmngcnv directory on the CD-ROM)
- Aid 15.2 Sample Period Table Rows (prdtable.xls and prdtbl97.xls in the \other directory on the CD-ROM)

Chapter 16: Data Staging

The following tools for data staging are located in the \chapters\ch16 directory:

- Checklist 16.1 Data Staging (c-16-01.doc)
- Checklist 16.2 Data Validation (c-16-02.doc)

Chapter 17: Building End User Applications

The following tools for building end user applications are located in the \chapters\ch17 directory:

- Template 17.1 End User Application Template Definition (t-17-01.doc)
- Template 17.2 End User Application Template Layout (t-17-02.doc)
- Checklist 17.1 Application Development Guidelines (c-17-01.doc)

Chapter 18: Planning the Deployment

The following tools for planning the deployment are located in the \chapters\ch18 directory:

- Checklist 18.1 Desktop Installation Readiness (c-18-01.doc)
- Checklist 18.2 Deployment Readiness (c-18-02.doc)

Using the CD-ROM

The CD-ROM includes an HTML file to be used with any HTML browser, such as Microsoft Explorer 4.0 or Netscape Communicator 4.0, to support navigation between the files on the CD-ROM. Instructions for using a browser in conjunction with the CD-ROM are detailed below.

If you do not have an HTML browser, the CD-ROM includes a readme.txt that guides you through the organization of the CD-ROM's contents.

CD-ROM Browser Instructions

Starting the CD-ROM browser page is straightforward. Place the CD in your computer, navigate to the CD drive and run the file named index.htm. To run it, either double-click on the index.htm file, or type D:\index.htm from the Run file selection (where "D:" is the drive letter for your CD-ROM drive).

Software Requirements

Most of the Business Dimensional Lifecycle Toolkit templates, checklists, figures, and other aids are provided in Microsoft Office 95 file formats (Word version 6.0/95, Excel 5.0/95 and PowerPoint 95). The architecture figures are Visio documents embedded in PowerPoint. The dimensional model diagrams were constructed using the ABC Snap-Graphics version 2.0 module of Micrografx's ABC FlowCharter version 6.0 product.

Index

NOTES

NOTES

NOTES

NOTES

NOTES

NOTES

NOTES

NOTES